THE JESUITS
& ITALIAN
UNIVERSITIES
1548–1773

Paul F. Grendler

THE JESUITS & ITALIAN UNIVERSITIES 1548–1773

THE CATHOLIC UNIVERSITY OF
AMERICA PRESS *Washington, D.C.*

The paper used in this publication meets the minimum requirements of
American National Standards for Information Science—Permanence
of Paper for Printed Library Materials, ANSI Z39.48–1984.
∞

Cataloging in Publication data available from the Library of Congress
ISBN 978-0-8132-2936-2

To past and present members of the Society of Jesus

CONTENTS

LIST OF TABLES,

FIGURES, AND MAPS

Tables

Figures and Maps

Heliogravure portrait of Possevino from: Alfred Hamy, Galerie Illustrée de la Campagnie de Jésus. Vol. 6 (Paris, 1893), 37. Courtesy of Rare Books and Special Collections, The Catholic University of America.

Portrait by an unknown artist in the early seventeenth century. University of Padua, Palazzo centrale dell'Universita, Sala della Facolta di Lettere e Filosofia. With permission of the University of Padua and thanks to Francesco Piovan.

ASB, Assunteria di Studio 89, Stampi e duplicati 1576–1660. With permission of the Ministero per I Beni e le Attivita Culturali, Archivo di Stato di Bologna.

ASR, Archivio dell'Universita di Roma 195, c 23. With permission of the Ministero per I Beni e le Attivita Culturali, Archivio di Stato di Roma.

ASR, Archivio dell'Universita di Roma 195, c 384.With permission of the Ministero per i Beni e le Attivita Culturali, Archivio di Stato di Roma.

ACKNOWLEDGMENTS

It is a pleasure to thank the individuals and institutions that helped bring this book to completion. First and foremost, I wish to thank Joseph De Cock, Brian Mac Cuarta, Paul Oberholzer, James Pratt, and Francesco Stacca who facilitated my visits to the Archivum Romanum Societatis Iesu in 1999, 2001, 2009, 2010, 2011, and 2013. I am especially grateful to Mauro Brunello. Several of the above also eased physical access during an episode of osteoarthritis in September 2011.

Maria Alessandra Panzanelli Fratoni graciously identified and obtained copies of documents from the Archivio Storico dell'Università di Perugia for me. Alessandro Leonicini and Patrizia Turrini searched for and made copies of documents for me at the Archivio Storico dell'Università di Siena. Giuliana Adorni and her colleagues Roberto Leggio and Paola Ferraris did the same at the Archivio di Stato di Roma. Daniela Ferrari and her staff at the Archivio di Stato di Mantua were very helpful. I am grateful to many other Italian archivists and librarians whose names are unknown to me for their assistance over the years. Ugo Baldini, Robert Bireley, Emanuele Colombo, William Connell, Piero Del Negro, Thomas Deutscher, Mark Lewis, Robert Maryks, John O'Malley, Francesco Piovan, Erika Rummel, Maurizio Sangalli, and Piotr Stolarski answered questions, provided materials, or checked translations. I am particularly grateful to Nelson Minnich who did all three activities on many occasions. Cristiano Casalini and Christoph Sander generously sent me pre-publication copies of their scholarship on Jesuit philosophy. An anonymous reviewer made a number of useful suggestions that I have tried to incorporate. A Franklin Research Grant from the American Philosophical Society in 2003 and a Renaissance Society of America Research Grant in 2010 made possible visits to various archives and libraries in Italy. I thank Gian Paolo Brizzi and his colleagues at the Centro interuniversitario per la storia delle università italiane who invited me to present a paper at a conference, which took place during a snowstorm, at Parma in December 2001, followed by invitations to conferences at Padua and Bologna in 2006, Padua in 2009, and Sassari in 2012. The invitations made possible side trips to archives and libraries in other towns.

On this side of the Atlantic, the University of North Carolina at Chapel Hill library, especially its interlibrary loan department, and the Duke Divinity School library have been most helpful. A visit to the Woodstock Theological Library of Georgetown University was useful. I am grateful to the Archive of the Jesuits in Canada for an extended loan of three volumes. Lenore Rouse of Rare Books and Special Collections, The Catholic University of America, graciously photographed an illustration. I thank Trevor Lipscombe, director of the Catholic University of America Press, for his willingness to publish a large and complex book. I thank Theresa Walker and Tanjam Jacobson for guiding the book into print. All of the above made the book better; the shortcomings are mine alone.

Jesuit attempts to found universities or to teach in civic universities is the topic of the present work. A second volume on Jesuit pre-university schools in Italy is in preparation.

This book is dedicated to three groups of Jesuits. The Jesuits of the sixteenth, seventeenth, and eighteenth centuries created voluminous records. The Jesuits of the late eighteenth and the nineteenth centuries preserved a great deal of that material despite suppression, confiscations, and the predations of Italian governments. And the Jesuits in Rome at the Archivum Romanum Societatis Iesu and the community of San Pietro Canisio welcomed a researcher into their midst.

ABBREVIATIONS

Citation Elements

bu.	busta
c. (cc.)	carta
f. (ff.)	folio (folios)
sig.	signature

Archival and Library

AAUP	Archivio Antico dell'Università di Padova
APUG	Archivio Storico della Pontificia Università Gregoriana
ARSI	Archivum Romanum Societatis Iesu
ASB	Archivio di Stato di Bologna
ASCTo	Archivio Storico della Città di Torino
ASM	Archivio di Stato di Mantova
AG	Archivio Gonzaga
ASMc	Archivio di Stato di Macerata
APCM	Archivio Priorale del Commune di Macerata
ASPr	Archivio di Stato di Parma
ASR	Archivio di Stato di Roma
AST	Archivio di Stato di Torino
ASUP	Archivio Storico dell'Università di Perugia
ASUS	Archivio Storico dell'Università di Siena
BAB	Biblioteca Archiginnasio, Bologna
BAP	Biblioteca Augusta, Perugia
BPP	Biblioteca Palatina, Parma

Printed Sources

AHSI *Archivum Historicum Societatis Iesu*

CHRP *Cambridge History of Renaissance Philosophy* (ed. Schmitt et al.)

DBI *Dizionario biografico degli italiani*

DHCJ *Diccionario Histórico de la Compañia de Jesús: Biográfico-temático* (ed. O'Neill et al.)

DSB *Dictionary of Scientific Biography* (ed. Gillispie et al.)

ER *Encyclopedia of the Renaissance* (ed. Grendler et al.)

Gesuiti e università 2002 *Gesuiti e università in Europa (secoli XVI–XVIII)* (ed. Brizzi and Greci)

MP *Monumenta Paedagogica Societatis Iesu* (ed. Lukács)

OER *Oxford Encyclopedia of the Reformation* (ed. Hillerbrand et al.)

Sommervogel 1960 *Bibliothèque de la Compagnie de Jésus* (Sommervogel)

THE JESUITS
& ITALIAN
UNIVERSITIES
1548–1773

INTRODUCTION

Italian States and Their Universities

In the middle of the sixteenth century Italy had ten major states, a number of smaller states, and fourteen universities. The majority of the states remained independent for the following two centuries. Although a few were ruled by Spain, they retained considerable self-rule in local affairs and had a rich enough history that contemporaries rightly saw them as distinct states. If a city or state had a university, this was an important part of its political identity.

The Duchy of Piedmont-Savoy was a state in northwestern Italy.[1] It consisted of one ruler over two states, the Italian-speaking Principate of Piedmont and the French-speaking Duchy of Savoy, which extended into mountains that are now part of France. Although Savoy was the larger territory, Piedmont was more important, because Duke Emanuele Filiberto Savoia made Turin, in Piedmont, his capital in 1562. Furthermore, Turin had a university. Founded in stages between 1411 and 1413, it became a medium-sized institution of modest academic stature. The city council of Turin paid most of the bills and made proximate decisions, while the dukes made ultimate determinations. The Jesuits attempted to become professors at the University of Turin. In the seventeenth century the rulers of Piedmont-Savoy tried to create a second university in Chambéry, the capital of Savoy, for their French-speaking subjects, enlisting Jesuits in the endeavor.

On the eastern border of Piedmont-Savoy was the Duchy of Milan, which ruled most of Lombardy. Although it had been a powerful state that tried to conquer its neighbors in centuries past, it was now part of the Spanish Empire with a viceroy, often an Italian military commander, appointed by Madrid. Milan's university was Pavia, founded in 1361 and located south of Milan. It had been the third most important Italian university, after Padua and Bologna, in the late fifteenth century, but was often closed during the Italian wars (1494 to 1559). It now sought to regain its size and prestige. The Senate of Milan made appointments and decided other matters with

---

1. In what follows, the information about Italian states is well known. The material about universities comes from Grendler 2002, which has much additional bibliographical data.

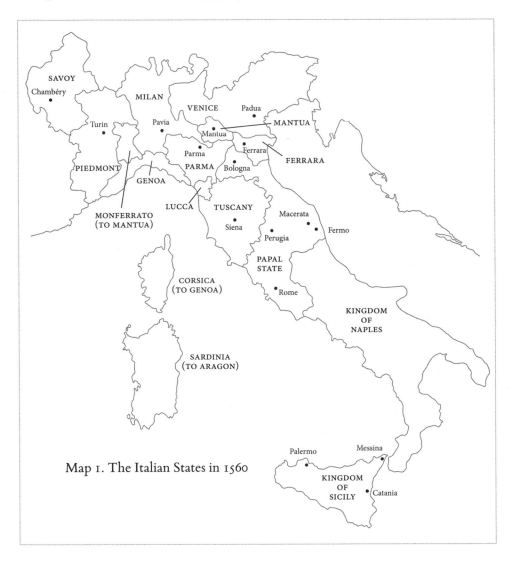

Map 1. The Italian States in 1560

little interference from viceroys. The senators wondered if a Jesuit mathematician might be added to the University of Pavia.

East of Lombardy stood the Republic of Venice, which occupied all of
northeastern Italy. A legendary maritime state, the Republic of Venice was
now also a major land power in the peninsula and heavily involved in its
politics. Venice was an aristocratic republic with democratic and monar-

chical tendencies, making it a living example of ancient Roman political theory. In the middle of the sixteenth century approximately 2,500 adult noble males elected a Senate of about 230 voting members plus executive councils. The same 2,500 nobles indirectly elected a doge, the head of state. Although more than an elderly figurehead, the doge took instructions from the Senate.

The University of Padua was the university of the Republic of Venice. The traditional account states that the University of Padua began with a migration of teachers and students from the University of Bologna in 1222. Limited evidence confirms the presence of professors and students in Padua in the 1220s and 1230s. At that time Padua was an independent city; it then fell into the hands of a local family in 1318. In 1405 the Republic of Venice conquered Padua. The Venetian government strongly supported and ruled the University of Padua. Thanks to distinguished and innovative professors, Padua competed with Bologna for intellectual leadership among Italian universities and had the second largest enrollment. Men from all over Europe, including Protestants from Germany and England, came to study there. Nevertheless, professors and students worried about the growing Jesuit school in Padua.

Two smaller duchies—Parma, ruled by the Farnese family, and Mantua, ruled by the Gonzaga—are located south of Milan and the Republic of Venice. Both had splendid courts and patronized artists, writers, and scholars. Neither had a university. Both wanted one and enlisted the Jesuits in their quests.

South of the Republic of Venice stands the Duchy of Ferrara, which included Modena, ruled by the Este family. An Este created the University of Ferrara in 1442. It was a second-tier university, with some famous professors and an enrollment smaller than Bologna and Padua. While the duke exercised ultimate authority, the city appointed professors and paid the expenses. When the last Este duke in the direct line died without an heir in 1597, the Duchy of Ferrara became part of the papal state and was governed by a papal legate. A papal legate considered appointing a Jesuit mathematician to the university.

The Duchy of Tuscany (raised to a Grand Duchy in 1569) was a large state in north-central Italy that stretched to the Tyrrhenian Sea on the west and shared a border with the papal state on the south. Its capital was Florence, famous for its art. The Medici family ruled Tuscany with an authoritarian hand. Its university was Pisa, founded in 1343. However, because the Jesuits never had a college in Pisa, they did not interact with the university. In 1557 Tuscany purchased the Republic of Siena from Spain, after troops of the Spanish Empire had starved Siena into surrender in 1555, and incorporated it into the Duchy of Tuscany. In this way Tuscany acquired the University of Siena, founded in 1246.

The University of Siena had a good reputation in law but stopped teaching during the Spanish siege. It recovered very slowly because Duke Cosimo I de' Medici favored the University of Pisa and blocked complete restoration of the University of Siena. However, his successor, Francesco I de' Medici (ruled for his father from 1567, and was grand duke in 1574–1587) allowed the institution to recover fully. It became a medium-sized second-tier university important as a destination for ultramontane students. A later grand duke entertained a request from a Jesuit to teach mathematics in the university.

Next came the large papal state that dominated central Italy from the Tyrrhenian Sea on the west to the Adriatic Sea on the east, north to the border with the Duchy of Ferrara, and south to the border with the Kingdom of Naples. The papal state comprised several units acquired over two centuries. The pope was the civil ruler of the papal state but had very little to do with the affairs of individual towns and territories. He left that to cardinal legates. In practice cities enjoyed a considerable amount of self-rule. City councils dominated by nobles made most local decisions, and legates tended to support civic aspirations. Because it was an ecclesiastical state, local bishops took a more active role in the educational affairs of cities than in states and cities ruled by princes. The papal state had five universities within its boundaries. The most important by far was Bologna, known as *Alma Mater Studiorum* (Nourishing Mother of Universities).

Bologna vied with Paris for the honor of being the first university. The traditional account states that sometime in the late eleventh century students began to come to Bologna to gather at the feet of jurists who looked to ancient Roman law for legal principles that would enable them to adjudicate between the laws and rights of empire, papacy, states, cities, and citizens. Over time others began to teach, including Gratian, a monk who made a compilation of church council decrees, papal letters, and extracts from patristic writings for the study of canon law. The presence of teaching legists attracted scholars and students in other disciplines to Bologna.

Because the law students had little or no legal existence away from their homelands, they organized themselves into an association in order to assert legal rights—they were law students, after all. An imperial document of 1158 recognized such an association (*universitas*). The arts students also organized and were recognized. These and other developments between 1150 and 1200 are usually taken as the beginning of the University of Bologna.

The University of Paris came into being in the same half century but with a different structure.

The next important step was the decision in the 1220s of the city government (the commune) of Bologna to pay salaries to law teachers. The reason was to guarantee the stability of the university. If professors stayed in one place to receive salaries, students would as well. Although the commune stopped paying salaries to the legists in the 1230s, it resumed doing so in 1280, and it began to pay salaries to teachers in other disciplines in the first decade of the fourteenth century. These were the most important decisions in the early history of Italian universities because they determined governance. Paying professorial salaries meant that the civil government controlled universities, which eventually meant making appointments and issuing regulations. Every other Italian city with a university followed the Bolognese example.

Bologna, always tumultuous, slowly and grudgingly accepted papal overlordship, which produced internal peace. In the sixteenth and later centuries, the commune, dominated by local families holding hereditary seats, and the papal legate acting for the pope, ruled together. They united to support the university, the city's most important intellectual and economic asset. Bologna had the largest enrollment of any Italian university and attracted students from everywhere in Europe. It competed with Padua for the title of most distinguished Italian university. And like Padua, it kept a watchful eye on the Jesuit school in Bologna.

The second university that came into the papal state through the political decline of its host was Perugia. Medieval Perugia, the independent and prosperous leading city of Umbria, founded a university in 1308. The commune made appointments, paid salaries, and promulgated regulations. The University of Perugia had the great good fortune that Bartolus (Bartolo da Sassoferrato, 1313–1357) and Baldus (Baldo degli Baldi, 1327?–1400), the two most famous and influential legal scholars of the late Middle Ages, taught there most of their careers. Their method and works set the pattern for Italian legal education for the next several centuries. But Perugia never reached comparable heights in other disciplines, and over time law professorships went to local men of limited accomplishments.

Internal divisions caused the commune of Perugia to begin to lose its political independence in the late fourteenth century. In 1424 the papacy took direct control of the city and appointed a papal legate to rule it, although Perugia remained tumultuous. As the legate's power grew, he played a direct role in appointments, something that did not happen at Bologna. In the middle of the sixteenth century and beyond, the University of Perugia was a small university still dominated by law. And its difficulties caused some Perugians to consider asking for assistance from the Jesuits.

The third university in the papal state was the University of Rome. It began in the 1240s but remained a very minor institution until the second half of the fifteenth century. It then grew. It had a large and talented faculty, especially in the humanities, from the 1470s until the sack of Rome in 1527. After 1535 it settled into the lesser position of a middle-rank university educating men from the papal state for careers as lawyers, civil servants, physicians, and teachers. It differed from all other Italian universities because it had many professors of theology drawn from the ranks of medieval mendicant orders with headquarters in Rome. As the civil ruler of Rome, the pope ultimately governed the University of Rome. But authority for appointments and other matters rested with the city government and the university itself. A few blocks away stood its rival, the Jesuit Roman College, which had excellent teachers and more students than the university.

The fourth and fifth universities of the papal state were new. Macerata was a relatively large town on the eastern side of the papal state in the land known as the Marches. As usual, a papal legate ruled the city but did not interfere in local affairs so long as the town paid the required taxes into the papal treasury. Macerata wanted a university and secured a papal bull for one in 1540. Unlike the lay rulers of other Italian states, the popes were pleased to sanction new universities even when they competed with others in the state. The commune of Macerata created a small university of eleven or twelve professors, about two-thirds in law, who began teaching in 1540 and 1541. Its major purpose was to educate men from the surrounding territory in law so that they might obtain positions in the papal bureaucracy. The fifth university of the papal state was Fermo, founded in 1585, also located in the Marches but separated by mountains and two river valleys from Macerata. It was slightly larger than the University of Macerata. The Jesuits secured a significant presence in both institutions.

The Kingdom of Naples occupied the lower third of the Italian peninsula. However, it lost its independence to Spain in 1503 and was ruled by viceroys. Its universities were Naples, founded in 1224, and Salerno, founded around 1592. Neither had collaborations or altercations with the Jesuits and, hence, will not be part of this story.

It was different in the Kingdom of Sicily, which was ruled by viceroys from the united Kingdom of Aragon and Castile since 1479 and Spain since 1504. The tiny University of Catania, founded in 1445, was the sole university in Sicily due to the fact that Spain would not authorize any other Sicilian institution to confer degrees. However, Messina and Palermo, the two largest and most important cities of Sicily, and intense rivals, wanted universities. They tried to break Catania's monopoly with the help of the Jesuits. Thus, the Jesuits became heavily involved in university disputes in all three cities.

Despite their political and historical differences, Italian states and cities made decisions in similar ways. The prince, legate, viceroy, or commune ruled. In the case of the Venetian Senate, a hereditary nobility ruled. Although princes, legates, and viceroys enjoyed absolute authority in theory, they took into account the wishes of local elites. More often than not, they employed a mix of threat, persuasion, compromise, and/or concession to get their way. The local nobility acting through city councils employed the same tactics plus bureaucratic delay to thwart the ruler, and sometimes prevailed. Finally, there were some instances where prince, viceroy, legate, and city elite were in total agreement.

Italian universities shared some common features. They were civic institutions, because a prince or commune founded and ruled them. Ruler and subjects viewed the local university as "our university." The vast majority of students sought doctorates in law or medicine, while logic and philosophy were usually, but not always, viewed as preparation for law or medicine. The majority of professors who taught these subjects were laymen. On the other hand, except for Rome, Italian universities taught little theology.

"Professor" is the best American English word to describe a man who taught in Italian universities. University rolls (lists of lectures offered) did not give titles to those who lectured. Instead, they listed the subject matter of the lectureship, such as "Ad lecturam Theoricae Medicinae" followed by a name. Sometimes it was qualified as "Ad Philosophiam extraordinariam" or shortened to "Ad Logicam." Given the multiple meanings of lecturer in American English and the fact that the vast majority of Italian university teachers held doctorates, professor is the best term.

All of the above states except the Kingdom of Naples interacted with the Jesuits on university matters. They either wanted to include the Jesuits in their universities or were determined to keep them out.

The Jesuits

On September 27, 1540, Pope Paul III approved the Society of Jesus as a religious order of clerics regular with the bull *Regimini militantis Ecclesiae*. At that time the Society consisted of ten men who had pledged to serve God when they were students at the University of Paris. Five were Spanish; four were French, two were French-speaking Savoyards, and one was

Portuguese. None was Italian. This was not surprising, because very few Italians attended the University of Paris.

In addition to the customary vows of poverty, chastity, and obedience, the Society added a fourth vow, a special vow of obedience to the pope concerning missions. This simply meant that individual Jesuits would go on missions to convert non-Christians if the pope asked. The rules and practices of the Society differed from those of medieval mendicant religious orders in several ways. The most important was that Jesuits were not required to pray together. That is, they did not have to recite or chant in common the divine office, the prayers that Benedictines, Dominicans, Franciscans, et al., did together in the monastery in which they lived. It meant that canon law did not tether Jesuits to a monastery. They might travel freely to convert non-Christians, preach, catechize, hear confessions, or undertake any other task. This facilitated a key goal of the new order, which was to serve God and neighbor in the world. These ten former students, none with degrees higher than the master of arts, had ambitious goals.

The next steps were to elect a superior general and to draft preliminary constitutions, normal tasks for new religious orders. Other orders limited the superior general to a term of years; the Jesuits decided that he would serve for life. As expected, they elected Loyola as superior general on April 29, 1541. Except for a handful of brief trips to nearby towns, Ignatius spent the rest of his life in Rome dictating letters of instruction and exhortation to Jesuits throughout the world. After election, he and another first Jesuit began to draft permanent constitutions. When the other Jesuit died a few months later, the task fell to Ignatius. He wrote and rewrote the constitutions in the light of Jesuit experiences until his death in 1556. The Society adopted them in 1558.

Ignatius Loyola and the first Jesuits laid sturdy foundations. While Ignatius attracts the most attention, many other Jesuits played major roles before his death and long after. Three factors were essential to the success of the Jesuits and enabled them to avoid most of the pitfalls of new religious orders. First, they attracted an astounding number of dedicated and talented men into their ranks. When Loyola died in 1556, there were a thousand Jesuits. Ten years later there were three thousand. And the order continued to grow. Moreover, by the early 1560s the Jesuits had fully embraced their destiny as teachers.

Second, the Jesuits had a spirituality rooted in Loyola's *Spiritual Exercises* to sustain them through successes and failures, martyrdoms and lapses into sin. It is perhaps difficult at first to grasp the effect of the *Spiritual Exercises*, because as a book it is a dull read. It simply offers directions to the person guiding an individual through thirty days of intense meditation and prayer. But the evidence is that when given by an able spiritual director to a receptive soul, the effects were transformative. Recipients found and embraced God's will as they saw it and reshaped their lives accordingly. The *Spiritual Exercises* gave the Jesuits a strong and distinctive spirituality sometimes lacking in other Catholic Reformation orders.

Third, the Jesuits built well. Ignatius and his successors made wise organizational decisions, and when they made mistakes, they almost always corrected them. What emerged from the trial and error of the first twenty-five years was an effective organization of strong individuals and structures. Individual Jesuits were novices, scholastics (younger Jesuits studying philosophy or theology), priests, and temporal coadjutors, sometimes called brothers. Temporal coadjutors were the cooks, tailors, buyers, and custodians of churches and buildings who kept colleges functioning.

A Jesuit college was an established community of Jesuits in a town. A college had a building in which the Jesuits lived, a church that they owned or was set aside for their exclusive use, and sufficient continuing financial support, preferably an endowment.[2] Almost all colleges had a school (in another building) which offered free Latin education to boys and men who met the academic requirements. Although scholars often use "college" and "school" synonymously, they were not the same. Some of the Jesuits in a college carried on non-teaching ministries, including preaching, hearing confessions, ministering to the sick, and catechizing.

From 1578 onward every Italian college was a unit in one of the five Jesuit provinces of Milan, Venice, Rome, Naples, and Sicily, whose territories were not coterminous with political states. The college and province in which a Jesuit studied, taught, or carried on other ministries were the most important parts of the Society to him. Each province had a superior appointed by the general. The five Italian provinces were part of the Italian assistancy, led by an assistant superior elected by a General Congregation. When a superior general dies, a General Congregation consisting of delegates from all parts of the Society meets to elect a successor and to discuss issues related to the Constitutions or other matters of importance. For example, the Thirty-Sixth General Congregation met from October 3 to November 12, 2016. Between general congregations the superior general rules the Society.

The most important ministry of the Jesuits in Europe was education, and Jesuit schools developed a strong curriculum and pedagogy that they

2. I am grateful to John O'Malley for this succinct definition.

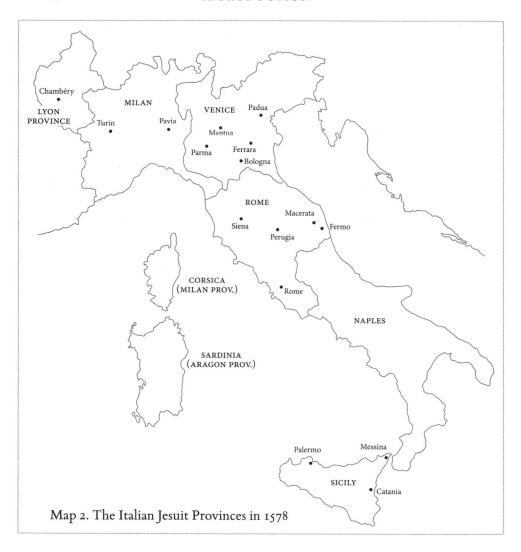

Map 2. The Italian Jesuit Provinces in 1578

codified in the Ratio Studiorum (Plan of Study) of 1599. At the age of ten or older a boy, who already knew how to read and write and had learned the rudiments of Latin grammar (morphology and very elementary reading), entered the Jesuit Latin grammar class. This was often divided into three classes: lower grammar, middle grammar, and upper grammar. He spent the next six or more years studying grammar, the humanities, and rhetoric. It was a very intense program of reading, writing, and speaking classical Latin, along with some Greek, based on the classics of ancient Rome and Greece. Jesuit schools also taught Catholic doctrine and tried to inculcate good moral habits through attendance at Mass, devotional activities, good example, and exhortation.

At the age of sixteen or older, the student moved to the upper school where he attended three successive year-long courses in logic, natural philosophy, and metaphysics, usually meeting twice daily, based on the appropriate texts of Aristotle. In addition, the largest and most important Jesuit schools offered optional lectures in mathematics. All four competed with Italian university courses. The final part of the Jesuit upper school consisted of four years of lectures in scholastic theology plus limited lectures in cases of conscience. All Jesuits preparing for the priesthood attended these lectures, but only a limited number of non-Jesuit students did.

Civil Governments and the Jesuits

It was one thing to teach university subjects in their own schools, it was quite another for the Jesuits to create their own universities or to seek professorships in existing universities. Nevertheless, that is what the Jesuits did in northern Europe. They played major roles in the universities of Prague, Vienna, Coimbra, Évora, and several Spanish universities. They created the small French universities of Billom, Pont-à-Mousson, and Tournon. They had their greatest successes in what is now Germany, where between 1549 and 1648 they founded or became a significant presence in fourteen universities.[3] But what happened in Italy when the Jesuits tried to found universities or teach in existing universities?

The answer depended on the reactions of civil governments. If the prince, legate, viceroy, bishop, and/or city council wanted the Jesuits to be part of the local university, they were welcomed and given financial support. If the prince, legate, viceroy, bishop, and/or city council did not want them, the Society was rebuffed. And if they disagreed with each other, or with the Jesuits over terms and conditions, a battle raged until a decision was reached.

Between 1548 and 1773 the Jesuits tried to found new universities or to become professors in existing universities. They fought attempts by universities and civil governments to shut down their schools when they were seen as threats to the local university. These events occurred in sixteen cit-

---

3. They were Bamberg, Cologne, Dillingen, Erfürt, Freiburg im Breisgau, Heidelberg, Ingolstadt, Mainz, Molsheim, Münster, Osnabrück, Paderborn, Trier, and Würzburg (Hengst 1981). This is a model study of which there is no equivalent for Italy.

ies and towns ruled by Italian states and are little known. This book is the
history of the interactions between the Jesuits and Italian universities and
governments. Interactions is a neutral word for encounters that ranged
from serene collaborations to pitched battles.

An American political adage, attributed to Thomas P. "Tip" O'Neill, a
former Speaker of the U.S. House of Representatives, is that all politics is
local politics. A corollary is that all Jesuit educational history is local history. Although outside influences affected events, the local response always
determined the outcome, and each encounter between the Jesuits and a city
or prince concerning a university was a distinct story. To understand the
whole history, all episodes must be studied.

This book is organized by place. Each chapter narrates the history of Jesuit attempts to become professors in one city, and occasionally two or three
when there were strong similarities. Each chapter begins with the establishment of the Jesuits in a city. It concludes with the date of the final interaction
between the Society and the local university or 1773. While the book generally proceeds chronologically, it sometimes moves forward and back.

The political boundaries of Italian states at the time determine the geographical range. The attempt to found a civic-Jesuit university at Chambéry in French-speaking Savoy is included because Chambéry was part of
the Italian Duchy of Piedmont-Savoy. The universities of Cagliari and Sassari in which Jesuits taught are not discussed because Sardinia was part of
the Kingdom of Aragon.[4]

Although each local story is unique, there are links and similarities.
Events in one city or university sometimes influenced events and people
in other places. Failure taught the Jesuits to change tactics. This book attempts to track the connections from city to city and across changes of
policy and tactics. Opponents of the Jesuits made many charges and accusations against them, and sometimes the Jesuits replied in kind. Whenever
possible, the accuracy of the accusations and responses is evaluated. Chapter 14 summarizes the sharp differences between the Jesuits and civil universities concerning the teaching of philosophy, while chapter 15 discusses
what the Jesuits contributed to theological education in Italy.

The story begins with the university studies of the first Jesuits, because
their student days shaped their approach to Italian universities.

4. In addition, the Jesuit colleges of Sardinia were part of the Jesuit Province of Aragon and
the Spanish Assistancy. There is considerable excellent scholarship on the Jesuits and the universities of Cagliari and Sassari. See Zanetti 1982; Turtas 1986; Turtas 1988; Turtas, Rundine, and
Tognotti 1990; Sorgia 1986; Turtas 1995; Battlori 2012; and *Le origini dello Studio generale sassarese*
2013. In 1718 Sardinia became part of Piedmont-Savoy.

I

THE FIRST JESUITS AS
UNIVERSITY STUDENTS AT
PARIS AND PADUA

The Jesuits were predestined to become university professors. The original Jesuits were the best-educated founders of a religious order to that date in history.[1] They bonded at the University of Paris, and their Paris experiences strongly influenced the curricula and pedagogy of Jesuit schools and universities. After the Society was approved, the first Jesuits wanted their new recruits to receive university educations. But when they came into contact with Italian universities, the Jesuits found them lacking.

A dozen Jesuits created the Society. The ten cofounders of the Society were Ignatius Loyola, Nicolás Bobadilla, Pierre Favre, Diego Laínez, Simão Rodrigues, Alfonso Salmerón, Francis Xavier, Claude Jay, Paschase Broët, and Jean Codure. The first seven swore vows together in a tiny chapel on the Montmartre hill in Paris on August 15, 1534; Jay did the same exactly one year later, and Broët and Codure on August 15, 1536. Jerónimo Nadal and Juan de Polanco must be added, because they were next in importance only to Ignatius Loyola in the early Society. Polanco served as a sounding board for Ignatius, after which he dispensed directives and advice to Jesuits across Europe and the world through his letters written in the name of Ignatius and the next two generals, or on his own authority. Nadal implemented Ig-

---

1. The next best-educated order was the Clerics Regular of St. Paul (Barnabites), founded in 1530 and recognized by the papacy in 1533. Two of the three cofounders were university-educated. St. Antonio Maria Zaccaria (1502/3–1539) studied arts and medicine at the University of Padua, Venerable Bartolomeo Ferrari (1499–1544) studied law at the University of Pavia, while Venerable Antonio Morigia (1497–1546) did not study at a university. The Barnabites dedicated themselves to catechetical instruction as well as pastoral and preaching ministries in the sixteenth century, and became educators in the seventeenth.

natius' instructions and Jesuit policies and made many decisions as a roving commissary with wide powers.[2] Both played key roles in the development of Jesuit educational policy. Of these dozen key early Jesuits, seven were Spanish, four were French, and Rodrigues was Portuguese. Most important, all twelve studied at the University of Paris, and some of them studied at the University of Alcalá de Henares earlier. At least five, and possibly seven, lived and studied at one college in Paris. They obtained bachelor of arts, licentiate of arts, and master of arts degrees. All studied theology, and Nadal obtained a doctorate in theology. Their university experiences, especially at Paris, exercised an enormous influence on Jesuit educational policy.

The University of Paris

The University of Paris was a vast institution of many parts held together by a well-defined curriculum and rigid degree requirements. It had somewhere between twelve to twenty thousand students, making it the largest university in Europe. Another thousand members of medieval religious orders (Dominicans, Augustinians, Franciscans, Carmelites, and others) studied in the *studia* (upper-level schools) in the Parisian monasteries of these orders.[3] Possibly the majority of arts students lived in private rooms and hospices. A large number also lived in and studied in residence colleges. The last were relatively small and intimate institutions in which teachers and students lived, taught, and learned in close proximity.

The University of Paris had approximately forty secular colleges, all located in the Latin Quarter. Although their students and teachers were subject to the degree requirements imposed by the university, the colleges were

2. For the importance of Nadal and Polanco in all aspects of the first quarter century of the Jesuits, see O'Malley 1993, 10–14. Although any list of the most important twelve early Jesuits is arbitrary, historians have documented the importance of the men listed here. Juan Jerónimo Doménech (Valencia 1516–1592 Valencia), and Peter Canisius (Nijmegen 1521–1597 Fribourg) would come next in a list of important early Jesuits in educational matters. Doménech began to study at the University of Paris in 1535, just missing meeting Ignatius there. On a trip to Rome in 1538 he met several of the founders and became a Jesuit in 1539. He helped establish the Jesuits in Paris and Louvain, and helped prepare the way for the Jesuits in Messina. He was also rector of the Roman College, the Roman Seminary, and the German College, and provincial superior of Sicily three times for a total of nineteen years. See Medina 2001. Peter Canisius is omitted because he spent most of his career as a Jesuit in German-speaking lands.

3. Farge 1999, 404. Schurhammer 1973, 79 and 79n30, adds other mostly contemporary estimates of the number of students. Farge 1985, 11n12, estimates that there were between 1,500 and 2,100 members of mendicant orders, "largely students," living in Paris in the first half of the sixteenth century. It should be noted that the number of students was very high because many of them were boys aged nine to eighteen learning or perfecting their Latin. Nevertheless, they were enrolled as university students. Italian universities, by contrast, did not enroll students this young.

otherwise autonomous. Some had pious foundations and enjoyed small or large endowments; others were privately owned and lived on student fees. The eighteen largest were self-contained public colleges with the right to enroll fee-paying students. Each had a *magna aula* (great hall) for formal events, classrooms, refectory, chapel, and rooms for masters and students. Colleges taught preparatory humanities instruction and the arts curriculum. Students attended lectures in individual colleges taught by the teachers of that college.[4] The Collège de Montaigu, later mocked by former student Desiderius Erasmus, and the Collège de Sainte-Barbe (College of St. Barbara) were the best known and largest colleges. They had high reputations in humanistic studies and philosophy.[5]

The Collège de Sainte-Barbe played a large role in the education of the first Jesuits. Founded in 1460, it occupied a building that had seen better days across the street from the College of Montaigu and adjacent to other colleges and gardens in the Latin Quarter. Because it was privately owned and lacked an endowment, the students paid fees. In 1520 a Portuguese scholar named Diogo de Gouvea (or Gouveia), who had a doctorate from the University of Paris, leased the college, became its principal, and persuaded the Portuguese king to endow some bursaries for Portuguese students. It became the preferred college for students from the Iberian peninsula. It enrolled about two hundred resident students and masters and an unknown number of day students, most of them from Spain and Portugal, in the 1520s.[6]

Although colleges accepted students as young as nine or ten, thirteen to fifteen was the normal age of entry. Others arrived in their late teens, and a few were older. The students were lay boys and young men or young clerics in minor orders expecting to become secular clergymen. The most important act of the new college student was to choose a teacher who would lecture to him, supervise his academic exercises, correct his compositions, and share lodging with him. Teachers were required to be celibate. A teacher and three or four students commonly lived together in one room, sometimes sharing beds.[7]

---

4. Schurhammer 1973, 79–85; Farge 1985, 11–12. There is a great deal of information on the colleges of the University of Paris, including their teachers and students, scattered through Schurhammer 1973. See also Codina Mir 1968, 50–150.

5. Codina Mir 1968, 61–62; and Lécrivain 2011, 56–57.

6. Codina Mir 1968, 50, writes that the Collège de Sainte-Barbe constituted "une veritable fief ibérique." See also Schurhammer 1973, 81–85, including a plan of the college, 101–2; and Lécrivain 2011, 64–65, and illustration 19 that locates the Collège de Montaigu and the Collège de Sainte-Barbe in Paris.

7. Schurhammer 1973, 80–81, 81n50, 95–96, 141; Farge 1985, 11–12; Farge 1992b, 231n42; and Farge 1999, 404.

The youngest college students typically studied the Latin humanities as preparation for arts. In the 1520s they studied a mix of traditional medieval grammatical authors and the ancient classics. The students heard lectures, wrote compositions, and participated in drills and repetitions (review exercises). Latin students at the College of St. Barbara were divided into ten classes, and rose from one class to another by proving that they had mastered the material. The length of time that a student spent in humanities study depended on his preparation and progress; a year or two was common, while others needed more time. The student had to pass an examination before beginning to study arts.[8]

Arts meant the study of logic, natural philosophy, and metaphysics based on Aristotelian texts, with a smattering of mathematics and moral philosophy. Students were expected to hear three years of lectures and spend part of a year preparing for degree examinations.[9] But there was no predetermined length for these studies, and some students devoted five or more years to the arts curriculum. It began with one to two years of the study of logic based on Aristotle's *Organon* and traditional medieval supporting manuals.[10] Next came metaphysics and natural philosophy. The most important part of the philosophy program, usually done in the third year, was natural philosophy, which meant hearing lectures on the *Physics* of Aristotle, a work of basic science. The *Physics* offered a broad discussion of the physical world, and how various parts of it could be understood by examining their conditions and causes, rather than through measuring phenomena.[11]

The arts curriculum culminated in the conferral of one or more of bachelor of arts, licentiate of arts, and master of arts degrees. A student might present himself for the examination for the bachelor of arts degree at the end of his second year of study, or he might wait until he had studied for several years.[12] If successful, he was expected to wait a year before presenting himself for the licentiate of arts degree, although there were exceptions. He might devote that time to more study and/or teaching Latin.[13]

The licentiate was more significant. The candidate had to be twenty-one years of age (although dispensations were granted), possess a bachelor's degree, have studied logic and philosophy for three years, have attended lectures on the required texts, disputed twice, and passed an examination.

8. Schurhammer 1973, 81, 113–14.
9. Farge 1985, 12; García-Villoslada 1990, 368.
10. Schurhammer 1973, 113–14; García-Villoslada 1990, 372–73.
11. Schurhammer 1973, 143–44.
12. Farge 1985, 12.
13. Schurhammer 1973, 114, 145.

This won him the licentiate (*licentia docendi*) which conferred on him the right to teach and exercise other magisterial functions in Paris and beyond. To celebrate his success, the new licentiate was expected to host an expensive banquet for his teachers and friends.[14]

The master of arts degree at Paris did not require additional course work or another examination. The only conditions were possession of a licentiate and being twenty-one years of age, although, as usual, dispensations from the age requirement could be obtained. At Paris a candidate for the master of arts degree delivered an inaugural lecture, after which the presiding master asked the other masters present if the candidate should receive the master's biretta. The answer was invariably yes. He was thus enrolled in the list of the masters of the university. The expenses for the master's degree were considerably higher than for the licentiate, as the candidate was expected to dress well for the occasion, pay fees to those involved, and provide a lavish banquet. A master of arts was eligible to teach in the university, to vote in some matters, and to hold some university offices.[15] This was the apex of arts education. After obtaining the master of arts degree, the recipient could become a regent master teaching philosophy in a college, for which he would receive payment and usually lodging. This enabled the young master to support himself while attending lectures in the higher faculties of theology, canon law, or medicine if he wished.[16] This was the degree path at the University of Paris. Alcalá de Henares and other universities outside of Italy copied Paris, with minor deviations.

The First Jesuits at Paris

All ten founding Jesuits, as well as Nadal and Polanco, studied at the University of Paris between 1525 and 1538. They came at different ages and from different lands. Although no two people ever have exactly the same educational experience, even when they study the same curriculum under the same teachers at the same time, the early Jesuits shared a great amount of similar educational experiences. Their later educational decisions demonstrated how much they were influenced by the University of Paris and its practices.

Francis Xavier (Navarre 1506–1552 Shangchuan, China) was the first to arrive. Born in the castle of his noble Basque father, he arrived at the University of Paris in 1525 at the age of nineteen, already a cleric in minor

---

14. Schurhammer 1973, 145; Farge 1985, 12.
15. Schurhammer 1973, 147; Farge 1985, 12–13.
16. Schurhammer 1973, 148–49; Farge 1985, 12–13.

orders. He enrolled in the Collège de Sainte-Barbe where he shared a room with his teacher and Pierre Favre. After passing the Latin competency examination, Francis began his philosophical studies in October 1526. He obtained the bachelor of arts degree in early 1529 and both the licentiate and the master of arts degrees in March 1530. Francis then taught philosophy as a regent master for the next three-and-a-half years at the Collège de Beauvais while continuing to live in the Collège de Sainte-Barbe and studying theology. He left Paris for Venice in late 1536.[17]

Pierre Favre (Villaret 1506–1546 Rome), the son of poor peasants of Savoy, also arrived in Paris in 1525 at the age of nineteen. After briefly studying at the Collège de Montaigu, he moved to the Collège de Sainte-Barbe where he shared a room with Francis Xavier and their teacher. In 1530 he received the bachelor of arts and licentiate of arts and began to study theology, which he continued for six years. In October 1536 he received the master of arts degree and left with other founding Jesuits for the intended rendezvous with Ignatius in Venice.[18]

Ignatius Loyola (Loyola 1491–1556 Rome), possibly the most famous late blooming student in history, followed a similar path once he came to Paris. He studied Latin, logic, and theology at the universities of Barcelona and Alcalá de Henares for short periods of time, and for a few days at the University of Salamanca. He found none of them satisfactory because their unstructured curricula permitted a student to attend any course he wished whether or not he was prepared, a policy that served students poorly, in his view. He decided to go to Paris, arriving there on February 2, 1528. Now thirty-seven years of age, he first improved his Latin by attending Latin grammar classes alongside much younger students for eighteen months at the Collège de Montaigu.[19] In September 1529 he crossed the street to the Collège de Sainte-Barbe to study philosophy. He shared a room with Francis Xavier, Favre, and Juan de la Peña, who taught all three.[20] He acquired the bachelor of arts degree in 1532 and the licentiate of arts degree on March 13, 1533. Like Favre, he postponed receiving the master of arts degree until he could beg

17. Schurhammer 1973, 108, 137, 141, 148–49, 171, 216; García-Villoslada 1990, 366; and López-Gay 2001, 2140. Schurhammer 1973 provides the best account of the experiences of the first Jesuits at Paris. Bernard-Maître 1950 and García-Villoslada 1990, 346–421, which concentrate on Ignatius, are also useful.

18. Schurhammer 1973, 106n247, 108n3, 110–12, 146, 269–70; and Donnelly 2001d, 1369.

19. Farge 1992b, 230. All biographies describe the career of Ignatius at Paris. The best are Schurhammer 1973, index; García-Villoslada 1990, 346–421; and the short account in Donnelly 2004b, 38–53.

20. Schurhammer 1973, 140–41.

the funds to pay its expenses; he became a master of arts on March 14, 1535.[21] In the interim he studied theology. Throughout his years in Paris Ignatius devoted much time and energy to giving the Spiritual Exercises and counseling those who gravitated to him. He also made trips to Bruges, Antwerp, and London to beg funds from Spanish merchants for himself and other poor students. Ignatius left Paris in early May 1535.

Diego Laínez (Almazán 1512–1565 Rome), the son of a wealthy landowner in Old Castile, was a gifted student. He began his university studies at the University of Alcalá de Henares in 1527 at the age of fifteen and obtained the bachelor of arts there in June 1531 at the age of nineteen, the licentiate on October 13, 1532, and the master of arts on October 26, 1532, when he was twenty years of age. Laínez arrived at Paris to study theology by the end of 1532, where he met Ignatius. Laínez studied theology at Paris for nearly four years before leaving with other first Jesuits in November 1536.[22]

Alfonso Salmerón (Toledo 1514–1585 Naples) was the son of a merchant of Toledo. He showed a gift for learning at an early age and was a brilliant student of Latin and Greek at the University of Alcalá de Henares, where he began his studies about 1527. There he became a friend of Laínez and heard about Ignatius. Salmerón and Laínez set off for Paris to meet Ignatius, arriving in late 1532. Salmerón studied Greek, philosophy, and theology in Paris in the next four years, followed by Hebrew and Syriac in subsequent years. After studying with regent Francis Xavier, he obtained his master of arts on September 4, 1536, which meant that he had earlier obtained the licentiate of arts. He left Paris in November 1536.[23]

Nicolás Bobadilla (Palencia ca. 1509–1590 Loreto, Italy) was the son of poor parents of Old Castile. He showed great academic ability at an early age and became a tonsured cleric at the age of nine. He won a place reserved for poor students at Alcalá de Henares and began studying there at the age of thirteen and received his bachelor of arts degree in 1529. He also attended theology lectures, and continued to do so when he went to Valladolid to teach logic. Still penniless, he went to Paris in the autumn of 1533 where he obtained a regency in philosophy at the Collège de Calvi and heard lectures in theology. He studied with regent Francis Xavier, received

21. Schurhammer 1973, 146–47, 236–37, 243; Dalmases 1985, 116–17; García-Villoslada 1990, 372–77; Farge 1992b, 232; Donnelly 2004b, 44–45; and Lécrivain 2011, 67–71.

22. Copies of the letters patent confirming his master of arts from Alcalá de Henares and the certificate that he studied theology at Paris are found in *Lainii Epistolae* 1912–1917, 8:633–35. See also Scaduto 1964, 125–27; Schurhammer 1973, 187n262, 203–5, 254; and Scaduto 2001b, 1601–2.

23. Schurhammer 1973, 187n262, 205–6, 269; Bangert 1985, 149–50, 153–62; Scaduto 2001e.

a licentiate at an unknown date, and a master of arts in October 1536. He departed Paris the next month.[24]

Simão Rodrigues (Vouzela 1510–1579 Lisbon), a nobleman from northern Portugal, arrived at the University of Paris in fall 1527. He lived in the Collège de Sainte-Barbe as a stipendiary of the Portuguese king. After spending a short time improving his Latin, he began to study philosophy. He became part of Ignatius' circle in 1532. Rodrigues was one of the seven who on August 15, 1534, vowed themselves to perpetual poverty and chastity and to make a pilgrimage to the Holy Land or, that failing, to place themselves at the disposition of the pope.[25] Rodrigues obtained his licentiate in March 1536 and his master of arts degree in October 1536, and studied theology. He left Paris in November 1536.[26]

The Savoyard Claude Jay (Vers-lez-Jay 1500/04–1552 Vienna), a friend of Favre, arrived in Paris in October 1534 and lived with Favre at the Collège de Sainte-Barbe. He took his licentiate in March 1535 and his master of arts degree in October 1536. He probably also heard theology lectures. He left Paris for Venice with other first Jesuits in November 1536.[27]

Paschase Broët (Bertrancourt 1500–1562 Paris), from Picardie in northern France, was ordained a priest in 1524, and came to Paris at the end of 1532 or the beginning of 1533. He lived in the Collège de Calvi, as did Bobadilla, and met Favre, who guided him through the Spiritual Exercises. He studied philosophy and theology and obtained his licentiate on March 14, 1536. He left Paris in the middle of November 1536 for the planned meeting with Ignatius and the other first Jesuits in Venice.[28]

Jean Codure (Seyne 1508–1541 Rome), from the village of Seyne in the French Alps, enrolled in the University of Paris at the end of 1534, and studied philosophy and heard theology lectures. He made the Spiritual Exercises under Favre's guidance and pronounced the Montmartre vows on August 15, 1536. He obtained the licentiate of arts on March 14, 1536, and the master of arts on September 4, then left Paris in November 1536.[29]

Juan de Polanco (Burgos 1517–1576 Rome), the son of a wealthy merchant in Burgos in Old Castile, came to the University of Paris to study Lat-

24. Bobadilla 1970, vi–vii; Schurhammer 1973, 206–8, 256, 269; García-Villoslada 1990, 410–11; Dalmases 2001a; and Lewis 2004, 442–43.

25. The other six were Ignatius, Francis Xavier, Bobadilla, Favre, Laínez, and Salmerón. Jay did the same on the same date in 1535 and Broët and Codure in 1536. For brief accounts, see Dalmases 1985, 120–22; and García-Villoslada 1990, 413–15.

26. Schurhammer 1973, 189–90, 269; Vaz de Carvalho 2001b.

27. Schurhammer 1973, 259–61; Bangert 1985, 1–5, 9–16; Dalmases 2001e, 2142.

28. Schurhammer 1973, 261–63, 269; Bangert 1985, 1–5, 9–15; and Donnelly 2001b.

29. Schurhammer 1973, 263, 269; Dalmases 2001c.

in in 1530 when he was thirteen. He also studied philosophy for three years (1535–1538), and obtained a licentiate of arts and master of arts in 1538. His family then obtained for him an appointment as apostolic notary in Rome. There he met Ignatius and made the Spiritual Exercises under his direction. In 1541 he decided to become a Jesuit. He went on to become secretary and alter ego to Ignatius and secretary to the next two generals, Laínez (1556–1565) and Francisco de Borja (1565–1572). His influence on the Society went far beyond that of a secretary.[30]

Jerónimo Nadal (Palma de Mallorca 1507–1580 Rome) was born in the Balearic Islands. He went to the University of Alcalá de Henares in 1526 to study Latin, Greek, Hebrew, and philosophy, then to Paris in 1532 where he studied theology and mathematics. Although it is possible that he obtained one or more degrees at Alcalá de Henares and Paris, documentary evidence has not been found. Nadal was acquainted with Ignatius and other first Jesuits at Alcalá de Henares and Paris but resisted joining them. He left Paris in the autumn of 1536 during an outbreak of anti-Spanish hostility fueled by the renewal of war between France and Spain. He went to Avignon, ruled by the papacy, where he was ordained and received a doctorate of theology on May 11, 1538, becoming the only Jesuit in the group of twelve with a theology degree. Nadal then returned to Palma de Mallorca until invited to Rome in the autumn of 1545. There he renewed acquaintance with Ignatius and other Jesuits and entered the Society on November 29, 1545.[31] He went on to become a roving commissioner who visited Jesuit colleges throughout Europe implementing and interpreting Jesuit directives from Rome and dispensing advice.

The educational biographies of the Jesuit founders plus Nadal and Polanco demonstrate the extraordinary uniformity of their university educations. They all studied at the University of Paris for periods of two to eleven years, and an average of nearly six years.[32] Ten of them obtained licentiates of arts, and nine received both licentiate of arts and master of arts degrees from the University of Paris. Several lived and studied in the College of St. Barbara. The University of Alcalá de Henares was also important: five of the twelve

30. Dalmases 2001f, 3168; and *Year by Year* 2004, x.

31. Codina Mir 1967; Schurhammer 1973, 241–42; Bangert and McCoog 1992, 4–8, 17–26; Ruiz Jurado 2001a, 2794. For his doctorate at Avignon see chap. 14, "Quick Doctorates for the First Jesuits."

32. Twelve Jesuits spent a total of about 70 years of study in Paris; hence, 5.8 years per Jesuit. This is an approximate figure for several reasons. Classes did not meet twelve months of the year, the month in which a Jesuit arrived in Paris is not always known, and some of them spent indeterminate periods of time outside Paris.

TABLE 1-1. The University Educations of the First Jesuits

Jesuits	University Education Prior to Paris	Years/College in Paris	Degrees in Paris
Ignatius Loyola, 1491–1556	Barcelona, Alcalá, Salamanca	1528–1535, Montaigu, St. Barbe	BA 1532, LicA 1533, MA 1535
Nicolás Bobadilla, ca. 1509–1590	Alcalá 7 years, BA 1529; Valladolid	1533–1536, Regency at Calvi	LicA ?, MA 1536
Paschase Broët, ca. 1500–1562		1532/33–1536, Calvi	LicA
Jean Codure, 1508–1541		end of 1534–1536, Lisieux	LicA 1536, MA 1536
Pierre Favre, 1506–1546		1525–1536, Montaigu, St. Barbe	BA 1530, LicA 1530, MA 1536
Claude Jay, 1500/04–1552		1534–1536, St. Barbe	LicA 1535, MA 1536
Diego Laínez, 1512–1565	Alcalá 1529–1532, BA 1531, LicA 1532, MA 1532	1532–1536, St. Barbe?	
Simão Rodrigues, 1510–1579		1527–1536, St. Barbe	LicA 1536, MA 1536
Alfonso Salmerón, 1514–1585	Alcalá, possibly 1527–1532	1532–1536, St. Barbe?	LicA ?, MA 1536
Francis Xavier, 1506–1552		1525–1536, St. Barbe, 1530–1533, Regency Beauvais	BA 1529, LicA 1530, MA 1530
Jéronimo Nadal, 1507–1580	Alcalá 1526–1532, possible BA, LicA, MA	1532–1536, unknown	
Juan de Polanco, 1517–1576		1530–1539, unknown	LicA 1538, MA 1538

studied there, and three obtained at least one degree there. None of them studied anywhere except in Alcalá de Henares and Paris, with the very limited exceptions of Nadal's eighteen months at Avignon, the spotty study of Ignatius at Barcelona and Salamanca, and Bobadilla's brief time at Valladolid. The uniformity of their university experiences will inspire and limit the Jesuit educational vision.

Philosophical and Theological Choices

The instruction that the first Jesuits received in Paris and the choices that they made there shaped the philosophical and theological curricula of their future upper schools and universities.[33] Ignatius, Favre, Rodrigues, Francis Xavier, and possibly other first Jesuits, studied philosophy under the guidance of Juan de la Peña. From Castile, Peña enrolled at the University of Paris in 1522, obtained his master of arts degree in 1525, then taught philosophy as a regent master at the Collège de Sainte-Barbe. Since Peña came from a conservative tradition, it is very likely that he taught a conservative scholastic approach to Aristotelian philosophy.[34] Indeed, the curriculum and degree examination requirements of the University of Paris left little room for anything else. Hence, the first Jesuits at Paris learned scholastic Aristotelian logic and philosophy, and adopted it in their future upper schools and universities.[35]

But the major reason that the future Jesuits went to Paris was because it was the leading theological school of Europe. There they heard theology lectures for periods of time ranging from about two years to between five and six. Although Paris had over a hundred theologians, according to Nadal, and they held different views, the Jesuits decided to attend only the lectures of traditional scholastic theologians.[36] Two disputes roiling the University of Paris influenced the decision.

The first centered on biblical humanism, which meant the application of humanistic philological scholarly principles to the study of the Bible. Humanists argued that scholars should study the holy book in its original languages in order to understand better God's Word. Jacques Lefèvre d'Étaples (ca. 1460–1536), who taught at the Collège de Cardinal Lemoine before 1508, and Desiderius Erasmus (1467–1536), who was a student at the Collège de Montaigu for less than a year in 1495 and 1496, were pioneering biblical humanists whose works attracted considerable attention in Paris. Biblical humanists were ready to use Greek or Hebrew manuscripts to cor-

---

33. This is not the place to discuss the influence of the Paris colleges on the curriculum and pedagogy of the classes in Latin grammar, humanities, and rhetoric in the Jesuit lower schools in Italy. Farrell 1938; Codina Mir 1968, 300–330; and esp. MP vols. 1–3 provide much material. However, it should be noted that the Renaissance humanistic curriculum developed by fifteenth-century Italian pedagogical humanists also had a major influence on Jesuit schools, especially in Italy. For example, Jesuit lower schools in Italy discarded medieval grammar manuals such as the *Doctrinale* (ca. 1199) of Alexander de Villedieu, which was still taught in Paris, in favor of humanist manuals, such as those of Guarino Guarini (1374–1460) and Erasmus. And they emphasized direct and intense reading of the ancient classics themselves. In general, grammar and humanities classes in Italian Jesuit schools adopted the sequential courses and pedagogical exercises of Parisian colleges but emphasized classical texts and humanist manuals more than their Paris teachers had. See Grendler 1989, 377–81; and O'Malley 1993, 215–25.

34. Schurhammer 1973, 108–10.

35. See Grendler 2009b, 200–209, for a summary.

36. Lécrivain 2011, 156, 159. Nadal wrote in 1557.

rect the traditional Vulgate (Latin translation) when necessary. They relied on newly edited and printed versions of the Bible based on manuscripts, especially Erasmus' Greek New Testament accompanied by a revised Vulgate first published in 1516. Biblical humanists also believed that studying ancient religious texts with the aid of information gleaned from other authors and texts from the early Christian era helped explain them. Thus, theologians inspired by humanism assigned higher priority to the early Church Fathers than to medieval and contemporary scholastic authors, whom they criticized for a sterile methodology.[37]

The Faculty of Theology of the University of Paris viewed matters differently. In 1523 it began an assault on what it considered to be theologizing humanists and humanistic theologizing, an assault that continued through the next twenty years and beyond.[38] The Faculty of Theology censured Lefèvre's commentary on the Gospels in 1523. In 1525, just as Francis Xavier arrived, the Faculty of Theology denounced Erasmus' scriptural exegesis. It condemned new Latin translations of the Bible based on Greek and Hebrew texts, an action directed especially at Lefèvre d'Etaples and Erasmus. It censured passages from the works of Erasmus that commented on, often satirically and negatively, fasts, oaths, celibacy, and the indissolubility of marriage. It did the same with books and passages written by other biblical humanists. Led by Erasmus, the biblical humanists fought back with their pens. They especially criticized Noel Beda (ca. 1470–1537), the deeply conservative syndic and leading voice of the Faculty of Theology.

Despite the opposition, biblical humanists found places in Paris. Francis I in 1530 created five royal lectureships, two in Greek and three in Hebrew, with additional appointments in subsequent years. Some in Paris saw this as royal endorsement of humanistic studies, but this was an exaggeration. Although lacking precise institutional status, the royal lecturers delivered their lectures in colleges and attracted university students. These endowed royal lectureships came to be called the Collège Royal in the seventeenth century and were renamed the Collège de France later.[39]

The royal lecturers argued that the Vulgate needed to be emended to make it conform with the Greek and Hebrew texts. But altering the Vulgate might have theological implications. Hence, the Faculty of Theology con-

37. There is a large bibliography on biblical humanism. Good recent works include Rummel 1995, esp. chap. 5; Jenkins and Preston 2007; the studies in *Biblical Humanism* 2008; and Rummel 2009.

38. Farge 1985, 170–219; Farge 1992a, 40–42, 117–31, for documents; Farge 1992b; Farge 2008; and Bedouelle 2008.

39. Farge 2014.

cluded that they were teaching theology, and bad theology at that, without permission. Therefore, in 1534 it brought suit in the Parlement of Paris against the royal lecturers of Greek and Hebrew for teaching theology without permission of the Faculty, although it did not oppose the teaching of Greek and Hebrew that did not involve the Bible. The Parlement of Paris agreed; it forbade the royal lecturers from criticizing the Vulgate.[40] Although it was a victory for the Faculty of Theology, the war continued. The royal lecturers and some philosophy teachers in the colleges embraced humanism to a greater or lesser degree, while the overwhelming majority of theologians and most regent masters did not.

The first Jesuits encountered the dispute between scholastic theology and biblical humanism in the College of St. Barbara. Diogo de Gouvea, the principal, was hostile to humanism and condemned Erasmus.[41] However, during his absence in Portugal from November 1529 to September 1531, André de Gouvea, his nephew, became principal. He disliked scholastic theology, favored humanism, and brought in some like-minded controversial figures. When Diogo de Gouvea returned, he reasserted a conservative scholastic direction.[42] Indeed, he judged those who knew Greek and philosophy to be Lutherans.[43]

The second matter that roiled the University of Paris was Protestantism. Some Protestants and their sympathizers moved in the same circles as the first Jesuits. In 1530 Principal André de Gouvea brought Nicolas Cop (ca. 1501–1540), a friend of Jean Calvin, into the College of St. Barbara as a regent in philosophy. In October 1533 Cop was elected rector of the university for the usual three-month term, and on November 1, he preached a controversial sermon in a church considered to be part of the university. He denounced scholasticism, endorsed justification by faith alone, decried the forceful suppression of heresy, and generated an uproar. The Faculty of Theology uncovered six heretical opinions in his sermon and presented its findings to the Parlement of Paris. The latter ordered an investigation; this produced lengthy meetings and much rhetoric from members of the university community, the usual response of academics of all centuries. André de Gouvea defended Cop; many did not. Parlement ordered Cop to appear before it on November 20, 1533. Warned that Parlement intended to arrest him, Cop fled to Basel.[44] The

40. Farge 1985, 205–6; Farge 1992a, 40–42, 117–31; and Farge 2008, 162–64.

41. Schurhammer 1973, 101–2, 134–36, 137n239, 171, and the index.

42. Bernard-Maître 1950, 822; Schurhammer 1973, 162–67, 171, 192.

43. Codina Mir 1968, 79.

44. Schurhammer 1973, 192–200, gives a good account. See also Farge 1992b, 236; and Farge 1996a.

affair of the placards that came on the night of October 17/18, 1534, was far more unsettling. Broadsheets attacking the Mass appeared throughout Paris. In the following months and years the crown with the concurrence of Parlement retaliated by arresting and executing by burning or strangulation numerous men and women judged to be Protestants.

The nearly simultaneous appearance of biblical humanism and Protestantism, followed by the strong condemnations of the Faculty of Theology, persuaded many in the university community to conclude that the humanist approach to sacred studies led to heresy. They included the first Jesuits. Bobadilla noted that the Lutheran presence in Paris had resulted in many burnings and concluded that "qui graecizabant, lutheranizabant" (those who were fond of Greek were fond of Luther). Although Bobadilla probably read some of the works of Erasmus while at Alcalá and had come to Paris to study Greek and Hebrew, Ignatius counseled him to avoid the royal professors and to study scholastic and positive theology with Dominican and Franciscan professors. That is what he did.[45]

In 1530 Ignatius advised Francis Xavier to attend the theological lectures of the Dominicans or Franciscans rather than those of the royal lecturers.[46] Ignatius and the other first Jesuits therefore went to the Dominican monastery near the Pont Saint-Jacques and, to a lesser extent, to a Franciscan monastery of the strict observance for theology. They heard scholastics who generally endorsed the condemnations of biblical humanism and Erasmus' works by the Faculty of Theology.[47]

45. "Eo tempore incipiebat grassari Parisiis haeresis lutherana, et multi comburebantur in platea Mumbert, et qui graecizabant, lutheranizabant." Bobadilla 1970, 614–15 (quotation at 614). It comes from his autobiography, in which he referred to himself in the third person. Lécrivain 2011, 150–51, provides an English translation of the whole paragraph with a slightly different translation of this sentence. See also Codina Mir 1968, 79; and Schurhammer 1973, 171n187, 208, 256. The charge that the study of Greek led to heresy was uncommon but not unknown. Erasmus in *The Antibarbarians* of 1520 wrote "these latter are persuaded by the successful tricksters that to know Greek is heresy" (CWE, 23:32). I am grateful to Erika Rummel for this reference. For the report that Bobadilla probably read Erasmus at Alcalá de Henares, see Lewis 2004, 442. One caution: Bobadilla wrote his autobiography after he reached the age of eighty, and after the Jesuits had decisively turned against Erasmus. People who write autobiographies late in life do not always remember the past perfectly. Two recent accounts of the complex story of the attitudes of the first Jesuits toward Erasmus are O'Malley 1993, 260–64, and the index; and Grendler 2014.

46. Schurhammer 1973, 171.

47. Favre provided the names of seven theologians who taught the Jesuits in Paris. They were two Dominicans (Jean Benoît and Thomas Laurent), the Franciscan Pierre de Cornet (Cornibus), plus Jean Adam, Jacques Barthélemy, François Picart, and Robert Wauchope (or Wancob). See the letter of Pierre Favre to Diogo de Gouvea of November 23, 1538, Rome, in *Ignatii Epistolae*, 1964–1968, 1:133–34; English translation in Ignatius of Loyola 1974, 105. For further information on them see Farge 1992b, 232–33, who adds the Dominicans Matthieu Ory

The first Jesuits were unanimous in their preference for scholastic theology and distrust and hostility toward biblical theology. Ignatius advised Nadal not to study Greek without theology, presumably scholastic theology, because this would lead to novelties in the faith. Nadal agreed, and included what Ignatius had said in his commentary (*scholia*) on the Jesuit Constitutions that he wrote years later.[48] In another work Nadal strongly endorsed scholastic theology because it provided certainty and avoided perplexity in doctrine, which he saw as a grave danger. He endorsed humanistic studies and the study of Greek and Hebrew, but not as part of theology.[49] In 1542 Jay noted Erasmus' scriptural errors and concluded that he was a pagan.[50] Salmerón praised traditional scholastic philosophy and lamented the harm done by Erasmus' erroneous annotations and paraphrases of the New Testament.[51]

Ignatius codified his choice of scholastic theology by adding a new section to the Spiritual Exercises entitled "Rules on Thinking with the Church." He probably wrote most of the rules in Paris in 1534 or 1535, and the rest in Rome shortly after November 1537.[52] The eleventh rule endorsing scholastic theology was probably the result of his experiences in Paris.

We ought to praise both positive theology and scholastic theology. For just as it is more characteristic of the positive doctors, such as St. Jerome, St. Augustine, St. Gregory [the Great], and the rest to stir up our affections toward loving and serving God our Lord in all things, so it is more characteristic of the scholastic teachers, such as St. Thomas, St. Bonaventure, the Master of the Sentences [Peter Lombard], and so on, to define and explain for our times the matters necessary for salvation, and also to refute and expose all the errors and fallacies. For the scholastic teachers, being more modern, can avail themselves of an authentic understanding of Sacred Scripture and the holy positive doctors. Further still they, being enlightened and clarified by divine influence, make profitable use of the councils, canons, and decrees of our Holy Mother Church.[53]

---

and Gilles Binet, the Franciscans Michel Foullon and Richard DuMans, plus Marial Mazurier to the list. For a little additional information, see Codina Mir 1968, 261–62; Bobadilla 1970, 614; Schurhammer 1973, 134, 184–85, 194, 208, 247–51, 256, and the index; García-Villoslada 1990, 381–82; and O'Malley 1993, 245–48.

48. Nadal 1976, 102–3. Nadal wrote the *scholia* between 1556 and 1561 and revised it later. Both Codina Mir 1968, 79n107; and Schurhammer 1973, 169n166, quote some of Nadal's words from an earlier edition.

49. Nadal 1898–1962, 5:828–29. This was part of an unfinished *exhortatio* on sections of the Constitutions, written between 1573 and 1576. O'Malley 1993, 257, also notes this.

50. Schurhammer 1973, 261n108.

51. Schurhammer 1973, 255; Bangert 1985, 157–62; O'Malley 1993, 263–64.

52. O'Malley 1993, 49.

53. The English translation is that of George E. Ganss in Ignatius of Loyola 1991, 212. The eleventh rule (of eighteen) is par. 363 of the *Spiritual Exercises*.

The eleventh rule presented two different theological approaches and why Ignatius preferred one of them. Positive theology, a term just coming into use, meant the study of scripture, patristic authors, and other foundational texts for theological doctrines. Ignatius endorsed reading scripture and the Church Fathers because they "stir up our affections toward loving and serving God our Lord." This was the classic humanist view that words should move and persuade. But he relied on scholastic theology to interpret and explain scripture and the ancient Fathers. Thomas and the other scholastics, "being more modern," had "an authentic understanding" of them and could extract what was necessary for salvation "for our times." And in a bow to the religious disputes of the century, Ignatius added that the scholastics would also expose and refute errors. His intent was to elevate scholastic theology above positive theology; the Jesuits would turn to the scholastics to understand and interpret the sacred texts. They were "more modern."

Despite the title, the "Rules for Thinking with the Church" were not rules to be strictly observed, but principles or cautions for Jesuits to keep in mind in pastoral practice.[54] They help to explain why Ignatius chose scholastic theology. He wanted theology that would inform and prepare members of the Society to be effective caretakers of souls in the world. He did not believe that study of the foundational texts of Christianity in their original languages would do this so well as the study of scholastic theology, which had a record of success. The eleventh rule is also important for the scholastics omitted, above all, John Duns Scotus (ca. 1266–1308) and William of Ockham (ca. 1285–1347). The Jesuits did not adopt Scotism or nominalism, even though the latter was the strongest philosophical current at the University of Paris, and they had attended the lectures of several Franciscans who usually followed Scotus.[55] The Jesuits would develop and teach a modified Thomism enriched by new insights and the Renaissance emphasis on the individual conscience.

Ignatius did not rule out studying scripture and the ancient Fathers in their original languages. Nor were the first Jesuits ignorant of Greek and other biblical languages or humanistic scholarship. Salmerón studied Greek, Hebrew, and Syriac, and later wrote sixteen volumes of commentary on the New Testament in which he put to use his knowledge of ancient languages and used editions of the Church Fathers that Erasmus edited.[56] Nadal knew Hebrew well enough to teach it in Messina. The Jesuits

---

54. O'Malley 1993, 49–50, makes this point.

55. Farge 1992b, 224.

56. Schurhammer 1973, 254–56; Bangert 1985, 328–29, 334–44; and the overview of Jesuit theological culture and humanism in O'Malley 1993, 243–64.

did not ban Greek from their schools. On the contrary, they integrated Greek grammar and reading into all three classes (grammar, humanities, and rhetoric) of the lower school. A few larger Jesuit schools in Italy had professorships of Greek now and then. Future Jesuit theologians showed themselves to be variegated, complex, and full of original comments on issues and controversies unknown to the medieval scholastics.

But the Jesuits made a choice. In their schools and universities they will name their professorships of theology "Scholastic Theology" and decree that the teachers must follow Thomas Aquinas, with permission to differ with him on some points.[57] The Jesuits endorsed scholasticism, as did the University of Paris, other Catholic universities, religious orders, and theologians across Europe. In most cases religious orders and universities simply continued a commitment to scholastic theology begun centuries earlier. In Italy a promising biblical humanist movement in the first third of the sixteenth century petered out in part because of the lack of institutional support.[58] In embracing scholastic theology the Jesuits conformed to the approach and curriculum of Italian universities, which taught a small amount of Thomist scholastic theology, or Scotist scholastic theology, or a little of both.

The First Jesuits at Italian Universities

When the first Jesuits came to Italy they encountered Italian universities, and they did not like what they saw.

In November 1537 Pope Paul III appointed Favre and Laínez to teach theology at the University of Rome. Their appointments came about because Paul III was impressed when he heard them debate as he dined. Laínez taught scholastic theology by lecturing on the *Sacri canonis missae . . . expositio* (first edition 1488), an explanation of the canon of the Mass by the German nominalist theologian Gabriel Biel (ca. 1410–1495). This was not a nominalist treatise but an often-printed manual of practical pastoral theology. Although he was the best theologian of the first Jesuits and an excellent disputant, Laínez by his own admission was not a successful teacher at first. But he steadily improved until all who heard him, even members of the Roman Curia who showed up at his lectures, approved.[59] This was his only known comment about his experience at the University of Rome. Fa-

---

57. *Ratio Studiorum* 2005, 62–95.

58. Grendler 2008.

59. Letter of Polanco, written for Laínez, to Giulio Onofrio, Rome, November 21, 1556, in *Lainii Epistolae* 1912–1917, 1:102; Tacchi Venturi 1951a, 102; Scaduto 1964, 129; and Schurhammer 1973, 411.

vre taught positive theology in which he focused on the Bible. Laínez and Favre taught two years at the University of Rome, leaving in the summer of 1539.[60] And a single source states that Salmerón lectured and preached at the University of Rome, possibly in the academic year 1539–1540.[61]

In April 1542 the Jesuits established a college of eight Jesuits at Padua, the fourth college of the young order. Ignatius immediately sent Juan de Polanco and André des Freux, also known as Frusius (Chartres ca. 1515–1556 Rome), two of his most promising young recruits, to study at the University of Padua.[62] Polanco was told to review philosophy and then study theology, while André des Freux would study philosophy.[63]

In May 1542, shortly after his arrival, Polanco reported to Laínez that the lectures in natural philosophy and metaphysics were good. But there were not enough of them, and the students had little opportunity to practice arguing and disputing, the kind of academic exercise of their wits, memory, and tongue that would solidify and make permanent in their minds what they had learned. And he criticized the theology professors for their slow pace. They lingered so long on single questions that he feared that they would not cover the theological course in his lifetime. Polanco's solution was twofold. He decided to do most of his theological study on his own, and he would find private philosophy lectures for André des Freux. If he could not find good private teachers, Polanco himself would teach him logic and dispute with him.[64]

60. Carafa 1971, 2:451–52; Renazzi 1971, 2:99; Salmerón 1971–1972, 2:734–35; *Fontes narrativi* 1943–1960, 1:122–23; Tacchi Venturi 1951a, 93, 102; and Schurhammer 1973, 411.

61. In 1557 Nadal wrote "M. Salmerón Romae legebat in academia Sapientiae et concionabur." *Fontes narrativi* 1943–1960, 2:94. This was part of Nadal's unpublished "Apologia contra censuram Facultatis Theologiae Parisiensis," his long and passionate response to the condemnation of the Society of Jesus by the Faculty of Theology of the University of Paris on December 1, 1554. However, notes 125 and 127 on the same page indicate that no other source confirms this. Schurhammer 1973, 496; and Bangert 1985, 165, repeat the statement that Salmerón taught at the University of Rome without additional documentation, and Bangert calculates that he taught there in the academic year 1539–1540.

62. Born into a poor family, des Freux obtained a master of arts at the University of Paris at an unknown date. After ordination he became a parish priest in a village near Versailles, then entered the service of Cardinal Rodolfo Pio da Carpi, nuncio to Paris. He came to Rome with Pio, met Ignatius, and entered the Society of Jesus in 1541. The best classical scholar of the early Jesuits, Des Freux edited Martial, Horace, and Terence for school use, wrote orations, and translated the *Spiritual Exercises* into elegant Latin. He taught at Messina, then played key roles in the early years of the Roman College and the German College. Scaduto 1964, 7–9; Lukács 2001b.

63. Martini 1952, 229, 234; and *Year by Year* 2004, 13–14. García de Castro Valdés 2012, 95–102, also describes Polanco's studies at Padua.

64. See Polanco's letter to Laínez of May 18, 1542, Padua, in Polanco 1969, 1:2–3; it is reprinted in MP 1:358–59. See also Martini 1952, 234; O'Malley 1993, 203; and Brizzi 1994, 473.

The University of Padua offered considerably more instruction in theology and metaphysics than any other Italian university at this time. In 1542 it had two professors of theology, a Dominican who taught theology "in via S.ti. Thomae" and a Franciscan Conventual who taught "in via Scotti." It had another Dominican who taught Thomist metaphysics and another Franciscan who taught Scotist metaphysics. All four were conservative scholastics, and none was distinguished.[65] Most of the students who attended their lectures were members of medieval mendicant orders. Dominicans and members of other religious orders that followed Thomas, such as the Carmelites, normally attended the Thomist theology and metaphysics lectures, while Franciscans and Augustinians heard Scotist theology and metaphysics lectures. This was the theological instruction that Polanco found wanting.

Despite Polanco's criticism, the leadership in Rome continued to send young Jesuits to study at the University of Padua. Themselves university men, they still hoped that universities could educate new members of the Society. By 1546 there were fourteen Jesuits at Padua. At least eleven of them, including three priests, were students at various levels.[66]

The Jesuit leadership in Rome, probably in the person of Laínez expressing the views of Ignatius, sent strict instructions concerning what was expected of young Jesuits at the University of Padua. The Jesuit students were told to learn what was necessary so that they would be prepared to teach grammar, dialectic, logic, philosophy, and theology; to hear confessions; to exhort; and to preach the word of God for the health of souls.[67] Rome had precise ideas about the educational program that would accomplish these goals. Those studying Latin grammar were to attend "scole delli putti" (classes for children); they should choose the best teacher that

---

65. For the artists' roll (at Padua theologians were listed with the professors of philosophy, medicine, logic, and humanities) for the academic year 1543–1544 of the University of Padua see AAUP, Inventario 320, no foliation. The artists' roll for 1542–1543 is missing. However, the names of the four theologians and metaphysicians who taught in 1542–1543 can be found in Simioni 1934, 60, 63, 67, 68; and in Facciolati 1978, part 3, 251–52, 256, 259, 263. For more on the teaching of theology and metaphysics at the University of Padua, see Grendler 2002, 366–72.

66. Martini 1952, 232.

67. "Circa il modo de studiare li nostri scolari di Padova" in MP 1:3–17, and 1:6 for the opening sentence stating the educational goals, which lists both "dialectica" and "logica." The anonymous document lacks a date, and the Italian is awkward, which suggests that the author was not an Italian. Lukács, in MP 1:3–5, believes that Laínez wrote it. However, he has identified the hand as that of one of the Italian Jesuits at Padua, which means that the document is a copy of the original. In any case, this was the first known attempt to draft procedures and rules for educating Jesuits. Lukács assigns the date of 1546. It must be after September 1, 1546, when Polanco left Padua, because the text would have mentioned him if he were still there.

they could find, preferably one who taught for free. Four better-prepared Jesuits, including Pedro de Ribadeneira (Toledo 1526–1611 Madrid), future biographer of Ignatius and historian, were directed to attend the lectures of Lazzaro Bonamico (1477/78–1552), professor of Latin and Greek humanities at the University of Padua.[68] A fervent Ciceronian, Bonamico had an enormous scholarly reputation in his lifetime, even though he wrote little. Ribadeneira was still attending Bonamico's lectures in the academic year 1547–1548.[69]

Jesuits studying logic and philosophy were told to attend classes at the university, or in convents, or from good private teachers, the choice to be made by the Jesuit superior at Padua.[70] Jesuit students were expected to hear lectures on the entire logic of Aristotle plus some material from Porphyry in one year. (The *Isagoge* or *Introduction* of Porphyry [234–ca. 305] was often used to help teach Aristotle's logic.) They were to devote another two-and-a-half years to natural philosophy, metaphysics, mathematics, and moral philosophy, depending on the availability of lectures. Finally, the two most senior Jesuits at Padua, Fathers Pierre De Smet (Brussels ca. 1518–1548 Padua) and Elpidio Ugoletti (Parma 1516–1580 Palermo) were allowed to study as they wished, which meant that they might study privately or attend lectures from anyone they chose.[71]

Above all, the Jesuit leadership exhorted and ordered the Jesuits at Padua to participate in academic exercises, including repetitions, declamations, and disputations, as much as possible. They were to do repetitions immediately after hearing a lecture and for an hour in the evening. They were told to engage in public disputations every Sunday after the midday meal with non-Jesuits invited to participate. All the academic exercises should take place in the Jesuit college unless a university professor joined them, in which case they might dispute in his house.[72] The 1546 instructions from Rome showed the direction of Jesuit thinking about higher education before the first Jesuit school in Italy was established. The leadership wanted

68. "Circa il modo de studiare ... di Padova," in MP 1:6–7. Bonamico taught at the University of Padua from 1530 until his death; for more, see Avesani 1969 and Grendler 2002, 40, 166, 233–34. The other three Jesuits were Giovanni Battista Tavona (Modena ca. 1520–1573 Bivona); possibly Henricus Hucker of whom very little is known; and Fulvio Cardulo (Narni 1529–1591 Rome), who taught rhetoric at the Roman College for many years. For Tavona, see Scaduto 1968, 144; for Cardulo, see Scaduto 1968, 37; Lukács 2001a; and Maryks 2010, 137n91.

69. MP 1:46.

70. "Circa il modo de studiare ... di Padova," in MP 1:8–9, 11–12.

71. "Circa il modo de studiare ... di Padova," in MP 1:8, 11, 13. On 1:8 the time allowed was four years. For De Smet and Ugoletti, see Scaduto 1968, 46, 149.

72. "Circa il modo de studiare ... di Padova," in MP 1:7–13.

young Jesuits to attend university lectures that taught Aristotelian philosophy. That was no surprise. At the same time, they strongly endorsed pedagogical exercises, a feature of the Paris colleges. By contrast, students in Italian universities engaged in academic exercises, especially disputations, spontaneously rather than as a requirement, and probably less frequently.

On the other hand, the Jesuits studied theology privately at Padua rather than hearing lectures. Polanco did this for four years, 1542 to 1546, as he sought a theology that had clear doctrinal definitions and was pastorally useful. He apparently found it in Thomas Aquinas and his major Renaissance interpreter, Tommaso de Vio (called Cajetan, 1469–1534), because they dominated his reading. He also read Scotist theologians, but not the nominalists, and he studied commentaries on the Bible. He did not read the few works written by Paduan theologians. His spiritual reading was broad, except that he practically ignored the Church Fathers.[73] None of the Jesuits who studied at Padua took any degrees there. Polanco, André des Freux, and a third Jesuit, Girolamo Otello (Bassano ca. 1520–1581 Verona), completed their private theological study at Padua and left for pastoral ministries at Bologna and elsewhere just before September 4, 1546.[74]

The cumulative judgment of the Jesuits about the University of Padua was unfavorable. In 1549 Polanco repeated his earlier criticism that few university lectures were useful or stimulated fervor. Even good university lectures did not prepare Jesuits adequately for working in the vineyard of the Lord. Therefore he had looked to private lectures and Jesuit house lectures to supply what was missing.[75] Ignatius agreed that Italian universities did not provide good lectures.[76]

Nevertheless, the Jesuits gave the University of Padua a second chance. On October 23, 1557, Polanco, now an important figure in the Society, wrote to the rectors of the Jesuit colleges at Padua and Venice telling them that Jesuit scholastics then at Padua should attend university lectures, as Pedro de Ribadeneira and other Jesuits had done earlier. This would yield several benefits, Polanco opined. Young Jesuits would learn from good teachers, and through their conversations with university students they might bring some of them to Christ. Attending lectures would also earn the goodwill of professors, which would lead to invitations to the Jesuits

73. Martini 1952. See also Polanco's letter to Bernardino da Salina of October 28, 1549, Rome, in Polanco 1969, 1:50–51.

74. *Year by Year* 2004, 43.

75. MP 1:517–18.

76. Letter of Polanco, written for Ignatius, to Nadal of July 6, 1549, Rome, in *Ignatii Epistolae*, 1964–1968, 2:463.

to participate in public disputations. In such an atmosphere of cooperation and goodwill, the Jesuit school in Padua might attract more students.[77] This last was important, because it was struggling.[78]

This second attempt ended eighteen months later because the university was "too depraved." In the spring of 1559 two Jesuits were attending university lectures there, although not continuously, with the approval of the new rector at the Jesuit college at Padua. On May 4, 1559, Benedetto Palmio (Parma 1523–1598 Ferrara), the new superior of the Jesuit Province of Lombardy, which embraced all of northern Italy at that time, wrote to Laínez to object: the university was too depraved and the Jesuit students were too young. He did not want Jesuits to converse with or engage in disputations with the "intristi" (evildoers) of a university that was "che è più depravata che mai" (more depraved than ever). He forbade Jesuit students from attending university lectures.[79]

More than likely the evildoers to which Palmio referred were Protestant students; his personal experience at Padua influenced him in this regard. In August or September 1557 Laínez had sent Palmio to Padua to preach.[80] Palmio discovered that there were heretics in Padua. This was no surprise, because the Republic of Venice allowed German Protestant students to attend the university. He wanted to denounce them in his sermons, but Laínez ordered him to proceed cautiously. He should not denounce them unless he was sure that they had proven themselves heretics in word or deed, and he should take counsel from a confessor in these matters. Most

77. "L'altra cosa è che li nostri sentano le lectioni publici di Padova come già fece Pietro Ribadeneira et altri. Il che sarà causa a loro de imparare da maestri valenti et anche essendo bene instruendi del modo di conversare potriano tirar alcuni buoni suppositi alle cose spirituali et per questa via guadagnare alcuni a X.o et essendovi occasione guadagnata la benevolentia deli mastri potriano fare alcune nostri in publico et altre demostrationi et con questo forsa si tirarà più gente alle schole nostre." Letter of Polanco to Cesare Elmi of October 23, 1557, Rome, in ARSI, Italiae 61, f. 4v. See also Scaduto 1974, 425. The letter does not indicate whether Polanco, now secretary to Laínez, spoke for him. (After the death of Loyola, Laínez was elected vicar general on August 4, 1556, and general on July 2, 1558.) Nevertheless, one wonders if this second attempt to send young Jesuits to study at the University of Padua originated with Laínez. Widely-read, he was more open to different scholarly views than Ignatius.

78. The Padua Jesuits had opened a lower school for external students in 1552. For its fortunes, see chap. 5, "The Jesuit School at Padua."

79. Letter of Palmio to General Laínez of May 4, 1559, Ferrara, in ARSI, Italiae 114, f. 260v; and Scaduto 1974, 425. No response from Laínez has been located. The new rector at Padua who approved of Jesuits attending university lectures was probably Father Lucio Croce (Tivoli ca. 1532–1596 Rome) about whom little is known. Scaduto 1968, 39.

80. See the letter of Polanco writing for Laínez to Giovanni Battista Tavona of August 7, 1557, Rome, and the letter of Polanco, possibly written for Laínez, to Andrea Lippomano of August 21, 1557, Rome, in Lainii Epistolae 1912–1917, 2:346, 381.

important, Laínez told Palmio that he should exhort rather than denounce in his preaching.[81]

The Jesuits concluded that Italian universities were depraved places that placed young men at grave moral and spiritual risk. In 1572 Michele Lauretano (Recanati 1537–1587 Rome), prefect of studies for the humanities at the German College in Rome, denounced Italian universities in strong language. They were full of rascals who devoted themselves to games of chance, questions, factions, and dishonesties and indecencies in word and deed. They led men to reject the Catholic faith and to become atheists. A youth of sixteen to eighteen who attended an Italian university was alone and vulnerable. He had money to spend and a thousand opportunities to get into trouble. Because fathers could no longer watch over them, university students fell under the influence of madmen (*pazzi*) and evildoers (*tristi*) of the worst kind, because they were learned as well as evil. When youths imbibed corrupt habits and engaged in sacrilegious and nefarious actions at an impressionable age, it was very difficult to cure them later, Lauretano warned. Such youths, so badly educated at universities, will damage the community when they become the rulers of civil and ecclesiastical institutions.[82] Although Lauretano's diatribe was written in the context of another dispute, it expressed the dominant Jesuit view at this time, especially the fear that youths who attended Italian universities would become atheists.[83]

81. Letter of Laínez to Palmio of February 19, 1558, Rome, in *Lainii Epistolae* 1912–1917, 3:138. For more on Palmio, see chaps. 5, 6, 14, and the appendix. For a brief biography, see Zanfredini 2001f.

82. "L'università d'Italia et l'academie che sono sparse in diversi luoghi ... per la maggior parte sono piene de discoli che non attendono se non a giuochi, questioni, fattioni, disonestà et sporcitie di fatti et di paruole, le quali così insieme con la vanità delle scientie conducono gli huomini all'ateismo, et li fanno reprobi circa fidem." MP 2:996–97 (entire memorandum 994–1004). "Accademia" had many meanings: a university, a school, a society of learned men, even an informal debating society, in sixteenth-century Italy. For Lauretano, see Jacobs 2001.

83. Lauretano wrote because he wanted to keep the German College in Rome open to Italian lay students. Founded by the Jesuits in 1552, the Collegium Germanicum was intended to be a boarding school for the education of German youths preparing for the priesthood. Jesuits in Germany chose likely candidates who were sent south to live for several years free of charge at the German College while attending classes at the Roman College. After ordination, they were expected to return to their homelands to help restore Catholicism. However, the German College got off to a rocky start and nearly closed for the lack of financial support. To keep it open General Laínez in 1558 permitted it to accept secular boarders who paid high fees. The solution created new problems. By about 1570, the German College had some 250 boarders, of whom 80 to 90 percent were Italian secular youths, many of them sons of powerful noble families. And some of them behaved badly. An intense debate among the Jesuits about the future of the German College ensued. Lauretano wanted to keep the doors open to Italian lay boarders in order to keep them out of Italian universities. The crisis passed in 1573 when Pope Gregory XIII provided

The verdict was in. Polanco and Ignatius criticized Italian universities for their alleged pedagogical insufficiencies, while Palmio and Lauretano saw them as dens of iniquity and seedbeds of atheism. The leaders of the Society did not send any more young Jesuits to study at Italian universities after Palmio's veto.[84] Their disillusionment with Italian universities was not unique. Between 1540 and 1544 the Society established its first nine residences and colleges in Alcalá de Henares, Coimbra, Cologne, Lisbon, Louvain, Padua, Paris, Rome, and Valencia, all university towns except Lisbon. The Jesuit leadership hoped that young Jesuits might study at the universities in these towns. But they were found wanting.[85] Disappointment with the instruction and dismay at the perceived immoral culture of Europe's universities was a major reason that the Society decided to create its own universities.

Conclusion

Their own university educations had a huge impact on the ten founding Jesuits (as well as Nadal and Polanco) and the educational policies of the Society. All of the first Jesuits studied in colleges in the University of Paris for a number of years, and some of them studied in Spanish universities as well. All twelve acquired more than one university degree. The first Jesuits warmly endorsed the experience of learning and living in collegiate universities such as Paris, and they believed in and accepted the curriculum and pedagogy of Paris. After the foundation of the Society in 1540, the Italian Jesuits also believed that they could send their recruits to the University of Padua to be educated. Disillusioned with Padua, they decided to create their own universities. Their first attempt was at Messina.

---

substantial financial and moral support. An increasing number of German youths enrolled, the Italian lay boarders were eased out, and the college began to fulfill its original purpose. Scaduto 1974, 325–33; Schmidt 1984. For the history of the German College as a whole, see Scaduto 1992, 186–90; O'Malley 1993, 234–36; Gerhartz 2001; and Cesareo 2004, 621–29.

84. Older scholarship states that Robert Bellarmine (Montepulciano 1542–1621 Rome) attended lectures at the University of Padua when he was at the Jesuit college in Padua from 1567 to 1569 where his primary duty was Sunday preaching. Then he discovered that a Dominican professor "was taking everything word for word from a commentary on St. Thomas which he could read more profitably for himself." So he stopped attending lectures. Brodrick 1961, 21–22. However, recent scholarship does not see him as hearing lectures at all. Rather, he studied theology privately by following a commentary on the *Summa Theologica* of Aquinas written by the Jesuit Francisco de Toledo (Córdoba 1532–1596 Rome) that he had copied with his own hand earlier at Rome. Galeota 2001, 387.

85. See Lukács 1960–1961, part 1, 199; Codina Mir 1968, 256–57, 259–60; and Gonçalves 2004, 713.

2

THE BATTLE

OF MESSINA AND THE JESUIT

CONSTITUTIONS

The Jesuits and the city of Messina attempted to create a new university in Messina in 1548. But they had different visions. The Jesuits wanted a collegiate university under their control, and the city desired an Italian law and medicine university of shared governance. At a time when the negotiations were at a stalemate, Ignatius Loyola (with the assistance of Nadal) wrote for the Constitutions of the Society prescriptions for Jesuit universities that codified the collegiate university model. Because the Society adopted the Constitutions in 1558, its recommendations influenced future Jesuit policy.

A University for Messina

The Jesuits opened a school in Messina in 1548. Several people worked hard to achieve this result, including the viceroy, Juan de Vega (1507–1558). He had previously served as Spanish ambassador to the pope (1543 to 1547) at which time Ignatius became a friend and informal spiritual adviser to the viceroy, his wife Leonor Osorio de Astorga (d. 1550), and their children. Moreover, Osorio had helped Ignatius establish a house for wayward women in Rome.[1] In late December 1546 King Charles I of Spain appointed Vega as viceroy of Sicily. Vega and Osorio arrived in Messina on Septem-

---

1. In addition to Messina, several members of the Vega family strongly supported the Jesuits elsewhere in Sicily. Viceroy Vega and Osorio de Astorga played key roles in establishing the Jesuit college at Palermo in 1549. Daughter Isabel de Vega y Luna (d. 1558) provided financial assistance and political support for the foundation of the college at Bivona in 1556. Two sons helped the Jesuits establish colleges in Siracusa (1554) and Catania (1556). Rahner 1960, 462–68; Tacchi-Venturi 1951b, 364–67.

ber 9, 1547, and immediately urged the Messina Senate to invite the Jesuits to come to Messina. Vega also appealed personally to Ignatius.[2] The only Jesuit in Sicily at the time was the energetic Juan Jerónimo Doménech, who became Vega's confessor. He also encouraged Vega, Osorio, and Ignatius to establish a school in Messina.[3] Their task was aided by the fact that the leading citizens of Messina wanted a Jesuit school. On December 17 and 19, 1547, the Senate of Messina sent two letters formally asking Ignatius Loyola to establish a school in Messina to teach lay boys, that is, boys not intended to become clergymen.[4] The city promised to provide a residence for the Jesuits, a church, and an annual income of 500 scudi (200 gold ounces).[5] Ignatius accepted the invitation in a letter of January 14, 1548.[6] His acceptance launched the prototypical Jesuit school.[7]

While Ignatius and other leaders of the Society were considering making education a ministry, Messina was a surprising choice for the first Italian school.[8] The city was certainly large enough to support a school. With 40,000 to 45,000 souls at mid-century, it was the second-largest city in Sic-

2. Novarese 1994, 29–32.

3. Tacchi Venturi 1951b, 331–32; Lukács 1960–1961, part 1, 18; and *Year by Year* 2004, 62–64.

4. Letter of the city of Messina to the viceroy of December 17, 1547, which was passed on to Ignatius, and letter of the Senate to Ignatius Loyola of December 19, 1547, Messina, in *Epistolae mixtae* 1898–1901, 1:450–52, 454–56. The invitation came from "li Jurati nobili et populani dela nobile città de Messina" (450, 456). The *jurati* or *giurati* (sworn ones or sworn officials) were the six members of the highest executive magistracy of the city, *la Giurazia* (the sworn body). The sworn duty of the giurati was to govern and defend the city, and to represent it to outside powers such as the Spanish crown, the viceroy, and other cities. The viceroy, who ruled all of Sicily for the crown, could not overturn a decision of la Giurazia, but he might impose his will by force. The Giurazia consisted of three noble giurati and three popular giurati from the merchant elite, and sometimes four nobles and two popular giurati, each group elected by its class in a very restricted franchise. While there had been much conflict between nobles and *popolani* in the past, mutual economic and political interests plus intermarriage had produced a unified governing elite in the sixteenth century. See Salvo 1995. That is not to say that they always agreed. Annual elections on May 1 always produced six new giurati who sometimes rejected the policies of their predecessors. In 1517 the Spanish crown authorized la Giurazia to call itself the Senate of Messina and its members senators. These more familiar titles will be used in the following discussion.

5. Polanco provides the financial details; see MP 1:506 (Latin); and *Year by Year* 2004, 64–65 (English translation). See also Scaduto 1948, 102–3; and Novarese 1994, 35–36. The Sicilian money of account was the gold ounce worth 2.5 scudi at this time. Ounces will be converted into scudi in what follows.

6. Letter to the city of Messina of January 14, 1548, Rome, in *Ignatii Epistolae* 1964–1968, 1:679–81; Tacchi Venturi 1951b, 332–33; and Novarese 1994, 36–37.

7. Messina was not the first Jesuit school. In 1543 a few Jesuits began to teach boys and youths at Goa. And there was a school at Gandía in 1545; see below.

8. This is not the place to rehearse the broader reasons why the Jesuits decided to become educators. O'Malley 1993, 200–242, provides an excellent overview of the origins and impact of the schools on the Society in its first twenty-five years.

ily, behind Palermo's 60,000.[9] But it was in far-off Sicily in a city separated from the rest of Italy by the treacherous Straits of Messina. At this time the Jesuits only had colleges without schools in Rome, Padua, and Bologna (founded in 1546). Of course, the strong support from Juan de Vega and his consort was a major factor. Nevertheless, if the Spanish Jesuits who led the Society wanted to found their first Italian school in a state ruled by Spain, Milan and Naples looked more promising.

The key reason for the choice of Messina was that the city expected that a Jesuit school would quickly become a university. Polanco's account of the invitation makes this clear: "The city gave thought to setting up a *studium generale* or university at Messina and required the Society to provide only four teachers."[10] Doménech also wrote to tell Ignatius that everyone in Messina expected that a Jesuit school would soon be converted into a university.[11]

Although the letters of invitation did not mention a university, the city made it clear that it had in mind much more than teaching Latin to boys. The city wanted four or five "magistri in theologia" to lecture daily in theology, cases of conscience, philosophy, and rhetoric and grammar. The first three were university-level courses, while rhetoric was both a university course and the apex of humanistic studies. The second letter twice describes the teachers as *doctori*.[12] One did not need a doctorate to teach Latin grammar to boys, but almost all professors in Italian universities possessed doctorates. The second letter also invited Ignatius to send five non-teaching Jesuits and suggested that they would study as well as engage in Catholic works and exercises.[13] Since Jesuit scholastics already possessed Latin fluency, the appropriate subjects to study would be the university subjects of philosophy and theology.

Messina had long wanted a university but could not create one because of the opposition of Catania. Both cities tried to found universities in the early fifteenth century, and Catania won. Moreover, the University of Catania, founded in 1445, was the only institution in Sicily empowered to con-

9. Ginatempo and Sandri 1990, 183, 192, 228, 241.

10. MP 1:506 (Latin); *Year by Year* 2004, 65 (English translation and quotation); Novarese 1994, 35.

11. Sáinz y Zúñiga 1957–1958, 2:171, citing an ARSI document; and Novarese 1994, 35n29.

12. Literally "che in questa città con la venuta de li detti religiosi et doctori" and "li detti doctori et religiosi." Letters of the city of Messina to Juan de Vega and Loyola, December 17 and 19, 1547, Messina, in *Epistolae mixtae* 1898–1901, 1:450–52, 454–56, quotations at 455. Farrell 1938, 26, provides an English translation of the letter of December 19 that is not quite literal and does not translate *doctori*. This may be the only miscue in an admirable book.

13. *Epistolae mixtae* 1898–1901, 1:455.

fer degrees, and it fiercely defended its monopoly.[14] The united Kingdom
of Aragon and Castile that took control of Sicily in 1479 confirmed Catania's monopoly and refused to grant permission for a second university, as
did subsequent Spanish governments.[15] The refusal may have been part of
Spanish policy to prevent one city from dominating the island. Messina
and Palermo were larger and more important economically, and viceroys
resided for half the year in each. But Catania had the island's sole university. As events will show, the civic leaders of Messina calculated that the
introduction of a Jesuit school with the warm support of the viceroy might
offer a way to overcome Catania's monopoly.

   Ignatius sent an international group of ten Jesuits. The rector (superior)
was Jerónimo Nadal from Palma de Mallorca. The others were André des
Freux from northern France, Peter Canisius from the Netherlands, Cor-
nelius Wischaven from Flanders, Isidoro Bellini from Rome of German
parents, Benedetto Palmio from Parma, Annibal du Coudret (1525–1599)
from Savoy, Raffaelo Riera from Barcelona, Martino Mare from France,
and Giovanni Battista Passari (or Passarino, d. after 1557) from Brescia.[16]
The first four were priests; the others were scholastics. Sending Nadal, one
of the four most important men of the Society at this time, underscored the
importance that Ignatius placed on the Messina venture.[17] The considerable intellectual abilities of the group confirms that Ignatius saw Messina as
more than a school. No Jesuit temporal coadjutors (brothers) accompanied
them, which meant that the ten would have to take care of themselves.

   They left Rome on March 18, 1548, with the expenses of their trip paid
by the city of Messina, and arrived in Messina on April 8. The city, the viceroy, and his wife received them warmly. The city rented temporary housing for the Jesuits, repaired the church assigned to them, purchased a house
and garden for the Jesuits, and renovated a building to serve as the school,
although it was not yet ready.[18] The Jesuits began teaching on April 26.[19]
But after a month or two, they stopped because of the summer heat.

   They resumed teaching in the fall and scheduled the ceremonial opening of the school for October 1, 1548. In preparation the Jesuits distributed a prospectus advertising the school. They inaugurated the school with
Latin orations by Peter Canisius and Benedetto Palmio, with Viceroy Vega

---

14. For a brief summary and additional bibliography, see Grendler 2002, 106–8.

15. Cesca 1900, 6–7; Tropea 1900, 85–86; Novarese 1994, 24–28; and Grendler 2002, 106, 121.

16. Scaduto 1948, 104n9; Novarese 1994, 41n42.

17. The others were Ignatius Loyola, Diego Laínez, and Juan de Polanco.

18. *Year by Year* 2004, 75–76; *Jesuit Writings* 2006, 49.

19. Cesca 1900, 6; Scaduto 1948, 105. Novarese 1994, 42, states that the Jesuits did not begin
teaching until October.

and local notables in attendance. Once begun, they slowly introduced the method of Paris. Disputations, sometimes in competition with the Dominicans, followed in the academic year.[20]

Although the city had requested only four or five upper-level teachers, the Jesuits initially offered seven classes. They added three Latin classes because students needed good Latin skills before advancing to the higher classes. Benedetto Palmio taught the lowest Latin grammar class, Annibale Coudret taught the middle Latin grammar class, Giovanni Battista Passeri taught the highest Latin grammar class, and Peter Canisius taught rhetoric. In what will later be called the "upper school," Isidoro Bellini taught logic, André des Freux taught Greek, and Nadal taught Hebrew. All classes were free of charge. But the Jesuits did not teach theology or cases of conscience as the city had requested.[21]

Immediately after the formal opening of the Jesuit school, the Messina Senate urged Viceroy Vega to ask Ignatius to obtain a papal bull creating a university in Messina.[22] A bull was necessary because by custom and legal tradition only the pope and emperor were viewed as transnational authorities with the authority to empower a town, organization, or individual to confer degrees recognized throughout Christendom. A bull or charter was not a university, because teachers, students, and instruction were needed. Rather, it provided the legal foundation on which to build a university. Ignatius agreed to try to get a university bull. His acquiescence to this request signaled a policy change: the Society would help create a new university in which Jesuits would teach their own members and external students.

It was customary that a very substantial "free gift"—in reality a payment or bribe—accompanied a request for a university bull or charter. Hence, the Messina Senate made a contribution of 500 gold ducats toward the curial expenses of obtaining a bull.[23] On November 16, 1548, Pope Paul III issued the bull *Copiosus in misericordia Dominus* authorizing a University of Messina (Messanense Studium Generale).[24] The extraordinary speed with which the bull was issued testified to the excellent relations of the Jes-

20. "Parisiensis universitatis in docendo modum paulatim induxit." MP 1:509–10 (quotation at 509); *Year by Year* 2004, 76; Bangert and McCoog 1992, 59–60.

21. MP 1:509–10; *Year by Year* 2004, 76; Bangert and McCoog 1992, 59–60.

22. Scaduto 1948, 106–7; Novarese 1994, 43–47. Polanco wrote "At length the city magistrates came to the viceroy, Juan de Vega, and easily obtained his consent (which was necessary) and letters requesting both Father Ignatius and the ambassador of Emperor Charles V at Rome to obtain from the Supreme Pontiff whatever authorization was necessary for a university." *Year by Year* 2004, 65, except that Polanco put the date as 1547.

23. Novarese 1994, 45.

24. Cesca 1900, 7; Scaduto 1948, 107; and Novarese 1994, 48. The bull is found in Tropea 1900, 87–92; and *I capitoli dello Studio di Messina* 1990, 3–8.

uits with Paul III, who had already conferred many benefits on the Society. No doubt the 500 gold ducats also helped.

The bull authorized the erection of a university (*studium generale*) in the city of Messina that would have the power to confer bachelor, master, licentiate, and doctoral degrees recognized throughout Christendom. The bull stated that its graduates would enjoy the same rights and privileges as graduates of the universities of Bologna, Paris, and Salamanca, common reference points in university charters.[25] Invoking existing universities was designed to claim for a new university and its graduates the same legal status and prestige as established universities.

The bull decreed that all authority in the university would be invested in two people, the superior general of the Society of Jesus and a local Jesuit. The superior general would name a Jesuit to be the rector of the university; he would also serve as chancellor of the university and rector of the Jesuit college in Messina. The Jesuit rector-chancellor would confer degrees and decide curriculum matters. Because the university would be completely subject to the Society, the superior general, acting for the Society, would have the authority to write and amend the statutes of the university. He might determine what subjects would be taught, the number and kind of lectures, and he might expand or restrict privileges. The city would have only the authority to determine the stipends of professors and, presumably, to pay them. Finally, the bull rejected the claim of the University of Catania that it was the only institution in Sicily empowered to grant degrees.[26] The papal bull wrote the legal framework for a Jesuit university to be located in Messina. The University of Messina bull of November 16, 1548, was practically a carbon copy of the bull authorizing the creation of the University of Gandía of November 4, 1547. Both were entitled *Copiosus in misericordia Dominus*, and the Messina bull simply inserted the new name, "Messina," when necessary.[27]

The University of Gandía was the creation of Francisco de Borja (1510–1572), duke of Gandía and the third general of the Society (1565–1572).[28] Located about forty-seven miles south of Valencia, Gandía is a small coastal city that was the capital of the hereditary lands of the Borja family. Noting that the Jesuits had just established a college, but no school, at Valencia in

---

25. Tropea 1900, 89–90; *I capitoli dello Studio di Messina* 1990, 5–6.

26. Tropea 1900, 88–91; *I capitoli dello Studio di Messina* 1990, 4–8; Scaduto 1948, 108; Novarese 1994, 53–55.

27. Novarese 1994, 54–57.

28. There is a large bibliography on Borja. Start with Scaduto 1992; Dalmases 2001b; and *Francisco de Borja* 2011.

1544, Borja decided to use some of his wealth to create a Jesuit college and school in Gandía. The school opened its doors in 1545 with a handful of Jesuits and scholastics. At Borja's request they also taught the sons of his converted Muslim subjects.[29] Because Borja wanted to raise the Gandía school to a university, Ignatius obtained the 1547 bull from Paul III. It made the rector of the Jesuit college the rector of the university.[30] Of course, there was no competition, because only Jesuits taught at Gandía. Thanks to the bull, the University of Gandía conferred doctorates of theology on Borja and four other Jesuits, none of whom spent much time studying theology, in 1550.[31]

Much Jesuit historiography sees Gandía as the first Jesuit school to teach non-Jesuits in Europe and as a model for future schools.[32] That overstates its importance. Gandía was little more than a paper university because it did not offer significant instruction in philosophy or theology, or any other subject for that matter. In 1548 it had thirteen Jesuits, which meant that a handful of Jesuit teachers taught a handful of Jesuit scholastics and a small number of external students. After his wife died, Borja gravitated to the Jesuits, and entered the Society in February 1548. When he moved to Rome in 1550, the Gandía school declined further. Instruction in philosophy and theology was gone by 1555, at which time the Jesuit community had shrunk to ten, only four of them priests. They taught two lower school Latin grammar classes and cases of conscience.[33] In 1574 Gandía taught few or no classes, and in 1600 it had only one upper school class and two lower school classes.[34] Gandía was the anomalous creation of Francisco de Borja. Nevertheless, the bull for the proposed University of Messina copied the Gandía bull.

29. Perry 2011.

30. "Since the university had already been built and confirmed by the authority of the Apostolic See ... the rector of our college was also the future rector of the university. Thus, the first rector of the first university possessed by the Society was Father Andrea de Oviedo ...." Polanco in *Year by Year* 2004, 84; for the Latin, see MP 1:512.

31. See chap. 15, "Quick Doctorates for the First Jesuits"; and Scaduto 1992, 24.

32. Polanco wrote "This was the first university that the Society possessed." *Year by Year* 2004, 67; for the Latin see MP 1:507 and 507n46. Modern histories echo this statement. See Farrell 1938, 16–17 and 22n57; MP 5:2*–6*; and Lukács 1999, 18, 20, 22, a condensed English version of the previous work. O'Malley 1993, 203, more accurately calls it an "exceedingly modest institution."

33. For the history of the school at Gandía from 1546 through 1555, see MP 1:8*, 50–64, 373–75, 502, 507n46, 512–13; *Year by Year* 2004, 52, 58, 67, 83–84, 89, 109, 135, 185, 344–46, 359, 388, 451–52; and Scaduto 1992, 23–24.

34. Lukács 1960–1961, part 2, 54.

The Collegiate University

The real models for the proposed University of Messina were the collegiate universities found everywhere in Europe except Italy and, in particular, the collegiate University of Alcalá de Henares and its dominant college, the Colegial Mayor de San Ildefonso. Their structures and constitutions shaped what the Jesuits hoped to create in Messina.[35] Cardinal Francisco Jiménez de Cisneros (1436–1517), archbishop of Toledo, ecclesiastical reformer, and one of the most powerful men in Spain, created the University of Alcalá de Henares in 1508.[36] It began teaching Latin, philosophy, theology, medicine, and canon law in the academic year 1509–1510. It did not teach civil law because Cisneros forbade it, and he made provision for only two professors of medicine and two for canon law. The university had many more professors and regent masters to teach theology, arts, rhetoric, Greek, and Hebrew. It added a little more law and medicine in the second half of the sixteenth and in the seventeenth centuries.[37]

Cisneros also created and endowed the Colegial Mayor de San Ildefonso to be the head, heart, and largest component of the university. Named for an archbishop of Toledo who died in 667, it was a quasi-monastic combination residence and teaching institution whose members were the elite teachers and students of the university. They taught and studied philosophy and theology. Disputations, examinations, and Sunday lectures took place in San Ildefonso under the authority of its rector. Even some medical instruction was delivered in the infirmary of San Ildefonso. Minor colleges (sometimes called *colegios pobres* or poor colleges) housed other students and teachers, most of whom concentrated on Latin and philosophy.

35. Lukács, the editor of MP, provides many footnotes pointing out the similarities between Jesuit documents concerning university and college organization and passages in the constitutions of the University of Alcalá de Henares and the Colegio Mayor de San Ildefonso. See MP 1, index (Complutum). See also A. Romano 1992, 43, 51–52.

36. For this and the following two paragraphs, see Sáinz y Zuñiga 1957–1958, 1:378–83; 2:291–308, 407–14, 416–18, 422–28; Codina Mir 1968, 15–49; and García Oro 1992. Novarese 1994, 54–55, also argues for the influence of the Spanish *colegio universidad* and the Colegio Mayor de San Ildefonso on the Jesuit conception of a university and on the Gandía and Messina foundation bulls.

37. In the second half of the sixteenth century the university added three professors of medicine and three canonists, as well as additional professors and teachers in other subjects. In 1606 there were six professors of medicine, six of canon law, seven of theology, eight of grammar, four of rhetoric, three of Greek, and two of Hebrew, plus an unknown number of regent masters who taught philosophy and possibly other subjects. After decades of struggle, the university finally changed its statutes to add civil law in the 1620s. Pellistrandi 1990, 126, 133; Garcia Oro 1992, 342–53.

Following the direction of Cisneros, the constitutions of the university, issued by Pope Julius II in 1510 and elaborated in other bulls, made the rector of the College of San Ildefonso the dominant figure of the university. A regular clergyman, the rector, assisted by three councillors from San Ildefonso, organized the curriculum, inspected the teaching, and chaired degree examinations. In some circumstances he might confer degrees, which was normally done by the chancellor, the archbishop of Toledo. Finally, the rector was charged with defending the rights of the university.

The first Jesuits were well acquainted with the University of Alcalá de Henares and its Colegio Major de San Ildefonso because several of them had studied there. Ignatius studied logic, natural philosophy, and the *Sentences* of Peter Lombard at Alcalá de Henares from about March 1526 to June 1527, either through attendance at university lectures or with a private teacher. However, the local inquisition interrupted his studies with extended questioning and imprisonment of seventeen days, so he left.[38] Other first Jesuits had tranquil and successful careers at the university. Bobadilla, Laínez, Nadal, and Salmerón studied at Alcalá de Henares between 1526 and 1532. Bobadilla and Laínez obtained degrees there, and Nadal may have.

In addition, the Jesuits had established a very active college (without a school) in Alcalá de Henares in 1546. Some Jesuit scholastics studied at the university, other Jesuits guided numerous people in making the Spiritual Exercises. The Society pursued an active ministry to university students with the result that many university students abandoned their licentious behavior, Polanco wrote. So many young men wanted to become Jesuits that they had to be sent to other Jesuit colleges or turned away. Relations between the Jesuits and the university were good.[39]

Alcalá de Henares was one example of the collegiate university found everywhere in Catholic and Protestant Europe except in Italy. All of them were dominated by colleges which were a combination of teaching and residence institutions.[40] They concentrated on the humanities, philosophy, and theology, but taught little law and medicine. For example, Oxford, the quintessential collegiate university with many colleges and other student

38. Dalmases 1985, 93–101; García-Villoslada 1990, 309–37; and especially Sanz de Diego 2012, 676–94.

39. For Jesuit activities in Alcalá de Henares see *Year by Year* 2004, 31, 39–40, 52–53, 57, 81, 89, 105, 108, 113, 137, 183–84, 236–37, 295–96, 301, 313, 349, 395, 455; O'Malley 1993, 54–55, 129; and Sanz de Diego 2012, 694–713.

40. On collegiate universities see Sáinz y Zúñiga 1957–1958, vol. 2; Farge 1985, 11–13; *The Collegiate University* 1986; *I collegi universitari* 1991; Müller 1996, 333–39; Pedersen 1996, 463–64; and *Vocabulaire des collèges* 1993. No attempt is made to describe all the complexities and nuances of collegiate universities.

residences, had numerous regent masters and student theologians teaching the humanities, philosophy, and theology. But it had only a single professor of law and one or two in medicine in any given year in the sixteenth century.[41] The University of Paris, a collegiate university on a grand scale, had several hundred regent masters of arts and theologians, but only a few professors of medicine and canon law. And it did not teach civil law. The University of Vienna, a modified collegiate university, had sixteen professors of arts and theology, but only four professors of law and three of medicine in 1554.[42]

In the terminology of twenty-first century North American and, to a lesser extent, European education, a collegiate university was a combined secondary school and undergraduate university topped by a limited amount of graduate-level and professional training in law and medicine. Sixteenth-century collegiate universities were clerical and religious in culture because the majority of the teachers were clergymen, and because of the quasi-monastic rules of the colleges in which students and teachers lived, taught, and studied. The Messina bull authorized a collegiate university dominated by the Jesuits.

The Italian University

No Italian university resembled the university described by the Messina bull because Italy did not have any collegiate universities. The differences between Italian universities and collegiate universities were enormous. They were at the heart of the coming conflict at Messina and they influenced other Jesuit attempts to found universities in Italy.

All Italian universities were graduate professional universities.[43] They taught law, medicine, and theology at an advanced level. They did not teach Latin to boys aged thirteen to fifteen; students had to acquire Latin skills before they entered the university. Italian universities did not provide five years of logic, natural philosophy, and metaphysics lectures to students aged sixteen to twenty-one so that they might obtain bachelor of arts and master of arts degrees. Italian universities only awarded doctorates. The bachelor's degree had disappeared in Italian universities by the early fifteenth century and the licentiate, or authorization to teach, was conferred with the doctorate. Students normally began their studies at Italian universities at about the

41. For law, see Barton 1986; for medicine, see Lewis 1986.
42. Freedman 1985, 132–34. Such examples can be multiplied.
43. What follows is a summary based on Grendler 2002, which provides detail and much bibliography.

age of eighteen and emerged five to seven years later with doctorates in law or medicine.[44]

Because Italian universities taught only students pursuing doctorates, their enrollments were much smaller than those of collegiate universities. As noted in chapter 1, the total annual enrollment of the University of Paris has been estimated as 12,000 to 20,000 students in the sixteenth century.[45] Alcalà de Henares averaged 3,000 students between 1568 and 1618.[46] By contrast, estimated enrollments at Italian universities in the sixteenth century ranged from a low of 100 to 200 at the tiny University of Catania to 2,000 at the University of Bologna.[47]

Italian universities concentrated on teaching law and medicine at a professional level. In the middle of the sixteenth century, 67 to 75 percent of the degrees awarded by Italian universities were doctorates in law, usually *in utroque iure*, that is, in both civil and canon law. Civil law dominated; a student added canon law to his doctorate by attending another course or two and answering a few more questions in the doctoral examination. Another 20 to 25 percent of the degrees conferred were doctorates in medicine. A handful of students received doctorates of philosophy. And about 5 to 10 percent of the degrees conferred were doctorates of theology.[48] Although no matriculation lists have been located, it is likely that the percentage of students who studied law, medicine, or theology reflected the percentage of doctorates conferred in each discipline.

The portion of professors who taught each discipline roughly paralleled the distribution of decrees conferred. In the middle of the sixteenth century about 47 percent of the professors in Italian universities taught law, about 28 percent taught medicine, 20 percent taught natural philosophy, logic, mathematics, and the humanities, and 5 percent taught theology and metaphysics.[49] Large and small Italian universities demonstrated the same pattern. The number of professors of law and medicine in Italian universities dwarfed the number in collegiate universities. For example, in the academic year 1550–1551 the University of Bologna had 38 professors of law, 22 professors of medicine, 20 professors of philosophy, logic, mathematics and the humanities, one metaphysician, and no professors of theology, for a total of 81 professors, none of them regent masters.[50] (Theology did not

44. Grendler 2002, 172–74.   45. Farge 1999, 404.

46. Pellistrandi 1990, 137–43.   47. Grendler 2002, 515.

48. Grendler 2002, 50 (Siena), 104 (Ferrara), 116 (Macerata), 365 (Pisa). For Bologna see Guerrini 2005, 31.

49. For individual universities, see Grendler 2002, chaps. 1–4.

50. Dallari 1888–1924, 2:120–23.

secure a permanent place in the curriculum until the academic year 1566–1567.)[51] The University of Padua at mid-century had 25 professors of law, 13 professors of medicine, 13 professors of logic, philosophy, mathematics, and the humanities, two theologians, and two metaphysicians, for a total of 55 professors, again with no regent masters.[52]

Italian universities had a relatively large number of professors of natural philosophy, logic, mathematics, and the humanities despite the fact that they did not confer degrees in these disciplines.[53] With that said, these disciplines were considered useful preparation for the study of law or medicine. Law students often attended logic courses, and medicine students almost always heard natural philosophy lectures. Furthermore, some students attended humanities lectures because the attraction of the *studia humanitatis* was great. They came to hear an eminent humanist scholar analyze an ancient Latin or Greek text, not to perfect their Latin. Metaphysics was considered preparation for theology. Hence, theology students attended lectures in metaphysics, which was taught in the larger Italian universities, always by a Dominican, Franciscan, or member of another medieval order. But small Italian universities very seldom taught metaphysics. After the Council of Trent concluded in 1563, a handful of the larger Italian universities added professorships of biblical studies.[54]

Theology and metaphysics were not important in Italian universities. For example, Italian universities annually promulgated two rolls listing the professors, what they taught, and when they lectured. One roll was for those who taught law. The other, entitled "Arts," included everyone else, that is, those who taught medicine, logic, philosophy, mathematics, humanities, and theology. More telling, other members of the academic community often held metaphysicians and theologians in low esteem. One Bologna professor of natural philosophy judged Aristotelian metaphysics to be a simple and useless subject fit only for friars. Others criticized the scholastic approach to theology employed by practically all Italian theologians. They should lecture directly from the ancient sacred texts without mixing in human philosophy, a professor of philosophy at Pisa wrote.[55]

Other differences divided Italian universities and collegiate universities. Italian universities did not have regent masters. The vast majority of professors in Italian universities, and nearly all who taught law and medicine,

51. Grendler 2002, 381–83.
52. Grendler 2002, 33.
53. They did award a handful of degrees in theology and philosophy combined.
54. Grendler 2002, 353–92.
55. Grendler 2002, 387–89.

possessed doctorates. By contrast, only a small minority of teachers in collegiate universities held doctorates. Except for the medieval order clergymen who taught theology and metaphysics, almost all professors at Italian universities were laymen, often prominent in the city and sometimes famous for their scholarship. The vast majority of the students were also laymen, who lived in rented quarters, not in supervised student residences. Italian university towns had a few small student residences, but they did not offer formal instruction.[56]

Above all, Italian universities were civic institutions. City governments or princes founded Italian universities, paid the expenses, governed them, and chose the professors. The students did not select the professors, except for a handful of the lowest level professors at one or two universities. But even these choices had to be approved by the governments that paid professorial salaries.[57] The city, the prince, or the two together created civic magistracies that oversaw Italian universities. Most often called Riformatori dello Studio di [name] (Reformers of the University of [name]), they consisted of elected and/or appointed laymen, often influential men who had already filled important city offices. Some riformatori possessed doctorates, usually in law.[58] The riformatori discussed appointments, salaries, curriculum, and student misbehavior. They listened to the comments and complaints of professors, students, and governments. If the prince recommended someone for a professorship, the riformatori considered him, and usually concurred. The riformatori also discussed the creation of new professorships, adding an additional one in a discipline, reducing the number of professorships in another, and emending the statutes. The riformatori recommended actions, appointments, and salary figures to the city government or prince, which almost always followed their recommendations.

By contrast, the papal bull of 1548 conferred all authority over the proposed University of Messina to one clergyman, the Jesuit rector. No Italian university had such a rector or any other officer with such authority.[59] The

56. Grendler 2002, 166–72.

57. The students had the power to choose a few professors at Pavia in the fifteenth century and at Padua until 1560. Grendler 2002, 85, 158.

58. They were called Riformatori dello Studio at the universities of Ferrara, Padua, Parma, Pavia, and Turin, assunti of the Assunteria di Studio at Bologna, Savi dello Studio at Siena, and Ufficiali dello Studio at Florence. Grendler, 2002. For some of the actions of the Riformatori dello Studio di Padova see ibid., 32–33, 157, 234, 333–34, 348, 372, 491, 506.

59. There was one partial exception. In 1543 Duke Cosimo I de' Medici created the office of Provveditore dello Studio (overseer of the university) to supervise the University of Pisa. A civil servant, the provveditore initially visited the University of Pisa twice a year; from 1575 he resided in Pisa. He sent detailed reports to the duke and his advisers, who made decisions about

only rectors in Italian universities were student rectors, that is, the leaders of student organizations who defended the rights of students. Nor did Italian universities have administrative structures within the university. They did not have faculty senates.[60] A beadle came daily to each classroom to note whether the professor showed up to lecture, and that was it. Professors lectured, students listened, and then both went home. Professors had a great deal of autonomy and the freedom to lecture and write as they chose. Students had the freedom to attend or skip lectures and to learn as they wished.

In Italian universities colleges of men who held doctorates in law, medicine, or theology examined degree candidates and determined if they had learned enough to merit the doctorate.[61] Colleges of doctors were independent bodies legally separate from the university. For example, the membership of a college of law typically consisted of twelve to twenty-four local men possessing doctorates in law, almost always from the local university, plus a few of the most important professors. Colleges of doctors of medicine also examined degree candidates and had the same membership mix. The membership of a college of doctors of theology consisted of regular clergymen with doctorates of theology who lived in the local convents of the medieval mendicant orders (Augustinian Canons, Augustinian Hermits, Carmelites, Dominicans, Franciscan Observants, Franciscan Conventuals, etc.) including one or two of them who taught in the university.[62]

If the candidate received the approval of the appropriate college of doctors, the chancellor of the university, who was usually the local bishop, conferred the degree. The chancellor did not decide who merited a degree. He simply performed the ceremonial action of conferring it.

The features of Italian universities, including the dominance of law and medicine, the minimal presence of theology, civic governance, colleges of doctors, a lay professoriate, and a lay student body were very different from those of collegiate universities. These profound dissimilarities produced different atmospheres and cultures. For example, every rector of the University of Paris organized a grand procession toward the end of his rectorate, which meant four processions annually. In one of those of 1528, some

---

the university. The provveditore replaced the previous magistracy overseeing the university. But he served the ruler. He did not have the powers that the papal bull awarded to the Jesuit rector. Grendler 2002, 75.

60. Grendler 2004b, 10–12.

61. See Grendler 2002, 174–78, on colleges of doctors of law and medicine.

62. On colleges of doctors of theology and theology generally in Italian universities, see Grendler 2002, 353–92.

2,291 members of the university participated, including 845 mendicant friars, 132 other religious, 632 masters and regents, 62 doctors of theology, and so on.[63] The large number of clergymen was remarkable. Processions of that sort did not happen in Italian universities, not least because few clergymen taught in Italian universities. Instead, law professors interpreted Bartolus, and wealthy lay students wearing swords strutted around the town looking for a fight. Collegiate universities were quasi-clerical and semi-religious institutions. Italian universities were civic and lay enterprises.

The Messina Senate Wants an Italian University

Members of the Messina Senate must have been shocked when they saw the papal bull. It awarded complete authority over the proposed University of Messina to the Jesuits. The only privilege conceded to the city of Messina was that of paying the salaries of the professors of law and medicine. Since the city had committed itself to paying the expenses of the Jesuits as well, it would be paying all the expenses of the university without any authority over it. From the Middle Ages onward some members of Messina's elite had obtained doctorates of law from mainland universities, especially Bologna.[64] Hence, they knew what an Italian university looked like, and this was not it. But the Senate still wanted a university. So it immediately began efforts to get the bull modified.

At the end of 1548 or in early 1549 the Senate issued a document listing *ordini* (rules) for the proposed university.[65] The ordini embodied the changes that would have to be made to the papal bull for it and the university to be acceptable to the city. This was the beginning of a long struggle between the city of Messina and the Jesuits over the structure and governance of the proposed University of Messina.[66]

63. Lécrivain 2011, 62–63.

64. Salvo 1995, 65–66, 79, points out that from the Middle Ages onward, some giurati possessed law degrees. Guerrini 2005, index, lists 27 men from Messina who obtained doctorates in law from the University of Bologna in the sixteenth century. Another example: 189 Sicilians obtained doctorates from the University of Siena from 1484 to 1486 and 1496 to 1579, all but 17 in law. An indeterminate number came from Messina. *Le lauree dello Studio senese* 1998, xxiv, xxvi. And Sicilians regularly studied law at the University of Ferrara. See A. Romano 1995.

65. "Forma di lu ordini di li Studii" in ARSI, Sicula 197 I, f. 79r–v. It is printed in Novarese 1994, 435–36, and analyzed on 63. It carries the date "1548." However, as Novarese points out, it appears to follow the Incarnation-style calendar which changes years on March 25. Hence, it could have been written anytime between the arrival of the papal bull of November 16, 1648, and March 25, 1549, and Novarese suggests early 1549.

66. There has been a considerable amount of scholarship on the origins and first years of the University of Messina. The most useful studies are Cesca 1900; G. Romano 1900; Tropea 1900;

First, the city stated that it would choose the professors of civil law, canon law, medicine, and surgery. The Jesuits would name the other professors for the university and teachers for the lower school: four for logic, philosophy, and metaphysics; one each for theology, mathematics, Hebrew, Greek, rhetoric, and the humanities; and three for grammar. The city would pay the salaries of the Jesuit professors and teachers according to an agreement to be negotiated with the Society.[67]

Second, the city insisted that the university had to have a non-Jesuit student rector who would be elected by the majority of the students and confirmed by the rector of the Jesuit college. The student rector would enjoy the honors and privileges that student rectors received in other universities, with two exceptions. The city would exercise jurisdiction over professors and students involved in criminal and civil law offenses. The rector of the Jesuit college would have authority (*superiorità*) over, and might give advice to, professors and students in matters touching the order of the lectures and habits. However, his authority would only be spiritual.[68]

Third, the city would name a chancellor who would confer degrees. However, the chancellor might designate the rector of the Jesuit College as his surrogate in the college of doctors. Fourth, a college of doctors (never mentioned in the papal bull) would examine degree candidates. Citizens of Messina, foreigners who graduated from the University of Messina (which did not yet exist), and professors from the university would comprise the membership of the college of doctors.[69]

The city's demands expressed the essential elements of an Italian university with some concessions to the Jesuits. Although the ordini were a compromise, they leaned strongly toward the Italian university model. The Jesuits would have to give up most of the authority over the university that the papal bull granted them. To make this a reality, the papal bull would have to be revised. However, before going to the pope and curia for a revised bull, the Jesuits and the city would have to resolve their differences in order to present a united front, and thus intense negotiations began. Jerónimo Nadal, the rector of the Jesuit college in Messina, negotiated with the Senate, while the viceroy and another royal official intervened periodically. Ignatius Loyola in Rome would make the final decisions for the Jesuits.[70]

Scaduto 1948; *I capitoli dello Studio di Messina* 1990; Moscheo 1991; A. Romano 1992; and Novarese 1994. In the following account, which carries the story to 1552, only studies and pagination most relevant to the Jesuits will be cited.

67. Novarese 1994, 63, and the 1549 *ordini* printed on 435–36.

68. Novarese 1994, 63, 435–36.   69. Novarese 1994, 63, 436.

70. Scaduto 1948, 108–9; Bangert and McCoog 1992, 64–65; Novarese 1994, 60–62.

Ignatius was angry at the Messina senators and their ordini. He rejected the changes that the city wanted and explained his reasons for a unified university under a Jesuit rector in a letter to Nadal of July 6, 1549.[71] He began on a note of exasperation: the city had wanted the university and the Jesuits had agreed to it as a favor to Viceroy Vega. But now the lack of progress had become an embarrassment to the Society. He offered reasons why the university should have a single leader and why the Jesuits should provide that leadership. Strong and unified governance guaranteed that the university would be a serious enterprise with regular lectures, which was not the case in Italian universities, in his view.[72] A division of the university into two distinct bodies without a single head would foment discord. There could not be peace and unity among students and professors when some would be subject to the authority of the Jesuits and others to the city. Such a division would sow confusion and might even encourage the Jesuit college to meddle in public matters.

Ignatius then promised that pedagogical and religious benefits would flow from a single head and Jesuit dominance. Jesuit teachers would offer more pedagogical exercises and they would take better care of the sons of Messina, he wrote. A university in which religion and letters were imparted in tandem would be honored. If the Jesuit model were not followed the Jesuits would be limited to a few sermons and confessions. Finally, Ignatius promised that degrees would be granted in good conscience and at small expense.[73]

The letter demonstrated several things, beginning with the fact that Ignatius strongly believed that a collegiate university under the complete control of the Society in the person of the Jesuit rector was the ideal university form. He believed that this was the only way that the university could work well. He may have had in mind the College of St. Barbara, while ignoring the fact that it was only one part of a large and complex university. Second, Ignatius believed that the purpose of a university education was as much religious as intellectual. Students would profit spiritually as well as academically from a Jesuit university. And to make this happen, the Jesuits had to have complete control so that they might teach minds and help souls.

71. The letter is found in *Ignatii Epistolae* 1964–1968, 2:462–63. Although expressing the views of Ignatius, it was drafted by Polanco. Novarese 1994, 65–66, summarizes and quotes extensively from the letter; see also A. Romano 1992, 48.

72. "4.0 Es de creer que, governando otros, no avria lectiones tan assiduas, pues se vey cómo va la cosa en las universidades de Italia." *Ignatii Epistolae* 1964–1968, 2:463. It is also quoted in Novarese 1994, 66n95.

73. *Ignatii Epistolae* 1964–1968, 2:462–63; Novarese 1994, 65–66.

Next, Ignatius judged Italian universities negatively. He saw them as institutions that were chaotically organized, lacking a coherent curriculum,
and offering too few lectures. His comment that Jesuit leadership would
guarantee that university degrees would be awarded honestly suggested
that he was aware that the results of degree examinations in Italian universities were invariably positive. He may have believed that examinations
in a University of Messina under a Jesuit rector would be more rigorous.
He promised that degrees would cost little. He obviously knew that Italian
university degrees were very expensive. This was because the new doctor
was obliged by regulations to pay fees to his examiners and promoters and
forced by custom to host a lavish banquet for friends with gifts for all.[74]
Finally, Ignatius did not consider, or did not realize, that lay professors and
students of law and medicine would resent being ruled by a Jesuit priest.
Famous and very highly-paid professors of law and medicine who consort-
ed with princes were unlikely to pay much attention to a clerical rector.[75]

Ignatius followed with another letter in which he opined that in the face
of the city's intransigence, there were three options: to impose the Society's
will on the city, to ask the viceroy to intervene, or to cede control over
law and medicine to the city.[76] He opted for further negotiations with the
aid of the viceroy. In October 1549 Nadal asked the viceroy to pressure the
Messina Senate into accepting the papal bull. At this time Vega imprisoned
some men who had earlier served in the Senate and sent others into exile,
although it is not known if he was punishing them for refusing to accede to
the Jesuits.[77] In any case, the viceroy's mediation did not produce an agreement.

Despite the differences over the university the city continued to support
the Jesuits and their school. On December 22, 1549, Nadal took official possession of the church given to the Jesuits and the renovated houses for which
the city had paid.[78] There were now nineteen Jesuits in Messina, a substantial
commitment of human resources for a small order. The Jesuit school offered

74. Grendler 2002, 178–80, for a sampling of degree expenses.

75. For the high salaries and influence of some of the law professors from the Sozzini family
who taught at various universities, see Grendler 2002, 461–63. For another example, see the career of Giacomo Antonio Marta (1557/58–1628), a legist who taught at several Italian universities
and was fiercely independent. Grendler 2009b, 83–126, 149, 159–61, 240–45.

76. Letter of Ignatius to Diego Laínez, July 6, 1549, Rome, in *Ignatii Epistolae* 1964–1968,
2:467; A. Romano 1992, 48; and Novarese 1994, 66–67.

77. Letter of Nadal to Ignatius, October 29, 1549, Messina, in Nadal 1898–1962, 1:72;
Bangert and McCoog 1992, 65; Novarese 1994, 67; and *Year by Year* 2004, 123; repeated in *Jesuit
Writings* 2006, 52. The last two put the imprisonment of the senators in late 1550, which seems to
be a chronological error by Polanco.

78. Novarese 1994, 68.

eleven classes: scholastic theology, philosophy, logic, rhetoric, humanities, and three grammar classes. In addition, the extraordinarily energetic and learned Nadal taught Greek, Hebrew, and mathematics. The total enrollment of the Jesuit school in November 1549 was 260 to 264 students: 195 or 196 students in the grammar, humanities, and rhetoric classes, and 55 to 58 in the six upper school classes.[79] The city provided financial support of 500 scudi annually to the college as previously agreed.

The stalemate ended when Loyola abandoned his insistence that the Jesuits must rule the entire university. This was characteristic. Ignatius staked out strong positions, but when thwarted, sometimes accepted a pragmatic compromise in order to save his primary goal, in this case that the Jesuits would teach in a university. On February 5, 1550, he authorized Nadal to make an agreement with the Messina Senate.[80] In March and April 1550 the two sides inched toward agreement. The Jesuits would provide six professors for university classes and nine teachers for the Jesuit school. The Senate would provide additional financial support to pay for the Jesuit professors. It would also appoint and pay professors to teach law and medicine. The city accepted the papal bull of 1548 with the understanding that it would be amended.[81]

On April 25, 1550, the city announced the appointment of four professors, two for law and two for medicine, who would teach without compensation until the university opened.[82] On April 29, 1550, the city issued a proclamation announcing the beginning of the University of Messina. It would be a studium generale possessing all the rights and privileges of other universities in Italy and France. It would offer classes in theology, both laws, medicine, logic, natural philosophy, metaphysics, mathematics, surgery, Hebrew, Greek, rhetoric, humanities, and grammar. University lectures would take place in the Jesuit college of St. Nicholas.[83] With considerable fanfare the city

79. Scaduto 1948, 110; MP 1:515; *Year by Year* 2004, 91–92; *Jesuit Writings* 2006, 50. The individual class enrollments were lower grammar class 78, middle grammar 56, higher grammar 42, humanities 14, rhetoric 15 or 16, logic 16, natural philosophy 13, theology "only three in scholastic theology (since there was almost no mature student among the lay students, and religious were not as yet coming to our schools)," Greek 10, Hebrew 3 or 4, and mathematics (teaching Euclid) 10 to 12. *Year by Year* 2004, 92; and *Jesuit Writings* 2006, 50.

80. Scaduto 1948, 110; Novarese 1994, 69.

81. See the documents in Tropea 1900, 93–99; Viceroy Vega's approval of April 14, 1550, and Nadal's letter of May 5, 1550, in Nadal 1898–1962, 1:78–79, 83–84. See also Scaduto 1948, 110–11; Bangert and McCoog 1992, 66; Novarese 1994, 69–72; *Year by Year* 2004, 122; and *Jesuit Writings* 2006, 51.

82. Tropea 1900, 99; Novarese 1994, 72, 368–69, 489–90.

83. *I Capitoli dello Studio di Messina* 1990, note 10 on p. xv for the text of the proclamation; and Novarese 1994, 72.

proclaimed the inauguration of the university and a few lectures were delivered.[84] However, the full university, including the Jesuit lectures, would not begin until early November, the traditional opening of the academic year for Italian universities. Nadal believed that the Jesuits would attract a hundred students to their university lectures.[85] It looked like the Jesuits would become professors in the University of Messina.

It did not happen. The election of May 1, 1550, brought a new group of senators into office. They did not accept the accord to which their predecessors had agreed but not yet signed. The first dissent was financial. On June 11, 1550, the Messina Senate issued a document informing the Jesuits about the amount of money they would receive for their university teaching. The Senate acknowledged that the Jesuits had a need for 2,000 scudi annually. However, it would give the Jesuit college only 1,500 scudi for fifteen Jesuit teachers (university and school combined). The document also stated that the Senate projected that the total cost of the two parts of the university would be 6,000 scudi annually.[86] Because faculty salaries comprised almost all the expenses of a university, this meant that the Messina Senate expected to spend up to 4,500 scudi annually on a limited number of professors of law, medicine, and surgery for its half of the university, but provide only 1,500 scudi to the Jesuits for its school and university teaching combined. Since the city was already paying the college 500 scudi for nine teachers, it was offering the Jesuits only another 1,000 scudi for six more Jesuits, all of whom would teach university-level classes. The Jesuits did not believe that this was fair compensation.

A second blow came on the same day. The new Messina Senate had deputized a committee to draft university statutes. The Jesuits were not included and, so far as is known, were not invited to submit their views. The committee did its work, and on June 11, 1550, the Messina Senate promulgated statutes, which it called *capitoli*, for the new university.[87] The capitoli delineated the terms of the proposed contract with the Jesuits and described

84. *Year by Year* 2004, 122; repeated in *Jesuit Writings* 2006, 51.

85. "Et che in breve la Compagnia potrà in questa università alimentare 100 scolari." Nadal's letter to Ignatius Loyola of May 5, 1550, Messina, in Nadal 1898–1962, 1:84.

86. The senate document of June 11, 1550, is printed in Tropea 1900, 100–102. See also Scaduto 1948, 111; Bangert and McCoog 1992, 66; and Novarese 1994, 73–74.

87. The capitoli are printed in Tropea 1900, 102–9; and *I Capitoli dello Studio di Messina* 1990, 9–17. The latter is preferred, because it is more readable and because Novarese numbers the key paragraphs. Novarese calls them university statutes. However, they were never officially promulgated, and they omitted some material that university statutes normally included. See the brief comments on the capitoli of A. Romano in *I Capitoli dello Studio di Messina* 1990, xvi–xviii; and the good, full analysis of Novarese 1994, 75–83.

the structure of the university. The capitoli mostly followed the ordini that the Messina Senate had prepared at the end of 1548 or early 1549.

The capitoli of 1550 began by revoking the agreement that Nadal had made with the Senate. It then described a university consisting of what it called two bodies (corpi), Jesuit and civic. For the former the city agreed to pay the Jesuits 1,500 scudi for the services of fifteen teachers for the university and school. Seven Jesuits (an increase of one) would teach in the university. However, the city attached several conditions. No payment would be made until the papal bull had been changed and all fifteen were teaching. If any of the fifteen Jesuit teachers died, became ill, or was transferred, the Society had to provide another teacher of equal quality within three months. Otherwise, the payment would be reduced. The city also attached several conditions on the payment, the most important of which was the appointment of two provisori (provisioners or stewards) who would distribute the money to the Jesuits, keep accounts, collect receipts, and make sure that the money went toward pedagogical expenses. How the provisori would carry out these duties without entering into the internal affairs of the Jesuit college was not made clear.[88] The capitoli said little more about the Jesuit part of the university. The rector of the Jesuit college would be the rector of the Jesuit body of the university, but neither he nor any other Jesuit would have any jurisdiction over the law professors and students except for vague authority over the scheduling of lectures and undefined spiritual authority.[89] This part simply repeated the ordini of early 1549.

The larger part of the capitoli dealt with the other body of the university, the university for law and medicine to be governed by the city. The city promised to spend 4,000 scudi (rather than the 4,500 scudi it promised earlier) on salaries for the professors of this part of the university. The city would first hire four famous foreign (meaning not from Messina) scholars who had taught in other Italian universities to fill the major professorships of civil law, canon law, medicine, and surgery. These men would be the principal professors of the university and would receive four-year contracts. They would be obligated to teach according to the method and form of the universities of Bologna and Padua.[90] After the four distinguished outsiders were appointed, the Senate and the students would jointly choose the rest

88. Tropea 1900, 104–5, 107; I Capitoli dello Studio di Messina 1990, 11–12, 15; Novarese 1994, 75–77.

89. Tropea 1900, 107; I Capitoli dello Studio di Messina 1990, 15.

90. "Tutti li sopraditti letturi in iure canonico, civili, medicina et cirurgia, seranno obligati legere di lo modo et forma che si legi in li Studii Generali di Bologna et Padua …." I Capitoli dello Studio di Messina 1990, 13. Also Tropea 1900, 106.

of the professors. The Senate would propose to the students a list of *dotturi* (men with doctorates). Thirty-six students chosen by lot from the student body would vote on them. The dotturi receiving the most votes would become professors.[91] The Senate did not indicate how many professors would be chosen in this way, nor what positions they would fill.

The city's decision to appoint four distinguished outsiders copied the practice of the University of Bologna. In 1513 the Bolognese Senate decreed that the University of Bologna must have four non-Bolognese professors on its rolls, one each in law, medicine, philosophy, and the humanities. In practice these men were highly-paid distinguished scholars who were intended to garner prestige for the university and attract students. Almost all of the remaining professors at Bologna were local men of little reputation who received low salaries.[92] Messina intended to do the same. Permitting the students to choose the rest of the faculty from Messina Senate nominees was an innovative way of filling out the faculty with local men, because the unwritten assumption of the capitoli was that the Senate would nominate native sons. In short, the Messina Senate intended to have a faculty of four distinguished scholars along with an undetermined number of lowly-paid local men. Although seldom acknowledged, this was common Italian university practice.

The rest of the 1550 capitoli also aligned the university with Italian university practices. Indeed, the capitoli three times explicitly ordered that the University of Messina must follow the practices of the universities of Bologna and Padua.[93] The archbishop of Messina or his vicar would be the chancellor of the university and confer degrees. The chancellor and the college of doctors would examine doctoral candidates. The college of doctors would consist of citizens of Messina with doctoral degrees and some professors at the university. The capitoli referred to a single college of doctors; established Italian universities had one for law, a second for medicine and philosophy, and a third for theology. Doctoral recipients would not be obligated to pay more than 20 scudi for their degrees, a figure much lower than at other Italian universities.[94]

The students would elect a student to be rector of the civic part, with the rectorship alternating annually between a law student and a medicine student. The student rector would have all the honors, authority, and re-

---

91. Tropea 1900, 106; *I Capitoli dello Studio di Messina* 1990, 14.
92. Grendler 2002, 16, 18, with further bibliography.
93. Tropea 1900, 106–7; *I Capitoli dello Studio di Messina* 1990, 13–14.
94. Tropea 1900, 106–7; *I Capitoli dello Studio di Messina* 1990, 13–14, 17.

wards that student rectors at other universities received, except jurisdiction over students accused of crimes, which was reserved to the city. Most Italian towns hosting universities followed this policy, although strong student organizations were sometimes able to thwart city governments. The capitoli concluded by repeating that a new or revised papal bull that incorporated the provisions of the capitoli had to be obtained before the Jesuits would receive any money.[95] Thus, if the Jesuits wanted to be part of a University of Messina, they would have to use their influence in Rome to get a revised bull.

The Jesuits were deeply disappointed and angry. They had ceded overall control of the university and had agreed to accept a university of two parts, in return for which Ignatius and Nadal believed that the city had promised the Jesuits 2,000 scudi. Now it was going back on its word. Moreover, they believed that they had a legitimate need for 2,000 scudi, because the city's payment for education had to support all the Jesuits in the city, their church, and their other ministries, including preaching, visiting the sick, hearing confessions, and catechetical instruction, none of which generated revenue. Since the Jesuits had not been in Messina long enough to develop a strong donor base, substantial financial support from the city was needed. Indeed, the Senate's financial document of June 11, 1550, seemed to acknowledge this larger need of the Jesuits.[96] In addition, the Jesuits wanted to open a probation house, that is, a residence for Jesuit novices, and the Messina Senate knew this.

Nadal and Ignatius objected to two points in particular. They believed that 1,500 scudi was not enough for the services of fifteen teachers. And they objected to the financial controls that the city intended to impose on the delivery and expenditure of the money. Ignatius instructed Nadal to tell the city that it would provide no more than eight teachers for 1,500 scudi, adding that the Society's colleges elsewhere received greater financial support for less teaching. And he rejected civic oversight into how the Jesuits would spend the money as intolerable interference in the internal affairs of the college. The Jesuits did not budge from their position, and neither did the city.[97]

95. Tropea 1900, 106–7, 109; *I Capitoli dello Studio di Messina* 1990, 13–14, 17.

96. Tropea 1900, 101.

97. See letters of Ignatius and Polanco to Nadal, and Nadal to Ignatius, between May 17 and October 11, 1550, in *Ignatii Epistolae* 1964–1968, 3:46, 123–24, 189, 198–99, plus an undated (probably June 1550) letter of Ignatius in Novarese 1994, 439–40. See Nadal's letter to Ignatius of July 1, 1550, Messina, in Nadal 1898–1962, 1:84–87. See also Scaduto 1948, 111; and Novarese 1994, 83–85.

Once again, the Jesuits called on Viceroy Vega to exert pressure on the Messina Senate. But the viceroy was in north Africa commanding an imperial army besieging Tunis. Unable to move the Senate from afar, he urged the Jesuits to settle for what they could get. Eventually, the Senate and the Jesuits on January 4, 1552, signed an agreement in which the Jesuits agreed to provide five teachers for grammar, humanities, rhetoric, Greek, and Hebrew in exchange for 750 scudi annually. Noticeably absent were teachers of philosophy and theology, which were essential for a university. The city pledged 70 scudi toward the expenses of a probation house and the Jesuits received ownership of the house and building in which they lived and taught.[98] Nothing was said about the proposed University of Messina. Ignatius may have put the attempt to establish a university in Messina on hold because the Roman College, which opened on February 22, 1551, absorbed a great deal of the Society's intellectual and pedagogical talent.[99]

Reasons for Failure

The Jesuits in the sixteenth century and subsequent historians rightly view the Messina school open to external (non-Jesuit) students as a success and supremely important to the Jesuits. It demonstrated to the Jesuits and the world that the Society could be a successful teaching order. Moreover, the Messina school powerfully influenced Jesuit pedagogy. Annibal du Coudret, a teacher at Messina, and Nadal, the rector, drafted pedagogical treatises in 1551 and 1552 that prescribed a curriculum, method, and organization that the Jesuits practiced and refined for many years, and codified in the Ratio Studiorum of 1599.[100] But Messina was also a failure, because the Jesuits did not succeed in establishing a university or becoming part of one. The Messina Senate and the Jesuits could not agree on the structure, control, and finances of the proposed university. There were several reasons, some local and others more general.

The city wanted a university, which meant that it had to obtain a charter from the emperor or the pope. Obtaining an imperial charter was out of the question because Emperor Charles V was also King Charles I of Spain, whose monarchy enforced the Sicilian monopoly of the University of Catania. It would have been futile for the city to ask the papacy directly for a university bull, because the papacy would not have acted against the wishes of the Spanish crown. Asking the Jesuits to obtain a university bull from

98. Scaduto 1948, 112; Bangert and McCoog 1992, 67; Novarese 1994, 85–88.
99. A. Romano 1992, 55, makes this point.
100. They are found in MP 1:93–106 and 133–63. See also Codina Mir 1968, 262–336.

the papacy offered a way around the problem. Hence, the city asked Ignatius to obtain a bull creating a University of Messina, and he was successful. The Senate probably saw the Jesuits as a means to an end rather than as excellent university professors. This is understandable, because in 1548 the Jesuits had minimal experience as university professors. Their high reputation as scholars and teachers will come later.

The papal bull gave the Jesuits exactly what they wanted, which was a small collegiate university under their control in which students would reap the educational and spiritual benefits of Jesuit teaching and religious guidance. This was totally different from what the city wanted, which was an Italian law and medicine university ruled by the city. The city was not concerned about the spirituality of the students so long as they refrained from assaulting the honorable women of the town. The Jesuits proclaimed that they were following the method of Paris, while Messina wanted the organization of Bologna. The two very different conceptions of a university were the primary reasons for the failure to create a University of Messina.

Nevertheless, the two sides tried to overcome their differences. The Jesuits agreed to a university of two bodies. But a new group of senators rejected the compromise and enforced their demand for an Italian university by imposing new conditions. One wonders if reducing the subsidy and imposing intrusive financial oversight on the Jesuits were intended to exclude the Jesuits from the proposed university. In any case, that was the result.

The political and social elite of Messina were not of one mind concerning the Jesuits and their participation in the university. This was not surprising, because the Jesuits had supporters and detractors wherever they went. It was also very likely that the viceroy's forceful pressure on the Messina Senate to give the Jesuits what they wanted stiffened civic opposition to the Jesuits. Whenever the university negotiations reached an impasse, Ignatius instructed Nadal to call on the viceroy for help, and Vega always intervened on the side of the Jesuits until late 1551. The tendency of Loyola and other first Jesuits to rely on rulers to smooth the way for the Society was much in evidence in Messina.[101] But over time, calling on the viceroy proved counter-productive. The city initially welcomed Vega as a friend, but his actions caused them to reconsider. Although he built roads and hospitals, and listened to the complaints of the poor, he also cruelly punished individuals for small crimes. And he preferred coercion over persuasion in religious matters. For example, in 1555 Vega ordered all boys between the ages of six and twelve to gather in parish churches on Sundays and religious

---

101. Bangert and McCoog 1992, 102–3; O'Malley 1993, 71–72.

holidays for catechism lessons. Parents whose sons failed to attend were to be fined. He charged the Jesuits with overseeing catechetical instruction, and they responded with enthusiasm.[102] Given his methods, it is not surprising that many in Messina hated Vega by the time that he left in August 1556. Close association with the viceroy produced some hostility against the Jesuits after his departure.[103]

Nor could the Jesuits escape their Spanish origins. Loyola, Nadal, and Doménech, who played prominent roles in the negotiations with Messina, plus Diego Laínez who played a minor role, were Spaniards.[104] If the leaders of Messina saw the viceroy and the Jesuits as Spanish conquistadores, this was understandable. On the other hand, Ignatius and his fellow Jesuits seemed oblivious to the fact that they might be seen as representatives of Spanish rule. Overall, the Jesuits were somewhat naive and obtuse in their dealings with the Messina Senate.

A lesson from Messina was that a city sometimes wanted only part of what the Jesuits offered. The Senate was happy to have the Jesuits teach in a pre-university school and to exercise their other ministries. These contributed to the public good. But a university was another matter. A university was expected to educate the elite of the city, to train intellectuals who would play prominent roles in the life and government of the city. A civic-Jesuit university would have given the Jesuits a larger role in the intellectual life of the city than the governing elite of Messina was willing to allow. The contradiction between welcoming a Jesuit pre-university school and other ministries while rejecting Jesuit participation in a university will reappear in Italy. Finally, the city failed as well. It wanted a university, but when it took a hard line against the Jesuits, the possibility of creating a university disappeared. The city and the Jesuits will try again in the future.

The University in the Constitutions

Even though disagreement between the Jesuits and the Senate over control and the form of the university prevented the creation of a University of Messina, Ignatius and his lieutenants did not change their views. They continued to believe that a collegiate university dominated by the Jesuits was the best model.

In the second half of 1552 Nadal wrote a treatise on the organization of

102. *Year by Year* 2004, 376–77.
103. Bangert and McCoog 1992, 65–68; Scaduto 1948, 132–33; and A. Romano 1992, 49.
104. Scaduto 1948, 132; Bangert and McCoog 1992, 65–66, 89–90; A. Romano 1992, 38, 49.

universities, *De studii generalis dispositione et ordine*, in response to a request from Ignatius, who was soliciting comments from senior Jesuits on his draft of the Jesuit Constitutions.[105] The title is not completely accurate, because Nadal devoted two-thirds of his work to describing the curriculum and pedagogical practices for a pre-university school beginning with a class in which little boys learned to read and write.[106]

In the final third of his treatise Nadal discussed the qualifications and duties of the rector of a university, who would be a Jesuit appointed by the general. He should possess master of arts and master of theology degrees, but not a doctorate, a significant omission. The rector would oversee all studies with the aid of deans, beadles, and secretaries whom he would appoint. He would have the power to appoint and remove professors. While the teachers would ordinarily be Jesuits, if non-Jesuits had to be hired, they would receive appropriate salaries. The rector would enforce university statutes and be present at all examinations of degree candidates and disputations. He would also be chancellor for arts and theology and, in conjunction with the deans and teachers of arts and theology, would decide who received degrees.[107] In short, Nadal described an arts and theology collegiate university ruled by the Jesuits. He ignored law and medicine, and did not mention colleges of doctors.

Ignatius Loyola would soon write his plan for universities in the Jesuit Constitutions. He had begun, with the aid of Polanco, to write the Constitutions in 1547. Part 4 dealt with the education of Jesuits and external students. By 1551 he had drafted ten short chapters about schools and the education of novice Jesuits, but he had not written anything on universities. In preparation for this section, he asked the rector of the Jesuit college at Gandía to study the constitutions of the universities of Valencia, Alcalá de Henares, Salamanca, and Coimbra for him, and he wanted copies of the statutes of the universities of Paris, Louvain, Cologne, Bologna, and Padua.[108] And he soon had Nadal's *De studii generalis dispositione et ordine*.

At this moment Ignatius received another invitation for the Jesuits to be part of a new university. In July 1553 Juan Alvarez de Toledo, OP (1488–1557), cardinal and archbishop of Santiago de Compostela, proposed to Ignatius the establishment of a university there, and asked Ignatius if the So-

---

105. This is the title that Lukács gives it. It is printed in MP 1:133–63, based on the autograph manuscript. On the period of composition see also Farrell 1938, 54, and Bangert and McCoog 1992, 86.

106. MP 1:136–52. Farrell 1938, 55–58, provides a brief summary.

107. MP 1:153–63. Farrell 1938, 58–59, provides a partial summary.

108. Lukács in MP 5:5*–6*; an English translation is found in Lukács 1999, 22.

ciety would assume direction of it. The cardinal offered 2,000 scudi, while local nobles promised additional support. Ignatius' first response was to ask Diego Laínez how such a university should be organized.[109] Laínez sent a thoughtful response about a curriculum for a Jesuit school and university in Santiago de Compostela that mostly followed the lead of the Roman College. But he wrote nothing about the governance and structure of a university.[110]

After receiving Laínez' response in early August, Ignatius drafted a plan for a university in Santiago de Compostela. He mostly repeated what Laínez had written about the curriculum, but he added three items concerning governance. The rector of the Jesuit college would also be the rector and chancellor of the university. Cardinal Alvarez and other ecclesiastics might nominate students to study and possibly live under the guidance of the Jesuits in Santiago de Compostela. Ignatius proposed regulations for the spiritual formation of the students, which included catechetical instruction, prayers, obligatory attendance at Mass, and reception of the sacraments. In brief, he offered a plan for a small Jesuit collegiate university that would offer bachelor's and master's degrees in arts and theology. He did not mention law or medicine.[111] Ignatius alerted various Jesuits in Spain about the university plan. Nadal, then in Coimbra, went to Santiago de Compostela to negotiate further with the cardinal and the city about the university. He arrived on November 2, 1553.

Nadal left thirty-six hours later. Neither Cardinal Alvarez nor other strong supporters were there. Instead, Nadal had to negotiate with the city government which professed itself happy to have the Jesuits and to provide them with a building. But the city insisted that it would rule the proposed university. The city would appoint and dismiss Jesuit professors, and the Jesuits would be subject to the statutes of the university. Nadal rejected the city's terms and left.[112] The Jesuits eventually established a college, possibly

109. See the letter of Polanco written for Ignatius, to Laínez of July 29, 1553, Rome, in *Ignatii Epistolae* 1964–1968, 5:255; and reprinted in part in MP 1:433n1.

110. Letter of Laínez to Ignatius, August 5, 1553, Florence, in *Lainii Epistolae* 1912–1917, 1:228–29; and reprinted in MP 1:433–35. Polanco thought the letter was important enough to summarize it in his *Chronicon*; see MP 1:555–56. *Year by Year* 2004, 267, provides an English translation.

111. "En el collegio de Santiago," sent to Antonio de Araoz (1515–1573), superior of the province of Spain, on August 20, 1553, in *Ignatii Epistolae* 1964–1968, 5:273–75; and reprinted in MP 1:435–38. On 436.8, there should be a closed parenthesis after "canciller," which clarifies the meaning. For further references to the proposed university, see *Ignatii Epistolae* 1964–1968, 5:258, 371–72, 380–81.

112. Letter of Nadal to Loyola, November 7, 1553, Sancti Joannis de Longavares, in Nadal 1898–1962, 1:189–90.

with a school, at Santiago de Compostela in the 1570s.[113] But they never established a university there.

How much influence the Jesuit experiences in Messina and Santiago de Compostela had on the views of Ignatius and Nadal about universities is difficult to determine. In any case, the Jesuit leadership had two unhappy encounters with cities that wanted the Jesuits to be part of a university at a time when Ignatius was thinking about and drafting the section on universities for the Constitutions.

In late 1553 or early 1554 Ignatius wrote "De las universidades de la Compañía" as a separate fascicule.[114] It then became chapters 11–17 (paragraphs 440 through 509) of the final version of the Constitutions that the Society adopted as binding in 1558. It was only nine percent of the total Constitutions, fourteen pages in English translation.[115] These pages offered a plan for the organization and governance of either a Jesuit university or a university with a dominating Jesuit college.

Chapter 11 began by affirming that just as the Society can undertake the work of schools "for the improvement in learning and in living not only of our own members but even more of those from outside the Society," so it "can extend also to accepting charge of universities in which these benefits may be spread more universally," meaning by teaching and conferring degrees on non-Jesuit students. Degree recipients would then be able to "teach with authority elsewhere what they have learned well in these universities for the glory of God our Lord."[116] In short, Jesuit universities were an extension of the ministry of the schools.

The Constitutions stated that the rector of the university might be the rector of the local Jesuit college or might be another Jesuit. In either case, he would have complete authority over the university.[117] That included the power to appoint lecturers and the chancellor, also a Jesuit, so long as he

---

113. Dalmases 2001d, 1267, gives the date as 1573; Medina 2004, 959, makes it 1577; and Wright 2004, 923, offers 1578. Whether there was a school is unknown.

114. See MP 1:27* and 270–73 for the dating by Lukács, which is widely accepted.

115. See MP 1:274–325, for side-by-side Spanish and Latin versions collated from various manuscripts plus notes by Lukács. For what follows, the English translation of George Ganss is used. It is found in three places: Ganss 1956, 329–45; *Constitutions* 1970, 210–29 with notes; and *Constitutions* 1996, 177–90, without notes but with a slightly smoothed translation. In what follows the 1970 and 1996 English translations will be cited. It must be said that the *Constitutions* is a convoluted work.

116. *Constitutions* 1970, par. 440 (210–11, quotations at each page); *Constitutions* 1996, 177 (quotation).

117. "The complete charge, that is, the supervision and government of the university, will belong to the rector." Also "the office entrusted to him of directing the whole university in learning and habits of conduct." *Constitutions* 1970, par. 490 (225); *Constitutions* 1996, 187.

informed the provincial superior or the superior general of his choices. The chancellor would confer degrees and serve as de facto prefect of studies. He would represent the rector in organizing studies, overseeing disputations, and determining who would be awarded degrees. However, if the rector was able to perform the duties of chancellor in addition to his own, both functions might be invested in him.[118] This material nearly repeated what Nadal had written in *De studii generalis dispositione et ordine* in 1552.

The Constitutions added several other university officers, most of them Jesuits. Four Jesuit consultants or assistants would aid the rector. A Jesuit secretary would keep a list of the students and "receive their promise to obey the rector and to observe the Constitutions." There would be three or four non-Jesuit officers: a notary who would publicly certify degrees and two or three salaried beadles, one of whom might serve as a corrector who would administer corporal punishment as needed.[119] Other Jesuits would serve as academic officers. The university should be divided into three faculties, "languages" (meaning the humanities), "arts" (meaning philosophy), and theology, each with a Jesuit dean and two representatives from the faculty. When summoned by the rector, they would advise him on what was good for the faculty. Finally, there should be a "general syndic," also a Jesuit, who would offer information to the rector, the provincial superior, and the superior general about the persons and matters of the university.[120]

This bloated academic bureaucracy of an all-powerful rector, a chancellor, and three faculties, each with a dean and representatives, plus other officers, was similar to the structure of faculties of arts and theology in northern European universities, especially Paris. However, the University of Paris had hundreds of teachers and up to twenty thousand students, far larger than any Jesuit university would be. On the other hand, Paris had only a rector of limited powers, usually a regent master elected by the members of the faculty of arts, who served only three months.[121] What Ignatius prescribed was far more than what was needed for a Jesuit collegiate-university and was seldom, if ever, fully implemented before 1773.[122] His organizational prescriptions were completely different from Italian universities, which had no faculty structures.

118. *Constitutions* 1970, pars. 490–94 (225–26); *Constitutions* 1996, 187.

119. *Constitutions* 1970, pars. 490, 495, 498–500 (225–27, quotation at 226); *Constitutions* 1996, 187–88 (quotation).

120. *Constitutions* 1970, pars. 501–7 (227–29); *Constitutions* 1996, 188–89.

121. Schurhammer 1973, 80, 192–99, who indicates how limited were his powers.

122. This is a tentative statement, because I have not studied Jesuit universities outside of Italy.

Ignatius prohibited the Jesuits from teaching some subjects. The Constitutions stated that no Jesuit or Jesuit university would teach civil law, canon law, or medicine, because these disciplines were "more remote from our Institute."[123] (Institute meant both the founding documents of the Society and its ministries.)[124] Ignatius did leave a tiny loophole: Jesuit professors of theology might include some aspects of canon law, such as decrees of popes and church councils, in their teaching of theology. But they could not teach canon law in so far as it "is directed toward trials in court."[125] Since a major reason for studying canon law was to acquire the expertise to win cases in court, this meant that Jesuits could not teach canon law, nor would Jesuit universities include professorships of canon law. The Jesuits eventually ignored this prohibition (chapter 11).

Nadal's *De studii generalis dispositione et ordine* of 1552 and Loyola's organization of a university in the Constitutions documented that the Jesuits continued to endorse a collegiate university model dominated by a Jesuit college. One of the reasons that Nadal and Ignatius insisted that the rector be all-powerful and might also be the chancellor was that they saw educating Jesuit scholastics as a major purpose of a university.[126] They also saw a university as an element of Jesuit education that began with the lowest Latin class and concluded with theology. Despite the Messina and Santiago de Compostela disappointments, Ignatius and Nadal did not change their views. This was understandable, because Jesuit collegiate universities were rising in Germany and elsewhere. Nevertheless, the views expressed in the Constitutions will complicate attempts to found universities or to enter existing universities in Italy. Meanwhile, the effort to found a university at Messina had stalled because of disagreements with the city. The two sides will try again.

123. "The study of medicine and laws, being more remote from our Institute, will not be treated in the universities of the Society, or at least the Society will not undertake this teaching through its own members." *Constitutions* 1970, par. 452 (215); *Constitutions* 1996, 180.

124. *Constitutions* 1970, 43–45.

125. *Constitutions* 1970, par. 446 (213); *Constitutions* 1996, 179.

126. See the scholium of Nadal on the *Constitutions*, part 4, chap. 17, first sentence, on the words "qui idem esse poterit" (that the rector of the Jesuit college and the university may be the same person): "Si quidem sempre erit coniunctum collegium Societatis cum Universitate. Neque enim cura Universitatis suscipietur, nisi ubi simul poterit amplum collegium nostrorum scholasticorum institui, ea enim primaria pars Universitatis, praecipuum etiam propositum Societatis in Universitatibus suscipiendis." Nadal 1976, 307. This is also found in MP 1:313–14n2, quoted from a nineteenth-century edition. Nadal began writing a commentary on the Constitutions in 1556. Then the General Congregation of 1558 ordered Polanco and Nadal to prepare scholia (comments or explanations) to explain them better. Polanco was too busy, so Nadal wrote them, finishing in 1560, although he added more material later. See Nadal 1976, xi–xv.

3

MESSINA AND CATANIA,
1563 TO 1678

Even though the Jesuits and the Senate of Messina differed profoundly in their views about governance and organization, both parties were still interested in creating a University of Messina. This led to more negotiations. When the plague drove the Jesuits out of Messina in 1575, some Jesuits wanted to make Catania the major Jesuit school in Sicily. That provoked a debate in Catania and disagreement among the Jesuits. When the plague subsided, the Jesuits returned to Messina. There the Senate finally created an Italian law and medicine university without the Jesuits. Nevertheless, their supporters continued to try to bring the Jesuits into the University of Messina.

Negotiations Resume

The Senate of Messina did not abandon hope of establishing a university. Neither did local Jesuits, who saw Messina as the right place to educate the growing number of Sicilian scholastics. Discussions resumed in 1563 and 1564, as Pedro de Ribadeneira and Jerónimo Doménech, the provincial superior, negotiated with the Messina Senate. Doménech and Ribadeneira hoped to include six Jesuits, three to teach theology, and one each to teach logic, natural philosophy, and metaphysics, into the proposed university, for which the city would pay the Jesuits 600 scudi. On October 7, 1564, General Laínez noted some problems. He wondered if he could provide six Jesuits on short notice, and he doubted that there would be enough students for six classes. And he judged the promised payment to be inadequate. He pointed out that the Jesuits received 3,500 scudi to support their teaching at Coimbra, obviously for both university and pre-university classes.[1]

1. Scaduto 1948, 113–15, especially the long quotation from Laínez' letter written by Polanco to Doménech at 114, which is found in ARSI, Italiae 65, f. 197v. See also Novarese 1994, 88–95.

Doménech returned to the negotiating table; on November 24, 1564, he and the Messina Senate signed a scaled-back agreement. The Senate would appoint three Jesuits to teach logic, natural philosophy, and metaphysics in the university. They would be appointed to four-year terms and would receive salaries of 100 scudi each. Doménech acknowledged that this was not what he had hoped for, but believed that the terms might be improved over time. The contract was subject to the approval of Laínez, who had two months in which to respond.[2]

On December 17, 1564, Laínez rejected the contract as contrary to the principles of the Society.[3] The Society, not the Senate, had to name the Jesuits to teach. Moreover, individual Jesuits might not receive salaries for university teaching. In his eagerness to reach a long-desired Jesuit goal in Messina, Doménech had made an arrangement contrary to the principles of the Society, and Laínez pulled him up short.

But Laínez offered a very generous alternative. In order to serve the common good of the city (*servire al ben commune della città*), he was willing to send three Jesuits to Messina to teach logic, natural philosophy, and metaphysics without an increase in the subsidy that Messina was providing for the lower school. They would teach twice a day, employing the academic exercises that had proved so successful in Rome in "awakening the intellects and resolving the difficulties" that arose from the lectures. He meant the method of Paris that the Jesuits were using at the Collegio Romano.[4] The Jesuits inaugurated a course in logic in their college in Messina in the academic year 1564–1565.[5]

After Laínez died on January 19, 1565, his successor, Francisco de Borja, wished to continue the same policy in the hope that the Jesuits might become part of a University of Messina.[6] But the Senate thought otherwise. In 1565 it again sought to establish a university without the Jesuits by promulgating statutes that ignored the papal bull of 1548. Instead, they claimed that the Byzantine emperor Arcadius (r. 395–408) had crowned Messina "Siciliae caput" (leader of Sicily) because the city had rescued the Roman fleet in 407, and that this meant imperial approval for a university. They also stated that King Alfonso V of Aragon (r. 1416–1458) had given permission to the city of Messina for a university in 1434, and that King

2. The contract is printed in Novarese 1994, 371–74; Scaduto 1948, 115, provides excerpts.

3. Scaduto 1948, 115–16.

4. "Per svegliar li ingegni et risolver le difficultà che delle lettioni restanto sogliono adoperare," from Laínez' letter of December 17, 1564, Rome, as quoted in Scaduto 1948, 116.

5. Scaduto 1974, 360.

6. Scaduto 1948, 116–19; Novarese 1994, 89–90.

John II of Aragon (r. 1458–1479) had given permission to the city for a college of doctors to award degrees in 1459. The latter two claims were true.[7]

The rest of the 1565 statutes described an Italian law and medicine university whose professors would teach "iuxta modum Studiorum Italie" (according to the style of Italian universities), possibly an implied rejection of the *modus Parisiensis* of the Jesuits. The statutes listed the usual positions (civil law, canon law, medicine, philosophy, and theology) and assigned salaries ranging from 500 scudi for the leading professor of civil law down to 50 scudi for the professor of theology. The students would elect a rector, while the Messina Senate would appoint two officials called *riformatori* to oversee the university. The statutes never mentioned the Jesuits.[8] This was not the beginning of a university, because the Senate of Messina did not appoint professors nor had it overcome the objections of Catania. Rather, the Senate again made it clear that it wanted an Italian law and medicine university without the Jesuits.

Despite the Senate's snub, in 1567 General Borja approved upper school classes, and in the early 1570s the Messina school regularly offered two classes in scholastic theology, and one each in cases of conscience, metaphysics, natural philosophy, and logic, plus a lower school of about six classes. In 1574 the Messina Jesuits numbered 80 to 90, including about 15 scholastics and 20 novices, because the Society had opened a novice house in Messina.[9] Messina was the most important of the eight Jesuit colleges in Sicily.

To demonstrate its determination to strive toward a full university the Senate annually paid one to four men to teach law and medicine in the second half of the 1560s and in the 1570s. In any given year at least one man taught each discipline. The Senate sometimes added another one or two for other disciplines, including an Augustinian friar to teach metaphysics and a Dominican to teach theology, subjects that the Jesuits taught in their school. The men appointed to this skeleton university lacking the authority to award degrees usually taught for a few years, then left.[10]

The Senate did appoint a former Jesuit to teach metaphysics in 1568, but it was not a friendly move. This was Miguel Garzía (near Cuenca 1536–1571 Loreto), who became a Jesuit in 1558, studied at the Roman College and was ordained a priest about 1564. Considered a learned man, he began

7. The two very short and cryptic royal privileges are printed in Tropea 1900, 85–86.

8. The 1565 statutes are found in G. Romano 1900, 151–57 (quotation at 152), and *I Capitoli dello Studio di Messina* 1990, 18–25 (quotation at 19). See also the analysis in Novarese 1994, 95–102.

9. Lukács 1960–1961, part 2, 50; Scaduto 1992, 226–28.

10. Novarese 1994, 128–35, and the documents at 490–95.

teaching philosophy in the Jesuit school at Messina in or before 1566, but was not very successful. Nevertheless, the short-handed Jesuits decided to let him teach theology in tandem with a senior Jesuit. But Garzía mocked the theological approach of his colleague. Recalled to Rome, Garzía was dismissed from the Society. Although he had promised to return to Spain, he went back to Messina where, with the help of a former student who had been a Jesuit briefly before being dismissed, he persuaded the Senate to appoint him professor of metaphysics at a salary of 125 scudi. This was 25 scudi higher than the value that the Senate placed on Jesuit professors in previous negotiations. The Messina Jesuits were very angry at the favor shown a man who had been dismissed from the Society. In the uproar Garzía was forced to return to Rome where he was, surprisingly, readmitted into the Society in December 1568.[11] Although it is not likely that Garzía taught very long, if at all, in the Messina skeleton university, the episode documented the continuing friction between city and Society over the proposed university.

The Move to Catania

The scene shifted to Catania. Plague in Messina in 1575 forced the Jesuits to move their scholastics and upper school to Catania where a debate revealed how the leaders of that city viewed the Jesuits as university teachers.

The Jesuits already had a college with a school in Catania. In 1547 Viceroy Juan de Vega and some citizens began encouraging the city to invite the Jesuits while simultaneously urging the Jesuits to establish a college there. Although a college was not founded at that time, the Jesuits with the support of the viceroy did organize an orphanage and taught the catechism. Then in 1554 Hernando de Vega, eldest son of Juan and captain of the military force at Catania, renewed the quest for a Jesuit college. He had a further ambition: because he judged the University of Catania to be a weak institution in need of reorganization, he wanted direction of the university given to the Society.[12] This was a fruitful tactic in northern Europe. Requests inviting the Jesuits to enter small and/or weak universities in order to revitalize them had enabled the Jesuits to assume important positions in the universities of Ingolstadt, Prague, Trier, and Vienna.

Certainly the University of Catania was small and undistinguished. It

11. Scaduto 1948, 151–53; Scaduto 1968, 62–63, under the name "García, Michele"; Scaduto 1992, 224, 226; and Novarese 1994, 134.

12. Catalano 1916–1917, part 1, 53.

had only a dozen professors, none of them accomplished: three for civil law, two for canon law, three for medicine and surgery, and one each for natural philosophy, logic, the humanities, and theology. They were mostly Sicilians, many of whom had acquired doctorates at Catania. The university had about 200 students, the vast majority studying law. Nevertheless, it was the only educational institution in Sicily empowered to confer degrees.[13]

The Jesuits were amenable to this suggestion, not least because of their frustration in Messina. In September 1554, Jerónimo Doménech, the provincial superior, wrote to Ignatius to propose that the Jesuits should establish a college at Catania. He also reported Hernando de Vega's long term goal.[14] It is not likely that the city government knew about Vega's plan for the university. Ignatius poured ice water on the idea. He did not think that the time was right for another Jesuit upper school in Italy because the Society did not have enough teachers for advanced classes. He doubted that Catania would provide the necessary financial support. And he believed that Messina was the proper place for a university with Jesuit participation. The Jesuits had obligated themselves to do this in Messina, and with the help of additional income which he believed had been secured, he concluded that a University of Messina would come into being.[15]

The proposal for a college in Catania did not die. In early 1556 the bishop of Catania, with the support of Juan and Hernando de Vega, asked Ignatius to send some Jesuits to Catania to establish a college. Ignatius hesitated, because he was still worried about local financial support and the difficulty of finding Jesuits to send. But he reluctantly agreed, because Catania had a university.[16] Two Jesuit priests and two brothers arrived in Catania in late February 1556. They began preaching, teaching the catechism, hearing confessions, and, most importantly, negotiating with the city of Catania for financial support. The unenthusiastic city and the Jesuits eventually reached an agreement in principle on a subsidy of 210 scudi annually. The

13. For the history of the University of Catania in the fifteenth and sixteenth centuries, see Catalano 1934; Catalano-Tirrito 1975; and Sabbadini 1975. Grendler 2002, 106–8, 515, offers a summary and more bibliography.

14. "Estuue dos días en Çaragossa, y de allí me boluí donde estava el señor Hernando de Vega, y platicamos sobre Catania, que está á su cargo, y díxome que havía pensado, para reformar la vniversidad, que no havía otro medio que dar la sopraintendentia á la Compañía ..." Letter of Doménech to Loyola of September 23, 1554, Messina, in *Epistolae mixtae* 1898–1901, 4:353; and Catalano 1916–1917, part 1, 51.

15. Letter of Ignatius written by Polanco to Doménech of December 5, 1554, Rome, in *Ignatii Epistolae* 1964–1968, 8:138. Catalano 1916–1917, part 1, 54, quotes much of it.

16. Letters of Ignatius written by Polanco of February 29 and March 3, 1556, Rome, in *Ignatii Epistolae* 1964–1968, 11:71, 84; and Catalano 1916–1917, part 1, 55.

bishop also contributed money, and Hernando de Vega bought a house for the Jesuits.[17]

The Jesuit school began in the spring of 1558 with two lower school classes. It had an initial enrollment of 80 students which grew to 220, probably in three classes, in 1563. The number of Jesuits rose from nine in 1559 to nineteen, including a few scholastics, in the mid–1560s.[18] The Jesuits wanted to add a philosophy course in or about 1570. But the city was unwilling to increase its financial support, which would have meant subsidizing competition to the university.[19] In 1574 there were twenty-one Jesuits in Catania, and the school offered four lower school classes.[20]

Then in 1575 Catania became part of the story of the University of Messina. At the end of February 1575 General Everard Mercurian (1514–1580, general from 1573) appointed Juan de Polanco visitor to Sicily with wide powers. He arrived in March. On September 8, 1575, Polanco wrote to Mercurion that the plague was worsening in Messina. He was considering moving two of the Messina philosophy courses to Catania.[21] In early October Polanco wrote again. The plague had struck Messina in full force and the city had ordered some school closings. Moreover, the city had ceased paying its annual subsidy of 300 scudi to support the Jesuit upper school. Polanco and Doménech had decided to transfer the classes of scholastic theology, metaphysics, natural philosophy, and logic to Catania, which meant moving teachers, scholastics, and some brothers. Polanco saw some advantages to the move: Catania had better air than Messina and a university.[22] On October 17, 1575, some sixty Jesuits waited outside the gates of Catania for permission to enter.[23]

They received permission and entered Catania where the bishop welcomed them. For the time being the Jesuits lived in the episcopal palace and in nearby houses. There were now seventy Jesuits in Catania and they desperately needed more money. The bishop of Catania diverted the income

17. ARSI, Sicula 194 II C, ff. 8r, 17r–19v; Catalano 1916–1917, part 1, 56–80; part 2, 159; Tacchi Venturi 1951b, 480–81; and Scaduto 1974, 356–57.

18. Scaduto 1974, 355–56.

19. Scaduto 1992, 238.

20. Lukács 1960–1961, part 2, 108.

21. Letter of Polanco to Mercurian of September 18, 1575, Messina, in *Polanci complementa* 1969, 2:362.

22. Letter of Polanco to Mercurian of October 5–8, 1575, Messina, in *Polanci complementa* 1969, 2:368–69.

23. Letter of Giovanni Battista Carminata of October 17, 1575, Messina, in ARSI, Italiae 149, f. 24r.

from some benefices to support them and added an outright gift.[24] This sustained them for the time being.

The Jesuits prepared for the new academic year. They held public disputations and recited orations and verses in order to "wake up" the people of Catania and to attract students to the upper school classes.[25] Classes began immediately after November 2, with the four new upper school classes meeting in the bishop's house. The Jesuits were pleased that the classes attracted students.[26]

But they needed more money. Additional Jesuits had arrived from plague-stricken Bivona, bringing the total to eighty in Catania. Doménech had moved himself to Catania as well, adding to the importance of the Catania college. He wrote to Rome that this might be the time to make Catania the major Jesuit college in Sicily, because Catania had good air, more food, and cheaper housing than Messina. And because it had "an old university," he expected that upper school enrollment would be higher than at Messina. Doménech speculated that the Catania school could replace Messina for philosophy and theology, while Messina would teach the humanities and languages. And, of course, the Jesuits were disappointed that the Messina Senate had refused to create a university, although Doménech did not mention this.[27] But the pressing need was financial. Polanco spoke with the leaders of Catania about an increased subsidy from the city, and he hoped to have good news after Christmas.[28]

On December 27, 1575, the Consiglio Generale (General Council or Assembly) of Catania met to consider a proposal to support a Jesuit upper school in the city. The Consiglio Generale was a special legislative body that met when matters considered to be of great importance needed to be considered. Its membership consisted of about eighty men, including the captain of the city (the chief law enforcement and judicial official), the members of the major executive magistracy (called giurati), nobles, mer-

24. Letter of Jerónimo Doménech to Mercurian of October 19, 1575, Catania, in ARSI, Italiae 149, f. 28v.

25. "Si facessi con rumor de dispute publiche, et orationi, et versi, per animar et svegliar' i catanesi." Letter of Polanco to Mercurian of October 5–8, 1575, Messina, in *Polanci Complementa* 1969, 2:369.

26. See the letters of Polanco to Mercurian of October 30, 1575, Catania, in *Polanci Complementa* 1969, 2:387; and of Jerónimo Doménech to Mercurian of November 18, 1575, Catania, in ARSI, Italiae 149, f. 129r–v.

27. Letter of Doménech to Mercurian of November 18, 1575, Catania, in ARSI, Italiae 149, f. 129v.

28. Letter of Polanco to Mercurian of December 20–21, 1575, Catania, in *Polanci Complementa* 1969, 2:425.

chants, and artisans.[29] One of the giurati opened the meeting by describing the spiritual benefits that the town had already received from the Jesuits through their preaching, by hearing confessions, and other ministries. He reported that the Jesuit college had added many more preachers and priests; thus, it was appropriate to increase the subsidy.[30]

The captain, Cavalier Geronimo li Cutelli, then made the recommendation, which clearly was what the leaders of the city had worked out in advance, hoping that it would be endorsed by the General Council. The city had previously proposed to give the Jesuits 250 scudi with which to buy a house as well as an income of 165 scudi annually to support the school, he began.[31] This was now inadequate. Cutelli recommended that the city should give the Jesuits a one-time donation of 500 scudi for accommodations and pay them 250 scudi annually for the larger Jesuit school. In order to fund the annual payment he proposed that the city establish an endowment fund of 3,125 scudi that would yield eight percent in annual income, which would be 250 scudi. The money would come from the tax on food. In return the Jesuits would have to obligate themselves to stay in Catania and to maintain in perpetuity the lectureships of theology, metaphysics, natural philosophy, and logic. They would also have to promise not to offer these classes in any other school in Sicily. However, they could teach Latin, Greek, Hebrew, and one class of logic elsewhere.[32] The meaning was that Catania would be the major Jesuit school in Sicily with a full complement of upper-level courses. By contrast, the Messina Jesuit school would teach only Greek, Hebrew, and lower school classes, while the school in Palermo would teach logic and lower school classes, as it was doing at the time.[33] The following speaker endorsed what Cutelli proposed.

However, Pietro Colle (not further identified) offered an opposing view, which he said had the endorsement of a number of citizens. He argued that the city owed no obligation to the Jesuit professors and students who had just arrived. They were not part of the Catania college but came from elsewhere. He believed that other Jesuit colleges were better prepared

29. Catalano 1916–1917, part 1, 47, 58–59. The giurati functioned like the senators of Messina except that they were not called senators until 1608.

30. Catalano 1916–1917, part 2, 160–61, 182–83. The archival document with the entire discussion and vote of December 27, 1575, is printed in 182–86.

31. Catania, like Messina, used Sicilian ounces, a money of account worth 2.5 scudi. Again ounces have been converted into scudi for the sake of consistency and to facilitate comparisons. The Jesuits mostly wrote *scudi* in their correspondence.

32. Catalano 1916–1917, part 2, 161, 183–84.

33. See Grendler 2004a, 498. No other Jesuit school in Sicily taught any upper school classes in 1580.

financially to support the displaced Messina Jesuits. Catania was already overburdened with taxes and had to pay a substantial sum to the Spanish government for the defense of Sicily. Rather than adding a new and unnecessary financial burden, they should devote the city's scarce resources to the support of local monasteries and pious works.[34]

The fourth speaker was Giovanni Mercurio, who had earlier taught surgery and medicine at the University of Catania.[35] He argued that helping the Jesuits would not help the university, and that the Jesuits wanted to create their own university. Although the Jesuits claimed that their courses in theology, philosophy, and logic taught by pious professors would attract students from other parts of Italy, which would aid the University of Catania, he did not believe this to be true. Students came from afar to study law and medicine, which the Jesuits did not teach, he asserted. The Jesuits would be teaching only their own students. Nor could he resist pointing out that Messina had looked to its own needs at a time of crisis and had permitted the Jesuits to leave. Helping the University of Catania should be the city's greatest concern. Students did not come to the University of Catania from distant places now because the university lacked a distinguished professor of medicine. Further, no excellent medical professor was willing to come to Catania because the stipends were so low and because the university lacked a second professor of philosophy. Instead of giving money to the Jesuit college, Mercurio recommended that the commune use the 250 scudi to improve the University of Catania by appointing a second professor of philosophy and by raising the salaries of the professors of medicine.[36]

Other speakers endorsed the gift and increased annual payment to the Jesuits with conditions. One speaker objected to the fact that the tax to pay the annual subsidy to the Jesuits would fall most heavily on the poor. He believed that the wealthy should provide the subsidy and he volunteered 25 scudi.[37] In the end the original proposal of Cavalier Cutelli prevailed. It received 68 votes, Colle's proposal received 11, and a third proposal received a single vote.[38] It appears that Mercurio's recommendation was not put to a vote, possibly because self-interest tainted his argument. He wanted a pro-

34. Catalano 1916–1917, part 2, 161, 184.

35. Mercurio (life dates unknown) was professor of surgery, a position of low prestige, in the academic year 1569–1570. He moved up to afternoon professor of medicine in 1570–1571, returned to surgery for three years, 1571–1574, then was replaced by another man. Mercurio held no professorship when he spoke in December 1575. Catalano 1934, 75–76, 80.

36. Catalano 1916–1917, part 2, 161–62, 184–85.

37. Catalano 1916–1917, part 2, 161–63, 185–86.

38. Catalano 1916–1917, part 2, 186. However, Catalano also states (ibid., 163) that the proposal received 70 votes.

fessorship of medicine, which he received in 1578. Moreover, he wanted the university to add a second professorship of philosophy as a counterweight to the incumbent professor of natural philosophy with whom he had quarreled.[39]

Why did Catania agree to provide additional financial support for Jesuit upper school courses that had the potential of competing with the University of Catania? Probably because they saw this as a means of blocking a University of Messina. If the Jesuit theology, metaphysics, and natural philosophy classes were taught in Catania, they would not be taught in Messina. Protecting Catania's monopoly of Sicilian university education was always the primary issue for the city.[40] To that end it was willing to support the Jesuits even if they competed with its own university. On the other hand, the discussion also revealed negative attitudes toward the Jesuits. Some saw them as outsiders to whom the city owed nothing. And Mercurio did not believe that the Jesuits would attract more students to the University of Catania.

Despite the reservations of some, the city approved an increased subsidy to support the upper school classes of the Jesuits. Polanco expressed his pleasure in his letter of January 3, 1576, to Mercurian. He believed that the Catania school could and should become the most important Jesuit school in Sicily, the Society's "university." Catania had healthy air and offered comfortable living, while the Jesuit college in Messina was located in an unhealthy place. There were now eighty Jesuits in Catania and, by the grace of God, all were healthy. The students were well disposed, unlike those in Messina, a city afflicted by melancholy. If it were to be the will of God that the principal Jesuit house of studies should remain in Catania, he hoped that God would favor it.[41] Polanco then discussed ways of securing more money, including transferring bequests from other Jesuit provinces to

39. Catalano 1916–1917, part 2, 161; Catalano 1934, 74, 76, 81. Mercurio held the morning professorship of medicine from 1578 to 1595. And the university added a second professor of philosophy in 1580.

40. See the remarks of Catalano 1916–1917, part 2, 159.

41. "Et in vero, ci pare questo luogo con molta ragion eletto per far vniversità da questo regno, per la salubrità dell'aere et commodità del vivere; et anche per tener li studii nostri principali di questa provincia, ci pare questa città molto oportuna. Siamo qui intorno ad 80 persone, et tutti sani per la divina gratia, et di buona voglia li scolari, quali stavano in Messina in molto differente dispositione, perchè quella città è molto soggetta alla melancolia, et mal sano il sito del collegio nostro." "Et se sarà la volontà di Dio N. S. che il principale studio nostro resti in Catania, spero darà buon successo a qualchuno delli disegni che ci sono." Polanco's letter to Mercurian of January 3, 1576, Catania, in *Polanci Complementa*, 1969, 2:438–39 (quotations at both pages).

Catania, borrowing against future income, and selling annuities, because the funds from the endowment to be established by the city would not be available before August.[42]

The money never came. The city did not give the Jesuits the higher subsidy for which it had voted.[43] The reason is that General Mercurian did not approve making Catania the major Jesuit school in Sicily. In a letter of February 25, 1576, he told Polanco that he should not make any new plans for Catania. He sharply reminded Polanco of the gratitude and debt in conscience that the Jesuits owed Messina. When the plague ends, they should return there. He forbade Polanco from agreeing to the terms of the city. He told Polanco not to engage in any new building projects in Catania, and he denied permission for the Jesuits to enter into the money-raising ventures that Polanco had proposed.[44] Thus Mercurian scuttled the plan for Catania to replace Messina and sharply rebuked Polanco.

There was no love lost between Mercurian and Polanco. As explained in the appendix to this study, most Jesuits expected that Polanco would be elected general in 1573. However, Pope Gregory XIII vetoed all Spaniards, and some Jesuits opposed Polanco because of his *converso* ancestry. Hence, the Society elected Mercurian, who was born in Luxembourg. Mercurian then moved Polanco and some other prominent Jesuits of converso ancestry out of Rome.[45] It was shabby treatment for someone who had contributed so much to the Society.

In addition, Polanco and Mercurian were very different. By his actions in Sicily Polanco showed that he was a first Jesuit. He wanted to seize opportunities when they presented themselves and then scramble to make them succeed. Mercurian, by contrast, believed in caution, order, and regular procedures. He tried to impose this *modus operandi* on the Society while

42. Letter of Polanco to Mercurian, January 17, 1576, Catania, in *Polanci Complementa* 1969, 2:445–49.

43. Catalano 1916–1917, part 2, 163–64.

44. "20. Quanto alla permutatione degli studi di Messina a Catania per perpetuargli in quella città, non si deve dare alcuna intentione di questo, nè fare alcuno nuovo disegno. Et quando verrà il procuratore si potrà trattare il fatto con maggiore luce. Et conviene fra tanto che ci habbia molto riguardo alla gratitudine che dobbiamo alla città di Messina et al debito della conscienza; et cessato la peste non sarà necessario che alla città di Messina si dia alcuna significatione di tale permuta. Et sarà bene che qua si scriva se Catania ha dato o vuole dare alcuna cosa, et con che conditione. Et pensiamo che V. R. non haurà fatto cosa alcuna nè dato intentione di accettare niente; perchè sa che bisogna haverlo prima trattato qua, et presentate le conditioni." Letter of Mercurian to Polanco of February 25, 1576, Rome, in *Polanci Complementa* 1969, 2:481. In the rest of the long letter (477–82) Mercurian rejected all of the proposals for raising money in Catania and practically everything else that Polanco wanted to do.

45. Maryks 2010, 68–71, 117–18, 121–23.

invoking the example of Loyola as justification. Although Ignatius had also preferred Messina to Catania, in many other instances he had been a bold opportunist.

Polanco promised to obey. But then with the support of Doménech and other Jesuits, he continued to try to persuade Mercurian that Catania was preferable. They were prepared to return to Messina, but few would do so voluntarily, he wrote. Messina was an unhealthy place; the father provincial called it the "sepulcher" of the students. If the Jesuits had to return to Messina, they would need to find a new residence. By contrast, Catania was a healthy city, the students were doing well, and Polanco had the promise of more financial help.[46]

Mercurian responded decisively. He repeated his order, appointed a new provincial superior for Sicily, and relieved Polanco of his visitorship. He instructed him to go to Calabria for his health and to visit colleges there if he wished.[47] In a long letter to Mercurian of June 30, 1576, Polanco reviewed and justified his actions regarding Catania and Messina, then left for Calabria.[48] Now gravely ill with double tertian fever (malaria in which the fever occurs daily) he slowly made his way back to Rome where he died on December 20, 1576.

The plague subsided and the Messina Jesuits went back to Messina in autumn 1577, while the Bivona Jesuits returned to Bivona. The Jesuit college and school at Catania reverted to their previous dimensions of about twenty Jesuits and a lower school of three classes.[49] The Catania story had a brief epilogue. In 1579 the Catania Jesuits asked for positions in the University of Catania. Viceroy Marco Antonio Colonna (r. 1577–1584), rejected the request, but he also eliminated the humanities professorship in the university. Consequently, university students desirous of humanities instruction would have to attend the Jesuit school or go elsewhere.[50] Hence the Jesuits did not teach in the university, but did teach an unknown number of university students who came to their college classes.

46. Letters of Polanco to Mercurian of April 2, May 19, and June 15, 1576, from Palermo, Catania, and Carangino, in *Polanci Complementa* 1969, 2:509, 518–19, and 523–25, with the comment about the Messina college being a sepulcher on 523.

47. Mercurian's letter to Polanco of April 15, 1576, Rome, in *Polanci Complementa* 1969, 2:514–16. The Jesuits often repeated their messages because they assumed that not all letters would reach their destinations and others would be delayed.

48. Letter of Polanco to Mercurian of June 30, 1576, Tremilia (the Jesuit villa outside of Siracusa), in *Polanci Complementa* 1969, 2:528–33.

49. On January 1, 1581, there were 22 Jesuits in the Catania college and it offered three lower school classes. In May 1582 there were 18 Jesuits and the same three classes. ARSI, Sicula 183 I, ff. 10r, 35r.

50. Catalano 1916–1917, part 2, 166–67; repeated in Catalano 1934, 90–91.

So ended the Catania interlude. Hernando de Vega wanted the Jesuits to become part of the University of Catania in 1554 but nothing happened. Then the plague brought the Messina upper school classes to Catania in 1575. Dissatisfied with Messina, Polanco and Doménech sought to make Catania the major Jesuit school in Sicily. Although they did not mention entering the University of Catania in their letters, that would have been a logical future goal. The 1575 debate in the Consiglio Generale of Catania revealed strong support for the Society, plus some opposition and doubt that the Jesuit school would benefit the university. However, General Mercurian vetoed the plan. The Jesuits requested positions in the University of Catania in 1579 but were rebuffed.

The University of Messina

The city of Messina renewed its efforts and succeeded in founding an Italian university in 1596, in which the Jesuits were not included. After the Jesuits returned to Messina, things began well. Thanks in part to pressure from Viceroy Marco Antonio Colonna, the Messina Senate on March 11, 1578, renewed its contract with the Jesuits for their upper school for a period of six years.[51] The Jesuits were happy. On January 1, 1581, the provincial superior for Sicily reported that the Messina college had eighty Jesuits, including twenty-four scholastics. The school offered fifteen classes, the most ever, nine of them in the upper school: three for scholastic theology, plus a single class (and professor) for cases of conscience, metaphysics, natural philosophy, logic, Hebrew, and Greek. The lower school had six classes in Latin grammar, the humanities, and rhetoric. The school enrolled 400 non-Jesuits in fifteen classes.[52]

The city of Messina simultaneously moved against the Jesuits. On April 22, 1578, the Senate "nomine universitatis" (in the name of the university) began to pay the Dominicans in the city 250 scudi annually for offering public lectures in theology, philosophy, logic, and cases of conscience. What did this mean? The Messina Dominicans had had a school of theology and philosophy with the power to confer degrees for some time, and the next General Congregation of the Dominicans confirmed it in 1580. Now the Messina Senate was paying the Dominicans to open their lectures to all comers, alongside the three or four law and medicine lectures that

51. Novarese 1994, 105, 120, and especially the documents at 378–83.
52. ARSI, Sicula 183 I, f. 8v. The information is repeated in Grendler 2004a, 498, table 5. The provincial superior was Giovanni Battista Carminata (Palermo 1536–1619? Palermo). Scaduto 1968, 27.

the city sponsored. And since the Dominican school possessed the power to confer degrees in theology and philosophy, the implication was that it would be part of the University of Messina that the city was striving to establish. Since the city had practically designated the Dominicans as university lecturers, it no longer had to deal with the Jesuits or the papal bull of 1548. Thus the Messina Senate stopped paying the Jesuits for their upper school lectures in 1581. In the next few years the Jesuits took legal action and appealed to the viceroy in an effort to compel the Senate to honor its financial commitment.[53]

The city changed its mind in early 1590. Now the Messina Senate agreed to increase the subsidy to the Jesuits from 475 scudi to 750 scudi for three philosophy lectureships and three other positions (presumably in the lower school), and to support their other ministries.[54] There was a reason. In 1592 another General Congregation of the Dominican Order revoked the authority of its Messina school to confer degrees.[55]

This maneuvering took place as the city closed in on its long-sought goal of a university with the authority to award degrees. In 1590 the city of Messina made what it called a free donation of 500,000 scudi, an immense sum, to the Spanish monarchy. In return, the crown on October 21, 1591, authorized Messina to establish a university with the power to confer doctorates. The crown also permitted the city to impose a tax on wheat and flour entering the city to pay for the university.[56] Although the royal action never referred to the University of Catania, it meant the end of Catania's monopoly. The royal decree did not mention the papal bull of 1548 nor the Jesuits, which left their status unclear. In short, the crown gave Messina what it desperately wanted, a university charter, and left it to the city to create a functioning university and to deal with unresolved legal issues.

With permission to create a university empowered to grant degrees and with the Dominicans no longer in the picture, the Senate once again turned to the Jesuits to help staff the university. The negotiations went well. Even though General Claudio Acquaviva (Atri 1543–1615 Rome, general from 1581) believed that a university including the Jesuits should be unitary and have a Jesuit as rector and chancellor as the Constitutions stated, he quickly agreed that the University of Messina would be organized into two mostly

---

53. Novarese 1994, 120–24, and the documents at 469–77 (quotation at 469).

54. See the document of October 4, 1590, published in Novarese 1994, 383–84. See also Scaduto 1948, 124; and A. Romano 1992, 58.

55. Novarese 1994, 124.

56. The text of the decree of 1591 is found in *I capitoli dello Studio di Messina* 1990, note 25 on pp. xx–xxi. See also Cesca 1900, 18–19; Scaduto 1948, 124; and Novarese 1994, 104–5.

independent parts, Jesuit and civic. On the other side, the Senate promised the Jesuits an annual payment of 2,500 scudi, a generous sum, in addition to the 750 scudi that it already paid for the lower school. In return, the Jesuits would provide seventeen teachers for the university and the lower school combined.[57]

The preparations for the university then stopped for three years, because Catania challenged the decision of the Spanish crown to permit Messina to have a university with the power to confer degrees.[58] Because the papal bull of 1548 was at the center of the dispute, Catania took its case to the Sacred Roman Rota, the highest court in the Catholic church, consisting of twelve judges called auditors. To argue its side Messina hired the well-known legal scholar Giacomo Gallo (Naples 1544–1618 Padua), who obtained his doctorate in law at the University of Naples and taught law there for many years, becoming the highest paid professor. He then moved to Rome in 1591 where he argued cases before papal courts.[59]

Gallo made an ingenious but not always convincing presentation that swept away both Catania's monopoly and the Jesuits. Against Catania he argued that Messina had already received from King John II of Aragon in 1459 the privilege that created a college of doctors with the authority to award degrees. The University of Messina had not yet conferred any degrees, but this was due to viceregal and monarchical prohibitions that had protected the monopoly of Catania. They were now gone, while the University of Messina retained the privilege of awarding degrees. Then he faced the obstacle that the papal bull of 1548 awarded the Jesuits authority over a university in Messina. Gallo argued that although the University of Messina was associated with the Jesuits because of the papal bull, it really was an Italian law and medicine university (studium generale) because the papal bull had awarded a university not to the Jesuits but to the city. Why? Because of the previous existence of a college of doctors, and because law and medicine instruction were an integral part of a studium generale but not appropriate to the Society of Jesus.[60] He meant that the Constitutions prohibited the Jesuits from teaching law and medicine.

On May 23, 1593, the Sacred Roman Rota ruled that the papal bull of

57. Scaduto 1948, 125–27, which quotes most of Acquaviva's letter of 1592 (no month) and another letter of April 30, 1592; and Novarese 1994, 107–9, and 384–86 for Acquaviva's letter of 1592 detailing Jesuit demands.

58. For the dispute before the Sacred Roman Rota, see Cesca 1900, 19; Tropea 1900, 59; Scaduto 1948, 128; Novarese 1994, 108–19.

59. For a brief biography, see Buscemi 1900, 59–62. For Gallo's career at the University of Naples, see Cannavale 1980, 71–76, 82; and Cortese 1924, 318.

60. Novarese 1994, 108–15, summarizes Gallo's consilium which his son later published.

1548 conferred a university on the city of Messina, and it rejected Catania's monopoly. Catania appealed and the Rota confirmed its ruling in 1594 and 1595.[61] Nevertheless, Gallo's arguments and the Rota's ruling are hard to reconcile with the words of the bull, which clearly awarded a university and authority over it to the Jesuits. Several factors may have influenced the judges. Gallo based part of his case on the common definition of an Italian law and medicine university. This had a supporting legal tradition that all the auditors of the Rota must have understood well, because they possessed law degrees from Italian universities. Another reason may have been that the Jesuits took no role in the legal argument between Messina and Catania. When the dispute arose, General Acquaviva ordered the Messina and Catania Jesuits to remain neutral, because both cities supported Jesuit colleges.[62] So far as can be determined, the Jesuits did not present a brief in the case, which may have made it easier for the Rota to ignore the words of the papal bull.

Personal and political considerations may also have aided Gallo and Messina.[63] Gallo had excellent connections with some of the auditors of the Sacred Roman Rota and the higher clergy: his brother was the bishop of Nola (near Naples) and a relative was a cardinal. It is also possible that the Rota and, by extension, the papacy, did not wish to oppose the will of the government of Philip II, the most powerful monarch in Europe. It would not be the first time, nor would it be the last, that a court acceded to the wishes of a ruler rather than follow the words of a legal document, or that a papal court failed to support the Jesuits in a university dispute. Finally, in April 1596 Messina defeated another legal challenge brought by Catania, this time before the Spanish crown.[64] Messina was now free to inaugurate a university with the power to award degrees.

With the legal challenges from Catania overcome, the Senate and the Society returned to negotiating the role of the Jesuits in the university. On May 16, 1596, General Acquaviva named a Jesuit to be the chancellor of the university.[65] Although the Jesuits and the city discussed some of the same issues and differences that had first arisen in 1549, the city now had the upper hand, and opponents of the Jesuits were bolder. An initial document

---

61. Scaduto 1948, 128; and Novarese 1994, 115–16.

62. See Acquaviva's letter to the giurati of Catania of August 1, 1592, quoted in Scaduto 1948, 128; and Novarese 1994, 108n73. Moscheo 1991, 121, states that the refusal of the Jesuits to support Messina in the dispute poisoned relations with the Messina Senate in the 1590s.

63. Novarese 1994, 109–10, makes the points concerning Gallo's personal contacts in Rome. The rest of this paragraph consists of my speculations on the reasons for the Rota's decision.

64. Novarese 1994, 117–19, and the documents on 454–68.

65. Scaduto 1948, 129; Novarese 1994, 146.

with the title *Capitoli propusti* [sic] *la prima volta* (here called "the first *Capitoli*") indicated the state of the discussions in early summer 1596.[66]

The first Capitoli contained fifteen numbered paragraphs. Paragraph one affirmed that the rector of the Jesuit college would be the chancellor of the university. As chancellor he would assign the *punti* (the passages that degree candidates discussed in examinations), order candidates to make professions of faith before receiving degrees, confer the doctorate on all those admitted to the doctorate by a college of doctors, sign diplomas, and hold the seal of the university. Admission to the doctorate by a college of doctors meant that it, not the chancellor, would conduct the degree examinations determining who would become doctors. Paragraph eight stated that neither the Jesuit rector nor the chancellor would have any authority over the law professors or the law students.[67] In short, while a Jesuit would be the chancellor, he would be a ceremonial chancellor without power, like the local bishops who served as chancellors in all Italian universities except Rome.

Paragraph two gave the Jesuits limited authority in the choice of university professors but also inserted the Senate into the selection of Jesuit professors. For each of the first and second-position professors in law and medicine, the Senate would prepare a list of three candidates, and the general of the Society would choose one. In similar fashion, the Senate would name four Jesuits residing in Italy for every position in philosophy and theology, and the general would choose one.[68]

The Jesuits would provide ten lecturers for the university: two for scholastic theology, and one each for positive theology, cases of conscience, for a course on heresies (that is, controversial theology) or an alternate subject, metaphysics, natural philosophy, logic, mathematics, and moral philosophy. The Jesuits would also provide seven more teachers for grammar, humanities, Greek, and Hebrew, but these would not be part of the university.[69]

The Senate found the first Capitoli unacceptable. Hence, on July 13, 1596, the city presented to the Jesuits "li secondi Capitoli" (the second Capitoli), which contained stronger expressions of the city's wishes.[70] The

66. The "Capitoli propusti la prima volta" are published by Novarese 1994, 440–42, and 145–47 for analysis. *Capitoli* are terms or chapters.

67. Novarese 1994, 440–41.

68. Novarese 1994, 440–41.

69. Novarese 1994, 441–42. The only reference to payment to the Jesuits was par. 14 which obligated the Senate to pay the Jesuits 500 scudi. This was a much lower figure than the payment tentatively agreed to in 1592. Since par. 14 followed immediately after the paragraph listing the seven Jesuit non-university teachers, it is possible that this meant payment for these teachers only. Novarese 1994, 442.

70. The complete title of the document is "Capitoli offerti dalli giurati di Messina alla

city demanded that the Jesuits to be appointed to the University of Messina must be the most famous Jesuits in Italy. Moreover, they had to have already taught the subjects that they would teach in Messina for four years in the Jesuit schools of Milan, Padua, Rome, or Naples. The Roman College, and the Jesuit schools at Milan and Naples, were the most important Jesuit schools in Italy, while the school at Padua, although prohibited in 1591 from teaching non-Jesuits, was still important. If the Jesuit teachers lacked these qualifications, the city could appoint members of other religious orders, or secular priests, or laymen in place of the Jesuits.[71] And the payment to the Jesuits would be reduced or voided. Second, if the Jesuits wanted to change the statutes of the university, the city would create a commission that would decide what changes to allow. If the Jesuits did not accept the decision of the commission, the Senate would not pay the Jesuits for their teaching.

The second Capitoli were obviously unacceptable to the Jesuits, so the Senate drafted a third version, labeled *Li terzi et ultimi Capitoli* (third Capitoli) in September 1596. Most of it repeated the first Capitoli, which meant some retreat by the Senate. The section demanding that Jesuit professors at the University of Messina had to be the most famous Jesuits in Italy was deleted. But the Senate added a new section forbidding the Jesuits from creating any other "university," meaning an upper school with classes in theology and philosophy, in Sicily. The city would only permit other Jesuit schools in Sicily to offer one class in philosophy and one in cases of conscience. Further, no other Jesuit school in Sicily would be allowed to confer the doctorate, and all the Jesuit scholastics in Sicily had to study at Messina. Moreover, the third Capitoli retained the paragraph from the second Capitoli that a commission appointed by the Senate would rule on any changes to the statutes of the university that the Jesuits might want. If the Jesuits tried to create another major school in Sicily, or tried to change the statutes on their own, the city would stop payment.[72]

All three sets of Capitoli included unacceptable terms for the Jesuits, especially those provisions that interfered with Jesuit management of their personnel and schools in Messina, Sicily, and Italy. It was clear that the ma-

---

Compagnia per l'Università (li secondi Capitoli)." Located in ARSI, it is printed in Novarese 1994, 442–43; see 147–48 for discussion.

71. "E che non seli donando tali, la città possa conducere altri di qualsivoglia religione o secolari a luogo loro, deducendo la rata del salario che loro si dona o in tutto o in parte, secondo sarà lo mancamento." Second *Capitoli* in Novarese 1994, 443. "Secolari" could mean secular priests or laymen.

72. See Novarese 1994, 443–46, for the text from an ARSI document, and 148–49 for a summary.

jority of the members of the Senate did not want Jesuits in the University of Messina. Giuseppe Blundo, the Jesuit provincial superior for Sicily, offered several reasons.[73] First was the decision of the Sacred Roman Rota, which Gallo, now in Messina, was trumpeting. Gallo assured the senators that the city did not have to share control of the university with the Jesuits. Civic leaders agreed. They believed that the city should have authority over the university because it would bear the cost. Second, a number of people did not want the Jesuits for a potpourri of motives, including local pride, self-interest, complaints about Jesuit teaching, unrealistic expectations, and money. They wanted the archbishop of Messina, or a dignitary from the cathedral church, or someone else elected by the city, to be the rector. Members of other religious orders, secular priests, and local men wanted positions in the university. They claimed that some Jesuits were weak lecturers, and that they could teach better for less money.[74] Others wanted famous lecturers, and seemed to believe that star professors would come to a new university far from the major academic centers of Italy. Money was an issue to some: Father Blundo noted that the city was strapped for cash, and he urged Acquaviva to give ground on this. Although the Jesuits had friends in Messina, they were outnumbered, Blundo concluded.

It was a foregone conclusion that the Jesuits would not accept the terms. On September 28, 1596, General Acquaviva wrote to the Jesuit rector of the Messina college directing him to reject what the Senate wanted. Rather than responding to individual points in the three draft Capitoli, Acquaviva simply stated that the terms were counter to Jesuit procedures and would restrict the liberty of the Society in Sicily and elsewhere.[75] With that the negotiations ended, and the University of Messina went forward without the Jesuits. On December 1, 1596, teaching began. The ceremonial inauguration of the university occurred on December 22, with a speech by Giacomo Gallo followed by an oration by a professor of medicine the next day.[76] The Senate appointed a committee that included Gallo and another

73. Letter of Blundo to General Acquaviva of September 11, 1596, Messina, in ARSI, Sicula 197 II, ff. 299r–301v, also printed in Novarese 1994, 446–52, and with a brief summary on 149–50.

74. "Allegano che qualche volta hanno letto il corso persone che l'han fatto molto fiaccamente ...." Blundo went on to name three Jesuits against whom the accusations were directed. Blundo's letter of September 11, 1596, printed in Novarese 1994, 448.

75. Scaduto 1948, 129–30, quotes most of the letter of Acquaviva, but without the date. Novarese 1994, 150–51, also quotes excerpts and gives the date. Novarese 1994, 150, believes that Acquaviva was responding to the Second *Capitoli*. It is more likely that he responded to the Third *Capitoli*, because Blundo in his letter of September 11, 1596, referred to the latter. See the postscript to Blundo's letter in Novarese 1994, 451.

76. Novarese 1994, 125.

law professor to draft statutes for the new university. They were promulgated on March 21, 1597.

The 1597 statutes created an Italian law and medicine university.[77] In fact, they several times emphasized that the University of Messina would conform to the practices of other Italian universities. For example, the holder of the first-position professor of civil law was directed to teach the same texts as were taught at Bologna, Pavia, and elsewhere.[78] The statutes stated that the archbishop of Messina would be the chancellor of the university. Students would elect a student rector. The statutes prescribed the membership and procedures of colleges of doctors of law, medicine, and theology which would examine degree candidates.[79] The Senate would appoint two riformatori dello studio to oversee the university. The university would have fourteen professorships with designated salaries. The statutes praised Giacomo Gallo for his work in Rome on behalf of the university, and he was appointed first-position professor of civil law at 1,150 scudi, the highest salary.[80] But Messina could not hold him. The Senate sent him to Rome in 1602 to argue another case for the city. He won the case, but while in Rome accepted an appointment to the University of Padua. The angry Senate moved to confiscate his property in Messina but then let him go without retribution.[81]

The 1597 statutes made only one reference to the Jesuits, a sentence stating that they would receive 750 scudi for their teaching in their own school.[82] Dominicans mostly filled the professorships that the Jesuits would have held.[83] General Acquaviva waited two years until the upper school contract with the Messina Senate was completed. Then in 1599 he ordered the Messina upper school classes to move to Palermo.[84] Palermo replaced

77. The statutes of 1597 are printed in G. Romano 1900, 158–76, and *I capitoli dello Studio di Messina* 1990, 26–50. The latter is used because it is more accessible. See also Cesca 1900, 19–22, and Novarese 1994, 154–68.

78. "La prima catreda della lege si debba intendere conforme alli Studii di Bologna, Pavia et altri. Quella della sera nella quale s'ha da legere il digesto infor(tiato) et il digesto novo, conforme alli detti Studii." From the 1597 statutes in *I capitoli dello Studio di Messina* 1990, 41. There are similiar statements on 36, 47, and 59.

79. On the other hand, the paragraphs dealing with the colleges of doctor made no mention of the creation of a college of doctors by King John II of Aragon in 1459, even though this was a key part of Gallo's successful argument before the Sacred Roman Rota.

80. The 1597 statutes in *I capitoli dello Studio di Messina* 1990, 28, 42.

81. Buscemi 1900, 60; for Gallo's career at the University of Padua, see Facciolati 1978, part 3, 136.

82. The 1597 statutes in *I capitoli dello Studio di Messina* 1990, 43.

83. Novarese 1994, 124, and the documents on 477–87.

84. Moscheo 1991, 121–22n66.

Messina as the location of the largest and most important Jesuit college and school in Sicily. In 1600 there were 147 Jesuits in Palermo, which had a college, a school, a professed house, and a novice house.[85] The total included 28 Jesuit scholastics studying theology and philosophy. The Palermo school offered ten classes: five in the upper school (two classes of theology and one each in metaphysics, natural philosophy, and logic), and five in the lower school (humanities and four grammar classes).[86] By contrast, in 1600 Messina had only 89 Jesuits in its college, school, and novice house. The total included 13 scholastics who attended lower school classes. The Messina school offered only one upper school class, in Hebrew, plus seven lower school classes.[87]

The Messina school made a comeback. In 1605 the Messina college reopened its upper school in Messina and enrollment grew, as did the number of Jesuits there.[88] In 1649 Messina had 154 Jesuits in its college, professed house, novitiate, and boarding school. The school offered fourteen classes, eight in the upper school and six in the lower school.[89] But Palermo was larger. In 1649 Palermo had 234 Jesuits in its college, novice house, and professed house, and the Jesuits also operated a boarding school whose students attended the college school. Palermo's school offered twenty classes equally divided between upper school and lower school.[90] Although it trailed Palermo, Messina was still the second most important Jesuit college and school in Sicily by a very large margin.[91]

The events of the 1590s concluded negotiations between the Messina

85. A professed house was a residence for Jesuit priests who had professed their vows and now lived together in poverty while they engaged in spiritual ministries. It did not have a fixed income, but was expected to rely on gifts. Ignatius saw professed houses as places where Jesuits, at least for limited periods of time, might devote themselves to a higher standard of spiritual perfection in poverty, including begging, in a manner that Jesuits who lived in colleges and were involved in teaching and other mundane ministries could not. He put considerable emphasis on professed houses, but also realized before he died that colleges and schools were the future of the Society. Nevertheless, there were five professed houses in Italy, one in each Jesuit province, in the last quarter of the sixteenth century. The professed house of the Province of Sicily was in Palermo. Lukács 1960–1961, part 2, 4–19, 48–51; *Constitutions* 1970, 166n19, 251–59 (pars. 553–81); and *Constitutions* 1996, 226–38.

86. ARSI, Sicula 60, ff. 168r, 170r. Lukács 1960–1961, part 2, 50, makes the total as 151 Jesuits.

87. ARSI, Sicula 60, ff. 168v, 170r. See also Lukács 1960–1961, part 2, 50, who makes the total as 92 Jesuits at Messina.

88. Moscheo 1991, 122n68.

89. ARSI, Sicula 66, ff. 161r–64r.

90. ARSI, Sicula 66, ff. 157r–160r. Note that both Messina and Palermo now had professed houses, testimony to the intense rivalry (see below) between the two Jesuit communities.

91. ARSI, Sicula 66, ff. 168r–69r.

Senate and the Jesuits that began in 1548. The city originally saw collaboration with the Jesuits as a means to getting a university in Messina. Thanks to dogged determination, a huge payment to the crown, and successful legal actions, it got a civic law and medicine university in 1596 without the Jesuits.

Final Attempt

In a surprising development, the Messina Senate invited the Jesuits to become professors in the University of Messina in 1628, and they probably taught in the university between 1637 and 1640. This happened because the Messina Jesuits wanted to divide the Jesuit Province of Sicily into eastern and western provinces, in the expectation that the Messina Jesuits would dominate the former. Their lay supporters viewed adding Jesuit professors to the university as a means of raising the profile of the Messina Jesuits and, therefore, strengthening the case for the division. This was part of the larger competition between Messina and Palermo.

Observers noted that Sicilian Jesuits were just as full of *campanelismo* (exaggerated local pride) and as suspicious of outsiders as other Sicilians. Giulio Fazio (Naples 1534–1596 Monreale, Sicily) made an inspection visit to the Sicilian colleges in 1581 and 1582.[92] In May 1582 he reported that there were about 300 Jesuits in the province, almost all Sicilians. Jesuits from other regions did not come voluntarily to Sicily, because Sicilian Jesuits did not want outsiders to get the best of them, he reported. Fazio especially noted the hostility between "Messinesi" and "Palermitani" Jesuits. They brought these attitudes from secular life into the religious life and it affected the Society daily. Fazio praised many Sicilian Jesuits for their great intelligence, courage, virtue, and spirit. But others were unstable, melancholy, dissimulating, suspicious, and enveloped in "the smoke of their own self-esteem," making governing the province very difficult.[93]

92. Fazio was provincial of Sicily in 1576 and 1577, then became secretary to the entire Society from 1578 to 1583. He later served as superior of the provinces of Naples and Venice, then rector of the college of Monreale. For brief biographies see Scaduto 1968, 54–55, and Zanfredini 2001a.

93. "Sarano in questa provincia appresso 300 soggetti et quasi tutti siciliani, la caggione per le non vi si trova tanta meschina d'altre nationi, può essere così perche non vi son mandati, ne forse essi anco vengono volontieri; come perché questi di Sicilia non sopportano invero volontieri, che altri di altra natione prevalgono in essi, e fra loro stessi anche, tra Messinesi e Palermitani regna non so che di emulatione et contesa, che dal seculo hanno portato, et nella Religione ancora, alla occasioni predomina, come per manifesti effetti giornalmente si vede, sono universalmente belli ingegni, et coraggiosi, et se bene per gran [illegible word] non manca in molti di

By the early seventeenth century the rivalry between the Jesuits of Messina and Palermo was even more intense, because local recruits filled the colleges, an Italy-wide development. It is likely that the majority of Italian Jesuits of the seventeenth and eighteenth centuries were educated, lived, and died in the province in which they were born.[94] Even more important, provincialism often became localism. Boys enrolled in the town's Jesuit school, became Jesuits, and then returned to teach or perform other ministries in their home towns. This was certainly true in Messina: sons of the Messina elite who became Jesuits were often assigned to the Messina college.[95] And it was probably true in Palermo and elsewhere in Sicily. When this happened, campanelismo became part of the Jesuit way of proceeding. Municipal governments no longer saw Jesuits as members of an international religious order lacking local patriotism.

The Messina Jesuits had been campaigning to divide Sicily into two provinces from 1610 or earlier. They believed that this would enable them to escape what they saw as oppression by the Palermo Jesuits. And because the Messina college and school were far and away the largest and most important in the eastern half of Sicily, they knew that they would dominate an eastern province. But General Acquaviva consistently rebuffed the Messina Jesuits and had finally imposed silence on the issue. After his death in 1615, the Messina Jesuits renewed their demand, which the provincial superior, a native of Palermo, strongly opposed. The Messina Senate supported the cause; for example, when the provincial superior came to visit the Messina college in 1617, it barred him from entering the city.[96] The Messina campaign was crowned with success when General Muzio Vitelleschi (Rome 1563–1645, general from 1616) created the provinces of Eastern Sicily and Western Sicily in 1626. The announced reasons were the size of the island and distances between colleges.[97] This may have been true, but the lobbying of the Messina Jesuits brought it about.

The division of the Sicilian Jesuits into two was part of a larger political struggle. Because the viceroy resided six months of the year in Palermo and six months in Messina, the two cities functioned as half-capitals, nomi-

---

loro gran virtù, zelo, et spirito, purché in altri si vede non so che d'instabilità, melancolia, dissimulatione, suspetto, et fumo di propria estimatione, et alterezza." Visitation report of Giulio Fazio, [probably May] 1582, in ARSI, Sicula 183 I, f. 28v.

94. This is my impression based on reading Jesuit biographies in DHCJ and many documents.

95. Novarese 1994, 308–12, lists Messina Jesuits who came from the urban elite.

96. Novarese 1994, 314n23.

97. Fois 2001b, 2080–81, provides a succinct account; Novarese 1994, 306–7, 313–15, adds a few details, but gives the date of the division as 1628 on 306 and 315.

nally of equal weight, of the Viceroyalty of Sicily. However, Messina was convinced that Palermo had greater power, and that it used it to oppress Messina. It further believed that Palermo was scheming to become the sole capital of the viceroyalty, and that the Spanish crown favored Palermo. So the Messina Senate proposed to the crown that Sicily should be divided into two viceroyalties at the Salso River, which runs north to south in the middle of the island. Each viceroyalty would have its own viceroy and capital, Messina for the eastern viceroyalty and Palermo for the western viceroyalty. The Messina Senate believed that this would put the two cities on an equal footing and raise the importance of Messina. But Palermo opposed the division with the argument that Messina really wanted to be an independent republic.[98]

These developments spurred the controversial move that a pro-Jesuit Messina Senate unveiled on September 28, 1628. It dismissed several incumbent professors and gave the Jesuits seven professorships in the University of Messina. The Jesuits would fill two positions in scholastic theology and single professorships in cases of conscience, metaphysics, natural philosophy, logic, and mathematics. The Jesuits would not lecture in their own college but in a nearby building, probably rented. Jesuit students were required to attend university classes rather than classes in their own college. This may have been intended to impress on the Jesuits that their responsibility to the university took precedence over their own school. The Jesuit college would receive 1,000 scudi for its university teaching. A Jesuit was designated to deliver the lecture inaugurating the academic year on October 15, 1628, and classes would begin on November 3.[99]

The decision was very unpopular. Resistance to inserting the Jesuits into the university was strong, and the elite of Messina were not of one mind. The result was a confusing array of moves and countermoves in the next few years. The displaced professors and other religious orders, especially the Dominicans, protested. Some law and medicine students expressed their disapproval by throwing oranges and stones at Jesuit students.[100] Because of the uproar, it is not clear if the new agreement was put into effect in the academic year 1628–1629, and if it was, how long Jesuits taught in the university. In any case, in May 1629 a new group of senators was elected, and they denounced the agreement. In December 1629 the senators ordered the university beadles not to open the doors of the university

98. Cesca 1900, 23; Novarese 1994, 319 (esp. notes 38–39), 321–23.

99. Cesca 1900, 22–23; Tropea 1900, 66; Moscheo 1991, 135–36; Novarese 1994, 315–18, and especially the documents on 415–24.

100. Novarese 1994, 327n54.

building to Jesuit professors in order to prevent them from teaching. The Messina Jesuits wanted to fight back, but General Vitelleschi told them that the city was within its rights, and that the Messina Jesuits should accept the reversal and concentrate on teaching their own students in their own school. The Messina Jesuits were thwarted for the time being.[101]

The two larger Messina initiatives also failed at this time. The Spanish crown rejected the idea of two viceroyalties in Sicily. It was in Madrid's best interest to keep Messina and Palermo competing for crown favor. Nor did the two Jesuit provinces last. Many Sicilian Jesuits objected, criticizing the Messina Jesuits as restless, rebellious, and given to factionalism. At the end of 1631 the two provincial superiors began to meet, and they eventually reported to the general that a single province was the better way. In January 1633 General Vitelleschi reunited the Jesuits into a single Province of Sicily that lasted until the Jesuits were suppressed in Sicily in 1767.[102] For good measure, the Ninth General Congregation of the Society that convened in 1649 and 1650 sharply condemned Jesuits "who attempt to coerce the creation of new provinces by means of the help of externs" (non-Jesuits).[103]

However, the struggle over the university continued. Although the Jesuits had been forced out, they had an agreement. So the rector of the Jesuit college sought legal redress, and the Jesuits had supporters. In February 1630 the highest court in Messina ruled that the Jesuits had a valid contract with the city to teach in the university and ordered the city to honor it. The Senate refused and exactly what happened next is unclear. Eventually, in 1637, the viceroy ordered the city to honor the duration of the contract, with the result that seven Jesuits taught in the University of Messina from 1637 to 1640.[104]

That was the end. After 1640 no more attempts to insert Jesuits into the university have come to light. In 1660 the Senate did invite a Jesuit, Giuseppe Maria Mazzara (Scicli 1619–1661 Messina), to fill a theology professorship. But there was no controversy, because this was a single appointment, and because Mazzara enjoyed Sicily-wide fame as the author of works of religious history, accounts of Sicilian historical and current events, and poetry.[105] Like almost all Jesuits he lacked a doctorate, so the leadership in

101. Cesca 1900, 24–26; Tropea 1900, 67–69; Moscheo 1991, 137–38; Novarese 1994, 317–18, 326–28.

102. Fois 2001b, 2081; Novarese 1994, 324–25.

103. For Matters of Greater Moment 1994, 302, decree 5.

104. Cesca 1900, 26–29; Tropea 1900, 69–73; Moscheo 1991, 139–41; Novarese 1994, 329–34, and the documents on 421–24 and 587–88.

105. Mira 1964, 2:63.

Rome authorized the Messina college to confer one on him.[106] The general saw Mazzara's appointment as an honor to the Society. But he had little lasting effect, because he died in June 1661. There were no other Jesuit appointments to the university.

In 1674 Messina's long-time hostility toward Spain burst into an uprising in which some professors and students of the university played prominent roles. By contrast, the Jesuit general imposed neutrality and silence on the Messina Jesuits.[107] After the revolt was crushed in 1678, the Spanish crown suppressed the university. It was not restored until 1838.

The Jesuit college and school continued to flourish in Messina but as a distant second to Palermo. In 1696 there were 120 Jesuits in Messina distributed among the college, two boarding schools, a novice house, and a professed house. The school offered nine upper school classes (two for scholastic theology, and single classes in scripture, cases of conscience, Hebrew, metaphysics, natural philosophy, and mathematics) and six lower school classes in rhetoric, humanities, and grammar.[108] Palermo had about 300 Jesuits, and its school offered twelve upper school classes (three for scholastic theology, two for Greek, and single classes in scripture, cases of conscience, metaphysics, natural philosophy, mathematics, and moral philosophy), plus eight lower school classes (three for rhetoric, two for the humanities, and three for grammar).[109] The gap widened in the next half century. In 1749 Messina had 106 Jesuits, and its school offered eight upper school classes and seven lower school classes.[110] Palermo, by contrast, had 340 Jesuits, and its schools offered fifteen upper school classes and eleven lower school classes.[111]

Conclusion

Negotiations between Messina and the Jesuits to establish a University of Messina that had begun in 1548 resumed in the 1560s. The city proposed and the Jesuits reacted. When plague drove the Jesuits out of Messina to Catania, that city emerged as an alternative site for the major Jesuit school in Sicily with the potential to become a university. The city of Catania offered support, but General Mercurian vetoed the idea. After the Jesuits returned to Messina, the city continued to pursue a university. It achieved its goal of an Italian civic university without the Jesuits in 1596. Nevertheless, sporadic efforts were made to add the Jesuits in the next four decades, in part because the Jesuits and city of Messina made common cause against the

106. Novarese 1994, 335–36.
108. ARSI, Sicula 92 III, ff. 23r–29r.
110. ARSI, Sicula 139, ff. 14r–17r.

107. Novarese 1994, 337–42.
109. ARSI, Sicula 92 III, ff. 41r–47r.
111. ARSI, Sicula 139, ff. 22r–27r.

Jesuits and city of Palermo. None of the attempts had more than transitory success.

Over the course of nearly a century it became clear that the Jesuits never had the necessary strong and lasting civic support needed to overcome determined opposition to Jesuit participation in the proposed university. And the Messina Senate was craftier and more ruthless than the Jesuits. It used the Jesuits as a means toward its goal, which was to break the Catania university monopoly. It then dropped the Jesuits when they were no longer needed. The leaders of Messina viewed the Jesuit pre-university school and a university differently. They valued the Jesuit lower school and never withdrew its financial support. But a university intended to train the leaders and professional class of Messina was another matter. The Messina Senate created a civic university without the Jesuits to do this.

4

THE ATTEMPT TO
ENTER THE UNIVERSITY
OF TURIN

The Jesuits next tried to become professors of theology, philosophy, and the humanities in the University of Turin. For the first time, the Jesuits worked with an Italian prince. Duke Emanuele Filiberto and Achille Gagliardi created a plan in 1572 to insert Jesuit professors into the University of Turin. The plan failed in the face of intense opposition. A proposal to do the same in 1593 was not implemented.

Arrival of the Jesuits

The Jesuits came to Turin at a propitious moment. At the beginning of the sixteenth century the Duchy of Savoy was a bilingual state of many units stretching from the Ligurian Sea in the south to Geneva in the north. Chambéry, in French-speaking Savoy, was the capital but the dukes were ambulatory rulers who moved from town to town in the duchy. The Principality of Piedmont, the largest unit of the Italian-speaking part of the duchy, became the dominant part of the duchy; hence, it will be called Piedmont-Savoy. Religious division and the predations of larger states produced territorial losses, including Geneva, in the first half of the century. When war between France and Piedmont-Savoy broke out in 1535, the French captured Turin and several other Piedmontese towns in 1536 and stayed; the Spanish occupied some other towns.

Emanuele Filiberto Savoia (1528–1580, r. from 1553), the son of the exiled duke, became a military commander in the service of Spain and won the decisive victory over France at Saint-Quentin in 1557. This led to the Peace of Cateau-Cambrésis of 1559 that finally brought the Habsburg-

Valois wars to an end and obliged the French to leave Turin, but not immediately. Confirmed as duke of Piedmont-Savoy by both powers, Emanuele
Filiberto began to rebuild his state and its institutions. Although not loved
by his subjects, he proved to be an absolutist prince who ruled with an effective combination of pragmaticism and ruthlessness. Early in his reign he
sought the aid of the Jesuits in ridding the duchy of heresy and revitalizing
Catholicism.

A dynamic young Jesuit named Antonio Possevino (Mantua 1533–1611
Ferrara; see the appendix for his biography) established a strong relationship with Emanuele Filiberto. He had his first audience with the duke on
February 2, 1560, followed by many more in the next three years.[1] They
faced two groups of heretics. The long French occupation had made it easy
for French-speaking Calvinists to move into the duchy, including Turin,
where some of whom enjoyed the protection of the duke's consort, Duchess Margherita of Valois (1523–1574).[2] Waldensians lived in the mountains
and valleys of the duchy. Like almost all rulers at the time, Emanuele Filiberto believed that religious division threatened the security of the state.
He initially tried military suppression to rid the duchy of heretics, but then
realized that they could only be won over by concessions and religious instruction. On June 5, 1561, he granted the Waldensians freedom to wor-
ship in their valleys and freedom of conscience elsewhere. Possevino agreed
with the duke's goal of ridding the duchy of heresy but not his harsh initial
methods. He proposed an amnesty followed by preaching, missions, catechetical instruction, clerical reform, and education.[3] He arranged for the
printing and distribution of thousands of catechisms, especially those of Peter Canisius, with the duke bearing the cost. On Possevino's urging, Emanuele Filiberto ordered the male and female teachers in his state to teach the
catechism, and civic and rural authorities to enforce his will.[4] The attention
paid to female teachers may have been unique; clerical reformers usually
ignored the humble women who taught basic literacy and sewing to girls.

Possevino and Emanuele Filiberto agreed that introducing Jesuit colleges and schools into the duchy would strengthen Catholicism and help
counter heresy. Although the vast majority of Italian Jesuit colleges and
schools were not founded to fight heresy, Possevino emphasized this pur-

---

1. Scaduto 1959, 61–62, 93–98, for the first meeting.
2. See Possevino's memorandum of 1562 concerning the religious situation in Piedmont-
Savoy in Scaduto 1959, 174.
3. Scaduto 1959, 67–87. For Emanuele Filiberto's religious views, see Stumpo 1993, 560.
4. See Emanuele Filiberto's edict of January 15, 1563, in Scaduto 1959, 165–66. There are
many references to Possevino's efforts to distribute catechisms in Scaduto 1959.

FIGURE I. P. Antonio Possevino, SJ (1533–1611)

pose in Piedmont-Savoy, and the duke concurred. After discussing various towns and cities in which to locate colleges, they agreed that Mondovì would be the first.[5]

A major reason was that the city of Mondovì was in the process of creating the university of the duchy. This had been the University of Turin,

5. Scaduto 1959.

founded between 1411 and 1413. However, it barely functioned during the French occupation of Turin. It most likely did not teach in the years 1536–1538, 1546–1556, and after 1558, and it offered only a limited number of lectures in the years in which it did teach.[6] The city of Mondovì offered a considerable sum of money to the duke for the privilege of hosting and paying the expenses of a university. In December 1560, the duke accepted the offer. Mondovì was a logical choice. Although located fifty-six miles south of Turin in the southernmost part of the duchy, the city of 20,000 souls was the largest in Piedmont. The duke and the commune set about obtaining the necessary privileges, and assembling a faculty, including some who had previously taught at the University of Turin. A few professors began lecturing in March 1561.[7] Pope Pius IV authorized the granting of degrees on September 22, 1561, and Pius V confirmed the privilege in 1566. This was not the University of Turin translated to Mondovì, but a new university.[8]

The Jesuits established themselves at Mondovì at the same time as the university began. On January 4, 1561, Emanuele Filiberto offered them the annual sum of 400 scudi, most of it to come from raising the salt tax, plus privileges, immunities, and concessions if they would establish a college with a school in Mondovì. The Jesuits accepted. Both the Jesuits and the duke wanted a Jesuit college and school in Mondovì because it hosted a university and to combat heresy through learning. Twelve Jesuits arrived in Mondovì on April 15, 1561. Not everything was ready as promised, and the initial payment of the 400 scudi from the duke had not arrived. Hence, the Jesuits had to rent a building for their college, and were able to do so only because Cardinal Michele Ghislieri, archbishop of Mondovì and the future Pope Pius V, gave the Jesuits 200 scudi. Nevertheless, the Jesuits organized a school that opened on June 22, 1561, with an inaugural lecture in praise of human knowledge. It consisted of three classes, probably Latin grammar, humanities, and rhetoric.[9]

From the beginning Possevino and Emanuele Filiberto saw the Jesuits as joining the University of Mondovì. On January 19, 1561, Possevino wrote

6. For a brief survey of the University of Turin through 1600, see Grendler 2002, 93–99, with additional bibliography. See Chaiudano 1972c, 53, for the closings.

7. Possevino's letter to General Laínez of March 23, 1561, Fossano, in Scaduto 1959, 150; and Lerda, 1993.

8. Vallauri 1970, 1:152–96, 205–7; Chaiudano 1972c, 53–55; Lerda 1993.

9. Letters of Possevino of January 19 through July 8, 1561, in Scaduto 1959, 142–43, 145, 147, 150, 154, 156–57, 161; Laínez' letter to Duke Emanuele Filiberto of February 19, 1561, agreeing to establish a college in Mondovì, in *Lainii Epistolae* 1912–1917, 5:385–86; letter of Polanco to the entire Society of May 21, 1561, in *Polanci Complementa* 1969, 1:270; Monti 1914–1915, 1:106–20; and Scaduto 1974, 426–30.

to another Jesuit about the possibility of Jesuits teaching in the university. Since the university would begin teaching in March, he believed that the Jesuits should begin teaching scripture and Greek or Latin humanities. This would please the duke very much. It might also enable the Jesuits to take possession of these lectures. This would enhance the prestige of the Jesuit college, gain for it a larger subsidy, and be of greater service to God, he concluded.[10] Possevino reiterated these views in a letter to General Laínez of March 23, 1561. But Laínez was skeptical because of the duke's unfilled promises. He had not yet produced the first payments of the promised 400 scudi or a building. Hence, General Laínez did not send more Jesuits.[11]

Nevertheless, in July 1561 the University of Mondovì invited the Jesuits to provide someone to lecture on Greek and Latin in the university, in other words to fill the humanities professorship. The Jesuit rector proposed Michele Vopisco (Naples ca. 1539–?), who had begun teaching the rhetoric class in the Jesuit school. The university accepted him. Vopisco was certainly able; despite his youth he had previously taught Greek and Latin humanities in the Jesuit school in Padua, and he later published at least one book.[12] However, he was headstrong, disobedient, and disruptive. Called to Rome to explain himself, he refused to go. Worse, he remained near Mondovì criticizing the Jesuits and counting on influential friends to confirm him in the university lectureship. He asked Duke Emanuele Filiberto for permission to remain in Piedmont, but the duke deferred to Laínez and refused. Vopisco then went to Rome where he was dismissed from the Society.[13]

The Mondovì Jesuits did much better with a young rhetoric teacher. In late October 1564 General Laínez ordered Robert Bellarmine (Montepulciano 1542–1621 Rome), then in Florence and still a scholastic, to go immediately to Mondovì to teach rhetoric. He added that Bellarmine's class,

10. "Poiché cominciandosi questo marzo d'adesso lo Studio, si potrebbe, venendo, dare qualche principio ad una lettione di sacra Scrittura et a lettere greche o latine d'humanità: il che molto piacerebbe al s.r duca, et sarebbe un pigliare il possesso di tali letture, non senza modo forse di amplificare con destra occasione il collegio et acquistar qualche emolumento maggiore in maggior servitio di Dio." Possevino's letter to Gaspare Loarte, Genoa, of January 10, 1561, Vercelli, in Scaduto 1959, 143. See also Scaduto 1964, 425.

11. Possevino's letter to General Laínez of March 23, 1561, Fossano, in Scaduto 1959, 150–51; and Scaduto 1964, 425. The duke's slowness to honor his financial promises to the Jesuits, or failure to honor them in full, will prove to be a pattern.

12. For very brief biographical information on Vopisco, see Scaduto 1968, 157; for his teaching in Padua in December 1558, see MP 3:282; for his publication of an Italian-Latin dictionary, see Scaduto 1974, 427n9. Scaduto adds that the *governatore* of the university, a friend of the Jesuits, issued the invitation. He has not been identified.

13. Scaduto 1974, 427.

while part of the Jesuit school, would also be listed as a university lecture of rhetoric and Greek. And that this was being done as a favor to Emanuele Filiberto to whom the Jesuits owed a debt. Bellarmine began teaching in Mondovì on November 27; he taught Cicero's *Partitiones oratoriae* and *In Catilinam I*, Greek grammar, Demosthenes, and Isocrates. He also orated, preached, and taught some astronomy in the summer.[14]

However, neither Possevino nor the duke saw Mondovì as the permanent location of the university or the Jesuit school. On December 8, 1562, about a year and a half after the beginning of the university and the Jesuit school, Possevino recommended to General Laínez that the Jesuit college should move to Turin. Turin will be the head of all the affairs of Piedmont, he predicted. The university, the Senate, the archiepiscopal see, and the court much of the time will be there, he wrote. He believed that the duke would make Turin his residence.[15] In other words, Possevino had learned that the duke was planning to make Turin the capital of his state, and that he intended to revive the University of Turin.[16] Possevino added that he hoped to persuade the duke to transfer his financial support from the Jesuit college at Mondovì to one at Turin, and that his support would continue so long as Turin had a university. He had not yet spoken to the duke about this, but would shortly when he rejoined the ambulatory court. But he assured Laínez that the Jesuits would not move their college until financial support was secured.[17]

The letter revealed Possevino's goals and tactics. First, he pursued what he saw as the most advantageous position for the Society in Piedmont-Savoy, which he believed to be the establishment of a college and school in the most important city, which was going to be Turin. If the college and school at Mondovì had to be sacrificed, so be it. Second, Possevino intended to locate a Jesuit college wherever the university would be. And while he did not put it into writing, he hoped that the Jesuits might be a part of the

14. Letter of General Laínez to Bellarmine, October 28, 1564, Rome, in *Lainii Epistolae* 1912–1917, 8:280–81; Monti 1914–1915, 1:119–20; Scaduto 1974, 429; Scaduto 1992, 343–44; and Lerda 1994.

15. "Che invero io non so quale migliore città poteva presentare la bontà di Dio N. S. che quella di Turino, poiché ivi è il capo di tutti i maneggi del Piemonte, et ivi sarà lo Studio, il senato, la sedia archiepiscopale, et molte volte la corte, come si ha a credere; et penso hora v'anderà a stare sua altezza." Letter of Possevino of December 8, 1562, Fossano, to General Laínez, then at the Council of Trent, in Scaduto 1959, 163.

16. "Il signore duca inclinasse a tramutarlo, mutandosi lo Studio come si spera." Letter of Possevino of December 8, 1562, Fossano, to Laínez at Trent, in Scaduto 1959, 164.

17. Possevino's letter of December 8, 1562, Fossano, to Laínez at Trent, in Scaduto 1959, 164–65.

university. Third, Possevino would follow the duke's lead. The Jesuit leadership in Rome endorsed the anticipated move from Mondovì to Turin. In January 1563 Francisco de Borja, commissioner for Italy while Laínez was at the Council of Trent, wrote that it would be best to keep both colleges going. But if that was not possible, Turin was preferred, because it would produce greater benefits for souls and the Society.[18]

Events transpired as Possevino anticipated. The French finally left Turin in December 1562. The duke proclaimed Turin the capital of his state and the home of his court. Although he left the Senate of Savoy in place in Chambéry, its authority was limited to Savoy and subject to the duke's approval. Emanuele Filiberto made his official entrance into Turin on February 7, 1563.

The university followed. The commune of Turin begged the duke to restore the University of Turin. Their pleas fell on deaf ears. Then they offered the duke 4,000 scudi (at the high rate of one scudo per eight florins) plus an annual contribution of 1,000 scudi, double the subsidy from Mondovì. Now the duke heard them. Upon receipt of the payment, the duke reconfirmed the privileges of the University of Turin. The University of Mondovì stopped teaching in the summer of 1566, and many of its professors were appointed to the University of Turin. A few new scholars, some of them distinguished, were added. The restored University of Turin began teaching in the middle of November 1566.[19]

The Jesuits also moved. When, contrary to Possevino's expectations, the duke did not provide financial support, another man came to the rescue. In December 1565 Aleramo Beccuti promised 300 scudi in annual income if the Jesuits would establish a college in Turin. The Jesuits accepted his offer and in late February 1567 sent nine Jesuits to found a college in Turin. In addition, the Jesuits began to transfer some of their members from Mondovì to Turin.[20] The small Mondovì college lingered until it closed in 1576, though the Jesuits returned in 1596.[21]

The Jesuits initially agreed to teach only a class in logic at Turin. This was unusual. A Jesuit school ordinarily began with a lower school of classes in Latin grammar and the humanities. After several years, when students were prepared for advanced classes, and additional financial support was

18. Scaduto 1974, 430.

19. Vallauri 1970, 1:196–203, 209–12; Chiaudano 1972c; and Catarinella and Salsotto 1998, 523–31.

20. Monti 1914–1915, 1:153–59; Scaduto 1992, 329–30. Despite his importance, the sources do not give further information about Beccuti.

21. Monti 1914–1915, 1:121–29.

secured, upper school classes were added. The Turin Jesuits may have been thinking already about competing with or joining the university. And they had the right person to teach logic. In late December 1566 a Jesuit making arrangements for the Turin school suggested that Robert Bellarmine, still at Mondovì, should be transferred to Turin to teach the logic course. He then changed his mind: "If Messer Roberto would begin to teach logic here, I believe that many students would come, and that the lecture would be satisfying to the students. But I believe that the doctors who teach at the university would take it very badly and might raise complaints against the Society."[22] So in 1567 the Society sent Bellarmine to Padua where he preached and studied theology privately.[23]

The Turin Jesuits dropped the notion of beginning with a logic course. They decided to start a lower school in Turin and sought support for it. On July 1, 1567, the duke provided a subsidy of 200 scudi to the Jesuits for teaching Greek and Latin letters, humanistic studies, rhetoric, the fear of God, and Christian discipline.[24] The Jesuits asked the commune for another 100 scudi. Lacking the money, the commune borrowed the sum from a Jew and gave it to the Jesuits. With this support plus the 300 scudi from Alerame Beccuti, the Jesuits in 1567 established a college in Turin. The school formally opened on April 24, 1568, with orations on classical themes before local notables. Duke Emanuele Filiberto came the next day and there were more orations. The school initially consisted of three classes with 100 students.[25]

Emanuele Filiberto also viewed the Jesuit school as the provider of humanities instruction for students at the University of Turin. According to the rector of the Jesuit college, he did this for two reasons: he was dissatisfied with the meager progress that students were making under lay profes-

22. "Se M. Roberto incominciasse a leggere qui la logica, credo vi concorrebbero molti scolari e che sarebbe grata tale lezione per gli scolari; ma i dottori dell'università che la leggono credo l'avrebbero molto per male, per il che forse si eleverebbe qualche rumore contro la Compagnia." Letter of Father Gian Andrea Terzo of December 22, 1567 (sic), Turin, as quoted in Monti 1914–1915, 1:160. Although Monti assigned the year 1567 to the letter, it must be 1566 because Bellarmine left for Padua in the summer or autumn of 1567. For Terzo (Bergamo 1536–1613 Naples), see Scaduto 1968, 144–45.

23. See chap. 1, note 84.

24. "Insegnar et instruir la gioventù nelle lettere greche et latine et nelli studi di humanità et rettorica et nel timor d'Iddio buoni cristiani et cristiana disciplina." Quotation from the letters patent of Emanuele Filiberto of July 1, 1567, in Chiaudano 1972b, 93–94n5.

25. See Monti 1914–1915, 1:161; Grosso and Mellano 1957, 2:88–89n75; and *Polanci Complementa* 1969, 2:678. The last is from Polanco's "Commentariola rerum memoria dignarum in Societate nostra ab anno 1564," an account of noteworthy events of the Society from 1564 to 1573. Polanco states that the school began in 1567. However, Scaduto 1992, 330–31, writes that the school began on April 24, 1568.

sors and the dissolute lives they lived, and he had received good reports about Jesuit learning and teaching methods from the papal nuncio and the Venetian ambassador.[26] Hence, beginning in the academic year 1566–1567 communal financial documents listed an annual payment of 200 scudi to the Jesuits as a university expense alongside the salary payments to university professors.[27]

Since university students who needed and wanted humanities instruction could now obtain it at the Jesuit school, Emanuele Filiberto did not renew the contract of the star humanities professor in 1568. This was Giovanni Battista Giraldi Cinzio of Ferrara (1504–1573), author of many works in Latin and Italian.[28] He had taught at the University of Mondovì from 1563 to 1566 and then moved to the University of Turin, where he received a salary of 400 scudi per annum, one of the highest in the university.[29] After his dismissal, Giraldi Cinzio immediately found a new position as professor of Greek and Latin oratory at the University of Pavia.

From Pavia Giraldi Cinzio wrote an angry letter denouncing the Jesuits. He charged that they taught children the very obscure precepts and barbarisms of Despauterius.[30] He meant that the Jesuits taught Latin grammar from the medieval-style manuals of Jan Van Pauteren (ca. 1460–1520), a Flemish grammarian.[31] Like most Italian humanists, Giraldi Cinzio viewed Despauterius with disdain. Whether the Turin Jesuits did teach the grammars of Despauterius is unknown. Some Jesuit teachers in Italy initially used the manuals of Despauterius, probably because they had learned from them in northern Europe. They stopped when they encountered criticism from Italian parents and students.[32]

26. As reported in the letter of Achille Gagliardi to General Borja of September 13, 1570, Turin, in ARSI, Italiae 139, f. 219r. See also Scaduto 1992, 331, who gives the mistaken date of August 13, 1570.

27. The University of Turin rolls listed payments of 200 scudi per annum to the Jesuit college from the academic year 1566–1567 through the academic year 1573–1574. Chiaudano 1972b, 77–78, 93, 97, 99, 101, 103, 105, 107, 109.

28. For a brief biography, which does not mention why he left the University of Turin, see Foà 2001.

29. See his listing in the University of Turin rolls of 1566–1567 and 1567–1568 in Chiaudano 1972b, 90, 95.

30. See Giraldi Cinzio's letter to Pier Vettori, March 10, 1569, Pavia, in Giraldi Cinzio 1996, 425. Vallauri 1875, 199–200, also mentions Giraldi Cinzio's dismissal and angry letter. Monti 1914–1915, 1:160, follows Vallauri.

31. Despauterius wrote three textbooks: *Syntaxis* (published in 1511), *Prima pars grammaticae* (1512), and *Rudimenta* (1514). A combined edition entitled *Commentarii grammatici* appeared in 1537. These and other works on epistolary style, metrics, and orthography were frequently reprinted in the Netherlands and France, but seldom in Italy.

32. For another criticism of the Jesuits for using Despauterius, see chap. 12, "The Jesuits and

The larger issue was that Giraldi Cinzio and the Jesuit school taught different material. Giraldi Cinzio probably lectured on what he wrote, which was literary form and theory based on his study of ancient and modern tragedies and modern vernacular romances. By contrast, Jesuit lower schools taught students how to read, speak, and write Latin prose and poetry by means of many drills and exercises. In his letter Giraldi Cinzio did not denounce Duke Emanuele Filiberto, who dismissed him, because the duke had given him 400 scudi and another 100 scudi for moving expenses to Pavia.[33]

The Attempt to Enter the University of Turin

The next step was for the Jesuits to become professors in the university. The duke and the new rector of the Jesuit college in Turin designed a plan to do this. General Francisco de Borja appointed Achille Gagliardi (Padua 1537/38–1607 Modena; see the appendix for his biography) rector in 1568 to replace a Spaniard who spoke imperfect Italian.[34] This was his first major position in the Society.

Gagliardi arrived in March 1568 and immediately went into action. He preached to acclaim, then lectured on controversial theology in the Jesuit school, probably to confute Calvinism. Like Possevino, Gagliardi believed that there were Calvinists in Turin, including in the entourage of Duchess Margherita Valois. He brought two young Calvinists, who enjoyed the protection of the duchess, to the attention of the papal nuncio, who persuaded them to abjure.[35] The duke then asked Gagliardi to send a Jesuit to the court to teach the pages so that they would not fall under Calvinist influence. Gagliardi began a Marian congregation, and on September 1, 1568, he founded a small boarding school for nobles that quickly had twice as many applicants as places.[36]

Then on September 13, 1570, Gagliardi reported to the general an extraordinary development: Duke Emanuele Filiberto planned to introduce several Jesuits into the University of Turin. Taking advantage of faculty deaths, the duke intended to appoint three Jesuits to teach logic, natural

---

the University in the 1550s and 1560s." For more on the Jesuit experience with the grammars of Despauterius, see MP, vols. 1–3, indexes.

33. Giraldi Cinzio 1996, 425.

34. Scaduto 1992, 329–30.

35. *Nunziatura di Savoia* 1960, xxi, 171, 180, 188, 193, 210–11. The nuncio was Vincenzo Lauro (1523–1592), an experienced Vatican diplomat who was raised to the cardinalate in 1583.

36. Monti 1914–1915, 1:162–63; Scaduto 1992, 329–32.

philosophy, and metaphysics in the coming academic year. Next, when the three medieval mendicant order clergymen currently teaching theology reached the ends of their contracts, the duke planned to replace them with three Jesuits. The Society would be permitted to choose the Jesuits to teach in the university, who would schedule their lectures as they wished. The Jesuits would teach in the Jesuit school instead of the university building, and would not be subject to the authority of the Riformatori dello Studio di Torino, the city magistracy that oversaw the university. For their university teaching the duke promised to give the Jesuit college enough properties and securities to produce 1,000 scudi in annual income, a sum that Gagliardi believed would enable the Turin college to grow to more than sixty Jesuits.[37] A college of that size would be the sixth largest in Italy, just behind Milan and Palermo.[38] According to Gagliardi, the duke had informed the Riformatori, the grand chancellor (the duke's chief minister), the archbishop, and the city of his plan. The duke had encountered much resistance and many objections, including from the archbishop, but he was determined to do it.[39]

Gagliardi believed that teaching in the university would yield several benefits. The University of Turin had distinguished professors and the duke was an important figure. Hence, teaching in this Italian university would bring more prestige to the Society than teaching in an ultramontane university. Joining a university so near to foreign lands offered the opportunity to educate people to resist heresy, which was always growing. Because the duke and other gentlemen were horrified by secular philosophy that tended toward atheism, Gagliardi looked forward to introducing Christian philosophy into the university. Finally, he assured General Borja that the Turin college had enough able Jesuits to fill the three initial professorships without neglecting its other ministries.[40]

But nothing happened in the next sixteen months. On January 9, 1572, Gagliardi brought the general up to date. The move into the university had

37. Letter of Gagliardi of September 13, 1570, Turin, to General Borja in ARSI, Italiae 139, f. 219r–v, entire letter 219r–21r. Scaduto 1992, 331, summarizes and quotes part of the letter but misdates it as August 13.

38. The largest three were Rome, Messina, and Naples. For the size of Italian Jesuit colleges between 1574 and 1580, see Grendler 2004a, 488, 492, 495–98.

39. ARSI, Italiae 139, f. 219r. The anonymous memorandum of 1593 ("Raggioni 1593," described in note 64 and discussed below) stated that the archbishop did not support the plan to give professorships to the Jesuits. This was Girolamo Della Rovere (Turin 1530–1592 Rome, archbishop of Turin from 1564, cardinal from 1586). He had previously served the duke as a diplomat at Paris and had been instrumental in persuading the French to leave Piedmont. Stumpo 1989.

40. Letter of Gagliardi of September 13, 1570, in ARSI, Italiae 139, f. 220r–v. Scaduto 1992, 331–32, quotes several sentences of this part of the letter.

been delayed because the duke was not ready to provide the promised 1,000 scudi, and because of the *gran rumore* (great outcry) against the Jesuits that rose from professors of the university. They had waited, and now was the time to strike. The city no longer saw the Jesuits as meddling in its affairs, and the duke had reaffirmed his intentions. He pledged to give the Jesuits nine professorships: two in scholastic theology, and one each in scripture, logic, natural philosophy, metaphysics, mathematics, rhetoric, and Greek.[41]

Moreover, Gagliardi and the duke had refined the terms under which the Jesuits would teach in the university. First, the duke agreed that the Jesuits might teach theology and philosophy their way, which meant that each Jesuit philosopher would deliver a morning and an afternoon lecture, plus the students would engage in disputations and exercises as outlined in the Constitutions. Second, the law and medicine professors would not be permitted to "impacciarsi" (meddle) in the teaching of the Jesuits. The Riformatori dello Studio and other officials would not be allowed to appoint or remove Jesuit professors or to impose obligations on them.[42]

Third, the duke agreed that the Jesuits would have the right to correct the students according to part 4 of the Jesuit Constitutions, with the duke providing support.[43] Gagliardi probably referred to paragraphs 481 through 489, which enjoined the Jesuits to try to make sure that students who attended Jesuit universities acquired "good and Christian moral habits" (par. 481). Paragraph 486 added: "In the classes no cursing, nor injurious words or deeds, nor anything immoral, nor anything indecent or dissolute should be allowed on the part of externs [non-Jesuits] who come to classes from elsewhere." And paragraph 488 added that "there should be a corrector from outside the Society" to deal with "those who are derelict either in proper diligence in their studies or in what pertains to good moral habits, and for whom kind words and admonitions alone are not sufficient."[44]

Fourth, the Jesuits would have the authority to confer degrees in the

---

41. "Che di legger una lettione di retorica, una di greco, et le facoltà di philosophia et theologia secondo che a noi parerosi, pur che siano almeno sette lettioni oltre le lingue che già ho detto, includendovi la matematica, che verrano a essere tre corsi di philosophia, due lettioni di [teologia] scolastica, una della scrittura sacra et le due di latino et greco." Letter of Gagliardi of January 9, 1572, in ARSI, Mediolanensis 76 I, Historia 1554–1603, f. 15r–v, quotation at 15v, entire letter ff. 15r–18r. Grendler 2006b, Study VI, 18–21, quotation at 18, publishes the entire letter. In the following notes both the archival reference and the printed letter will be cited.

42. ARSI, Mediolanensis 76 I, f. 15r–v; Grendler 2006b, Study VI, 18.

43. "3.0 Haveremo liberta di correger i scolari di scole secondo che nella 4.0 parte delle constitutioni si contiene, et Sua Altezza dara gl'aiuto et favore che sara necessario." ARSI, Mediolanensis 76 I, f. 15v; Grendler 2006b, Study VI, 19.

44. *Constitutions* 1996, 185–87, quotations at 185–86.

subjects that they taught without the participation of other professors or doctors. In addition, students of the Jesuits would be permitted to present themselves as degree candidates to a college of doctors without any difficulty.[45] These promises had two purposes. They affirmed that the Jesuits might award degrees on their own authority, which was based on papal bulls granting Jesuit schools the power to confer doctorates in theology and philosophy after a serious examination. The Jesuits would not be dependent on the university. And the duke's promise would bar the college of doctors of theology and college of doctors of medicine and philosophy from putting obstacles in the way of students of the Jesuits who might seek degrees from them. This was important, because the Jesuits were not members of either college.

Unlike Ignatius and Nadal at Messina, Gagliardi did not insist on a role for the Jesuits in the governance of the University of Turin. Instead he secured for the Jesuits the promise of a largely autonomous unit within the larger university. As a student at the University of Padua Gagliardi had learned how Italian universities were structured and had acted accordingly. He won all these promised rights and privileges from the duke. Professors, colleges of doctors, and the Riformatori dello Studio would not have conceded them. Gagliardi reviewed the financial support that the Jesuits would receive. The duke was now promising payment of 900 scudi, down from 1,000, for the teaching of the Jesuits. Gagliardi was confident that this sum, added to the expected high yield from the coming legacy of Alerame Beccuti, would support a Jesuit community of seventy.[46]

Next came the duke's slightly revised plan to insert Jesuit professors into the university. The Jesuits would enter one by one as incumbents died or completed their contracts. Turin, like all other Italian universities, normally gave professors one- or two-year contracts, sometimes three- or four-year contracts. They were almost always renewed until the professor left or died. But now they would not be renewed. In 1572 there were vacancies in scholastic theology and metaphysics. Gagliardi would organize public disputations with much pomp and circumstance at Easter time (April 6). Two Jesuits would dispute brilliantly and win applause from university students. Riding this wave of approval they would be appointed to the university. The same procedure would be followed until there were nine Jesuit professors. As each Jesuit entered the university, the duke would assign 100 scudi to the Jesuits until the sum reached 900.[47]

45. ARSI, Mediolanensis 76 I, ff. 15v–16r; Grendler 2006b, Study VI, 19.
46. ARSI, Mediolanensis 76 I, f. 16r–v; Grendler 2006b, Study VI, 19.
47. ARSI, Mediolanensis 76 I, ff. 16v–17r; Grendler 2006b, Study VI, 19–20.

There was one potential problem. The first Turin Jesuits whom Gagliardi named as potential professors were not distinguished scholars, even
though Gagliardi averred that they were just as able as young university
professors.[48] The papal nuncio asked Gagliardi to remedy this by bringing
in two Jesuit stars. He wanted Juan Maldonado (Badajoz 1533–1583 Rome),
a pioneering positive theologian and the ablest Jesuit biblical scholar of the
century, then teaching to acclaim in the Jesuit school in Paris.[49] And he requested Benito Perera (or Pereira, Valencia 1536–1610 Rome), who taught
logic, natural philosophy, metaphysics, and theology at the Collegio Romano from 1558 to 1570.[50] Although Perera was highly esteemed by his students, the conservative Gagliardi saw him as an Averroist. Gagliardi passed
the requests on to General Borja without comment.[51] However, it was not
realistic to expect that the general would send such important scholars to
remote Turin.

It was a bold plan. The duke promised to give the Jesuits nine professorships in a university of twenty-nine.[52] Just as important, he would give
them considerable independence to teach and award degrees without reference to the statutes and customs. He was willing to permit the Jesuits
to create a theology, philosophy, and humanities unit within the law and
medicine university. He promised to support the Jesuits in their efforts to
improve the moral behavior of university students, which could only be realized if he was willing to enforce Jesuit exhortations. The most innovative
and provocative part was his plan to introduce the Jesuits into the university through disputations and refusal to renew contracts. He would discard
traditional employment practices in order to bring in the Jesuits.

Gagliardi believed that the duke's plan to insert the Jesuits into the university was "gentle" and would not provoke controversy.[53] He was very
wrong. The city government took the lead in opposition. At some point in
1572 it sent a delegation to the Jesuits to beg them not to teach certain sub-

48. They were Pierre Christin (Nice 1541–dismissed from the Society in 1573), Bartolomeo
Mucante (Rome 1548–1629 Genoa), and Francesco Prandi (Bologna 1542–after 1590). Scaduto
1968, 32, 103, and Scaduto 1992, 310. There are no biographies of them in DHCJ, and Sommervogel 1960, has no entries for them, which argues that they published nothing.

49. Tellechea 2001.

50. Sola 2001.

51. ARSI, Mediolanensis 76 I, ff. 17v–18r; Grendler 2006b, Study VI, 20–21. For Gagliardi's denunciation of Perera, see chap. 14, "Jesuit Christian Aristotelianism."

52. In the academic year 1571–1572 the University of Turin had 11 law professors and 18 for
medicine, medical botany, philosophy, logic, mathematics, theology, and the humanities. In the
academic year 1572–1573, the university had 12 law professors and 17 for all the other disciplines.

53. ARSI, Mediolanensis 76 I, f. 16v; Grendler 2006b, Study VI, 19.

jects, especially metaphysics, in their college, because this would seriously damage the university.[54] Gagliardi undoubtedly refused. The city went to Emanuele Filiberto on or before March 7, 1572. It petitioned him to maintain all the professorships of the university so that Turin would be a whole university, just like all the other universities in towns in which the Jesuits had schools. The city pointed out that the Jesuits did not lecture in universities in other states with Catholic princes, not even in the papal state. Although the city did not name the universities in the papal state, they were Bologna, Macerata, Perugia, and Rome at that time. All four towns had universities and Jesuit schools, but the Jesuits did not teach in the universities.[55] The city argued that maintaining all the professorships of the University of Turin was essential for university instruction. The city further asked that civil regulations and the statutes of the colleges of doctors of law and medicine not be changed in order to admit new members in violation of their ancient rules. The city was objecting to the duke's promise that the Jesuits might bypass the rules of the colleges of doctors and confer degrees on their own authority.[56]

The city was defending the university, itself, and the people of Turin. It did not want incumbent professors to lose their positions. It supported the doctoral colleges, because Turin physicians were members of the college of doctors of medicine, and medieval mendicant order clergymen from local monasteries filled the college of doctors of theology. The city government did not want to lose its limited authority over the university exercised through the Riformatori dello Studio. And the city had a major financial interest at stake, because it had given the duke a substantial sum to get the university restored, and it paid much of the university's expenses.

The duke surrendered. He agreed that the university would always have a full complement of professors. He further conceded that the magistrates must observe the statutes of the colleges of doctors.[57] It was victory and relief for the university, the city government, and those who would have lost

54. Grosso and Mellano 1957, 2:89n76.

55. This was true in 1572. However, two Jesuits had taught at the University of Macerata from 1561 to 1563, and other Jesuits taught there in the seventeenth and eighteenth centuries. See chap. 8, "The Jesuits Enter the University of Macerata."

56. ASCTo, Carte sciolte, no. 97, 7 marzo 1572 (no foliation). Vallauri 1875, 201n1, quotes the first part of the petition from a different archival document.

57. "4.o Provvederà che l'università sii sempre compita del numero dei lettori leggenti nelle scuole pubbliche. 5.o Concede, e (illegible), che i suoi magistrati facciano osservare li statuti, et leggi fatte per i Collegi dei Dottori della Università, non ostante le lettere accordate in contrario." ASCTo, Carte sciolte, no. 97, 7 marzo 1572, no foliation. This appears to be a short summary of the duke's decision.

their positions to Jesuits. For good measure, the university payment that went to the Jesuits for teaching the humanities ceased after the academic year 1573–1574. But this did not mean the restoration of the full university humanities curriculum. For most of the rest of the century, the university had only a single humanist, a professor of Greek.[58] Students who wanted more humanities instruction had to go to the Jesuit school or elsewhere.

The duke abandoned his plan because it would have taken a prolonged struggle to implement it. Gagliardi had to go because the episode had sparked hostility against the Jesuits. In August 1572 Cardinal Carlo Borromeo (1538–1584), archbishop of Milan, asked General Borja to send Gagliardi to Milan to teach scholastic theology at the Jesuit school there. Borja agreed. But Emanuele Filiberto did not want him to leave. He entrusted diplomatic missions to Gagliardi, forcing Borja to leave him in place. Gagliardi finally wore out his welcome with the duke in the legal battles that ensued when Alerame Beccuti died in the winter of 1574. Although he left everything to the Jesuits, the duke and others claimed part of the legacy. Gagliardi attempted to mediate but soon asked to be relieved of the thankless task. In 1575 General Mercurian brought him back to Rome to teach scholastic theology at the Roman College.[59]

Its university plans thwarted, the Jesuit college remained small. In 1574 it had seventeen Jesuits and the school offered four lower school classes.[60] But the Jesuits developed their noble boarding school with considerable success. In January 1580 it enrolled 90 to 100 noble youths who came from all of Piedmont.[61]

58. Teodoro Rendio, about whom nothing is known, taught Greek at the university from 1567 to 1585, and a Latin humanist taught for two years, 1575–1577. Chiaudano 1972b, 77–78, 101, 103–4, 107, 109, 112–14, 116; Chiaudano 1972a, 165–66, 168, 170. A gap in the records from 1585–1586 until 1600 follows. However, no Latin or Greek humanist was appointed after 1600.

59. See two letters of Polanco to Cardinal Borromeo and Duke Emanuele Filiberto, both of December 13, 1572, in *Polanci Complementa* 1969, 2:161–64. Polanco was vicar general of the Society between the death of Borja on September 30, 1572, and the election of Mercurian on April 23, 1573. See also Rurale 1992, 139–40; and G. Brunelli 1998, 259.

60. Lukács 1960–1961, part 2, 49.

61. "Quelli del collegio M. Nicolino di convittori; del quale si dovria far gran conto, perché vi sono ordinariamente 90 o 100 giovani della nobiltà di tutto il Piamonte." Visitation report of Sebastiano Morales of January 28, 1580, Turin, in MP 4:348. See also the letter of the Turin rector, Mariano Settineri, of July 22, 1575, Turin, in MP 4:595. For Morales and Settineri, see Scaduto 1968, 102, 138.

The Second Attempt

The Jesuits and their supporters did not give up. In 1593 the university was experiencing a financial crisis because funds intended to pay salaries had been diverted to other purposes. Supporters of the Jesuits proposed to Duke Carlo Emanuele I (1562–1630, r. from 1580) that the Jesuits be given all the philosophical and theological professorships at the university. They offered several reasons. There was a shortage of worthy and able Italian professors to teach these subjects, they argued. But it was not a good idea to appoint ultramontane scholars of uncertain religious views. Instead, the Jesuits should be brought in, because they were learned, proven, doctrinally reliable, and exemplary in their habits. They already did the holy work of education for other Italian princes. The duke should follow the example of Archbishop Carlo Borromeo who brought the Jesuits to Milan to teach at the Jesuit university (meaning the upper school classes of the Jesuit school there).[62] And substituting the Jesuits for the lay professors would greatly reduce costs.[63]

The reaction was negative. On October 8, 1593, an anonymous author, possibly a professor of natural philosophy at the university, wrote a memorandum presenting many reasons against appointing Jesuits.[64] The major argument was that giving philosophy and theology to the Jesuits would greatly damage the university. To support his case the author offered examples of other Italian governments that had allegedly restricted Jesuit teaching. Most of the examples were wholly or partially inaccurate. He

62. However, it was not a smooth relationship. Although Borromeo invited the Jesuits to come to Milan in 1563 and provided financial support, the Jesuits and Borromeo had pedagogical and other differences. The Jesuits had to struggle to maintain their independence in the face of the demands of the imperious Borromeo. See Rurale 1992.

63. Vallauri 1970, 2:87–88; Vallauri 1875, 257–58.

64. AST, Istruzione Pubblica, Regia Università, mazzo 1, no. 7.2, "Raggioni perché non sia bene che gli Rev. Padri Giesuiti leggano la filosofia tutta, et la teologia nel loro Convento, et si lasci di leggersi nello Studio e pubbliche scuole, come sempre insino a qui si è fatto. 1593. ottavo giorno di ottobre." Hereafter "Raggioni 1593." The document consists of seven unnumbered pages of text plus the title on the eighth page. Although written in the first person singular, it lists no author. However, the contents, which demonstrate considerable knowledge about professors of philosophy and sixteenth-century philosophical research, and make several references to other Italian universities, suggest that the author was a professor of natural philosophy at the University of Torino. Unfortunately, the gap in the university rolls from 1586 to 1600 makes it impossible to speculate on the author's identity. It is not addressed to an individual or magistracy. It is likely a document in support of a petition, which would explain the lack of an addressee and author. Vallauri 1970, 2:88–91; Vallauri 1875, 258–61; and Scaglione 1986, 140–43, have discussed the document. Monti 1914–1915, 1:176, mentions it in passing.

noted that the Republic of Venice had forbidden the Jesuits of Padua from teaching philosophy. This was a reference to the Venetian Senate decree of December 1591 ordering the Jesuit upper school in Padua not to teach non-Jesuits, as described in chapter 5. However, the Padua school continued to teach philosophy and theology to Jesuit students. He added that the Venetian government may have ordered the Jesuits not to teach anything except Latin grammar anywhere in its state.[65] This was not true. The Jesuit professed house in Venice taught cases of conscience, the Brescia school taught philosophy, and the Verona school taught cases of conscience. These three classes were open to all comers.[66]

The author next stated that the Jesuits had tried with all their might to take over the theology and philosophy lectures at the universities of Rome, Bologna, Cesena, and elsewhere in the papal state. The author was relying on inaccurate information or was lying. As noted in chapter 1, two Jesuits taught theology at the University of Rome from 1537 to 1539, and another may have in the academic year 1539–1540, before the Society received papal recognition. But the Jesuits did not seek teaching positions at the universities of Rome or Bologna after 1540. And since there were no Jesuits in Cesena, they could not threaten the town's tiny and incomplete university.[67] The author then restated his major point: if universities lost their philosophy lectures, they would lose their "grandezza" (greatness) and become imperfect and truncated institutions. He believed that students wanted to hear lectures by professors in the university, not endure the pedantry of Jesuits in their college.[68]

After describing what the author saw as the inadequacies of Jesuit philosophical teaching (see chapter 14, "The Jesuits Teach Philosophy Badly"), the writer returned to his major theme: giving the philosophy and theology lectures to the Jesuits would render the University of Turin divided and imperfect. It would eventually dissolve. In the past the University of Turin had produced eminent scholars who had gone on to teach at Padua and Pavia. The author lamented that the university had once had a profes-

65. Raggioni 1593.
66. ARSI, Veneta 37, ff. 97r–98r (Padua 1595), 251r–v (Venice 1600), 258r–v (Brescia 1600), 261r–v (Verona 1600).
67. In 1571 Cesena established a partial university consisting of five professors: three in civil law, one for logic, and one for natural philosophy. In 1576 the city council of Cesena invited the Jesuits to come to Cesena and teach in the university. But they never came: there was no Jesuit college in Cesena at any time through 1773. In the meantime, the tiny partial University of Cesena limped along. It had four professors in the academic year 1593–1594. See Brizzi 1989, esp. 242–43 and n73.
68. Raggioni 1593.

sorship of the humanities (perhaps a reference to Giraldi Cinzio), and "gentili spiriti" (noble spirits) of the city had attended the lectures. But humanities instruction had been given to the Jesuits, and now only "putti" (boys) came. He feared that the same would happen to philosophy if the lectures were given to the Jesuits.[69]

The author then predicted more disastrous consequences if the Jesuits were awarded the philosophy positions. The city would lose control over appointments. At present the city had the authority to dismiss an unsatisfactory professor, he wrote. But if the Jesuits taught philosophy, the city would lose this power. This was true. In civic-Jesuit universities the Society, rather than the city or the prince, chose and replaced Jesuit professors. For good measure the writer opined that the initial Jesuits to arrive in Turin had been better teachers than the current ones.[70]

The author believed that Jesuit professors would weaken the authority of the college of doctors of medicine and philosophy. He explained that at present a doctoral candidate chose as his promoter a professor whose lectures he had attended. (Promoters were professors who assisted candidates in doctoral examinations.) But if the Jesuits taught philosophy, candidates might choose Jesuit professors as promoters. Consequently, the Jesuit professors would little by little take over the college of doctors of medicine and philosophy.[71] The author's prophecy did not come true. In the future Jesuit professors became promoters and members of colleges of doctors in the civic-Jesuit universities of Parma, Fermo, and Macerata (chapters 6 and 8). But they never controlled the colleges. The memorandum concluded with more praise of learned Turin professors and scholars of the past.[72]

Nothing changed at the University of Turin. The Jesuits were not awarded any professorships in 1593 or later. And the Jesuit college and school remained modest in size. There were twenty-four Jesuits in Turin in 1600, and they taught cases of conscience and three lower school classes.[73] How seriously Duke Carlo Emanuele I considered awarding the philosophy and theology lectures to the Jesuits in 1593 is unknown.[74] In any case, the author of the memorandum, and those for whom he probably spoke, believed that the integrity of the university was at stake. They saw the civic University of Turin as a structure of interlocking parts: professors who taught, colleges of doctors who examined degree candidates, and duke and

---

69. Raggioni 1593.   70. Raggioni 1593.

71. Raggioni 1593.   72. Raggioni 1593.

73. ARSI, Mediolanensis 47, f. 153r; Lukács 1960–1961, part 2, 49.

74. Vallauri 1970, 2:91, and Vallauri 1875, 261, credit Carlo Emanuele I with rejecting the proposal. I have not found further information in ARSI, ASCTo, or AST.

city who governed the university. Any change would produce a damaged and incomplete institution. Of course, the memorandum did not mention other damage, that some professors would lose their positions. Instead, it animadverted on the need to protect the integrity of the university. The memorandum also demonstrated that opponents sought and used information against the Jesuits from other Italian universities, whether it was accurate or not.

Conclusion

From their first meetings Antonio Possevino and Duke Emanuele Filiberto looked toward the Jesuits becoming professors in the university of the duchy. This came closest to reality at Mondovì, a new university in 1561, as the troublesome Michele Vopisco and the brilliant Robert Bellarmine briefly taught the humanities course there. However, the duke saw Turin as his future capital and the Jesuits followed his lead. When the University of Turin was restored in 1567, the Jesuits founded a college and school in Turin, at which point the duke and the Jesuits saw the Jesuits joining the University of Turin. In preparation, the duke suppressed the humanities professorship in favor of the Jesuit school.

In 1570 and 1572 Duke Emanuele Filiberto and Achille Gagliardi conceived a plan to insert nine Jesuits into the University of Turin. Unlike Messina, where Loyola and subsequent generals made the key decisions, this was an initiative of the duke and Gagliardi. But strong opposition from the university, the city council, and the town forced the duke to abandon the plan. In 1593 it was again proposed that the Jesuits be given theology and philosophy professorships in the university. Again there was opposition, and the proposal was not pursued. The Jesuits never obtained any professorships in the University of Turin. Messina and Turin were early attempts by the Jesuits to become professors in Italian universities. In both places the Jesuits underestimated the opposition.

5

THE PADUA DISASTER

The Jesuits never tried to enter the University of Padua. Instead, they created a flourishing school which some professors and students saw as a threat to the university. They persuaded the Venetian Senate to order the Padua school to teach only Jesuits, which closed the Padua school to almost all students. In addition, the Jesuits had to contend with Venetian nobles who strongly believed that the Jesuits were enemies of the Republic of Venice enticing their students to serve the king of Spain. In 1606 the Jesuits were expelled from the Venetian state.

The Jesuit School at Padua

The Jesuits arrived in Padua in 1542. Then in 1546 Andrea Lippomano, a Venetian clergyman from a noble family, gave his benefice, the priorate and revenues of Santa Maria Maddalena in Padua, to the Jesuits. As often happened, a relative challenged the donation, complaining that the Jesuits were a foreign religious order. The Jesuits told doge and Senate that they intended to establish a college and school, which would teach for free. And they denied that they were a foreign religious order. They pointed out that of the eleven Jesuits in Padua in 1548, eight were Italians, four or five of them Venetian subjects. This satisfied the Senate. On September 20, 1548, Doge Francesco Donà approved the donation of the priorate and its revenues, with which the Jesuits founded schools in Venice and Padua.[1]

The Venice school did not flourish. It introduced a grammar class in March 1550 that attracted only 20 students. Even with the addition of another class or two, enrollment never rose higher than 40 to 60 in the next fifteen years. So, in 1570 the Venetian college became a professed house

1. Tacchi Venturi 1951b, 305–24, and documents 9 and 14–19 on 664–68, 672–79. See also Scaduto 1964, 143–44; Donnelly 1982, 46–47; and Sangalli 1999, 15–18, 20–22.

without a school. It continued the lectureship in cases of conscience introduced in 1563, which met once or twice a week, but that was all.[2]

The Padua school had greater but still modest success. As noted in chapter 1, in its first years the Jesuit college housed a few young Jesuits who studied at the university or privately, while other Jesuits carried on ministries. The Jesuits opened a school for external students in 1552. It began with a grammar class that enrolled 150 students in the following year, a figure that dropped to below 100 in subsequent years. The school added additional lower school classes with good but not large enrollments. In 1555 they added a class in logic but could not sustain it. In 1558 the school had only three lower school classes with 78 to 80 students. The single upper school class returned in 1567, and was dropped again in 1570 and 1571.[3]

The Padua Jesuits kept trying: the school added a theology class, then a second one, in the 1570s. Some sons of noble families attended the school, which pleased the Society. The number of Jesuits in Padua expanded modestly over the years: from eleven in 1548 to twenty-four, including five to seven Jesuit scholastics, in 1560; twenty-four again in 1574; but probably fewer during the plague years of 1575 to 1577. There were also reverses: the lower school, whose size varied from one to four classes of grammar, humanities, and/or rhetoric over the years, closed, possibly during the plague.[4] The Padua college and school were standing still.

Then several developments between 1577 and 1582 produced major expansion and a change in direction. In early 1577 Federico Corner (or Cornaro, 1531–1590, cardinal from 1585), became bishop of Padua. From a major Venetian noble family that produced doges and high churchmen, including a older brother who was a cardinal, Corner was a reforming bishop whose priorities coincided with those of the Jesuits. He began to visit all the parishes in his diocese, he implemented the decrees of Trent, and he expanded catechetical instruction, a ministry to which the Jesuits were very committed. Corner became a strong moral and financial supporter of the Jesuits and their school.[5]

The next change came in the Society. In 1578 it divided the Jesuit Prov-

2. For the history of the Venetian college, then professed house to 1606, see Scaduto 1974, 418–22; Scaduto 1992, 305–16; *For Matters of Greater Moment* 1994, 119, decree 25 after the election; Zanardi 1994, 95, 98–110, 136–38, 146–51, 160–72; and Sangalli 1999, 118–19, 125–31, 167, 172–73.

3. Letter of Émond Auger of December 2, 1558, Padua, in MP 3:281–82; Scaduto 1974, 422–26; Donnelly 1982, 47–48; and Sangalli 1999, 46.

4. Lukács 1960–1961, part 2, 50; Scaduto 1992, 307–12; Sangalli 1999, 23–50.

5. For Corner, see Frasson 1983; and The Cardinals of the Holy Roman Church (ww2 .fiu.edu/~mirandas/bios1585-ii.html#cornaro).

ince of Lombardy, which included all of Italy north of Tuscany, into two, the Province of Venice (northeastern Italy and parts of the papal state) and the Province of Milan (northwestern Italy)—see map 2. By this date the Society had developed a policy of establishing a major school in each province at which most of the Jesuits of the province did their philosophical and theological studies. Consequently, the major school had the best teachers and offered the most classes, which ensured that it had the highest number of external students. The Brera school in Milan had been the major school in the old Province of Lombardy and continued this role in the new Province of Milan. But the new Province of Venice lacked a major school. The Jesuit leadership in Rome and the provincial superior decided that the Padua school would fill this role.

The Padua school quickly expanded. As urged by many parents and students, it restored its philosophy class in May 1579 and immediately enrolled about 80 students.[6] The Padua Jesuit school now offered four upper school lectures: two in scholastic theology, one in philosophy (probably logic, natural philosophy, and metaphysics in succession over three years), and one in cases of conscience. The number of Jesuits rose to 28: 10 priests, 10 scholastics, and 8 temporal coadjutors and second-year novices.[7] But there was no lower school.

The Jesuits believed that their philosophy and theology classes moved university professors to teach more. In his annual letter of January 1, 1580, Mario Beringucci (Siena 1536–1604 Venice), the provincial superior, wrote that the courses in the Padua school had been scheduled so as not to compete with the university lectures. Nevertheless, the Jesuit philosophy lectures had galvanized university professors. In the past they had delivered only their required daily ordinary lectures. (He might have added that professors often failed to deliver all the lectures required by the statutes because of their own absenteeism and because students took unauthorized holidays.)[8] Hence, university students thirsting for more instruction had come to the Jesuit school. Now in order to retain their students, professors had to offer additional lectures, both extraordinary and private, to the point that they taught two or three times daily.[9] The students were quite

---

6. ARSI, Veneta 105 I, f. 57v. See also Donnelly 1982, 48; and Sangalli 1999, 52.

7. ARSI, Veneta 105 I, f. 57r.

8. Grendler 2002, 495–96. For Beringucci, see Scaduto 1968, 14.

9. Extraordinary lectures were mandatory lectures delivered on designated extraordinary teaching days or on vacation days by professors whose appointments were described as extraordinary. They were a statutory part of university instruction. However, it appears that here Beringucci simply meant non-statutory, non-required teaching.

happy with this new state of affairs, he concluded.[10] However, even though professors charged fees for private lessons, something Beringucci did not mention, he seemed oblivious to the fact that they might resent the Jesuits for forcing them to teach more.[11]

The Jesuits reached out spiritually to the university community. In 1578 they organized a Marian congregation for students and professors that met regularly to hear lectures that combined learning, prayers, and exhortations to live Christian lives. By the end of 1579 it had a hundred members. including nine professors. Father Beringucci praised Antonio Riccobono of Rovigo (1541–1599), professor of humanistic studies from 1572 until his death, and Girolamo Mercuriale of Forlì (1530–1606), first-position ordinary professor of medical practice from 1569 to 1587, for their orations to the congregation.[12]

In 1582 the Jesuit Padua school began a major expansion. Pressed by Bishop Corner, the Jesuits founded a boarding school for boys and youths of certified noble birth. Since the vast majority of noble boys were not academically prepared for philosophy classes, a lower school was needed. So it reappeared in 1582 in an expanded form of two grammar classes and two humanities classes, open to all and free of charge. Numerous Paduan non-noble parents also sent their sons to the Jesuit lower school, whose enrollment rose to about 200 in 1584. The Jesuits then added a second class in philosophy, this time in natural philosophy, and a class in Hebrew so that theology students might learn to read the Old Testament in its original language. The provincial superior's annual letter for 1589 reported that the Padua school enrolled about 470 students from all over the Catholic world. Four hundred external (i.e., non-Jesuit) students attended the grammar, humanities, and philosophy classes. Seventy of them were Venetian nobles, probably almost all of them boarders. The theology classes enrolled fifty external students. And about twenty Jesuit scholastics studied philosophy or theology.[13]

10. ARSI, Veneta 105 I, f. 57v, annual letter of Mario Beringucci. See also Donnelly 1982, 48; and Sangalli 1999, 193, who quotes part of Beringucci's letter.

11. Some professors taught individual students or small groups of students the same subject matter on which they lectured publicly, or material not covered in the lectures, in private lessons for which they charged fees. Some professors realized more income from private lessons than from their professorial salaries. This was the case with Galileo Galilei, professor of mathematics and astronomy at the University of Padua from 1592 to 1610, in some years. Universities denounced private teaching but were unable or unwilling to stop it. For details, including Galilei's income from private teaching, see Grendler 2002, 486–90.

12. ARSI, Veneta 105 I, f. 58r. Sangalli 1999, 192–93, quotes part of the letter.

13. Donnelly 1982, 48–49; Sangalli 1999, 213–14. The estimate of about twenty Jesuit scholastics is taken from the number there in 1590.

In 1590 the Jesuit school offered ten classes: two in scholastic theology, one in cases of conscience, two in philosophy (probably logic and natural philosophy), one each in mathematics, rhetoric, and humanities, and two for grammar. The Hebrew class had been replaced by a class in mathematics taught by Marc'Antonio De Dominis, who will play a role in the coming controversy. There were 60 or 62 Jesuits at Padua: 20 priests, about 20 scholastics, and the rest temporal coadjutors. The net annual income of the college was about 2,500 ducats, not a large sum for a college and school of this size.[14]

In 1590 the Padua college was by far the largest college and school in the Jesuit Province of Venice. Nearly one-fifth (60 or 62 of 322) of the Jesuits in the province were at Padua, and another 38 were in Venice. When the Jesuits at Brescia (33), and Verona (23), both with flourishing schools, and the Crete mission (6 Jesuits), are added, about one-half (160 or 162 of 322) of the Jesuits of the Province of Venice lived in the Republic of Venice. This was a high concentration, because the province also included the duchies of Ferrara (including Modena), Mantua, and Parma, the legation of Bologna, and additional parts of the papal state.[15]

There were more Jesuits in Padua, and the school enrollment was much higher, than in Jesuit colleges and schools in the university towns of Bologna, Catania, Ferrara, Perugia, Macerata, Siena, and Turin.[16] The University of Padua with an enrollment of 1,500 to 1,600 students (probably 800 or more in medicine and philosophy, 700 in law, and a very small number in theology) faced a Jesuit school of 470 students.[17] Even though two-thirds or more of the students in the Jesuit school attended the lower school, the number of classes and students in the upper school was large enough to be viewed as a threat.

14. ARSI, Veneta 37, ff. 15r, 17r, 32r–35v. The total number of Jesuits is reported as 60 at f. 15r, and 62 at ff. 32r–35v, including Antonio Possevino. Baldini 1994, 574–75, offers a partial list of the upper school teachers at Padua, and some of the Jesuits at the professed house in Venice, from 1582 through 1603.

15. ARSI, Veneta 37, f. 15r.

16. The sizes of the Jesuit colleges and school enrollments in these cities are given in the relevant chapters. It should be added that the Jesuits had larger schools than that of Padua in the university towns of Naples and Rome. But, so far as is known, there were no clashes between the University of Naples and the Jesuits. And the Roman College and the University of Rome coexisted peacefully until the 1690s.

17. Grendler 2002, 36, for the estimated enrollment of the University of Padua around 1600.

Attacks against the Jesuit School

Some members of the university did see the Jesuit school as a threat. Attacks began in 1589 when an unidentified person asked the Venetian Senate to close it. The Senate did not act. On another occasion in 1589 university students stormed into the Jesuit school, disrupting classes. Police officers under the command of the two Venetian governors of Padua forced the invaders to return to their residences and forbade them from leaving the city pending charges. This violation of the students' traditional liberty to come and go as they pleased generated strong protests from students and their organizations. But the Jesuits forgave the culprits and peace was restored.[18]

Attacks on the Jesuit school on consecutive days followed two years later. On the night of July 11, 1591, a gang of students went through the city breaking windows, shooting off arquebuses, and insulting people they encountered. They broke windows of the Jesuit school and hurled insults. The next morning some students gathered at the lodging of one of their number. They took off their clothes, wrapped themselves in sheets, and again marched through the streets, displaying their penises, and insulting women and children. They arrived at the Jesuit school as its morning theology lecture was ending. They forced their way inside, dropped the sheets, and shouted insults and obscenities at the Jesuits and their students, before leaving. The Venetian authorities were embarrassed and outraged. The governors quickly identified eight students, all Venetian nobles from prominent families, one of them a student at the Jesuit school, and reported what had happened to Venice. The Council of Ten, which was responsible for public order throughout the Venetian state, punished the miscreants with heavy fines of 100 to 300 ducats each.[19]

Whether the student invasions of the Jesuit school contributed to, or had any connection with, the subsequent legal attack on the Jesuit school is difficult to determine. A Paduan chronicler recorded that the students said that they invaded the Jesuit school because the Jesuits lectured at the same hours as university professors. It is also possible that the chronicler read the later dispute back into the July invasion.[20] In any case, students often behaved badly, and ecclesiastical bodies were frequent targets. For example,

18. Sangalli 1999, 214–15. Two Venetian nobles appointed by the Senate, a *capitano* (military governor) and a *podestà* (chief judicial officer), governed Padua with the assistance of a small band of policemen and other officials.

19. Favaro 1877–1878, 428–31, 472–82; Donnelly 1982, 51; Sangalli 1999, 216, 218–19.

20. Favaro 1877–1878, 473; Donnelly 1982, 51; and Sangalli 1999, 217n59. Sangalli 1999, 219–20, does not see a link between the events of July 1591 and the Senate action of December.

University of Padua students broke the windows of an abbacy at the same time that they invaded the Jesuit school.[21] Nevertheless, two invasions of the Jesuit school in three years demonstrated hostility toward the Jesuits.

Of greater long-term consequence to the Jesuits was the loss through death of three key supporters, two of them from the university. The first was Girolamo Capodivacca of Padua (d. March 4, 1589), who came from an old and prominent Paduan noble family. Author of many publications, he had taught medicine at the university since 1553 and shared the first-position ordinary professorship of medical practice at his death. Capodivacca left a substantial legacy to the Jesuits and was buried in the Jesuit church.[22] Cardinal Federico Corner, bishop of Padua, died on October 4, 1590.[23] His successor, nephew Alvise Corner, did not play a role in subsequent events involving the Jesuits. And most importantly, Jacopo (or Giacomo) Zabarella of Padua (born September 5, 1533) died on October 15, 1589, with Jesuits at his bedside.[24] From a Paduan noble family, he was the second-position ordinary professor of natural philosophy, a distinguished scholar, and a strong supporter of the Jesuits.[25] He may have been a half-brother to Achille Gagliardi and Ludovico Gagliardi (Padua 1543–1608 Modena), Padua-born Jesuits who will play prominent roles in the coming controversy.[26] Whether brothers or not, relations between Jacopo Zabarella and the Jesuits were close and warm.

Zabarella was replaced by Cesare Cremonini (Cento, near Ferrara, 1550–1631), who obtained his doctorate at the University of Ferrara, then taught

21. Sangalli 1999, 220.

22. Donnelly 1582, 50, who gives his name as Capizucchio, although this is clearly Capodivacca; and Sangalli 1999, 199n24. For his biography, see Gliozzi 1975. Sangalli 1999, 222, refers to him as Pietro Capodivacca, which must be an error.

23. Frasson 1983, 185; and Sangalli 1999, 222.

24. Sangalli 1999, 199.

25. Donnelly 1982, 52; and Sangalli 1999, 196–99, 210, 222. Both describe Zabarella as first-position ordinary professor of natural philosophy, which is inaccurate. Wallace 1999b, 337, has it right. The Venetian government almost never permitted Paduans to hold first-position ordinary professorships. This curbed localism in university appointments and reminded Paduans that they were subjects.

26. This is the view of Sangalli 1999, 197. But it is not certain. According to another account, Girolama Campolongo married Francesco Zabarella in 1525, a union that produced a son named Francesco in 1533. After the death of her husband, Campolongo married Ludovico Gagliardi in 1537, a union that produced Achille in late 1537 or early 1538, Leonetto (1540–1564), and Ludovico in 1543. The younger Francesco Zabarella, who became an archpriest, and the Gagliardi brothers were close. The three Gagliardi joined the Society of Jesus in 1559 and Francesco Zabarella did the same in 1562, although he was dismissed in 1572. Scaduto 1964, 290–92; Scaduto 1968, 61, 160. In addition, Schmitt 1981, 580; Wallace 1999b, 337; and other biographies state that Jacopo Zabarella, the professor, was the son of Giulio Zabarella, a count palatine, but do not identify his mother.

there from 1573 to 1590. He began teaching at Padua in late January 1591.[27] Neither Cremonini nor Francesco Piccolomini (Siena 1523–1607), who held the first-position ordinary professorship of natural philosophy from 1565 to 1598, and had engaged in a bitter philosophical dispute with Zabarella, had any love for the Jesuits.[28] Both saw theology and philosophy as separate disciplines and refused to argue that Aristotelian philosophy was able to demonstrate that the human soul was immortal. The Jesuits, by contrast, taught a form of Christian Aristotelianism that held that philosophy could demonstrate the soul's immortality.

The Senate Orders the Jesuits Not to Teach External Students

Members of the university began to move against the Jesuit school.[29] On November 30, 1591, about four weeks after the beginning of the academic year, the rectors and councillors of the arts and law student organizations met. Having concluded that the Jesuit school was an illegal university inflicting significant damage on the University of Padua, they decided to go to the doge and the Venetian Senate to demand action against it. They elected eleven professors, three from arts and eight from law, to accompany the two student rectors.[30] From arts they elected Francesco Piccolomini, Cesare Cremonini, and Ercole Sassonia of Padua (1551–1607), second-position ordinary professor of medical practice.[31] The three arts professors volunteered to pay the expenses of the trip.[32]

Their action stimulated a flurry of moves and meetings in an effort to

27. His inaugural lecture of January 27, 1591, is found in Cremonini 1998, 3–51. Schmitt 1984, provides a good introduction to Cremonini.

28. For Piccolomini's career, start with A. E. Baldini 1980.

29. The dispute has attracted a good deal of attention from scholars. The most important studies, many of them with documents and summaries of documents, are Favaro 1877–1878 and 1911; Cessi 1921–1922; Donnelly 1982; Sangalli 1999, 187–362; and Sangalli 2001, 1–35, 79–175. A recent brief account is Muir 2007, 24–34.

30. Eight law professors may have been elected because the organization of the law students had more divisions (twenty nations, each with representatives) than the organization of the arts students (seven nations). Donnelly 1982, 54. However, law professors and students played small or non-existent roles in subsequent events. They did not feel threatened because the Jesuits did not teach law.

31. On Sassonia, see Facciolati 1978, part 3, 306, 339; and Tomasini 1986, 301, 312, 328. He had taught at the university since 1573 and was known for his research on how to diagnose skin diseases and syphilis.

32. Favaro 1877–1878, 432–33, 482–85 (document xi); Donnelly 1982, 53–54; and Sangalli 1999, 227–30.

resolve differences without going to the Senate. However, one maladroit Jesuit organized a meeting that made matters worse. On December 3, the Jesuit mathematics teacher mentioned above, Marc'Antonio De Dominis (born in Arbe, a Dalmatian island, 1560/61–1624 Rome), met with the student rectors of arts and law and Piccolomini for the purpose of telling them about the contents of *brevi* (which he called "bulls") of Pius V (1567, 1571) and Gregory XIII (1579).[33] De Dominis asserted that the bulls gave the Jesuits the right to teach in any university, and that anyone who prevented them from doing so would be excommunicated. He also stated that the bulls authorized the Jesuits to award doctorates. Later in the day De Dominis brought in the Dominican friar who taught Thomist metaphysics at the university and the Franciscan friar who taught Scotist theology at the university to confirm his interpretation of the bulls.[34]

De Dominis and the two friars misinterpreted the bulls. They focused on Jesuits teaching in Jesuit universities. Although the bulls mentioned privileges and penalties generically, as all such documents did, they did not threaten excommunication against those who barred the Jesuits from teaching in non-Jesuit universities. The bulls empowered Jesuit schools to confer doctorates, but only in philosophy and theology.[35] Most important, what De Dominis discussed and threatened was not relevant to Padua. The Jesuits had not asked to teach in the University of Padua and their school had not conferred any doctorates. The foolish threat of De Dominis served only to heap up ammunition to be used against the Jesuits.

The Venetian governors of Padua tried to mediate between the university and the Jesuits. On December 5, 1591, they reported to Venice the results of a meeting with the leaders of the two student organizations and unnamed professors. The student leaders complained that the Jesuits had established a university in "concorrentia" (competition) with the University of Padua, because they delivered lessons on the same subjects "quasi all'istesse hore" (almost at the same hours) as the university lectures. Moreover, they published "il Rotolo del lor Studio" (the roll of their university) listing the teachers, subject matters, and hours of their courses, in imitation of the University of Padua. And they rang a bell for the beginning of lectures, as did the university. The student leaders also complained that the Jesuits used "moderni

---

33. A papal *littera brevis*, also called a *breve*, brief, letter, or papal letter, delivered instructions in a less solemn format than a papal bull. Whether a brief or bull was obeyed depended on its content and reception. Contemporaries used "bull," "brief," and the other terms indiscriminately. Because De Dominis used "bull," it will be used here.

34. Favaro 1877–1878, 433–34, 486–87 (document xii); Donnelly 1982, 54–55, who was the first to identify De Dominis as the Jesuit mathematician; and Sangalli 1999, 235–36.

35. Favaro 1877–1878, 468–71, documents i–iii with passages from the papal brevi.

Summisti" (modern summaries) when they taught logic and philosophy instead of the texts of Aristotle, which the statutes of the University of Padua
obligated professors to use. Moreover, the Jesuit teachers dictated their lectures, that is, they read or spoke the material in such a way that the students
could write it down. Because these inferior pedagogical methods attracted
students, the university professors had to do the same in order to retain
their students. Consequently, students skipped the university lectures and
sent servants to write down the dictated material.[36] Since university lectures
were delivered in Latin, one wonders about the truth of this assertion.

The governors then spoke to Ludovico Gagliardi, the rector of the Jesuit college. He promised that the Jesuits would change their class schedule
so as to avoid teaching the same subjects at the same hours as the university.
He agreed to stop printing and distributing rolls. The Jesuits would only
post handwritten notices just outside their school. They would not ring
bells.[37] The Venetian governors hoped that this would mollify the student
leaders and professors.

It did not. They wanted nothing less than to shut down the Jesuit school.
On December 17, 1591, the Venetian governors informed the doge that a delegation consisting of the two student leaders and six professors was coming
to Venice to present their grievances against the Jesuits. The arts professors
were Cremonini, Piccolomini, and Sassonia, and the law professors were
Angelo Matteazzi of Marostica (d. 1607), the first-position morning professor of civil law; Ottonello Discalzi of Padua (1535–1601), second-position
morning professor of civil law; and Sebastiano Montecchio (or Monticoli,
d. 1611), the first-position afternoon professor of canon law.[38] On December 20, 1591, they presented their petition to the doge and Senate. It made
five points. The Jesuits should not teach the same subjects that the university taught. The Jesuits came as humble and poor priests to Padua to teach
Latin, but little by little they had become rich, and began to compete with
the university. The Jesuits were breaking the law of the Republic that made
Padua the sole university of the state. The Jesuits used papal bulls to threaten
excommunication against professors who opposed them. And there could
not be two universities competing with each other.[39]

36. Favaro 1877–1878, 487–88; Donnelly 1982, 55. Chap. 14 will discuss summisti, differences between Jesuit and university pedagogy, and the accuracy of the pedagogical criticism
that university professors and Jesuits leveled against each other.

37. Favaro 1877–1878, 488–89; Donnelly 1982, 55.

38. Favaro 1877–1878, 489. For the appointments of the law professors and information on
their careers at the university, see Facciolati 1978, part 3, 94, 118, 124, and the index.

39. Favaro 1877–1878, 499–500, document xviii.

Cremonini then spoke for them in a formal session of the Senate. Present were the doge, the Pien Collegio (full college consisting of twenty-six senators holding higher elective office who served as the cabinet of the Senate with the power to propose legislation and speak first), and the Senate as a whole. Because senators had many other duties in magistracies, in the mainland state, and in the overseas Empire, about 150 to 190 (of 230 voting members) were normally present.[40]

Cremonini constructed his oration on the points that the petitioners presented. Then like a good prosecutor well acquainted with the forensic works of Cicero, he added emphases, insinuations, assumptions, and accusations designed to rouse anger against the Jesuits. He contended that the Jesuits had introduced a second university in competition with the University of Padua and in opposition to the laws of the Republic of Venice.[41] He repeatedly referred to the University of Padua as "your university," meaning the university of the doge and the senators. Cremonini contrasted "your university" with "their university," or the "other university," or the "counter university" (antistudio), which was the illegal university that the Jesuits had allegedly created. He argued that the antistudio was destroying the University of Padua, and the Jesuits were flouting Venetian law. Cremonini repeatedly invited the doge and senators to defend "their" university against the law-breaking Jesuits.

Cremonini argued that the Jesuit school was a university because it advertised its lectures in the same way as civic universities. He referred to a traditional practice: Italian universities prepared and promulgated rolls, which were large sheets of paper listing pertinent information about the coming academic year. One to several months before the beginning of each academic year, the civic magistracy overseeing the university prepared a roll listing the courses, professors, schedule of lectures, and the texts or subject matter on which they would lecture. Larger universities, such as Padua, had two rolls, one for law and one for arts, which at Padua meant all other

40. For a brief description of the Venetian government and more bibliography, see Lane 1973, 254–58; and Grendler 1990, 37–41.

41. Entitled "Oratione dell'Ecc.mo S. D.r Cesare Cremonini filosofo nel studio di Padova in favore di esso studio contro li Padri Gesuiti. Fatta alla Sereniss.ma Sig.ria di Venezia," it is printed in Favaro 1877–1878, 93–100, from a Biblioteca Marciana, Venice, manuscript. It is reprinted in Cremonini 1998, 53–69, which is cited here because it is more accessible. There are at least a dozen manuscript copies of the oration in Venetian libraries, ARSI, Paris libraries, and elsewhere, none of them autographs, so far as is known. It was also printed three times in Paris with a French translation. Donnelly 1982, 62, and Schmitt 1984, 621, provide some locations. There is no critical edition based on all the known manuscripts. The edition in Cremonini 1998, is short for a Renaissance oration; hence, it may be a condensed account of what Cremonini said.

subjects including theology. Rolls were hand written initially and, after the invention of movable type, printed with decorative material. They carried official approval. They were then posted in prominent places in the town and sent to other towns near and far in order to attract students.[42] Universities also rang bells to announce class hours throughout the day.

Cremonini charged that the Jesuits printed and distributed a roll labeled *In Gymnasio Patavino Societatis Jesu* (In the University of Padua of the Society of Jesus) as if their school was a second university in Padua. According to him, they promulgated their roll with an oration exhorting the youth of the city to come. They posted their rolls throughout the city so as to get better publicity and they rang a bell for their lectures and other public events. All of this was manifest competition with the university of the Republic of Venice, Cremonini declared. The competition lowered the dignity of the University of Padua and reduced the number of students who attended, he charged.[43]

Like the leaders of the student organizations, Cremonini found Jesuit teaching wanting. Whether it is superficial or well-founded, whether the teachers are youngsters or experienced, he orated, they all teach from those papers that produce "antidottrina" (antilearning). Or else they borrow material from others.[44] He meant that the Jesuits lectured from course summaries prepared by others instead of from Aristotle.

Cremonini took advantage of the action of De Dominis by charging three times that the Jesuits used papal bulls to threaten the University of

42. For a reduced-size reproduction of the printed arts roll of the University of Padua for the academic year 1594–1595, see Grendler 2002, 35. Although very useful to historians, most Italian rolls have not survived, and those that are seldom published. There are two major exceptions. Dallari 1885–1924 prints the rolls of the University of Bologna from 1384 to 1799, and *I maestri di Roma* 1991 prints the rolls for the University of Rome from 1514 to 1787.

43. "Ho io, per dimostrare che i padri Gesuiti hanno fatto un antistudio, da toccare un punto solo: questi Padri fanno il suo rottolo, lo stampano con titolo *In Gymnasio Patavino Societatis Jesu*, quasi debba esser in Padova altro Studio che quello della Repubblica di Venetia, lo pubblicano secondo la cerimonia dello Studio con una oratione esortatoria a tutta la gioventú che vada a loro con qualche tacito pregiuditio degl'altri. Né questo basta: lo affiggono per tutta la città, acciochè si pubblichi meglio. Hanno anch'essi le sue scuole deputate, suonano la sua campana, hanno le ore delle letioni in ordinanza, ogni cosa in pubblica forma, come lo Studio di Vostra Serenità. Veggasi, per gratia, se questo è fare, com'essi dicono, uno Studio per li suoi novitii o se pure egli è fare una manifesta concorrenza allo Studio della Repubblica, dalla quale concorrenza nasce diminuzione notabile della dignità d'esso Studio, mancando per questa cagione in lui la frequenza, che già vi soleva essere delli scolari." Cremonini 1998, 65.

44. "Dovrei dire alcuna cosa del loro modo di insegnare: s'egli è superficiale o fondato, se gli uomini posti da loro in cattedra sono giovani da esercitare sé stessi o provetti da istruir gli altri, se leggono su quelle carte che tengono in antidottrina, ch'essi intendono, o dottrina tolta imprestito da altri." Cremonini 1998, 66.

FIGURE 2. Cesare Cremonini (1550–1631)

127

Padua.[45] He called the Jesuits men who came from far away lands, a reference to the non-Italian origins of the first Jesuits, but which was no longer true of the Jesuits in Italy.[46] Cremonini claimed that the introduction of the Jesuit university had produced constant fighting between university students and Jesuit students: they fought like Guelfs and Ghibillines to the point that the Venetian governors of the city could not keep order. And because the university had many foreign students, the bad reputation of Padua was spreading throughout Europe. The solution was to suppress the Jesuit antistudio.[47]

Cremonini offered ancient Roman and contemporary Italian examples for the doge and the Senate to follow. Emperor Justinian (r. 527–565) had expelled from Alexandria some learned men who had begun a university without his permission. The doge should do the same.[48] And, according to Cremonini, the university towns of Bologna, Ferrara, Perugia, Pavia, and Pisa had not permitted the Jesuits to establish universities within their walls. By contrast, the founding of the Jesuit Roman College had "destrutto assolutamente" (absolutely destroyed) the University of Rome.[49] Because Cremonini did not mention Messina and Turin, he must have been ignorant of Jesuit activities there.

Cremonini described a conniving order. The Jesuits had created their university secretly and stealthily. The poor Jesuit fathers, seemingly so humble, had begun to teach Latin grammar to children. Then little by little and softly softly, they accumulated riches, Cremonini did not know how. They gradually insinuated themselves into Padua and had come to the point where they taught all the disciplines. They intended to become the kings of learning in Padua. They wanted to triumph over the university of the Venetian Republic and would destroy it just as they have triumphed over and extinguished the Latin schools of Padua.[50]

Cremonini's oratory soared to a conclusion. These are the reasons, most serene prince, that the students of the university have thrown themselves at your feet. Their adversaries have tried to frighten them with bulls. But the students know that the nobles of this Republic are most wise, most just, and prudent. They await action for the public good that will overcome the excuses (*pretesti*) of the Jesuit fathers. They look to the restoration of calm to the university. They know that you will apply most vigorously the laws

---

45. Cremonini 1998, 61, 66, 69.   46. Cremonini 1998, 62.

47. Cremonini 1998, 64–66.   48. Cremonini 1998, 62–63.

49. Cremonini 1998, 63–64, quotation at 64.

50. Cremonini 1998, 68. Whether this happened in Padua is unknown. But it was difficult for private teachers, who charged fees, to compete with the free Jesuit schools.

that protect the university. You will deal with the evil of two universities in competition. The statutes of the Republic will be applied. The antistudio introduced into the state by a foreign nation (*gente straniera*) will be eliminated.[51] Cremonini's oration was a tour de force.

What would the Senate do? On December 22, the Savi di Terraferma, the members of the Pien Collegio with primary responsibility for drafting legislation involving the mainland state, and the Riformatori dello Studio di Padova, three very senior Venetian nobles who oversaw the university, met to decide what action to recommend to the Senate. They were not persuaded by the petition from the students and professors or Cremonini's oratory. They decided that the Jesuits should be allowed to continue teaching, but should not print and distribute rolls or ring bells, which was the compromise worked out by the governors of Padua and Ludovico Gagliardi. The Pien Collegio made this proposal to the Senate on December 23.[52] Leonardo Donà (1536–1612, doge from 1606), the leader of the anti-papal party in the Senate, supported it.

It produced a seven-hour meeting and three ballots before a decision was reached. The mild measure failed twice.[53] Then a strong anti-Jesuit law stating that the Jesuits might teach only members of their order was proposed. Alvise di Paolo Zorzi (1535–1616), an anti-papal senator, delivered a fiery ninety-minute speech favoring it. After he finished, Leonardo Donà and others who opposed it were hooted down. The law passed by a substantial margin.[54] The Senate forbade the Padua Jesuits from teaching anyone except Jesuits.

What Zorzi said is unknown, because no text or summary of his speech has come to light. His actions in future years demonstrated that he was one of the most vehement opponents of the papacy in Venice. Since Zorzi had served as a Riformatore dello Studio di Padova from 1586 to 1588, he knew the university, and he endorsed the views of the petitioning students and professors. When he again served as a Riformatore in 1614 and 1615, he

51. Cremonini 1998, 69.

52. Favaro 1877–1878, 500–501, document xix.

53. The votes were 80 yes, 11 no, and 91 undecided; and 77 yes, 8 no, and 100 undecided. For the votes, see Favaro 1877–1878, 500–503. A law passed when it received an absolute majority of favorable votes. Voting undecided (*non sinceri*) was an option; it was a way of voting no and telling the Collegio that a different proposal was desired. The rules of the Senate required every senator present to vote, and they were forbidden to leave until a decision was reached. Maranini 1974, 255–57. The vast majority of measures presented to the Senate by the Pien Collegio received overwhelming approval. This was an exception.

54. The vote was 110 yes, 8 no, and 60 undecided. Favaro 1877–1878, 503. See also Donnelly 1982, 56–57; and Sangalli 1999, 245–46.

worked successfully to make it possible for university students to obtain doctorates from the university without professing Catholicism, a requirement since a 1564 bull of Pius IV. He supported Paolo Sarpi and he wrote fierce anti-papal pamphlets during the interdict battle of 1606–1607 (see below). Personal rivalry and a contrarian streak may also have moved him in 1591. Even though he shared the views of Leonardo Donà on most church-state issues, he saw himself, rather than Donà, as the leader of that group. And contemporaries noted that he enjoyed contradicting the majority.[55]

Jesuit Responses

The decision of the Senate provoked consternation among the Jesuits. Their first reaction was to assess why the majority of the senators had voted against them. Ludovico Gagliardi described the senators as divided into three groups. Some senators supported the Jesuits. The rest consisted of two camps. The first hated the very existence of the Jesuits and had done so from the beginning. The second group did not hate the Jesuits but at certain times had been jealous of their growth for political reasons (*per ragion di Stato*). Knowing this, those who hated the Jesuits had spread an infinite number of lies, along with some true statements, about the Jesuits in order to fan their jealousy. In this way they had turned the Senate against the Society.[56] Although it is impossible to determine the motivations of 110 senators, Gagliardi's analysis is persuasive.

Some Jesuits pointed to the obvious: they had failed to develop broad support in the Venetian patriciate. The Jesuits had sought and obtained the support of leading members of the government but not the majority of the Senate.[57] A combination of numbers and location hampered their efforts. Because 230 senators had the right to vote in the Senate, winning over a majority of them was a difficult task. That the school was in Padua and the

55. Sangalli, 1999, 249–51. For a brief summary of Zorzi's political career, see Grendler 1990, 85. He should not be confused with Alvise di Benetto Zorzi (1515–1593), who was one of the Savi Grandi who proposed the mild measure on the Padua Jesuit school to the Senate and was generally sympathetic to the papacy and the church. Grendler 1979, 321–22. For the comment about the contrarian streak of Alvise di Paolo Zorzi, see Cozzi 1958, 38n1. For Zorzi's anti-papal actions in subsequent years, see Cozzi 1958, index.

56. "Alcuni sono che odiano *ex instituto* il nome nostro *ob vivendi licentiam*, altri da certi tempi in qua per ragion di Stato pretendono gelosia di ogni nostro progresso, se bene *alioquin* non si odiano et li primi sapendo l'humor di questi spargono infinite cose false, mescolate con alcune vere, et aumentano molto la gelosia e volgono facilmente con questo il Senato contro di noi." Letter of Ludovico Gagliardi of January 11, 1592, Padua, in ARSI, Italiae 160, f. 211r, as quoted in Sangalli 1999, 279.

57. Donnelly 1982, 57–58; Sangalli 1999, 253–59.

senators lived in Venice made it more difficult. Because the professed house in Venice taught only cases of conscience to clergymen, there were no satisfied local parents to plead the case of the Jesuits. Some Venetian nobles sent their sons to the Jesuit boarding school in Padua, but they were a minority. Subsequent events will demonstrate that the Jesuit school had strong support in Padua, but the wishes of Paduan parents and city council did not matter to Venetian senators.

The Jesuits were furious at what they viewed as Cremonini's lies. Because written versions of his oration began to circulate almost immediately, they wanted to answer him. Although the Senate had made the decision, it was wiser to attack Cremonini than to criticize senators, and it might be the first step toward changing the mind of the Senate. Five senior Jesuits who had spent years in Padua and/or Venice responded.[58]

Ludovico Gagliardi, from a prominent Padua family and the rector of the Jesuit college in Padua from 1590 to 1592, wrote a dignified but firm response between December 27, 1591, and the middle of January 1592. Wiser and more prudent than his brother Achille, Ludovico had earlier taught philosophy and theology at Padua and had been superior of the professed house in Venice. In February 1592 he was transferred to Milan and then appointed rector at Mantua. He served in that capacity until August 1594, when he became superior of the Province of Venice, serving until 1596. He then returned to the professed house at Venice and later served as rector at Verona and Modena.[59]

Paolo Comitoli (Perugia 1545–1626 Bologna) composed a colorful, hostile, and pseudonymous reply to Cremonini between December 28, 1591, and the end of January 1592. He adopted the guise of a former student of the Padua school who was traveling through Lombardy when he learned what happened. He may have adopted this format because he lived at the Jesuit professed house in Venice from 1590 to 1599, where he taught cases of conscience at least part of the time. A published biblical scholar and theologian with a fiery temperament, he had previously taught in the University of Perugia for two or three years (see chapter 12, "The Jesuits and the University in the 1550s and 1560s"), the Roman College, and in Milan. After Venice he taught at several other north Italian schools. During the interdict crisis of 1606 and 1607 he wrote two anti-Venetian tracts.[60]

58. The fact that all five Jesuits accurately reported Cremonini's words argues that they had copies of his oration.

59. Scaduto 1968, 61; Donnelly 1982, 69–70; Baldini 1994, 565n105; Gorzoni 1997, 84, 87, 382; Sangalli 1999, index; and Sangalli 2001, 4–5 and index.

60. Sommervogel 1960, 2:1342–43; Scaduto 1968, 35; Donnelly 1982, 58–59, 67–68; Sangalli 1999 and 2001, indexes; and Donnelly 2001c.

Pietro Bonaccorsi (or Buonaccorsi, Messina 1540–1597 Venice) was in Venice when the Senate acted. He had earlier lived in the professed house in Venice where he tutored a Corner noble in Euclidian mathematics, then became rector of the Jesuit college at Mantua in October 1590. Doge Pasquale Cicogna invited him to preach at St. Mark's Basilica, which was legally the doge's chapel, during Advent and the Christmas season of 1591. He immediately began to write a response to Cremonini and finished it by the end of January 1592. It was a strong response that ridiculed Cremonini and called him a liar. Bonaccorsi may have remained in Venice for all or most of the rest of his life.[61]

The fourth response came from Benedetto Palmio (see the appendix for his biography), who was the rector of the Jesuit college at Ferrara in December 1591. In February 1592 General Acquaviva sent him to Venice with the charge of dealing with the Padua situation. Neither Acquaviva nor Palmio believed that they could change the mind of the Senate, but they hoped to ease tensions. In March and April 1592 he wrote the longest and least polemical response, one more addressed to the senators than to Cremonini. Palmio wanted to address the Senate, but was probably rebuffed. He may have presented his treatise to Doge Pasquale Cicogna.[62]

The last response came from Antonio Possevino (see the appendix for his biography), who wrote anonymously in the early months of 1592. He had been in and out of Padua and Venice for many years, including an extended stay at Padua between 1587 and 1591, where he may have taught theology for a short time. Although he wrote in Rome, Possevino had access to a copy of Cremonini's oration.[63]

The five Jesuits refuted or denied Cremonini's charges and disavowed the actions of De Dominis. They explained how the Padua school functioned, and argued that it aided the University of Padua and the Venetian nobility by attracting students from afar. They affirmed that they were not foreigners but loyal Venetian subjects. Because they lived in Venice, Padua, and Rome, and wrote their responses at slightly different times, it is not likely that they collaborated. While they made some of the same points, each included unique material, and each employed a different rhetorical style.[64]

61. Scaduto 1968, 23; Donnelly 1982, 68–69; Gorzoni 1997, 79, 83–84, 382; Sangalli 1999, 129–30, 244–45, 253, 257–60; and Sangalli 2001, 4–32.

62. Scaduto 1968, 110; Donnelly 1982, 60–61, 63–65; I gesuiti e Venezia 1994, index; Sangalli 1999, index; Sangalli 2001, 6–7 and index; and Zanfredini 2001f.

63. For his visits to and comments on the situation in Padua and Venice, see Donnelly 1982, 65–67, who was the first to identify Possevino as the author of this anonymous response. See also Sangalli 1999, index; and Sangalli 2001, 6–8 and index.

64. The five Jesuit responses, each entitled Apologia or Risposta, are found in ARSI, Veneta

Four of the Jesuits strongly denied that the Society had acted furtively and secretly. They pointed out that their college and school had been authorized and approved by both Paul III and the Venetian government. They cited the order of Doge Francesco Donà of September 15, 1548, which ordered the Venetian governor of Padua to implement the renunciation by Andrea Lippomano of the priorate of Santa Maria Maddalena and its revenues in favor of the Jesuits for the creation of schools in Padua and Venice.[65] Although the doge's order did not mention external students explicitly, the Jesuits pointed out that they had been teaching external students in Padua almost continuously since 1552.[66] Gagliardi, Bonaccorsi, and Palmio asserted that De Dominis had not acted with the permission of his superiors. Gagliardi and Bonaccorsi described De Dominis as a simple-minded Jesuit student who was duped by a malicious university student. He had misinterpreted the bulls; they did not threaten excommunication or any other action against the University of Padua.[67]

Although De Dominis was not simple-minded, it is impossible to believe that he acted with the approval or foreknowledge of his superiors. He was not a priest, but only a scholastic studying theology while he taught mathematics. Whatever his motivation in 1591, his subsequent career revealed him to be an unstable man of wavering religious views. He was ordained a priest in 1592, then left the Society in 1597 in order to acquire a Dalmatian bishopric with handsome revenues. During the Venetian interdict of 1606–1607 he denounced the papacy. He then accompanied the English ambassador back to England where he supported the Church of England. He wore out his welcome by embracing Puritanism, so he moved to the Calvinist Netherlands. He finally went to Rome, where he proclaimed

105 I, ff. 236–336. There are a few other extant manuscripts, mostly in the Biblioteca Ambrosiana in Milan, as Donnelly 1982, 63–70, notes 82, 85, 89, 94, and 97, mentions. The five Jesuit responses are conveniently printed from the ARSI manuscripts in Bencini 1970–1971; and in Sangalli, 2001, with Gagliardi's on 79–94, Comitoli's on 95–111, Bonaccorsi's on 113–28, Palmio's on 129–59, and Possevino's on 161–75. In what follows, the author's name and the pages in Sangalli 2001 will be cited. Donnelly 1982, 63–71, provides excellent summaries of the five Jesuit responses; and Sangalli 1999, 261–74; and Sangalli 2001, 21–33, also comment on them.

65. Sangalli 2001, 81–82, 85 (Gagliardi); 108 (Comitoli); 114–16, 120 (Bonaccorsi); 132, 135 (Palmio). The papal breve of September 7, 1548, and the doge's order of September 15, 1548, are printed in Tacchi Venturi 1951b, 677–78. The key phrase in the doge's order is "ut duo collegia studentium erigantur, alterum in urbe Patavina, alterum in hac civitate nostra Venetiarum" (678).

66. Donnelly 1982, 70, points out that the doge's order did not explicitly authorize the Jesuits to teach external students.

67. Gagliardi called De Dominis "un nostro simpliciotto fratello." Sangalli 2001, 84. Bonaccorsi described De Dominis as possessing the religious simplicity of a Jesuit student. Ibid., 117. For Palmio's comments, see ibid., 137. See also Donnelly 1982, 64, 69.

his return to Catholicism and that he had always sought Christian unity. Now in deteriorating health, he abjured Protestant beliefs and died before the Roman Inquisition reached a decision. It condemned him posthumously as a relapsed heretic.[68]

Comitoli and Palmio denied that the Padua college had become wealthy. On the contrary, Palmio explained that the college had had to borrow money for living expenses and to build; as a result it owed "many hundreds and some thousands." And prices were rising. The Padua college had to support about sixty persons including twenty-five scholastics because it was responsible for educating and preparing rectors, preachers, teachers, and confessors for the other twelve colleges in the Province of Venice. He reminded readers that the Jesuits never accepted payment for any of their ministries. And he declared that the Jesuits were good landlords who had reduced rents and improved conditions for the tenants on the agricultural properties that they owned.[69]

Bonaccorsi, Gagliardi, and Palmio agreed that the Padua school printed and distributed rolls listing their courses and rang bells. But they disputed that this was an attempt to compete with the University of Padua. They explained that the school posted rolls listing the schedule of classes and the texts to be taught for the convenience of students and parents, and so that booksellers could stock the books that students needed. Moreover, the Jesuit roll was a simple printed notice, while the university roll was a hand-written official document authenticated by a notary public and proclaimed in the cathedral at the beginning of the academic year. They acknowledged that the Jesuit college and school rang bells thirty times a day to change classes, for academic exercises, for catechism classes, for sermons on holidays, to call Jesuits to dinner, and to tell boarders that it was time to return to their rooms to study. Because the Jesuit school was distant from the center of Padua, the bells had to be loud. But the three Jesuits declared that they did not ring a bell so loudly that it competed with the bell of the university. They pointed out that the Padua school had been posting rolls and sounding bells since the school began without complaint, until now.[70]

68. These are the bare bones of his complicated life. For more see Cavazza 1987 and Korade 2001a, each with more bibliography. The most recent discussion, with new details concerning the Roman Inquisition's handling of De Dominis is Mayer 2014, 134–51, 295–309.

69. "Se ben non tanto mai che non sia stato bisogno più volte pigliar denari ad interesse, non solo per fabricare, ma anco per vivere, de' quali ne restano ancora in piedi al presente debiti di molte centinara, et qualche miliara." Sangalli 2001, 108–9 (Comitoli), 133 (quotation), 135 (Palmio). The Jesuits were rebuilding their church at this time.

70. Sangalli 2001, 86, 88 (Gagliardi); 128 (Bonaccorsi); 139–41 (Palmio).

What the Jesuits wrote was probably true. Sixteenth-century university rolls carried approvals from a representative of the university, ruler, or city. Whether Padua Jesuit school rolls bore any legal approval is unknown because none has survived. It was also true that Jesuit colleges and schools rang bells throughout the day. How loud they were is unknown. In Padua the Jesuit college and school were located at least a thousand meters from the center of the city where the university building stood.[71]

Palmio addressed the charge that the words *In Gymnasio Patavino Societatis Iesu* meant that the Jesuits touted their school as a university. He wrote that *gymnasium* was a word of Greek origin that meant a place for literary exercises, that they used *patavino* because the school was in Padua, and that they were the Society of Jesus.[72] All true. However, *gymnasium* had two meanings at this time. *Gymnasium*, plus *gymnasio* and *ginnasio* in Italian, meant a humanistic school that taught grammar, rhetoric, and philosophy based on their ancient Latin and Greek texts. It also meant university. Whether a *gymnasium* was a university depended on whether it had the authority to award degrees and exercised that authority. Like all Jesuit schools the Padua school had the authority to confer degrees in philosophy and theology. But it never used it.

Both Cremonini and the Jesuit responders ignored the fact that the Jesuits did not use in their rolls the more common and universally accepted words for university, namely *studium, studium generale, studio, studio generale*, and *studio pubblico*. These words always meant an institution of higher learning that taught university subjects, and whose lectures anyone might attend. *Generale* meant that the *studio* (university) taught and awarded degrees in all subjects. Palmio did refer to the Padua school as "nostro collegio o picciolo Studio" (our college or little studio) in his *Apologia*. He argued that the Jesuit little university was even more the doge's university than the University of Padua. This was because the Jesuit school had been erected and funded by the generosity of the Venetian nobility and the authority of a doge, while the University of Padua had not been founded by Venice.[73]

Palmio's comment was double-edged. He alluded to the fact that the

71. The long-gone priory and Jesuit church were probably located next to a branch of the Brenta Canal in the eastern part of Padua just within the old walls, approximately where the Ospedale Civile and medical clinics are now located. See also Donnelly 1982, 49–50.

72. Sangalli 2001, 141 (Palmio).

73. "Che il nostro collegio o picciolo Studio sia veramente non meno Studio della Serenità vostra di quello che è lo Studio dell'università, anzi tanto più quanto che quello non fu fondato da principio da questa republica, come è stato il nostro eretto, et dotato per liberalità della nobiltà veneziana et per l'auttorità dei predecessori della Serenità vostra." Sangalli 2001, 35, 136 (Palmio quotation).

University of Padua began in 1222 when Padua was an independent city. Only after Venice conquered Padua in 1405 did it become the university of doge and Senate. The other part of his comment pointed to a new vocabulary that Jesuits were soon to adopt. In a few years the Jesuits will make a distinction between *studio generale* or *università compiuta* (complete university), meaning Italian civic universities that taught all subjects, and *studio nostro* or *nostra università* (our university), meaning a Jesuit school that taught theology, philosophy, and the humanities (see chapter 6). But in 1592 Palmio's choice of words probably did not help the Padua Jesuits.

The Jesuits denied that they scheduled their lectures at the same hour as university lectures on the same subjects, and asserted that they worked to avoid this.[74] Without rolls it is impossible to verify this statement. Bonaccorsi pointed out that other religious orders in Padua taught university subjects without objection from the university.[75]

The Jesuits strongly denied that Jesuit schools had destroyed several Italian and European universities. They pointed out that there had been no disputes between the Jesuits and the universities of Bologna, Ferrara, Perugia, Naples, Rome, and Siena, and that they had no college or school in Pavia and Pisa. Nor had they damaged universities in other parts of Europe.[76] This was true in 1592, although there will be differences with the universities of Bologna and Rome in the seventeenth century. And university students and Jesuit students sometimes fought each other in Pavia when the Jesuits established a college and school there in the seventeenth century (see chapters 10, 11, and 13). On the other hand, the Jesuits never founded a college or school in Pisa. Nor had they destroyed any university outside of Italy. They did succeed over time in dominating the teaching of theology and philosophy in the universities of Ingolstadt, Prague, and Vienna. They did this mostly by replacing professors from other religious orders, thanks to the support of rulers. Although they did not become part of the University of Louvain, they sharply differed with Louvain's theologians in the seventeenth century.[77]

The Jesuits countered Cremonini's argument that ancient rulers had decreed that Athens, Alexandria, and Rome had only one institution of higher learning each by means of numerous references to ancient sources proving the opposite. Indeed, Ludovico Gagliardi listed seven gymnasii in

74. Sangalli 2001, 105 (Comitoli); 147 (Palmio).
75. Sangalli 2001, 120, 128 (Bonaccorsi).
76. Sangalli 2001, 89–90 (Gagliardi); 122–23 (Bonaccorsi); 153–54 (Palmio); 168–70 (Possevino).
77. Roegiers 2012.

Athens, and he wrote that ancient Rome had three institutions of higher learning.[78] Comitoli and Palmio ridiculed the idea that the modest Jesuit school of five upper-level classes could threaten the large University of Padua with its famous scholars and more than forty professors. Why should it worry about fifty students of philosophy and theology, and a few more in logic, when eighty to ninety percent of the university students studied law and medicine?[79]

This was technically correct but avoided the real issue. Eighty to ninety percent of university students did study and obtain degrees in law and medicine. However, a majority attended a logic course because it was considered useful preparation for both law and medicine. Practically all medicine students heard lectures in natural philosophy, because this was Aristotelian science, considered essential preparation for the study of medicine. And an unknown number of students attended humanities courses. The two natural philosophers and the humanist at the University of Padua led the fight against the Jesuit school because they were losing students to it.

The Jesuits strongly denied that the presence of the Jesuit school and their students sparked student violence. They attributed it to conflicts between student nations, bitterly-contested student elections, and the fact that many students carried firearms, all causes mentioned in the reports of Venetian governors of Padua.[80] Nevertheless, the events of 1589 and 1591 demonstrated that some students wanted the Jesuit school gone, whether or not students of the Jesuit school fought university students.[81] Possevino added two additional causes: depraved students and philosophical and religious differences between students. He referred to students who embraced secular Aristotelian positions such as the eternity of the world and the mortality of the human soul, and the presence of Protestant students at Padua.[82] The reports of the Venetian governors of Padua did not indicate that students fought over philosophical and religious differences, because Venetian authorities seldom acknowledged that the university had Protestant students.

Palmio responded to the charge that the Jesuits were foreigners by pointing out that the most important Jesuits in the Padua college beginning

---

78. Sangalli 2001, 91 (Gagliardi); 102–3 (Comitoli); 121 (Bonaccorsi); 167 (Possevino).

79. Sangalli 2001, 105 (Comitoli); 144 (Palmio); and Donnelly 1982, 64.

80. Sangalli 2001, 88–89 (Gagliardi); 105, 108 (Comitoli); 157 (Palmio); 171 (Possevino). One may add to the list of causes of violence student hazing, the reluctance of governments to confiscate weapons, and the failure to punish students for fear that they would leave. There is a growing literature on violence in Italian universities; start with Grendler 2002, 500–505; and Carlsmith 2012.

81. Donnelly 1982, 70, makes this point.

82. Sangalli 2001, 171.

with the rector, the *padovano* Ludovico Gagliardi, were Venetian subjects, and that many other Jesuits there, including scholastics, were also Venetian subjects.[83] Bonaccorsi wrote that except one from France and another from Portugal, all sixty Jesuits at Padua were Italians, almost all of them from northern Italy. Then he turned the accusation against Cremonini, who was not a Venetian subject. How can this mercenary philosopher from the mud and reeds of the Ferrara bog, a man of barbarous conceits and worse language, call Paduan nobles and members of old families foreigners?[84] The "pantano ferrarese" (the Ferrara bog) referred to Cento, Cremonini's birthplace, a town on the Reno River that regularly overflowed its banks. And "members of old families" referred to Jesuits such as Ludovico Gagliardi.

In addition to refuting Cremonini, the Jesuit writers emphasized the benefits that they believed the Jesuit school brought to the University of Padua. They argued that the Jesuit school functioned as a preparatory school for the university. Not only did the Jesuits teach the humanities, philosophy, and theology well, they did so in an atmosphere of peace and quiet, free from the danger of infection of heresy. They taught good habits and the fear of God, which were very important for the peace and security of the Venetian state. The good instruction of the Jesuits spurred the university professors to do more and better teaching. For these reasons the Jesuit school attracted out-of-town students, including Venetian nobles. Well prepared in the humanities, they went on to the university where they flourished. And Possevino promised that more students would come. Because the Jesuits had 30,000 students in their schools across Europe, they could easily persuade a thousand or more of them to come to Padua for their university studies. But if the Padua school was closed to external students, they would go to other universities.[85]

Palmio, who addressed his work more to the Venetian nobility than to Cremonini, argued that the Padua school served young Venetian nobles well. Those who came to Padua to study only philosophy could obtain excellent philosophical training at the Jesuit school in less time than if they studied at the university, he wrote. Hence, they would be able to return to Venice in ample time to prepare for their public careers, which began at the age of twenty-five.[86]

Palmio referred to an educational path that many young Venetian nobles traveled. Only male Venetians of certified noble birth could vote and

83. Sangalli 2001, 155; Donnelly 1982, 65.
84. Sangalli 2001, 120–21; Donnelly 1982, 68.
85. Sangalli 2001, 88 (Gagliardi); 107 (Comitoli); 142–47, 149 (Palmio); 172 (Possevino).
86. Sangalli 2001, 142 (Palmio).

hold legislative and administrative offices in the Venetian state, and they became eligible at the age of twenty-five with a favored few receiving this right at twenty-one. Hence, many came to Padua in their late teens to study at the university for a few years, sometimes to hear lectures in several disciplines. Very few of them obtained degrees, because they had no need of them. Instead, they returned to Venice at the age of twenty-one or twenty-five ready to begin their public careers. They served in offices of increasing importance for the rest of their lives.[87] Whether intended or not, the Padua boarding school was designed to attract and serve Venetian nobles in the way that Palmio described. Finally, the five Jesuits defended and explained in detail the practices of Jesuit teaching and the preparation of their teachers, which are discussed in chapter 14.

Attempts to Reopen the Padua School

The closing of the Padua school to external students made two groups of people acutely unhappy. A large number of Paduan parents who wanted their sons to study in the Jesuit school and a smaller number of Venetian nobles who wanted to send their sons to the noble boarding school if it were still there. Paduan parents pressured the Jesuits not to close their school, on the dubious conjecture that the Senate had not intended to close the lower school to external boys. Their request presented a dilemma to the Jesuits. While they wanted to retain the goodwill of Paduan parents by reopening the school to all, they feared the consequences if they disobeyed the Senate. They also concluded that approaching the Senate directly would do no good and might increase the Senate's hostility toward them. General Acquaviva made the only possible decision in January 1592. He told the Padua Jesuits that they should not reopen the school to external students without the Senate's permission.[88]

Nothing happened for two years. Then the leading citizens of Padua acted. On June 27, 1594, the city council of Padua, with the consent and collaboration of the Jesuits, voted 50 to 10 in favor of a petition asking that the Venetian Senate permit Jesuit classes in grammar, humanities, and rhetoric be

87. A classic example was Gasparo Contarini (1483–1542), who spent eight and one-half years at the University of Padua studying natural philosophy, theology, Greek, mathematics, and astronomy, but took no degree. He left at the age of twenty-five and one-half at a time of crisis for the Venetian state, and served it well as a diplomat until made a cardinal in 1535. Grendler 2006a, 138–42. Sangalli 1999, 214, also points out that Venetian nobles came to Padua to study the humanities and philosophy rather than to take degrees.

88. Donnelly 1982, 59–61; Sangalli 1999, 280–85.

opened to all students.[89] The city praised these classes and the Jesuit school. It had been founded on healthy moral and religious principles, was free of charge, and employed an effective pedagogy. The city council rejected the accusation that the Jesuits had been trying to establish an antistudio. And because the pupils in the Jesuit lower school would all be boys, there was no risk of fighting with university students. Indeed, the students at Jesuit schools lived disciplined lives and did not carry arms.[90] The city council argued that the Jesuit school had conferred a great benefit on the city, because it had taught students well and had prepared them for university studies. But now the city lacked good teachers. Parents had to send their sons to other towns to learn Latin well, which was inconvenient and expensive. Brescia and Verona had Jesuit schools; why should not Padua have one?[91]

The city council of Padua then obtained approval from two-thirds of the university professors for reopening the Jesuit lower school classes. This was conditional on the Jesuits not teaching the *Rhetoric* and *Poetics* of Aristotle, the *Topica* (a logical text) of Cicero, plus unnamed works, in the same year that Antonio Riccobono, the humanities professor, taught them.[92] The Jesuits agreed to these conditions. Thirty-three professors (twenty of twenty-one legists, and thirteen of twenty-eight from other disciplines) signed a memorandum of approval. This was two-thirds of all the professors who taught in the academic year 1594–1595.[93] The signers included Cremonini, Francesco Piccolomini, Girolamo Fabrici d'Acquapendente (a prominent professor of surgery and anatomy), and Riccobono initially, although he quickly changed his mind and vigorously opposed reopening the school. The Jesuits, including Possevino from Rome, worked with the city council to prepare the city's case.[94]

On August 10, 1594, an ambassador for the city presented the petition to the Pien Collegio. It went nowhere. Riccobono and the leader of the law students' organization spoke against it. The Pien Collegio voted against re-

89. Donnelly 1982, 71; Sangalli 1999, 286.

90. Sangalli 1999, 287–88, 291.

91. Much of this comes from a memorandum drafted by the man chosen by the city council of Padua as ambassador to the Venetian government. Sangalli 1999, 286–87. See also Donnelly 1982, 72–73, for the behind-the-scenes contributions of the Jesuits.

92. In the academic year 1594–1595, Riccobono taught the *Topica* of Cicero and *Oedipus tyrannus* of Sophocles. See the arts roll of the University of Padua for the academic year 1594–1595 in AAUP, Inventario 1320, no pag.

93. AAUP, Inventario 1320, arts and law rolls for the academic year 1594–1595, no pag. For an illustration of the arts roll, see Grendler 2002, 35. About half of the professors (13 legists and 12 in arts) were natives of Padua, which helps account for the strong support for reopening the Jesuit school. See also Sangalli 1999, 288–89.

94. Donnelly 1982, 71–72; Sangalli 1999, 288–99.

ferring the issue to the Venetian governors of the city of Padua, who probably would have approved opening the Jesuit school to external students. Nor did it recommend action by the Senate. The prohibition of 1591 remained in effect.[95]

That Padua wanted the Jesuit school reopened to external students did not matter to the Venetian patriciate, who had no love for the padovani. In 1509, when the Venetian army suffered the crushing defeat of the battle of Agnadello, the people of Padua had thrown off Venetian rule and welcomed the imperial army into the city. The Venetians remembered the events of 1509 and showed them no favor.

The petition of 1594 was the most significant attempt to reopen the Jesuit school to external students. The city of Padua, with the help of the Jesuits and sometimes with behind-the-scenes support of some Venetian nobles, tried again in 1596, 1597, 1602, and early 1606. Some were serious efforts, others did not go beyond wishful talk. Riccobono opposed the Jesuit school until he died in 1599; other professors shared his views. The main student opposition now came from the German nation, whose leaders repeated the charge that the Jesuits had destroyed the universities of Ingolstadt, Prague, and Vienna. More to the point, the German nation included many Protestants, possibly a majority of the 200 or more German students in Padua at the end of the sixteenth century.[96] While the Padua Jesuits wanted to reopen the school to external students, General Acquaviva was ambivalent. He did not want more difficulty with the Venetian government.[97]

Church versus State

Several church-versus-state disputes prepared the ground for hostility against the Jesuit school in 1591, and subsequent conflicts and accusations intensified it. A major shift in Venetian attitudes and policies began in the 1580s and solidified in the 1590s. It began with some constitutional changes in 1582 and 1583, after which men with different ideas occupied more and more of the highest offices in the Republic. The new leaders began to assert stronger civil jurisdictional authority over institutions and subjects at the expense of the rights and claims of the Venetian church and the pa-

95. Donnelly 1982, 73; Sangalli 1999, 299.

96. Grendler 2002, 193, esp. n164. Possevino gave the same number for German students. When he was in Padua in 1587, he wrote that 57 of the 60 German medical students and all of the 150 German law students were Protestants. But it is not likely that 99 percent of them were Protestants. Donnelly 1982, 51–52.

97. Favaro 1911; Donnelly 1982, 74–78; Sangalli 1999, 299, 313–33, 350–57.

pacy. And Venice turned its foreign policy in a new direction because it feared Spain. Some of these changes influenced Venetian perceptions of the Jesuits.

The first issue that roiled church-state relations was the development of public policy discouraging the accumulation of land by ecclesiastics and favoring lay acquisition of church lands. The Venetian government believed that monasteries and religious orders owned too much agricultural land. A food crisis in 1590 and 1591 provided the catalyst for new policies that severely restricted ecclesiastical institutions from acquiring land. Such laws, which continued to be enacted through 1605, were a major reason for the Venetian interdict of 1606–1607.[98] The Padua Jesuits did not escape criticism in this regard: some of their land deals, including one involving Jacopo Zabarella, provoked murmuring in the 1580s and the early 1590s.[99] Elsewhere in Italy the Jesuits acquired a great deal of property through gifts and legacies without much reaction. Venice was different.

Jesuit involvement in Venetian diplomacy created suspicion about the Society's politics. In 1589 the Protestant Henry of Navarre became King Henry IV of France. Venice, now pursuing pro-French and anti-Spanish policies contrary to papal wishes, offered Henry IV diplomatic recognition and possibly other forms of support because it saw France as a counterweight to Spain. But the papacy excommunicated him, and Spain sent an army to fight on the side of Henry's opponents. Before long Henry IV signaled his willingness to become a Catholic, and negotiations began to make this happen and for the papacy to lift the excommunication. In the meantime, the French civil wars continued, and many Italians feared that the conflict would spill over into Italy. In the midst of war and tension, Achille Gagliardi, who had been at the Padua college from 1579 to 1581 and was now in Milan, inserted himself into the diplomacy. Working closely with the Spanish governor of Milan, Gagliardi in 1593 and 1594 tried to persuade the Venetian government that it should send two extraordinary ambassadors to Paris, where they would mediate peace between Henry IV, Philip II, and the papacy. The Venetian government did send the ambassadors but with instructions limited to congratulating Henry IV on becoming a Catholic and entering Paris. Gagliardi's back-channel maneuvering

98. Grendler 1977, 203–5.

99. In 1575 Jacopo Zabarella purchased lands from the Jesuit college that the Gagliardi brothers had given the college when they became Jesuits. But when he sought to resell them in 1586, other members of the Gagliardi family claimed that the Jesuit college's title to the properties was not free and clear. See Sangalli 1999, 196–202, for this and other land disputes involving the Padua college.

came to nothing, except to convince Venetian senators that the Jesuits were political meddlers who leaned toward Spain.[100]

Other events in France further damaged the reputation of the Jesuits. On December 27, 1594, a twenty-year-old law student, who had previously studied with the Jesuits, tried to assassinate Henry IV. In reprisal the Jesuits were expelled from Paris and other cities, and a Paris Jesuit found in possession of materials advocating regicide was hanged in January 1595. Criticism of the Jesuits continued in France in the following years, and was echoed in Venice.[101]

Venetian church-state jurisdictional disputes became more frequent and more intense in the 1590s. Two of the most important involved the Inquisition and book censorship. Since the 1550s and 1560s the Venetian government and the Venetian Inquisition, a joint ecclesiastical and civil body consisting of three clergymen and three Venetian nobles chosen by the state, had worked together to suppress heresy and for effective prepublication press censorship.[102] But cooperation became conflict around 1590. Although the threat of Protestantism had eased, the Venetian government believed that some inquisitions in the mainland state were exceeding their authority. So it tightened supervision over them. And in 1596 Pope Clement VIII issued a revised Index of Prohibited Books with rules imposing greater ecclesiastical control over the publishing industry, which was economically very important in Venice. This caused a row with the Venetian government in which the papacy had to concede considerable ground.[103]

Despite the Senate action against the Padua school in 1591, the Jesuits continued to enjoy support from some leading nobles and their spouses. Noble families whose members included bishops and cardinals were more sympathetic to other clergymen than families lacking high clergymen in their ranks. And Jesuits served as spiritual advisers and confessors to some nobles, including Doge Marin Grimani (1532–1605, doge from 1595), and their wives. But proximity exacted a price. Jesuit confessors to influential Venetian nobles heightened fear that the latter would vote against the best interests of the state. Some feared that nobles close to Jesuits would spill state secrets to them. The concern was warranted, because Venice was a sieve. Despite prohibitions, senators often spoke freely to foreign diplomats and others.[104] In-

---

100. The complicated story is found in Cozzi 1963; for summaries, see Cozzi 1994, 75–76; and G. Brunelli 1998, 261–62. Fear and hatred of Spain dominated Venetian policy at this time. See Davidson 2015.

101. Mousnier 1973, 213–28 and index. 102. Grendler 1977, 145–69.

103. Grendler 1977, 201–85.

104. Cozzi 1994, 74–75, 79–82, and Sangalli 1999, 316. See Grendler 1990, 77, for a list of the high offices that Grimani held before becoming doge.

dividual Jesuits may have learned some state secrets, but there is no evidence that they used them to help Venice's enemies.

Paolo Sarpi (1552–1623) wielded considerable influence. Born in Venice, where he met some future leaders of the Venetian state when he and they were schoolboys, he became a Servite (Servants of Mary) priest, obtained a doctorate of theology at the University of Padua, and held responsible positions in his order at Mantua, Milan, and Rome. He returned to Venice to stay in 1588, at which time he became a leader of an informal circle of anti-papal nobles, academics, and amateur scholars. Whether he was a fideist Catholic, clandestine Protestant, skeptic, or atheist is a matter of dispute among historians. What is clear is that he was a fervent Venetian patriot and a strong proponent of state absolutism, the view that civil governments must command the total obedience of all individuals and institutions in the state, and that the claims of conscience, liberty, vows, religious doctrine, and ecclesiastical law were invalid or subordinate. Because he was neither a noble or a layman, he could not hold political office. But he did offer informal advice. Then in January 1606 he was appointed theological and canon law consultant to the Venetian state in which capacity he crafted intellectual justification for Venetian policies, including the assertion of civil jurisdiction over clergymen and ecclesiastical institutions.[105] His scholarship, intellect, and incisive prose made him a powerful anti-clerical and anti-papal force in Venice and abroad.

Anti-Jesuit Ideology

From this cauldron of disputes, politics, suspicion, foreign events, and Sarpi rose an anti-Jesuit ideology embraced by a significant number of senators. Ideology is the right word, because they held some virulently negative convictions about the Jesuits not based on fact that moved them to act. They saw the Jesuits spreading treason through education. They believed that Jesuit teachers seduced students from their loyalty to parents and *patria* and taught them to obey foreign clergymen and rulers. They invoked the specter of Jesuit approval of regicide. From this point of view keeping the Padua school closed to external students and ridding the Republic of the Jesuits was necessary for the security of Venice.

105. There is a large bibliography on Sarpi. Sarpi 1969 is essential, not only for the works but for the general introduction and comments on individual works of Gaetano and Luisa Cozzi. Bouwsma 1968 offers a broad study of Venetian history in which Sarpi is prominent. The most recent book on Sarpi is Kainulainen 2014, which emphasizes his political philosophy of state absolutism.

A tract, probably written in 1595, commenting on events in France articulated some of the anti-Jesuit ideology. According to its anonymous author, the Jesuits were Spanish agents who promoted Spain, hated France, and sought to weaken allegiance to the French king. As evidence, the author cited the fact that the first five generals were Spaniards or vassals of the Spanish king. Then the anonymous author accused Benedetto Palmio of arguing that it was permissible to kill any king who had been excommunicated, an attempt to link him to the attempted assassination of the excommunicated Henry IV.[106]

The first charge was true but meaningless. The first three generals, Loyola, Laínez, and Borja, were Spaniards. The fourth general was Everard Mercurian (1573–1580) who came from Luxembourg, ruled by Spain, and the fifth was the Italian Claudio Acquaviva (1581–1615), from the Kingdom of Naples, also ruled by Spain. But the Jesuit leadership had many differences with the Spanish monarchy over the years.[107] And whatever Palmio thought, it was very unlikely that he expressed such a broad regicide view publicly.

Another anonymous anti-Jesuit work written between February 1604 and April 1606 emphasized the nefarious role of Jesuit schools.[108] In 1601 Duke Ranuccio I Farnese of Parma founded a boarding school for boys and young men of certified noble birth, and on January 27, 1604, he awarded direction of the school and responsibility for teaching in it to the Parma Jesuits. It enrolled noble youths from many Italian and other states. The anonymous author claimed that thirty-four young Venetian nobles were attending the noble school of Parma with terrible consequences for the Republic of Venice.[109] In a rambling discourse full of colorful metaphors, the author described the damage caused by Jesuit education.

The author began by charging that the Padua Jesuit school had great-

106. Biblioteca Marciana, Venezia, Ms. It. VII 1221, ff. 1–4, as quoted and discussed in Sangalli 1999, 310–13.

107. *For Matters of Greater Moment* 1994, 10–13, 188, 191–94, 206–7; Bangert 1986, 98–103.

108. Entitled "Informatione intorno al Collegio di Parma nuovamente eretto da' PP. Giesuiti, in quanto concerne l'interesse della Serenissima Repubblic di Venezia," from ARSI, Fondo gesuitico 1487/I, n. 11, and printed in Brizzi 1980, 190–92, which is followed here. See also Brizzi 1980, 166–67. It can be dated between the end of January 1604 and April 1606. This is because the title and the first sentence refer to Jesuit control of the Parma College of Nobles which began on January 27, 1604 (see Capasso 1901, 13–15), and because the treatise did not mention the Venetian Interdict that Pope Paul V imposed on Venice in April 1606 and the banishment of the Jesuits from the Republic of Venice that soon followed. The author surely would have used these events in order to blacken further the reputation of the Jesuits had they occurred before he wrote.

109. "In questo College si trovano al presente 34 figlioli di Nobili Venetiani, dal che ne possono seguire notabili, et pernitiose consequenze per la Serenissima Repubblica." Brizzi 1980, 190.

ly damaged the University of Padua. But when the Venetian government closed it, the Jesuits had established themselves in Parma as an act of revenge for being deprived of their university (studio) in Padua. Now they were in a position to do even more harm, because these young Venetian nobles, after studying with the Jesuits at the Parma noble school, will attend the University of Parma rather than the University of Padua.[110]

The rest of the tract argued that Jesuit education made young Venetian nobles practically Spanish subjects. The subversion began when Venetian fathers delivered their sons to Parma. The duke of Parma, a stipendiary of the king of Spain, invited them to dine and "caressed" them. This was part of the Jesuit plan to promote the Spanish monarchy and the institution of monarchy. The tract prophesied that noble Venetian youths under the care of the Jesuits and the protection of the duke of Parma would learn to love and respect the king of Spain. Little by little the Republic of Venice will become Spanish. How so? A young man more readily obeys the wet nurse who suckled him than his own mother.[111] Like babes, young Venetian nobles nourished in Parma will drink in the ambitious, insolent, prodigal, and dissolute rites and habits of its court. They will bring courtly ways to Venice, and that will lead Venetians to dishonor God, scandalize their neighbors, change the laws of the Republic, and ruin houses and families by consuming their wealth.[112]

There was much more. Because they are allies of Spain, the Jesuits persuade their students that they are obligated in conscience to betray their patria for the universal benefit of Christendom.[113] The Jesuits already boast

---

110. Brizzi 1980, 190.

111. "La seconda conseguenza di maggior importanza è questa, che la Nobiltà Veneta contro il suo buon instituto si domestica troppo col Duca di Parma dipendente, et stipendiato dal Re di Spagna poi che per arte de Giesuiti subito che il Duca sa essere arrivato in Parma un Gentilhuomo Veneto che accompagni il figliolo al Collegio l'invita a desinar seco, gli fa insolite carezze.... Et ecco si scuopre un altro fine Giesuitico, cioè di convertir tutta la Nobiltà à poco à poco alla divotione di Spagna, per meglio facilitarle la strada alla Monarchia.... ch'essendo la gioventù attissima à ricevere le prime impressioni, ritrovandosi tanto numero di giovani sotto il governo de Giesuiti, et sotto la protettione del Duca, resteranno impressi dell'affettione verso il Re Cattolico per rispetto che si suole portare à simili sopra intendenti, et introducendosi l'habito difficile à mutarsi, ne seguita ch'à poco à poco la Repubblica non avvedendosi, diverrà Spagnola.... consideri che i giovani adulti bene spesso fanno maggior ossequio alla Nodrice, che alla propria madre per haver da quella succhiato il latte nella loro fanciullezza." Brizzi 1980, 190–91.

112. "La quarta. Quando le cose presenti non seguissero, ne seguirà almeno che la gioventù Veneta, nodrita, et allevata in Parma s'imbeverà de riti, et de costumi della Corte, ambitiosi, insolenti, prodighi, et dissoluti, onde riporterà le medesime usanze in Venetia con dishonore di Dio, scandalo del prossimo, alteratione delle santissime leggi, consumatione delle proprie sostanze,con evidente ruina della case, et delle familiglie." Brizzi 1980, 191.

113. "... è evidente quanto li Giesuiti siano partiali della corona di Spagna .... che si gran

that they command the old senators (*vecchi,* the colloquial name for senators more favorably disposed to the papacy). Nobles educated by the Jesuits in Parma will complete the Jesuit takeover. When these youths become the leaders of the Venetian Republic, they will concede the spice trade to Spain.[114]

The author continued. Venetian noble fathers are sending their sons to study under the guidance of unknown pedants (the Jesuits) in Lombardy, men who are uncultured in language and habits. These boys leave Venice as civilized beings and return as unkempt barbarians. The writer concluded with a call to arms against the Jesuits who desire the ruin of the Republic. They claim that the doge is the supporter of heretics. They want the lagoon of Venice to silt up so that Venice will become hard ground, leaving it helpless against the prince who is the Jesuits' confidant. Of course, the Jesuits do not say such things inside the Republic, because they fear the claws of the Lion of St. Mark. But permitting the Jesuits to educate Venetian youths is putting a sword into the hands of the enemy.[115]

In truth, the combination of the noble school and the calculated generosity of Duke Ranuccio I did exert a strong attraction on Venetian nobles. The duke projected the image of a magnificent prince. He founded a noble school that enabled Italian boys from Venice and elsewhere to live, study, hunt, and play with European aristocrats bearing more famous titles. As the denunciation mentioned, Ranuccio welcomed the noble boarders to his court. He gave them seats of honor at ducal functions and invited them to hunt in his park. All of this appealed to some Venetian nobles who, despite their privileged local position, did not rank very high compared to the landed nobility of Europe. At the time of the interdict the Venetian government barred its subjects from attending Jesuit schools. Nevertheless, significant numbers of noble boys from Venice and the Veneto attended the Parma school in the seventeenth and eighteenth centuries.[116]

In 1606, during the interdict struggle, Marc'Antonio Querini (1554– 1608), one of the leaders of the anti-papal senators, published a pamphlet defending Venice against the bull of excommunication of Pope Paul V.[117]

---

numero di giovani s'interessi con detti Padri li quali con mirabile artifico li persuaderanno essere obligo di conscienza il tradire la propria Patria, rivelando ogni importante segreto, quando si tratta del beneficio universale del Christianesimo." Brizzi 1980, 191–92.

114. Brizzi 1980, 191.   115. Brizzi 1980, 192.

116. Brizzi 1980, 161–65.

117. It is entitled *Aviso delle ragioni della Serenissima Republica di Venezia intorno alle difficoltà che le sono promosse dalla santità di Papa Paolo V, di Antonio Querini senator veneziano, alla sua patria et a tutto lo stato della medesima Republica.* It is printed in *Storici e politici veneti* 1982, 657–729, with the material on the Jesuits at 688–89. For more information on the circumstances of the work and

He included an attack on Jesuit education. Querini accused the Jesuits of forcing all students in their schools and all members of their Marian congregations (associations of students who met for religious exercises and pious works) to swear an oath to obey Jesuit teachers and congregation prefects (student leaders) in everything. They were obliged to defend the rules and constitutions of schools and congregations whatever the stance of civil authority, Querini wrote. This was the beginning of division and secret sedition (*sedizione secreta*) that will ignite fires hard to put out. With such means the Jesuits diminished the authority of the prince, Querini concluded. His pamphlet was printed five times in Italian and twice in French translation.

Paolo Sarpi criticized Jesuit schools in similar terms in late 1622. The issue was whether the Jesuits should be entrusted with the direction of, and teaching in, the Greek College in Rome. Founded in 1576 by Pope Gregory XIII, its purpose was to educate young Greeks so that they would become Latin-rite clergymen in Greek-speaking lands ruled by the Turks and islands governed by Venice. The number of young Greeks who lived and studied in the College ranged from twenty-five to sixty. Some of them were not future priests but fee-paying lay boarders, because the College needed money. Additional financial support came from benefice income diverted from bishoprics in the Venetian maritime empire. Cardinal protectors oversaw the college, drafted the rules, and chose rectors, teachers, and staff. They initially chose secular priests, followed by the Jesuits from 1591 to 1604, the Somaschans from 1604 to 1609, and then the Dominicans.[118]

The student boarders at the Greek College were unhappy about the quality of their education and other matters. When the cardinal protector who had given the Dominicans charge of the college died in 1621, the new cardinal-protectors proposed that the Jesuits be brought back. The Venetian government objected. Renier Zen (or Zeno), the Venetian ambassador to the Holy See and a good friend of Sarpi, went in person to the Greek College to talk to the Venetian subjects among the boarders, about a third of the total. He told them that they were being disloyal to Venice because they were plotting to bring in the Jesuits, a charge they denied. On October 30, 1622, the leading cardinal protector, Cardinal Ludovico Ludovisi (1595–1632), informed the students and staff of the College that the Jesuits would assume direction of the College. The Venetian government howled.

---

its manuscript and printing history, see *Storici e politici veneti* 1982, 645–55, 905–12. For Querini's views and actions during the interdict crisis see Cozzi 1958, index. For a brief summary of the high offices that Querini held in the Venetian government, see Grendler 1979, 337–38.

118. For the history of the Greek College, see Krajcar 1965, 1966, and 2001.

The Pien Collegio demanded an explanation from the papal nuncio. On November 29, 1622, the nuncio told the Pien Collegio that the major reason was that the Jesuits had no equals in education.[119] The Senate asked the advice of Sarpi. He gave it in a *Scrittura di F. Paolo Sarpi in materia nel Collegio de' Greci di Roma,* possibly the last consultation that he wrote.[120]

Sarpi began with a brief history of the Greek College according to his point of view. He asserted that its purpose was not to train priests to minister to Greek Catholics, but to prepare young Greeks to serve and promote the good of the papal court. He devoted most of his short work to refuting the statement of the nuncio that the Jesuits "non hanno pari dell'educazione" (have no equals in education).[121] One cannot make such a sweeping statement, he began, because education is not an absolute. Education is useful or not according to its relationship with the form of government of the state. The kind of education useful to a military state that is maintained and grows through violence is pernicious to a peaceful state that prospers through the rule of law. However, Jesuit education stripped the student of every obligation toward father, patria, and prince. Jesuit teachers turned all the student's love and fear toward a spiritual father whose commands he will obey. This kind of education promoted the greatness of clergymen and was useful for the subjects of a clerical state. But it was the wrong education for governments whose goals were liberty and true virtue.[122]

Sarpi declared that nothing was so important to governments as the principles that youths learned in school, because these guided them throughout their lives. But the Jesuits "have no equals" in alienating people from their fathers and princes. No son emerged from a Jesuit school obedient to his father, affectionate toward his patria, and devoted to his prince, although all three were essential for a free republic. Sarpi concluded that awarding direction and teaching in the Greek College to the Jesuits would be good for the Jesuits but not for anyone else. He advised the doge and Senate to oppose the move.[123] Nevertheless, the cardinal-protectors

---

119. Krajcar 1966, 14–18.

120. It is printed in Sarpi 1765, 143–46. Although the *Scrittura* lacks a date, it was written after November 29, 1622, and before Sarpi's death on January 15, 1623. In addition to his quoting the nuncio's words (see below), Sarpi referred to "Ambassador Zen" on 143. Bouwsma 1968, 524–25, translates and analyzes key passages from the *Scrittura*, some of which is repeated in Muir 2007, 34–35. Ulianich 1994, 257–58, and Del Negro 2006, 423–24, discuss the work briefly.

121. He quoted the phrase, attributing it to the nuncio, three times. Sarpi 1765, 144–46.

122. Sarpi 1765, 145.

123. Sarpi 1765, 146. Possevino had rejected all these charges in 1608. See Prosperi 2013. This was Sarpi's only extended comment on Jesuit education. Elsewhere he viewed the Jesuits

gave direction to the Jesuits and appointed as rector a Jesuit of Greek background. The Jesuits directed and taught in the Greek College until 1773.[124] Although arguments against Jesuit education appeared elsewhere in Italy, nothing compared with the accusations and damning characterizations that came from Venetian pens in these years.

Expulsion of the Jesuits

Although forbidden to teach external students, the Padua school continued to be the most important school in the Province of Venice because it taught the Society's members. There were 65 Jesuits in the Padua college in 1595. They included five teachers (two for scholastic theology, and one each for cases of conscience, philosophy, and the humanities), 12 scholastics studying theology, 11 studying philosophy (metaphysics that year), and 10 studying the humanities. The rest were priests carrying on other ministries and 16 brothers.[125]

From 1596 through 1599, the number of Jesuits fluctuated between 57 and 67. The teachers were always four: two for theology, one for cases of conscience or scripture, and one for philosophy. The number of theology and philosophy scholastics ranged from 25 to 34.[126] In 1602 there were only 36 Jesuits, including 13 scholastics, because the Province of Venice was in the process of moving its philosophy and theology students to Parma.[127] The province then established a probation (novice) house in Padua, in which new Jesuits spent their first two years in prayer and good works without formal study. There were 88 Jesuits in Padua in January 1603, compared to 60 in 1590. They included two teachers of scholastic theology, 15 theology students, 48 novices, priests carrying on various ministries, and brothers. The number of Jesuits remained at this level until 1606.[128] The Jesuits were still a significant and visible presence in the city.

Then came the interdict.[129] In December 1605 Pope Paul V issued an

---

as disloyal to Venice and as agents of the papacy and Spain, but did not write any other treatises against them. Ulianich 1994.

124. Krajcar 2001, 843.

125. ARSI, Veneta 37, ff. 97r–98r. The humanities teacher was described as "Mastro d'humanità per a' nostri fratelli" (f. 97r).

126. ARSI, Veneta 37, ff. 120r–21r, 123r (Possevino), 150r–53r, 186r, 208r–12r, 236r.

127. ARSI, Veneta 37, ff. 252r–53r (60 Jesuits in 1600), 267r–68v (36 Jesuits in 1602). Lukács 1960–1961, part 2, 50, lists only 53 Jesuits in 1600.

128. ARSI Veneta 38, ff. 12r–14r, 28r–31v, 53r, 122r. Although information on the number of Jesuits is lacking for 1604 and 1605, it had to have been about the same as in 1603, because the probation house was still there.

129. In what follows, no attempt is made to give a complete account of the Interdict,

ultimatum. If the Republic of Venice would not hand over for trial in ecclesiastical courts two clergymen accused of crimes, plus revoke laws asserting civil jurisdiction over clerics accused of crimes and laws concerning the disposition of ecclesiastical lands, he would excommunicate the Senate and impose an interdict on the Republic. The Venetian government, led by Doge Leonardo Donà, refused. The pope then laid Venice under interdict in April 1606. The terms of the interdict forbade clergymen from exercising almost all priestly functions, including celebrating Mass and administering the sacraments. The Republic ordered the clergy to disobey the papacy and to carry on their sacerdotal functions under pain of death. The majority did so willingly, while others yielded to the threat. The Jesuits, Capuchins, and Theatines refused, and the latter two were permitted to leave the Republic quietly.[130] By contrast, the Senate, in a harshly-worded decree that described the Jesuits as enemies of the state, expelled them on June 14, 1606, forbidding them ever to return.[131] On August 18, 1606, the Senate barred all its subjects, including women, from any contact with Jesuits by letter or other means. It also forbade all its subjects from sending family members or dependents to attend Jesuit schools outside of the state.[132] The Jesuits had to abandon their college and novitiate in Padua, their colleges with flourishing schools in Brescia and Verona, their professed house in Venice, their residence with no school in Vicenza, and their residence in Candia, Crete, which did a little teaching.[133]

The interdict attracted attention across Europe. Paolo Sarpi and other Venetians wrote pamphlets attacking the papacy and praising civil jurisdiction. Cardinals Robert Bellarmine and Cesare Baronio, Antonio Possevino, and other clergymen and laymen defended the papacy and attacked Venice. French Gallicans, Huguenot theologians, Catholic polemicists, and jurists from across Europe offered their views in the first great church-state confrontation of the post-Reformation era at a time of growing political absolutism.

Within a few months the Republic and the papacy reached an impasse and began to extend peace feelers. Paul V softened his position, and the unanimity of the Senate began to crack. In February 1607 Venice accepted mediation by a French cardinal, and on April 21, 1607, Paul V lifted the in-

---

because the focus is on what happened to the Jesuits. For the interdict, see Cozzi 1958, and Bouwsma 1968; for the Jesuits in the interdict, see Pirri 1959. Pastor 1891–1953, 25:111–83, describes the papal side of the interdict.

130. Pirri 1959, 24, 26.   131. Cozzi 1994, 77.

132. Pirri 1959, 27–28.

133. Pirri 1959 provides numerous documents concerning the expulsion of the Jesuits. Zanardi 1994, 95, provides a brief summary of Jesuit schools before and after 1606.

terdict. Venice handed over to Henry IV of France the accused clergymen sought by Rome, but retained the laws asserting civil jurisdiction over clergymen and church lands. Although much was left unsettled, the Republic and the papacy renewed diplomatic relations. The Capuchins, Theatines, and other clergymen who had left Venice during the Interdict were permitted to return quietly.[134] But not the Jesuits. Despite several attempts and much diplomacy, they were not permitted to return to the Venetian state until 1657.[135]

After readmission the Jesuits in Padua reestablished a school that enrolled external students. But the number of Jesuits in the college was low and the school taught only the lower school classes of grammar, humanities, and rhetoric.[136] The Jesuits did not risk angering the university by teaching upper level courses because they remembered what happened in 1591.

Conclusion

The size and success of the Jesuit school and strong hostility against the Society produced the Padua disaster. The Jesuits founded a school in Padua in 1552. It remained small until the Jesuit leadership decided to make it the major school of the new Jesuit Province of Venice. It expanded quickly and greatly in the 1580s and added a boarding school for nobles. The humanities, logic, and philosophy classes competed well with the university classes. Hence, professors teaching these subjects and some students reacted with anger. They wanted the Jesuit school closed. After rejecting a compromise, professors and students went to the Venetian Senate where Cremonini denounced the Jesuit school as an illegal competitor to the University of Padua. In late December 1591 the Senate ordered the Padua school to stop teaching external students, thereby closing the school to more than 95 percent of its students. The Senate's decision was extreme. It might have worked out a compromise, such as barring external students in some classes, or accepting the Jesuit promise not to print rolls and ring bells. It did not do this.

134. Pastor 1891–1953, 25:178.
135. Signorotto 1994; and Gullino 1994.
136. In 1660 the Padua school offered five classes: rhetoric, humanities, upper grammar, middle grammar, and lower grammar. ARSI, Veneta 97 I, f. 145r–v. In 1696 a college of fifteen Jesuits offered three classes: rhetoric, humanities, and grammar. ARSI, Veneta 49, f. 123r. In 1710 the Padua school offered the same three classes. Brizzi 1994, 509. In 1746 the Padua college had twenty-four Jesuits and a school of three classes: rhetoric, humanities, and grammar. ARSI, Veneta 59, f. 340r. In 1770 there were twenty Jesuits and the school taught the same three classes of rhetoric, humanities, and grammar. ARSI, Veneta 62, f. 311r.

There was more to the Senate decision than defending the University of Padua from competition. The majority of the senators embraced a very negative view of the Jesuits and their school. The rise of an anti-papal party, church-state jurisdictional conflicts, international tensions and events that could be linked, however tenuously, to the Society, and some maladroit maneuvers by Jesuits fueled an anti-Jesuit ideology holding that Jesuit education produced disloyal subjects. Although not shared by all senators, this view determined Venetian policy toward the Jesuits from 1591 through the interdict and beyond. While hostility to Jesuit education and hatred of the Jesuits existed to some degree elsewhere, they were particularly intense in Venice. There was nothing comparable in Italy until the middle of the eighteenth century, when non-Italian philosophers and civil rulers launched the campaign that culminated in the suppression of the Jesuits.

For their part the Padua Jesuits seemed oblivious to the impact that the rapid expansion of their school had on professors and university students. Their attitude was that if professors were losing students to the Jesuits, they should do more and better teaching. They did not realize that competing successfully with the university would produce a backlash. After the Senate action, five Jesuits wrote responses rebutting Cremonini's charges, some of which were untrue. But the responses were ineffective. The Jesuits lacked broad support among the Venetian nobility. If the Jesuits had had a school in Venice, they might have been able to build a foundation of support in the rank and file of the Venetian nobility. But they still would have had to contend with the anti-Jesuit ideology.

It was ironic that Cremonini and other members of the university successfully accused the Jesuits of doing what they had not done. They never tried to establish a Jesuit university in Padua. They did not attempt to force their way into the University of Padua as they tried to do in Turin. They never conferred degrees. Nevertheless, their large school was closed to external students in 1591 and the Society banished from the Republic of Venice in 1606. The Jesuits will next turn to Parma in their search for a place in Italian universities.

6

THE CIVIC-JESUIT UNIVERSITY
OF PARMA

A new approach was needed. After the failures in Messina and Turin and the forced closure of the Padua school, the Jesuits needed to find an uncontroversial way to enter Italian universities. Fortunately, an opportunity presented itself. The duke of Parma, the ruler of a city and state that had no university, invited the Society to join him in creating a new university in which the Jesuits would have a significant role. Although rulers and Jesuits had collaborated to create universities in northern Europe, this was a new development for Italy. Because it was a new university, the Jesuits did not have to contend with the traditions and entrenched interests of an existing university. And the University of Parma differed from the collegiate universities of northern Europe and the Hispanic Peninsula, because it was an Italian university in which law and medicine dominated. But a third of it was Jesuit.

The Jesuits had learned from their failures. In order to become part of the University of Parma they diluted the university principles articulated by Ignatius Loyola in the Constitutions. The University of Parma enabled the Jesuits to demonstrate that they could thrive as faculty members of an Italian university.

The Jesuits Come to Parma

The Duchy of Parma and Piacenza was a recent creation. Except for a few years of independence, Parma had been ruled by Milan since 1346. It then passed to papal control in 1521 during the Italian wars. In 1545 Pope Paul III (Farnese 1468–1549, pope from 1534) created the independent duchy of Parma and Piacenza. It consisted of the two cities, with nearly equal populations, about thirty miles apart, plus contiguous smaller towns and noble fiefdoms. He made his son, Pier Luigi Farnese (1503–1547), a military man of blemished character, its first duke. Pier Luigi made Piacenza the capitol and began a process of centralization and taxation that alienated a group of Piacenza nobles. With the encouragement of the governor of nearby Spanish-ruled Milan, they assassinated him in September 1547. After a period of uncertainty and negotiations between the pope and Emperor Charles V, the duchy remained in Farnese hands, ruled by Pier Luigi's son, Ottavio Farnese (1525–1586, r. from 1547). He enjoyed Spanish protection because he had married Margaret of Parma (1522–1586), illegitimate daughter of Charles V and a Dutch servant woman, and a powerful figure in her own right as governor of the Netherlands. Ottavio moved the capitol to Parma where it remained.

Two first Jesuits, Pierre Favre and Laínez, spent the years 1538–1540 in Parma, winning applause for their preaching and charitable ministries. They left behind a group of ardent supporters who formed a confraternity. And Laínez' preaching inspired the teenage Benedetto Palmio to consider becoming a Jesuit. However, Favre and Laínez had also criticized local clergymen, promoted some devotional practices such as frequent communion, and had served as confessors to a controversial local woman seen as a saint. These actions provoked suspicion and hostility from the Parma clergy that lasted for years.[1]

Nevertheless, in 1559 a Jesuit began negotiating with a dubious Duke Ottavio to establish a college. Duchess Margaret favored the Jesuits, and Duke Ottavio eventually overcame his doubts and local opposition, and invited the Jesuits to come. The city council and the duke provided financial support, and the Jesuits were given the Oratorio of San Rocco, then under construction, plus three contiguous houses to be renovated for classrooms. Twenty-three Jesuits, a sizeable number for a new installation, founded the Parma college in October 1564. On November 6 the school began with four classes teaching rhetoric, humanities, grammar, and a beginner's class of reading, writing, and the rudiments of Latin. Sons of nobles and other prominent townspeople initially flocked to the school, producing an enrollment of 300.[2]

They did not stay. Enrollment dropped to 150 in three classes (rhetoric, humanities, and grammar) in 1569, and about 100 in 1583. Most troubling to the Jesuit rector, few sons of nobles and other important families

---

1. Brizzi 1980, 139–41.

2. Scaduto 1964, 431–35; D'Alessandro 1980, 27–30; Scaduto 1992, 316–21; and ARSI, Veneta 94, ff. 51r–52r, September 20, 1569, which reported four classes.

attended, while many sons of "low persons" and artisans did. The Jesuit rector blamed the poor quality of Jesuit teachers for the low enrollment. But the Jesuits persevered. From the early 1570s through 1597 the Jesuits continued to teach rhetoric, humanities, and grammar, although the size of the Jesuit community dropped to a range of fourteen to nineteen, some of them Jesuit scholastics.[3]

Ranuccio I and the Jesuits Create the University of Parma

In 1586 Ranuccio I (1569–1622) became de facto ruler for his absent father, Duke Alessandro Farnese (1543–1592, r. from 1586), a military commander for Philip II in the Netherlands who seldom, if ever, visited Parma. Ranuccio became duke in his own right in 1592. Sincerely Catholic, as well as superstitious and afraid of witches, he followed and affirmed the Farnese family policy of strong support for the Jesuits. It had begun with Paul III, who had shown them much favor, and continued with Ranuccio's parents. Ranuccio's great uncle, Cardinal Alessandro Farnese (1520–1589, cardinal from 1534), warmly supported the Jesuits including financing the construction (1568 to 1584) of the Church of the Gesù where he is buried.[4]

Ranuccio dismissed a lay tutor of his younger brother Odoardo (1573–1626, cardinal from 1591), and appointed a Jesuit to teach him philosophy. Odoardo then became a strong supporter of the Jesuits and a friend of Robert Bellarmine. He built the Rome professed house of the Jesuits adjacent to the Church of the Gesù, where he is also buried.[5] Ranuccio later appointed Jesuits to tutor his two sons, the illegitimate Ottavio (1598–1643) and the legitimate Odoardo (1612–1646, duke from 1628). Ranuccio and his consort took Jesuit confessors, as his grandfather Ottavio had done. And in the seventeenth century Ranuccio supported financially the Jesuit mission to China.[6]

Duke Ranuccio I sought to create a strong absolutist Catholic state. He pursued that goal with single-minded determination, intelligence, cultural politics, avoidance of war abroad, and ruthlessness at home. By absolutist

3. ARSI, Veneta 36, ff. 25r–26v (March 1573); Veneta 105 I, f. 53r (February 10, 1578), f. 145v (ca. May 1, 1581); Lukács 1960–1961, part 2, 51 (1574); Brizzi 1980, 145–46, 169–70, and 203–4nn56–59.

4. Scaduto 1964, index; Scaduto 1992, index; and Andretta and Robertson 1995, 63, 68.

5. Zapperi and Robertson 1995, 116, 118, and Cadoppi 2013, 31. The Jesuit who taught philosophy to Cardinal Odoardo was Giulio Negroni or Negrone (Genoa 1554–1625 Milan), author of a number of rhetorical works including an oration congratulating Cardinal Odoardo. Sommervogel 1960, 5:1615; and Ruiz Jurado 2001b.

6. Brizzi 1980, 154–57, 206–7n84, 210n116.

state is meant a state in which there was no theoretical limitation on the ruler's authority except that imposed by a small number of divine, natural, and/or fundamental laws. The ruler controlled all the levers of power, including other organs of government, police, army, and bureaucracy.[7] In practice an absolute ruler might choose to, or be forced to, negotiate and compromise with other groups in the state, especially the nobility, to reach his goals. Not Ranuccio, who saw the nobility, especially the Piacenza nobles, as enemies to be brought to heel. In 1594 and 1595 he promulgated new constitutions that lasted for a century and a half and he began to build a massive ducal palace. He also decided to found a university.

The people and commune of Parma had wanted a university for a long time. The city had tried to create one between 1412 and 1417 when it was temporarily free of the rule of the Visconti of Milan. It obtained a university charter from a schismatic pope and hired a handful of scholars, some of them distinguished, to come to Parma. They did a limited amount of teaching, some degrees were conferred, and Parma boasted that it had a university. It did not last. When the Visconti regained control over Parma, they closed the nascent University of Parma, decreeing that the University of Pavia would be the only university in their state. Parma became a paper university. The local colleges of doctors of law, medicine, and theology conferred degrees without offering university instruction beyond some theology taught in the medieval mendicant order monasteries.[8]

Parma tried again in the middle of the sixteenth century. The commune of Parma petitioned Duke Pier Luigi Farnese for a university and he agreed. In 1547 the commune hired three teachers for *Institutes,* logic, and Greek and Latin humanities. The assassination of Pier Luigi and the subsequent diversion of university funds to military spending ended this attempt.[9] The dream lived on. In 1568 the commune petitioned Duke Ottavio to "reopen" the university by renewing the lectureships.[10] And in 1580, Galeazzo Cusani del Monacis (1523–1604), a native of Parma who served as secretary to Emperors Maximilian II and Rudolf II Habsburg and had become wealthy, wrote a testament expressing his wish that Parma should have a university equal to the best in Italy that would attract ultramontane students. He mentioned the Jesuits as possible professors, and he offered

7. This is a slightly modified version of the definition of French absolutism found in Major 1994, xxi.

8. Piana 1963, 307–24, 333–502; Piana 1986; Greci 1998; and Grendler 2002, 127–28.

9. D'Alessandro 1980, 20–25, 39, 44–52; and Grendler 2002, 126–29. Brizzi 1980, 136, views the attempt to revive the university between 1547 and 1551 as "ephemeral."

10. Di Noto Marrella 2002, 192.

to erect a handsome building, comparable to the Archiginnasio building (erected 1562–1563) of the University of Bologna.[11] His offer was not accepted.

The closing of the Padua school to external students offered a fresh opportunity for Parma. When Benedetto Palmio, now sixty-four years of age, visited Parma in the summer of 1597, the duke asked him how things were going in Padua. Palmio was forced to answer: not well. Ranuccio then suggested that the Padua school, its financial support, and the noble school should move to Parma. Palmio consulted the provincial superior and went to Venice to assess the situation. Upon his return he told the duke that the Jesuits could not move the Padua school or its financial support without negative repercussions in the Republic of Venice, because the Jesuits still had strong supporters. The duke then suggested that a university (studio) might be established in Parma without any assistance from Padua. Palmio replied that he could not think of a better city for this.[12] It soon became clear that Ranuccio had more than just a Jesuit upper school in mind. He wanted to found an Italian law and medicine university in which the Jesuits would play a major role. Given Ranuccio's favorable view of them and the high scholarly reputation they now enjoyed, this was not surprising. In addition, Jesuit professors might cost less than lay professors.

Although no document revealing Ranuccio's motives for creating a university has come to light, there were sound reasons. The most important was that a university in Parma would benefit many parties. It would earn visibility and prestige for the duke, his family, and his state. A small Italian duchy and its ruler were practically invisible in Italy and Europe. One with a university would attract favorable attention from afar, because non-Italians would come to study law and medicine. The prince who founded the university would be hailed as a patron of learning. Ranuccio would also advance a local political goal, that of elevating the prestige of Parma and its people over Piacenza and its nobility, some of whom remained hostile to him (or so Ranuccio thought).

It is not likely that Ranuccio wished to found a university in order to create a new governing class.[13] It is sometimes assumed that Renaissance rulers founded new universities in order to educate administrators, to fill

11. Arrigoni Bertini 2002, 269.

12. "Et perché quel buon Prencipe [Ranuccio I] si dimostrava desideroso, che in Parma si potesse mettere tale studio, con dire che facilmente col tempo si potrebbono offerire ocasioni di stabilirlo senza l'aiuto di Padova." Letter of Palmio to General Acquaviva of August 6, 1597, Ferrara, in Brizzi 1980, 175–82, at 176–77. See also Brizzi 1980, 142–43.

13. As D'Alessandro 1980, 31, and Cadoppi 2013, 31, argue.

the expanding bureaucracies and councils of their centralizing states.[14] This might have been true for national monarchies such as England, or for German Protestant princes who wanted pastors and civil servants of the new faith. But not for small Italian duchies. They needed few administrators and members of major local noble families, men who seldom attended universities, were eager to serve the prince and reap courtly rewards. Only loyalty was required.

The people of Parma knew that a university would generate economic benefits, because wealthy out-of-town students would spend generously on lodging, food, servants, tutoring, and other needs. Parents would save money because their sons would be able to study at Parma rather than a university in another state. Some fortunate men from Parma and the duchy would win professorships at the university. In short, a university would enable the city to realize its dream, and it would thank Ranuccio and his descendants.

The Jesuits of the Province of Venice were eager to become part of a new university in Parma, so serious negotiations began. A member of the government represented the duke. Palmio, until his death on November 1, 1598, and Antonio Lisio (Fondi 1546–1618 Naples), the provincial superior, spoke for the Jesuits. General Claudio Acquaviva worried about securing adequate funding and the drain on Jesuit human resources.[15]

The Jesuits, chastened by what had happened at Messina, did not seek a collegiate university dominated by the Jesuits. They now recognized that the Italian-style university, in which law and medicine dominated, was the only university form that Duke Ranuccio I or any other Italian prince or city council would accept. Perhaps Acquaviva, who had studied canon and civil law at the University of Perugia before he became the first Italian to lead the Society, understood this better than the three Spaniards and one Luxembourger who preceded him.[16]

A sign of Jesuit acceptance of the Italian university reality came with the terminology that the Jesuits began to employ. Acquaviva used the words studium generale (university or general university), or università compita or università compiuta (complete university), to describe the Italian-style university.[17] By contrast, he and other Jesuits used terms as Studio nostro or nostra Università (our university) or picciolo studio (little university) to

---

14. This idea may have originated in an article entitled "The Education of the Aristocracy in the Renaissance" of J. H. Hexter, conveniently found in Hexter 1961, 45–70, esp. 63–69.

15. Brizzi 1980, 142–43, 147, and 200–201n42; D'Alessandro 1980, 31–32.

16. Coniglio 1960, 168; Fois 2001a, 1614. It is likely that Acquaviva acquired a doctorate in both laws at Perugia, but neither biography states this as a certainty.

17. "Se ben penso per le lettere passate haver assai chiaramente esplicato il concetto mio

describe a collegiate university in which the Jesuits dominated or a Jesuit school that taught only theology and philosophy.[18]

On August 4, 1599, General Acquaviva told Lisio to accept the duke's offer to include the Jesuits in his university so long as the terms did not violate the Society's rules.[19] The Jesuits then sent Antonio Possevino, who had already negotiated with the king of Sweden, the tsar of Muscovy, and other crowned heads, for face-to-face discussions with Duke Ranuccio I.

Possevino and the duke reached an agreement in late 1599. The Jesuits would provide all the instructors for theology, philosophy (meaning logic, natural philosophy, and metaphysics), mathematics, and the humanities in return for annual payment of 1,000 ducatoni (large ducats of account worth 7 lire 6 soldi instead of the normal 6 lire 4 soldi) to the college. The Jesuits would choose which Jesuits would teach in the university. The duke and commune would appoint and pay the professors of law and medicine.[20]

The end result was that a Jesuit studio or university would be part of a larger University of Parma. Jesuit instruction would be combined with the teaching of law and medicine to create a complete university (Università compiuta).[21] The University of Parma would teach law, medicine, theology, philosophy, logic, mathematics, and the humanities, with law and medicine dominating. The civic University of Parma would include the

---

intorno alli Studi generali che s'è trattato di mettere in Parma tuttavia hora che V[ostra] R[everenza] mi scrive haverne S[ua] A[ltezza] [= Ranuccio I] ragionato col P[adre] [probably Ludovico] Gagliardi et essersi dichiarata che desidera università compita." Acquaviva's letter to Father Ottavio Bulgarini of February 20, 1599, Rome, in ARSI, Veneta 4, f. 380v, as quoted in Brizzi 1980, 200n42. See also Acquaviva's letter to Antonio Lisio of August 4, 1599, Rome, quoted in Brizzi 1980, 205n70.

18. "Il nostro collegio o picciolo Studio." Palmio in his response to Cremonini of March and April 1592, in Sangalli 2001, 136. These were tendencies; the Jesuits were not always consistent in their terminology.

19. "Il primo è che per quel che tocca a studij generali et università compita sempre che siano le cose in ordine et la fundatione bastante noi accetteremo il carico et faremo quanto possiamo conforme a nostri decreti et sempre siamo stati di quest'ultimo animo sin dal principio di questo trattato et ciò offerse il P. Palmio buona memoria a S[ua] A[ltezza, i.e., Ranuccio I] in nome nostro sin dallhora." Letter of General Acquaviva to Antonio Lisio of August 4, 1599, quoted in Brizzi 1980, 205n70. As Brizzi points out, this marked a change from Acquaviva's earlier view seen in his letter to Lisio of January 9, 1599. At that time Acquaviva referred to "al negotio del nostro Studio in quella città," which was Parma. Quoted in Brizzi 1980, 205n70.

20. Brizzi 1980, 144, 183–84, statement of Antonio Possevino of late 1599; and D'Alessandro 1980, 32.

21. "Et che quel nostro Studio sia incorporato con gli altri di leggi et medicina come parte per fare Università compiuta con li privileggi annessi." A memorandum of the Parma Jesuits addressed to Ranuccio I, no date, but ca. 1602, in ARSI, Veneta 37, f. 256 r–v, and printed in D'Alessandro 1980, 73.

Society, making it a civic-Jesuit university. This was a major innovation for Italy and for the Italian Jesuits. They agreed to enter a university run by the state whose major purposes were to create new knowledge and to prepare laymen for positions in secular life.

After agreeing on the number of Jesuit professors and financial matters, the duke and Possevino turned to other issues.[22] At this point Possevino articulated additional Jesuit goals. Although the Jesuits would not have educational, moral, or spiritual authority over the university as a whole, Possevino tried to persuade the duke to draft rules for students and professors that would help them achieve Christian spiritual and moral ends. He wanted the University of Parma to be a model Catholic university, so he made requests and recommendations based on his knowledge of universities in Italy and abroad. His knowledge was extensive. Before joining the Society he had heard philosophy lectures at the universities of Ferrara and Padua, and he knew well the current situation in Padua. In his diplomatic travels he had observed universities in northern Europe, eastern Europe, and France.[23]

Possevino insisted that heretics should not be permitted to enroll; if they did, they should not be permitted to live openly or privately as heretics.[24] Possevino knew that Protestants, especially Germans and Englishmen, attended Italian universities. While they seldom flaunted their religious views, some behaved as Protestants behind closed doors, for example, by eating meat on Fridays. And they occasionally engaged in surreptitious provocative actions, such as writing anti-Catholic slogans on walls. Italian inquisitions seldom tried to find and prosecute Protestant students, even when they engaged in provocative actions, because rulers and city governments did not want to chase away foreign students who spent freely and added to the prestige of the university.[25] Duke Ranuccio promised that no heretic or converso would be permitted to enroll. If one did, he would immediately be handed over to the inquisitor.[26]

However, Possevino had not asked that conversos (New Christians of

22. The document entitled "Proposte fatte al Serenissimo Signor Duca di Parma .... Ragionamento con Sua Altezza di Parma. Intorno allo stabilimento et buon ordine di quella Università. P. Antonio Possevino," is found in ARSI, Veneta 116, Fundationes Collegiorum, ff. 76r–81r, and is printed in Brizzi 1980, 183–89.

23. For the lectures that Possevino heard at Ferrara and Padua in the late 1550s, see chap. 14, "Jesuit Christian Aristotelianism."

24. Possevino, "Proposte," in Brizzi 1980, 185.

25. Grendler 2002, 190–95.

26. "Prima non piaccia a Dio, che io [Duke Ranuccio] permetta, che heretico veruno conversi in questo studio, anzi se alcuno vi venisse lo darà subito all'Inquisitore." Possevino, "Proposte," in Brizzi 1980, 185, 187 (quotation).

Jewish or Muslim ancestry, often thought to be lukewarm Christians or secretly practicing Judaism) be barred from the university. The duke's stance
must have saddened him, because the place of conversos in the Society was
a lacerating issue for him and the Society as a whole.[27] Loyola had considered himself a spiritual Semite and had welcomed recruits of Jewish ancestry, with the result that some of the most important early Jesuits, including
Laínez and Polanco, had converso ancestors.[28] But beginning in 1573 some
influential Jesuits demanded that the Society should not admit men with
converso pasts. Palmio, a leader of this group, wrote a vehement denunciation of Jesuits of Jewish ancestry. Possevino strongly disagreed. He vigorously defended converso Jesuits and their contributions to the Society and
Christianity in four memorials.[29] But the anti-converso Jesuits prevailed.
In 1593 the Fifth General Congregation barred admittance into the Society
of applicants of converso ancestry, and the prohibition was not completely
reversed until 1946.[30] Although Possevino did not write about university
students of converso ancestry, it is impossible to believe that he agreed with
Duke Ranuccio.

Given Ranuccio's association with Palmio, his promise is not surprising. But it contrasted with the reality of Italian universities. Students of
converso ancestry and many Jews studied, and some professors of converso
ancestry probably taught, in Italian universities in the sixteenth, seventeenth, and eighteenth centuries.[31]

Possevino worried about possible confrontations between the lay professors of law and medicine and Jesuit professors, and their respective students. In his view conflicts might occur if lay professors claimed superiority or parity with the Jesuits, or when law and medicine students and Jesuit
students encountered each other in the street. And he did not want lay professors teaching philosophy. He argued that if someone who was not first a
good theologian taught philosophy, he might introduce "pestilential errors
about the mortality of the soul."[32] Possevino here alluded to the fact that
Jesuits had to finish their theological studies before they were permitted to

27. Maryks 2010 tells the story well.

28. Maryks 2010, 42–76.

29. For Palmio's views, see Maryks 2010, 129–43, 219–56. For Possevino's opposition, see
Donnelly 1986; Cohen 2004; Maryks 2010, 159–82 and index; and Colombo 2014. See also the
biographies of Palmio and Possevino in the appendix.

30. *For Matters of Greater Moment* 1994, 12, 204, 635; Maryks 2010, 149, 213.

31. Ruderman 1995, 100–117, with a large bibliography.

32. "Altri potrebbono pretendere letture di filosofia benché fossero secolari, la quale quando
è letta da chi non è prima buon Teologo, serve spessisimo per introdurre pestilenti errori della
mortalità dell'anima, o di altro." Possevino, "Proposte," in Brizzi 1980, 188.

teach philosophy. The duke responded that the lecture venues and hours could be arranged so that all students would have the opportunity to attend any lectures that they wanted to hear with little risk of hostile encounters. And he assured Possevino that there would never be any changes in the professorships of philosophy and the other subjects that the Jesuits would teach, because the Society would last as long as the world endured.[33]

The duke told Possevino that he intended to prohibit students from carrying arms. Possevino also wanted him to stop students from engaging in "public dishonesties, illicit games, and indecent disturbances."[34] He also urged the duke to punish students who wrote obscenities on walls. He wanted the duke to prevent students from shutting down lectures through noisy demonstrations or by extending or inventing vacation days, as often happened at Italian universities. He reminded the duke that at some universities professors delivered only 70 lectures annually, in contrast to the 100 to 135 lectures that university statutes mandated. Again, this was true. By contrast, Possevino said that Jesuit philosophy professors delivered 400 lectures in the same time period.[35] While they did not teach 400, some did teach 300 lectures annually, because they often lectured twice daily, and the Jesuit academic year was longer than the Italian university year.[36] The duke agreed to everything.

In addition, Possevino offered advice about attracting students that was a combination of the obvious, the widely practiced, and the unrealizable. He told the duke to hire professors who lived good lives, were learned, had taught many years in distinguished universities, possessed many languages, and were both theologians and philosophers. The last was irrelevant for law and medicine professors. Possevino advised the duke to prepare printed rolls listing the courses and professors and to distribute them far and wide before the academic year began. All Italian universities did this. The duke should encourage pages and nobles at his court to enroll in the university. He should guarantee reasonable rents to students needing accommodations, and he should erect a residence for poor students, as the Jesuits had done at Prague. Governments of Italian university towns and states sometimes regulated rents and provided free or low-cost residences for poor students.[37]

33. Possevino, "Proposte," in Brizzi 1980, 188–89.

34. "Ma tanto più, quanto insieme si lieverà ogni occasione di publiche disonestà, di giuochi illeciti, o disturbi indecenti a chi studia." Possevino, "Proposte," in Brizzi 1980, 185.

35. Possevino, "Proposte," in Brizzi 1980, 185.

36. For more on the number of lectures that Jesuits and university professors delivered, see chap. 14, "Jesuit Criticism of University Pedagogy."

37. Grendler 2002, 76, 168, 170–71.

Possevino wanted the duke to grant students exemptions from various taxes. This was customary in Italian university towns. He wanted the duke to make arrangements so that students would have the books that they needed at reasonable prices. Some governments promised to do this; it could be done by making arrangements with local booksellers. And the duke should clean the streets of Parma of mud and garbage in order to make a good impression on students. Possevino even offered advice about how to organize the garbage collection. The duke promised to do everything that Possevino asked.[38] Possevino wanted a Catholic university in a city of clean streets in which students and professors would teach, learn, and behave well. Above all, he wanted the University of Parma to succeed.

On June 8, 1601, Duke Ranuccio I promulgated privileges and rules for the professors and students of the new university.[39] They included a great deal of what Possevino asked. Several paragraphs admonished students to behave well and threatened punishment for misbehavior that included disrupting lectures. The university banned *spupillazione*, a form of hazing and extortion of money from new students by older students that produced violence in Italian universities.[40] Possevino had not mentioned spupillazione. Students would not have to pay taxes on the food that they purchased and were assured that landlords would not overcharge them. The duke promised that every year four poor students would receive free doctorates, again going beyond the requests of Possevino. On November 5, 1602, the duke promulgated new regulations requiring thorough and regular removal of mud and garbage from the streets.[41] He also wrote letters encouraging prospective students to come to Parma rather than go to Bologna or elsewhere.[42]

But the duke did not keep all his promises. The university did not bar heretics and conversos. The rules permitted students and their servants to carry arms under the same terms (not explained) under which the duke's subjects might do so.[43]

The University Begins

The university began in three stages. Two or more Jesuits began to teach courses, including philosophy, in 1599. Four Jesuits taught theology, natural philosophy, logic, and mathematics in the university in December

---

38. Possevino, "Proposte," in Brizzi 1980, 185–87.
39. *Sanctiones* 2001, 11–21.
40. On *spupillazione* see Grendler 2002, 503–6.
41. Cadoppi 2013, 122–24.   42. Cadoppi 2013, 91–94.
43. *Sanctiones* 2001, 14.

1600.[44] The theologian was François Remond (Dijon 1561–1631 Mantua).[45] Famed as an orator, Remond delivered the inaugural lecture for the entire university on November 5, 1600. In the meantime, Duke Ranuccio and members of his government devoted a good deal of effort to recruiting professors of law and medicine. A few of them began teaching in the academic year 1600–1601.[46] Duke Ranuccio formally proclaimed the refoundation of the University of Parma, a term that nodded to the earlier attempts, and the privileges and rules of the university, in a decree of June 8, 1601.[47] The complete university began to teach in the autumn of 1601. The first roll of the University of Parma listed seventeen professors teaching eighteen subjects; six were Jesuits.

Six men taught civil law and one taught canon law. Almost every Italian university had a star civil law professor whose reputation was expected to attract students, and Sforza degli Oddi filled that role in Parma. Four men offered five daily lectures in medicine, as the anatomist also taught medical botany. Six Jesuits taught scholastic theology, metaphysics, natural philosophy, logic, mathematics, and rhetoric, and the unfilled theology professorship was intended for a Jesuit. One Jesuit was a native of Parma. Six of the eleven lay professors were also native sons, while the other five came from elsewhere in northern Italy. Unlike most Italian universities at this time, the University of Parma had two non-Italians in its faculty, both of them Jesuits.

The roll included a professorship of rhetoric filled by a Jesuit. The negotiators had not discussed this because it was not a new position. The Jesuits had taught rhetoric since 1564, because it was part of the original contract that they had made with city, not the duke, to teach grammar, humanity, and rhetoric.[48] It was now listed as a university course.

The move highlighted rhetoric's awkward place in the Jesuit curriculum but better fit in a university. The Ratio Studiorum made rhetoric the highest class in the Jesuit lower school. This did not mean that rhetoric was less demanding than logic, natural philosophy, metaphysics, mathematics, and theology of the upper school. The reason was that the lower school taught the humanities based on the ancient classics, while the upper school taught philosophy and theology based on Aristotle and Aquinas. Students who attended the philosophical, theological, and mathematics classes needed good Latin but not the ability to read, speak, and write eloquent classical

44. ARSI, Veneta 37, f. 256r–v; Brizzi 1980, 170.
45. For biographical information, see Grendler 2009b, 253.
46. Cadoppi 2013, 49–91, 94–99.
47. *Sanctiones* 2001, no pag., introduction by Sergio Di Noto Marrella.
48. Brizzi 1980, 169–70.

TABLE 6-1. University of Parma Roll 1601–1602

Texts	Lecturer
Scholastic Theology (de Deo)	François Remond of Dijon, SJ
Moral Theology (de iure et iustitia)	Unfilled[a]
Canon Law	Teodoro Testa of Parma
Civil Law, ordinary p.m.	Sforza degli Oddi of Perugia[b]
	Vincenzo Francolino of Fermo
Civil Law, ordinary a.m.	Annibale Marescotti of Bologna
	Innocenzo Canoso of Parma
Institutes [civil law]	Gaspar Trincadino of Parma
	Marco Antonio Bottone of Parma
Metaphysics	Ottavio Trecca of Parma, SJ[c]
Natural Philosophy	Vittoriano Premoli, SJ[d]
Medical Practice	Alberto Sanseverino of Parma
	Alessandro Recordati of Bologna
Medical Theory	Giovanni Talentono of Fivizzano
Mathematics	Jean Verviers of Belgium, SJ[e]
Anatomy	Pompilio Tagliaferri of Parma[f]
Logic	Marco Garzoni of Venice, SJ[g]
Rhetoric	Paolo Bombino of Cosenza, SJ[h]
Simples [medical botany]	Pompilio Tagliaferri of Parma

From ASPr, Istruzione pubblica farnesiana, bu. 1, no foliation. It is accurately printed in D'Alessandro 1980, 60–61, but without the additional information provided here. The professorships are listed in the order given in the document. The Latin names and descriptions have been converted into Italian, French, and English. Jesuit professors have been identified.

a. This position was intended for a Jesuit, as subsequent rolls demonstrated.

b. Sforza degli Oddi had previously taught at the universities of Perugia, Macerata, Pisa, Pavia, and Padua, and had written several legal and other works. See Grendler 2002, 113–14, 178–80.

c. Trecca or Treccani (Parma 1562–1622 Ferrara) taught metaphysics the following year, then served as prefect of studies for the Jesuits at least from 1616 through 1618. Brizzi 1980, 170–71; Baldini 2002, 294 and 294n38.

d. Premoli (Crema 1566–1630 Castiglione) published a confessor's manual, and taught philosophy and theology at Jesuit schools at Parma, Padua, Rome, and Bologna. Sommervogel 1960, 6:1203–4; Brizzi 1980, 170–71; and Baldini 2002, 294 and 294n37.

e. Verviers (Giovanni Verbieri in the roll; Mons, Belgium 1561–1627 Parma) taught mathematics at the University of Parma, including many Jesuit mathematical students, through the academic year 1604–1605 but was not a significant scholar. He was also the confessor of Duchess Margherita Aldobrandini Farnese from 1600 to 1627, and Duke Ranuccio I from 1605 until 1622. Baldini 2000, 191–92; Aricò 2002; and Baldini 2002, 294–95, 310.

f. From a Parmese noble family, Tagliaferri (ca. 1560–1639) had a long teaching career at Parma and was the first to detect the plague in Parma in 1630. He received several honors from the commune. Rizzi 1948, 27; Affò 1969, 19–20.

g. Garzoni (Venice 1571–1630 Parma) later taught theology, then was rector at Parma where he interacted with Ranuccio I, and superior of the Province of Venice. He published little or nothing. Sommervogel 1960, 3:1250; Aricò 2002, 223–24, 226; Baldini 2002, 294–95 and 294–95n36.

h. Bombino (Cosenza 1575–1648 Mantua) published an expurgated edition of Catullus, various orations, and lives of Ignatius Loyola and Edmund Campion. He later served as theologian to two Gonzaga dukes of Mantua. He became a Somaschan in 1629, but continued to serve as a consultant and teacher to members of the Gonzaga family. Sommervogel 1960, 1:1682–84; Baldini 1992, 95, 95n100, 199–200.

Latin or the capability of analyzing Latin and Greek literary texts. Jesuit grammar and humanities classes taught more than enough Latin to enable students to read philosophical and theological texts. Students and Jesuits knew this; consequently, the rhetoric class always had a much smaller enrollment than the grammar and humanities classes, and many Jesuit schools did not offer a rhetoric class. By contrast, a rhetoric class fit well into the university curriculum. Most Italian universities had one or more professorships entitled rhetoric, rhetoric and poetry, humanistic studies, humanities, or Greek and Latin humanities.[49] University rhetoric professors typically analyzed classical texts in detail, which was what the two Jesuit rhetoric professors at the University of Parma may have done in the academic year 1617–1618 (see below).

Neither the Jesuits nor the duke viewed the 1599 accord, the 1601–1602 roll, or the duke's initial support of 1,000 ducatoni as the last word. The Jesuits pressed Ranuccio for more money and offered to provide additional teachers. In 1600 the duke added another 300 ducatoni. On December 5, 1602, he added 700 more, bringing the total to 2,000 ducatoni. In exchange, the Jesuits agreed to provide two professors of scholastic theology, and one each for moral theology, cases of conscience, metaphysics, natural philosophy, logic, mathematics, and scripture, a total of nine.[50]

The duke also added more professors of law and medicine, so the number of professors of law and medicine and Jesuit professors expanded at about the same rate. Thus, the Jesuits continued to account for about a third of the teachers but a higher percentage of the lectures, since some Jesuits lectured twice daily. The roll for the academic year 1617–1618 listed 27 professors who offered 31 daily lectures. They included eleven legists, seven medical professors, and nine Jesuits. The latter offered six lectures in the morning: two in scholastic theology, and one each in metaphysics, natural philosophy, logic, and rhetoric. In the afternoon the Jesuits offered seven: single lectures in scholastic theology, moral theology, mathematics, metaphysics, natural philosophy, logic, and humanities. However, there was no scripture lecturer or cases of conscience lecturer. The Jesuits did provide a scripture professor for the academic year 1621–1622, but he was not there the following year.[51] The following table lists the Jesuits, their professorships, and the texts that they taught in the University of Parma in 1617–1618. It does not include the professors of law and medicine.

49. See Grendler 2002, 199–248, for a survey of rhetoric professorships and teaching in Italian universities.

50. See D'Alessandro 1980, 32, and the documents on 59, 71, 74–76.

51. Brizzi 1980, 172.

TABLE 6-2. Jesuit Professors at the University of Parma in 1617–1618

Lecture, Hour, and Texts	Lecturer
Morning	
Scholastic Theology, hour 16, Aquinas, de sacramentis in genere et de Eucharistia	Girolamo Serravale of Bologna[a]
Metaphysics, Aristotle, *De generatione, De anima, Metaphysics*	Giacomo Filippo Trezzi of Innsbruck[b]
Natural Philosophy, Aristotle, *Physics* bk 8, *De caelo, De generatione* bk 1	Francesco Rossano of Forlì[c]
Logic, Aristotle, *Organon*	Niccolò Zucchi of Parma[d]
Rhetoric, Cicero, *Partitiones oratoriae*	Francesco Milanino of Parma
Scholastic Theology, hour 17, de sacramentis minoribus	Bernardo Cesi of Modena[e]
Afternoon	
Moral Theology, hour 20, Ten Commandments	Domenico Zanetti of Ferrara[f]
Mathematics, Euclid *Elements, Sphaera*	Giuseppe Biancani of Bologna[g]
Scholastic Theology, Aquinas, de vitiis et peccatis	Vittorio Premoli of Cremona
Metaphysics, same texts	Giacomo Filippo Trezzi of Innsbruck
Natural Philosophy, same texts	Francesco Rossano of Forlì
Logic, same texts	Niccolò Zucchi of Parma
Rhetoric, Cicero, *Verrines* bk 1, Virgil *Aeneid* bk 2	Francesco Milanino of Parma

From ASPr, Archivio del Comune di Parma, Studio, bu. 1909, no foliation. The complete roll including the law and medicine lectures is printed in Grendler 2002, 134–35. The document does not indicate the titles of the Jesuit professorships, only the texts to be taught. From these it is easy to infer the professorships. A comment on the teaching hours: it is not likely that five Jesuits lectured at the same hour in the morning, or that seven Jesuits lectured at the same hour in the afternoon. It is more likely that the morning lectures were spread through hours 16, 17, and 18, and the afternoon lectures spread through hours 20, 21, and 22, and that the document did not note this. Italian universities used a twenty-four hour clock in which hour 1 was one hour after sunset, hour 2 was two hours after sunset, and so on.

a. Serravale (Bologna ca. 1577–1645 Parma) earlier taught metaphysics and natural philosophy at Parma and continued to teach theology there at least through 1622. He later served as rector and confessor to Duke Odoardo Farnese and his mother. Brizzi 1980, 171–72; Baldini 1992, 193; Baldini 2002, 295n44.

b. Trezzi (Innsbruck ca. 1580–1633 Piacenza) taught at Parma at least from 1616 to 1618, then taught theology from 1624 to 1628 at the University of Mantua. Baldini 2002, 296 and 296n51; and Grendler 2009b, 81, 162, 170, 254.

c. Rossano (Forlì 1583–1647 Piacenza) taught moral philosophy, logic, natural philosophy, metaphysics, and theology at Parma through at least 1622, then theology at Mantua from 1624 to 1628 and later served as rector at Parma. Brizzi 1980, 171–73; Baldini 2002, 196 and 196n50; Grendler 2009b, 81, 163, 168, 253–54.

d. Zucchi (Parma 1586–Rome 1670) is known for his research on optics which enabled him to construct a reflecting telescope allowing a closer examination of Mars and Jupiter. He was also known for his preaching and ascetic works. He taught logic, natural philosophy, and metaphysics at the University of Parma from 1614 to 1620, and later taught mathematics and served as rector at the Collegio Romano. Brizzi 1980, 171–72; Zanfredini 2001h; and Baldini 2002, 295–96.

e. Cesi (Modena 1582–1630 Parma) taught logic, natural philosophy, metaphysics, and scholastic theology at the University of Parma from 1614 through 1622 and perhaps beyond. He also wrote a book on minerals and tutored an Este princeling. Brizzi 1980, 171–73; Baldini 2002, 295–96 and 295–96n46.

f. Zanetti (Ferrara 1585–Reggio Emilio 1670) taught logic and cases of conscience in alternation at the University of Parma between 1616 and 1622. Brizzi 1980, 171–73; Baldini 2002, 296n53.

g. Biancani (Bologna 1566–1624 Parma) was the most important Jesuit mathematician in the Province of Venice and teacher of numerous other Jesuit mathematicians. On the whole, he supported Galilei. He taught mathematics at the University of Parma from 1605 until his death. Grillo 1968; Mellinato 2001b; Baldini 2002, 295–97, 310–11; Grendler 2009b, 66–67.

The 1617–1618 roll of twenty-six professors was the full size of the University of Parma. It remained at twenty-six or twenty-seven, occasionally thirty to thirty-two, one third of them Jesuits, through most of the seventeenth and eighteenth centuries.[52]

The city agreed to pay the law and medicine professors, while Ranuccio I paid the Jesuits.[53] In the academic year 1609–1610 the University of Parma had twelve law professors, seven medical professors, and four student lecturers paid tiny stipends, who received a total of 4,757 ducatoni.[54] The duke paid the Parma Jesuit college 2,000 ducatoni for eight Jesuit teachers, and the city paid the Jesuit college 300 ducatoni for the four-class lower school that included rhetoric.[55] Together Ranuccio I and the commune of Parma laid out about 6,832 ducatoni (4,757 + 2,000 + 75 for rhetoric) for professorial salaries, a substantial amount, of which the city paid 71 percent. If Duke Ranuccio or the city had had to pay laymen to teach the subjects that the Jesuits taught, the total cost would have been higher, because some natural philosophers commanded high salaries.

For the first time, the Society, not just a lone Jesuit, was part of an Italian law and medicine university. It had a fixed statutory position teaching the humanities, mathematics, philosophy, and theology. Jesuit superiors, not the duke, selected the Jesuits who would teach in the University of Parma. The University of Parma was a civic-Jesuit university, a significant innovation for Italy.

Joined but Separate

The Jesuits were incorporated into the University of Parma, but they also wanted to be separate and autonomous. They asked to teach their classes in

52. This is a tentative statement, because few university rolls have been located. There are several for the 1670s and 1680s and for the eighteenth century in ASPr, Istruzione pubblica farnesiana, bu. 1, and Archivio del Comune di Parma, Studio, bu. 1909.

53. Cadoppi 2013, 47–48.

54. ASPr, Archivio del Comune di Parma, Studio, bu. 1913, a ledger entitled "Delli lettori e altri provisionati nel Studio rifformato," ff. 1r–22r, which listed payment records for the non-Jesuit professors for the period October 1609 through October 1610. This list of individual professors and their salaries is printed in Grendler 2002, 131, table 4.7. The total seems to have been typical. An undated document from about this time listed 4,910 ducatoni paid to law and medicine professors. With 2,075 ducatoni for the Jesuits, the total was 6,985 ducatoni. ASPr, Istruzione pubblica farnesiana, bu. 2, document entitled "Nota delle provisioni che ogni anno si devono alli ss.ri. lettori nel studio di questa città di Parma."

55. "Ad superiorum classium praelectiones tenetur collegium ex obligatione contractus cum Seren. Duce. 2000 aureorum. Inferiorum vero cum civitate circiter. 300." ARSI, Veneta 38, f. 205r–v (1618).

their own building, to be located at some distance from where the "seculars," the law and medicine professors, taught. This would produce greater quiet and discipline for their students, the Jesuits argued.[56]

They got their wish. In January 1601, Galeazzo Cusani de Monacis, who in 1580 had volunteered to leave a bequest to erect a university building, now offered to sell his palace to the commune of Parma for classroom use. It was located next to the thirteenth-century Church of San Francesco del Prato (now deconsecrated) in the northeast quadrant of the half of the old walled city located on the eastern side of the small stream (Torrente Parma) that bisects Parma. The commune bought it from him on June 1602 for 7,500 ducatoni, a price fixed by Ranuccio I. A garden of simples (medicinal herbs) was added for the teaching of medical botany, and the building became the venue for the law and medicine lectures.[57]

The Jesuits, on the other hand, taught in their own school, which was located in some small buildings very near the Oratorio of San Rocco, their church. San Rocco was also situated on the eastern bank of the walled city, but in the south-central quadrant and much closer to the Torrente Parma.[58] Today the two sites are about a fifteen-minute walk distant from each other. The roll for the academic year 1617–1618 explained the two venues in this way: the professors of law and medicine taught "in scolis novissimis" (in the newest schools) and the Jesuits taught "in scolis veteribus" (in the old schools).[59]

The Jesuits followed university practices and traditions when they coincided with the mandates of the Ratio Studiorum of 1599 and did not when the Ratio Studiorum differed. Philosophical texts presented no difficulties. Both university statutes and the Ratio Studiorum stated that lectures in logic, natural philosophy, and metaphysics must be based on the appropriate texts of Aristotle. However, the four Jesuits who taught logic, natural philosophy, and metaphysics, plus rhetoric, taught twice daily as decreed

56. "Finalmente, che già che la Compagnia piglia il carico di leggere le sudette facoltà non vi possano essere altri concorrenti nè ordinarii nè straordinarii di quelle scienze ch'ella insegnerà et che quel nostro Studio sia incorporato con gli altri di leggi et medicina come parte per fare Università compiuta, con li privileggi annessi. Ma per il bisogno poi presente bisognerà prima si faccia la separazione delle nostre scuole da quelle de i secolari, con lasciare a noi libero il palazzo per la quiete maggiore et disciplina de nostri scolari." Submission by the Parma Jesuits to Ranuccio I, ca. 1602, printed in D'Alessandro 1980, 72–73.

57. D'Alessandro 1980, 34; and Arrigoni Bertini 2002, 269–70.

58. Dossi 1964, no pag.; and D'Alessandro 1980, 34. B. Adorni 1978, 161, 171, 191, provides maps of Parma that show the locations of these buildings and the old walls, plus additional information and illustrations.

59. ASPr, Archivio del Comune di Parma, Studio, bu. 1909, roll of 1617–1618, no pag.

by the Ratio Studiorum. This was a departure from university practice, as Italian university professors almost never delivered two daily lectures on the same subject, and very few taught two subjects. Jesuit professors at Parma continued to teach twice daily. For example, in the academic year 1677–1678 the Jesuit professors of the above four subjects delivered two lectures daily, at hour 16 (late morning) and hour 21 and a half (late afternoon). On the other hand, in the academic year 1617–1618 the Jesuits who taught scholastic theology, moral theology, and mathematics delivered only one daily lecture as the Ratio Studiorum dictated, as did the Jesuits who taught these disciplines in 1677–1678.[60] In other words, although the Jesuits were part of the University of Parma, they followed the practices for Jesuit upper schools as dictated by the Ratio Studiorum.

All large Italian universities had concurrents, that is, two or more professors teaching the same subject and text at the same hour. They had them for the major professorships of civil law, *Institutes*, canon law, medical practice, medical theory, and natural philosophy, and the lesser professorship of logic. Large universities also had metaphysics and theology concurrents, friars who taught metaphysics and scholastic theology at the same hour, albeit different traditions: Dominicans taught Thomist metaphysics and theology (*in via s. Thomae*) and Augustianians or Franciscans taught Scotist metaphysics and theology (*in via Scoti*). Anatomy, mathematics, and humanities, deemed less important, typically had only a single professor. Small universities had few or no concurrents in any subject.[61] As a medium-sized university the University of Parma had concurrents teaching civil law, *Institutes*, canon law, medical practice, and medical theory.

However, the Parma Jesuits did not want any concurrents.[62] Hence, single Jesuits taught metaphysics, natural philosophy, logic, mathematics, and rhetoric without concurrents. Nor did the Jesuit theologians teach at the same hour. And although they all followed the *Summa Theologica* of Aquinas, they did not teach the same material.[63] For example, in the academic year 1617–1618 three Jesuits taught scholastic theology. Girolamo Serravale lectured on the sacraments in general and the eucharist, Bernardo Cesi lec-

60. See the roll of 1677–1678 in ASPr, Archivio del Comune di Parma, Studio, bu. 1909, no pag.

61. Grendler 2002, 145, 147–49, for the rolls of some large and small Italian universities with and without concurrents.

62. See the quotation in note 56.

63. The Ratio Studiorum provides detailed instructions about how Jesuit theologians should approach and teach specific parts, questions, and articles of the *Summa Theologica*. *Ratio Studiorum* 2005, 69–95.

tured on the lesser sacraments, and Vittorio Premoli lectured on vices and sins. Domenico Zanetti taught moral theology by lecturing on the Ten Commandments.[64]

The Jesuits had practically their own arts and theology university within the larger university, a new arrangement for Italy.[65] The Parma arrangement was similar to, although not identical with, the structure of some northern European universities, such as Catholic Prague and Vienna and Lutheran Wittenberg. However, because the number of law and medicine professors was much smaller in northern universities, philosophers and theologians in northern Catholic and Protestant universities had a larger relative position and profile than the Jesuit professors at Parma.

While founding a university, Duke Ranuccio also pondered creating an educational institution for noble youths. He first considered a military school for noble boys. Then he thought about erecting a university student residence. He finally decided to create a boarding school for boys of certified noble lineage. Named Collegio per Nobili di Santa Caterina, it opened its doors on October 28, 1601, with secular priests serving as teachers and administrators.[66] In January 1604, he awarded direction and teaching responsibilities to the Jesuits.[67] The Society now had three educational enterprises in Parma.

The Santa Catarina school enrolled noble boys aged eleven to twenty who boarded in the school's building (no longer extant) and attended academic classes in the Jesuit school at San Rocco. The majority of the boys studied the rudiments of Latin grammar, Latin literature, and humanities. A small number of older and abler boarders attended the Jesuit classes in rhetoric, logic, natural philosophy, metaphysics, and mathematics. This was only part of their education. Students at the noble school performed theatrical productions with music and dancing under the guidance of Jesuit teachers. And the Jesuits hired laymen to teach riding, fencing, designing fortifications, vernacular languages, singing, dancing, and how to play musical instruments. Numerous lay employees, many of them de facto servants, provided for the needs and wishes of the noble boys. As noted

---

64. I am classifying Premoli's lectureship as scholastic theology rather than moral theology because it was based on a section of Thomas' *Summa Theologica* that dealt with the nature of vices and sins. By contrast, I am classifying Zanetti's professorship as moral theology because it is likely that he discussed issues arising from violations of the Ten Commandments, which was common subject matter for moral theology.

65. See also the comments of D'Alessandro 1980, 40–41.

66. Brizzi 1980, 150, 152, 208.

67. Brizzi 1980, 157–68. For more information, see Capasso 1901, Brizzi 1976, and Turrini, 2006. The school for nobles has attracted more scholarly attention than the University of Parma.

in chapter 5, Duke Ranuccio I and his successors showered favors on the boarders. The Jesuit Latin instruction was free of charge. But parents of the boys paid high fees for room, board, services, lessons in the other subjects, and the cachet of attending the school.

The Parma noble school generated a culture that combined elite self-identification, spiritual formation, bonding with fellow nobles, the security of a future leadership role, the rules of civil life, an ethic of responsibility, many activities and recreations, and academic achievement. And if a young noble was not academically gifted, Jesuit scholastics tutored him. The Parma noble school was the best known of the boarding schools for nobles or citizens that the Jesuits administered and staffed in Italy in the seventeenth and eighteenth centuries. In 1605 it had 64 boarders, followed by thousands more in the future.[68] Twenty-three percent of its enrollment for the years 1601 through 1770 came from outside of Italy.[69] The Parma noble school reached its highest enrollment of 285 noble boys in 1700.[70] The noble boarding school greatly boosted both Ranuccio's prestige and the reputation of the Jesuits as teachers and mentors to the ruling class.

However, the duke and the Jesuits agreed that the noble school and the University of Parma were distinct institutions. The duke decreed that noble college students and university students should not have any contact with each other, with the exception of public college disputations in which priors of the university student arts organization might participate.[71] The duke wished to emphasize the exclusivity of the noble school, while the Jesuits feared that university students would corrupt the noble boys. This widened an existing educational division. Young nobles no longer attended universities, as some had in earlier centuries. But the sons of professionals did, in order to obtain the degrees enabling them to follow in their fathers' footsteps.

Although the Jesuits were part of the University of Parma and wanted all university students to behave in a moral and upright fashion, some had other ideas. In or about 1602 a student addressed a petition to the duke asking for various concessions. He wanted the magistrates and policemen to deal leniently with dissolute students. And he wanted the city authorities to grant permits allowing "prostitutes and similar paid women" to come to the students.[72] Since it was not likely that the duke allowed this, students probably made their own arrangements.

---

68. ARSI, Veneta 105 II, f. 550v. 69. Brizzi 1976, 38.

70. Capasso 1901, 102.

71. D'Alessandro 1980, 40–41, 80 (letter of Ranuccio I to the governor of Parma of December 6, 1605).

72. "Ultimamente vorrei supplicare l'A[ltezza] V[ostra] a fare che non meno di lei siano

The authorities did respond when Jesuit classes and students suffered harassment. In 1621 the bishop of Parma and his vicar issued a proclamation against anyone who disturbed the San Rocco school. It barred games in or near the school; writing on its walls; carnivalesque noise; harassment of students who came and went; throwing stones, tomatoes, and eggs; selling food without permission; fighting and name-calling directed against students of the Jesuits; and defamatory placards, pasquinades, and other writings against the Jesuits. It empowered the rector of the Jesuit college to order unauthorized students to leave the school and its courtyard. The bishop threatened a series of penalties beginning with fines and three drops of the rope (*strappado*) and ascending to perpetual galley service or death.[73] Many similar proclamations in the next 150 years argue that the Jesuits and their students had to endure some harassment.[74]

On at least one occasion the Jesuits complained that law and medicine students disturbed their classes.[75] However, it was not likely that the Jesuits were special targets. It was more likely that this was the typical boorish behavior of university students that targeted fellow students, townspeople, and clergymen indiscriminately. Moreover, even though the 1621 decree listed multiple forms of harassment and was repeated, it should not be concluded that the Jesuits and their students suffered from all these actions. Such proclamations typically threatened punishment for many kinds of misbehavior, whether or not they had just occurred, in the hope of discouraging future bad behavior. Some harassment was part of the price of operating a Jesuit school in a university town.

The Jesuits in the University

From 1618 to 1768 the Jesuits provided eight to ten teachers for the university except for a period of plague and war in the 1630s and 1640s.[76] Most

---

amorevoli li officiali in concedere certi favori o licenze a scolari se ne ricercano, come in dimandare licentie per puttane et simili pagatelle che molto obligano il scolare così anco li sono di grandissima consolatione et poco o nulla rilevano a V[ostra] A[ltezza], che però anco se le vengono negate molto li disgustano." Printed in D'Alessandro 1980, 67–68 (quotation at 68).

73. "Bando contra quelli che disturbano lo Studio de Padri della Compagnia di Giesù," dated January 7, 1621, and printed in D'Alessandro 1980, 82–85; see also 41.

74. Di Noto Marrella 2002, 196–97.

75. "Ult.o che si ponga rimedio al disturbo, che danno alle nostre schole gl'scholari dell'Università, i quali sono causa, ch'i Padri non possono fare il debito loro co' qual decoro e disciplina, ch'à religiosi conviene." ASPr, Istruzione pubblica farnesiana, bu. 1, a package of documents labeled "S. Rocco," no foliation and no date, but probably seventeenth century.

76. The history of the University of Parma in the seventeenth and eighteenth centuries has

often nine Jesuits taught. Eight lectures remained constant. Two Jesuits taught scholastic theology, and one Jesuit each taught cases of conscience (sometimes called moral theology), metaphysics, natural philosophy, logic, mathematics, and rhetoric. Through most of the seventeenth century a ninth Jesuit taught moral philosophy. Beginning in or about 1696 the Jesuits substituted a professorship of scripture for moral philosophy, and it continued through the eighteenth century.[77]

Since some Jesuits were now faculty members of the University of Parma, they hoped and expected to participate in examining degree candidates and awarding degrees. Professors could do this in two ways. Many served as promoters for degree candidates. Some were members of the colleges of doctors that examined degree candidates and determined whether they merited degrees.

Obtaining a doctorate in an Italian university required several steps.[78] After hearing lectures for a number of years and disputing, the student presented himself to the appropriate college of doctors to be examined for the doctoral degree (*laurea*).[79] University towns normally had three colleges of doctors: law, medicine (including philosophy), and theology. They were not part of the teaching university, but independent bodies, all of whose members possessed doctorates.[80] Colleges of doctors decided who would receive doctorates from the university.

At the preliminary meeting with the appropriate college of doctors the candidate was asked to provide certificates (*fedi*) from professors stating that he had studied for the required number of years (four to seven for law, medicine, and philosophy, longer for theology) at this and/or other uni-

---

yet to be written. Rizzi 1948 and Berti 1967 provide information about many of the professors and their publications, but that is all that has been done.

77. For the details, see ARSI, Veneta 38, f. 253r–v (1619), Veneta 39 I, f. 40r (1622), 64r–67r, 130r (1625), 196r (1628), Veneta 71, f. 158r (1628), Veneta 39 I, f. 281v (1633), Veneta 71, 248r–49v (1636), Veneta 39 II, 377r (1639), Veneta 71, ff. 299v–300r (1639), Veneta 39 II, 472r (1642), Veneta 71, 386r–87r (1645), Veneta 125, no pag. (1646), Veneta 40, f. 165r (1649), Veneta 97 I, 162r (1661), Veneta 49, 122r (1696), Veneta 59, f. 338r (1746), Veneta 91, printed catalogue for 1767, 13r–14r. In addition, Baldini 2002, 294–309, lists all the teachers of metaphysics, natural philosophy, logic, and mathematics at the Parma school between 1600 and 1768 plus biographical information.

78. This and the following three paragraphs are a shortened version of Grendler 2002, 174–77, which offers additional bibliography. Count palatine doctorates and doctorates by examination without years of university study are not discussed here.

79. As noted in chapter 2, Italian universities awarded only doctorates, possibly because students did not want to pay the expenses for lesser degrees. This was a major difference between Italian universities and universities in the rest of Europe.

80. For more information on the composition and size of colleges of doctors, see chap. 2, "The Italian University."

versities, and that he had disputed once or twice. Then three or four, occasionally five professors, some chosen by the candidate, others named by
the college, were assigned to represent and help the candidate throughout
the process. Called promoters, they testified that the candidate was ready to
be examined. The college fixed the date and informed the candidate of the
cost, which was substantial, because payments to members of the college
and others were mandatory.

The candidate had to surmount two examinations. The first determined whether he would win the doctorate, and this was followed by a
second pro forma examination. Historians call them the private and public
examinations. On the first day of the private examination the prior of the
college gave the candidate the points (*puncta*) on which he would be examined. These were two, three, or four brief passages selected at random
from the statutory texts in the subject matter of the desired degree. In civil
law, they came from the *Corpus juris civilis;* for medicine from the works of
Avicenna, Galen, or Hippocrates; for philosophy from the works of Aristotle; for theology usually from Peter Lombard's *Sentences.* The candidate
had twenty-four hours to prepare, with the assistance of his promoters. The
examination was conducted by the full college or a limited number of its
members. The candidate expounded on the puncta. The doctors of the college then proposed counter-arguments or raised new issues. Throughout
the private examination the promoters sat with the candidate and prompt-
ed him when necessary. After the examination was finished, the candidate
and his promoters withdrew while the college voted. A two-thirds favorable vote was required.

If the candidate received the necessary votes, within two or three days
he proceeded to the second (public) examination and the conferral of the
degree. The same procedure was followed. But since the examiners had already satisfied themselves as to the candidate's competence, the public examination was invariably successful. Then the chancellor of the university
conferred the degree as members of the college, promoters, and friends of
the candidate looked on.

The Parma Jesuits became part of the degree examination process. Like
their law and medicine colleagues, Jesuit professors at Parma signed numerous fedi confirming that students had attended their lectures.[81] Jesuit theologians were promoters for successful candidates for doctorates of theology
almost from the beginning. One, two, or three Jesuit professors served as

---

81. There are numerous such fedi, some signed by Jesuit professors, in ASPr, Archivio del
Comune di Parma, Studio, bu. 1903.

promoters for 18 of the 34 known recipients of doctorates of theology conferred by the University of Parma from 1604 through 1646.[82] The majority of the new doctors were secular priests, a minority were members of
medieval mendicant orders. The surviving documentation for the other 16
doctorates of theology does not list any promoters. Hence, it is possible that
Jesuits served as promoters for additional new doctors.

In addition, a Jesuit served as a promoter, alongside four non-Jesuit promoters, for a man who obtained a doctorate in "arts, philosophy, and medicine" in 1606. Another Jesuit was a promoter, alongside three non-Jesuit
promoters, for a man who obtained a doctorate in "arts and philosophy"
in 1641.[83] Although university rolls for these years have not been located,
it is likely that these two Jesuits taught logic or natural philosophy in the
university. In short, Jesuit professors played a major but not exclusive role
as promoters of degree candidates in theology and a very small role as promoters for degree candidates in philosophy and medicine.

Gaining entry into the Parma college of theologians was another goal.
The membership of all Italian colleges of doctors of theology consisted of
theologians from the local monasteries of medieval mendicant orders and,
very rarely, the secular clergy. When the new orders of the Catholic Reformation (Barnabites, Jesuits, Somaschans, and Theatines) appeared in the
sixteenth century, Italian colleges of doctors of theology did not accept
them into their ranks. This was the case in Parma. Although there was no
teaching university, Parma had a college of doctors of theology that awarded doctorates of theology in the fifteenth and sixteenth centuries, but it had
no members from the new religious orders.[84]

This changed for the Jesuits alone in the seventeenth century, thanks to
the dukes. In 1603 Duke Ranuccio I reconstituted the college of doctors of
theology. Because details are lacking, it is not known if he added Jesuits to
the college. In 1629 Duke Odoardo Farnese promulgated a new constitution for the college of doctors of theology that added four Jesuits: the rec-

---

82. Cadoppi 2013, 189, 191, 193, 196–204. The list of doctorates comes from notarial records
and, as Cadoppi states on 151–52, has chronological gaps and is far from complete. Many documents do not indicate the discipline. As always in Italian universities, the majority (64 percent)
of the doctorates for which the discipline is known were in law, which was not relevant for the
Jesuit professors.

83. Cadoppi 2013, 191 (Antonio Maria Zucchi Panighetti), 203 (Carlo Boni). The university
conferred 46 known doctorates in arts, arts and medicine, and medicine between 1602 and 1646,
and undoubtedly others for which documentation has not been found.

84. Piana 1963, 363–502, and Piana 1966, 515–61, provide a list of doctorates conferred 1432
through 1522; and Cadoppi 2013, 175–87, offers a list of 136 doctorates conferred between 1527
and 1598.

tor of the Jesuit college, the prefect of studies of the Jesuit school, and two Jesuit professors of theology.[85] Because the college of doctors of theology probably had about twelve members, the Jesuits had a significant, but not dominating, presence in it. Still, it was a major breakthrough for the Jesuits in Parma and Italy.

Despite these successes, the number of Jesuits who taught in the University of Parma declined between 1636 and 1650. In December 1634 there were nine: two taught scholastic theology, and one each taught cases of conscience, metaphysics, natural philosophy, logic, mathematics, moral philosophy, and rhetoric.[86] On January 1, 1636, there were only five: two teaching scholastic theology, plus one each for metaphysics, logic, and moral philosophy. From that date through the academic year 1649–1650, the number fluctuated between five and seven, once rising to eight.[87]

There were two reasons. The first was the terrible plague in northern Italy between 1630 and 1633. An anonymous Jesuit historian wrote that it appeared in Parma in April 1630 and soon was claiming 120 victims daily and similar numbers in other towns in which the Jesuits had schools.[88] The death toll on the Jesuits was not so drastic but still significant. The Province of Venice had 428 Jesuits in December 1628 and only 344 in November 1633, a drop of 20 percent.[89] Recovery was slow. In 1645 the province still had only 402 Jesuits, about 94 percent of the number in 1628.[90]

Jesuit deaths caused a shortage of teachers. The Province of Venice coped by reducing the number of teachers rather than by closing schools. But the upper school teacher shortage lasted much longer than the three to four years of the plague, because it took many years to prepare a Jesuit for upper school teaching. He typically did not begin to teach the philosophical trio, mathematics, or theology until he had spent a dozen years or more

85. Del Monte 1948, 18–21.

86. ARSI, Veneta 71, ff. 237r–38r (December 1634).

87. ARSI, Veneta 71, ff. 248r–49v (five upper school teachers on January 1, 1636); Veneta 39 II, f. 377r (five teachers in 1639); Veneta 71, ff. 299v–300r (eight teachers on November 1, 1639); Veneta 39 II, ff. 412r–13r (five teachers in 1642); Veneta 71, ff. 386r–87r (six or seven teachers in 1645); Veneta 125, no foliation (six teachers in 1646); Veneta 40, f. 165r (seven upper school teachers on September 8, 1649).

88. ARSI, Veneta 125, a brief history of the Province of Venice between 1626 and 1762, no foliation. It goes on to say that the population of "questa città" (either Parma or Piacenza) was 33,000 in 1628 but only 14,000 at the end of 1630. See also Smeraldi, "De' principii," 147. Orazio Smeraldi, SJ (Parma 1592–1672), who came to Parma in September 1637 and later served as rector of the college, wrote a history of the noble school from 1601 to 1670 that remains in manuscript. For similar plague mortality estimates, see Hanlon 2014, 44, 207.

89. ARSI, Veneta 71, ff. 174v (1628), 224r–31v (1633).

90. ARSI, Veneta 71, ff. 382r–92r.

in the Society: two years as a novice, humanities study if he was deficient, three years of philosophical study, three to five years teaching in a lower school, four years of theological study, and ordination to the priesthood. Most Jesuits did not begin teaching upper school courses before the ages of thirty-one to thirty-five.[91]

The second reason was the foolish diplomatic and military adventures of Duke Odoardo Farnese (ruled 1628 to 1646) that began in 1633.[92] In a reversal of his father's policy, Odoardo sought to free his state from what he saw as bondage to Spain, so he allied himself with France. Egged on by Cardinal Richelieu and his emissaries, Odoardo, together with the dukes of Mantua and Modena, raised troops and invaded Spanish-ruled Lombardy. The military campaign went badly; Spanish troops routed Odoardo's forces and occupied Parma. Odoardo sued for peace, which was arranged in 1637, with the result that Odoardo was once again under Spanish influence.[93]

This was followed by the even more foolish wars of Castro of 1641–1644 and 1649 between Parma and the papacy for which Duke Odoardo and Pope Urban VIII shared responsibility. The Duchy of Castro and Ronciglione, in Lazio, was a Farnese enclave deep inside the papal state. The Duchy of Castro was a patch of land located about 50 miles north of Rome. It consisted of a territory 31 miles long by 25 miles wide extending from the shores of Lake Bolsena south to the Tyrrhenian Sea. Ronciglione and some nearby towns were a noncontiguous part of the duchy located about 30 miles north of Rome. Pope Paul III had awarded Castro and Ronciglione to Pier Luigi Farnese in 1545 as part of the Duchy of Parma and Piacenza, a fief that made the dukes of Parma vassals of the pope. Castro's economy depended on growing grain and selling it in Rome.

Duke Odoardo had borrowed heavily against the Castro harvest to finance his failed military campaign in Lombardy, thereby incurring large debts to Roman creditors. Strongly encouraged by his bellicose nephews, Pope Urban VIII (1623–1644) wanted to incorporate the Duchy of Castro

91. Baldini 2002, 317–18, and Grendler 2016, 23–24.

92. The comments of Orazio Smeraldi, who was in Parma throughout this period, summarize the situation for the Jesuits. "Non durò molto tempo quest'allegrezza; perche sopra giungendo gli garbugli bellici l'ann. 1633 che seguitarono fino al 1644 e turbandosi perciò la quiete publica molto restò turbato la privata ancora del Collegio e si ridusse a molto pochi." "Seguitarono li medesima causa de strepiti militari, che tenero l'Italia tutta sospesa o sollevata, come è noto sino al 1644." Smeraldi, "De' principii," 147, 85.

93. Pastor 1888–1953, 28:348–49; Quazza 1950, 482–85; Tocci 1979, 267–68; and especially the detailed account of Hanlon 2014.

into the papal state. He took advantage of Odoardo's debts and the duke's diplomatic insults to the Barberini nephews to demand the Duchy of Castro in lieu of payment. Odoardo refused, both sides mobilized, the pope excommunicated Duke Odoardo, and papal forces captured Castro in October 1641. Urban VIII also seized Farnese possessions in Rome, including the Farnese palace. Duke Odoardo marched south, seized some towns at the northern perimeter of the papal state and then Castro from the inept papal army. Other Italian states became involved; the French threatened to intervene, which drew Spain's interest. The war ground on at enormous expense; but little action occurred until March 1644 when a Venetian army routed a papal army near Ferrara and nearly captured Cardinal Antonio Barberini, nephew of Urban VIII. At this point the papacy and Parma made peace, which restored the status quo before the war, including removal of the excommunication. Castro remained part of the Farnese state.[94]

The second Castro war began when the newly appointed bishop of Castro was assassinated en route to Castro on March 18, 1649. Since the young Duke Ranuccio II (1630–1694, r. from 1646) had not recognized the appointment and had refused to pay the Roman debts owed by his late father, suspicion fell on him and his court. Pope Innocent X (Pamphili, 1644–1655) took immediate action. His army besieged Castro and captured it on September 2, 1649. It then razed the town, destroying every building including the churches and the Farnese palace. Abandoned by other Italian states, Ranuccio II was forced to cede the Duchy of Castro to the papacy.[95]

The Parma Jesuits took precautions and maintained a lower profile during the wars. One reason for caution was that some saw the Jesuits as papal agents, even though they were close to the Farnese. From about 1620 through 1635 the college of San Rocco had 60 to 70 Jesuits, including 20 to 30 scholastics studying philosophy and theology. The noble school had an additional eight Jesuits.[96] In 1636, during the military campaign in Lombardy, the Jesuits moved their philosophy scholastics to Mantua and their theology scholastics to Bologna.[97] This lowered the number of Jesuits at San Rocco from 25 to 30 because, with the scholastics gone, fewer priests and temporal coadjutors were needed. After the wars ended, the Jesuits returned only a few scholastics to Parma because the Jesuit schools at Bologna and Mantua had grown in importance. On the other hand, the number of

94. Pastor 1888–1953, 29:382–401; Tocci 1979, 268–70; Nussdorfer 1992, 203–27 with maps; and Hanlon 2014, 211–14.
95. Pastor 1888–1953, 30:369–71; Tocci 1979, 278–80.
96. See the relevant references in note 77.
97. Baldini 1992, 405, 432–33.

Jesuits at the noble school, the pride of the Farnese dynasty, remained at eight. When the first Castro war began, the Jesuits had moved the noble school to Carpi, thirty miles east, for the academic year 1641–1642, but returned it the following academic year.[98]

After losing Castro, Duke Ranuccio II avoided war during the rest of his long rule. The Jesuit community returned to its previous numbers minus some scholastics. The University of Parma continued to be a medium-sized Italian university through the seventeenth and eighteenth centuries with 25 to 32 professors in most years, typically 10 to 12 legists, 8 to 11 professors of medicine, and 8 to 10 Jesuits.[99] For example, in 1696 there were 71 Jesuits at Parma, including nine teachers for the university (two for scholastic theology, and one each for cases of conscience, scripture, metaphysics, natural philosophy, logic, mathematics, and rhetoric) and three lower school teachers. Another Jesuit taught the duke's children. The annual income of the Jesuit college was 4,325 Roman scudi, a substantial sum. Eighteen Jesuits lived in the noble school, including five scholastics who studied and served as tutors (called *ripetitori*) to noble boys.[100]

Around 1660 the Jesuits requested several changes in the teaching schedule and pedagogical practices of the university. The Parma Jesuits petitioned the duke to change the daily lecture schedule of the university to give them ninety minutes for their classes.[101] They wanted an hour-long lecture followed by a half-hour of review (*ripetitione per mez'hora*).[102] This was what the Ratio Studiorum recommended, and what the Jesuits did in their schools unconnected to an Italian university.[103] But it would be a significant change, because almost all Italian universities allowed only one hour for lectures. At the same time the Jesuits wished to avoid schedule conflicts with, and ill will from, the professors of law and medicine who

98. Baldini 2002, 298n77.

99. See, for example, rolls of 1666–1667 (25 professors) and 1677–1678 (21 professors delivering 25 daily lectures) in ASPr, Archivio del Comune di Parma, Studio, bu. 1909, no foliation; and salaries for 20 legists and 9 medical professors in 1697, and 10 legists and 12 medical professors for 1707 in ASPr, Istruzione pubblica farnesiana, bu. 1, no foliation. Payments to the Jesuits are not listed.

100. ARSI, Veneta 49, ff. 45r–v, 122r.

101. ASPr, Istruzione pubblica farnesiana, bu. 1, no foliation, undated (probably early 1660s) petition.

102. ASPr, Istruzione pubblica farnesiana, bu. 1, no foliation, point one of the undated petition.

103. "Review [Repetitio] in the classes. When the lessons are over, some should go over them for a half-hour among themselves in groups of about ten, with one of their Jesuit fellow students put in charge of each of these groups, if possible." *Ratio Studiorum* 2005, 106 (par. 230), instructions for teachers of philosophy.

lectured for one hour. So the Jesuits proposed that the university's lecture timetable be changed. In the morning the law and medicine professors should teach from hour 15 and one-half to hour 16 and one-half (about 9:30 to 10:30 a.m. in November), and Jesuits would teach from hour 16 and one-half to hour 18 (10:30 a.m. to noon in November). Then the law and medicine professors would lecture at hour 18. The Jesuits proposed a similar timetable for the afternoon.[104] Subsequent rolls demonstrated that the university adapted a variation on the Jesuit proposal by scheduling some lectures to begin on the half-hour. The Jesuits had also made an accommodation. They scheduled all their lectures in the late morning (hour 16, at 10 a.m.) and the late afternoon (hours 20 and one-half and 21 and one-half, at 2:30 and 3:30 p.m. in November). That left the law and medicine professors free to lecture on the hour in the early morning and in the early afternoon and mid-afternoon.[105]

In practice, probably few students experienced schedule conflicts before or after the changes. It is not likely that many law and medicine students attended lectures in metaphysics, mathematics, or theology. They might attend rhetoric, logic, and/or natural philosophy lectures in their first year in preparation for the study of medicine or civil law. But after the first year they probably attended law or medicine lectures exclusively. And some students attended lectures only in their major subject, one or two a day, throughout their university careers.[106] Moreover, the thirty-minute review sessions after Jesuit lectures might be seen as structured circular disputations. These were meetings of a professor and students in the piazza after the lecture in which the professor and his students disputed informally the material of the lecture. Some Italian universities required daily or weekly circular disputations; in other universities they were an optional practice that professors ignored.[107]

The Jesuits also petitioned the duke that Jesuit professors be allowed to use Saturdays (an ordinary lecture day) for student disputations that focused on the week's lectures. They wanted monthly disputations involving all their teachers and students. They further pointed out that the Jesuit academic year was considerably longer than the university academic year: the

---

104. ASPr, Istruzione pubblica farnesiana, bu. 1, no foliation.

105. See the university rolls of 1666–1667 and 1677–1678 in ASPr, Archivio del Comune di Parma, Studio, bu. 1909, no foliation.

106. For example, the famous historian and political writer Francesco Guicciardini attended only law lectures, one or two daily, in six years of study at the universities of Pisa, Ferrara, and Padua, from 1498 to 1505. Grendler 2002, 148–49.

107. Grendler 2002, 156.

Jesuit academic year lasted from November through August, while the university academic year was November through June, and sometimes shorter in practice.[108] The requests came directly from the pages of the Ratio Studiorum.[109] Although the duke's response is unknown, the Jesuits did follow their own vacation schedule.[110]

The petitions and responses suggest that over the years Jesuit pedagogical practices had some power over the university. Moreover, the Jesuits obtained more autonomy for their classes. But more autonomy may also have produced greater isolation and a smaller role in the larger university. And a major question is, did the Jesuits teach more or fewer university students over time? Unfortunately, the documents do not provide an answer.

The Jesuits embarked on a major building program in the second half of the seventeenth century. It began when Giovanni Federico Cusani (Parma 1624–1692 Parma), the grandson and heir of Galeazzo Cusani de Monacis, decided to become a Jesuit. While in the St. Ignatius novice house at Bologna between 1646 and 1649, he offered all of his worldly goods to the Parma Jesuits for a building in which the Jesuits would live and teach. He did it "for the love of St. Ignatius." Many details had to be resolved and a building planned, all subject to the approval of the Jesuit general in Rome, before the donation was formally approved in 1662. Part of the initial payment of 80,000 lire in 1656 was invested in order to provide future income. Other donors, including Cusani's brother, Giovanni Carlo Cusani, also a Jesuit, and his uncle, Giovanni Paolo Cusani, a Barnabite in Bologna, contributed their patrimonies. Properties and houses around the Oratorio of San Rocco and Jesuit school were purchased, and construction of the immense building began in 1662.[111]

In an unusual move, the Jesuit general in 1694 placed Cusani in charge of construction, reasoning that rectors sometimes had their own ideas and failed to honor the wishes of donors and predecessors, words that could not have pleased the Parma rector. Construction slowed in 1729 and halted in 1733, with the building not quite finished. The Jesuits then lived and taught in this imposing structure, a new Collegio di San Rocco. By this date many in the city were complaining that the Jesuits had erected a grandiose build-

108. ASPr, Istruzione pubblica farnesiana, bu. 1, no foliation and no date.

109. *Ratio Studiorum* 2005, 26, 106–7, 110, 145, 149 (pars. 60, 231, 241, 350, and 357).

110. The Jesuits at the University of Parma stopped teaching on the vigil of St. Bartholomew (August 23), while the rhetoric class continued until September 8. ARSI, Veneta 94, Consuetudines ed ordinationes di Venetia 1569–1667, ff. 5v–6r, no date but clearly between 1601 and 1667.

111. Arrigoni Bertini 2002.

ing but had neglected the "cult of God" and the people of Parma, who needed a larger church. So in 1737 the Jesuits began to tear down the Oratorio of San Rocco and replace it with the elegant late Baroque church of San Rocco. Completed with a campanile around 1754, it was a part of the College of San Rocco but with its own entrance.[112]

The size of the Parma Jesuit community remained steady in the eighteenth century. In 1746 there were 55 Jesuits in the College of San Rocco, which provided the same nine university teachers and three lower school teachers as in 1696. Another 12 Jesuits oversaw 85 boarders in the noble school.[113] In 1751 the Jesuits added a second mathematician who taught at the court, probably for the benefit of pages and others interested in mathematics.[114] In 1767 there were 52 Jesuits at the College of San Rocco, including three lower school teachers and the same nine upper level teachers as in 1746, plus the second mathematician.[115]

Some of the Jesuits who taught the three philosophical subjects and mathematics were distinguished scholars who explored new fields and published many works.[116] For example, Jacopo Belgrado (Udine 1723–1789/90 Udine) taught mathematics from 1738 to 1750, then became court mathematician and confessor to Duke Ferdinando di Borbone, which gave him more time for research. He published extensively on mathematics, mechanics, archeology, and especially electricity. Exiled with the other Jesuits in 1768, he became rector at the Jesuit college in Bologna where he continued his scholarship. There he strongly resisted the policies of the cardinal archbishop of Bologna, Vincenzo Malvezzi, a virulent enemy of the Jesuits, and was arrested and deported in 1773. He then retired to Udine and was honored with memberships in several scientific societies including that of Paris.[117]

112. Arrigoni Bertini 2002. See also Dossi 1964, no pag.; and Cardinali and Galanti 1992.

113. ARSI, Veneta 59, ff. 338r, 339r.

114. Baldini 2002, 307–9 and 307n175. In 1767 the Jesuit catalogue for Parma described the second mathematician as "leg. mathe. in acad. Reg.," thus calling the venue a royal academy. ARSI, Veneta 91, printed catalogue of the Province of Venice, 13r.

115. ARSI, Veneta 91, 13r–14v in a printed catalogue of the Province of Venice. Unfortunately, there is no information on the Parma noble school in this document.

116. Baldini 2005, provides a good overview.

117. Cappelletti 1979; Mellinato 2001a; and Baldini 2002, 306–8, all with more bibliography.

Suppression

The direct line of the Farnese lost the Duchy of Parma and Piacenza in the eighteenth century.[118] Francesco Farnese (1678–1728, r. from 1694), second son of Duke Ranuccio II, succeeded his father. In 1696 Francesco married the widow of his elder brother Odoardo, Dorothea Sophia of Neuburg, a union contracted in order to hold on to her rich dowry, which the debt-ridden duke needed, and to preserve good relations with the Vienna Habsburgs, to whom she was connected. Dorothea Sophia, who was eighteen years older than Francesco, did not produce an heir. The duchy passed to his younger brother Antonio Farnese (1679–1731, r. from 1727), a man devoted to idleness, pleasure, and prodigious spending. He quickly married, but the union produced no children. With his death the direct line of the Farnese ended.

The Duchy of Parma and Piacenza became a pawn on the chessboard of Europe to be pursued, captured, or sacrificed for greater gain by the great powers. After a spirited diplomatic competition with France and Austria, Spain won. It was decided that Carlo I Bourbon-Parma (1716–1788) would become duke of Parma and Piacenza in 1732. He was the son of King Phillip V Bourbon of Spain and his queen, the very ambitious Elisabetta Farnese (1692–1766), who was the daughter of Odoardo Farnese and Dorothea Sophia of Neuberg. The new dynasty was named Bourbon-Parma (Borbone-Parma or di Borbone in Italian). Parma was a prize but not the highest prize. After becoming duke of Parma and Piacenza, Carlo immediately mustered an army, conquered Naples, and became king of Naples in 1734. When Philip V died in 1759 he became King Carlos III of Spain. However, Parma and Piacenza were ceded to Austria in 1735 and then returned to the Spanish Bourbons in 1748 at the Treaty of Aix-la-Chapelle which ended the War of the Austrian Succession. In 1748 Filippo di Borbone (1720–1765, r. from 1748), the second son of Philip V of Spain and Elisabetta Farnese, became duke of Parma, Piacenza, and Guastalla, a nearby territory that had been ruled by a cadet branch of the Gonzaga of Mantua. When Duke Filippo di Borbone married a daughter of King Louis XV of France, Parma came under French influence.

The most important event in the rule of Duke Filippo di Borbone was the arrival of Léon Guillaume du Tillot (1711–1774), a Frenchman of modest lineage and strong Enlightenment views. He quickly became first minister of the government and wielded enormous power that continued

118. For what follows, see Gencarelli 1961; Tocci 1979, 283–316; Romanello 1993, 1996, 1997a, and 1997b, each with additional bibliography.

with the next duke, Ferdinando di Borbone (1751–1802, r. from 1765), son of Filippo di Borbone. Tillot pursued an aggressive policy of limiting the rights of the church in the duchy and separating the Parma church from the papacy, which the weak Ferdinando accepted.[119]

The Jesuits maintained their position for a while. All the above dukes strongly supported the noble school which the Jesuits directed. But the number of boarders declined. Like his predecessors, Ferdinando di Borbone had a Jesuit tutor but only until the age of seven. Other tutors with strong *philosophe* and anti-clerical views followed. Etienne Bonnot de Condillac (1715–1780), who articulated a philosophy of sensationalism, that is, the theory that everything depended on the senses, became Ferdinando's most important teacher.

The attack on the Jesuits came in 1768. King Carlos III of Spain expelled the Jesuits from Spain and Spanish territories on April 1 and 3, 1767. The Kingdom of Naples, also ruled by a Spanish Bourbon, followed suit in November 1767. Tillot persuaded Duke Ferdinando di Borbone, the nephew of Carlos III, to do the same. Without warning, Duke Ferdinando expelled the Jesuits from the duchy of Parma and Piacenza on the night of February 7/8, 1768. All the Jesuits in the duchy were ordered to gather their personal possessions and were escorted to the borders of the duchy.[120] While most Jesuit properties were sold at auction, the large Collegio di San Rocco building became the home of the University of Parma, now deprived of Jesuits. Its curriculum and structure were reorganized along Enlightenment and anti-Jesuit principles.[121] The direction of the noble boarding school was entrusted to the Piarists (Poor Clerics Regular of the Mother of God of the Pious Schools). They were soon replaced by other clergymen, who failed to halt its decline. It closed in 1830.

In 1771 Duke Ferdinando di Borbone partially repented of his actions and dismissed Tillot. After the suppression of 1773 he began to invite back some former Jesuits, especially Spanish Jesuits, an early step on the long road to the restoration of the Society of Jesus. Some of the Spanish ex-Jesuits assumed important positions in the duchy, including teaching at a boarding school in Piacenza. But they were not invited back into the University of Parma nor permitted to open a school.[122] Duke Ferdinando di Borbone conferred a title on Jacopo Belgrado, his former confessor, but did not persuade him to return to Parma.[123]

119. Pastor 1888–1953, 37:264–73, 275; Venturi 1976, 214–36.
120. Pastor 1888–1953, 37:249–59; Tocci 1979, 306–7.
121. Tocci 1979, 309–15.   122. Bangert 1986, 422; Olmi 2010.
123. Mellinato 2001a.

Today the Collegio di San Rocco building is the administrative center of the state University of Parma; it houses the office of the rector, the Aula Magna, natural history collections, and classrooms. The Church of San Rocco passed through the hands of several religious orders until it was restored to the Jesuits when they were permitted to return Parma in 1844, only to be expelled again in 1848. The Jesuits returned permanently to Parma in 1916 and regained possession of the Church of San Rocco.[124]

Conclusion

The University of Parma came into being because both the Jesuits and Duke Ranuccio I wanted a university. Together they created the civic-Jesuit University of Parma, a new model for Italy. In so doing the Jesuits abandoned the quest to create their own collegiate university. This marked a significant change from the goal of Loyola, Nadal, the Constitutions, and the effort at Messina. The Jesuits did not need to try to insert themselves into an existing university, as at Turin. Nor did they build a large school that an existing university might see as a threat, as at Padua.

At Parma the Jesuits accepted the smaller but still substantial role of teaching theology, philosophy, mathematics, and the humanities in a medium-sized law and medicine civic university. They filled one-third of the professorships but delivered more than a third of the lectures. The duke and the Society split governance. The duke appointed the professors of law and medicine, while the Jesuits decided which of their number would fill the other positions. The Jesuits were integrated into the university. For the first time a group of Italian Jesuits were able to teach the full Jesuit curriculum to university students, to participate in degree examinations, and to become members of a college of doctors of theology. The creation of the University of Parma in 1601 was a major gain for the Jesuits of the Province of Venice reeling from the forced closure of the Padua school to external students and the approaching banishment from the Republic of Venice. Subsequent dukes and Jesuits at Parma continued to honor the pact that Ranuccio I and Possevino forged. Jesuit participation in the University of Parma continued until 1768, when they were banished from the duchy.

Although part of the university, the Jesuits were also separate and autonomous. They taught in a building somewhat distant from the building in which law and medicine lectures were delivered. The Jesuits introduced many of their own pedagogical practices that differed from university tra-

---

124. For the history of the Jesuits in Parma after 1768, see Dossi 1964.

ditions. They wanted to create a Catholic spiritual environment in the university, but their degree of success is impossible to measure.

Over time, relations between the Society and the Farnese dynasty became quite close. Jesuits heard the confessions of Farnese dukes and their consorts, tutored Farnese sons, went on minor diplomatic missions for Ranuccio I, praised him and other Farnese dukes as Christian rulers, received gifts, and enjoyed the hospitality of the court.[125] The Parma Jesuits were seen, accurately, as supporters of the regime. And much scholarship views the Jesuits as inevitable allies of the absolutist rulers of small Catholic states, even though Jesuit political theory presents a mixed attitude. However, the agreement that created the University of Parma was the product of circumstances and timing. At a certain moment Ranuccio I and Jesuits wanted something that the other side offered, and thus they made a pact that benefited both.

While he strongly supported education, Ranuccio I was also a ruthless despot. In 1612 he arrested, tortured, and executed thirteen men and women accused of conspiring to overthrow him, while another man died during torture. Others spent years in prison, and both the executed and imprisoned saw their lands confiscated. Even worse, some of his victims were probably innocent. Ranuccio's actions provoked international criticism.[126] They must also have caused dismay and moral repugnance among members of the Society. Ranuccio's crimes inevitably tainted the reputation of the Jesuits because of their partnership. This was the price they paid for an association that permitted them to teach in a university and run a famous noble boarding school.

The civic-Jesuit University of Parma was the first university collaboration between the Jesuits and an Italian ruler. A second duke and another Jesuit community will soon follow.

125. Aricò 2002.
126. Solari 1968, 163–201; Hanlon 2014, 7–8.

7

THE CIVIC-JESUIT UNIVERSITY

OF MANTUA

Duke Ferdinando Gonzaga created the Peaceful University of Mantua in 1625. It was an Italian law and medicine university in which the Jesuits taught theology, philosophy, mathematics, and the humanities. It quickly became a medium-sized university with an innovative curriculum. But war closed it in the autumn of 1629, and plague and a sack devastated Mantua in 1630.

University law and medicine instruction never returned to Mantua. However, the Jesuits slowly rebuilt their school, including scholastic theology in 1684. They believed that they had restored their part of the University of Mantua. With the consent of another Gonzaga duke, they began to award doctorates in theology and philosophy. This Jesuit partial university lasted until laws against religious orders in the 1760s and the suppression of the Society in 1773 closed it.

The Jesuits Come to Mantua

The Jesuits founded a college and school in Mantua in 1584.[1] Cardinal Ercole Gonzaga of Mantua (1505–1563), de facto ruler of Mantua as regent for two underage dukes, had persuaded General Laínez that the Jesuits should establish a college with a school in Mantua in early 1563. But Cardinal Gonzaga suddenly died on March 2, 1563, and the Jesuits did not come. He did leave a substantial legacy for a Jesuit college in Mantua that went unclaimed. Then Duke Guglielmo Gonzaga (1538–1587), regent after 1550 and

1. The first four sections of this chapter provide a condensed history of the Jesuit school in Mantua and the Peaceful University of Mantua to 1630. In order to conserve space, the notes provide only the most important archival and other references. For details and full documentation see Grendler 2009b.

ruler in his own right after 1559 of two duchies—Mantua and Monferrato, the latter in northwestern Italy but separated from Mantua by Spanish-ruled Lombardy—and his consort, Duchess Eleonora Habsburg of Austria (1534–1594), decided to activate Ercole Gonzaga's will. After negotiations in which Antonio Possevino, a native of Mantua, spoke for the Jesuits, agreement was reached. The Jesuits received Ercole's legacy, plus gifts and income-bearing lands deeded to the Jesuits by Duke Guglielmo, and a substantial gift from Duchess Eleonora. A church and a building were found for the Jesuits. Fourteen Jesuits arrived, and the school formally opened on November 21, 1584. It offered the usual three classes of rhetoric, humanities, and grammar. A class in cases of conscience was added in or about 1586.[2]

The short, holy life of Luigi Gonzaga brought the Gonzaga family and the Jesuits very close. Luigi (Aloysius in English) Gonzaga (1568–1591) was the eldest son of a cadet branch of the family that ruled Castiglione delle Stiviere, a town about twenty-two miles northwest of Mantua guarding the southern end of Lake Garda. His father was the signore and later marquis of Castiglione delle Stiviere and a professional soldier who fought for Philip II of Spain. Consequently, the boy Luigi spent time at the Spanish and other courts far above his family's modest rank. In 1584 he informed his father that he wished to renounce his right of succession in order to become a Jesuit. After receiving his father's blessing, he entered the Jesuit novice house in Rome on November 25, 1585, and studied in Rome and Naples. He devoted himself to prayer, fasting, and caring for the sick. Members of the Jesuit community in Rome increasingly saw him as a saint.[3]

Because of his perceived holiness, he exerted influence in Mantua as well. In July 1585 he undertook Loyola's Spiritual Exercises while living in a little room in the Jesuit college in Mantua. In 1589 and 1590 General Acquaviva ordered Luigi, still a Jesuit scholastic, back to Mantua, where he resolved a fierce quarrel between Duke Vincenzo I Gonzaga of Mantua (1562–1612, r. from 1587) and Luigi's violent brother, who had become marquis of Castiglione delle Stiviere. While in Mantua he again lived in the Jesuit college. For his peacemaking and piety, many in Mantua and Castiglione viewed him as a holy man.[4] Back in Rome, he devoted himself to caring for the sick during a period of raging disease. He fell ill on March 3, and died on June 21, 1591.

2. Grendler 2009b, 24–25, 29–32, 48–49.
3. Grendler 2009b, 41–45.
4. Grendler 2009b, 44–45.

A cult of Luigi sprang up in Rome, Castiglione delle Stiviere, and elsewhere, as people began to see him in visions. Requests for beatification and canonization arose spontaneously. Duke Vincenzo I, additional Gonzaga family members, Roman Jesuits, and others pleaded his cause in Rome. On June 21, 1605, Pope Paul V proclaimed him "blessed." He was only the second Jesuit so honored, preceded by Stanislaus Kostka (1550–1568) in 1602. Ignatius Loyola had to wait until 1609.[5]

The Mantua Jesuits and the Gonzaga rejoiced together in Luigi's beatification. The Gonzaga were proud that their house had produced a holy man, and the Jesuits were proud that he was "one of ours." The Jesuits set aside the room in their college that he had briefly occupied as a shrine and a place of meditation, and declared Luigi patron of the Mantuan college. His life and the aftermath produced a bond between Jesuits and Gonzaga, even when Gonzaga dukes did not act in righteous ways. No other Italian ruling family had such strong public, emotional, and spiritual links with the Society of Jesus.[6] Luigi Gonzaga and Stanislaus Kostka were canonized together on December 31, 1726, and Luigi was declared a patron of youth.

In the meantime the Jesuit school in Mantua added a course in logic in 1595, and the number of Jesuits slowly grew to twenty in 1600. When the Society was expelled from the Republic of Venice in 1606, some Jesuits came to Mantua, a natural destination because the Duchy of Mantua and the Venetian Republic had a common border. The Jesuits added a philosophy class, probably natural philosophy, in 1607. There were twenty-two Jesuits in Mantua in 1622.[7]

The next, audacious goal was a university. The rulers and leading citizens of Mantua had long desired one. Marquis Gian Francesco Gonzaga (1395–1444, r. from 1407) asked Emperor Sigismund I of Luxembourg (r. 1410–1437) for a university charter when the emperor visited Mantua, and the emperor responded on September 27, 1433. Emperor Albert II (r. 1438–1439) confirmed the university privileges on January 1, 1439. So did Emperor Frederick III (r. 1440–1493) on December 21, 1442, and again on August 27, 1455. University privileges were also conferred on a Mantuan monastery and an academy of learned men by Charles V (r. 1519–1556) and Pope Pius IV (1559–1564).[8] But nothing happened. Obtaining a charter was easy. Creating a functioning university by recruiting professors to teach, finding the money to pay them, and attracting students was difficult. No Gonzaga marquis or duke attempted to found a university in the fifteenth

5. Grendler 2009b, 46–47.

7. Grendler 2009b, 48–49, 52.

6. Grendler 2009b, 48; Logan 2011.

8. Grendler 2009b, 54–59.

and sixteenth centuries. Nevertheless, the Gonzaga dukes in the second half of the sixteenth and the early seventeenth centuries strongly supported learning. They hired university professors to tutor their sons. They supported major scholars, authors, artists, and musicians, as well as alchemists and others of dubious learning.

Duke Ferdinando Gonzaga

Ferdinando Gonzaga (1587–1626, regent from 1613, duke from 1616) was the second son of Duke Vincenzo I Gonzaga and Duchess Eleonora de' Medici (1567–1611). He had a thirst for learning and was the most intellectually gifted Italian ruler since Lorenzo de' Medici (1449–1494). And he esteemed the Jesuits. Ferdinando and his elder brother Francesco (1586–1612) often visited the Jesuit college as boys. Ferdinando made his first confession to a Jesuit and, after preparing himself with the aid of the Spiritual Exercises, made his first communion at about the age of nine.[9] Because he was a second son, his destiny was to serve his family in the church. Because he was a Gonzaga of Mantua, he would be a cardinal. Hence, he needed to be educated well.

His most important tutor was Giovanni Antonio Magini (1555–1617), a long-time professor of mathematics and astronomy at the University of Bologna. He published several works, corresponded with Johann Kepler and Tycho Brahe, and was both a friend and critic of Galileo Galilei. He argued that Copernicus had devised hypotheses that fit the positions of the stars and the planets very well. But he rejected heliocentrism and esteemed Aristotle. Thus, he was open to new ideas but retained a conservative core, a position that Ferdinando and the Jesuits found congenial. Beginning in 1599, Magini taught mathematics to Ferdinando and Francesco, then twelve and thirteen respectively, for about two years.[10]

When Ferdinando was fourteen, his father sent him to the University of Ingolstadt in Bavaria for the academic year 1601–1602 because he wanted him to learn German. Ingolstadt at that time was a part Jesuit, part civic university: Jesuits taught arts and theology, while a small number of lay professors taught law and medicine. The Jesuits also taught in the paedagogium, the secondary school that prepared students for university studies. There students, some eighteen percent of them nobles, studied the standard Jesuit lower school curriculum plus a little logic. Ferdinando was a student

---

9. Grendler 2009b, 59.
10. Grendler 2009b, 59–60. For Magini, see Baldini 2006b.

in the *pedagogium* and may have heard some university lectures as well. As the son of a ruling family he lived in a house with tutors and several priests, and the rector of the Jesuit college at Ingolstadt heard his confessions.[11]

After the year at Ingolstadt, Ferdinando returned to Mantua for about eighteen months where he received more instruction from Magini and probably others. In fall 1603 he enrolled in the University of Pisa. Very few princes from Italian ruling families attended universities. Those who did were usually second sons with the necessary intellectual capacity who were intended for the church, which exactly described Ferdinando. And there was a family precedent. Ercole Gonzaga studied at the University of Bologna for two and a half years, during which time Pietro Pomponazzi was his mentor.[12] Ferdinando arrived at Pisa at the age of sixteen and a half, twelve to eighteen months younger than the average entering student in Italian universities. He studied at Pisa through the first half of 1607, nearly four years.

Ferdinando wanted to study natural philosophy. But his great-uncle Grand Duke Ferdinando I de' Medici (1549–1609, r. from 1587), who oversaw his university education, insisted that he study law. This was customary and sensible advice for a future prince of the church, because the vast majority of Italian popes, cardinals, papal diplomats, and bishops studied law rather than theology. Ferdinando Gonzaga bowed to the wishes of his great uncle and studied law. But he also read natural philosophy as time allowed. On February 19, 1605, Ferdinando Gonzaga participated in an informal disputation in his house in Pisa. For two hours he put forward twenty-two arguments in the process of defending six legal and six philosophical propositions against two other students and nine *dottori*, men with doctorates who might or might not have been professors. Ferdinando's minders sent glowing accounts of his intellectual prowess to Duke Vincenzo I, which others, not beholden to the Gonzaga family, confirmed.[13] And he continued to demonstrate wide-ranging curiosity. He applied to the Congregation of the Holy Office in Rome for permission to read Paracelsus (Theophrastus Philippus Aureolus Bombastus von Hohenheim, ca. 1493–1541), whose works combined theories of chemical medicine with alchemy, anti-church sentiments, and much else, and were prohibited by the 1596 Index of Prohibited Books. The Holy Office denied his request in May 1606.[14]

11. Chambers 1987, 116–18.
13. Chambers 1987, 118–24.
14. Baldini 2001, 175n14.

12. Murphy 2007, 5–13.

Ferdinando wanted a doctorate, but his advisers advised against it because it would be expensive and politically inappropriate. The 1544 statutes of the University of Pisa required all recipients of doctoral degrees to swear an oath of allegiance to the grand duke of Tuscany, an unusual requirement in Italy.[15] Even though the oath had an escape clause and was not universally enforced, the son of the duke of Mantua could not swear fealty to the ruler of another state, even his friendly great-uncle. Thus Ferdinando did not get a doctorate.

He returned to Mantua in June 1607, and Pope Paul V named him a cardinal on December 10, 1607, when Ferdinando was twenty years and seven months old. The Mantuan Jesuits marked his elevation by inviting him to their college for a celebration.[16] His affection and admiration for the Jesuits was genuine. At some point in his youth he vowed to become a Jesuit. But his father obtained a release from the vow from the Sacred Penitentiary in Rome.[17] The vow must have been more than a pledge to himself if it caused Vincenzo I to apply to Rome for release. After becoming a cardinal, Ferdinando remained in Mantua for the next two years, studying botany, composing madrigals, and organizing musical and dramatic events.

Cardinal Ferdinando took up residence in Rome in early 1610. His Vatican duties were minor, although his appointment to the Congregation of Rites, which evaluated candidates for beatification and canonization, gave him the opportunity to urge the canonization of (then Blessed) Luigi Gonzaga. He had ample opportunity to pursue his intellectual and artistic interests. He created a laboratory where he engaged in alchemical experiments under the guidance of Magini. He haunted the Vatican Library where he spent hours in discussion with scholars and notables; after becoming duke he continued to visit the Vatican Library when in Rome. In 1610 he obtained a papal pardon for the painter Caravaggio (Michelangelo Merisi) who had killed a man. He composed more music and lyrics. And he ran up large bills. Partly to avoid his creditors he retreated to Mantua in early 1611.[18]

In Mantua he continued his engagement with contemporary scientific matters and the Jesuits. In May 1611 he arranged for a public mathematical presentation on the height of the mountains on the moon based on telescopic observations and mathematical presentations by the Jesuit mathematician Giuseppe Biancani, then teaching at the University of Parma. Biancani repeated his presentation privately for Ferdinando.[19]

15. Chambers 1987, 122n63. On the oath, see Cascio Pratilli 1975, 140, 142–43; and Mango Tomei 1976, 38–39.

16. Gorzoni 1997, 101–2, 107.   17. Chambers 1987, 126–27.

18. Grendler 2009b, 65–66.   19. Grendler 2009b, 66–67.

In fall 1611 Ferdinando went further. During a visit to Florence he participated in a luncheon dispute about the buoyancy of waters. On one side of the table sat, figuratively and maybe physically, Galileo Galilei and Cardinal Maffeo Barberini (b. 1568), the future Urban VIII (1623–1644). On the other side were Cardinal Ferdinando and Flaminio Pappazoni (ca. 1550–1613), who had just been appointed ordinary professor of natural philosophy at the University of Pisa after teaching at the universities of Bologna and Pavia. Pappazoni and Ferdinando defended Aristotelian views, which Galilei and Barberini rejected. Galilei looked at buoyancy as a matter of dynamics and mechanics, and followed Archimedes to some degree.[20] Given Ferdinando's Jesuit schooling and university study, it was to be expected that he would be an Aristotelian and differ from Galilei. Nevertheless, to participate in the luncheon debate he had to have some specialized knowledge and be agile enough verbally to dispute the immensely learned and sharp-tongued Galilei, even if Galilei treated him gently.

Ferdinando's life of freedom with few responsibilities abruptly ended. His father died on February 18, 1612, and Ferdinando's older brother became Duke Francesco III Gonzaga. But he suddenly died on December 22, 1612, apparently of smallpox. He left only a three-year-old daughter. Ferdinando became regent for his niece, then had to fight off Piedmont-Savoy which tried to seize the Duchy of Monferrato. He successfully petitioned the papacy for permission to renounce his cardinalate and to be allowed to marry. Since he had taken only minor orders and was not a priest, his petition was granted. Ferdinando was formally crowned duke of Mantua and duke of Monferrato on January 6, 1616. He then married, taking as his bride his second cousin Caterina de' Medici (1593–1629). This marriage solidified the Gonzaga-Medici alliance. He settled down to governing the two duchies of Mantua and Monferrato, rich and important north Italian states.[21]

As duke he continued to seek out the company of the Jesuits. In the words of the Jesuit historian of the Mantuan college, Ferdinando came at any hour and became "a familiar presence in our house." To make his visits easier and more private, Ferdinando built an elevated passageway from his palace to the houses next to the Jesuit college. Once inside the college, he donned the informal dress that Jesuits wore at home and participated in their recreations and exhortations. He made the Spiritual Exercises.[22] And

---

20. Grendler 2009b, 67. 21. Grendler 2009b, 68–73.

22. "S'era egli [Ferdinando] fatta famigliare la nostra casa, dove egli per strade private segretamente ad ogni hora veniva. Fece egli perciò far un passaggio o corridore di legno in aria che,

he became the leader of the congregation of nobles organized by the Jesuits. There was more. In 1618 Blessed Luigi Gonzaga was declared the protector of the city of Mantua, an event celebrated in grand style on his feast day, June 21. Ferdinando arranged for civic celebrations. And he placed himself, his family, and all his subjects under the protection of Blessed Luigi.[23]

The Peaceful University of Mantua

Ferdinando had larger plans that would include the Jesuits. In roughly 1622 he revealed his resolve to found a university in Mantua, and that the Jesuits would be part of it. Only two personal comments, uttered in passing, have come to light about his reasons. In June and July 1624 he wrote that a university would benefit the public, and he wanted the Jesuit part of it to begin in November of 1624, so that the city would quickly realize the benefits.[24]

This was undoubtedly true, but the larger reason was that he was a prince-savant who prized learning. He had studied law and natural philosophy at the University of Pisa, did alchemical experiments, and displayed an interest in Paracelsian chemical medicine, astronomy, astrology, and mathematics. He had agents seek out new books that might interest him.[25] He enjoyed participating in academic events, such as the debate with Galilei. In contrast to so many Gonzagas who were military commanders, Ferdinando was happiest in the company of scholars.

Ferdinando's close association with and high respect for the Jesuits meant that they would be included in his university and that the University

---

partendo dal suo palazzo, attraversava la strada detta del Zuccaro ed inoltrandosi per quelle case immediate arrivava copertamente fin al nostro collegio. Suo gusto era intervenire alle nostre ricreationi, alle nostre fonzioni di casa, alle nostre essortationi. Anzi, egli stesso, vestendo una nostra vesta da camera che noi chiamiamo vesta grossa, così faceva a' padri dotte e spiritu[ali] essortationi et a' suoi, et anzi facea gl'essercitii spirituali di sant'Ignatio." Gorzoni 1997, 120. Giuseppe Gorzoni (1637–1713) was the Jesuit historian. Although born in Mantua, he spent his career as a Jesuit elsewhere until sent to the Mantua college in 1695, where he served as the *economo*, the Jesuit in charge of the college's financial affairs. He wrote his history of the Mantua college between 1700 and his death. It is immensely valuable because Gorzoni had access to the memories of Jesuits and college documents now long gone. When his history can be checked against ASM records, it has proven to be very accurate. See Flavio Rurale's introduction in Gorzoni 1997, 34–37.

23. Grendler 2009b, 74.

24. "[A] beneficio publico." Duke Ferdinando to his brother Vincenzo, June 10, 1624, Florence, in ASM, AG, bu. 2176, Lettere originali dei Gonzaga 1624 e 1625, f. 52r. "Potrà V[ostra] I[llustrissima] far intimare à i Padri Gesuiti che debbano principiare lo studio à quatro novembre, acciò quanto più presto la città possa godere del beneficio." And Duke Ferdinando to his brother Vincenzo, July 9, 1624, Florence, in ibid., f. 109r.

25. Grendler 2009b, 72.

of Parma would be the model. He moved forward on parallel tracks to create his university. He recruited professors of law and medicine.[26] And he wanted the Society to expand the Jesuit school in Mantua into the arts and theology part of the university. The Mantua Jesuits welcomed the proposal.

Ferdinando searched for the financial means to support the Jesuits. He first tried in 1623 to persuade Pope Gregory XV (Alessandro Ludovisi, 1554–1623, pope from 1612) to permit him to use income from a very rich abbey to support the Jesuit part of the university. When Gregory XV and his successor, Urban VIII, said no, he realized that he would have to do it with his own resources. Ferdinando and the Mantua Jesuits reached agreement in principle in July, and signed a contract on December 19, 1624. Father Orazio Ferrari (Modena 1575/76–1630 Modena), rector of the Mantuan college who had previously taught philosophy at the University of Parma, signed for the Jesuits, and Duchess Caterina de' Medici, procurator general for her husband when he was absent from the city, signed for the duke.[27]

The 1584 contract had funded the original Jesuit college, a lower school, and other ministries.[28] The 1624 contract was designed to support the additional Jesuits needed to teach in the university. For this Ferdinando created a land endowment. He deeded to the Mantua Jesuits numerous agricultural properties near the village of Fabbrico in the extreme southern part of the Duchy of Mantua. The agreement stated that these properties were worth a little less than 60,000 scudi, calculated at 6 Mantuan lire equals 1 scudo. To bring the value of the endowment up to 60,000 scudi, the duke added an annuity funded by another member of the Gonzaga family. The combined annual income from the properties and annuity was expected to produce 5 percent in annual income, which would be 1,500 scudi. This was deemed enough to support twenty-five Jesuit professors and scholastics at the rate of 60 scudi each per annum. This was a minimum figure; there were forty to fifty Jesuits in Mantua in the years in which the university taught. In addition, the duke gave the Jesuits a house either contiguous with or near to the college, and he pledged to renovate it for the Jesuit university lectures.[29]

The Jesuits agreed to provide professors to teach scholastic theology, cases of conscience, metaphysics, natural philosophy, logic, mathematics,

26. This account focuses on the Jesuit presence in the University of Mantua. For Ferdinando's recruitment of scholars to teach law and medicine and his taxation schemes to pay for that part of the university, see Grendler 2009b, 82–148, 154–58.

27. For a later copy of the contract see ASM, AG, bu. 3366, ff. 28r–37v. See also the summary in Gorzoni 1997, 144–45. See Grendler 2009b, 75–78, for the negotiations, and 252 for a short biography of Ferrari. The very capable Duchess Caterina often acted for her husband.

28. Grendler 2009b, 29–32.

29. ASM, AG, bu. 3366, ff. 28r–37v. Most of the contract listed the properties.

rhetoric, and the humanities at the university. In addition, they agreed to maintain in perpetuity a minimum of twenty-five Jesuits, divided between professors and scholastics, in the Mantua college.[30] Since Ferdinando wanted the university, had ample resources, and never worried about how much he was spending, he was generous. On the other hand, the Fabbrico properties never produced the expected income. The land was not very fertile and was subject to flooding. It was relatively distant from Mantua, which made transporting produce to Mantua time-consuming and expensive. And the Jesuits lost some of the fields to local people as a result of monetary and legal disputes that Ferdinando had left unresolved. By 1628 the Jesuits wanted to exchange the Fabbrico properties for others, but the devastation of the countryside caused by war and plague that came in the following years made this impossible. The Jesuits were stuck with the Fabbrico properties, which over time yielded average annual income of 2.5 to 3 percent, about half of what was expected.[31]

On October 25, 1624, Duke Ferdinando proclaimed that the Jesuit part of the university would begin teaching in November. He named it the Public Academy of Mantua (Publica Academia Mantuana) for the time being. A roll was printed and promulgated. As at Parma, the superior of the Jesuit Province of Venice in consultation with the general in Rome chose the Jesuit professors. Nine Jesuits delivered twelve daily lectures. In addition, the roll promised that disputations on philosophical and theological questions would take place practically daily and weekly, plus more solemn disputations every month and on the afternoons of non-teaching days.

None of the Jesuits teaching at the Public Academy in 1624–1625 was a native of Mantua. Only three of them (Francesco Rossano, Cesare Moscarelli, and Giacomo Filippo Trezzi) had previously taught at the University of Parma. The Jesuits of the Province of Venice did not raid Parma for teachers for the new university, which suggests that they had a deep pool of scholarly talent.

With the Jesuit part of the university launched, Duke Ferdinando intensified his efforts to recruit law and medicine professors, especially a star

---

30. The agreement did not name the professorships that the Jesuits would fill. Instead, it stipulated that they would teach "all the disciplines usually taught in other universities of the Society" (e mantener un Studio nella città di Mantova di tutte le scienze solite leggersi nelle altre università di detta Compagnia). ASM, AG, bu. 3366, f. 37r. Gorzoni clarified that the Jesuits were obliged to fill the professorships of "teologia scolastica e morale, filosofia, matematica, retorica, belle lettere e lingue." Gorzoni 1997, 144. ARSI, Veneta 115, ff. 191r–93r, dated February 20, 1720, confirms Gorzoni's account.

31. Gorzoni 1997, 148–49, plus the introduction of Flavio Rurale in ibid., 25, 45n55; and ARSI, Veneta 115, f. 192v.

TABLE 7-1. Public Academy of Mantua Roll 1624–1625

Hour	Lecture and Texts	Jesuit Professor
	Morning	
XV	Rhetoric: Cicero, *Partitiones oratoriae* and *Pro Milone*	Giacomo Accarisi of Bologna
XVI	Theology: quaestiones de Incarnatione Verbi Divini and Sacramentis in genere	Francesco Rossano of Forlì
XVI	Natural Philosophy and Metaphysics: *De generatione*, bk. 2; *De anima*; and *Metaphysics*	Vincenzo Serugo of Forlì
XVI	Logic: Porphyry, *Isagoge*; Aristotle, *Categories*, *On interpretation*, and *Analytics*	Antonio Morando of Piacenza
XVII	Moral Philosophy: Aristotle, *Nicomachean Ethics*	Matteo Torto of Verona
	Afternoon	
XX½	Poetry: Aristotle, *Poetics*; Virgil, *Aeneid*, book 12, and Seneca, *Medea*, in alternation	Giacomo Accarisi of Bologna
XX½	Cases of Conscience: Ten Commandments	Emilio Zucchi of Parma
XX½	Mathematics: Euclid, *Elements*; Clavius, *Sphaera*; and sundials★	Cesare Moscatelli of Bologna
XXI½	Theology: questions on angels, blessedness, and human actions	Giacomo Filippo Trezzi of Innsbruck
XXI½	Natural Philosophy and Metaphysics: same texts as taught in hour XVI	Vincenzo Serugo of Forlì
XXI½	Logic: same texts as taught in hour XVI	Antonio Morando of Piacenza
XXII½	Scripture: Gospel parables	Giovanni Battista Noceto of Genoa

From *Ad Maiorem Dei Gloriam. Catalogus Patrum Societatis Iesu, qui in Publica Academia Mantuana a Serenissimo Ferdinando Gonzaga Duce VI Montisq. Ferrati IV liberaliter erecta docebunt à mense Novembri Anno domini MDCXXIV & MDCCV.* ASM, AG, bu. 3366, f. 103. The table conveys the information of the roll but is not a translation. Latin personal and place names have been rendered into Italian. Biographical information for most of the above Jesuits is found in chapter 6 and in Grendler 2009b, 251–54.

★*In Sphaeram Ioannis de Sacro Bosco commentarius* (1581 with many reprints) of Christoph Clavius is a commentary on the *De sphaera* (written ca. 1220) of Johannes de Sacrobosco (d. 1244 or 1256), the most used and commented-upon astronomical work in medieval and Renaissance universities. Clavius rejected the heliocentric system of Copernicus as physically incorrect. Sundials did a better job of measuring time than other instruments at this time; hence, mathematicians taught students how to construct and use them.

professor of law and a star professor medicine. He sought established scholars from other universities for these two positions and landed two well-known, much-published, and innovative scholars. He then filled out the rest of the law and medicine faculty with lesser-known scholars. They were men from northern Italy lacking university positions, plus local legists and physicians, some of them with publications to their credit, who had served the ducal court and/or the city. Hence, the duke was familiar with them and their achievements.[32]

Duke Ferdinando was much more generous than Ranuccio I. At Parma the duke supported the Jesuits, while the city paid the salaries of the law and medicine professors, by far the largest expense. At Mantua Ferdinando paid the law and medicine salaries, although he did raise the tax on butchered meat, a tax that mostly spared the poor, with the proceeds to go toward university expenses.[33] He also paid the Jesuits by donating from his personal holdings the properties for the land endowment. Legacies and gifts from other members of the Gonzaga family also helped.

Ferdinando named his new university the Pacifico Gymnasio Mantuano (Peaceful University of Mantua). The star legist delivered the inaugural oration on November 5, and ordinary lectures began on November 7, 1625. The roll for the academic year 1625–1626 listed twenty-nine men who filled thirty-six positions as ordinary and extraordinary professors plus two demonstrators.[34] The first explained medicinal plants in the botanical garden and the other demonstrated the distillation and preparation of chemical medicines, a position that showed a commitment to Paracelsian chemical medicine. Eleven men taught law, with four positions still vacant. Eight men filled eleven medical positions, with two places vacant. A non-Jesuit taught metaphysics. And nine Jesuits taught thirteen lectures daily: two scholastic theologians, and one Jesuit each for scripture, cases of conscience, natural philosophy, mathematics, moral philosophy, logic, and humanities. The natural philosopher and logician delivered two lectures daily.[35] The Jesuit humanities professor delivered three lectures daily, the first on texts of Cicero and Q. Curtius Rufus, the second on Horace and book 8 of Virgil's *Aeneid*, and the third on a Greek text of Basil the Great.[36]

The Jesuits taught their university classes in a building adjacent to the

32. Grendler 2009b, 83–148.

33. Grendler 2009b, 154–58.

34. *Rotulus Excellentissimorum Dominorum Doctorum legentium in Almo* Pacifico Gymnasio Mantuano *infrascriptas lecturas, quas aggredientur die v. mensis Novembris anni instantis MDCXXV.* Mantuae, Apud Aurelium & Ludovicum Osannam fratres, Ducales Impressores, 1625. ASM, AG, bu. 3366, f. 64, a large printed sheet 36 x 50 cm. It is transcribed and analyzed in Grendler 2009b, 162–65.

35. The Jesuit provincial superior failed to provide a Jesuit to teach metaphysics, which angered Ferdinando's chief minister. Hence, a secular priest was appointed to teach metaphysics. In the following academic year, 1626–1627, the Jesuits provided a metaphysician. Grendler 2009b, 152, 163–64.

36. Grendler 2009b, 164, 254.

Jesuit college. The professors of law and medicine taught in another building that had once belonged to another Gonzaga and was described as a palace with large rooms appropriate for lectures. It was contiguous with the building in which the Jesuits taught. Thus, unlike Parma, the Jesuits and the law and medicine professors lectured in side-by-side buildings. The Jesuit church of Santissima Trinità, the Jesuit college, the building for Jesuit lectures, and the building for the law and medicine lectures were four contiguous or near-contiguous buildings along the street now named Via Ardigò in a central part of Mantua.[37] The complex was sometimes called the Jesuit island.

Two years later the Peaceful University of Mantua expanded to its full projected size. It was a larger and more ambitious university in size, curriculum, and scholarly ambition than the University of Parma. It now had thirty-seven professors delivering forty-two lectures. Fourteen legists delivered sixteen lectures with two second-place positions in canon law vacant. Twelve medical scholars filled thirteen medical professorships with no unfilled positions. Ten Jesuits delivered twelve lectures daily in theology, philosophy, and the humanities. And one layman taught Tacitus, a very unusual professorship.[38] Thus, the Jesuits accounted for a little more than one fourth of the professors and the lectures.[39]

In the academic year 1627–1628 the Peaceful University of Mantua was a medium-sized Italian university, about the size of the universities of Rome and Siena, and a little larger than Parma and Turin.[40] It was intellectually innovative and vigorous. It was the first Italian university to create a professorship of chemistry at a time when only two other universities (Marburg and Jena) had them, and more than one hundred years before other Italian universities did. Two professors of medicine at Mantua practiced and taught Paracelsian chemical medicine.[41] Its star professor of medicine made some original discoveries, while its star civil law professor was a prolific scholar with new ideas.[42]

Although the Jesuits were part of the university they could not participate in the examination of doctoral candidates in medicine and philosophy.

---

37. See *Il palazzo degli studi* 1998, 20–29; and Grendler 2009b, 34–35, 161–62. Much has changed since 1625 because of the construction of the Palazzo degli Studi in the eighteenth century, the suppression of the Jesuit college, the deconsecration of the Jesuit church, and the renovation of buildings for other uses.

38. Grendler 2009b, 167–69, 195–97.

39. To be precise, the Jesuits comprised 27 percent (10 of 37) of the professors, and 29 percent (12 of 42) of the professorships.

40. Grendler 2002, 54, 61, 97–98, 132, 515.   41. Grendler 2009b, 164, 169, 178–84.

42. Grendler 2009b, 117–22, 184–91.

TABLE 7-2. Peaceful University of Mantua Roll 1627–1628

Hour	Professorship and Texts	Jesuit Professor
	Morning	
1st	Civil law (two concurrent professors)	
	Feudal law, extraordinary, holidays	
	Medical theory (two concurrents)	
2nd	Canon law (one plus one vacancy)	
	Pandects (humanistic jurisprudence)	
	Civil law, *De regulis iuris*	
	Criminal law, extraordinary, holidays	
	Theology, questions on God three and one	Francesco Rossano of Forlì
	Logic, Porphyry, *Isagoge*; Aristotle, *Categories, On Interpretation, Prior* and *Posterior Analytics*	Orazio Fontana of Bologna
	Natural Philosophy, 8 books of the *Physics*, 4 books of *De Caelo*; *De generatione* book 1	Francesco Manfredini of Modena
	Medical theory, extraordinary (two concurrents)	
3rd	Civil law, *Institutes* (two concurrents)	
	Medical botany	
	Moral philosophy, Aristotle, classes of moral virtues	Matteo Torto of Verona
	Surgery	
	Afternoon	
1st	Civil law (two concurrents)	
	Civil law, *Institutes,* extraordinary, holidays	
	Medical practice (two concurrents)	
	Logic, same texts	Orazio Fontana of Bologna
	Mathematics, Euclid, *Elements*; Clavius, *Sphaera*; pseudo-Aristotle, *Mechanics*	Cesare Moscatelli of Bologna
2nd	Canon law (one plus one vacancy)	
	Civil law, *Institutes*, extraordinary, holidays	
	Theology, questions on justice and law	Giacomo Filippo Trezzi of Innsbruck
	Cases of conscience, ecclesiastical censures	Lorenzo Megli of Sarzana
	Metaphysics, Aristotle *De anima*, *Metaphysics* book 12, *De generatione* book 2	Vincenzo Serugo of Forlì
	Natural philosophy, same texts	Francesco Manfredini of Modena
	Medical practice, extraordinary (two concurrents)	
3rd	Civil law, *Institutes* (two concurrents)	
	Sacred Scripture, *Genesis* chap. 1	François Remond of Dijon

table continues

TABLE 7-2. (*cont.*)

Hour	Professorship and Texts	Jesuit Professor
	Indeterminate	
	Chemistry (to begin January 9, 1628)	
	Greek and Latin humanities (alternate days and various hours), Cicero, *Orator, Pro Milone*; Aristotle, *Rhetoric*	Giovanni Francesco Natta of Monferrato
	Virgil, *Aeneid* book 6; Isocrates, *To Demonicus*	
	Anatomy (to begin January 17, 1628)	
	Medical botany demonstration (to begin May 2, 1628)	

From *Rotulus Excellentissimorum Dominorum Doctorum legentium in Almo PACIFICO GYMNASIO Mantuano infrascriptas lecturas, quas aggredientur die v. Novembris MDCXXVII*. Mantuae, Ex Officina Typographica Fratrum de Osannis, Ducalium Impressorum, 1627. ASM, AG, bu. 3366, f. 109. It is a large printed sheet, 36 x 50 cm. Latin names and place names have been rendered into Italian. This table focuses on the Jesuit professors and their lectures; for biographical information on them, see Grendler 2009b, 251–54. The table does not include the names of other professors, nor give complete information on the courses taught by non-Jesuits. For a full version of the roll with additional information, see Grendler 2009b, 167–69. All of the Jesuits were ordinary professors, which meant that they taught on the ordinary teaching days (Monday, Tuesday, Wednesday, Friday, and Saturday). Concurrents taught the same texts at the same hour. Extraordinary and holiday lecturers taught on Thursdays and holidays, of which there were many. They were considered less important than the ordinary professors and received lower salaries. For further explanation, see Grendler 2002, 143–48.

In November 1626 the rector of the Jesuit college complained that the medical professors had passed a decree stating that they would confer doctorates without the participation of the Jesuit professors of philosophy, meaning without them as promoters or examiners.[43] The rector pointed out that Jesuit professors in other universities participated in such exercises (which was true in Parma and Fermo) and that the Jesuit professors were equal in status with other professors.[44] This would have become a contentious issue had the university lasted longer.[45]

The Mantuan Jesuits and their students also endured some harassment. In December 1625 law students came to the logic and natural philosophy lectures and made derogatory remarks. Then they forced their way into

43. While little is known about the Mantua college of physicians, a list of members in the sixteenth, seventeenth, and eighteenth centuries does not include any Jesuits. Carra, Fornari, and Zanca 2004, 137–40.

44. Girolamo Furlani to Duke Vincenzo II, November 19, 1626, Mantua, in ASM, AG, bu. 2775, f. 539r.

45. No information about doctorates of theology or the existence of a college of doctors of theology at this time has come to light. Had the Peaceful University of Mantua endured, some procedure for conferring doctorates of theology would have had to be arranged, and it would have had to include the Jesuits.

the humanities class, grabbed a book out of the hands of the Jesuit teacher, allegedly made filthy and insulting remarks, and left, but threatened to return. The Jesuit vice-rector immediately asked Duke Ferdinando for protection, noting that the students in the class were the sons of the highest-ranking nobles of Mantua.[46] And in June 1627 some men, not necessarily students, left a pasquinade with a list of alleged sodomites in one of the Jesuit classes.[47]

War Destroys the Peaceful University

The Peaceful University of Mantua was the personal creation of Duke Ferdinando. And his untimely death on October 29, 1626, at the age of thirty-nine, initiated a chain of events that destroyed the university. Since the marriage of Duke Ferdinando and Duchess Caterina de' Medici had not produced any children, the next ruler was his younger brother, Vincenzo II (1594–1627, r. from 1626), who was feckless, morally obtuse, and in bad health. After Ferdinando had discarded his cardinal's hat to become duke of Mantua, Vincenzo had become the family cardinal in December 1615. But in August 1616 he secretly married Isabella Gonzaga di Novellara (1578–1630), the widow of Ferrante Gonzaga from a cadet branch of the family. When news of the marriage emerged, he lost his cardinal's hat. Far worse for Mantua, Isabella, who had borne eight children previously, did not produce any more. Hence, Duke Vincenzo II was the last male member of the direct line of the Gonzaga of Mantua. As it became known across Europe that Duke Vincenzo II was ailing, members of cadet branches of the large Gonzaga clan schemed to succeed him when he died, which happened on December 25, 1627. France, Austria, and Spain also paid close attention.

Two claimants to the duchies of Mantua and Monferrato emerged. The first was Carlo Gonzaga-Nevers (1580–1637, r. from 1628), sometimes called "the French Gonzaga," because he had served the French monarchy as a soldier and had acquired small territories in northern France. Learning of the death of Vincenzo II, he dashed to Mantua, arriving on January 17, 1628. He seized power with the support of holdovers from the administra-

46. Letter of Giovanni Battista Tiberio to Duke Ferdinando, December 10, 1625, Mantua, in ASM, AG, bu. 2768, f. 358r. Because he wrote "entrati nella scuola d'Humanità," and referred to sons of the highest nobility of Mantua as students, this may have been the humanities class in the lower school rather than a humanities lecture at the university. On the other hand, a single class may have served both. For Tiberio (Brescia 1578–1630 Novellara), see Sommervogel 1960, 8:18.

47. Antonio Porta, captain of justice, to Duke Vincenzo II, June 25, 1627, in ASM, AG, bu. 2777, f. 107r–v. Porta arrested four men, all of whom denied writing the pasquinade.

tions of dukes Ferdinando and Vincenzo II. Duke Carlo I Gonzaga-Nevers promised continuity, and he strongly supported the university. The second claimant was Ferrante II Gonzaga (1563–1630), duke of Guastalla, a small territory on the southern border of the Duchy of Mantua. He had an equally strong hereditary claim and vague support from the Habsburgs of Austria and Spain.[48]

Piedmont-Savoy saw Carlo I Gonzaga-Nevers as weak, so it invaded the Duchy of Monferrato with the goal of seizing the fortress city of Casale Monferrato, a key military installation in northwestern Italy. Because a change of ownership of Casale Monferrato would affect the military balance between the major powers of Europe, now fighting the Thirty Years' War (1618–1648), they took sides in earnest. France supported Carlo I Gonzaga-Nevers, while the Habsburgs supported Ferrante II Gonzaga. Eventually an Austrian Habsburg army of German-speaking troops came to Lombardy; it then invaded the Duchy of Mantua in October 1629. Carlo I's small army offered little resistance, and the Austrian army marched toward Mantua. Carlo I prepared for a siege by taxing the Mantuans, including the clergy, in order to pay for supplies. The Jesuit college had to contribute hundreds of scudi.[49] The imperial army attacked Mantua from December 22 to 24, 1629. But thanks to the preparations and Mantua's natural defenses, which included lakes on three sides and a canal on the landward side, the city held. The imperial army withdrew for the winter.[50]

But lakes and a canal could not stop the plague. It first appeared in Lombardy, and German soldiers may have brought it into the Duchy of Mantua. Refugees or Gonzaga troops probably carried it into the city of Mantua. The first verified case of malignant fever and buboes in the city was discovered on November 2, 1629; the plague then swept through the city, which was filled with weak and malnourished refugees. Nearly 1,200 died in Mantua in January, 2,200 in April, and 4,000 in May. The imperial army again laid siege to Mantua in May 1630, and this time it overwhelmed the disease-reduced defenders on the causeways between the lakes on July 18, 1630. Sacking was the customary punishment for cities that resisted sieges, in this case two sieges in a period of eight months. Hence, for three days, July 18–20, the commander permitted imperial troops to kill, loot, and destroy.[51]

48. Grendler 2009b, 232–35.

49. Gorzoni 1997, 160.

50. This is a condensed account of a complicated story. For details and full bibliography, see Grendler 2009b, 235–37.

51. Grendler 2009b, 238–39.

The Jesuits boarded the doors and windows of their college during the sack and suffered only limited forced entries and minor damage.[52] After military order was restored, three thousand soldiers occupied the city for another fourteen months. To support the soldiers, the military government levied taxes on the parishes of the city. Although the Jesuit church was not a parish church, they also had to pay. They lacked the money, partly because their income-producing properties at Fabbrico had been devastated. The soldiers had destroyed houses, farm buildings, and livestock, then forced the impoverished farmers and villagers to feed and lodge them for weeks and months. The Mantua Jesuits were fortunate to be able to borrow money from the Province of Venice.[53] Peasants and townspeople were not so fortunate.

A peace treaty dictated by the great powers was signed in April 1631, and the soldiers left Mantua in September. Carlo I Gonzaga-Nevers was confirmed as duke of Mantua and Monferrato (his rival, Ferrante II Gonzaga, had died of the plague in June 1630), and he ruled until his death in 1637. But substantial parts of Monferrato, although not the fortress city of Casale Monferrato, were given to Piedmont-Savoy, and bits of the Duchy of Mantua assigned to others.[54]

As the city prepared to defend itself in the autumn of 1629, professors and students fled and the university ceased to function. As the Jesuit historian put it, "the university dissolved like salt in water."[55] The Jesuits sent most of their professors and scholastics out of the city to avoid the plague. But others stayed and died, as the Jesuits continued their ministries and tried to keep the lower school open. Three Jesuits died in 1629, ten Jesuits including the rector died in May and June 1630, and two more died in 1631.[56] One of them was François Remond of Dijon, the professor of scripture, who had delivered the inaugural lecture for the University of Parma in 1600. He remained in the city, hearing the confessions of those stricken by the plague, especially French soldiers, all through the siege and its aftermath. He died on November 14, 1631.

---

52. Gorzoni 1997, 184–85.   53. Gorzoni 1997, 169–71, 179, 182, 184.

54. Grendler 2009b, 238–40.

55. "Con quest'ocasione lo studio si disfece come sale nell'acqua, absentandosi maestri e scolari, sì che al principio del novembre le catedre e le scuole amutolirono. Anche li nostri lettori, anche li nostri giovani scuolari partirono di qua." Gorzoni 1997, 160.

56. Gorzoni 1997, 159, 165–68, 190.

A Jesuit Partial University

Although Mantua was devastated and the university closed, the dogged Jesuits slowly rebuilt their college and school. In the academic year 1631–1632 there were seventeen Jesuits in Mantua (compared with forty to fifty in 1627 and 1628), and the school offered only three classes: cases of conscience, humanities, and grammar.[57] The number of Jesuits and classes remained at this level through the next several years.[58] Then the Jesuits revived the upper school. It restored the metaphysics, natural philosophy, and logic classes in the academic year 1639–1640 and added a mathematics class in the academic year 1641–1642.[59] On May 1, 1642, the Mantua Jesuit school had forty-four Jesuits and offered seven classes: metaphysics, natural philosophy, logic, mathematics, rhetoric, and two grammar classes.[60] In other words, it had brought back nearly half of the classes that it had taught at the University of Mantua between 1625 and 1629, but not theology. Just as important, the bond between the Gonzaga and the Jesuits remained strong. The Jesuits tutored Gonzaga princes. And when the court moved to its summer residence at a villa about ten miles north of Mantua, individual Jesuits were often invited to accompany them.[61]

The Jesuit school then took another major step in 1683: it claimed that it was reviving the University of Mantua. Duke Ferdinando Carlo (1652–1708, regency of his mother 1665–1669, r. 1669–1707), who had a Jesuit tutor from the age of ten, issued a proclamation. He announced that the University of Mantua, founded in the Jesuit college many years ago, was now restored.[62] In the words of the happy Jesuit historian, negotiations between the Jesuits and the duke had restored to "our University of Mantua its own rights [propri diritti] to teach in it all the disciplines according to our Institute and then to empower us to promote to the doctoral degree those that through the merit of knowledge have been approved by us."[63] Accord-

---

57. ARSI, Veneta 71, f. 216r; and Grendler 2009b, 246–47n75.

58. ARSI, Veneta 39 I, f. 278r, August 15, 1633; Veneta 71, f. 251r–v, January 1, 1636.

59. Baldini 2002, 293, 311.   60. ARSI, Veneta 39 II, f. 478r.

61. Gorzoni 1997, 216, 242–43, 249.

62. ASM, AG, bu. 3366, "Notizie spettanti alla Università di Mantova dalla sua prima erezione nel 1625 all'Anno 1747," f. 196v. The "Notizie" (ff. 196r–99r) is an anonymous and undated (but probably 1747) short history of the University of Mantua that focuses on the events from 1683 to 1747. For his Jesuit tutor, see Gorzoni 1997, 242.

63. "La prima fu il negoziato intrapreso, proseguito e felicemente conchiuso di rimettere questa nostra università di Mantova ne' suoi propri diritti, di leggervi tutte le scienze giusta il nostro instituto, e poi di poter noi promovere alla laurea dottorale quelli che per merito di sapere fossero da noi approvati." Gorzoni 1997, 268–69.

ing to the proclamation, the restored university had all the privileges of the original university. The Jesuits could use the name University of Mantua, although they never used the original name, the Peaceful University of Mantua. They claimed the power to confer doctorates in theology and philosophy in the name of the university.

Even with the proclamation, the Jesuits did not see their school as a university unless it taught theology. So the school added two professors of scholastic theology who began teaching in November 1684.[64] These were the first lectures in scholastic theology that the Mantua Jesuits offered since the Peaceful University of Mantua closed in 1629. The Mantua school now had seven upper school teachers who offered two classes in scholastic theology, and one each in cases of conscience, metaphysics, natural philosophy, logic, and mathematics. There was also a rhetoric class, considered a university-level course, plus one humanities and two grammar classes in the lower school.[65] The Province of Venice then sent a group of theology scholastics to Mantua, They replaced philosophy scholastics who were moved to another Jesuit college. Non-Jesuit clergymen began to attend the classes with the goal of obtaining doctorates.[66]

In 1688 the Mantua Jesuit school, claiming to be a university, conferred its first doctorate or doctorates in theology. That it occurred four years after the scholastic theology instruction began was not accidental, because four years of theology had become the norm for theological study in the Society.[67] The Mantua Jesuit historian described the ceremony in detail.[68] It imitated that of Italian universities except that the Jesuits dominated the proceedings.

The bell in the public tower of the piazza rang for a half-hour, followed by the bell in the Jesuit college tower, to announce the event. People gath-

64. Gorzoni 1997, 269. The two professors of scholastic theology were Giovanni Battista Salvatico and Giulio Beltrami. There is no information about them in the usual sources. A later report also noted the addition of the two scholastic theology classes in 1684 and stated that the Jesuits began calling their school a university at this time. Report of Ludovico Biscossa of March 18, 1747, in ASM, AG, bu. 3366, f. 184r (entire report at ff. 183r–88r). See below for more information on Biscossia and his report.

65. ARSI, Veneta 49, f. 118r (1696). There were 44 Jesuits in Mantua and the college had annual income of 3,384 Roman scudi less some expenses at this time.

66. Gorzoni 1997, 269.

67. *Ratio Studiorum* 2005, par. 15 (10). For more information, see chap. 15, "Four Years of Theology."

68. Gorzoni 1997, 277–78. It should be remembered that Gorzoni wrote his history between 1700 and 1711 in part to provide information and instruct current and future Jesuits. Hence, while he provided much detail, he did not give the name or names of the candidates and participating Jesuits or how many decrees were conferred. But it is likely that it was only one or two.

ered in the Jesuit church for the public examination. The Jesuit promoter presented the candidate with a short oration extolling his merits. The candidate, Jesuit professors, and doctors of theology entered the church. A beadle carrying a silver mace emerged from the sacristy. Three Jesuits, the rector of the college, the prefect of studies, and the Jesuit promoter, a professor of theology, came and sat at a small table. The candidate sat at another small table. An examining committee of six voting doctors, three non-Jesuit members of the regular clergy and three secular clergymen, sat in a circle near to the two tables. Other doctors of theology were in attendance. The Jesuit promoter praised the merit of the candidate. The candidate then analyzed two puncta from the *Summa Theologica* of Thomas Aquinas. Three of the examining doctors offered competing arguments to which the candidate responded. Then all six doctors voted on the candidate. Because this was the public examination, the vote was favorable. When the beadle announced the result, trumpets sounded. The candidate received gloves and gave a ducat to each of the examiners, but not to the Jesuits involved. Sonnets praising the candidate were declaimed. The candidate genuflected before a crucifix and made his profession of Catholic faith. The prefect of the Jesuit school declared that the candidate was a doctor and authorized to teach. The new doctor then explained briefly a theological point, and received the doctoral ring and biretta. Trumpets again hailed the new doctor.[69]

The Jesuit doctoral procedure included in a subordinate position doctors of theology who were not Jesuits. They questioned the candidate and voted for or against him. But the description did not state that they were members of a Mantuan college of doctors of theology, if such a body existed. Nevertheless, the procedure resolved a problem for the Jesuits. Since very few Italian Jesuits possessed doctorates, an examination in which Jesuits lacking doctorates voted for or against awarding a doctorate would have raised eyebrows. The inclusion of non-Jesuit doctors of theology as examiners added legitimacy and conformed to Italian university tradition.[70]

In August 1698 the rector of the Mantua Jesuit college reported that the Jesuits had conferred two more doctorates in theology on non-Jesuits. And they expected to confer another one on a priest from Brescia who had studied with the Jesuits and had publicly defended theological propositions.[71]

---

69. Gorzoni 1997, 277–78.

70. See chap. 15, "The Italian Jesuits Do Not Want Doctorates."

71. "Da due dottoramenti in teologia fatti in chiesa nostra con molta solennità, essendo promotore uno de' nostri lettori teologi, e dando la laurea il P[adre] Prefetto de' Studi, conforme a' privilegj che gode l'università." Letter of Ludovico Pagello of August 7, 1698, Mantua, in ARSI, Veneta 97 II, f. 355v.

It is clear that the Mantua Jesuits did not confer very many doctorates, no more than one or two annually, and probably none in some years. Participating in lengthy and formal public disputations, called Special Acts and General Acts by the Ratio Studiorum, was the conclusion of four years of theological study for the vast majority of students. The doctorate was considered to be an unusual honor reserved to the ablest students.[72] And it is likely that few non-Jesuits studied theology for the four years that the Jesuits deemed necessary.

The Mantua public examination and conferral of the doctorate had some resemblance to the Roman College doctoral procedure.[73] But there was a major difference. The Roman College and all other Jesuit schools possessed the authority to award doctorates in theology and philosophy, thanks to a series of papal bulls and privileges issued between 1552 and 1578.[74] However, the Mantua doctorates were conferred on the authority of the privileges of a revivified University of Mantua as proclaimed in the decree of Duke Ferdinando Carlo.

That privilege gave the Jesuits a powerful position in Mantua, which they exploited. They insisted that anyone seeking a doctorate from their University of Mantua had to attend Jesuit philosophy and theology lectures. They would not confer doctorates on candidates instructed by Dominicans, who taught their own version of Thomism, or by Franciscans and Augustinians who taught the Scotist philosophical and theological tradition. Other religious orders could teach their own members in their own monasteries and, thanks to papal bulls favoring them, confer doctorates on their own members under certain conditions. But such in-house doctorates would not carry the name of the University of Mantua. And, as will be seen, the Jesuits claimed more powers. They asserted that, because of their university privileges, only they might teach external students, meaning students not from their own order. And only they might sponsor public disputations. These monopolistic claims angered the other religious orders. But they did not challenge the Jesuits for the time being.

In the meantime, Gonzaga rule over Mantua and Monferrato went from bad to imbecilic. Gonzaga dukes of the second half of the seventeenth century increasingly devoted themselves to foolish pleasure instead of prudent governance. Ferdinando Carlo was the worst example of this tendency. His mother, Duchess Isabella Clara Habsburg, regent during his minority (1665–1669), left the duchy to him in excellent condition. She had

---

72. *Ratio Studiorum* 2005, pars. 16–17, 105–13 (11–12, 40–42).
73. Grendler 2011b, 89–90.
74. *Institutum Societatis Iesu* 1892, 29–30 (1552), 34–37 (1561), 45 (1571), 76–77 (1578).

nourished the alliance with the Austrian Habsburgs on which the security of Mantua ultimately depended, while preserving considerable freedom of action. And she arranged for a marriage for Ferdinando Carlo that added two small territories and a large dowry.[75] But instead of following his mother's good example, Ferdinando Carlo devoted himself to festivities such as the Venetian carnival which he seldom missed, many extramarital affairs, restless travel, and playing at fighting the Turk in eastern Europe, all at enormous expense. Chafing at Habsburg influence and in need of money, he sold the dynasty's most important strategic asset, the fortress town of Casale Monferrato, to Louis XIV of France in 1681, thus allying himself with the French and infuriating the Habsburgs in both Vienna and Madrid. Other missteps followed, as the major European powers lurched toward the War of the Spanish Succession.[76]

France, Spain, and Austria waged the war in order to determine who would be the new king of Spain and to decide whether all Habsburg lands would be united under a single ruler. Although the dispute focused on Spain, some of the fighting took place in northern Italy. When the war broke out in April 1701 a French army occupied Mantua, ostensibly to support Ferdinando Carlo, and Louis XIV gave Ferdinando Carlo a large sum of money. Austrian Emperor Leopold I, who considered the Gonzaga duke to be his vassal, declared that Ferdinando Carlo had broken his oath of fealty by favoring France. He declared Ferdinando Carlo a traitor and released the people of Mantua and Monferrato from their obedience to him in May 1701. Austrian Habsburg troops then entered the Duchy of Mantua and blockaded Mantua in December 1701.[77] During this period the Jesuits were suspected of being spies for the Spanish, and a handful of Mantua Jesuits who were sons of families with feudatory allegiances to the Habsburgs were expelled from the city.[78]

As always, war was bad for learning. Only a few students attended the Jesuit school at the beginning of the new academic year in November 1702. Because of the low enrollment, the Jesuits asked Duke Ferdinando Carlo for permission to reduce the number of teachers, including the temporary suppression of one of the two professorships of scholastic theology. They needed his permission because the University of Mantua was predicated on the Jesuits offering two daily lectures in scholastic theology. And because

75. See Tamalio 2004.

76. For Ferdinando Carlo and his reign, see Fochessati 1930, 191–264; Mazzoldi 1963, 139–92; Coniglio 1967, 460–70; Benzoni 1996; and Pescasio 2000.

77. Coniglio 1967, 467–68.

78. Rurale 2002, 63–64.

the university contract between the Jesuits and the Gonzaga signed in December 1624 stipulated that the Jesuits had to teach a certain number of classes in order to receive financial support. Ferdinando Carlo granted their request, then fled to Casale Monferrato, the capital of the Duchy of Monferrato, for safety. He left a council of six knights in charge of Mantua.[79]

The troubles of the Jesuit school and the flight of Ferdinando Carlo emboldened the Dominicans to challenge the Jesuit monopoly of higher education in Mantua. The Dominicans quickly added many more students to their classes in logic and theology, leaving the remaining Jesuit theology class practically empty. Then they prepared for a solemn and elaborate disputation in which two laymen who had studied with the Dominicans would perform. The goal was to demonstrate to the city that the Jesuit university was an empty shell while the Dominican school was real. Both the Jesuits and the Dominicans appealed to the duke and duchess in Casale Monferrato for support, with the Dominicans sending financial gifts to accompany their pleas. On June 21, 1703, the duke decreed that the Dominicans might continue to teach secular students at their monastery, but they were not allowed to proclaim that they were teaching "publicly," meaning as a university with rights and privileges and open to all. And they were to abstain from conducting public disputations. He also appointed a committee consisting of his consort, Duchess Anna Isabella Gonzaga di Guastalla, and some senators, to examine the issue.[80]

Both the Jesuits and the Dominicans sought to influence the committee and the court. The Jesuits restored the second scholastic theology professorship and the mathematics professorship in November 1703. This nullified a major Dominican argument. The Jesuits emphasized that their rights rested on the historical privileges conferred on the University of Mantua, the university founded by the Gonzaga. Their political point was that the Dominicans were undermining the university of the Gonzaga family. They cited their international scholarly reputation, and they argued that permitting the Jesuits and Dominicans to teach two different traditions of philosophy and theology in the university would produce antagonistic student factions, whose brawling would disturb the city. The Dominicans countered with their own arguments. However, the committee produced a report favoring the Jesuits. Acting on the report, Ferdinando Carlo on January 4, 1704, told the Dominicans to stop teaching non-Dominican students and not to hold public disputations. A brief coda followed. In 1706 the Dominicans asked

79. Rurale 2002, 64.
80. Rurale 2002, 64–65.

for one or two professorships in the university. They were rebuffed.[81] The Jesuits won a clear victory that confirmed their monopoly position in the University of Mantua. The Dominicans were angry and embittered.

The Jesuit University under the Habsburgs

In the eighteenth century civil governments and their representatives slowly moved to embrace new ideas about universities and their governance. Nevertheless, the Jesuits held on to their dominant position in the partial University of Mantua despite efforts to weaken it. But neither the Jesuits nor the university could survive the devastating anti-clerical legislation of the 1760s and 1770s.

Duke Ferdinando Carlo's reign did not last much longer. He had allied himself to the losing side in the Italian military campaigns of the War of the Spanish Succession and paid the price. When the French army was crushed at the battle of Turin in September 1706, Ferdinando Carlo went into exile in Venice and died in Padua in 1708. In 1707 the Duchy of Mantua became one of the many units of the Austrian Empire, while Piedmont-Savoy and France divided the Duchy of Monferrato. Gonzaga rule that had begun in 1328 ended in ignominy.

Austrian rule had no immediate impact on the Jesuits and their school because the Habsburg government decided to support them. In 1722 a committee appointed by Emperor Charles VI Habsburg (1684–1740, r. from 1711) accepted the Jesuit claim to be a university and forbade other religious orders from teaching external students. His decree of February 9, 1725, went further. It stated that the University of Mantua, chartered by Holy Roman Emperors, existed in the form of the Jesuit school, and that it was close to the emperor's heart. He threatened financial punishment against anyone who created difficulties for the Mantuan Jesuits.[82] This was a strong endorsement.

But protests against the Jesuit claim that their school was a university and its monopoly position in the teaching of external students continued. In 1744 the Theatines began to teach philosophy to external students. The Jesuits went to the Senate of Mantua to protest that this violated their privileges, again arguing that different religious orders teaching different philosophical traditions would produce dissension among the students. On

81. Rurale 2002, 65–66.
82. ASM, AG, bu. 3366, f. 184r (report of Ludovico Biscossia of March 18, 1747), and f. 197r ("Notizie spettanti alla Università di Mantova dalla sua prima erezione nel 1625 sino all'Anno 1747").

June 13, 1744, the Senate affirmed the monopoly of the Jesuits. All the other religious orders reacted by refusing to participate in any public academic functions (disputations and degree-granting ceremonies) involving the Jesuits.[83]

In these same years the Jesuits became even more important in the religious and educational life of Mantua. Antonio Guidi di Bagno, bishop of Mantua from 1719 to 1760, decreed that all diocesan seminarians must study the humanities, philosophy, and theology at the Jesuit school. In the seminary they would study only Gregorian chant and "ecclesiastical discipline," that is, learning how to administer the sacraments, celebrate Mass, and the duties and rules of parish priests. Further, the Jesuits were invited to participate in the episcopal conferences of diocesan priests that resolved cases of conscience and advised diocesan confessors. And Bishop Guidi di Bagno inserted the Jesuits into the examining committees that judged the qualifications of priests competing for parish assignments, an important matter in a century in which there were more priests than benefices. In the examinations the candidates were obliged to expound upon a biblical passage, explain a decree from the Council of Trent, and to resolve three cases in moral theology, all material that they would have learned in the Jesuit school.[84]

The Jesuit college and school grew. In 1746 there were 53 Jesuits in the Mantua college: 21 priests, 4 teachers not yet ordained, 15 scholastics, and 13 temporal coadjutors. The school offered twelve classes: two in scholastic theology, and one each in scripture, cases of conscience, metaphysics, natural philosophy, logic, and mathematics in the upper school. The lower school offered courses in rhetoric, the humanities, and two in grammar. The net annual income of the college was 4,400 scudi, a good figure.[85]

In 1740 Maria Theresa Habsburg (1717–1780) became the ruler of the Holy Roman Empire, which included Lombardy and the Duchy of Mantua. In 1745 she made the duchy part of Lombardy, which meant that the imperial governor of Lombardy ruled it through surrogates. This administrative action cancelled or called into question traditional Mantuan rights and privileges. It offered another opportunity for opponents to challenge the Jesuit claim to be a university conferring degrees, its monopoly on teaching external students, and its control over public academic exercises.

On September 28, 1746, the Habsburg government commissioned Lu-

83. ASM, AG, bu. 3366, ff. 184v, 185v, Biscossia's report of 1747. See also Rurale 2002, 67, especially n41.

84. R. Brunelli 1988, 156.

85. ARSI, Veneta 59, f. 334r.

dovico Biscossia to examine the Jesuit claim to be operating a University of Mantua. The government acted at least in part in response to the denial of the Theatine request to teach philosophy.[86] Born in Pavia at an unknown date, Biscossia taught canon law from 1709 to 1719, then civil law from 1719 to 1744, at the University of Pavia. Maria Theresa's government made him a senator of Milan in 1744, then appointed him prefect of Mantua for four years. He died in Milan on July 10, 1756.[87] His report, dated March 18, 1747, reviewed the history of the University of Mantua and Jesuit claims.

Biscossia presented a mixture of accurate and false statements, hostility toward the Jesuits, and his own views concerning the history of the University of Mantua. Given his years as a professor at the University of Pavia, which insisted that it was the only university in the Habsburg territories in northern Italy, it was inevitable that Biscossia would reject Jesuit claims. His report also revealed fresh attitudes concerning scholarly differences and university foundations.

Biscossia rejected the Jesuit claim that its school of 1683 and beyond was the revival and continuation of the Peaceful University of Mantua founded in 1625. He confirmed that the decrees and events of 1683, 1684, 1688, 1703–1704, and 1744 had all favored the Jesuits. But he challenged their historical foundation. In his view the University of Mantua had died as a result of the disastrous events of 1629 and 1630 and was still in its coffin. Only after a long interruption had the Jesuits once again begun to teach philosophy, theology, and mathematics, he wrote.[88]

This last statement was not completely accurate and failed to do justice to Jesuit fortitude during and after Mantua's catastrophes. They had remained in Mantua during war, sack, plague, and occupation by German troops, despite a heavy personal toll. They had continued limited teaching through many difficult years, and had restored classes in metaphysics, natural philosophy, logic, and mathematics when the city was still sparsely populated and poor. They had added theology in 1684.

Biscossia wrote that the Jesuits had restored classes in philosophy and theology for financial rather than educational reasons. In his view, they feared losing the income from the 60,000 scudi in properties assigned to them by Duke Ferdinando and Duchess Caterina Gonzaga on December

---

86. ASM, AG, bu. 3366, ff. 183r–88r, Biscossia's report of March 18, 1747, Mantua (hereafter Biscossia). The first sentence refers to the decision of June 13, 1744, that rejected the request of the Theatines.

87. The biographical information comes from *Memorie di Pavia* 1970, part 1, 95. Mazzoldi 1963, 217, states that he was appointed *podestà* of Mantua in 1742.

88. Biscossia, f. 185r.

19, 1624, for not fulfilling their contracted teaching obligations.[89] Biscossia further asserted that the Jesuits brought back theology because Ferdinando Carlo, always in debt, threatened to reclaim the grant to the Jesuits on the grounds that they were not fulfilling their contract.[90] His statements about Jesuit motives cannot be verified or denied. If true, they were not the only motives.

Biscossia's weightiest argument was that the Jesuit school of the eighteenth century was not a university. Therefore, it was not allowed to confer degrees, or enjoy a monopoly over teaching, or control public academic exercises. He offered several reasons. He argued that the Jesuits could not confer degrees on the authority of imperial privileges given to the University of Mantua because those privileges had been conferred on the entire University of Mantua and had not mentioned the Jesuits.[91] This was correct. In his proclamation of the Pacifico Gymnasio Mantuano of November 4, 1625, Duke Ferdinando Gonzaga cited as his legal authorization the charters for a university in Mantua issued by Emperor Sigismund I of Luxembourg on September 27, 1433, and by Emperor Frederick III on December 21, 1442, and August 27, 1455.[92] For good measure Emperor Ferdinand II Habsburg (1578–1637, r. from 1619) issued another charter on July 17, 1627, as the Pacifico Gymnasio Mantuano approached its third year.[93] Neither Duke Ferdinando's proclamation nor the four charters mentioned the Jesuits or their school. Instead, they discussed the usual matter of university charters: the right to confer degrees in all university subjects and the rights and privileges of teachers and students. On the other hand, Biscossia wrote that the entire body of the University of Mantua in the years 1625 to 1630 was completely separate from the Jesuit college, which was not true.[94] The Jesuits were an integral part of the Peaceful University of Mantua.

Bicossia further pointed out that the original University of Mantua had forty-two professorships, of which the Jesuits filled only ten.[95] His count of the number of professorships and Jesuit professorships in the original University of Mantua was accurate. He also mentioned more than once that the revived university of the 1680s did not teach law and medicine. He was

89. Biscossia, f. 185r; Grendler 2009b, 78–79.

90. Biscossia, f. 185r.

91. Biscossia, ff. 185r–86r.

92. See the handwritten copy in ASM, AG, Decreti 55, ff. 1r–3v; and Grendler 2009b, 54, 158, with further bibliography.

93. See the handwritten copy in ASM, AG, bu. 3366, ff. 97r–100r.

94. Biscossia, f. 185v.

95. Biscossia, f. 185r.

making the undeniable point that an Italian university consisted of three parts: law, medicine, and everything else. This was what the University of Mantua had been between 1625 and 1629, with the Jesuits providing only the third part. Hence, he argued that the Jesuit school that taught and awarded degrees in only theology and philosophy was not a university. By contrast, the Jesuits believed that their school was a university, even though it did not teach law or medicine. Once again the contrast was between two university models, the Italian law and medicine university and the collegiate arts university of northern Europe. Biscossia added that the Jesuits claimed to have a university, but it was without a head, regulations, or rules for its governance.[96] Although the Jesuit school certainly had a head in the rector, plus a prefect of studies and rules, it did not have a bishop as chancellor, or the same rules and regulations, as an Italian law and medicine university.

Biscossia rejected the Jesuit claim that it should have a monopoly of the public teaching of philosophy and theology. The basis of the Jesuit claim was the traditional right of universities to regulate (that is, to permit or forbid) public instruction (lectures open to all students) in a university town. Biscossia also pointed out that when in 1744 the Theatines wanted to teach philosophy to external students, the Jesuits had argued that two schools teaching different traditions of philosophy and theology would sow discord and dissensions, foment libertinism in youth, and encourage insolence.[97] Although Biscossia probably exaggerated the words of the Jesuits, this was true.

By contrast, Biscossia praised differences. He believed that a teaching monopoly was contrary to "libertà naturale" (natural liberty). Celebrated universities encouraged diversity in instruction, he wrote. They had many teachers so that students could choose those that they deemed most able. Contrasting views helped bring forth truth.[98] Biscossia returned to this theme at the end of his report. He lauded the benefits accruing from a variety of views. Students could choose the instruction that pleased them. "These virtuous wars," as he called scholarly differences, fired youthful minds, and advanced the search for truth.[99] Biscossia's depiction of Italian

---

96. Biscossia, f. 185r.

97. "fossero capaci di seminare zizanie e discordie colle loro dottrine, e di fomentare il libertinaggio della gioventù con aprire franchigie alla sua insolenza." Biscossia, f. 184v.

98. Biscossia, f. 185v.

99. "All'incontro quando diverse sono le scuole, chiascheduno scieglie quella che più gli aggrada, e che stima più conforme al buon gusto, nascendo poi colla varietà delle opinioni, che direvano dalla diversità de' sistemi, quelle virtuose gare, che accendono l'ingegni della gioventù a sempre più inoltrarsi nella ricerca del vero." Biscossia, f. 188r.

university teaching was correct. Professors drew different conclusions from the texts of Aristotle, Galen, and the *Corpus juris civilis* that they all taught. Whether this produced true knowledge, endless arguments, or some of both, is an open question.

Both the Jesuits and Biscossia placed considerable emphasis on the authority of the local civil ruler to decide what was a university and what was not. Ferdinando Carlo had decreed that the Jesuit school was a university and Biscossia did not deny the duke's power to do this. The emphasis on the local ruler marked a significant change from past centuries. Noticeably absent in the statements of both the Jesuits and Biscossia was any reference to the papal authority to charter a university or school empowered to confer degrees. Biscossia did not mention it because it would not have helped his argument, and the Jesuits did not refer to it, possibly because they relied on the decree of Ferdinando Carlo. The medieval and Renaissance tradition that a university was an international institution, chartered by the supranational authority of emperor or pope, that gave students extraterritorial privileges and conferred degrees recognized throughout Christendom, had faded. Princes now decided whether a university existed in their states.

The most contested claim of the Mantua Jesuits was their insistence that only they had the right to teach theology and philosophy to external students and to hold public academic exercises. They clung to this position. An important reason was policy: the Jesuits never permitted members of other religious orders to teach these subjects in their own universities or in civic-Jesuit universities unless forced to do so. Part IV of the Constitutions had enunciated this policy and the Jesuits followed it whenever possible. They believed that they did the best job teaching these critical disciplines.

In addition, the Jesuits were copying the exclusionary practices of Italian universities, colleges of doctors of theology, and the medieval mendicant orders. Italian universities did not appoint Jesuits to teach theology and philosophy.[100] The only exceptions were the civic Jesuit universities of Parma, Mantua, and Fermo, plus Macerata in which the Jesuits taught philosophy regularly and theology briefly.[101] Colleges of doctors of theology, which were completely dominated by the medieval mendicant orders, did not admit Jesuits as members except in towns with civic-Jesuit universities. And at Parma the duke made the decision to admit the Jesuits.

But by the eighteenth century the Jesuit monopoly position in Mantua was a serious political mistake for three reasons. First, it turned the other

---

100. As noted in chap. 1, Pierre Favre and Diego Laínez taught theology at the University of Rome from 1537 to 1539 before the Society of Jesus received papal approval in 1540.

101. See the appropriate chapters.

religious orders of the city against them. In his report Biscossia revealed that, under instructions from the Habsburg government, he had tried to broker a peace agreement between the religious orders in the city that would have permitted the other religious orders to teach external students and to hold public academic disputations under certain circumstances, but had failed.[102] The divisions were too deep and too bitter. Second, the Jesuit monopoly differed from the Italian university practice of offering some diversity in theological and philosophical instruction through the concurrent system. Third, the position of the Mantua Jesuits was contrary to the view, held by a growing number of intellectuals imbued with Enlightenment values, that truth emerged from the clash of opinions.

However, Biscossia's report did not result in any changes being imposed on the Jesuits, as the Habsburg government took no action. Instead, the Mantua Jesuits used bricks and mortar to expand their physical presence in the city. In 1753 they began to erect a very large new building adjacent to the existing college. Substantial local financial support and the endorsement of Maria Theresa made it possible.

But the conviction that the state should control higher education throughout the Habsburg state was growing in Vienna. Between January and June 1755, as the new building progressed, the Italian president of the Council of Italy in Vienna wrote to the Habsburg governor of Mantua several times about the University of Mantua, always with messages to be conveyed to the Jesuit rector. The Council of Italy disapproved of Jesuit control over the University of Mantua. The Jesuit rector should not be the head of the university. Degrees should be conferred only in the university and according to an imperial privilege. The bishop and his vicar should be the chancellor and vice-chancellor of the university and confer degrees. However, the Council of Italy conceded that the Jesuit rector should be allowed to continue to play a role in the conferral of degrees even though this was contrary to the practice of universities. Some academic exercises such as disputations not under the control of the university should be permitted. The Jesuits should be allowed to continue to hold all their current professorships. However, members of other religious orders should be given professorships as well.[103] The Council of Italy told the Jesuits that the new university with an altered structure would benefit the public.

102. Biscossia, f. 186r–v.

103. See ARSI, Veneta 115, ff. 270r–74v, consisting of copies of letters and other material from Vienna including "Riflessioni sopra il Progetto della nuova Università di Mantova col nome di Teresiana" of March 1755, by a Baron Palazzi, an official of the Council of Italy not further identified, at ff. 272r–73v. The Jesuit rector at Mantua forwarded this material to Rome along with his letter of June 2, 1755. Rurale 2002, 67–68, summarizes the "Reflessioni."

Both Habsburg officials and the Jesuit rector referred to "the new university." However, the Jesuits meant the new building, while the Council of Italy meant "the new university of Mantua with the name of Teresiana" that would be housed in the new Jesuit building.[104] Although the proposals of the Council of Italy were not radical and would permit the Jesuits to continue to play a leading role in the university, they indicated that Vienna intended to affirm its authority over the university and to make some changes. But nothing happened in 1755.

Maria Theresa's government returned to the issue in 1760, 1761, and 1762. This time it imposed new regulations. They were a compromise that gave members of other religious orders a slightly larger role, brought the university closer to the Italian university model, but still permitted the Jesuits to play the largest role. The new regulations made the bishop of Mantua the head of the university. Nevertheless, they authorized the Jesuits to continue to confer doctorates in philosophy and theology using the same examination process as before with a minor adjustment. Now eight clergymen would vote on the candidate, and these regular order clergymen were called members of a faculty of theology.[105]

In a surprise development, the new rules brought the colleges of medicine and law under the umbrella of the Jesuit university for the limited purpose of doctoral examinations. Members of the colleges of medicine and law had been conferring doctorates on the basis of imperial charters of earlier centuries even though the colleges offered no formal instruction in law and medicine. Degree candidates studied elsewhere or offered themselves for examination without university study. The colleges wanted to continue to award degrees and were permitted to do so. The new rules stated that the University of Mantua might award doctorates in law and medicine with the Jesuit rector and another Jesuit participating in the examination of candidates.[106]

Maria Theresa's government also asserted its authority through name changes. It renamed the Jesuit University of Mantua the "Regio Arciducale

104. The translated quote comes from the title of the "Riflessioni" given in the previous note. ARSI, Veneta 115, f 272r.

105. ARSI, Veneta 108, ff. 230r–34r. There are three printed documents. The first is "Regole da osservarsi nella collazione della Laurea Teologica e Filosofica nel Regio Arciducale Ginnasio de' PP. della Compagnia di Gesù in Mantova in conformità del Decreto di S. E. di 17 Dicembre 1761" (ff. 230r–31r); the second is entitled "Regole per la Collazione della Laurea in ambe le Leggi, da osservarsi nel Regio Arciducale Ginnasio de' PP. della Compagnía di Gesù di Mantova, prescritte da S. E. sotto li 4 Maggio 1762" (232r–v); and the third has no title but carries the place and date "Mantova. 6 Novembre 1762" (233r–34r). See also Pinotti 1983, 93–94.

106. ARSI, Veneta 108, f. 232r–v; and Pinotti 1983, 93.

Ginnasio de' PP. della Compagnia di Gesù in Mantova" (Royal Archducal Gymnasium of the Fathers of the Society of Jesus in Mantua). At times it inserted Pubblico before Ginnasio. The bishop of Mantua, the rector of the Jesuits, and the prior of the appropriate college would sign doctoral diplomas. Maria Theresa's name was added to the university seal and to documents. In other words, the Habsburg government affirmed the Mantua school as both the Jesuit university and Maria Theresa's university. Finally, those who taught were admonished not to teach anything against the dogmas of the church, against good habits, and the laws of the ruler.[107]

But other state actions overwhelmed the moderate university measures. Maria Theresa's government launched a massive assault on the independence and property of the church, especially the religious orders. Although the directives came from Vienna, the imperial governor of Lombardy and the Mantovano carried them out vigorously. This was Carlo Gottardo, Count of Firmian (1718–1782). Imbued with English and Italian Enlightenment ideas, and Jansenist religious views, Firmian was strongly anti-Jesuit. Named minister plenipotentiary of Milan and vice-governor of Mantua in 1758, he ruled Lombardy and the Duchy of Mantua absolutely, unless checked by Vienna, which did not happen in the area of church reforms.[108]

The attacks began in 1762 with a decree that required state approval for any instructions from Rome to dioceses in Habsburg lands. In 1765 a government commission was established in Milan to draft and implement measures against the church. In the next few years the government barred the clergy from involvement in civic affairs, ordered that a representative of the government must be present at any clerical assembly, restricted clerical transfers, and closed small monasteries.[109]

A series of laws struck at the financial foundations of Jesuit colleges. Most damaging were the edicts eliminating church mortmains that began to appear in 1761. A mortmain was the transfer of land or any other immovable property to a corporate body, such as a church or a school. The law declared as null and void all property acquisitions by religious institutions made since October 1, 1752. They had to be liquidated within two months, which produced quick forced sales. No doubt the sales produced low returns to the Jesuits, but windfalls for those who bought church lands

107. ARSI, Veneta 108, ff. 230r–34r; and Pinotti 1983, 93–94.

108. Garms-Cornides 1997, provides a good summary of Firmian's life. Although the ecclesiastical reforms in Lombardy are a large topic with considerable bibliography, this discussion is limited to the Jesuits in Mantua.

109. Mazzoldi 1963, 229–32; R. Brunelli 1988, 162; Carpanetto and Ricuperati 1987, 165–66; and Beales 2003, 186–92.

at a fraction of their worth and sold them at market value. Future land and property donations to religious institutions were forbidden. Any bequest after 1722 for the foundation of a new ecclesiastical body had to be sold within one year. Those who entered the religious life were forbidden to give their property to a religious order. And much else. The edicts had an immediate impact on the Jesuits of Mantua. For example, they were forced to sell a large property to a prince in 1768, while a 1764 contract with a widow was declared null and void.[110] The latter was likely a living bequest; that is, she gave her worldly goods to the Jesuits in exchange for a fixed annual income for the duration of her life. These had been common; they were now illegal.

The Jesuits were universally suppressed in 1773, which meant the closing of the Jesuit school in Mantua. The Jesuit church and the original Jesuit college were given to the local Augustinians. The church was deconsecrated sometime in the 1790s and became a barn for animal fodder. Today the original Jesuit college is the home of the Archivio di Stato di Mantua and the former church is empty except for the part that shelves archival documents.

Maria Theresa's government obtained permission from the papacy to use Jesuit properties and the proceeds from the sale of Jesuit lands for the establishment of a state school system. When the new Jesuit building was completed in 1763, it was called Il Palazzo degli Studi. It had classrooms, a library, an observatory, rooms for the meetings of Marian congregations, bedrooms for the lay staff, and much else.[111] With the suppression, it became the Reale Arciducale Ginnasio and the home of the Reale Accademia di Scienze, Lettere ed Arti. Favored by Firmian and Vienna, the Accademia sought to promote philosophical, scientific, technical, and economic learning. However, neither the Accademia nor the Reale Arciducale Ginnasio conferred degrees, because in 1779 the Habsburg government limited this right to the University of Pavia.[112] The last trace of the civic-Jesuit University of Mantua was gone.

---

110. A printed decree bearing the names of Maria Theresa, Count Firmian, and Duke Francesco Este of Modena, the nominal Habsburg ruler of Lombardy and the Duchy of Mantua, of September 5, 1767, presents in much detail the mortmain restrictions as of that date. ARSI, Veneta 108, ff. 249r–52v. Vaini 1980, 17–25, offers specific information about its effects on the church in Mantua including the Jesuits.

111. See the many diagrams and illustrations in *Il Palazzo degli Studi* 1998, 38–57.

112. Pinotti 1983, 94; *Il Palazzo degli Studi* 1998, 76.

Conclusion

The Mantua Jesuits and the Gonzaga family forged a partnership that lasted until the end of Gonzaga rule in 1707. Duke Ferdinando Gonzaga, who had a close and warm relationship with the Jesuits, created the Peaceful University of Mantua in 1625. The Jesuits provided a little more than one-fourth of the professors and lectures. This marked the upper limit of the size of the role that the Jesuits might assume in an Italian university that taught law, medicine, arts, and theology. The Peaceful University of Mantua was an innovative institution that showed great promise. But it lasted only four years, the victim of Duke Ferdinando's death, war, and plague.

The creation of the civic-Jesuit universities of Parma and Mantua located only thirty-eight miles from each other in the same Jesuit province demonstrated the initiative, educational popularity, and scholarly strength of the Jesuits at that time and place. The two universities more than compensated for the closure of the Padua school and expulsion from the Republic of Venice. Indeed, those reverses freed Jesuit scholarly resources to staff the universities of Parma and Mantua.

The revived Jesuit University of Mantua of 1683 was another story. Here the Jesuits overreached. Another Gonzaga duke endorsed their claim that they constituted the revival of the University of Mantua and might confer degrees and monopolize university teaching of theology and philosophy. But it was only a partial university controlled by the Jesuits. Their claim that it was the revival and continuation of the original University of Mantua was an exaggeration. Nevertheless, the Mantua Jesuits held on to their partial university and its powers for eighty years against opposition from other religious orders and Enlightenment critics. In the end the attacks on the church as a whole in the 1760s and 1770s swept away the Society and the university.

8

TWO NEW UNIVERSITIES
IN THE MARCHES: FERMO
AND MACERATA

The Jesuit positions in the new universities of Fermo and Macerata were similar and different from their roles in the universities of Parma and Mantua. Fermo and Macerata were two small civic universities separated from each other by twenty-five miles of hills and valleys in a remote part of the papal state. They were founded in the middle and late sixteenth century and served men from the region who needed degrees, especially law degrees, to pursue their ambitions. Fermo and Macerata presented new challenges for the Jesuits, because they were ruled by city councils instead of a prince and dynastic family. Nevertheless, the Jesuits succeeding in becoming professors in both universities. Despite some disagreements, the Jesuits prospered in the universities and managed relations with the two city governments fairly well.

The University of Fermo and the Jesuit College

Fermo is a picturesque hill town in the Marches in central Italy located about four miles inland from the Adriatic Sea. Its population ranged from 6,000 to 10,000 in the sixteenth century. A papal census counted 8,300 inhabitants in 1656, and the population grew to roughly 10,500 by the end of the eighteenth century.[1] The ultimate sovereign of Fermo was the pope, whose representatives in Fermo were a governor and a vice-governor who oversaw justice and the financial solvency of the city and its territory. In addition, Fermo had a city council which governed the city and an arch-

---

1. Cecchi 1979, 154; Ginatempo and Sandri 1990, 241.

bishop, often a cardinal, who wielded much local influence when he chose to do so.

Legend endowed Fermo with an illustrious educational heritage. The city claimed that Lotario I, king of Italy from 820 to 855, had established a university there in 825, that Pope Boniface VIII issued a bull for a University of Fermo on January 16, 1303, and that Pope Eugenius IV in 1446 and Pope Calixtus III in 1455 confirmed the university's privileges. The reality was that there was no university in the ninth century, that the little-known Boniface IX issued a bull in 1398 that produced nothing, and the privileges of Eugenius IV and Calixtus III did not mention a university.[2]

Yet the city of Fermo wanted a university and worked hard to create one in the late sixteenth century. It ordered new members of the local college of doctors of law to teach *Institutes.* It authorized the expenditure of 2,000 scudi for academic salaries, the money to come from tolls and custom taxes. In 1580 it sent an emissary to Rome to ask the pope for a university charter, though Pope Gregory XIII (1572–1585) did not respond.[3]

When Gregory XIII died, the cardinals elected Sixtus V on April 24, 1585. This was Felice Peretti (1521–1590), a poor boy from Montalto (now Montalto delle Marche), a village about twenty miles southwest of Fermo. He became a Franciscan Conventual novice at the age of twelve, then studied in several Franciscan monasteries including that of Fermo, where he obtained a doctorate of theology in 1548. Known for his preaching and learning, Fra Peretti came to the attention of Cardinal Michele Ghislieri, the future Pius V (1566–1572), who entrusted him with several difficult charges. Pius V raised Peretti to the cardinalate in 1570 and sent him back to Fermo as bishop in 1571, which office he held until 1577.[4]

The former bishop came to the rescue. After his election, the commune of Fermo renewed its request for a university. Sixtus V, who remembered Fermo fondly, issued a bull of September 13, 1585, creating the University of Fermo.[5] It finessed the difference between legend and reality by both restoring non-existent ancient privileges and founding a studium generale (university). The grateful city commissioned a metal statue of Sixtus V and placed it in a prominent position in the Palazzo dei Priori, the seat of government, in 1590.[6]

---

2. Curi 1880, 7–38, states the case for the tradition, while Brizzi 2001, 9–25, demonstrates that no university existed before 1585.

3. Curi 1880, 45; Brizzi 2001, 25–26.

4. Curi 1880, 43–44; Pastor 1891–1953, 21:24–39; De Feo 1987, 7–53.

5. The bull is printed in Curi 1880, 135–44, though see also 45–47; and Brizzi 2001, 26.

6. Curi 1880, 52–53. See Brizzi 2001, 11, for a photograph of the statue.

The city government hired faculty from nearby universities to fill law professorships and invited students to come. The inaugural oration was delivered and lectures began on November 4, 1585.[7] Before the end of 1585 the University of Fermo conferred its first doctorate on a local man, who immediately began to teach law in the university.[8] This became the pattern, as local men replaced the initial legal appointees. On the other hand, men from Fermo and its territory filled most of the medical, philosophical, and theological professorships from the beginning. The University of Fermo probably had an average of fourteen professors in its first quarter century.[9]

The commune created a residence to house students from beyond the walls of Fermo and its nearby territory. In 1589 Censorio Marziale, a wealthy canon, bequeathed a considerable amount of money for a university student residence, while leaving implementation to the commune. The latter bought two houses, founded the Collegio Marziale, opened the residence to six students in 1594, and promulgated rules on February 1, 1595. Students who wished to reside in the Collegio Marziale were required to come from towns at least thirty miles distant from Fermo and might live in it for six years while attending the university. It had some success in attracting students from afar. Even though about seventy percent of the students at the Collegio Marziale came from the papal state, the rest came from other parts of Italy, and a few from Habsburg territories and Switzerland.[10] For example, five men from Graz, Austria, who resided in the Collegio Marziale, obtained doctorates from the University of Fermo between 1667 and 1724.[11]

The Jesuits arrived in the early seventeenth century. In 1584 an itinerant Jesuit preached so effectively in Fermo that the city council instructed its representative in Rome to try to persuade the Jesuit leadership to leave him in place in the hope that the Jesuits might establish themselves in the city.[12] But the Jesuits did not arrive until 1601, when a handful of them established a Jesuit residence, that is, a temporary community. A residence was often a trial run to ascertain whether there was enough support for a college with church, building, and school.

Cardinal Ottavio Bandini (1558–1629), the archbishop of Fermo, played

---

7. Curi 1880, 53, 67; Brizzi 2001, 22, 34, 39.

8. Brizzi 2001, 113; Curi 1880, 48, gives the mistaken date of April 1586.

9. The statement is tentative because no rolls from the early decades have been located.

10. Curi 1880, 55–57; Brizzi 2001, 47–51.

11. See the list of doctorates in Brizzi 2001, 154, nos. 1898 (1667), 1899 (1668); 161, no. 2280 (1680); 170, nos. 2752 and 2753 (both in 1698); 174, no. 2952 (1707); and 182, no. 3504 (1724).

12. Brizzi 2001, 56.

the key role in bringing the Jesuits to Fermo and persuading the city council to insert them into the university. From a Florentine noble family, Bandini earned a doctorate in civil law and canon law at the University of Pisa and was known for his eloquence. He moved to Rome where Sixtus V named him vice-governor of Fermo in 1586, in which office he served for about a year, then became president of the Marches in 1590. He was appointed archbishop of Fermo in June 1595 and made a cardinal in June 1596. Bandini resigned the see of Fermo in favor of his nephew before April 1606 and moved to the curia where he was a candidate for pope in successive conclaves.[13] But he still exercised influence in Fermo.

Prodded by Bandini, the commune of Fermo and the Jesuits moved to establish a college with a school and add Jesuits to the university. Pope Paul V provided a breve of September 1605 that awarded the Jesuits 250 scudi annually from a tax on salt sold in Fermo and its territory, although the income from this tax rose and fell over time. The pope also arranged for the Jesuits to receive 100 scudi annually from the Apostolic Camera, the Vatican department that collected and disbursed revenues in the papal state. In December 1605 the city and the Jesuits reached agreement. The Jesuits contracted to open a lower school and teach philosophy, plus scholastic theology or moral theology without remuneration.[14] A second contract of March 23, 1609, moved the Jesuits into the University of Fermo where they would fill four positions: scholastic theology, metaphysics, natural philosophy, and logic. The city agreed to pay the Jesuits 500 scudi annually to support the college and lower school, plus 335 scudi annually for its university teaching.[15] As was often the case, commune and Jesuits will differ over some aspects of the contracts in the future.

On March 23, 1609, the Jesuit school opened its doors. In 1611 the Jesuits moved into their college building, which provided living quarters and classrooms. It was located near the church of San Salvatore which the papacy awarded to the Jesuits. The Jesuit college was three to five minutes' walk to the university building in the Piazza Grande (now Piazza del Popolo) in the center of the city.[16] In 1609 or 1611 the Jesuits began to teach scholastic

13. Merola 1963; *Legati e governatori* 1994, 242; and The Cardinals of the Holy Roman Church at www2.fiu.edu/~mirandas/bios1596.htm#Bandini.

14. An Italian summary of the contract of "Natale 1605" is found in ARSI, Roma 121 I, f. 22r. See also Curi 1880, 74–75, and Brizzi 2001, 57.

15. A copy of the lengthy and complex 1609 contract, with the confirmation of Paul V, dated June 23, 1609, is found in ARSI, Roma 121 I, ff. 17r–20v.

16. See the reproduction of an eighteenth-century map of Fermo which identifies these and other buildings in Brizzi 2001, 58–59.

theology, metaphysics, natural philosophy, and logic in the University of Fermo.[17] The 1725–1726 roll of the University of Fermo explains the organization of lectures and the position of the Jesuits.

The University of Fermo had twenty professorships at this time: ten for law, four for medicine, three in theology, and one each for logic, natural philosophy, and metaphysics. The Jesuits filled four of them. The 1725–1726 roll was typical for the eighteenth century when all positions were filled. The only variation came about 1750 when a third professor of medical theory was added.[18] All the legists and medical professors were natives of Fermo; none of the Jesuits was.

The presence of the Jesuits at the University of Fermo differed from their position in Parma and Mantua in several ways. First, it was smaller. The Jesuits occupied only one-fifth of the teaching positions, not one-fourth to one-third as at Parma and Mantua. Noticeably absent was a second Jesuit teaching scholastic theology and a Jesuit teaching moral theology or cases of conscience. It was not for the lack of a moral theologian. The Fermo college always had a moral theologian who lectured in the college, but his lectures were not listed as university offerings. Second, the Jesuits taught a class in either rhetoric or the humanities or both in the universities of Parma and Mantua, but not at Fermo. Again, the Jesuit college in Fermo offered a class in either rhetoric or the humanities throughout the seventeenth and eighteenth centuries, but it was not a university lecture. Third, neither the university nor the Jesuit school taught mathematics. This was not unusual, as small universities and small Jesuit schools normally did not teach mathematics.

Fourth and most important, the Jesuits had to share the teaching of theology with the medieval mendicant orders. The Fermo Jesuits insisted on, and initially achieved, a theological monopoly in the university, as they had in Parma and Mantua. But it did not endure. In 1647 a Franciscan friar armed with letters of recommendation from many cardinals appeared before the city council and asked for a theology appointment. The city granted it. The Fermo Jesuits objected. They believed that it would divide the small number of students who attended theology lectures, and would open the door for members of other religious orders to teach logic,

17. ARSI, Roma 250, f. 23, states that the Jesuits began teaching in the university in 1609; Curi 1880, 74–75, is ambiguous on the date; and Brizzi 2001, 36, 56–57, states that the Jesuits began teaching in the university in 1611. Roma 250 is a booklet with a vellum cover bearing the title "Diario Vecchio." An archivist has given it the title "Historia del Collegio Fermeno (Series Rectores et eorum qui in Coll. docuerunt 1609–1744)." Written in several hands, it records events considered noteworthy in the history of the Fermo college.

18. See the rolls of 1747–1748, 1750–1751, 1752–1753, 1754–1755, 1756–1757, and 1757–1758 in Brizzi 2001, 42, 48, 93–94, 96–97.

TABLE 8-1. University of Fermo Roll 1725–1726

Hour	Professorship and Texts	Jesuit Professor
	Morning	
First bell	Civil law extraordinary	
	Medical theory	
Hour 1	Civil law, *Institutes*	
	Logic, *Organon*	Ferdinando Bagnesi[a]
	Natural Philosophy, *De caelo, Meteorology*	Pietro Francesco Rossignoli
Hour 2	Civil law, *Institutes*	
	Metaphysics, *De generatione, De anima*	Giovanni Battista Giovannini
Hour 3	Canon law ordinary	
	Dogmatic theology	Franciscan Minorite priest
	Medical theory	
After Hour 3	Civil law ordinary	
	Afternoon	
First bell	Civil law ordinary	
Hour 1	Civil law *Institutes*	
	Medical theory	
Hour 2	Civil law *Institutes*	
	Theology, "De Sacramentis in specie"[b]	Filippo Antonio Orlandi[c]
Hour 3	Canon law ordinary	
	Moral theology, sacrament of penance	Dominican priest
	Medical theory	
After Hour 3	Civil law	

From a photograph of the roll in Brizzi 2001, 92.

a. Bagnesi (Florence 1689–1769 Florence) was the author of a hagiography. Sommervogel 1960, 1:773.

b. "The sacraments individually" is the translation. That is, Orlandi intended to discuss the sacraments one by one. The opposite approach was to teach "De Sacramentis in genere" (The sacraments in general), which the Ratio Studiorum recommended should be part of second-year theology instruction. *Ratio Studiorum* 2005, pars. 182, 185 (64–65). Although the roll named the position "theology," this was Jesuit scholastic theology.

c. Orlandi (Città delle Pieve 1683–1753 Rome) taught philosophy, theology, and scripture for many years and published a hagiography in 1731 which he dedicated to the archbishop of Fermo. Sommervogel 1960, 5:1934.

natural philosophy, and metaphysics. They further argued that the friar's supporters had obtained the appointment in high secrecy. And they emphasized their own generosity: although the original contract obligated them to teach only the three philosophy courses, they taught theology free of charge. The Jesuit rector threatened to halt all Jesuit teaching in the university. The city rescinded the appointment, and the friar did not teach in the university.[19]

The Jesuits won the battle but lost the war, as the 1725–1726 roll demonstrated. Other eighteenth-century rolls always listed a Jesuit professor of theology and usually listed one or two more theologians drawn from the ranks of the medieval mendicant orders.[20] Approximately the same number of Jesuits and non-Jesuits taught theology in the eighteenth century.[21] On the other hand, only Jesuits taught metaphysics, natural philosophy, and logic in the university in the seventeenth and eighteenth centuries.

The Jesuits in the University of Fermo

Some disputes and arguments arose between the Jesuits and the city or other members of the university community. Not everyone was pleased to have the Jesuits in the university, while the Jesuits only grudgingly conformed to some university customs and sought to maintain their independence.

In the first decades after 1611 the Jesuit theologian taught in the university only two days a week instead of the five that ordinary professors taught. He taught Monday or Tuesday, then Friday or Saturday; whether he taught the other three days in the Jesuit college is unclear. It was the task of the university beadle to visit every class daily to make sure that professors came and lectured the full hour. He kept track of the missed and short lectures and reported this to the appropriate magistracy. At Fermo, as at other Italian universities, professors were assessed a financial penalty, called a *puntatura,* for each missed or shortened lectures. The total assessed was then deducted from a professor's salary at the next payment. Again like most universities, salaries at Fermo were paid in three installments, each

19. ARSI, Roma 250, ff. 87–88. Fra Gagliardo, the Franciscan, does not appear on the list of men who taught at the University of Fermo in the seventeenth century compiled by Curi 1880, 90–101.

20. See table 8.1 and Brizzi 2001, 42, 48, 93–94, 96–97.

21. Sixteen Jesuits and twenty members of other religious orders taught theology at the University of Fermo in the eighteenth century according to the list of all the known professors at the university compiled by Curi 1880, 102–13. An exact comparison for the years 1700 to 1773, when the Jesuits left, is not possible because Curi's list does not indicate when and for how long individuals taught.

called a *terzeria,* that is, salary for one-third of the year.[22] On December 23, 1624, the beadle reported to the city council that the Jesuit theologian was subject to the puntatura.[23] Whether the beadle acted on his own, or at the instigation of others who were unhappy about the absences of the Jesuit theologian, is not known. Since the Jesuit theologian had lectured only two days out of five, for six to seven weeks from the beginning of classes on November 3 or 4 to late December, the financial penalty was probably a good deal of money. But because the Jesuits received no compensation for his teaching, this may have been a means of attacking the Society.

The Jesuit rector protested to the city council. He argued that the puntatura had to be reversed because the Jesuits were teaching theology in the university *gratis,* thanks to the "grace" or favor that the superior general (Acquaviva) had granted to Cardinal Bandini at the time of the original agreement, and that general Muzio Vitelleschi had confirmed in 1622. When they did not receive a reply, the Jesuits decided that their theologian would no longer go to the university to teach.[24]

When the puntatura was assessed against the next terzeria, the rector pointed out to the city council that Jesuits were not permitted to teach for pay, which was true. He declared that the Fermo Jesuits would not teach under threat of the puntatura. The city council would have to revoke the puntatura before any Jesuit would resume teaching theology in the university. In June 1625 the city council agreed that the theology lecturer would not be subject to the puntatura. But there was grumbling. Some in the city complained that the original agreement of 1605 was null and void because the pope had misrepresented the views of the city.[25]

A Jesuit theologian continued to teach only two days a week at the university in the next few years.[26] But it is very likely that he eventually taught five days a week because the surviving eighteenth-century rolls listed the Jesuit theologian in the same way that it listed all the ordinary professors, including non-Jesuit theologians.[27] The Jesuits no longer had a monopoly of theology instruction in the university in the eighteenth century. Hence, if the Jesuit theologian did not teach five days a week he would have been at a disadvantage in the competition for students with the non-Jesuit theologians.

22. Grendler 2002, 10, 161.
23. ARSI, Roma 250, ff. 41 (December 23, 1624), 44 (July 31, 1627).
24. ARSI, Roma 250, f. 41, December 23, 1624.
25. ARSI, Roma 250, ff. 41–42. The account does not indicate how the pope allegedly misrepresented the views of the city.
26. ARSI, Roma 250, f. 44, July 31, 1627.
27. Brizzi 2001, 42, 48, 92–93, 94, 96–97.

The puntatura issue did not go away. In June 1636 the university levied a puntatura of five scudi on the Jesuits because the professors of logic, natural philosophy, and metaphysics had not taught on March 31 when heavy rain fell on the city. Again the rector of the Jesuit college appealed to the city government to revoke it, and the council agreed by a vote of twenty to two. The rector also obtained a promise from the city that the Jesuits would not be subject to the puntatura in the future, this time by a vote of fifteen to six. Even though the Jesuits again succeeded in overturning the puntatura, the Jesuit diarist noted that this was not well received in the city. General Vitelleschi took a different approach: he ordered the Jesuit rector to make sure that the Jesuit professors delivered every required lecture and followed the rules of the university strictly.[28] Since penalizing Jesuits for not lecturing on a very rainy day seems petty, trying to impose a puntatura may have been an expression of continuing hostility against Jesuits in the university.

The Fermo Jesuits were members of the college of doctors that examined degree candidates in theology, medicine, and philosophy. It was unusual. While most universities had a college of theology and another for medicine and philosophy, Fermo had a combined college of doctors of theology, medicine, and philosophy. Although they lacked doctorates, the Jesuits who taught at the university were members of this college and participated in examinations and ceremonies.[29] When a dispute arose over precedence in the seating of members of the college, the city decreed that the prior of the college would be given the most important seat, followed by the rest of the members in alternation: a non-Jesuit, a Jesuit, a non-Jesuit, and so on.[30]

It was inevitable that there would be disputes in a college of doctors whose membership included mendicant order clergymen, Jesuits, and laymen, who taught the quite different disciplines of theology, philosophy, and medicine. In December 1696 some members argued that Jesuit professors of philosophy should not participate in theology examinations, but should cede their places to "dottori secolari" (secular doctors), meaning either secular priests or laymen. Jesuit philosophers should be allowed to participate only in fortuitous circumstances (*per accidens*), such as the ab-

28. ARSI, Roma 250, ff. 64 (June 25 and 28, 1636), 65 (marginal note about the superior general's letter adjacent to the date of July 4, 1636).

29. "Essendo nata controversia se li nostri lettori di filosofia i quali godevano già il jus suffragij nel coll.o de filosofia e medicina e theologia." ARSI, Roma 250, ff. 29 (entry of 1618), and 146 (early 1690s).

30. ARSI, Roma 250, ff. 62 (November 21 and 28, 1635), 63 (May 25, 1636).

sence of other members. And Jesuit professors of philosophy should defer
to regular members, a condition not further explained. The dispute was
referred to the city council, which in a vote of twenty to two awarded the
Jesuits complete victory. It ruled that Jesuit professors of philosophy were
full members of the college and must participate in doctoral examinations.
Indeed, the city council awarded them the same priority over secular doctors that they had enjoyed in the past.[31]

Even though Jesuit professors were members of the doctoral college,
they tried to avoid some of its ceremonial functions. In 1724 the university
decreed that all the professors were obliged under a heavy puntatura to accompany new doctors to the church to attend Mass and receive the sacraments. The procession was an elaborate affair, as the new doctor, his friends,
and professors paraded through the city accompanied by trumpeters and
drummers. The Jesuit professors of logic, natural philosophy, and metaphysics dutifully joined the procession of the next new doctor, whose degree was
in medicine, and attended the Mass. But they complained that they lost an
entire morning of teaching and were unavailable to hear confessions. (They
may have heard confessions before and during the Mass.) So the rector of
the Jesuit college posed a rhetorical question to the university and the city
council. Which was the greater service to the city, attending the ceremonies for a new doctor, or assisting penitents, lecturing, and preparing for
both teaching and hearing confessions? Nevertheless, many in the university
and city council wanted the decree to be obeyed; hence, various proposals
and counter-proposals were aired. In the end the city council decided that
the Jesuit professors would be required to attend the doctoral Mass only in
those mornings in which no classes met or their assistance was not needed in
church. The rector opined that such mornings would be few.[32]

Although some Fermo Jesuits were members of a college of doctors of
the university, the Jesuit school also possessed the right to confer doctorates
in philosophy and theology on its own authority. In 1633 two men asked

---

31. "Nel Xbre del 1696 fù mossa lite contro de' nostri lettori di filosofia, cioè che dovessero
nelli dottorati di teologia cedere il luogo e la mano alli dottori secolari che sono del Collegio
Teologico, con allegare per ragione, che i nostri lettori filosofi non siino del Collegio Teologico,
e che però non debbano intervenire per se nelli dottorati di teologia, mà solo per accidens, cioè
in supplemento et in mancanza di soggetti che sono del Collegio Teologico, che però debbano
cedere à questi. Si portò la controversia in Adunanza, ove si dibatte il punto controverso, et
si risolvè, che i nostri lettori di filosofia sono del corpo del Collegio Teologico, e che devono
intervenire iure loro nelli dottorati di teologia, e perciò devono precedere alli dottori teologi
secolari, come si era sempre fatto per il passato, e di 22 voti dell'Adunanza due soli furono con-
trarij." ARSI, Roma 250, f. 149.

32. ARSI, Roma 250, f. 233.

the rector of the Jesuit college, who also served as the prefect of studies at its school, to be examined for doctorates in theology and philosophy respectively. When the university college of doctors of theology, philosophy, and medicine heard about this, it objected and took the issue to the city council. The latter made a provisional and limited decision: the rector might award a doctorate in philosophy to the man who requested it, and a doctorate of theology to the other. But the city council would address the larger issue of the authority of the Jesuit college to award doctorates only after hearing arguments from both sides. The rector examined the candidate in philosophy and the school conferred a doctorate on him on April 30, 1633. However, the diary of the Fermo college offered no further information about the man who sought a doctorate in theology or the city's decision on the larger issue.[33] Since the diary did not mention any similar cases in the next one hundred years, it is likely that the Fermo Jesuits decided not to award any more doctorates on their own authority in order to avoid conflict with the university and its college of doctors, a policy that Jesuit schools throughout Italy generally followed.

Two Disputes

Two larger quarrels roiled relations between the Jesuits and city of Fermo around 1700.

A long financial dispute led to a new contract in 1713 that sharply lowered the financial contribution of the city. In the early 1680s the annual income of the Fermo Jesuit college looked good on paper. It included 500 scudi from the city to support the living expenses of the Jesuits, its lower school, and other ministries of the Society. The college also received 335 scudi as payment for the four Jesuits who taught in the university. It received 100 scudi from the Camera Apostolica, and 140 scudi from the salt tax. The salt tax amount was much lower than contracted in 1605, because the Jesuits had agreed to accept less because of the straitened circumstances of the city. This was a total of 1,075 scudi from government sources. In addition the Jesuits received 376 scudi in income from their properties, interest-bearing shares in a monte (savings and investment bank), and annuities, for a total income of 1,451 scudi. This sum had to support sixteen Jesuits and three paid employees (garzoni), the upkeep of the Jesuit church and college building, and the expenses of other ministries. The Jesuits calculated that the living expenses of the sixteen Jesuits and three employees amount-

---

33. ARSI, Roma 250, ff. 60–61.

ed to 1,210 scudi, while another 388 scudi in expenses brought the total to 1,598 scudi. Hence, expenses exceeded income by 147 scudi.[34]

But the reality was far worse. The city did not pay the college the full annual amount of 500 scudi.[35] Further, it had been failing to meet its contractual obligations for many years.[36] The documents do not indicate the total amount of the arrears, but it was clearly very large. Part of the reason was that the city had financial difficulties of its own. For example, it was spending about half as much on law and medicine professorial salaries as it spent early in the seventeenth century.[37] The city justified its refusal to pay the contracted amount to the Jesuits on the grounds that the Fermo Jesuits no longer needed 500 scudi because they had recently come into three substantial legacies which should be used to support the Jesuit college and its ministries. The Fermo Jesuits responded that the terms of the legacies barred unrestricted use of the money: they had to spend it on the church and the college building. The Jesuits were convinced that the city was refusing to honor the terms of the contract. The two sides quarreled over the missing payments from the early 1680s until 1713.

In early 1684 the Jesuit provincial superior asked for help from Cardinal Decio Azzolini (1623–1689, cardinal from 1654), a native of Fermo, graduate of its university, and one of the most powerful men in the papal government.[38] Azzolini praised the Jesuit contribution to the university. Without them it would be empty, because the students would go to the universities of Macerata or Perugia, he wrote. But he cautioned the provincial superior not to pursue litigation, because it would hurt the reputation of the Jesuits in the city. He advised him to come to an agreement with the city.[39]

34. ARSI, Roma 121 I, ff. 37r–38r, an anonymous and undated (but early 1680s) memorandum entitled "Entrata del Collegio." It is a statement from the Fermo college of its income and expenses with comments. This is the initial document of many concerning the financial dispute with the city filling ff. 37r–120r in this busta.

35. Curi 1880, 75. One ARSI document indicated the amount of an annual shortfall. In 1711 the city paid 387 scudi (of the contracted 500). ARSI, Roma 68, f. 143r. All the other income and expense statements summarized in the Fermo catalogues that appeared every three to five years listed the city's contractual obligation of 500 scudi, not how much was received.

36. At one point a disillusioned Jesuit suggested that it was sixty years. "Tantoche solamente si verrebbe a perder la speranza, che fosse per crescer l'entrata per l'impositione sopra del sale: la quel speranza sopra si è debole e remota, con l'esperienza di anni sessanta." ARSI, Roma 121 I, f. 50r, an undated and anonymous memorandum written by a Jesuit urging acceptance of a deal with the city because there was no hope of getting what was owed.

37. See the table in Brizzi 2001, 84.

38. For his life and career see Pastor 1898–1953, vols. 30–32, indexes; and De Caro 1962.

39. Letter of Azzolini to the provincial of April 29, 1684, Rome, in ARSI Roma 121 I, ff. 52r–53r.

The dispute dragged on. In 1701 another provincial superior decided to give the city what it wanted, that is, to forego the 500 scudi per annum financial support. The Fermo Jesuits were outraged. On March 25, 1701, Father Agostino Maria Doria, the rector of the Jesuit college, wrote to the general. How can we support a theologian, a casuist, and three philosophers on so little money, he demanded. He wanted to sue. The expenses of litigation will not be greater than the loss of income, he wrote. The best tactic is not to show that we are afraid of litigation; we should make it clear that we are willing to fight for our rights. Moreover, he feared that if the Jesuits made one concession, the city would demand others. All but one of the Jesuits in the college agree with me, he concluded. The exception was a son of Fermo who was too partial to the city.[40]

Nevertheless, the provincial superior made a tentative agreement with the city. This provoked an angrier letter to the general. Every Jesuit in Fermo condemned the agreement, Doria wrote. They blamed Cardinal Baldassare Censi (see below) and another churchman for it. Of course, they blamed the provincial as much or more, but Doria did not write this.[41] Perhaps the letters had the intended result, because the agreement did not become final, and the dispute continued. Obviously, the differences between college, provincial, and general complicated the Jesuit position.

The years following 1701 brought new developments. The Jesuits tentatively resolved another internal division, how to use the proceeds from three major legacies. They decided that the Fermo college might use the proceeds of one for living expenses, while a portion of another one could be invested and the income used without restrictions. However, this emboldened the city to demand that the Jesuits forego the entire 500 scudi annual payment. It threatened to bring suit in the Sacred Roman Rota in Rome, the highest court in Catholicism. This gave the Jesuits pause, because they realized that the Rota would insist on reviewing the accounts of the college. This would be bad for the college and the Society, because the Fermo Jesuits had not kept good financial records. While the Jesuits were convinced that they had not done anything wrong, they were not certain that this truth would emerge clearly.[42] The provincial superior, Gabriele

40. Letter of Agostino Maria Doria to General Tirso González of March 25, 1701, Fermo, in ARSI, Roma 121 I, ff. 94r–96r.

41. Letter of Agostino Maria Doria to General González of March 28, 1701, in ARSI, Roma 121 I, f. 98r–v.

42. "Questo caso, quando debba seguire, assolutamente sarà di sommo disonore del Collegio e della Compagnia, perche i libbri non sono tenuti à dovere, et il perito, ancorche fosse nostro amorevole, non potendo ricavare il vero alle partite, che sono confuse." ARSI, Roma 121 I,

Maria Grassi, called a meeting with his consultors, and they decided to give the city what it wanted.[43]

On December 30, 1713, the Jesuits reached a new accord with the city. The Fermo Jesuits, now led by a different rector, relinquished their claim to the unpaid arrears, and agreed that in the future the city would not be obligated to pay them 500 scudi per annum to support the college. That part of the agreement of March 23, 1609, was nullified. In return the Jesuits received a lump sum of 3,000 scudi to invest and spend as they wished. Moreover, the general and provincial authorized the Fermo college to use the income from the three legacies as they wished.[44] The new pact did not affect other parts of the contract of March 23, 1609. The city continued to pay the Jesuit college 335 scudi per annum for their university teaching. The Fermo college continued to receive 100 scudi per annum from the Camera Apostolica and 190 scudi from the salt tax.[45] Indeed, the income from the salt tax rose to 285 scudi in the 1730s and 1740s.[46]

The results were not terrible for the Fermo college. If it invested the 3,000 scudi and received an annual return of five percent, the amount would have been 150 scudi, considerably less than 500 scudi. But they had not received full payment for many years. The combination of assured income from the 3,000 scudi, continuation of the other payments, greater proceeds from the salt tax, and unrestricted use of legacy income may have given the Fermo college as much or nearly as much income after 1713 as before. In any case, the financial agreement of 1713 endured until 1773.

At no time during the thirty years of the dispute did the Jesuits reduce their teaching; they always provided teachers for nine classes.[47] They were

---

ff. 113r–17r (quotation at 116v). This is a long anonymous memorandum to the general (probably Michelango Tamburini) explaining why the Jesuits settled with the city, probably written by or for the provincial superior Gabriele Maria Grassi. Although undated, it was written shortly after December 30, 1713, because it gave the date of the accord.

43. ARSI, Roma 121 I, ff. 119r–20r, anonymous undated memorandum listing seven Jesuits who met and what they decided. The meeting took place on November 23, no year, but probably 1713. The Constitutions obliged provincial superiors to appoint consultors and to seek their advice on matters of importance. After they were heard, the provincial made the decision. *Constitutions* 1996, par. 810 (398).

44. ARSI, Roma 121 I, f. 106r–v. See also Curi 1880, 75.

45. ARSI, Roma 69, ff. 155r (1717), 315r (1720).

46. ARSI, Roma 71, f. 314r (1734); Roma 72, ff. 149r (1737), 325r (1740); Roma 73, ff. 143r (1743), 319r (1746).

47. ARSI, Roma 59, f. 75r (1649); Roma 62, ff. 105r (1669), 303r (1672); Roma 63, f. 169r (1675); Roma 64, ff. 53r (1678, 17 Jesuits, 9 classes), 267r (1681, 16 Jesuits, 9 classes); Roma 66, f. 299r (1696, 17 Jesuits, 9 classes); Roma 67, ff. 142r (1700, 16 Jesuits, 9 classes), 304r (1705, 16 Jesuits, 10 classes); Roma 68, f. 143r (1711, 15 Jesuits, 9 classes).

scholastic theology, metaphysics, natural philosophy, and logic for the university, plus moral theology, rhetoric or the humanities, two grammar classes, and the rudiments of grammar in their own school. Jesuits taught the first eight, a secular priest paid 35 scudi per annum by the Jesuits taught the rudiments of grammar class. The number of Jesuits remained steady at 16 or 17. After the new pact was signed, the number of classes and Jesuits in Fermo remained at the same levels until the suppression.[48]

The long dispute revealed the financial vulnerability of a successful college. It attracted legacies that improved its financial health, but generous legacies signaled to governments that they might reduce their support. And if the city did so, the college had no good options. Taking legal action risked damaging the favorable reputation of the college, the goodwill that attracted donations. Pursuing litigation might mean permitting outsiders to examine its internal records, something no organization enjoys. It is not likely that the Fermo Jesuits falsified accounts; it is more likely that they failed to keep complete records and/or did not follow to the letter the terms of legacies. Moreover, papal courts seldom ruled in favor of the Jesuits. The last resort was to reduce the number of teachers. The Fermo Jesuits were loath to do this, because it would have created a backlash. In the end, the provincial superior with the approval of the general surrendered to the town, and the Fermo Jesuits had to accept it.

The second quarrel arose because the Jesuits wanted to direct and control the Collegio Marziale that the city founded and ruled. Even though the voluminous Jesuit documentation concerning the financial dispute did not mention the Collegio Marziale, the Jesuit wish to take control of it must have contributed to the city's determined stand on finances.

The Jesuits argued that the bad conduct of the students in the Collegio Marziale necessitated better direction, which the Jesuits could provide. In order to demonstrate how the Collegio Marziale should be run, the Jesuits proposed a new residence school for students modeled on Jesuit noble boarding schools. The new Jesuit school would offer a complete range of courses from Latin grammar through law and medicine, plus Italian, geography, horsemanship, fencing, and music. In the summer the students

---

48. ARSI, Roma 68, f. 314r (1714, 14 Jesuits, 9 classes); Roma 69, ff. 155r–v (1717, 15 Jesuits, no information on classes), 315v (1720, 15 Jesuits, no information on classes); Roma 71, ff. 144r (1730, 16 Jesuits, 9 classes), 314r (1734, 17 Jesuits, 9 classes); Roma 72, ff. 149r (1737, 17 Jesuits, 8 classes), 325r (1740, 17 Jesuits, 8 classes); Roma 73, ff. 143r (1743, 22 Jesuits, 9 classes), 319r (1746, 17 Jesuits, 9 classes); Roma 74, f. 157r (1749, 17 Jesuits, 9 classes); Roma 75, ff. 155r (1758, 15 Jesuits, 9 classes), 332r (1761, 15 Jesuits, 9 classes); Roma 77, f. 308r (1770, 16 Jesuits, 9 classes). It is not known why there were 22 Jesuits in Fermo in 1743.

would fish and hunt by the sea. Students would come from wealthy and dignified families; they would live more regulated and upright lives than those at the Collegio Marziale. Indeed, the rules for the proposed school would limit the contacts of its students with other university students. Cardinal Baldassare Cenci (1647–1709, cardinal from 1695), archbishop of Fermo, offered his protection and patronage to the new Jesuit boarding school, and it opened its doors on November 1, 1701.[49]

Cenci warmly supported the Jesuits and their ambitions in Fermo. A native of Rome, he acquired a doctorate in both laws from the University of Rome, and then became a papal administrator and diplomat. He had a strong interest in education, which he manifested by becoming protector of the Collegio Capranica in Rome, a boarding school for future priests whose students attended classes at the Jesuit Roman College. Appointed archbishop of Fermo in November 1697, he immediately moved there and rarely left. He threw himself into improving the lives of clergy and laity. He founded a diocesan seminary, a hospice for penitents, and another for young women at risk. He enthusiastically endorsed the Jesuit boarding school and offer to assume direction of the Collegio Marziale.[50]

The proposal ran into vehement opposition in the city council and across the city. The heart of the objection was civic control and pride: the Jesuits should not control an institution so important to the city and essential to the well-being of the university. An anonymous printed pamphlet went further: it alleged that the Jesuits had a plan to take over the university. When the Jesuits offered to house and teach without charge ten local boys in their new boarding school, the anonymous author saw this as a scheme to take the boys hostages in order to get their way. In the face of such determined opposition, the Jesuits and the cardinal abandoned the quest to direct the Collegio Marziale. The new Jesuit boarding school lasted until 1704 and then disappeared. Economic difficulties and declining university enrollment eventually led to the closure of the Collegio Marziale in 1770.[51]

A Degree Mill

Despite the contribution of the Jesuits, the University of Fermo remained a small and undistinguished university lacking accomplished scholars, either laymen or Jesuits.[52] Localism in law and medical appointments was a

---

49. Brizzi 2001, 51–52. 50. Stumpo, 1979.
51. Brizzi 2001, 52–53; and Lupi 2005, 44–45.
52. Although Curi 1880, 58–67, 90–113, made a valiant effort to note the literary and sci-

major reason. Another was low faculty compensation. Not high in 1585, salaries dropped over time, making it difficult to retain good faculty. To make matters worse, some men appointed to law professorships lacked legal experience or did not bother to show up to teach.[53] University appointments were sometimes a way of distributing favors and money, rather than a means of providing good instruction.

The University of Fermo was a degree mill. A total of 4,083 men, an average of 22 per year, received doctorates, some more than one, from 1585 through 1773. The university conferred 53 doctorates in 1635, the peak year. And it conferred about 30 doctorates per year from 1630 through 1719, after which the number declined steadily to only four or five a year in the last decade of the century. About seventy percent of the doctorates were in law, almost always in both civil and canon law, about twenty-six percent in medicine, and three percent in theology. Many degrees were two-subject degrees, such as philosophy and theology or philosophy and medicine.[54]

The University of Fermo enthusiastically debased the doctorate. For example, Domenico Spinucci (1739–1823), the son of a local count and a feudatory of the king of Poland, received a doctorate of civil and canon law (*in utroque iure*) in 1751 when he was only twelve years and seven months old. He became a bishop and cardinal.[55] A number of men obtained two, and even three, doctorates on the same day or within two or three days. Since the private examination determined whether a degree would be conferred and friendly examiners might waive requirements, such as lecture attendance, this was possible. For example, on October 13, 1641, Decio Azzolini received two doctorates: in philosophy and theology, and in both laws, at the age of 18 years and 6 months.[56] One Giuseppe Olivieri of Fermo, a layman, obtained a doctorate of philosophy and a doctor of theology (separate degrees) on November 27, 1724. He then obtained a doctorate in both laws on November 29.[57] Others did the same.[58] Of course, Fermo was not the only Italian university that conferred easy doctorates in these centuries.

---

entific accomplishments of the men who taught at the University of Fermo, the list is short. A few went from Fermo to other universities or to positions in the papal bureaucracy where they did well.

53. Brizzi 2001, 84.

54. See the list in Brizzi 2001, 113–44, 153–84, 193–203, and the analysis of the degrees on 66, 70–73, 75–77, 80–81.

55. Brizzi 2001, 83, 187 (no. 3826); and The Cardinals of the Holy Roman Church, www2 .fiu.edu~mirandas/bios1816.htm#Spinucci.

56. Brizzi 2001, 132.

57. Brizzi 2001, 181 (no. 3339). For another example, see 172 (no. 2878), August 19 and 21, 1704.

58. See Brizzi 2001, 155 (no. 1958) (1670); 172 (no. 2866) (1703); 178 (no. 3168) (1716); 182 (no. 3437) (1729); 193 (no. 3590) (1739); 194 (no. 3620) (1741); 195 (no. 3712) (1746).

Laymen and clergymen obtained doctorates in both theology and law in order to improve their career options. A law doctorate was normally a prerequisite for a layman seeking a position in civil and ecclesiastical administrations. If after joining the bureaucracy of the papal states, a layman decided that ordination would enable him to rise to higher office, the prior possession of a doctorate of theology helped. It would permit him to shorten or bypass the theological education expected of a priest.

Careerist clergymen sought doctorates in both theology and law for the same reason. A theology doctorate was appropriate training for a future cleric. But a doctorate in both laws was essential for higher positions, because noble birth, a law degree, and patrons were de facto prerequisites for high ecclesiastical office. Consequently, numerous future Italian bishops, cardinals, and popes of the sixteenth, seventeenth, and eighteenth centuries obtained doctorates in both laws before they began to climb the ecclesiastical ladder.[59] In a degree mill such as the University of Fermo the Jesuits were a stable pedagogical element. They conscientiously taught Aristotelian logic, natural philosophy, and metaphysics and Jesuit Thomistic theology.

This came to an end in 1773. After the suppression a few ex-Jesuits were hired to teach in the university, but neither the Jesuit building nor income from the sale of Jesuit properties went to the university, as happened in Macerata. The French invasion led to periodic closures of the university plus a plan for its reorganization. The university reopened in 1807 under a new plan but did not flourish. When the papacy reorganized the universities of the papal state in 1826, it suppressed the University of Fermo.[60] Fermo has no university today.

City officials and archbishops brought the Jesuits into the University of Fermo where they filled four positions: scholastic theology, metaphysics, natural philosophy, and logic. Their role was small but very stable over nearly two centuries. There was some hostility toward the Jesuits, while they did not easily accept all university customs. And the city would not give control of the Collegio Marziale to the Society. However, the differences were not important enough to halt Jesuit teaching. The city council almost always supported the Jesuits in various petty disputes. But it unilaterally reduced payments to the Society, thereby reneging on the original contracts. The city and its archbishops saw Jesuit instruction as a competent and reliable part of an undistinguished regional university.

59. This statement is based on perusing the biographies of numerous popes, cardinals, and bishops in a variety of sources over the years. For cardinals, the biographical entries in The Cardinals of the Holy Roman Church website amply document the point.

60. Brizzi 2001, 83–98.

The Jesuits Enter the University of Macerata

The Jesuits also taught in the nearby University of Macerata. The hilltop town of Macerata is located above the Potenza River valley on the Adriatic slope of the Apennine Mountains some forty miles inland from coastal Ancona. The city was a regional agricultural center and an administrative hub because a legate ruled the Marches for the papacy from there. Like Fermo, the city enjoyed a good deal of local autonomy. Macerata's population was probably about 10,000 in 1550, may have risen to 13,000 in 1600, but dipped to 8,800 in 1656 because of the lingering effects of the plague of 1630 to 1633, then gradually rose to 12,500 in 1782.[61]

The city and townspeople had long wanted a university, and Pope Paul III granted their wish in a bull of July 1, 1540. The commune immediately began to hire professors and the university began teaching in the fall of 1540, reaching full size in the academic year 1541–1542. In the next two decades the roll of professors stabilized at ten to twelve professors, typically five, six, or seven teaching law, plus one each for theology, medicine, philosophy, logic, and the humanities. The university drew three-quarters or more of its students from the Marches.[62]

The Jesuits made a very favorable impression when they came to Macerata to preach in 1556. The commune invited them to establish a college in 1559, but did not provide enough support to persuade the Jesuits to come. The city persisted. The Consiglio di Credenza, the supreme legislative organ of Macerata, offered annual funding of 200 scudi, while individuals promised additional financial aid. Temporary arrangements for a church and building were made. When everything was ready, the commune on May 7, 1561, again wrote to General Laínez formally requesting a college with a school. The response was positive. Thirteen Jesuits arrived in Macerata on May 13, and the school began in late May with orations in Latin and Greek. By late 1561 it enrolled 140 to 150 students, most likely in two classes, grammar and humanities.[63] Parents and townspeople were pleased. The commune informed Laínez that even those who had opposed inviting the Jesuits were now their warm friends.[64] Only one notable incident inter-

61. Cecchi 1979, 154.

62. For the origins and early history of the University of Macerata, see Marongiu 1948; Adversi 1974b, 1–17; and Grendler 2002, 109–17. See also the collections of documents: *Studium maceratense 1541 al 1551* 1998; *Studium maceratense 1551 al 1579* 1999; Serangeli 2003; and Serangeli, Ramadù-Mariani, and Zambuto 2006.

63. Scaduto 1964, 429; Scaduto 1974, 393.

64. "Li mastri che insegnano li putti hanno sin qui talmente dimonstrato il loro procedere

rupted Macerata's enthusiasm for the Jesuits in the next forty years. In 1596 a man fired an arquebus against the windows of the Jesuit college, allegedly at the instigation of two nobles.[65]

The city saw the arrival of the Jesuits as an opportunity to strengthen humanities instruction in the university. In June 1561 it asked the Jesuits to provide two humanities teachers for the university, one to teach rhetoric and a second to teach Greek. The Jesuits agreed, and two Jesuits taught in the university for two years, 1561–1563. Giovanni Domenico Fiorenza (born in Rome ca. 1539 and left the Society in 1564) taught Latin humanities with lectures on the pseudo-Ciceronianan *Rhetorica ad Herennium* in the academic year 1561–62 and the *Rhetoric* of Aristotle in the next. Giovanni Catalano or Blet (Tarragona ca. 1523–after 1564), who had delivered the Greek oration at the opening of the Jesuit school in May, taught Greek texts.[66] This was gratis teaching, a quid pro quo for the financial support received from the commune and a bid for civic goodwill.

In 1562 the commune also wanted a Jesuit to fill the professorship of natural philosophy in the university because the incumbent was about to leave, and the Jesuits agreed. But then the cardinal legate for the Marches strongly recommended another person for the position. The commune was forced to rescind its invitation to the Jesuits and offer the position to the legate's nominee. But the latter asked for a higher stipend than the city was willing to pay. In the end the position went unfilled in the academic year 1562–1563, and a non-Jesuit was appointed the next year.[67]

The Macerata Jesuits had their own teacher difficulties. Fiorenza left the Society in 1564. Then the young and brilliant, but also sickly and neurotic, Giovanni Botero (1544–1617), who taught the grammar class in 1562–1563 in the Jesuit school, had to be transferred for health reasons.[68] They were not

con carità e dottrina, che tutti quelli oppugnavano questa santa opera, hoggi sono deventati loro amorevolissimi." Letter of the deputati of the Consiglio di Credenza of the Commune of Macerata to Laínez of May 24, 1561, Macerata, in *Lainii Epistolae* 1912–1917, 5:529. See other positive evaluations of the Jesuits by the commune in letters to Laínez of May 7 and 21, 1561, Macerata, in *Lainii Epistolae* 1912–1917, 5:505–6, 522–23. For more on the arrival and early years of the Jesuits in Macerata, see Scaduto 1964, 412–13, 426–29; Scaduto 1974, 392–96; and Paci 1977, 183–91.

65. Paci 1977, 190n270.

66. The appointment notice for the two Jesuits is printed in Serangeli, Ramadù-Mariani, and Zambuto 2006, 82–83. For the rolls of professors of 1561–1562 and 1562–1563, see ASMc, APCM vol. 794, ff. 79v–80r, 83v. These rolls are also printed in Marongiu 1948, 56–57. For more information on Catalano and Fiorenza, see Scaduto 1968, 16, 29, 57; and Scaduto 1974, 394–95, 399n17.

67. Serangeli and Zambuto, 2005.

68. Letter of Laínez, then at the Council of Trent, written by Polanco, to Cristóbal Madrid

easily replaced because the Society was desperately short of teachers, the consequence of the rapid expansion of its schools.[69] The Macerata Jesuits were able to keep their school going but could not expand. Nevertheless, they had one pupil who became famous. Matteo Ricci (1552–1610), from a prominent local family, attended the Macerata Jesuit school until 1568 when he left for Rome to study law.[70] Instead, in 1571 he entered the Society of Jesus, and in 1578 left for India and China.

The Jesuits came close to obtaining the university theology professorship in 1578. The Augustinian Hermits had enjoyed a near monopoly on it. Then the prior general of the order removed the incumbent from his university post because he suspected him of heresy. The commune decided to award the position to the Jesuits in June 1578, then changed its mind in September and appointed another Augustinian.[71] In 1593 the Macerata Jesuits asked General Acquaviva to permit them to add a logic class to their school. They offered several reasons, including that it would earn goodwill.[72] But no logician came to Macerata. Although the Jesuit community had fifteen to eighteen Jesuits in the last quarter of the sixteenth century, the school continued to offer only two classes, grammar and humanities, whose combined enrollment had declined to 80 in 1574.[73] The college introduced a class in cases of conscience in its church in 1602, but it did not last.[74]

Then the Jesuits aimed higher. In 1608 they offered to fill the professorships of theology, philosophy, logic, and humanities in the university in perpetuity, that is, to teach everything except law and medicine. The commune was very interested.[75] Fearing that the Jesuits would take their offer

---

in Rome, of November 8, 1563, in *Lainii Epistolae* 1912–1917, 7:480–81. See also Donnelly 2001a, 503; and Firpo 1971, 353.

69. On the teacher shortage during the generalate of Laínez, see Scaduto 1974, 448–50, 803–4; Grendler 1989, 370; and Grendler 2015, 654–57.

70. Sebes 2001.

71. Paci 1977, 162–63.

72. ARSI, Roma 122 II, f. 315r–v, dated "1593" on f. 316v.

73. ARSI, Roma 126b I, ff. 78r (1574, with the enrollment figure of 80 students), 100v (1576), 214r (1579); Roma 54, f. 51v (1600), repeated in Lukács 1960–1961, part 2, 48; Roma 128 I, f. 104v (1602); Roma 130 I, ff. 84v (1610), 212r–v (1611). See also Grendler 2004a, 488 (1574).

74. ARSI, Rom 128 I, f. 104v.

75. "Perche li reverendi Padri Gesuiti possano leggere teologia, filosofia, logica et umanità che la città debba dare provisione ciascun'anno scudi ducentocinquanta, et per questo si intendano applicati gli scudi ducento che il publico spende per la teologia filosofia et logica et per lo restante si applichi il salario che si da all'offitiale del Monte giaché detto offitiale può esser' pagato dalli frutti di detto Monte et ad effettuare questo negotio si eleggano quattro deputati per lo proseguiscano." ASMc, APCM, vol. 102, f. 14r, April 26, 1608, printed in Serangeli, Ramadù-Mariani, and Zambuto 2006, 118. The Consiglio di Credenza often deputized officials or prominent citizens to negotiate for it or to implement decisions in specific areas, including the university.

elsewhere for the benefit of another university, the commune sought the permission of the cardinal legate to discuss the matter further.[76] That other university was Fermo. Thus, in 1608 the Jesuits simultaneously offered to fill four positions each in the rival universities of Fermo and Macerata. It is also possible that the offer to Macerata was a bargaining ploy in negotiations with Fermo. In any case, the Jesuits achieved their goal in Fermo.

The Jesuits did win one position in the University of Macerata. The Jesuits added a logic class to their school at Macerata in 1612,[77] and the city decided to appoint the Jesuit logician to teach in the university. Only three members of the Consiglio di Credenza voted against the appointment, while the city greeted the news with great applause, according to the rector of the Jesuit college.[78] From 1613 through 1628 four different Jesuit priests taught logic in the university.[79] The stipend was always 50 scudi per annum, paid to the college. Although the salary was at the low end of the pay scale, logicians were never paid very well in Italian universities, and this figure was about average. The 50 scudi stipend for the logic professorship was in addition to the 200 scudi that the commune of Macerata paid the Jesuits annually to support the lower school and their other ministries.[80]

The Jesuit logician disappeared from the university in 1628.[81] In his

76. "Et havendo già un pezzo li Padri Gesuiti offerto di voler leggere perpetuamente teologia, filosofia, logica et umanità con le provisioni che saranno ordinate in publico per la cui parte non essendovi ancora nata risoluzione con pericolo che detti Padri non impieghino tal'offerta in benefitio d'altro Studio in Provincia si supplica vostra signoria illustrissima a nome delli Priori et deputati dello Studio di Macerata a compiacersi che possa congregarsi il Consiglio di Credenza per trattarvi di questo negocio." ASMc, APCM, vol. 102, f. 15r, April 26, 1608, printed in Serangeli, Ramadù-Mariani, and Zambuto 2006, 117. Although the Consiglio di Credenza made decisions concerning the university, it was prudent politics to consult the papal legate for the Marches, who resided in Macerata.

77. ARSI, Rom 130 II, f. 326r.

78. "Quest'anno è eletto uno di nostri per leggere logica nello studio publico con tanto applauso universale della città ... multitudine che concorreva a ballottare, apena tre [illegible word] di contrario parere." ARSI, Roma 130 II, f. 457r. The number of voting members of the Consiglio di Credenza at this time is not known. In 1740, thirty-nine members voted on a measure involving the Jesuits. Serangeli, Ramadù-Mariani, and Zambuto 2006, 167.

79. ASMc, APCM, vol. 206, f. 44r; vol. 209, f. 53v; vol. 212, f. 46r; vol. 214, f. 44r; vol. 216, f. 44r; vol. 217r, f. 45r. See also Adversi 1974b, 40; and Serangeli 2010, 92–94, 96, 100, with additional bibliography. Livio Donati taught from 1613 to 1616, Bernardino Saraceno from 1616 to 1620, Giorgio Bustroni (or Bostroni) from 1620 to 1622, and Giovanni Antonio Ciccardi from 1622 to 1628.

80. For example, in early 1620 the commune assigned a two-month payment of 8 florins 33 bioacchi to Giorgio Bustroni, the logic lecuturer (which went to the college), which came to 50 florins or scudi for the year. The Jesuit college received a two-month payment for the "provision delle scuole" of 33 florins 33 bioacchi, which came to 200 florins or scudi annually. ASMc, APCM, vol. 212, ff. 46r, 47r.

81. While documentation has not been located, the city must have made the decision.

place the city appointed a local clergyman who filled the position until 1655, except for the four years between 1635 and 1639, when two Dominicans taught for two years each.[82] The city was parceling out university positions to several medieval mendicant religious orders at this time. Then in 1639 the commune changed course. It gave the Jesuits four positions in the university: scholastic theology, metaphysics, natural philosophy, and logic (which meant that both a Jesuit and a medieval mendicant order clergyman taught logic in the university for a time), for which it paid the college 200 scudi.[83] There were 18 Jesuits in Macerata, and they also taught cases of conscience, humanities, and grammar in their own school in 1639.[84] From that year until 1773, the Jesuits filled three, and for a short time four, positions in the University of Macera with one brief exception. While differences rose, the city and the Society resolved them.

In 1645 the city informed the Jesuits that it was reducing payment for the four Jesuits in the university to 150 scudi. The Macerata Jesuits objected that they could not support four men for the reduced sum. Hence, in or about 1646 they stopped teaching theology in the university but continued to teach metaphysics, natural philosophy, and logic.[85] The commune appointed an Augustinian to teach theology.[86] The differences escalated in 1652. Angry with the Society because of a dispute with the Roman College concerning "the mill of the Abbey of Farfa," the commune stopped paying the Jesuits for teaching metaphysics, natural philosophy, and logic.[87] The Jesuits were no longer part of the university.

The decision displeased some leaders of the Consiglio di Credenza. In 1655 they wrote to the new Pope Alexander VII (Fabio Chigi, 1655–1667) asking that "for the public good," and "for the benefit of the city," the Jesuits be returned to the professorships of metaphysics, natural philosophy, and logic. Jesuit General Goswin Nikel (1652–1664) was willing, and the Con-

---

82. Serangeli 2010, 107, 110–11.

83. ARSI, Roma 122 II, f. 319v. This is an anonymous and undated (but March 1670) memorandum summarizing some of the history of the contracts between the Society and city.

84. ARSI, Roma 57, f. 287r.

85. ARSI, Roma 122 II, ff. 319v–20r; and Roma 59, f. 80r (1649).

86. Serangeli 2010, 115.

87. "Nel 1652 diversi della città sdegnati per la lite vertente trà la medesima città e il Collegio Romano in materia del molino dell'Abbadia di farfa, oprorno che di fatto si rivocasse la sopradetta perpetuità delle tre letture concessa à nostri." ARSI, Roma 122 II, f. 320v. There is an abbey on the Farfa River near Rieti on the western slope of the Appenine Mountains, much closer to Rome than to Marcerata. Communes and other civic bodies regularly taxed mills and those who used them, and the Collegio Romano owned extensive properties in the papal states. But what connection there was between the commune, a mill so far away, and the Roman College is unclear. And the dispute may have involved a different mill and abbey.

siglio di Credenza extended an olive branch. It offered to bring back the Jesuits and to give them a twelve-year contract at the sum of 150 scudi per annum on condition that the dispute between the city and the Roman College be resolved.[88] Alexander VII ordered the dispute settled in a letter to the governor of the Marches of September 18, 1655.[89]

Alexander VII's action was consistent with his views and policies. A learned man with university degrees, he had many friendly contacts with the Jesuits before and after becoming pope. He made the Spiritual Exercises, read the works of Francisco Suárez, and was a friend and admirer of several Jesuits, especially the theologian and historian Sforza Pallavicino (1607–1667), whom he raised to the cardinalate.[90] He strongly supported higher education, especially the University of Rome. It was not surprising that he helped the Jesuits regain their professorships in the University of Macerata.

The city and the Society implemented the twelve-year contract through a series of two-year appointments. Thus, the Society nominated three Jesuits and in September 1655 the city council of Macerata appointed them to teach metaphysics, natural philosophy, and logic for two academic years. All three appointments were renewed in October 1657 for two additional years and subsequently.[91] In 1658 and 1661 the Jesuits were teaching metaphysics, natural philosophy, and logic in the university, and cases of conscience, the humanities, and grammar in their own school.[92]

Although the twelve-year contract expired in 1667, the Jesuits continued to teach metaphysics, natural philosophy, and logic in the university for 150 scudi per annum.[93] In or about 1673 the Jesuits and the city signed a six-year renewable contract for the university teaching.[94] From that year

---

88. "... li principali cittadini di Credenza ... sottoscrissero un memoriale da dare al Sommo Pontefice supplicandolo per beneficio publico d'ordinare che per la restitutione delle letture alla Compagnia per beneficio della città." "Onde la città in detto anno 1655 con tutte le debite solennità di nuovo concesse alla Compagnia per dodeci anni le dette tre letture di logica, fisica e metafisica con la solita provisione di scudi 150 annui." "Vi aggiunsero però conditione espressa che non havesse effetto tal concessione se non terminata prima la lite trà il Collegio Romano e la città." ARSI, Roma 122 II, f. 320v. See also the letter of Father Sebastian Bellucci, rector of the Macerata college of September 13, 1655, Macerata, in ARSI, Roma 118, ff. 33r–34v.

89. "Questa conditione perche non haveva che fare con le letture fù d'ordine espresso di Papa Alesandro Settimo levata da tal concessione come appare per lettere della Sacra Consulta scritte al Governatore della Marca date alli 18 di settembre 1655." ARSI, Roma 122 II, f. 320v.

90. See Pastor 1898–1953, 31:14, 18, 130; and O'Neill and Viscardi 2001a, 2986–87.

91. Serangeli 2010, 118–19.

92. ARSI, Roma 60, f. 309r (1658); and Roma 61, f. 131r (1661).

93. ARSI, Roma 62, f. 308r (1672); Roma 63, f. 179r (1675).

94. "Ad lectiones Philosophiae habet obligationem ex contractu con publica universitate ad

through 1746, the Jesuits taught the three university courses for 150 scudi
on the basis of six-year contracts, plus cases of conscience, the humanities,
and grammar in their own school. The college, with 14 or 15 Jesuits, also
received 200 scudi per annum for their lower school teaching and other
ministries, plus income from donations, legacies, rents, and annuities.[95]

The Jesuits in the University of Macerata

The roll of 1725–1726, the only known surviving roll from the seventeenth
and eighteenth centuries, listed fifteen professors: eight for law, two for
medicine, a Dominican friar who taught theology, and a Franciscan who
taught philosophy (not further defined). It also had three Jesuits who taught
logic, natural philosophy, and metaphysics in the first, second, and third
hours of the afternoon.[96]

Three professorships of fifteen, one-fifth of the total, was a modest but
significant presence in the university. It was the same fraction as the Jesuits
had in the University of Fermo, where they filled four of twenty professorships. In reality the impact of the Jesuits was smaller, because they did
not teach theology and did not monopolize philosophy instruction. Like
the University of Fermo, the University of Macerata had no humanities or
mathematics professors. Again like Fermo, the University of Macerata had
a college of doctors of theology, philosophy, and medicine, and the Jesuits
who taught in the university were members of it. Hence, they served as
promoters and examiners of candidates for degrees.[97] This produced additional income for the Jesuits for a while.

As in all Italian universities, rules and tradition obliged successful doctoral candidates to pay fees to examiners, promoters, and other members of
colleges of doctors. A 1622 contract between the city and the Jesuits concerning the logic appointment stipulated that from that date forward the

---

sexennium, et anno proxime futuro expirabit tempus concessionis." ARSI, Roma 64, 135r–v
(1678). Since the six-year contract was due to expire the next year, then it must have been signed
in or about 1673.

95. ARSI, Roma 64, f. 278r (1681); Roma 66, f. 305r (1696, 22 Jesuits); Roma 71, f. 152r
(1730); Roma 71, f. 322r–v (1734); Roma 72, ff. 157r (1737), 333r (1740); Roma 73, ff. 151r (1743),
326r (1746). Why there were 22 Jesuits in 1696 is unknown. Serangeli 2010, 125–26, 130–31, 137,
139, 142, 144, 146, 150–51, 153–54, 163–65, 167, 170, lists Jesuits who taught in the university in
these years. There were probably others who have escaped notice.

96. Its content is reproduced in Serangeli, Ramadù-Mariani, and Zambuto 2006, 163–66.

97. For Jesuits who examined degree candidates or served as promoters for candidates, see
Serangeli 2010, 126, 137, 139, 142, 144, 187. Undoubtedly, other Jesuit professors participated
in doctoral examinations and meetings of the college, but the archive of the college has not
survived.

Jesuit college would receive the fees that accrued to any Jesuit who participated in doctoral procedures. This had the potential to involve a significant
amount of money because the University of Macerata conferred a large
number of doctorates in theology, philosophy, and medicine. Of the 2,951
known doctorates conferred by the university from January 1623 through
1772, 845 (28.9 percent) were in medicine and philosophy, and 379 (12.9 percent) were in theology, making a total of 1,224 doctorates.[98] Although the
number of doctoral ceremonies in which Jesuits participated must have been
small, perhaps a tiny fraction of 1,224, their actions still produced income.

The Jesuits received doctoral fee monies until 1647. In that year a Jesuit
provincial visitor, that is, a Jesuit empowered to make a detailed spiritual and
material inspection of every college in a province and to issue binding recommendations for improvement, arrived.[99] He ordered the Macerata Jesuits
to renounce the income from doctoral examinations. He concluded that the
Macerata college had sufficient income without the doctoral fees, because
taxes on the college were not onerous. Most important, he believed that
without the doctoral fees the Macerata Jesuits would be able to live in closer
observance of the Jesuit Institute, the collective term for the set of documents
that set down the basic principles of Jesuit life. In this case, he meant living
a life of poverty in so far as was possible. The Macerata Jesuits were obliged
to obey. Then in March 1670 the rector sent a letter and memorandum to
the general. Taxes and expenses had increased so much since 1647 that the
college was running a deficit, he wrote. Expenses exceeded income by 1,003
scudi in 1668 and by 1,545 scudi in 1669. He begged the general to permit the
Jesuits to accept doctoral fees.[100] The general's response is unknown.

Far more important, the Macerata Jesuits became part of the cultural
leadership of the city. At least sixteen Jesuits became members of the Accademia dei Catenati, the most important literary and scientific organization
of the town, in the eighteenth century.[101] This was not surprising because
the Macerata Jesuit professors were aware of scientific developments far
from Macerata. On March 16, 1663, Giuseppe Francesco Sozzifanti (Pistoia 1628–1700 Pistoia), who taught natural philosophy in the university

98. This is based on the list of doctorates and the statistics found in Serangeli 2003, 8–9,
92–172.

99. ARSI, Roma 122 II, ff. 319r–20r. The visitor was Valentino Mangioni (Perugia 1573–1660
Roma), a moral theologian, canonist, and expert on the interpretation of the Jesuit concept of
apostolic poverty. After serving as rector in three Italian colleges, including Fermo from 1617 to
1621, he served in the high office of assistant for Italy from 1653 until his death. Donnelly 2001f.

100. ARSI, Roma 122 II, ff. 321r–v, 323r–24v.

101. Adversi 1974a, 142–45. There were probably more, because the surviving documentation has many lacunae.

from 1655 to 1659 and was probably still there in 1663, wrote to the General Giovanni Paolo Oliva. He asked permission to read Galileo Galilei's *Dialogue Concerning the Two Chief World Systems* (1632) and Daniel Sennert's *Hypomnemata Physica* (1636), because he needed them for his research.[102] Sennert (1572–1637) was a German Lutheran physician who taught medicine for many years at the University of Wittenberg and published numerous works. He endorsed chemical medicine, sought to reconcile Galenic medicine and Paracelsianism, and wrote about corpuscular theory and atomism. He also practiced alchemy and believed in the occult to a limited degree.[103] The Congregation of the Index banned Galilei's work in 1632 and Sennert's work in 1639 pending correction, which was never done.[104] On March 31, 1663, Oliva granted Sozzifanti permission to read Galilei's *Dialogue*, but said that permission to read Sennert's book would have to come from the Inquisition.[105] One can only speculate on the nature of Sozzifanti's research.

As they did elsewhere, the Macerata Jesuits organized Marian congregations for different social and professional groups of the laity, including noble men, noble women (for a short time), students, and merchants and artisans.[106] In 1660 the lay leaders of the congregation of nobles wrote to the Jesuit general to praise a Father Marchini who taught philosophy at the university and was the moderator of the congregation of male nobles. This was Giovanni Marchini (Rome 1624–1694 Rome), who wrote a theological work that was published in Macerata.[107] The congregation of nobles praised his virtues and singular merits, which had captivated the souls of citizens. In the course of two years he had renewed the fervor of learning in the university and elsewhere. He had brought dignity to the university and glory to the Society, and the same to the congregation of nobles. Although Father Marchini was designated for assignment to another college, the congregation of nobles begged that he be permitted to stay in order to continue his good work in the confraternity and university.[108] Such praise was further proof that the elite of the Macerata endorsed the Jesuits.

102. Letter of March 16, 1663, Macerata, in ARSI, Rom 118, f. 140r. See Sommervogel 1960, 7:1413–14; and Serangeli 2010, 118. For his life dates, see Fejér 1985–1990, 5:121.

103. For Sennert see Debus 1977, 1:191–200, and Kangro 1978, each with additional bibliography.

104. For the prohibitions see *Index* 2002, 368, 828.

105. For Oliva's response, see ARSI, Roma 32 II, f. 381r. I am grateful to Ugo Baldini for this reference. Jesuit frustration with the censorship of scientific publications is a story that cannot be pursued here. But see the reactions of Francesco Ferroni in chap. 10, "A Limited Jesuit Victory, 1670 to 1673," and chap. 13, "The University of Siena."

106. Paci 1977, 190–91.

107. Sommervogel 1960, 5:531; Fejér 1985–1990, 3:229.

108. Letter to the general of September 27, 1660, Macerata, in ARSI, Rom 118, f. 105v.

Another Jesuit who taught at the University of Macerata attracted attention because he became a Protestant. Archibald Bower (Arcibaldo Bover in Italian, 1686–1766) was born in or near Dundee, Scotland.[109] After studying at the Scottish college at Douai, France, he went to Rome, where he entered the Society in 1706. He taught in the Jesuit lower schools at Fano and Fermo, studied theology at the Roman College between 1717 and 1721, taught philosophy at the Jesuit college in Arezzo, then began teaching logic at the University of Macerata in the fall of 1725.

In June or July 1726 Bower fled to England and became a Protestant. He wrote that he left the Jesuits and Italy because of the "hellish proceedings," including torture, of an inquisition at Macerata which he had witnessed as a consultant to the tribunal. However, nothing is known about an inquisition in Macerata at that time, and the Jesuits since the time of Loyola avoided any connections with Italian inquisitions. By contrast, Bower's English enemies said that he fled Macerata because his love affair with a nun became public knowledge. In the 1740s Bower made peace with the Jesuits and was readmitted into the Society in England. But he left them again; his enemies said that it was because the Society wanted him to return to the continent. Bower stayed in England where he married a wealthy widow. He wrote a multi-volume history of the popes and an account of his reasons for abandoning the Jesuits and Italy.

Opposition to the Jesuit professors rose in the eighteenth century. In March 1740 the Consiglio di Credenza voted twenty-nine to ten to eliminate the three Jesuit professorships.[110] The Jesuits were still there through 1746, the length of the six-year contract, but were gone in 1749.[111] But they returned in the 1750s to teach the same three subjects for 150 scudi per annum on the basis of fresh renewable six-year contracts, plus 200 scudi for teaching cases of conscience, humanities, and grammar. This continued until 1773.[112]

When the Society of Jesus was suppressed, the commune and the bishop fought over the spoils. The commune wanted the college, properties, and income in order to support and expand the university, while the bishop, a Barnabite, wanted them for his diocese and order. Pope Clement XIV ruled in favor of the commune. It transferred the college building to the university for classrooms, and the Jesuit library became the university li-

109. For this and the following paragraph, see Cooper 1886; and Serangeli 2010, 163–65.
110. Serangeli, Ramadù-Mariani, and Zambuto 2006, 167–68.
111. ARSI, Roma 73, ff. 151r (1743), 326r (1746); Roma 74, ff. 56r–v, 164r, 344r (1749).
112. ARSI, Roma 75, ff. 163r (1758), 340r (1761); Roma 77, 315r (1770); Roma 109, f. 227r–v (1773).

brary. The college building eventually became the home of the Biblioteca Comunale Mozzi-Borgetti and the civic museum of Macerata. The commune also used part of the income from Jesuit properties to pay faculty salaries.[113] The University of Macerata survived the Napoleonic period and reorganization of higher education in the papal state after 1815. Today it is a thriving regional university with a large law school.

The Jesuits were eager to teach in the University of Macerata and the city government believed that they would strengthen a small regional university. At the same time the city had to balance the desires of the Jesuits and other religious orders for positions. The Jesuits did well in this competition. They taught logic, then metaphysics, natural philosophy, and logic, from 1612 until the suppression. The Jesuits dominated these positions but did not quite have a monopoly over them. The Jesuits taught theology in the university for a few years, but other religious orders, especially the Augustinian Hermits, taught it most of the time. The Jesuits were accepted into the college of doctors of theology, philosophy, and medicine, which enabled them to participate in doctoral examinations. There was some opposition to the Jesuits and short term interruptions. But because they had built up goodwill in the city, the opposition had no long-term consequences.

Conclusion

Jesuit participation in the universities of Fermo and Macerata was similar. In both cases the city council and powerful churchmen collaborated to bring the Jesuits into small and young regional universities. Once part of the universities the Jesuits dominated or monopolized instruction in metaphysics, natural philosophy, and logic, but had a limited role in theology. In neither university did the Jesuits teach humanities or mathematics courses. In both Fermo and Macerata the Jesuit professors were members of a college of doctors of theology, philosophy, and medicine. At Fermo the Jesuits refused to participate fully in university customs, which caused some friction. The Jesuits at Macerata avoided this pitfall. As elsewhere, the Jesuits maintained some independence from the rest of the university. There was sporadic hostility toward the Jesuit presence in the two universities, and both city governments reduced payments to the Jesuits over time. Nevertheless, the disputes did not prevent the Jesuits from continuing to teach in the universities.

113. Adversi 1974b, 16–17; Serangeli, Ramadù-Mariani, and Zambuto 2006, 36–37, 173–75 (Clement XIV's breve of June 11, 1774).

Jesuit participation in the universities of Fermo and Macerata differed from their much larger roles in the universities of Parma and Mantua. There were fewer Jesuit professors and they comprised a smaller fraction of the professoriate. With one exception, the Jesuits at Fermo and Macerata did not seek to expand their roles. When the Fermo Jesuits wished to take control of the Collegio Marziale, the city rebuffed them. Jesuit participation in the universities of Fermo and Macerata demonstrated that they could thrive in Italian law and medicine universities governed by city councils.

9

THE BISHOP SAYS NO:
PALERMO AND CHAMBÉRY

The Jesuits tried to found a complete Italian law, medicine, philosophy, and theology university under their exclusive control in Palermo in the 1630s. The Duchy of Piedmont-Savoy was determined to found a civic-Jesuit university in Chambéry for the benefit of its French-speaking subjects in 1679. Everywhere else in Italy the local bishop either strongly supported the efforts of the Society and civil rulers to create a new university or acquiesced in the decision of prince or city council. But not in Palermo and Chambéry. The cardinal-archbishop of Palermo and the French bishop whose diocese included Chambéry demanded to be chancellors and rulers of the proposed universities. When the Palermo Jesuits refused, as did the Chambéry Jesuits and the ruler of Piedmont-Savoy, the two bishops used their political influence in foreign courts to block the creation of a University of Palermo and a University of Chambéry.

Palermo

The Jesuits arrived in Palermo in 1549. After receiving an invitation from the city with a promise of financial support, and the approval and encouragement of Juan de Vega and his consort, Ignatius Loyola agreed on June 1, 1549, to establish a college and school at Palermo.[1] Palermo was the second Italian college to include a school for external students from the beginning, which indicated the importance that Ignatius placed on Palermo. At the end of August he dispatched eleven Jesuits to Palermo and a twelfth in

---

1. Letter of Ignatius to the Senate of Palermo of June 1, 1549, Rome, and of Juan de Vega to Ignatius of May 14, 1549, Palermo, in *Ignatii Epistolae* 1964–1968, 2:425–28. See also Tacchi Venturi 1951b, 299–302.

October.[2] They included Diego Laínez and the young and brilliant Pedro de Ribadeneira. To announce the school the Jesuits presented a full day of orations by five Jesuits, including Laínez and Ribadeneira, on Sunday, November 24, 1549. The school began on Tuesday, November 26, with seven classes, a very large number for a new school: scholastic theology, logic, rhetoric, two humanities classes, and two grammar classes.[3]

Laínez did not stay to teach, but others did and the Palermo college and school rapidly expanded. Thirty-four Jesuits resided in the Palermo college in 1556, at which time the Jesuits taught five classes with an enrollment of 280. In 1580 the Palermo college had 64 Jesuits and taught six lower school classes plus logic to about 400 external students.[4] In 1600 there were 147 Jesuits in Palermo in its college, professed house, and novitiate combined. The college alone had 75 Jesuits including 28 scholastics.[5] In the first third of the seventeenth century the Palermo college with its school was far and away the most important Jesuit establishment in Sicily. In 1630 the Palermo school offered ten classes: scholastic theology, cases of conscience, scripture, metaphysics, natural philosophy, logic, rhetoric, two classes in humanities, and three in grammar, whose total enrollment was 1,140 students or more.[6]

The success of the Palermo school attracted the attention of those who dreamed of a university. Like many other Italian cities, Palermo had long wanted one. In 1312 it petitioned the king of Sicily, Federico III (r. 1296–1337) for a university, and in 1494 and 1495 it asked King Ferdinand II of Aragon (r. 1479–1516), who was agreeable. But nothing happened. The city kept trying; it appointed a physician to teach medicine, a legist to teach law, and three Dominican friars to teach theology and logic in the 1550s. However, these positions disappeared in the last quarter of the century. Although Palermo was the largest city and co-capital of Sicily, and the meeting place of the Parliament of Sicily, it had no university.[7]

The Jesuits sought to provide one. On January 6, 1632, Father Pietro Salerno (Palermo 1598–1666 Palermo), a Jesuit at the college of Palermo, made an offer to the Jesuit community there. He would provide the mon-

2. Letters of Ignatius and Polanco of August 17, August 31, and October 12, 1549, in *Ignatii Epistolae* 1964–1968, 2:515, 523, 577.

3. MP 1:516–17, from Polanco's *Chronicon*. See also Sampolo 1888, 29–31.

4. For the first half century of the Jesuit college and school in Palermo, see Sampolo 1888, 32–36; Lukács 1960–1961, part 1, 242, and part 2, 108; Scaduto 1974, 345–47; Scaduto 1992, 229–33; *Year by Year* 2004, 163, 282–83, 332; and Grendler 2004a, 498.

5. ARSI, Sicula, 60, f. 192r.

6. ARSI, Sicula 184 I, Sicula Historia 1626–1644, f. 53v. Although the individual class enrollments added together come to 1,140 students, the text states that there were 1,350 students.

7. Sampolo 1888, 12–23; Novarese 1998, 321.

ey to pay the salaries of professors of civil law, canon law, and medicine if the Jesuits would establish a University of Palermo. Although born in Palermo, Salerno came from a family of wealthy merchants from Nice. He entered the Society of Jesus in 1613 in Palermo, did his philosophical and theological studies, was ordained in 1626, and taught philosophy and theology in Palermo. When his father died in 1626, he inherited a large fortune. He made his offer on the occasion of his profession of solemn vows, which took place on January 11, 1632.[8]

Father Salerno's proposal, presented in the form of a legal document, was original, carefully crafted, very generous, and conditional.[9] He would give all of his wealth for the establishment of an Italian law, medicine, philosophy, and theology university under the authority of the Society of Jesus.[10] In order to receive the money, the general of the Jesuits, the provincial superior, and the rector of the Palermo college were obligated to establish a university in Palermo within six years of January 1, 1632. Lectures in civil law, canon law, and medicine would be added to the lectures in theology, metaphysics, natural philosophy, logic, and other subjects that the Jesuit college already taught. The professors of civil law, canon law, and medicine had to be laymen with doctorates. Salerno's gift would provide income of 2,000 scudi annually to be spent on their salaries. If the full amount was not disbursed in this way, the rest would not go to the Jesuit college. Instead, it would have to be spent in ways that would support the disciplines to be taught by the lay professors, such as purchasing legal and medical books for a library. While the Jesuit college would have custody over the library, it had to be open to the lay professors. Salerno also inserted safeguards against the city reneging on its financial support to the Jesuits for its college and instruction in other disciplines. If the city for any reason did not continue to fulfill its commitment, the Jesuits would be permitted to refuse to pay the lay professors until the city restored the missing funds.

The Jesuits would have complete authority over the university.[11] Saler-

---

8. Sommervogel 1960, 7:463; and Salvo 2001b.

9. For the following discussion, Sampolo 1888 is the best source, because it includes major documents. Aguilera 1737–1740, 2:854–60, offers a generic account that states that the "jealousy of a few blocked" (interpellaret invidia paucorum) the project without naming Cardinal Doria (856). Novarese 1998, 327–28, and Salvo 2001b, are based on Sampolo. Sanfilippo 1992, does not mention the University of Palermo proposal.

10. Salerno's notarized document of January 6, 1632, Palermo, is printed in Sampolo 1888, xi–xix; and is very briefly described in Sampolo 1888, 37, and Novarese 1998, 327.

11. "Cioè che di tutta la detta Università sua fabbrica, ne devano havere il totale governo e reggimento e dominio li Padri della Compagnia di Gesù senza subordinatione o dipendenza da altri in detto governo, e che li Maestri ancora secolari habbiano da riconoscere per loro Rettore

no spelled out what this meant. The Jesuits would select the lay professors according to norms that the general, the provincial superior, and the rector of the Palermo college drafted. The Jesuits would determine the salaries of the lay professors. "In matters pertaining to teaching" the lay professors would be required to recognize the rector of the Palermo Jesuit college as their rector and superior. They would have to recognize the prefect of studies of the Palermo college as chancellor of the university. The Jesuits would prescribe the norms for academic study. Although not elaborated, this probably meant the power to schedule lectures, arrange for disputations, and possibly naming the texts to be taught. Choosing the law and medicine texts to be taught would not be controversial, because in order for the university to be credible, it would have to teach the same authors and texts that law and medicine professors taught in other Italian universities. The document granted the lay professors the right to assemble in colleges of doctors of law and medicine in order to examine for the doctorate students who had diligently studied and fulfilled requirements.[12] Again this followed procedures found in other Italian universities and would render credible the proposed University of Palermo.

Salerno's legal document authorized the Jesuits to spend some of the promised money on the expenses of obtaining a university charter. While not explained, this might include the expenses of journeying to Madrid in order to present the petition for a university charter and to pay for the "free gift" that traditionally accompanied a request for a university charter. Other clauses discussed buying a piece of property and erecting a university building on it. Finally, the document imposed conditions and a deadline. The Jesuit college was barred from spending the money on anything other than the proposed university. And if after six years (January 1, 1638) a university charter was not obtained, the money would go to pious works for the public good, the choice of works to be made by the provincial superior in consultation with Father Salerno.[13]

It was a remarkable plan. Salerno and the Palermo Jesuits had done their homework. They had obviously consulted the Senate of Palermo and had received a favorable response. For the city of Palermo it would be what

---

e Superiore nelle cose appartenenti all'insegnare il P. Rettore *pro tempore* esistente del detto Collegio della Compagnia di Gesù, e per loro Cancelliero il P. Prefetto delli Studj di detto Collegio perche sa detto P. Salerno, che lo studiare sotto le leggi e regole che detti Padri prescriveranno sia per apportare maggiore utilità a scolari tanto nella dottrina quanto nei costumi, e perchè così, vuole et non *aliter*." Sampolo 1888, xii–xiii.

12. Sampolo 1888, xiii.

13. Sampolo 1888, xiii–xix.

they had long desired, a university, and at no expense to the city. The condition was that the Jesuits would have complete authority over the entire University of Palermo. Indeed, the proposed governance rules were nearly identical to the original plan of Ignatius Loyola for the governance of the University of Messina. For the Jesuits, the rules for the proposed University of Palermo would enable the Jesuits to sail over the governance and financial compensation rocks that had sunk the proposed civic-Jesuit university in Messina eighty years earlier.

The Jesuit rector and the Palermo Senate asked King Philip IV of Spain (1605–1665, r. from 1621), the ruler of Sicily, for a charter authorizing a University of Palermo with the same rights and powers as the existing Sicilian universities of Catania and Messina. A gift of 5,000 *reali* accompanied the request. The king consulted his advisors, the Council of Italy, the viceroy of Sicily, and various Sicilian authorities. He received complaints from Catania and Messina. As expected, Catania strongly opposed the establishment of another university and voiced dire threats against the Jesuit community in Catania for daring to propose it. On the other hand, the Senate of Palermo weighed in with letters assuring the monarchy that it accepted the terms of Father Salerno and the Jesuits, and that the city wanted the university. The Spanish administration moved at its customary glacial pace. Finally, on September 15, 1637, five years and nine months after the original petition, the crown granted consent for a University of Palermo.[14] Just as the monarchy had overruled Catania's objection to chartering the University of Messina in 1591, so it now ignored the objections of Catania and Messina.

But a new obstacle arose in the person of Cardinal Giannettino Doria (1573–1642, cardinal from 1604), the archbishop of Palermo. He demanded to be the chancellor of the university, the supreme authority who would oversee the university and confer degrees. He argued that bishops had this authority in universities founded under the auspices of popes, an argument that does not seem relevant in a university chartered by a king. The Jesuit rector responded that a Jesuit would be the rector of the university and that Jesuits would govern the university, because the Jesuits would create it, and the crown had agreed to this.[15]

More important than the differences over the charter was the fact that Cardinal Doria was the most powerful churchman in Sicily and a valued

14. Sampolo 1888, 39–40, xix–xxiv; Novarese 1998, 327–28.
15. Sampolo 1888, 40–41; Novarese 1998, 328. There were other differences between Cardinal Doria and the Jesuits that did not involve the proposed university. See ARSI, 184 I, ff. 133r–45v.

servant of Spain. Giannettino Doria was the son of Giovanni Andrea Doria (1540–1606) of Genoa, prince of Melfi, a naval commander in the service of Spain who won battles for the crown and commanded Spanish galleys in the Battle of Lepanto. Intended for the clergy from an early age, Giannettino was introduced into the Spanish court as a boy and studied at the University of Salamanca. He obtained the cardinal's hat through the patronage of Philip III in 1604 and became archbishop of Palermo in 1608. He became the preeminent ecclesiastic of Sicily, leader of the first estate of the Parliament of Sicily, and president of the viceregal government of Sicily. He served as temporary viceroy and lieutenant of the king of Spain four times for periods of up to two years when a viceroy died or was absent. Indeed, when a viceroy died of the plague in 1624, Doria was the de facto ruler of Sicily until 1627, during which time he fought the plague and secured grain for the starving island. His efforts won him considerable goodwill from Sicilians and much credit in Madrid.[16]

The dispute over the rectorship of the university was given to three crown ministers who ruled in favor of Cardinal Doria and against the Jesuits.[17] That was the end of the proposed University of Palermo. The Jesuits withdrew their offer, and the university was not established. Nor is it likely that the crown returned the 5,000 reali to the Jesuits. Father Salerno's donation went to pious causes and charitable works. He continued to live in the Palermo college, teaching logic, natural philosophy, metaphysics, scholastic theology, and cases of conscience over the years. He wrote two books of saints' lives, and served as librarian, prefect of studies, and twice as rector, until death claimed him in 1666.[18] But the cardinal's ego and selfishness, indulged by the crown, prevented the Jesuits and the Senate from creating a university. Palermo did not get a university until 1805.[19]

Chambéry

Chambéry (Ciamberi in Italian) was the capital of both Savoy and the entire state of Piedmont-Savoy in the fifteenth century. The Duchy of Savoy was the French-speaking northernmost territory of Piedmont-Savoy; it bordered France on the east and Lake Léman and the territory of the city of Geneva on the north. Then, as noted earlier, in 1563 Duke Emanuele Filiberto transferred the capital of his state to Italian-speaking Turin. In

16. Sanfilippo 1992.
17. Sampolo 1888, 40–41.
18. Salvo 2001b; and Sommervogel 1960, 7:463.
19. Sampolo 1888, 187–210, lxxiv–lxxix; and Novarese 1998, 330–31.

another move that confirmed the precedence of Turin and Piedmont over Chambéry and Savoy, he brought the Holy Shroud, believed by many to be the burial shroud of Jesus of Nazareth, which had come into the possession of Duke Ludovico Savoia in 1452, from Chambéry to Turin in 1578.

The Savoyards, who constituted about a quarter of the subjects of the duchy of Piedmont-Savoy, were not happy about their diminished importance.[20] Nevertheless, they continued to enjoy considerable autonomy in judicial, fiscal, and administrative matters, because Savoy had its own governing structures, always subordinate to the ruler. The Senate of Savoy functioned as a judicial court to ratify legal decisions.[21] Savoy also had its own senior financial body, the Chambre des Comptes, which (along with the Senate) had the right to protest against actions of the sovereign and occasionally did. Because Chambéry hosted both the Senate of Savoy and the Chambre des Comptes, it was the second most important town in Piedmont-Savoy state. It had a population of 13,000 in 1679.[22] Powerful families from Chambéry dominated the Senate and Chambre des Comptes and exercised influence over the city and Savoy as a whole through them.

However, neither Chambéry nor the rest of Savoy had a university.[23] All subjects of the dukes of Piedmont-Savoy were obliged to attend the University of Turin, but many did not. They attended French universities; indeed, the University of Valence was much closer to Chambéry than Turin.

The Jesuits arrived in Chambéry in 1565. Louis du Coudret (1523–1572), who was born in Sallanches, Savoy, discussed founding a Jesuit college in Chambéry with Duke Emanuele Filiberto in 1561, and Antonio Possevino did the same in 1562.[24] Possevino argued that a college in Chambéry, so close to heretical Geneva, would yield great fruit. General Diego Laínez offered to establish a college in Chambéry if the duke would provide adequate financial support. The duke agreed that the proximity to Geneva was a good reason to bring the Jesuits to Chambéry. But even more important, he believed that the Jesuits would teach his subjects to obey church and state authorities. He promised to provide a house and strong financial

20. In 1700 Savoy had 27.5 percent of the population of Piedmont-Savoy (330,000 of 1,200,000). Devos and Grosperrin 1985, 440.

21. Symcox 1983, 55–57, provides a succinct description of the governing structures of the two parts of the state. See also Merlin 1994, 106–7.

22. This is the figure given by Bishop Etienne Le Camus (see below) in his letter to Pasquier Quesnel of March 13, 1679, in Le Camus 1892, 330.

23. The rest of this chapter is an expanded version of Grendler 2012a.

24. For the origins and history of the Jesuit college in Chambéry to 1729, see Monti 1914–1915, 1:133–52, and Demoment 1949, 1228–57. On the origins alone see Scaduto 1992, 334–39. See also Martin 2004, 277–78, 288, who summarizes the story to 1580.

support.[25] Agreement was reached in October 1564, and a group of Jesuits arrived in August 1565. The school was up and running by the end of the year.

However, the first dozen years were very difficult, because the duke did not keep his word.[26] The Jesuits did not have their own church or building for college and school, and had to share a monastery with Franciscans, an arrangement that produced friction and hampered their ministries. Financial support came from a tax that had to be collected personally from the people of Chambéry, who resented it. The Jesuits struggled until 1577 when a bequest gave them a large property whose income enabled them to erect a college building. After that, their situation improved; in the next century they finally were able to build a church, thanks to financial aid from the ducal government. In 1606 Duke Carlo Emanuele I (1562–1630, r. from 1580) assigned the college 300 ducatoni annually to support the teaching of philosophy, which began with classes in logic and natural philosophy. In 1664 a donor gave the college 2,000 ducatoni to support two teachers of scholastic theology and one for cases of conscience beginning in 1674.[27]

In 1675 the Chambéry college had 44 Jesuits (15 priests, 11 scholastics, and 18 temporal coadjutors or brothers) and a school of 12 classes. The upper school had seven teachers: two for scholastic theology; one each for scripture, cases of conscience, and mathematics; and two for philosophy. The lower school had a rhetoric class, a humanities class, and three grammar classes.[28] The Chambéry Jesuits had the resources to teach theology and philosophy in a small university.

A University at Chambéry

The ruler of Piedmont-Savoy decided to create a university at Chambéry. Marie Jeanne-Baptiste Savoie-Nemours (Maria Giovanna Battista Savoia-Nemours in Italian, 1644–1724), ruled Piedmont-Savoy from 1675 to 1684 as regent for her underage son Vittorio Amedeo II (1666–1732, r. from 1684,

25. See the letter of Duke Emanuele Filiberto to General Lainez, on or about October 3, 1564, Avignon, in *Lainii Epistolae* 1912–1917, 8:229. Monti 1914–1915, 1:134–35, quotes two other letters of the duke with similar sentiments.

26. Martin 1988, 19, 52–53, 56–58, 62, 164, 207, 214; and Martin 2004, 253, 277–78, 288, 290, emphasize the difficulties of the early years. See also Monti 1914–1915, 1:137–44; and Demoment 1949, 1230–32.

27. Monti 1914–1915, 1:147; and Demoment 1949, 1238, 1241–42.

28. ARSI, Lugduni 21, Catalogi triennales 1665–1675, f. 428v. See also ibid., ff. 93r (1665), 180r (1669, but no information on the school), 322r–v (1672); and ARSI, Lugduni 22, f. 119r (1678, no information on the school).

abdicated 1730). The widow of Duke Carlo Emanuele II (1634–1675, r. from 1663) was a Frenchwoman from a distant branch of the Savoia family that had established itself in France in the early sixteenth century, but maintained strong connections to the Savoia of Piedmont-Savoy. An intelligent ruler who enjoyed the exercise of power, she was called Madame Royale (Madama Reale in Italian) by contemporaries and historians. In her nine years of power, she had to deal with a fractious court and French military threats. Unable to expand the boundaries of her state, she pursued a program of academic and cultural expansion that sometimes included the Jesuits.

Madame Royale decided to found a university at Chambéry. The dukes of Piedmont-Savoy had long wished to establish a university there for the benefit of their French-speaking subjects living in mountainous Savoy. But they had had to focus their attention and resources on defending their state against the aggression of France and especially Louis XIV.[29] She had in mind a civic-Jesuit university modeled on Parma and Mantua in which the crown and/or the city would appoint and pay the professors of civil law and medicine, while the Jesuits would teach the rest of the classes.

On July 21, 1679, Madame Royale wrote to the Chambre des Comptes informing them that she intended to establish a university at Chambéry.[30] Even though the annual cost would be 400 *pistoles* (doubloons), she believed that the benefits would be far greater. She urged the Chambre to move quickly because she wanted the university to open by November 11, the Feast of St. Martin of Tours.[31] She wanted no delay in the execution of an enterprise so glorious for her regency and so useful to the public. She directed the Chambre to rent space in the Franciscan monastery for the lectures at a cost of 50 ducats per year.[32] This was the same monastery that the Franciscans and Jesuits had been forced to share when the Jesuits first

29. "Il y a longtems que nos souverains ont connu de quel avantage il seroit a leurs estats de de [sic] la les monts, d'establir une université a Chambery, Charles Emanuel 1er, Victor Ame[deo], et Madame Chrestienne de France en ont formé le dessein en divers temps, et ne l'ont suspendu qu'a cause des guerres, qui les ont obligé d'appliquer leurs soins et leurs finances ailleurs." AST, Istruzione pubblica, Regia Università di Torino, Mazzo 1, no. 18, undated memorandum of President Joseph Delescheraine, who was a councillor of state and secretary to Madame Royale. See also Vallauri 1970, 2:34–35.

30. The story of the attempt to create the University of Chambéry is very little known. Vallauri 1970, 2:134–39, 267–75; and Demoment 1947, 1244–45, offer the most information. Other accounts mention it only in passing and not always accurately: Saint-Genis 1978, 515–17; Lovie 1979, 106; and Devos and Grosperrin 1985, 370. Modern histories of Piedmont-Savoy provide no information.

31. Why she chose this date is unknown. Italian universities traditionally began teaching on November 3 or 4.

32. "Que pouvoient empecher ou retarder l'esecution d'une entreprise si glorieuse pour

came to Chambéry. The Chambre des Comptes responded with enthusiastic gratitude.[33]

Things moved quickly. On August 19, 1679, the Franciscans agreed to a three-year lease of the ground floor of their monastery at an annual rent of 50 ducats (worth 7 florins each). In addition, the Franciscans promised to furnish two more rooms for the use of the professors of medicine, because Madame Royale intended that the university would teach medicine.[34] On the same day the Chambre des Comptes and the Franciscans entered into an agreement for extensive renovations of the monastery: erecting and eliminating walls, enlarging doors, plastering and painting, adding large glazed windows, preparing a room for the professors, and adding a garden. The Chambre des Comptes promised to pay the Franciscans 7,000 florins, half in advance, and the Franciscans would arrange for the renovations. If the renovations were not finished by November 11, the Franciscans would be obliged to find alternate quarters for the new university.[35]

Madame Royale and the Jesuits of Chambéry simultaneously discussed the terms under which the latter would be part of the University of Chambéry. She wanted the Jesuits to fill nine professorships at the beginning: one each in moral theology (i.e., cases of conscience), mathematics, Hebrew, and canon law, and an unspecified number in scholastic theology.[36] The Chambéry Jesuits already taught several of these subjects plus two classes in philosophy.[37] Hence, she was asking the Jesuits to add two to four

---

nostre Regence et si utile au Public." AST document of July 24, 1679, with the signatures of Marie Jeanne Baptiste (Madame Royale) and Joseph Delescheraine, printed in Vallauri 1970, 2:267–68.

33. Letter of the Chambre des Comptes of July 29, 1679, Chambéry, in AST, Istruzione pubblica, Regia Università di Torino, Mazzo 1, no. 16.

34. Document of the Chambre des Comptes of August 19, 1679, no place but Chambéry, from AST, printed in Vallauri 1970, 2:268–71.

35. Contract between the Franciscans and the Chambre des Comptes of August 19, 1679, no place but obviously Chambéry, signed by representatives of each side plus Councillor Delescheraine, printed in Vallauri 1970, 2:272–75.

36. "Comme les Peres Jesuites du College de Chambery fournizont un Professeur de Mathematique, un de Theologie morale, et un de la langue hebraïque qui ne sont point fondez; et que d'ailleurs ceux de la Theologie Scholastique." AST, Istruzione pubblica, Regia Università di Torino, Mazzo 1, no. 23, an undated and untitled document in which the Jesuits addressed the regent with their financial demands in exchange for providing professors. In another document, the Jesuits again mentioned one professor each for mathematics and casuistry, "des Professeurs de Theologie," plus a professor of canon law: "Pour cequi regarde le droit Canonique" and "un Professeur de droit canonique." AST, Istruzione pubblica, Regia Università di Torino, Mazzo 1, no. 20, a document entitled "Memoire des Peres Jesuites touchant l'université," no date, a five-page unsigned and unpaginated memorandum addressed to Madame Royale.

37. AST, Istruzione pubblica, Regia Università di Torino, Mazzo 1, no. 23, an unlabelled

more teachers: canon law, perhaps another philosopher, possibly another scholastic theologian, and Hebrew, although the Jesuit school already had a scripture class, and Jesuit scripture teachers often had expertise in Hebrew. If the number of Jesuit philosophers was increased to three, the university would be able to offer courses in logic, natural philosophy, and metaphysics simultaneously, which is what universities expected, rather than teaching them in rotation.

Claude Martin, the rector of the Jesuit college, negotiated with Madame Royale and her representatives over the financial compensation the Jesuits would receive for their contribution to the university.[38] The Jesuits first wanted assurances that past financial promises to support their college and its ministries, especially the school, would be fully honored. These included guarantees of perpetual ownership of lands assigned to them, revenues from properties, and tax exemptions. Next, noting that Madame Royale proposed to pay the lowest-ranking professor of law 100 ducats, Martin argued that the Jesuit college should receive at least 50 ducats for each of the Jesuit professors of mathematics, moral theology, and canon law, and that the minimum total for the Jesuit contribution to the new university should be 400 ducats of new annual income.[39]

After consulting with the provincial superior and the general in Rome, Father Martin also made several academic and governance demands.[40] He would permit Madame Royale to name the Jesuit professors in the first year, but insisted that the provincial superior would name them in the future. The Jesuits who would teach philosophy, theology, and mathematics had to receive doctorates from the university without undergoing examination or paying the customary fees. This was an effort to put Jesuit professors, who very seldom had doctorates, on an equal footing with the

and undated document. It is a memorandum to Madame Royale signed by Father Claude Martin, Jesuit rector at Chambéry. It begins "Les professeurs de Philosophie, Theologie, Langue Hebraïque, mathematique et autres sciences divines." See also ARSI, Lugduni 21, f. 428v.

38. Martin was appointed rector on October 7, 1678, and served until sometime in 1682. Demoment 1949, 1254.

39. For the demands of the Jesuits, see two unsigned and undated Jesuit memoranda addressed to Madame Royale in AST, Istruzione pubblica, Regia Università di Torino, Mazzo 1, nos. 20 and 23.

40. This paragraph and the following one are based on AST, Istruzione pubblica, Regia Università di Torino, Mazzo 1, no. 23, memorandum from the Jesuits signed by Father Martin. See also ARSI, Lugduni 33, Fundationes B-C, ff. 377r, 378r, 443r–44r, and 446r–47r. These folios contain three unsigned Latin and French, complete and partial, versions (one of them dated 1679), with minor differences from the memoranda in AST, plus a brief commentary on some of the articles. They demonstrate that the Society considered the Chambéry proposal carefully at the provincial level and in Rome.

lay professors of law and medicine, almost all of whom would possess doctorates.[41] The rector and the general feared that lay professors and students
would not respect Jesuit professors lacking doctorates.

Martin also insisted on other conditions designed to ensure that the Jesuit professors and the rector of the Jesuit college would be considered full
members of the university. The names of the Jesuit professors, along with
lists of the texts that they would teach, would be presented every year to
the conservator (conservateur) of the university so that they might be listed
in the faculty roll alongside the lay professors.[42] The Jesuits would have
the right to evaluate the level of preparation of the students who presented
themselves for their classes, as they did in their college classes.[43] This would
be contrary to the practice of Italian universities, in which the lectures
were public, meaning open to anyone who wished to attend and without
prerequisites. Students in Italian universities made their own decisions concerning their readiness for lectures.

Martin then addressed the relationship between Jesuit theologians and
other theologians in Chambéry. He wanted to create a faculty of theology that would include both the Jesuits and the theologians of the medieval
mendicant orders in the town. In order to make the university more notable
and to render the faculty more accomplished, Martin proposed that friars
and monks from the local convents—he named the Dominicans, Franciscans, Antonines, and the Observants, probably the Franciscan Observants—
should be brought into the faculty of theology of the university.[44] By "faculty of theology" he meant an Italian-style faculty of theology, which was
a loose confederation of all the religious order theologians in a university
town.[45] He did not mean a faculty of theology in the style of northern Europe, which was an organized teaching faculty inside the university.

41. For more on this, see chap. 15, "The Italian Jesuits Do Not Want Doctorates."

42. A conservateur was the personal representative of the ruler who oversaw day-to-day
operations of a university. Practically unknown in earlier centuries, they appeared under various titles in the seventeenth century. For example, the University of Turin had a conservator
who exercised jurisdiction over the students and professors in civil and criminal matters. Fisicaro Vercelli 1972, 350.

43. Ratio Studiorum 2005, pars. 259–63, 467 (117–19, 199).

44. AST, Istruzione pubblica, Regia Università di Torino, Mazzo 1, no. 23. memorandum
of the Jesuits signed by Claude Martin. The Antonines (Canons Regular of St. Augustine of
St. Anthony) were a hospitaller order founded in the Dauphiné about 1100. Its members followed the rule of St. Anthony the Abbot (ca. 250–350), credited as the founder of Christian
monasticism. The Antonines had had a convent in Chambéry for several centuries. They were
absorbed by the Knights of Malta in 1775. See Ruffino 1975, 134–41; and Lovie 1979, 101. The
Observant Franciscans were active in Chambéry. Lovie 1979, 68.

45. For further explanation, see Grendler 2002, 357–60.

Father Martin went on. Each of the medieval mendicant orders in Chambéry would be obligated to maintain a teacher of theology in its own monastery who would teach only members of his order. And the monasteries (whether each or collectively is unclear) would provide two doctors of theology to participate in degree examinations. In other words, they would constitute a college of doctors of theology. Further, the monasteries, their theology teachers, and the monks and friars who participated in degree examinations would all be considered part of the university.[46] In short, the Jesuits offered the medieval mendicant orders membership in a faculty of theology. He was more welcoming to them than they were normally to the Jesuits. But only the Jesuits would teach theology in the university.

Most of the rest of the Jesuit demands were intended to ensure that the new university would follow established practices and that the Jesuit professors and their students would be accorded appropriate respect. Martin wanted degrees to be awarded in the name of the chancellor of the university, which was normal university practice. The chancellor would enjoy the highest place of honor among the members of the university on ceremonial occasions, again the norm. And the father rector would precede the Jesuit professors on ceremonial occasions. This was unusual, because the rector of the Jesuit college was not expected to be a professor in the university. This appears to have been insistence on recognition of the institutional presence of the Jesuits in the university. Martin also insisted that members of religious orders who earned degrees should receive them in the same room where law and medicine students received their degrees. And professors should have the power of participating with the conservator in writing statutes and regulations, including those pertaining to degree expenses, for the university.[47]

Madame Royale agreed to a number of financial concessions and promised the Jesuits an income of 500 ducats for their university teaching.[48] Although her response to the academic and governance demands has not been located, she must have agreed, because she went forward in her plans. On August 23, 1679, on her orders, Commendatore Emanuele Pancalbo, a prominent figure at the ducal court, petitioned Rome for a papal bull for the new university. An abbot from Chambéry also requested a university

46. AST, Istruzione pubblica, Regia Università di Torino, Mazzo 1, no. 23, memorandum of the Jesuits signed by Claude Martin.
47. AST, Istruzione pubblica, Regia Università di Torino, Mazzo 1, no. 23, memorandum of the Jesuits signed by Claude Martin.
48. AST, Istruzione pubblica, Regia Università di Torino, Mazzo 1, no. 23, unpaginated document labeled "graces promises par ordre de M. R. aux pp. jesuites du college de Chambéry pour porter les charges del'université," dated July 24, 1679, Turin.

bull with all the privileges enjoyed by the universities of Bologna, Turin, and elsewhere. He informed the pope that the city of Chambéry had many "belli spiriti" with the capacity to learn.[49]

The final step was choosing the chancellor of the university, a largely ceremonial office usually filled by the local bishop. But there was a difficulty. Although Chambéry was the capital of Savoy, and earlier had been the capital of the entire Piedmont-Savoy state, it was not a diocese. Hence, it had no bishop or cathedral. Instead, Chambéry and Savoy were part of the Diocese of Grenoble in the Kingdom of France on the other side of the French Alps.

Chambéry did have a quasi-cathedral and a clergyman who acted like a bishop as the result of some complicated ecclesiastical and political history. In 1408 Duke Amedeo VIII (1383–1451, r. from 1391) began to construct a chapel in his palace in Chambéry, his capital, in order to manifest his authority and to promote Savoia family influence over the church in Savoy. Called La Sainte Chapelle, it became the home of the Holy Shroud shortly after mid-century. In 1467 Pope Paul II authorized the formation of a chapter consisting of twelve canons, six benefice holders, four additional clergymen, six choir boys, and an organist, with the dean of the chapter named perpetual vicar. This was a substantial ecclesiastical establishment. Moreover, La Sainte Chapelle absorbed the parish of St. Pierre and was directly subject to the pope, like a diocese. Sixtus IV (1471–1484) then united the chapter with the deanery of Chambéry (a major administrative unit of the Diocese of Grenoble), thus giving the chapter authority over a number of parishes in Savoy. On May 21, 1515, Leo X raised the deanery of Chambéry to the Archdiocese of Chambéry with La Sainte Chapelle as the cathedral church. He did this on request of Duke Carlo II of Piedmont-Savoy at the time of the marriage of the duke's sister, Filiberta Savoia, to the pope's brother, Giuliano de' Medici (1478–1516), a marriage designed to promote Medici and Savoia political interests.[50]

---

49. "Memoria del commendatore Panealbo [sic] per scrivere a Roma per l'ottanimento della bolla per l'Università di Chambéry," in AST, Istruzione pubblica, Regia Università di Torino, Mazzo 1, no. 18. Vallauri 1970, 2:136, mentions this document, but places it in fascicle no. 10. "Commendatore Panealbo" must be Commendatore Emanuele Filiberto Pancalbo (d. 1699), a professor of canon law, then civil law, at the University of Turin from the academic year 1659–1660 to at least 1689, after which there is a gap in the university records. Pancalbo was a ducal councillor who undertook a number of journeys for the rulers and was named commendatore in 1669. Fisicaro Vercelli 1972, 423–24. AST, Istruzione pubblica, Regia Università di Torino, Mazzo 1, no. 18, also contains an undated memorandum of one "Abbate Cagnolo" (not further identified) petitioning for a university charter for Chambéry.

50. Lovie 1979, 59–61.

However, King Francis I of France, the son of Luisa Savoia, another sister of Carlo II, objected. His objections mattered, because he had considerable power over the French church thanks to the Concordat of Bologna of 1516, and because French troops had been occupying Savoy for several years. The papal bull became a dead letter. Chambéry and Savoy remained part of the diocese of Grenoble even though La Sainte Chapelle and its dean reported directly to the pope.[51]

Nevertheless, Chambéry and Savoy were in practice autonomous, because geography divided them from the bishop and diocese of Grenoble. Although Grenoble and Chambéry are only about forty miles apart as the crow flies, high mountains and deep valleys separate them. The bishops of Grenoble seldom visited Chambéry because the journey meant riding a horse along rocky mountain paths, skirting precipices, fording mountain streams, and enduring the Alpine cold. Visiting the parishes of Savoy in the mountains and valleys north and east of Chambéry was even more difficult. Hence, the clergy and laity of Savoy looked to the dean of La Sainte Chapelle as their ecclesiastical leader and de facto bishop, and the Savoia dynasty exercised influence on the church in Savoy through La Sainte Chapelle and Chambéry.

Madame Royale chose the dean of La Sainte Chapelle, Abbé François de la Pérouse, to be the chancellor of the proposed university.[52] Given the confluence of political, ecclesiastical, and geographical factors, it would have been astonishing had she done anything else. Influential in his own right, he was also the son of François de la Bertrand de la Pérouse, the first president of the Savoy Senate. Father and son were members of a powerful family which held many important positions in Savoy.[53] Everything seemed ready to launch the new university for the French-speaking subjects of Piedmont-Savoy.

51. Lovie 1979, 60–61. Pastor 1891–1953, 8:416, notes that one of the consequences of the Concordat of Bologna was "the suppression of two sees created in Savoy." Chambéry must have been one of them.

52. See the letter of Bishop Etienne Le Camus to Pasquier Quesnel of August 31, 1679, in Le Camus 1892, 340.

53. There are several references to the influence and wealth of François de la Bertrand de la Pérouse and his family in Devos and Grosperrin 1985, 135, 184, 188, 192, 195, 210, 348. He is sometimes called the president of the Senate and other times president of the Chambre des Comptes in the documents; he obviously held both positions at one time or another. Bishop Le Camus called him "[le] commandant en Savoie." Le Camus 1892, 216.

Bishop Etienne Le Camus

The bishop of Grenoble strongly objected. He opposed the university because he saw its organization as an infringement on his authority and also because he hated the Jesuits, a hatred tinged with paranoia. His passion, energy, and powerful friends made him a formidable opponent.

Etienne Le Camus (1632–1707) was born in Paris into a prominent and wealthy *noblesse de robe* family. He obtained a doctorate of theology in 1658, was ordained a priest at an unknown date, and became an almoner of the court and a favorite of Louis XIV.[54] The young priest spent his time carousing rather than praying, including orgiastic Holy Week revelry that led to his temporary exile from Paris. Then in 1659 Le Camus underwent a conversion under the influence of prominent Jansenists at Port Royal and the Oratory in Paris. Now his rigorous penances rivaled his earlier partying. Louis XIV, who enjoyed his company, offered him the bishopric of Grenoble, which he accepted while vowing that he would continue his regimen of penances. Le Camus was named bishop on January 5, 1671, and consecrated on August 24. But he delayed entry into Grenoble until November 4, the feast day of St. Charles Borromeo, the rigorous and confrontational reforming archbishop of Milan whom Le Camus took as his model.[55] He was raised to the cardinalate in 1686 and died in 1707.

Le Camus never subscribed publicly to any condemned Jansenist doctrines, so far as is known, and he published in his diocese the 1705 papal condemnation of Jansenism. Nevertheless, the Paris Jansenists who had converted him continued to be his mentors. He poured out his heart to them in dozens of eloquent letters in which he reported on his reform efforts, complained about the sinful clergy and laity of his diocese, justified his stern actions, and looked to them for inspiration and advice.

Le Camus tackled the task of reforming his international diocese with energy and commitment; some historians see him as a prototypical Catholic Reform bishop.[56] Even though France never accepted the canons of the Council of Trent, Le Camus did, and he took further guidance from the reform decrees of Carlo Borromeo. Le Camus tried to make the parish the center of religious life. He wanted educated and celibate pastors who

---

54. Important studies of Le Camus include *Le cardinal Le Camus* 1974; Emery 1979, 135–49; Lovie 1979, 104; the excellent study of Luria 1991, who concentrates on his reform efforts in Grenoble and the other French parts of his diocese; and Gay 2011, 185, 227, 300n2, 480–90, 714–15, 735.

55. See Le Camus 1892, 56, 243; and Luria 1991, 1, and the index for evidence of his respect for Borromeo.

56. See the references in note 54.

would administer the sacraments in sober and devout services devoid of excessive display, and who would avoid the secular habits of their parishioners. To train them Le Camus established two seminaries in Grenoble. He made a determined effort to root out clerical abuses and to bring order and discipline to communal religious celebrations that he believed contained superstition and too much worldly frivolity. Le Camus favored austere religious observances stripped of Baroque piety. He sought to prune saints' cults and to limit the confraternities. He wanted the men and women under his spiritual authority to live righteous lives, and he believed that harsh public penances would help bring them to that end. His ideal church was grounded in the austere moral discipline of the ancient church in which absolution for sins was not easily granted. Le Camus imposed reform from above: he issued decrees and expected total obedience from clergy and laity. He viewed any dissent as seditious rebellion. The Catholic Reform that Le Camus embodied was austere, authoritarian, censorious, and joyless.

Le Camus first visited Chambéry and its deanery at the end of July 1673, and stayed through November in order to visit the fifty-five parishes of Savoy. According to Le Camus' own account, he was the first bishop of Grenoble to visit Savoy in forty years, and he followed with eight more visits in the next thirty years.[57] Le Camus did not have a high opinion of either his French or Italian subjects. After only five months as bishop he concluded that the debauchery of the monks and priests in his diocese was as bad as that in Italy, even though he had no personal knowledge of the latter.[58] At the end of his first pastoral visit, he wrote that Savoy contained the bilge of the priests of France and of Italy, and that the people did not know Jesus Christ.[59] In another letter he railed against the impurities, debaucheries, libertinism, usury, immodest dress, dances, balls, and vanities of the people of both Chambéry and Grenoble.[60]

Le Camus often clashed with the ecclesiastical and political leaders of Chambéry. He appointed a Savoyard representative in Chambéry to speak in his name to the clergy and people of Savoy, and the Senate of Savoy ac-

---

57. Lovie 1979, 72, 176.

58. "La débauche des moines et des prêtres est comme en Italie." Letter to Sébastien de Camboust de Pontchâteau of March 26, 1672, no place, in Le Camus 1892, 55. Pontchâteau (1634–1690) was a monk and author at the convent of Port Royal. Very hostile to the Jesuits, he was a key figure in what is sometimes called second Jansenism. Le Camus wrote many letters to him.

59. "Si bien que ce petit coin est la sentine des prêtres de France et d'Italie et le peuple n'y connâit point J.-C." Letter to Pontchâteau, no date but early 1674, in Le Camus 1892, 116. However, the editor of Le Camus 1933, 13n19, argues that it was written at the end of 1673, immediately upon his return from Savoy.

60. Letter to Father Pasquier Quesnel of March 13, 1679, in Le Camus 1892, 331.

cepted the nomination. But François La Pérouse, the dean of La Sainte Chapelle, did not. He claimed to be subject only to the guidance of the pope
and, in the words of Le Camus, acted as if he were the bishop of Savoy.[61]
Many battles followed. Le Camus issued directives, but the clergy of Chambéry and Savoy, tacitly or openly supported by the Senate, dragged their
feet. The differences over jurisdiction and what constituted true Catholicism prepared the way for the confrontation over the planned university.

Le Camus Opposes the University

Le Camus believed that the impetus for the new university came from the
Jesuits who would use it to fight Jansenism. At one point he complained that
the Jesuits were masters of doctrine who went from house to house labeling
as Jansenists those who did not love them.[62] On August 31, 1679, Le Camus
expressed his opinion about the proposed university and the role of the Jesuits in a letter to his friend and confidant, Father Pasquier Quesnel. An Ora-
torian, Quesnel (1634–1719 Amsterdam) was, next to Antoine Arnauld "the
Great" (1612–1694), also a correspondent of Le Camus, the most important
figure in second Jansenism. Le Camus claimed that the Jesuits, using the pretext that all of France was Jansenist, wanted the university at Chambéry as
a base from which to oppose them and himself.[63] He feared that Jesuit theology and canon law at Chambéry would result in extensive censorship of the
best books, meaning Jansenist books. This would produce lawsuits and con-
tinuous fights for himself and his successors. He feared that Jesuit opposition
would be so strong that he would be unable to overcome his opponents in a
foreign country as independent and opinionated as Savoy.[64]

Le Camus was mistaken in his idea that the initiative for the university
came from the Jesuits.[65] As indicated above, the idea originated with ear-

---

61. Letter of Le Camus to Pontchâteau of December 2, 1674, in Le Camus 1892, 172. See also
Lovie 1979, 173–74.

62. "Ils se rendent maîtres de la doctrine et allant de maison en maison, ils décrient qui il
leur plaît et font passer pour jansénistes ceux qu'ils n'aiment pas." Letter of Le Camus to Etienne-
François de Caulet (1610–1680), bishop of Pamiers, May 22, 1679, Rives, in Le Camus 1933, 205.

63. "Vous savez que les Jésuites veulent établir une université à Chambéry, sous prétexte
que tout est janséniste en France." Letter of Le Camus to Pasquier of August 31, 1679, Herbeys,
in Le Camus 1892, 340. There are 38 letters from Le Camus to Pasquier in Le Camus 1892.

64. "Et les Jésuites régents en théologie et en droit canon de cette université, il y aura tous
les jours des censures des meilleurs livres, et des formulaires nouveaux qu'on fera signer, et ils
me feront et à mes successeurs des procès et contestations continuelles auxquels je ne pourrai re-
médier dans un pays étranger, indépendant et aussi opiniâtre qu'est celui-là." Letter of Le Camus
to Pasquier of August 31, 1679, Herbeys, in Le Camus 1892, 341.

65. Lovie 1979, 106, following Le Camus, states that the university was the project of the

lier dukes of Piedmont-Savoy and Madame Royale acted on it. And if the Jesuits were primarily concerned to counter Jansenism in France, founding a new university outside of France was a bizarre way to do it.

One point was primary: Le Camus was convinced that the Jesuits taught bad theology, especially bad moral theology, and he was determined to stop them. He felt obligated to exert every effort at home and at the court in Paris to prevent the Jesuits from teaching their "new" theology. Le Camus believed that stopping the Jesuits was an opportunity to honor his vow to God; in so doing he would come as close as he could in this life to martyrdom in defense of the truth.[66]

Le Camus wrote that if it were not for the Dominicans, the Jesuits would have ruined all theological principles during the last sixty years.[67] He meant that the Jesuits had introduced deleterious changes into Thomism. And the last sixty years probably referred to the period in which Jesuit probabilism developed. In its simplest form probabilism argued that when clear choices were lacking, one might do what was morally probable, even if another action was more probable. Le Camus believed that the scandals and disorders of the church came principally from the evil moral theology of casuists, plus the laxity, cowardice, and ignorance of confessors.

Le Camus was convinced that Jesuit casuistry produced confessors who forgave sinners too easily, and so he tried to prevent the teaching of Jesuit casuistry. In 1671 the Jesuit college in Grenoble received a bequest to support a class in cases in conscience, and the general designated a very able Jesuit for the position. But Le Camus refused to permit the Jesuits to teach cases of conscience at Grenoble. The dispute dragged on until 1691 when General Tirso González surrendered, by ruling that the bequest could be used for a position in positive theology.[68] Le Camus also believed that Jes-

Jesuits, while Gay 2011, 484, sees the idea of a university at Chambéry originating with the Chambéry Senate and the Jesuits, which is also inaccurate.

66. "Il est vraie que je me suis trouvé obligé de faire tous mes efforts à Grenoble et à la Cour pour empêcher les Jésuites d'enseigner ici la théologie nouvelle. La leur est si corrompue en ces quartiers que j'ai cru que c'etait pour moi une occasion indispensable de témoigner à Dieu la fidélité que je lui ai vouée, et que c'était le seul martyre que je pouvais à présent endurer pour la défense de la vérité." Letter of Le Camus to Abbé François Dirois of January 17, 1674, Grenoble, in Le Camus 1892, 119. Dirois, who had a doctorate in theology from Paris, was at this time secretary to Cardinal César d'Estrées (1653–1714), bishop of Laon and currently in Rome representing Louis XIV. Ibid., note 2 on pp. xi–xii.

67. "Sans les Jacobins [= Dominicans], les Jésuites auraient ruiné tous les principes de théologie depuis soixante ans." Letter of Le Camus to Pontchâteau of May 25, 1674, Lavaldens, in Le Camus 1892, 132.

68. "Les Pères Jésuites continuent de vouloir enseigner les cas de conscience à Grenoble. Je m'y suis opposé il y a deux ans." Letter of Le Camus to Antoine Arnauld of December 12, 1673, Grenoble, in Le Camus 1892, 112. Le Camus wrote to Arnauld frequently. See also Gay 2011, 480–81.

uit moral theologians permitted usury, which he opposed.[69] And he complained that the Jesuits at Chambéry taught a version of ethics that had been banished on "this side of the Loire."[70] He may have meant that the Chambéry Jesuits did not teach the austere Jansenist moral theology found at Port Royal and elsewhere in France.

Le Camus also objected to Jesuit outreach to the laity through public religious exercises. He barred them from exposing the consecrated host in churches or outdoors on saints' days.[71] He disapproved of religious processions unless undertaken with his permission, which he rarely granted. Nor did Le Camus approve of Jesuit Marian congregations. He saw them as the means by which the Jesuits had won over the political leaders of Chambéry and Savoy.[72] He charged that the Jesuits used their multiple ministries in order to exert pernicious power throughout society. They had many friends in princely courts. They ruled adults through congregations, and children through their schools. They mastered women and the people through preaching and by hearing confessions.[73] For Le Camus, eliminating Jesuit theology and practices was a key part of true Catholic Reform.

Most of the time the Jesuits offered passive resistance to Le Camus by

69. "Car il ne se peut dire comment l'usure est autorisée en ces quartiers, surtout par les Jésuites." Letter of Le Camus to Pontchâteau of June 30, 1674, no place, in Le Camus 1892, 137.

70. "Les jésuites y dominent, et à Chambéry y enseignent toute la morale qui a été reléguée deça la Loire." Letter of Le Camus to Pontchâteau of March 26, 1672, no place, in Le Camus 1892, 55–56. He never wavered in his opposition to the Jesuits teaching theology; see his letter to Abbé Canel of April 2, 1700, in Le Camus 1892, 600.

71. Le Camus often barred or complained about Jesuit processions and expositions of the eucharist at Chambéry. See letters of December 12, 1673, through July 6, 1675, in Le Camus 1892, 113–14, 119, 137, 157, 172, 216. In processions the consecrated host was placed in a monstrance, which was a glass-faced ornate holder usually made of costly metals and sometimes decorated with precious stones. The priest carried the monstrance with the eucharist while the people knelt in adoration. Inside churches the eucharist was placed in a monstrance on the altar during such devotions as the Forty Hours. Worshipers came and went in relays, thus ensuring that someone was always praying in the presence of the sacrament.

72. "Ils ont une congrégation composée de tout le Sénat de cette ville [Chambéry]." Letter to Antoine Arnauld of December 12, 1679, Grenoble, in Le Camus 1892, 113; and "Les Jésuites gouvernent toutes les personnes de condition de l'un et de l'autre sexe et sont autorisés par les magistrats de ces deux Parlements [Grenoble and Chambéry], qui sont de leurs congrégations." Letter of Le Camus to Pasquier Quesnel, March 13, 1679, in Le Camus 1892, 330–31. Le Camus sometimes called the Senate of Savoy "parlement." This was French nomenclature; when the French occupied Chambéry they renamed the Senate "parlement."

73. "Vous savez le crédit qu'ils ont dans toutes les cours; comme ils son autorisés dans les villes où ils sont établis; comme ils tiennent les grands et les petits par les congrégations et par les collèges; per les prédications et les confessions, il se rendent les maîtres et des femmes et du peuple; par leur théologie et par les religieux qui leur sont attachés, comme les Capucins et autres." Letter of Le Camus to Etienne-François de Caulet (1610–1680), bishop of Pamiers, of May 22, 1679, Rives, in Le Camus 1933, 205.

ignoring his orders, delaying implementation, then apologizing, and finally conceding. They also fought back. In 1673 a Jesuit who had lived at the colleges in Chambéry and Grenoble told Duke Carlo Emanuele II in Turin that Le Camus was a Jansenist and a heretic. Le Camus angrily denied the charges. He went to Turin to assure the court that he was not a Jansenist; he protested vigorously to the Jesuit general about what he called a calumny; and for years he complained of Jesuit "persecution" to his Jansenist friends.[74]

The struggle continued. In 1678 and 1679 the Jesuits and the Senate of Chambéry sent three memoranda to the Congregation of the Holy Office in Rome. One was written by a Jesuit from Chambéry, another may have come from the provincial superior of the Province of Lyon, and the Senate of Chambéry sent the third. The first denounced Bishop Le Camus as a Jansenist and a crypto-Calvinist. All three added other charges: he encouraged the circulation of Jansenist tracts; he exaggerated the powers of bishops; he promoted confessional practices that did not preserve the secrecy of the confessional; he supported public penances; and he discouraged Marian and other public devotions.[75] Le Camus defended himself in person before the Senate of Chambéry and in Turin, and with letters to Madame Royale. He also appealed to the secretary of state of the government of Louis XIV. This was Simon Arnauld d'Andilly, marquis of Pomponne (1618–1699), secretary of state for foreign affairs from early 1672 through November 1679, and a nephew of Antoine Arnauld. Indeed, Pomponne was a regular correspondent of Le Camus.[76] Paris took up the bishop's cause with the ambassador of Piedmont-Savoy, and Le Camus wrote to Rome.[77] The papacy took no action against Le Camus.

Given the hostility between Le Camus and the Jesuits, it was inevitable that he would try to block the proposed University of Chambéry. He had several objections. He told Madame Royale that the university should be located in Thonon-les-Bains, a tiny town on Lake Léman at the extreme northern edge of Savoy.[78] Thonon had no Jesuits, and it was more than 80

74. The Jesuit was a Father Chapius. See letters of Le Camus of May 2, 1673, through October 13, 1679, in Le Camus 1892, 80, 254, 261, 350; and Le Camus 1933, 18–19, 155, 160.

75. Gay 2011, 484–88.

76. See Le Camus 1892, 53n1; and Le Camus 1933, 81, 209n107. It is clear from numerous references to Pomponne in his correspondence that Le Camus wrote many more letters to him than the four printed in these two volumes.

77. Le Camus 1892, 163, 173, 187, 207, 253; Le Camus 1933, 36–43, 79, 157–62, 166–67, 175.

78. "Je lui ai représenté que l'université serait mieux à Thonon, où saint François de Sales l'avait voulu était et où il y avait cinquante mille livres de rente de bénéfices unis pour fonder des collèges. Cela étant à trois lieues de Genève." Letter of Le Camus to Quesnel of August 31, 1679, Herbeys, in Le Camus 1892, 341.

difficult miles north of Chambéry and only 20 miles from Geneva. If the purpose of the proposed university had been to counter the Calvinist Geneva Academy, placing it in Thonon would have made some sense. But the purpose was to provide accessible university education to the young men of Savoy, for which Chambéry was the obvious best location.

When it became clear that the University of Chambéry would go forward, Le Camus changed tactics: he insisted that he should be named a combination of chancellor, "superior," and "visitor" of the university, with the right to "correct" the professors and what they taught.[79] Le Camus wrote a memorandum to Madame Royale setting out with copious legal references why he, as the bishop of the diocese in which the proposed university would be located, must be its chancellor. He referred to the canons of the Council of Trent and other ecclesiastical and legal sources.[80]

Madame Royale's legal advisers responded with two legal briefs arguing for civil authority over schools and universities. The first advanced a broad jurisdictional argument.[81] It began with the statement that it was imperative to find the right balance between civil and ecclesiastical jurisdiction. Providence has created spiritual and temporal jurisdictions in Christian states, and it was not good if they should be in disaccord, or for one to usurp the other. This would have deadly effects on *la vie civile* (civic life). One must render unto God what is God's and to Caesar what is Caesar's. It might at first glance appear that the governance of universities pertained to spiritual jurisdiction, because the goal of universities was to give youths a Christian education, the brief continued. However, because universities also had an impact on the utility of the sovereign and the good of the state, they were subject to Caesar's jurisdiction as well.

The brief moved to the consequences flowing from a division between temporal and spiritual jurisdiction. It asked rhetorically: since the goal of temporal jurisdiction was civil peace, should not the institutions where knowledge of the morality of arts and the law was acquired be subject to

79. "Enfin, ces raisons ne l'ayant pas touché, j'ai demandé d'en être le supérieur, visiteur avec droit de visite et correction, tant sur les régents que sur la doctrine, et même d'en être le chancelier, ou quelqu'un de ma cathédrale." Letter of Le Camus to Quesnel of August 31, 1679, Herbeys, in Le Camus 1892, 341.

80. This undated memorandum is found in AST, Istruzione pubblica, Regia Universitá di Torino, Mazzo 1, no. 15.

81. The first brief of eight pages is unsigned, undated, and unpaginated. It begins "La Providence ayant composé les Estats du Christianisme de deux differentes iurisdictions," and will be called "La Providence" in what follows. It is found in AST, Istruzione pubblica, Regia Universitá di Torino, Mazzo 1, no. 15. Vallauri 1970, 2:137, gives a very short summary of a few arguments of the two briefs.

civil jurisdiction? Moreover, since sovereigns founded universities, they had the right to govern them. The brief cited as examples that Emperor Theodosius II (r. 401–450) had founded the University of Bologna, and Charlemagne (r. 768–814) had founded the universities of Paris and Pavia.[82] Since sovereigns founded universities, and God has given them the power to establish laws for the common good, and learning is a common good, rulers had the right to found and govern universities independently of, and without interference from, the spiritual power.[83]

The brief next cited canons of the Council of Trent to argue for civil authority over universities. It noted that the council exhorted Catholic sovereigns to establish scripture lectureships in universities that lacked them.[84] This exhortation could not have the desired result if temporal and spiritual jurisdictions were at odds with each another, and if the civil authority lacked the means of implementing the wishes of the council. The brief also noted that the Council of Trent had authorized an exception to the right of bishops to visit schools. This was correct. In its broad Decree of Reform of September 17, 1562, the Council gave bishops "the right of visiting hospices, colleges of any kind ... but not those under the direct patronage of kings without their permission."[85]

The brief reached three major conclusions. Sovereigns had the right to found and govern universities without interference. Second, because emperors and other rulers had been founding and governing universities since the early Christian era, their seventeenth-century successors had the power to do the same. Third, the Council of Trent had removed from the jurisdiction of bishops colleges and universities under the protection of civil rulers, as the University of Chambéry would be.[86] At this time in European history, civil states were increasingly asserting authority over universities, in effect, treating them as organs of the state, at the expense of traditional

82. These so-called foundations were legends. The universities of Bologna and Paris slowly developed in the second half of the twelfth century and Pavia was founded in 1361.

83. AST, Istruzione pubblica, Regia Università di Torino, Mazzo 1, no. 15, "La Providence."

84. AST, Istruzione pubblica, Regia Università di Torino, Mazzo 1, no. 15, "La Providence." For Trent see chap. 6 of the second decree on instruction and preaching of the fifth session (July 17, 1546) in Decrees 1990, 2:668–69*. This edition has the Latin and English translation on facing pages. It translates "gymnasiis etiam publicis" as "public schools," which is correct but too broad. "Universities" is the better translation, because in the Italian context "gymnasium" normally meant "university." The adjective "publicis" confirms this.

85. Decrees 1990, 2:740–40*.

86. AST, Istruzione pubblica, Regia Università di Torino, Mazzo 1, no. 15, "La Providence."

claims that universities were part of a supranational Respublica Christiana. The Turin brief presented legal arguments for viewing universities as state institutions.

The second legal brief dealt with the specific issue of a bishop's authority in a university. It argued that the decrees of Trent and papal concessions limited the authority of bishops over universities that included the Jesuits.[87] It conceded that in the normal course of events bishops might examine the morals and doctrines of professors appointed to teach scripture. However, this would not be the case at Chambéry, because the professors of scripture and theology would be Jesuits, members of a religious order that already had the authority to teach in universities, and whose schools had the legal status of universities. The brief noted that Pope Sixtus V in 1585 had awarded the Jesuits university powers and privileges, and that Pope Paul V in 1615 had conferred a university privilege on the prince-bishop of Paderborn empowering him to govern the new Jesuit university at Paderborn.[88] The point was that Chambéry would be a university like Paderborn, that is, ruled by a sovereign and with Jesuit professors. Because the Society of Jesus possessed university privileges independently of its participation in the University of Chambéry, its members would not be subject to the jurisdiction of the local bishop when they taught.

The second brief added arguments of geography, convenience, and allegiance. It conceded that the local bishop normally awarded degrees, but added that there was no episcopal law or canon codifying this as a right. And it was better and more convenient that the person who awarded degrees should reside in the town of the university, which Le Camus did not. Moreover, it was inappropriate that a university founded by a prince should have as its highest officer a foreigner, that is, a chancellor who was the subject of a foreign sovereign, as Le Camus was the subject of the king of France.[89]

Madame Royale and her ministers also informed Le Camus that having a chancellor with such broad powers as he demanded was contrary to the custom in Italy, where universities were completely independent of the bishop of the diocese except in matters of faith.[90] They accurately described

---

87. It is an unsigned, undated, and unpaginated nine-page legal brief that begins "Il ne semble pas que Mons.r de Grenoble ait raison." AST, Istruzione pubblica, Regia Università di Torino, Mazzo 1, no. 15. It will be called "Il ne semble pas." See especially ff. [1r–v, 5r].

88. Paul V's bull of April 2, 1615, is found in Hengst 1981, 331–34.

89. AST, Istruzione pubblica, Regia Università di Torino, Mazzo 1, no. 15, "Il ne semple pas," f. [5r].

90. "Ils m'ont répondu que ce n'était pas l'usage d'Italie où les universités étaient toutes

the limited role of the chancellor in Italian universities. By tradition and statute the local bishop was the chancellor, but his duties were mostly ceremonial.[91] He presided at the pontifical high Mass in the cathedral inaugurating the academic year. He accepted professions of faith from professors and degree candidates, because the papal bull *In sacrosancta beati Petri* of November 13, 1564, obliged professors and degree candidates to make professions of adherence to Catholicism as a condition for holding professorships and receiving degrees.[92]

But the bishop as chancellor did not have any other legal or practical authority. The civil government appointed and paid professors. The bishop-chancellor did not determine what professors taught, nor did he monitor lectures. He conferred degrees only after colleges of doctors decided who would receive them. The bishop-chancellor simply presided over the public ceremony in which graduates received the doctor's biretta, ring, and books. Even that authority did not embrace all graduates. If a student did not wish to profess Catholicism or receive a degree from the college of doctors and chancellor, he could obtain a degree from counts palatine at lower cost.[93]

Le Camus wanted to be much more than a ceremonial chancellor. He wanted to be able to control what would be taught, at least in theology and canon law, and to censor professors who deviated. He had already become embroiled in censorship disputes with the Savoy Senate and the ducal government of Turin. Le Camus had demanded the right to bar the distribution of some theological and devotional works written by French Catholic theologians that professed views about piety and the frequent reception of the sacraments with which he disagreed.[94] He would certainly have told Jesuit professors what they might and might not teach.

Madame Royale and her advisors rejected his arguments and went forward with their plans. They produced drafts of a constitution for a law,

---

indépendantes des ordinaires, à la réserve des points de foi, etc." Letter of Le Camus to Quesnel of August 31, 1679, Herbeys, in Le Camus 1892, 341.

91. There were two partial exceptions. The archdeacon of the cathedral of St. Petronius was the chancellor of the University of Bologna as decreed by a papal bull of Honorius III in 1219. But his powers were as limited as those of bishop chancellors. And Pope Urban VIII in 1625 conferred on the bishop chancellor of the University of Perugia the right to participate in the selection of professors and determination of salaries in conjunction with colleges of doctors and the Savi dello Studio.

92. See Grendler 2002, 75, 191. However, the extent to which the bull was enforced on professors and students outside of Italy, in France for example, is unknown.

93. See Grendler 2002, 183–86, 507.

94. See letters of April 25, 1674, through November 24, 1678, in Le Camus 1892, 128–29, 304, 319–21; and Le Camus 1933, 158–59, 167, 175–76.

medicine, philosophy, and humanities university with Jesuit professors. The drafts provided for law professorships, a college of doctors of law to examine degree candidates, some indication of the number of law professors, that they would teach humanistic jurisprudence, degree requirements, rules for a chancellor of limited powers, and everything else needed for a university. Most important, the drafts made a provision for a conservator who would be the most important figure in the university with many powers, including correcting the professors.[95]

Failure

Thwarted, Le Camus sought external political support. As he had done in earlier disputes, he wrote to Pomponne, the French secretary of state, in order to enlist the support of the government of Louis XIV.[96] It produced the desired result. The government of Louis XIV told Madame Royale that it supported the demands of Bishop Le Camus. This was decisive. Although university practice, historical precedent, and probably canon law were on her side, Madame Royale could not afford to offend the most powerful monarch of Europe, who made no secret of his desire to seize Savoy by force. She had to give Le Camus everything that he wanted. In January 1681 the commandant of Savoy wrote to Le Camus offering to make Le Camus the chancellor of the university. He further conceded that Le Camus and his successors would have the rights of "superiority" and "inspection" over the university.[97]

A papal charter (bull), either unpromulgated or a draft, for a University of Chambéry confirmed this.[98] It proclaimed that Duke Vittorio Amedeo II,

95. See AST, Istruzione pubblica, Regia Università di Torino, Mazzo 1, no. 19, labeled by an archivist "Progetti d'editto del Duca Vittorio Amedeo 2.0 per il stabilimento dell'Università di Ciamberi. 1681." It contains three drafts of a constitution for the university, always in French. Each runs 15 to 22 pages and has about 38 articles. They were written in 1679 or 1680, because the contents parallel the arguments and discussions that took place in 1679.

96. Letters of Le Camus to Quesnel of August 31 and September (no day) 1679, in Le Camus 1892, 340–42.

97. "M. l'évêque de Grenoble écrit qu'il a reçu une lettre de M. le marquis de Saint-Maurice, commandant en Savoie, qui lui offre de le faire chancelier de l'université de Chambéry, dont Sa Majesté a empêché jusqu'à présent l'établissement, et de lui donner et à ses successeurs la supériorité et l'inspection dont on conviendra." Memorandum of January 10, 1681, from the Archives des affaires étrangères, Dauphiné, Paris, quoted in Le Camus 1892, 365–66.

98. ARSI, Lugduni 33, Fundationes B-C, ff. 367r–70r (quotation 368r). Although it carries the heading "Innocentius XI," pope from 1676 to 1689, the document lacks a date, formal closure, signature, and seal. It might be a draft of a charter never issued. The most likely date is 1681, perhaps between January and April. See the memorandum of January 10, 1681, mentioned

for whom Madame Royale was acting as regent, had determined to establish a university for the utility and prosperity of the duchy. It praised Chambéry as the historical capital of Savoy and said that the university would be there. The charter then stated that Vittorio Amedeo II had named Bishop Le Camus the "perpetual chancellor" of the University of Chambéry with "ius visitandi, correngendi" (the right of visiting and correcting) both regular and secular clergy who were part of the university without any exceptions. Future bishops of Grenoble would also be chancellors of the university with the same powers. In addition, Bishop Le Camus might name a vice-chancellor to act for him, and the latter would have the same authority to confer degrees and exercise oversight over the university. As if to underscore the capitulation, the papal charter named Le Camus three times, but never mentioned the Jesuits. The university would not include them. It was impossible for the Jesuits to be part of a university in which Le Camus would exercise draconian powers over them.[99]

Madame Royale attempted to reclaim some authority by naming a conservateur who would oversee the finances and other aspects of the university for the sovereign.[100] And she continued to try to inaugurate a university at Chambéry. In April 1681 she announced that letters patent from her son, Vittorio Amedeo II, creating the university were on the way. She expected that the formal inauguration would occur in late April 1681.[101]

It did not happen. While the capitulation may have satisfied Le Camus, this was not enough for the government of Louis XIV. Its attention having been drawn to the proposed university, France concluded that a university in Chambéry would draw students away from the French universities of Valence and Cahors. It judged that the ease with which students would be able to obtain doctorates at Chambéry would produce much revenue for Chambéry but lead to the abandonment of these two small French universities.[102] Hence, it did not want a university at Chambéry under any circumstances.

in the previous note, and the desire of Madame Royale to inaugurate the university in late April 1681 (see below).

99. I have not located any documents indicating that the Jesuits formally withdrew from the proposed university. The end of a failed initiative often leaves no documentary trace.

100. This was a "President Ducrest" not further identified. Vallauri 1970, 2:138.

101. Vallauri 1970, 2:138.

102. "Il croit que pour l'intérêt de son évéché cela suffirait, mais que pour celui de Sa Majesté, il y a quelque réflexion à y faire; par cet établissement l'université de Valence et de Cahors seront entièrement abandonnées, et que la fecilité que l'on aura à Chambéry de faire des docteurs y attirera bien du monde et y fera porter beaucoup d'argent; n'a répondu qu'en termes généraux jusqu'à qu'il su les intentions de Sa Majesté." Memorandum of January 10, 1681, in the Archives des affaires étrangères, Dauphiné, Paris, quoted in Le Camus 1892, 366.

Madame Royale did establish law instruction in April 1681 through a ducal decree and promised that a university charter would follow. This attracted some law students. But their number dwindled to just a few by 1683, because she was unable to establish a university with the power to confer degrees.[103] Discussion about a University of Chambéry disappeared from the records. Chambéry and Savoy were annexed by France in 1792, returned to Piedmont-Savoy in 1815, but ceded to France in 1860. Today Chambéry has a graduate engineering program. It has never had a university.

A French bishop and the French government blocked the creation of a civic-Jesuit university in the Italian state of Piedmont-Savoy. The government and the Jesuits could not overcome the opposition of a bishop who hated the Jesuits and had the ear of the most powerful monarch in Europe. The Jesuits could only watch as France enforced its will on Piedmont-Savoy.

Conclusion

Although Palermo and Chambéry were as far apart geographically as they could be, their stories were the same. Local Jesuits and the civil authority sought to create civic-Jesuit universities in cities lacking them. The Jesuits took the lead in Palermo, the ruler of Piedmont-Savoy in Chambéry. In both cases planning went smoothly until the local bishop demanded control of the proposed university, a domination that would have been unprecedented in Italy. Cardinal Doria and Bishop Le Camus wanted absolute control over the proposed universities, including the power to censor Jesuit teaching in the case of Le Camus. When the Palermo Jesuits and Madame Royale of Piedmont-Savoy rejected their demands, Doria and Le Camus appealed to the governments of Spain and France, which ruled in their favor. The Jesuits withdrew, and neither university came into existence.

103. Devos and Gorsperrin 1985, 370. How many law professors taught between 1681 and 1683, and how many students attended their lectures, is unknown.

IO

THE JESUITS

AND THE UNIVERSITY

OF BOLOGNA

Members of the University of Bologna viewed the Jesuit upper school as an illegal competitor. Since Bologna was the oldest university in Italy and very conscious of its standing, it took a dim view of the Jesuits and their growing educational role in the city. Some members of the university and their supporters in the city government demanded that the Jesuits be barred from teaching theology and philosophy because the university had the exclusive right to teach these subjects. Although the Jesuits never tried to enter the University of Bologna, they wanted and needed to teach theology and philosophy. This led to prolonged quarreling, albeit without the dramatic confrontation that occurred in Padua. After several lengthy disputes, the university, the city government (also called commune), the papacy, and the Jesuits reached a de facto compromise that permitted the Society to teach theology and philosophy to Jesuit scholastics and a limited number of external students.

First Contacts between the Jesuit College
and the University

Francis Xavier planted the seeds of the future Jesuit college during his visit to Bologna from October 1537 to April 1538. After securing permission from the bishop, he preached in public squares, heard confessions, taught the catechism to children, comforted the sick, and begged his daily bread. He impressed the rector of the parish church of Santa Lucia, a large and important parish with a small and ugly church on Via Castiglione, who gave Xavier and Nicolás Bobadilla two rooms adjoining the church in which to live. Francis kindled the admiration of a pious and wealthy widow, Violante Casali Gozzadini, who lived in a palace contiguous with the parish house of Santa Lucia. She was the daughter, sister, and widow of three of the most important men of Bologna.[1]

Gozzadini, her relatives, the parish priest of Santa Lucia, and others campaigned for a Jesuit college in Bologna. So did a young priest named Francesco Palmio (Parma 1518–1585 Bologna), the older brother of Benedetto Palmio, who came to study at the University of Bologna in 1541.[2] Ignatius Loyola granted their wish in 1546, and in the next few years sent several first Jesuits to Bologna for short periods of time. Francesco Palmio became a Jesuit in 1547 and the rector of the college in 1551, a position that he held until 1571. He felt privileged to live in the room that Francis Xavier had occupied, a room that eventually became a chapel. Pius IV assigned the church of Santa Lucia to the Jesuits in 1562. Thanks to benefactors, the Jesuits acquired the Gozzadini palace and bought and remodeled houses between Via Castiglione and Via Cartoleria Vecchio in close proximity to Santa Lucia. They were not in the center of the city where the university building was located but were well within the city walls.[3]

In 1551 the Jesuits founded a lower school of three classes, grammar, humanities, and rhetoric, with an initial enrollment of 100 students.[4] Growth was slow by Jesuit standards. In 1554 the school had only 115 students, and in the academic year 1557–1558 it added a class in logic, which soon disappeared. There were 13 Jesuits in the Bologna college in the years 1562 through 1564.[5] In 1569 there were 16 Jesuits at Bologna and they taught three classes, rhetoric and humanities combined, plus two grammar classes. Francesco Palmio lamented that the college still lacked secure income.[6] The number of Jesuits grew to 18 to 20 in early 1580, although the school still enrolled only 150 students in three lower-level classes.[7]

Cardinal Gabriele Paleotti (1522–1597) became bishop of Bologna in January 1567 and archbishop in 1582. He worked closely with the Jesuits and Father Palmio, who became his confessor, to implement Catholic Reform measures. Paleotti founded a seminary in 1567, and put the seminarians in a building contiguous with the Jesuit college building. He arranged for a

---

1. Tacchi Venturi 1951a, 126–28; Schurhammer 1973, 374–90.

2. Scaduto 1968, 110; Scaduto 2001c. In contrast to his brother, Francesco Palmio was a gentle and eternally optimistic man.

3. Schurhammer 1973, 374–90; De Angelis and Scannavini 1988, 13–14; Angelozzi and Preti 1988, 131; and Zarri 1988.

4. Tacchi Venturi 1951b, 412–17.   5. Scaduto 1974, 397–99.

6. ARSI, Veneta 94, ff. 48r–v, end of August 1569.

7. ARSI, Veneta 105 I, f. 59r.

door to be cut between the two buildings and asked the Jesuits to teach the seminarians. The first group began to study in the Jesuit school in 1569.[8]

However, the seminarians dragged down the school. The provincial superior visited in 1574 and found much to criticize. He found the rhetoric teacher to be good, but because he only attracted four or five students, the class had been abandoned. Humanities had only twenty-eight students, and grammar had only thirty. One reason was the competition from the university. Because it had several excellent professors of rhetoric, students left for the university rhetoric lectures as soon as they acquired some Latin competence. However, the provincial superior continued, the competition from the university has always been there. The major reason for the mediocre record of the school was that the Jesuits had lowered their standards to accommodate the "thick wits" of the seminarians. They wanted to be priests, but did not want to learn anything beyond a little Latin and the catechism. Worse, they answered the teachers with insolence and resisted being chastised. Because their attitude infected the other students, the classes were "spoiled."[9] Nevertheless, the Jesuits continued to teach the seminarians until 1598.[10]

The Bologna Jesuits were keenly aware of the university. In November 1556, Francesco Palmio was pleased to report that university students were attending the humanities and rhetoric classes.[11] In 1561 he believed that the Bologna school had turned the corner toward success, because the majority of the students were sons of nobles and other prominent figures, including the son of Francesco Robortello (1516–1567), humanities professor at the university and a well-known scholar.[12]

In the 1570s the Jesuits joined Paleotti in a ministry to the university. Paleotti knew the University of Bologna well. A native of Bologna, he obtained a doctorate in civil and canon law from the university in 1546, immediately began teaching *Institutes,* and was promoted to morning ordinary professor

8. Prodi 1959–1967, 2:139–41; Scaduto 1992, 281.

9. "Quello pare a questi padri è: prima, l'esser Bologna città di studio, dove sono eccelenti professori di retorica, et chi la vol servir, va là. 2. Perché chi ha un pocho di latinità per le pratiche de lettori, è subito tirrato a servir le lettioni publiche. Ma queste raggioni sono sempre state impiedi, et pure altre volte li nostri hanno havuto bone schole. A me par che sia la cagione di questa ruina principale l'haver accomodato il nostro modo d'insegnar alli chierici del seminario. Li quali dovendo esser preti, altro non vogliono che saper un pocho di latino et il catechismo che si legeva ex professo." He later wrote "li chierici del seminario sono d'ingegni per lo più grossi." Letter of Francesco Adorno to the Jesuit general, Everard Mercurian, of October 12, 1574, Forlì, in MP 4:552–54 (quotations at 552 and 553).

10. Fabrini 1941, 15.

11. Scaduto 1974, 398–99n10.

12. Letter of Palmio of May 16, 1561, Bologna, in *Litterae quadrimestres* 1932, 328; and Dallari 1888–1924, 2:147, 150.

of civil law in 1549. He taught at Bologna until 1556, when he was appointed to a high judicial position in Rome.[13] Now back in Bologna as bishop, he worked with officers of the student nations and representatives of the commune to found a Compagnia della Perserveranza in 1574. He placed it under the spiritual direction of the Jesuits, especially Francesco Palmio. The Compagnia promoted piety and learning, and helped students find lodging. In its meetings the members studied early church history, a humanistic emphasis, and the "mysteries of Christian philosophy," but avoided scholastic theology. As its numbers grew, the Compagnia divided into three groups according to student interests: law, medicine, and humanistic studies.[14]

The Bolognese Jesuits wrote glowing reports about the activities of the Compagnia della Perseveranza. Francesco Palmio reported on May 7, 1575, that a recent meeting had attracted more than eighty attendants, twelve of them university professors, including a major legist and an important philosopher.[15] A report of 1580 added more information. The Compagnia had a membership of more than one hundred professors and students, the majority of the latter nobles.

At the beginning of the academic year Cardinal Paleotti celebrated Mass for the Compagnia. In the middle of the service a professor from the congregation delivered a Latin oration to the satisfaction of all. Officers of the student organizations confessed and received the eucharist from the cardinal. After Mass a Jesuit offered a learned and spiritual discourse in the presence of the student rector of the university, professors, and students. Latin and vernacular compositions in prose and verse were posted. Throughout the academic year members of the Compagnia met every Sunday, and received the eucharist in the Jesuit church once a month. The report concluded by affirming that it was a great consolation to see noble and rich students who earlier had joked about "spiritual persons" now talking about the things of God.[16] In 1608 the Jesuits merged the Compagnia della Perseveranza into their own Congregation of the Assumption which enrolled

13. Dallari 1888–1924, 2:110, 112, 115, 118, 121, 123, 126, 129, 132, 134; and Prodi 1959–1967, 1:54–95.

14. Prodi 1959–1967, 2:215–20; Brizzi 1976, 76, 114–15.

15. ARSI, Italiae 147, f. 131r. The legist was Giovanni Angelo Papio, at that time first-position afternoon ordinary professor of civil law teaching part of the Corpus juris civilis. The philosopher was Federico Pendasio (ca. 1525–1603), first-position afternoon ordinary professor of natural philosophy. Dallari 1888–1924, 2:189–90; for Pendasio, see Lohr 1988a, 305–11. In early July 1575 Paleotti preached a sermon in Latin and distributed communion to 400 teachers and students. See Prodi 1959–1967, 2:129n192.

16. ARSI, Veneta 105 I, f. 59r–v.

university students and older students from the Jesuit school.[17] In 1622 the Congregation of the Assumption had 112 members.[18] It continued at least through the middle of the seventeenth century and probably beyond.[19]

In 1591 the Jesuits opened a class in logic for the benefit of the seminarians but it did not last.[20] At an unknown date the Jesuits began to teach cases of conscience to the local secular clergy and this became permanent. And in 1600 the Bolognese Jesuits told Rome that the Jesuit who lectured on cases also heard the confessions of Germans.[21] Since most of the Germans in Bologna were university students, this was another ministry to the university community. In 1622 the Bologna Jesuit school offered five classes: two grammar classes, humanities, rhetoric, and cases, with a total enrollment of 296.[22]

To this date the Jesuits did not attract criticism from the university or the city government. Even a public disputation at the Jesuit church in which four participants disputed philosophical and theological issues with many dottori and clergymen in attendance did not draw criticism from the university.[23] The reason was that the Jesuit school did not teach courses in logic, natural philosophy, metaphysics, mathematics, or theology that would have competed with university courses. The Jesuits limited themselves to trying to improve the spiritual lives of university students.

Novitiate and Noble School

In the 1630s the good relations between the Jesuits and the university and its supporters in the city government deteriorated. Several developments

17. Fabrini 1946a, 17–18; Brizzi 1976, 94–95. Prodi 1959–1967, 2:219–20, 439, states that the Compagnia della Perseveranza did not last beyond Paleotti's move to Rome in 1586. Although it may have declined after Paleotti's departure, documents in ARSI demonstrate that it continued under a new name and Jesuit direction.

18. ARSI, Veneta 39 I, f. 59r. While the congregations were not listed by their given names, the college at Bologna had a "prima congregazione de' scolari," most likely the Congregation of the Assumption, with 112 members. How many of them were university students is unknown. Two other congregations of students described as "seconda" and "terza" had memberships of 60 and 90.

19. Angelozzi 1988, 127.

20. Fabrini 1941, 7.

21. "P. Pietro Fracario confessore legge, et decide i casi in arcivescovado et confessa i Tedeschi." ARSI, Veneta 37, f. 259r, December 1600.

22. ARSI, Veneta 39 I, f. 58r. The rhetoric class had 43 students, the humanities class had 54, the upper grammar class had 70, the middle grammar class had 79, and the cases lecture drew 50.

23. "Et finito si diede principio alle dispute, con molto concorso di dottori et religiosi: li sustenti furono quattro, e ciascuno fece le conclusioni in teologia et filosofia." ARSI, Veneta 105 I, f. 59v, annual report for 1580.

caused the university to conclude that the Jesuits were planning to add an upper school teaching scholastic theology and philosophy. The first two were the addition of a novitiate and the St. Francis Xavier School for Nobles.

It began in the late 1620s. Marquis Alberto Serpa Angelelli, who came from a prominent Bolognese family, was a Jesuit novice for a short time in 1616, then left and inherited a fortune. Because he continued to admire the Society, he decided in 1625 to give a large sum for an upper school to teach philosophy and theology in Bologna. The rector of the Jesuit college in Bologna dissuaded him on the grounds that the Province of Venice already had an upper school at Parma. There was the university at Mantua as well. He encouraged Angelelli to give money for a novice house that would also serve as a retreat house for clergy and lay persons wishing to make the Spiritual Exercises. Angelelli agreed and Cardinal Ludovico Ludovisi, the archbishop of Bologna and a patron of the Jesuits, endorsed it. The Bolognese Jesuits accepted the gift in 1626.[24] Since this would be a new building, the approval of the city was needed. This was the beginning of disputes that lasted into the early 1670s.

The complexity of the governance of Bologna made resolution of any issue involving the university and the Jesuits time-consuming and difficult.[25] The supreme legislative body was the Senate of Bologna consisting of fifty men from powerful local families who were elected for life; indeed, some seats were de facto family seats. A series of committees called *assunterie* did much of the administration of the city. They had this name because they were composed of *assunti* (appointed or nominated ones), usually five or six senators and/or other men. Assunterie made recommendations to the Senate which rendered final decisions. One of the most important was the Assunteria (or Assunti) di Studio which oversaw the university. In addition, the pope appointed a legate, almost always a cardinal with diplomatic and administrative experience, with authority over the city. The Senate and the legate had to agree on measures before they became law and, surprisingly, they did agree most of the time. But the city also had a direct channel to Rome. It had an ambassador, always someone from a Bolognese oligarchical family, to the pope, the only unit within the papal state with this privilege. Like diplomats from sovereign states, the ambassador had the right to take the city's case to the pope, the cardinal secretary of state, and other papal officials. And Senate and Assunteria di Studio frequently ordered him to do exactly that.

24. Fabrini 1941, 8–9.
25. For what follows, see De Benedictis 1995; Terpstra 1995, 176–78, 192–94; Terpstra 2005, 22–23; Lines 2013, 665–67.

The presence of a renowned university added more complexity. Much of the city's identity, reputation, and economy depended on it. Hence, if a group from the university, some senators, the Assunteria di Studio, or another body declared that a proposed measure would harm the university, the claim was taken seriously. Discussions then took place in several venues, sometimes at cross purposes. The papacy also recognized the importance of the university. Although in previous centuries popes had rarely interposed themselves into university matters, popes and Vatican cardinals intervened, or tried to intervene, more often in the seventeenth century. Finally, because the Jesuit general also lived in Rome, the Bolognese ambassador and cardinals spoke to him as well.

Members of the university and the government were particularly sensitive to any perceived threat to the university because it was weak. In disputes with the Jesuits, members of the university and its supporters frequently cited the illustrious history and reputation of the University of Bologna. They did not mention its long list of problems.[26] The university had many professors, almost all of them Bolognese men of little distinction. While the government reserved four positions (in law, medicine, natural philosophy, and the humanities) for distinguished non-Bolognese scholars, the positions were seldom filled in the seventeenth and eighteenth centuries. One reason was that the city did not provide the money to attract distinguished scholars. Instead, it filled positions with Bolognese men who had recently acquired doctorates from the university. Indeed, any Bolognese citizen who obtained a doctorate from Bologna was practically guaranteed a professorship. Such appointments were a way of distributing favors and income, a form of patronage.[27] Many of these professors did not bother to teach.

The students created further difficulties. While seventeenth-century matriculation numbers were not as high as in the sixteenth century, they did not decline precipitously until the end of the century. The problem was that many matriculated students did not attend lectures; some did not even reside in Bologna. Instead, they paid fees for private instruction from university professors, leaving lecture halls empty. Professors did not teach

---

26. For this and the following paragraph, start with *Ordinationi* 1641. This was a list of university abuses and the threatened punishments for them issued on February 8, 1639, then reissued and printed by Cardinal Legate Stefano Durazzo and five Assunti di Studio on July 12, 1641. Additional secondary sources include Costa 1912; Simeoni 1987, 81–102; Grendler 2002, 477–508; Brizzi 1988b; Brizzi 2008, 69–87, 107–12; and Lines 2011, 2012, and 2013. These same problems were found in other Italian universities to greater or lesser degree in the seventeenth and eighteenth centuries.

27. Lupi 2005, 34–35.

when no one came. Another issue was the shrinking academic calendar. While Bologna's statutes mandated about 135 ordinary lectures in the academic year, there were fewer than 100, perhaps only 70 or 80, because of unauthorized holidays, student turbulence and absenteeism, and other reasons. Student violence was another chronic problem that disrupted teaching and study. Although the University of Bologna conferred more than 5,000 degrees in law between 1600 and 1796, and an unknown but large number in other disciplines, teaching and research at the University was not healthy.[28] The weakness of the university was a major reason why members of the university community, the Assunteria di Studio, and the Senate opposed any group that might effectively compete with the university.

In 1626 Cardinal Legate Ludovisi put the matter of the new novitiate before the Bolognese Senate, which was not pleased.[29] Some senators, relatives of Angelelli, disapproved on the grounds that the proposed novitiate would be used as a wedge to create a university. While this was not Angelelli's original desire, he had wanted an upper school. It was also true that disappointed relatives almost always objected when large gifts went to the Jesuits rather than to themselves. The petition of the Jesuits for the novitiate moved from committee to committee, including the Assunteria di Studio. The cardinal and the Senate accused each other of ignoring procedure and failing to communicate. So, with the approval of Cardinal Ludovisi, Angelelli went ahead: he purchased and renovated a house for the novitiate. The first Mass was celebrated there in April 1627. The Bolognese government then protested to the pope, who expressed surprise and referred the Bolognese ambassador to Jesuit General Vitelleschi, who professed that he was unaware that the novitiate building was completed and promised satisfaction. Indeed, he pointed out that the Jesuits already had two novitiates in the Province of Venice and suggested that the money might have been better spent enlarging the church of Santa Lucia. But the novitiate was a fait accompli, and the controversy disappeared from communal records.[30] Although a small dispute conducted with reasonable politeness, it left a residue of ill will. Most important, the view that the Jesuits wanted to add an upper school that would compete with the university was aired.

---

28. Guerrini 2005.

29. There are several accounts of the disputes between the university and the Jesuits from 1626 through 1673. Costa 1912, 59–72, is strongly anti-Jesuit; as is Zaccagnini 1930, 162–65. Simeoni 1987, 91–92, provides a brief neutral account. The most complete study is Fabrini 1941, which corrects Costa and provides a great deal of new research and documents. Brizzi 1976 is very useful.

30. Fabrini 1941, 9–14.

A sharper clash came a few years later over the Jesuit desire to provide upper school classes for the students in their boarding school for nobles. The noble school came into existence in a circuitous way. In the late sixteenth century a boarding school for boys under the name St. Prisca opened its doors in Bologna.[31] It differed from other student residences in Bologna because it only accepted boys of noble birth. In the academic year 1600–1601 Don Sinibaldo Blondi, a secular priest, became rector with complete academic and custodial responsibility. The school put itself under the protection of successive cardinal legates, and powerful local men supported it.[32] The school had 53 boarders in 1616 and 21 in 1620, the only years for which information is available.[33]

Since the boarding school did not have its own teachers, the noble boys attended classes at the Jesuit school at Santa Lucia, which was only steps away. Relations between the Jesuits and Don Blondi and his boarders were warm. The boys participated in Jesuit celebrations at the anniversaries of the beatifications of Ignatius Loyola and Luigi Gonzaga. Some noble boys joined the Congregation of the Assumption, and the Jesuits gave them prominent places in meetings. The noble boarders expressed their affection and gratitude to their Jesuit teachers through gifts to the Jesuit college.[34]

Then things changed. Father Blondi died of the plague in 1630. Some leading local men with strong connections to the Senate took control of the school. They insisted that students meet stricter proofs of nobility and they severed ties with the Jesuits. The boarders left the Jesuit school and studied with secular priests who lived in the school. The new authorities added some instruction in Italian literature but did not otherwise change the curriculum.[35]

The Jesuits decided to open their own boarding school for noble youths. This was a new venture for Bologna but not for the Jesuits of the Province of Venice who directed the Parma noble school. They named it the Collegio Nuovo de' Nobili di S. Francesco Saverio (New College for Nobles of St. Francis Xavier). The name invoked the link between the saint and Bologna, and told parents and students that it was a Jesuit school. The Jesuits used their school network to invite noble youths from Ferrara, Verona, and elsewhere to enroll. A wealthy supporter deeded some houses to serve as

---

31. St. Prisca (dates unknown) was a young Roman woman who refused to renounce Christianity and was martyred.

32. Brizzi 1976, 99–100.   33. Brizzi 1976, 132–33.

34. Brizzi 1976, 100–102.

35. Brizzi 1976, 103–9, 127–30, with copious quotations from documents from ARSI and elsewhere.

residences for the boarders in February 1634. The Jesuits appointed a secular priest as rector and he hired other personnel. The boarders would attend academic classes at the Jesuit school of Santa Lucia for free, but pay fees for food, lodging, and other instruction. The St. Francis Xavier New School for Nobles opened its doors on October 4, 1634.[36]

In 1644 Count Carlo Zani made a major contribution. A very wealthy Bolognese, he had entered the Society as a youth. But after finishing his theological studies, he had to leave the Society "for just reasons."[37] He bought the large building that housed the St. Prisca school, evicted the boarders, and gave the building to the Jesuits, who moved their noble boarders into it. Although the St. Francis Xavier School for Nobles was a Jesuit school, a secular priest continued to be the rector. Not until 1662 did the Jesuits appoint one of their own as rector.

A Transfer from Parma to Bologna

The second development was the transfer of Jesuit scholastics and some of their teachers from Parma to Bologna. The Jesuit school at Santa Lucia continued to teach only grammar, humanities, and rhetoric, while a Jesuit lectured on cases of conscience at the cathedral. Meanwhile, Marquis Alberto Serpa Angelelli reentered the Society of Jesus, was ordained, and died a Jesuit in 1648 or 1649.[38] In 1630 he left almost all of his substantial remaining wealth to the Bolognese Jesuits for an upper school. His aunt, the widow of a Bolognese senator, also gave money. In 1635 General Vitelleschi agreed that the Bolognese Jesuits might use Angelelli's bequest and his aunt's donation for an upper school in Bologna.[39]

There was a local reason and a provincial reason for the change of policy of the Bolognese Jesuits and the general. The former wanted to expand their school, and the Province of Venice desperately needed a second upper school to teach philosophy and theology to its scholastics. There had been two upper schools, in Mantua and Parma. But the terrible events of 1630 had closed the Mantua upper school. Then, as noted in chapter 6, Spanish troops invaded the Duchy of Parma. The Jesuits decided to move their phi-

---

36. Fabrini 1941, 24n1.

37. "Anche questo per opera del Conte Carlo Zani. Era questo fin de giovanetto entrato nella Compagnia over passò molti anni; ma pel finir della Teologia per giusti motivi ottenne la dimissione con intenzione di rientrarvi composte le sue cose. Ma la morte lo impedì." ARSI, Veneta 125, f. [2v].

38. ARSI, Veneta 40, f. 153r; and Fabrini 1941, 9, 10n2, 16.

39. Fabrini 1941, 16–17.

losophy and theology scholastics out of Parma.[40] But where would they go? Bologna was the obvious choice. It was the largest city in the province, and the Jesuits already had a college, a lower school, a boarding school, and a novice house there. Teachers of philosophy and theology could be brought in from Parma.

Members of the university community viewed the proposed upper school as a threat and launched a campaign against it. The arts students organization drafted a petition that was read in the Senate on October 3, 1635.[41] The students began with a grandiloquent statement: it has been 1,225 years since the university and the arts students have encountered obstacles to their privileges. This was an allusion to the foundation legend of the University of Bologna, according to which the Eastern Emperor Theodosius II destroyed the city of Bologna in a fit of anger. Then, thanks to the intervention of St. Petronius, bishop of Bologna from 432 to 450, he made reparation by rebuilding the city and founding the university.[42]

The arts students continued: the only threats to the university in that span of 1,225 years occurred in 1591 and 1615, when the Jesuit Fathers wished to teach philosophy and other university disciplines. Mindful of the damage that would have ensued, especially the loss of income from fees, as has occurred in many cities in Europe where the Jesuits have introduced their universities, the city prohibited the Jesuits from doing so. (The Jesuits did introduce a short-lived logic course in 1591, but the 1615 reference is unclear. Whether the Senate intervened on either occasion is unknown.) Now against every obligation and reason, the Jesuit fathers have begun to teach and to give certificates (fedi) to the students who attend their classes, just as the university notary does when he prepares the matriculation list.[43] There

40. Both Costa 1912, 62, and Fabrini 1941, 16–17, give as the reason for the transfer of scholastics and teachers from Parma to Bologna the war between Parma (Duke Odoardo Farnese) and the papacy (Urban VIII) over the enclave of Castro discussed in chap. 6. But that war did not begin until 1641 and it ended in 1644. The Jesuits transferred the scholastics around 1636, not in the 1640s.

41. ASB, Assunteria di Studio 92, fascicule "Gesuiti," which contains several unpaginated documents. There are two copies of this petition of the organization of the arts students, one of them with the notation "3 ottobre 1635. Letto in Senato." Since the petition is short and lacks references, the document is probably a summary or abbreviated version made by a secretary of the Assunteria along with a brief notice as to what action was taken. The same will be true for the other petitions from the Assunteria di Studio records cited below.

42. Sorbelli 1987, 12–13.

43. The meaning may have been that the Jesuits were giving students certificates stating that they had attended classes, just as university professors gave fedi to the students who attended their lectures. The students then had to present the fedi to prove that they had attended lectures the required number of years before undergoing doctoral examinations. Grendler 2002, 490.

is no doubt that students will go from the humanities class (in the Jesuit lower school) to the speculative disciplines, that is, Jesuit philosophy classes. That will cause damage and a loss of income to the university. In order to maintain the rights and privileges of the university, the Jesuits must be denied permission to teach higher courses.

Another protest addressed to the Assunteria di Studio made a more succinct claim. It charged that the Jesuits, who have never succeeded in obtaining professorships in any university of Europe since their foundation in 1540, now intend to become professors at Bologna.[44] Despite the inaccuracies, the two petitions conveyed dire warnings. Jesuit classes in philosophy and theology will attract students who would otherwise attend the university, and the Jesuits were trying to become part of the University of Bologna.

Members of the government became more concerned as the transfer of the scholastics approached. In a letter of November 14, 1635, Agostino Hercolani, the Bolognese ambassador to the papacy, reported that General Vitelleschi had told him that he had given the order, or was about to give the order (the ambassador was not certain which), to move, in the words of Hercolani, the "studio di filosofia e teologia" (university of philosophy and theology) of Parma to Bologna. Opining that this would harm Bologna, Hercolani passed on the information to the Assunteria di Studio.[45]

The Assunteria di Studio discussed his letter on November 22, 1635. It was not very concerned. It noted that the Jesuits taught only members of their own order with no outsiders in attendance. The Assunteria also observed that other religious orders, such as the Franciscans and the Dominicans, taught philosophy and theology to their own members and to outsiders, which was prejudicial to the university. On the other hand, they did not put on the long robes of the professors but wore clerical dress, meaning that they did not present themselves as university professors. The Assunteria di Studio took no action.[46]

This did not satisfy the arts students, who returned to the Assunteria di Studio and the Senate on December 4, 1635, and January 2, 1636, with two more memoranda arguing that Jesuit teaching was prejudicial to the university.[47] In one of them the officers of the arts students organization

---

44. ASB, Assunteria di Studio 91, "Gesuiti," no pag., no date, but late 1635.

45. ASB, Assunteria di Studio 92, "Gesuiti," no pag.; and Assunteria di Studio 10 Atti (1635–1639), f. 20r. See also Costa 1912, 62; and Fabrini 1941, 17.

46. Assunteria di Studio 10 Atti (1635–1639), ff. 20v–21r (November 22, 1635).

47. Assunteria di Studio 10 Atti (1635–1639), ff. 22v–23r (December 4, 1635), 25r–v (January 2, 1636).

protested that the Jesuits wanted to teach logic and philosophy publicly (meaning as a university) in their school contrary to the constitutions and privileges of this most noble and ancient university. This will sow dissension and cause the ruin of scholars, as has happened in Italy and beyond. Hence, they asked the Assunti to obtain a perpetual pontifical order forbidding the Jesuits from teaching the disciplines that university professors chosen and paid by the government of Bologna taught.[48] The Assunti discussed the memoranda of the arts students on January 7 and 10, and ordered its secretary to review the bull of Pope Honorius III (1219). They noted that the bull had established Bologna as the only university in Italy, and wondered what it said about its privileges.[49]

Most important, the Senate supported the university. In a letter of January 9, 1636, it wrote to Ambassador Hercolani. Referring to memoranda from the student organization and dottori of the university, it repeated some of their arguments, including the charge that the introduction of the Jesuits had harmed the University of Padua as well as the universities of Rome, Parma, Pavia, and Ferrara. The Senate invoked the privileges that Emperor Theodosius II had allegedly awarded the University of Bologna and the brief of Innocent VI (see below). It expected the ambassador to obtain some satisfaction or reassurance.[50]

The college of doctors of theology followed with its petition against the Jesuits on or about January 19, 1636.[51] The theologians argued that the Jesuits intended to damage the university by allowing students to teach philosophy and theology, the same accusation that Cesare Cremonini and the University of Padua made in 1591. And they charged that the Jesuits awarded doctorates to their own students, which violated the rights of the college of doctors of theology. The petition then offered four reasons why the Jesuits should not be permitted to teach philosophy and theology.

First, wherever the Jesuits teach, disorders follow, as has been the case

48. Assunteria di Studio 92, "Gesuiti," no pag. and no date. The second memorandum has not been located.

49. Assunteria di Studio 10 Atti (1635–1639), ff. 27r (January 7, 1636), 28r (January 10, 1636). The reference was to the decretal *Super speculam* of 1219 in which Honorius III charged the archdeacon of San Petronius with conferring the doctorate on candidates who passed examinations. The pope intervened at a time when commune and students were contesting control of the university. Bellomo 1995, 119–20.

50. The letter is cited by Costa 1912, 63; and Fabrini 1941, 19. Fabrini substitutes the University of Fermo for the University of Ferrara.

51. The petition of the college of doctors of theology along with a shorter version are found in ASB, Assunteria di Studio 92, "Gesuiti," no pag., no dates. The Assunti discussed some points made by the theologians on January 19, 1636. Hence, the petitions were presented on or just before that date. See ASB, Assunteria di Studio, 10 Atti (1635–1639), f. 30v.

in Italy and beyond. Second, because we Bolognese theologians are not permitted to teach in the universities of Parma, Mantua, Fermo, and other places occupied (*occupati*) by the Jesuits, the Jesuits should not be permitted to teach in our city of Bologna. Third, Pope Innocent VI in his breve of June 30, 1362, founding the college of doctors of theology of Bologna, had made the bishop the chancellor of the college and decreed that no one might receive a doctorate of theology in Bologna without permission of the chancellor and college of doctors of theology. Fourth, Pope Pius V in his breve of June 1, 1568, prohibited anyone external to the university, whether individual, religious order, or college, from conferring doctorates of theology in Bologna. This was the exclusive right and privilege of the college of doctors of theology of Bologna, the petition concluded.[52]

The college of doctors of theology was wrong on two points and correct on a third. Not students, but only ordained Jesuit priests who had completed three years of philosophical study and four years of theology taught philosophy or theology. Second, while Jesuit colleges with schools had papal authority to confer doctorates of philosophy and theology, the Italian Jesuits conferred very few doctorates on their own members after the 1560s.[53] Third, it was true that the Jesuits excluded members of other religious orders from teaching theology in the universities of Parma and Mantua. On the other hand, out-of-town theologians were never permitted to teach in the local university unless first admitted into the local college of doctors of theology, which did not easily accept outsiders.

Behind the words of the college of doctors of theology was the reality that they were losing university teaching positions. Other clergymen had broken the monopoly of university instruction in theology and scripture that the medieval mendicant religious orders had enjoyed. In 1587 the first secular clergyman was appointed to teach theology in the University of Bologna. In 1625 a Spanish clergyman from the Collegio di Spagna was appointed to teach scripture in the university.[54] Other secular clergymen and Spanish theologians followed. It is not surprising that the college of theologians saw the Jesuits as yet another threat.

The Assunteria di Studio discussed the memorandum of the theolo-

52. ASB, Assunteria di Studio 92, "Gesuiti," petition of the college of doctors of theology, no pag., no date.

53. See chap. 15, "Quick Doctorates for the First Jesuits," and "The Italian Jesuits Do Not Want Doctorates."

54. Turrini 2008, 448, 455–56; and Dallari 1888–1924, 2:228 (Giovanni Battista dall'Orto in 1587), 366 (Antonio Camón y Cerezuela in 1625). Founded in 1364, the Collegio di Spagna was a residence for Spanish students, almost all of them clergymen, and a handful of Spanish theologians who taught in it. Thanks to Spanish royal patronage, it was legally independent of the university.

gians. They read the briefs of Innocent VI and Pius V, and instructed their secretary to give copies to the college of doctors of theology.[55] Then on January 29, 1636, a group of "professors of theology, philosophy, and medicine" petitioned the Senate. The Jesuits, it began, were not content to teach in their own schools "although with little fruit," but were now teaching external students. This threatened the public lectures and the matriculation of students into the university.[56]

This petition was superfluous, because Ambassador Hercolani had already spoken with General Vitelleschi and obtained what the university and city wanted. On January 26, 1636, Vitelleschi wrote to the rector of the Jesuit college in Bologna ordering that no external student, whether clergyman or layman, was to be admitted into the theology or philosophy classes at the Jesuit school whatever the pretext or reason. The Bolognese Jesuit rector pledged his unconditional obedience in a return letter of February 9.[57] Complaints about the Jesuit school stopped.

In 1636 it was enough for the Jesuits that they had permission to have an upper school teaching only Jesuits. They could now move their philosophy and theology scholastics from Parma to Bologna, which probably happened in 1636. On January 1, 1636, the Parma college had 60 Jesuits including 25 theology and philosophy scholastics. On November 1, 1639, there were only 40 Jesuits at Parma, including two scholastics serving as *ripetitori* (tutors or coaches) for the students at the noble school.[58] By contrast, there were 65 Jesuits, including 8 theology scholastics and 15 philosophy scholastics, in Bologna in 1639. The Bologna school now taught two classes in scholastic theology; single classes in cases of conscience, natural philosophy, rhetoric, the humanities; and two in grammar.[59] The transfer had been accomplished.

55. ASB, Assunteria di Studio 10 Atti (1635–1639), ff. 30v (January 19, 1636), 31r (January 23, 1636).

56. "Havendo li Illi. RR. PP. Gesuiti non sol col leger attualmente nelle lor scuole come altre volte, sè ben con poco frutto." "Perciò li professori di theologia, filosofia, e medicina." ASB, Assunteria di Studio 92, "Gesuiti," no pag., with the notation "29 gennaro 1636 letto in Senato." It is likely that this was a petition from an ad hoc group of professors.

57. See a copy of the letter of Vitelleschi of January 26, 1636, Rome, in ASB, Assunteria di Studio 93, "Gesuiti," no pag. The letter is printed along with the reply of Father Fabio Albergati of February 9, 1636, Bologna, in Fabrini 1941, 18n2. The interesting thing is that both letters indicate that Vitelleschi had written the same thing to Albergati's predecessor as rector. The Assunteria noted Vitelleschi's letter on February 7, 11, and 14. ASB, Assunteria di Studio 10 (Atti 1635–1639), ff. 32v–34r.

58. ARSI, Veneta 71, ff. 248r–49v, 299v–300r. The Jesuits at Parma reduced the number of teachers only slightly because they were committed to teaching courses in the University of Parma.

59. ARSI, Veneta 71, ff. 294r–95v. There is no information for 1637 and 1638 because the

Although the university objected to competition from the Jesuits, it decided to compete with the Jesuits in a discipline that was a signature feature of Jesuit education. In 1577 Cardinal Paleotti instituted a twice-weekly lectureship on cases of conscience at the cathedral and gave the assignment to an Augustinian Hermit.[60] At some point in the 1580s or 1590s the Jesuits assumed responsibility for teaching cases of conscience. In 1600 a Jesuit was lecturing on cases and serving on the archdiocesan board that resolved difficult matters of conscience.[61] In 1622 a Jesuit was lecturing on cases of conscience to a class of fifty.[62]

In 1637 the University of Bologna created a lectureship in cases of conscience (which it sometimes called moral theology), the first continuing professorship of cases of conscience in an Italian university lacking Jesuit participation.[63] It appointed Giacomo Pistorini, a secular priest and member of the college of doctors of theology, who had been teaching cases privately. He held the position until his death in 1649, when another secular priest replaced him. The Assunteria di Studio gave as the reason for the new position the expectation of attracting clerical students to the university so that they might hear these sought after, fruitful, and necessary lectures.[64] The unstated reason was to draw students away from the Jesuit lecturer.

Urban VIII Checks the Jesuit School

The criticisms of 1635 and 1636 were only the beginning. When the war between Parma and Spanish-ruled Lombardy ended in 1637, the Jesuit scholastics did not move back to Parma. Of course, the university noticed this and was suspicious. The arts students organization raised the possibility of a complete ban on Jesuit theology and philosophy instruction. This now became the goal of the university and its supporters in the government.

---

catalogues summarizing the activities of every college in a province were compiled every third year at this time. Later in the century they became quadrennial.

60. Prodi 1959–1967, 2:125. Fabrini 1941, 49, states that Paleotti gave the charge of teaching cases of conscience to Francesco Palmio, the long-time rector of the Jesuit college. And that Palmio held the position until his death in 1585, after which other Jesuits taught cases. However, no Jesuit was teaching cases of conscience in Bologna in 1579. See Grendler 2004a, 495.

61. "P. Pietro Fracario confesse e legge, et decide i casi in Arcivescovado et confessa i Tedeschi." ARSI, Veneta 37, f. 259r, December 1600. Fracario has not been further identified.

62. ARSI, Veneta, 39 I, f. 58r.

63. For more see chap. 15, "Cases of Conscience."

64. "Allettar gli scolari ecclesiastici alla frequenza dello Studio publico per udir una lettione tanto desiderata, tanto fruttuosa e tanto necessaria." Quoted from an Assunteria di Studio document by Turrini 1990, 227; see also 236. For Pistorini's appointment, named "Ad lecturam Casuum conscientiae," see Dallari 1888–1924, 2:414, 418, 422, 426, 430, 434, 438, 442, 446, 450, 454, 458.

The protests began anew in 1639. According to their critics, early in 1639 the Jesuits persuaded some "foreign" (non-Bolognese) students at the St. Francis Xavier School for Nobles to ask the legate to allow the Jesuits to teach them logic. Cardinal Legate Giulio Sacchetti (1587–1663, cardinal from 1626), legate for Bologna from 1639 to 1640, granted permission.[65]

This was true. The Jesuits had begun teaching logic to two noble boarders who were not Jesuits. They did this because of their concern for the St. Francis Xavier noble school, which had only 23 to 25 students in the winter of 1638–1639. The Jesuits concluded that the boarding school would not grow unless they taught logic and the other parts of the philosophical trio. If they could do so, they believed that it would attract 60 boarders. So they spoke with some prominent members of the city government about teaching logic, and they did not object. They then obtained permission from the cardinal legate to teach logic to their own boarding students. And the Bolognese Jesuits were well aware of the criticism coming from the university and its supporters.[66]

Whether the initiative came from students, parents, or the Jesuits does not matter, because it was inevitable. Parents of noble boarders wanted their sons to study logic, because it was considered important and would give them an advantage if they attended university. The Parma noble school taught logic and natural philosophy, and sometimes metaphysics, and other Jesuit noble schools probably did as well, if they had the teachers. But teaching logic to non-Jesuits violated the agreement of January 1636.

The university swung into action. The college of doctors of canon law and the college of doctors of civil law charged that the Jesuits were abusing Sacchetti's permission by incrementally teaching more students and university subjects and asked the Assunteria di Studio to act.[67] The Assunteria asked Sacchetti and the Bolognese ambassador to the papacy to look into

---

65. Fabrini 1941, 22–23. For a short biography of Sacchetti see The Cardinals of the Roman Church, www2.fiu.edu/~mirandas/bios1626.htm#Sacchetti. Sacchetti had previously been papal nuncio to Spain and legate for Ferrara. Beyond this episode, his attitude toward the Jesuits is unknown.

66. Letter of Father Vincenzo Maria Bargalini to the general of February 9, 1639, Bologna, in ARSI, Veneta 97 I, ff. 64r–65v, at 64v–65r. Bargalini, who may have been an official visitor, reported on a meeting of eleven Jesuits in Bologna concerning the noble boarding school. They also discussed whether the Jesuits should take over complete governance of the school, and the consensus was no. As noted above, secular priests continued to govern the noble school until 1662.

67. Fabrini 1941, 22–23. The majority of Italian universities had a single college for both laws. The University of Bologna had separate colleges for canon law and civil law, a sign of the importance of law at Bologna. See Grendler 2002, 174, for their size and composition.

the matter.[68] The priors of the two law colleges also wrote directly to the ambassador.[69] On January 22, 1639, a delegation from the arts professors protested to the Assunteria di Studio that the Jesuits were trying to create their own public university under the pretext of teaching logic.[70] From this will follow damaging consequences to the university, as has happened in other universities in Italy and beyond, they argued. In their battles against the Jesuits university groups repeated past accusations and arguments, some of them demonstrably false, again and again. They believed that determined and repeated protests would eventually bring victory. And they had to persuade a new cardinal legate every two or three years.[71]

More petitions followed through 1639 and in the first half of 1640. The Assunteria di Studio and the Bolognese ambassador saw the Jesuits as a serious threat and were determined to "knock to the ground this innovation of the Jesuit Fathers," in the words of the ambassador.[72] But Cardinal Sacchetti was not very concerned, because the Jesuits were teaching logic to just a handful of students. Those opposed to the Jesuits decided to pin their hopes on a new set of regulations for the University of Bologna.[73]

Cardinal Stefano Durazzo (1594–1667, cardinal from 1633) replaced Sacchetti as legate in June 1640 and served until November 1642.[74] The Assunteria di Studio and the university continued the campaign with him. Durazzo was not initially helpful; indeed, he had ordered the Bologna Jesuits to teach philosophy to his nephew and two other young nobles.[75] The Assunteria refrained from criticizing him, but suggested that a Jesuit should

68. ASB, Assunteria di Studio 92, "Gesuiti," no pag., read in the Senate on January 18, 1639. It is also printed in Fabrini 1941, 23n2. See also ASB, Assunteria di Studio 10 Atti (1635–1639), f. 142v, January 19, 1639.

69. Fabrini 1941, 23n1, February 12, 1639.

70. "Alcuni giovani secolari del loro colleggio habbino dato principio di legger logica." ASB, Assunteria di Studio 92, "Gesuiti," no pag., January 22, 1639.

71. And the historian needs to repeat the protests to some extent in order to convey the determination and intensity of the opposition.

72. "Buttare a terra la novità de' PP. Giesuiti." Letter of Ambassador Agostino Hercolani of February 9, 1639, Rome, in ASB, Assunteria di Studio 77, Lettere dell'Ambassadore agli Assunti di Studio 1637–1693, no pag.

73. ASB, Assunteria di Studio 10 Atti (1635–1639), ff. 143r–v (January 22, 27, 1639), 144v–45r (February 1), 150v (March 29, 1639); and Fabrini 1941, 27–30.

74. For a brief biography, see Sanfilippo 1993.

75. While Sanfilippo 1993, gives no information concerning Durazzo's views about the Jesuits, earlier he had been a reforming archbishop of Genoa who promoted catechetical instruction, disciplined wayward parish priests, and reformed female monasteries. Since the Jesuits had a flourishing college and school at Genoa, and devoted much effort to catechetical instruction, he may have formed a favorable opinion of them there.

teach the nephew and his friends in the palace in which the nephew lived.[76] The Assunteria and other members of the government also made the larger case to Cardinal Durazzo that the Jesuits had "destroyed" the universities of Padua, Parma, Pavia, and Rome.[77] Bowing to pressure, Durazzo ordered his nephew to cease attending the Jesuit class. Opponents of the Jesuits also complained that the Jesuits who had come from Parma sounded a bell and left the door open when they taught theology, thus encouraging external students to attend in violation of the rules.[78] The bell-ringing charge was familiar; members of the University of Padua had complained about Jesuit bell ringing there. In this case the inference was that the Jesuits from the civic-Jesuit University of Parma were trying to create the same in Bologna.

Once again the Jesuits acquiesced. On July 10, 1640, General Vitelleschi wrote a letter to the rector of the Bolognese Jesuit college ordering him not to admit any *forestiere* (foreigner) into the philosophy and theology lectures in the Jesuit school.[79] The letter was nearly identical to his letter of January 1636 except for the substitution of *forestiere* for *esterno* (extern) in the earlier letter. The Bologna rector acknowledged it, as did the Assunteria di Studio.[80]

Not satisfied, the opponents of the Jesuits asked for two measures to halt any and all Jesuit upper school teaching. First, they wanted a prohibition against the teaching of university subjects by regular and secular clergymen lacking appointments in the University of Bologna. They wanted this to be done through a new set of university regulations, entitled *ordinationi* (orders), which were periodically revised and reissued. These consisted of procedures, rules, and qualifications for professors, students, and the operation of the university. Ordinationi always included prohibitions against, and punishments for abuses.[81] Cardinal Legate Sacchetti had promulgated ordinationi of 1639 that included a paragraph prohibiting clergymen lacking appointments in the university from teaching university subjects. But the university and commune wanted a new set of ordinationi with explicit approval from Rome.

76. Fabrini 1941, 31–32, esp. 32nn1–2.   77. Fabrini 1941, 33.
78. Fabrini 1941, 34.
79. "E le raccomando strettamente che non permetta che niuno forestiere, né scolare, ne religioso si ammesso à sentire detta lettione." Vitelleschi's letter of July 10, 1640, Rome, in ASB, Assunteria di Studio 92, "Gesuiti," no pag.
80. The Assunteria noted the letter from General Vitelleschi on August 12, 1640, and the Jesuit rector pledged obedience to the general in a brief letter of August 22. ASB, Assunteria di Studio 11 Atti (1639–1647), ff. 24v–25r; and Assunteria di Studio 92 "Gesuiti," no pag.
81. New ordinationi appeared periodically, e.g., in 1586, 1593, 1602, 1609, 1639, 1641, and 1713. See Costa 1912, 76–82; Simeoni 1987, 85–86; Grendler 2002, 488–89; and Lines 2011.

Second, and more importantly, the university and commune wanted a papal pronouncement barring the Jesuits from teaching university subjects. In support of these dual goals the Assunteria di Studio gathered information, including a copy of Cremonini's oration against the Jesuits of 1591, and a copy of the 1634 papal brief supporting the University of Krakow against the Jesuits.[82] The discussions in Rome were lengthy and slow, because Bologna sought two goals and because a papal brief was a significant undertaking. The ambassador eventually won over various individuals, including the very powerful Cardinal Francesco Barberini (1597–1679), nephew to Pope Urban VIII and arbiter of matters concerning learning and universities.[83]

The university and city got both. On July 12, 1641, Cardinal Durazzo promulgated new ordinationi for the university consisting of forty-seven short chapters, each dealing with a regulation or an abuse. Chapter 31 banned anyone without a university appointment from teaching university subjects. It began with a justification, the need to maintain high and frequent student attendance at the lectures of the university professors who are supported at very great expense by the government of the city. Then it prohibited anyone, whatever his status or qualification, even if worthy of nomination to the university, not listed in the rolls of the public university from teaching publicly or privately in Bologna and its territory any of the arts, faculties, or disciplines taught or customarily taught in the university. It threatened violators with very grave punishment to be determined by the cardinal legate. It allowed one exception: the regular clergy might teach members of their own orders in their own monasteries, but no other students.[84] Chapter 31 was aimed at the Jesuits, although they were not mentioned.

82. "Ho di già fatta pratica per havere copia del breve ottenuto dall'Ambassadore straordinario del Re di Polonia a favore dell'Università di Cracovia." Letter of Ambassador Agostino Hercolani of February 16, 1639, Rome, in Assunteria di Studio 77, Lettere dell'Ambassadore agli Assonti di Studio 1637–1693, no foliation. For the brief favoring the University of Krakow, see below.

83. ASB, Assunteria di Studio 11 Atti (1639–1647), ff. 25v, 33r, 46v; Assunteria di Studio 75, no pag., letter of Ambassador Ludovico Facchinetti of January 26, 1641; Assunteria di Studio 76, no pag., letters of Facchinetti of December 29, 1640, June 5 and 15, July 3 and 25, and August 14, 1641; and Fabrini 1941, 31–38. For Francesco Barberini, see Merola 1964, and Pastor 1891–1953, vols. 28–29.

84. "Capitolo 31. E per mantenimento maggiore del numero de' Scolari alle dette publiche lettioni et acioche con maggior frequenza de' Scolari li publici Lettori, quali si conducono in tante professioni, con tanta spesa da questo Illustriss. Regimento, con maggior gusto possino insegnare, Sua Eminenza vieta, et espressamente prohibisce a qual si voglia persona di qualonque stato, grado, e conditione ancorchè degna di specifica nominatione, che non sia descrittione nelli

The prohibition did what the university community wanted. However, a closer look suggests that the practical effect was not going to be as severe as threatened. Chapter 31 threatened punishment of violators but did not name the penalty, as some other provisions of the ordinationi did. Second, punishment depended on Cardinal Durazzo, who had wanted the Jesuits to teach philosophy to his nephew. He was not likely to punish the Jesuits severely, if at all. Third, university regulations were not always rigorously enforced, which is an understatement if there ever was one. Finally, there already was a conspicuous exception to the prohibition. The Collegio di Spagna, which opened its doors in 1368, was a student residence open to a limited number of lay and clerical students from Spain and Portugal studying law and theology. In the middle of the seventeenth century it had four lecturers teaching law and theology to its students, although they were not appointed to the university. Both the ordinationi and the papal brief (see below) forbade this teaching. However, the Spanish monarchy supported the Collegio di Spagna.[85] And so the four lecturers in the Collegio di Spagna continued to teach at least through 1747.[86]

Another regulation of the ordinationi might have been aimed at the Jesuits. Opponents of the Jesuits lamented that university professors had fallen out of the habit of dressing appropriately. Professors with doctorates were expected to wear a black gown with wide sleeves (con maniche larghe, also called le vesti dottorali or doctoral robes). But many professors dressed no differently from those who did not hold doctorates or teach, which confused students and damaged the university, according to the Bolognese ambassador. He hinted that the Jesuits took advantage of this.[87] Indeed,

---

Rotoli publici di questo Studio il poter, sotto qual si voglia pretesto legger publicamente, ò privatamente in questa Città, suo Contado, o Legatione alcuna delle arti, facoltà, ò scienze, che si leggono ò sogliono leggere nello Studio publico, sotto gravissime pene, ad arbitrio di Sua Eminenza, eccettuando però li Regolari, a quali si permette leggere nelli loro Claustri alli loro Religiosi, et non ad altri." Ordinationi fatte, et stabilite per conservare la dignità & riputatione dello Studio di Bologna publicate in Bologna alli 12 di Luglio 1641. In Bologna, per l'Herede del Benacci Stampatore Camerale, f. A7v. This is a small octavo booklet of twenty pages with the shelf mark Gozzadini 105, number 4, in BAB. Fabrini 1941, 27–28n4, also quotes chap. 31; as does Brizzi 1976, 119n52.

85. Ludovico Facchinetti, Bolognese ambassador to the papacy, reported that representatives of the king of Spain wanted expansion of the statutes of the Collegio di Spagna, which would likely conflict with the ordinationi. ASB, Assunteria di Studio 76, no pag., letter of July 3, 1641. The ordinationi did not mention the Collegio di Spagna.

86. Marti 1966, 90.

87. Letters of Ambassador Ludovico Facchinetti of May 11, June 5 (quotation) and 15, July 3, and November 27, 1641 (quotation), in ASB, Assunteria di Studio 76, Lettere dell'Ambasciatore agli Assunti di Studio 1599–1698, no pag.; and Fabrini 1941, 37.

although the Society did not have a prescribed dress, many Jesuits wore black flowing robes and a biretta or a wide-brimmed hat somewhat similar to academic gowns and the doctoral biretta. Augustinian, Dominican, and Franciscan canons and friars, by contrast, wore brown, black, or grey robes with cowl and cincture.[88] The ordinationi of 1641 insisted that lay professors must wear "la Toga Dottorale" (the doctoral gown) when lecturing and when going about in the city.[89] The goal was to enable people to recognize who were university professors and who were not.

On November 10, 1641, Urban VIII issued the desired papal brief against the Jesuit school. This was more important than the ordinationi because it came from the pope and it named the Jesuits. The brief threatened excommunication against anyone in Bologna teaching university subjects who was not an appointed professor of the university.[90] It began with praise for Bologna as the "Studiorum Mater" (mother of universities) and for being always faithful to the Holy See. It noted the determination of the city to preserve the health of the university. The brief prohibited any clergyman or layman, whatever his status, from any (other) university, and any order, congregation, college, confraternity, the "Societatis etiam Jesu" (Society also of Jesus), or institute, from teaching university subjects publicly or in secret in Bologna or its territory under pain of excommunication.[91] The brief named the Society of Jesus three times, but did not name any other religious order.

The papal brief was similar to Urban VIII's brief against the Jesuits of Krakow. The Society founded a college and school for their own members in Krakow in 1622. It wanted to be affiliated with the University of Kra-

88. See the illustrations in Dall'isola alla città 1988, 120, 122, and 144.

89. The key phrase describing the appropriate dress was "la Toga Dottorale con le maniche larghe aperte alla Ducale." Ordinationi, 1641, chaps. 36–37, sig. A8v (quotation)–A9r.

90. There are several print copies of the papal brief bearing both the original date and a reprint date of December 13, 1649, in ASB, Assunteria di Studio 89, no pag. The text is also given in Fabrini 1941, 39–40n2.

91. "Omnibus et singulis personis, tam saecularibus, quam Ecclesiasticis, etiam Regularibus cuiuscumque status, gradus, conditionis, dignitatis et praeminentiae ac cuiusvis Universitatis, Ordinis, Congregationis, Collegij, Confraternitatis, Societatis etiam Jesu, et Instituti, quantumlibet qualificatis, et privilegiatis, ac speciali nota et individua expressione dignis .... In Civitate praedicta, eiusque Comitatu, Territorio, et Legatione quamcumque ex Scientijs, Artibus, et Facultatibus quae in Publico eiusdem Universitatis Gymnasio docentur, et praeleguntur seu doceri et perlegi solent publice vel secreto docere seu legere ac profiteri audeant seu praesumant: nisi personae huismodi in publico eiusdem Universitatis cathologo seu Albo Rotulis vulgo nuncupatis descriptae sunt, sub Excommunicationis maioris eo ipso absque alia declaratione incurrendae, aut indignationis Nostrae aliisque arbitrii nostri poenis Apostolica auctoritate tenore praesentium interdicimus et prohibemus." Papal brief of November 10, 1641, Rome, in ASB, Assunteria di Studio, 89, no pag.; and Fabrini 1941, 39–40n2.

SENTENZA DI SCOMMVNICA

Contro coloro, che non defcritti ne' Rotoli del publico Studio leggeffero le Scienze, Arti,
e Facultà folite leggerfi in effo.

Publicato nouamente in Bologna li 13. di Decembre 1649.

VRBANVS PAPA VIII.

AD PERPETVAM REI MEMORIAM. Vberes fructus, quos in Vinea Domini Vniuerfitas
Studij Generalis in Ciuitate Noftra Bononien. ab antiquiffimis temporibus inftituta, & Studiorum Mater meritò nuncupata produxit, & in dies producit ; ac fummam erga hanc San-
ctam Sedem, fidem, & deuotionem, qua ipfa Ciuitas femper enituit, attentè confiderantes,
dignum reputamus, & rationi confentaneum, vt dictæ Vniuerfitatis conferuationi, vndè non modica in
in ipfam Ciuitatem dignitas, & vtilitas redundat, propenfis Studijs intendamus. Supplicationibus itaque
dilectorum filiorum Regiminis dictæ Ciuitatis Nobis fuper hoc humiliter porrectis inclinati : Omnibus,
& fingulis perfonis, tàm Sæcularibus, quàm Ecclefiafticis, etiam Regularibus cuiufcunque ftatus, gradus,
conditionis, dignitatis, & præeminentiæ, ac cuiufuis Vniuerfitatis, Ordinis, Congregationis, Collegij, Confraternitatis, Societatis etiam Iefu, & Inftituti quantumlibet qualificatis, & priuilegiatis, ac fpeciali nota,
& indiuidua expreffione dignis ; ne quocunque prætextu, vel ingenio, aut quæfito colore, vel quorumcũq.
Priuilegiorum, Conceffionum, Indultorum, & Gratiarum, tàm in genere, quàm in fpecie à felice record.
Pio Quinto, vel alijs Romanis Pontificibus Prædecefforibus noftris, & Sede prædicta etiam Motu proprio,
& Confiftorialiter, ac fub quacunque verborum forma, & ex quacunque caufa quantumuis pia, publica,
& fauorabili, ac aliàs quomodolibet, & quandocunquè Concefforum obtentu, feù vigore : in Ciuitate,
prædicta, eiufquè Comitatu, Territorio, & Legatione quàcumque ex Scientijs, Artibus, & Facultatibus,
quæ in publico eiufdem Vniuerfitatis Gymnafio docentur, & præleguntur, feù doceri, & prælegi folent
publicè, vel fecretò docere, feù legere, ac profiteri audeant, feù præfumant: nifi perfonæ huiufmodi in publico eiufdem Vniuerfitatis, Cathalogo, feù Albo, Rotulis vulgò nuncupatis defcriptæ fint, fub Excommunicationis maioris eo ipfo abfque alia declaratione incurrendæ, aut indignationis Noftræ, alijfquè ar-
bitrij Noftri pœnis Apoftolica auctoritate tenore præfentium interdicimus, & prohibemus; ficquè, & non
aliter in præmiffis per quofcunquè Iudices Ordinarios, & delegatos, etiam Caufarum Palatij Apoftolici
Auditores, ac S. R. E. Cardinales, etiam de Latere Legatos, fublata eis, & eorum cuilibet quauis aliter
iudicandi, vel interpretandi facultate, & auctoritate: iudicari, & diffiniri debere, irritumquè, & inane fi fe-
cus fuper his à quoquam quauis auctoritate fcienter, vel ignoranter contigerit attentari decernimus.
Non obftantibus Conftitutionibus, & Ordinationibus Apoftolicis, ac quorumuis Locorum, Ordinum,
Collegiorum, Confraternitatum, Societatum etiam Iefu, aliorumq. Inftitutorum Regularium, & gene-
raliter quibufuis etiam iuramento, confirmatione Apoftolica, vel alia quauis firmitate roboratis, ftatutis,
& confuetudinibus, priuilegijs quoq. indultis, & litteris Apoftolicis quibufuis locis, & Ordinibus, Congre-
gationibus, Collegijs, Confraternitatibus, Societatibus etiam Iefu, & Inftitutis, ac eorum Superioribus, &
perfonis quibuslibet fub quibufcunquè tenoribus, & formis, ac cum quibufuis derogatoriarum deroga-
torijs, alijfq. efficacioribus, & efficaciffimis claufulis, ac irritantibus, & alijs decretis in genere, vel in fpecie,
ac alias in contrarium præmifforum quomodolibet conceffis, approbatis, & innouatis. Quibus omnibus,
& fingulis etiamfi pro fufficiëti derogatione de illis, earumq. totis tenoribus fpecialis fpecifica, & expreffa,
ac de verbo ad verbum, non autem per claufulas generales idem importantes mentio, feù quæuis alia ex-
preffio habenda, aut aliqua exquifita forma adhoc feruan. foret; illorum tenores præfentibus pro fuf-
ficienter expreffis, & ad verbum infertis haben. illis aliàs in fuo robore permanfuris fpecialiter, & expreffè
derogamus, cæterifquè contrarijs quibufcunque. Datum Romæ apud S. Petrum fub Annulo Pifcatoris
die 10. Nouembris 1641. Pontificatus Noftri Anno 19.

M. A. Maraldus.

Bononiæ Typis Hæredis Victorij Benatij Impefforis Cameralis 1649.

FIGURE 3. Brief of Urban VIII of November 10, 1641

304

kow and the Polish king gave permission. However, from the beginning the Jesuits were the target of considerable hostility, and they competed with the Dominicans for noble favor and in other ways. At first the Jesuits taught only their own members and other clergymen. Then in 1628 they began to teach philosophy to external students. The university objected, arguing that the Jesuits damaged the university by offering unlawful competition in violation of the legal rights and privileges of the university, the same argument presented by the University of Bologna. The University of Krakow appealed to the Sacred Roman Rota which approved the Jesuit college and its classes in a series of decrees between 1626 and 1630. But a new king, Ladislaus IV (r. 1632–1648), took the side of the university. He obtained a brief from Urban VIII of March 22, 1634, which ordered the Jesuits "for the love of peace" to stop teaching external students, while permitting them to teach theology to their own members.[92]

The words of Urban VIII's brief of 1641 against the Jesuits were strong and threatening, but were not necessarily going to be enforced. It was not likely that the papacy was going to excommunicate the most effective religious order in the church for teaching philosophy to a few external students. Urban VIII gave the city and university what it wanted but would not do more, partly because he and the cardinal nephews were embroiled in the first Castro war.

The Assunteria di Studio arranged for printed copies of Urban VIII's brief to be posted around the city, including close to the Jesuit school. But the university did not achieve the total victory that it wanted. Both the ordinationi and the papal brief still allowed religious orders to teach university subjects to their own members. And the Jesuits were given to understand that they might consider the noble youths who attended the St. Francis Xavier School for Nobles to be guests (*commensali*) of the Society.[93] Hence, the Jesuits were permitted to teach them without incurring excommunication. Behind this quiet concession stood the political reality that the Jesuits had strong supporters in Bologna's ruling class. While the town took pride in the university and was determined to protect it for reasons of loyalty and the income it generated, many wanted the Jesuit school to succeed as well.

92. Grzebień 2001, 3176; Stolarski 2010, 28–41, 71–75; and Stolarski 2011.
93. Fabrini 1941, 41–42.

Jesuit Expansion

In the next decades the Bolognese Jesuits expanded their institutions, human resources, and buildings. In 1645 the Jesuits added another boarding school. Early in the seventeenth century a secular priest established a boarding school for a small number of boys of citizen and merchant status. In some Italian cities, "citizen" was a separate class for whom certain governmental offices were reserved, while merchants received tax concessions. Citizens were below nobles but above commoners. These citizen boys attended classes in the Jesuit school and joined Jesuit student congregations. In 1645 Carlo Zani again acted. He moved the school to a location near the Jesuit church of Santa Lucia and gave it the name Il Collegio dei Cittadini di Beato Luigi Gonzaga (The College of Citizens of Blessed Aloysius Gonzaga). The Jesuits assumed direction of it.[94] The majority of the students were sons of Bologna, a few came from elsewhere.

The College of Blessed Luigi Gonzaga and the St. Francis Xavier School for Nobles were for the wealthy. Students in both schools paid twenty-five doubloons per month for room and board. In the morning all attended the free academic classes at the Jesuit school at Santa Lucia. Most studied grammar, humanities, and rhetoric; a very small number studied philosophy. Both noble and citizen boys also received instruction in fencing, music, and dancing, for which they paid fees to non-Jesuit teachers.[95] Both schools had enrollments that normally fluctuated between 50 and 100 in the second half of the seventeenth century. The St. Francis Xavier School enrolled 76 boarders in 1662, 49 in 1680, 41 in 1689, 90 in 1693, and 126 in 1699.[96] The Blessed Luigi Gonzaga school had 100 boarders in 1645 and more than 70 in 1683.[97] Both continued into the eighteenth century.

Bologna now had many Jesuits. In 1649 there were 73 Jesuits at the Santa Lucia college: 24 priests, 33 scholastics, and the rest temporal coadjutors. The school offered twelve classes, five of them open to all: two in grammar and one each in humanities, rhetoric, and cases of conscience. The other seven classes were restricted to Jesuits and boarders at the St. Francis Xavier and Blessed Luigi Gonzaga schools. These were two classes in scholastic theology and one each in scripture, metaphysics, natural philosophy, logic,

94. Brizzi 1976, 85–86; Brizzi 1988a, 149–50.

95. Fabrini 1946b, 23–25, 41.

96. Brizzi 1976, 108–10, 128–33; Brizzi 1988a, 149, 152; ARSI, Veneta 106 II, f. 414r (90 boarders in 1693). Unfortunately, these are the only enrollment numbers that have been located.

97. ARSI, Veneta 125, f. [2v] (1645); Veneta 126 I/II, f. 335v (1683). Again these are the only known enrollments.

and mathematics. There were another 28 Jesuits in the novice house.[98] Bologna now had at least 101 Jesuits, compared to 27 or 28 in 1600.[99]

Nevertheless, enrollments in the upper school classes were tiny because of the restrictions. In 1646 the logic class had 8 Jesuits and 3 boarders from the St. Francis Xavier School for Nobles. The natural philosophy class had 5 Jesuits. The metaphysics class had 6 Jesuits and 2 noble youths, and the mathematics class had five Jesuits. There were 2 scholastic theology classes with an enrollment of 15 Jesuits and no one else. Hence, the number of students in these 6 classes of restricted enrollments was 44 of whom 39 were Jesuits. The enrollments were much higher in the classes open to all. The cases of conscience class had 80 students, rhetoric had 28, humanities had 47, upper grammar had 85, lower grammar had 95, and a class for beginners taught by a secular priest had 65 students. The enrollment for these 6 classes open to all was 400. The combined enrollment was 444.[100]

In the early seventeenth century the Jesuits began a construction program that continued well into the eighteenth century. The Jesuits decided as early as 1580 that the church of Santa Lucia was small, old, and ugly.[101] By the early seventeenth century they had accumulated enough financial resources to lay the cornerstone for a grand Santa Lucia in 1623. Enough had been accomplished for liturgical services to be held there in 1659, although construction continued until about 1732. The two boarding schools moved into new buildings. Construction of a new college building that included some classrooms began in 1697. More classrooms and a handsome library building were added in the first half of the eighteenth century. All these buildings were contiguous or within steps of each other, making the Santa Lucia complex one of the most impressive Jesuit urban islands in Italy.[102] The Jesuits did not receive financial assistance from the city, so far as can be determined, but relied on a wealthy donor base. The building program demonstrated strong community support but also heightened the fears of the university and its allies.

In March 1642 the Bolognese ambassador to Rome complained to General Vitelleschi that the Jesuits were violating the rules by teaching philosophy to external students in what he derisively called their "little school" (la scoletta). The general promised to make sure that this was not happening.[103] In 1649 the Jesuits asked permission of the city for a university law profes-

98. ARSI, Veneta 40, ff. 153r, 154r.

99. ARSI, Veneta 37, f. 259r–v (28 Jesuits). Lukács, 1960–1961, part 2, 51, counts 27 Jesuits.

100. ARSI, Veneta 125, f. 3r, "Stato de Studij del Collegio di Bologna."

101. This was Francesco Palmio's judgment. Schurhammer 1973, 377, and 374n1 for the date.

102. See the articles in Dall'isola alla città 1988.

103. ASB, Assunteria di Studio 75, letter of Ambassador Ludovico Fachinetti to the Assun-

sor to come and teach *Institutes* to students of the St. Francis Xavier College
of Nobles. The city said no. This produced a minor flurry culminating in
the reprinting on December 13, 1649, of Urban VIII's brief of November
10, 1641. It was posted throughout the city, including on the door of the St.
Francis Xavier Noble School.[104] After 1649 the members of the university
stopped complaining about the Jesuits to the Assunteria di Studio and the
Senate for about twenty years.

In May 1661 class enrollments demonstrated that the Jesuits were following the rules. The single class of scholastic theology had only 12 Jesuit
scholastics. The three classes of metaphysics, natural philosophy, and logic
had a total enrollment of 22 Jesuits and 10 boarding school students, for
a total of only 44 students in four upper school classes. The cases of conscience class at the cathedral had 60 students. The lower school, which was
open to everyone, had 325 students in 6 classes: rhetoric had 31 students,
humanities 68 students, upper grammar 76 students, lower grammar 80,
and two classes for beginners taught by secular priests hired and paid by the
Jesuits had a combined enrollment of 70 students.[105]

A Limited Jesuit Victory

The Jesuits were doing even better in the early 1670s. In 1672 the Jesuit
school offered 13 classes. There were two classes in speculative theology
(scholastic theology under a different name), plus single classes in metaphysics, natural philosophy, logic, and mathematics, the last "taught privately to
ours."[106] The total number of students in the upper school was 140 or a few
more. The rest of the classes, open to all, had many more students. Francesco Adorni taught cases of conscience to 80 to 90 clergymen.[107] Jesuits

teria of March 19, 1641, no pag. See also ASB, Assunteria di Studio 11, Atti (1639–1647), ff. 64r,
65v, 66v.

104. The reprint of Urban VIII's brief has a new title: "Sentenza di scommunica. Contro
coloro, che non descritti ne' Rotoli del publico Studio leggessero le Scienze, Arti, e Facoltà solite leggersi in esso. Publicato novamente in Bologna li 13 di Decembre 1649." ASB, Assunteria
di Studio 89, no pag. See also ASB, Assunteria di Studio 92, "Gesuiti," no pag., documents of
November 24, 1649, and "1649"; and Fabrini 1941, 42.

105. ARSI, Veneta 97 I, f. 175r, May 6, 1661. Baldini 2002, 311–12, provides evidence that
Father Francesco Maria Grimaldi (Bologna 1618–1662/63 Bologna), astronomer and mathematician, taught mathematics at the Santa Lucia school from 1648 through 1662. However, the
1661 document does not mention a mathematics class. It may have been omitted because it was
viewed as informal private instruction for a handful of Jesuits and/or boarders. See the next
paragraph. On Grimaldi, see Ziggelaar 2001; and *Giambattista Riccioli* 2002, index.

106. "La mate[matic]a privatamente a nostri." ARSI, Veneta 106 II, f. 234v.

107. He should not be confused with the sixteenth-century Jesuit Francesco Adorno (Genoa

taught rhetoric, humanities, and two grammar classes, while two secular priests paid by the Jesuits taught two classes for beginners. The enrollment in the six lower school classes was about 400.[108] The total school enrollment was 620 to 630 students, about 200 more than in 1661. Half of the increase was in the upper school. The Jesuits were proud of the fact that their disputations and other academic exercises attracted large audiences.

In fact, a disputation triggered another campaign against the Jesuit school. On June 10, 1668, the Jesuit college sponsored a grand public disputation in their church to which they invited the legate Cardinal Carlo Carafa (1611–1680, cardinal from 1664, legate from 1665), city officials, and university professors. The church was decorated and an orchestra provided musical interludes. A student at the St. Francis Xavier School for Nobles, a young count who was a subject of Emperor Leopold I of Austria, defended philosophical propositions against all comers. In anticipation of a brilliant performance, the emperor sent a gold chain. When the young man performed well, the cardinal legate presented him with it. The rector of the Jesuit college then hosted a dinner honoring the disputant. This very public disputation rekindled the anger of the university community and its supporters. But they held their fire, because Cardinal Carafa had participated in the festivities.[109] They correctly saw him as a friend of the Jesuits. As a Roman seminarian he probably attended classes at the Jesuit Roman College; as papal nuncio to Venice he negotiated the 1657 reentry of the Jesuits into the Republic of Venice; and when he died, he was buried in the Gesù church in Rome.[110]

In September 1670 Carafa was replaced by Cardinal Lazzaro Pallavicino (1602–1680, cardinal from 1669, legate from 1670 to 1673), who was not seen as favoring the Jesuits.[111] Groups from the university and its supporters sent a new round of accusations and petitions to the Assunteria di Studio. They had four major complaints. They objected to Jesuit mathematical instruction and the dissemination of mathematical conclusions; they did not like the fact that the Jesuits were advertising and holding public disputations; they did not want the archiepiscopal cases of conscience lecturer, a Jesuit, to teach cases in the Jesuit school; and they did not want the Jesuits to provide limited legal instruction to their boarding school students. The opponents of the Jesuits claimed that all of these violated the prohibitions of the ordinationi and the papal brief of 1641.[112]

1532–1586 Genoa). Scaduto 1968, 2, and Scaduto 2001a. For more on Francesco Adorni (d. 1688), see below.

108. ARSI, Veneta 106 II, f. 234v.   109. Fabrini 1941, 45–46.
110. Cammarota 1976.   111. Giordano 2014.
112. Costa 1912, 66–70, provides many anti-Jesuit quotations from Assunteria di Studio documents but is not nearly so complete as Fabrini 1941, which will be followed.

Beginning in late 1670 and continuing through 1671 and 1672 the Assunteria di Studio bombarded the cardinal legate and the ambassador to Rome, Camillo Paleotti, with denunciations of the Jesuits for subverting the university. It demanded that the brief of Urban VIII be enforced to the hilt. In Rome the ambassador made the city's case. The ambassador won over Cardinal Paluzzo Altieri, the most powerful man in Rome after the pope, Clement X (Emilio Altieri, 1590–1676, pope from April 29, 1670). Born Paluzzo Paluzzi degli Albertoni, Cardinal Altieri (1623–1698, cardinal from 1664), took the name Altieri and managed the affairs of the papacy because of the advanced age and memory lapses of Clement X.[113] On December 2, 1671, Cardinal Altieri wrote to Cardinal Legate Pallavicino to tell him that the pope agreed with the city. The pope wanted the mess to be fixed through full observance of the brief of Urban VIII and punishment of the transgressors.[114]

On December 30, 1671, the legate issued an "Edict against those not listed in the Rolls of the Public University of Bologna who have taught the Sciences, Arts, and Faculties usually taught in it." It had two parts. The first part proclaimed (in Italian) that it was the mind of the pope and the will of the government of the city that anyone who violated the brief of Urban VIII should be punished with the penalties stipulated in it. It then stated that city authorities would pursue transgressors and impose the penalties. The second part was entitled "Sentenza di scommunica" (Sentence of excommunication). It reprinted Urban VIII's brief threatening excommunication. Large printed copies of the edict were prepared and posted throughout the city, no doubt on or near Jesuit buildings.[115]

That was not the end of it. On April 29, 1672, the leaders of the arts students organization and the theologians teaching in the university came to the Assunteria di Studio, this time to complain about the mathematics teaching of the Jesuits. They charged that the Jesuits were teaching the same advanced mathematics as the three professors of mathematics at the university. Even worse, they were posting mathematical conclusions in the courtyard of the Archiginnasio, the university building in the center of the city. The Jesuits should be excommunicated because they were violating the brief of Urban VIII.[116]

113. Pastor 1891–1953, 31:443–45; and Stella 1960.

114. "Riparo al disordine con essigere universalmente l'intera osservanza di detta Bolla e castigare i transgressori." Fabrini 1941, 52–54 (quotation at 53).

115. "EDITTO Contro coloro, che non descritti ne' Rotoli del Publico Studio di Bologna leggessero le Scienze, Arti, e Facoltà solite leggersi in esso." There is a copy measuring 29 x 42 cm. in ARSI, Veneta 126 II, f. 227r. The text of the first part is also found in Fabrini 1941, 53–54.

116. Fabrini 1941, 54–57, most of which quotes from the letter of the Assunti of April 30, 1672, to the Bolognese ambassador to the papacy.

That the students at the Jesuit school were studying university-level mathematics and doing well is not surprising, because their teacher was Giuseppe Ferroni (Pistoia 1628–1709 Siena). He had studied mathematics under the very able Jesuit Niccolò Cabeo (Ferrara 1586–1650 Genoa). He also studied with the non-Jesuits Giovanni Alfonso Borelli (1608–1679), a mathematician best known for his pioneering research on biomechanics (the movements of animals), and Vincenzo Viviani (1622–1703), a Florentine disciple of Galileo Galilei. Ferroni taught mathematics in the Roman College from 1657 to 1660, the Jesuit school in Mantua from 1660 to 1666, and at Bologna from 1667 to 1686. He was an able mathematician who accepted the heliocentric views of Copernicus and Galilei, but did not say this in his own name.[117]

Instead, Ferroni hinted at his views in an anonymous work. In 1680 an anonymous dialogue appeared in Bologna: *Dialogo fisico astronomico contro il sistema copernicano tenuto fra due interlocutori Sig. Francesco Bianchini veronese, sotto il nome di Adimanto, Sig. Ignatio Rocca piacentino, sotto il nome di Silvio, convittori del Collegio del Beato Luigi Gonzaga della Compagnia di Gesù in Bologna* (A physical and astronomical dialogue against the Copernican system between two interlocutori Signore Francesco Bianchini from Verona, under the name of Adimanto, Signore Ignatio Rocca of Piacenza, under the name of Silvio, boarding students of the College of Blessed Luigi Gonzaga of the Society of Jesus in Bologna). Per Giuseppe Longhi, Bologna, 1680. Although Bianchini and Rocca were fictitious names, Longhi was an active publisher. Although no author was listed, Ferroni immediately sent a copy to a friend who knew his true views. Scholars do not doubt his authorship.[118]

In an introduction addressed to his fellow boarding school students, Bianchini stated that he has been studying mathematics, and he and Rocca decided to discuss why Nicolaus Copernicus and his followers were so wrong. Hence, both interlocutors ostensibly rejected the views of Copernicus. However, they presented Copernicus in a favorable light. One of the interlocutors commented that Copernicus had studied in Bologna, lectured on his *fantasie* (fantasies) in Rome before two thousand listeners, and dedicated his book to Pope Paul III.[119] All true. Copernicus studied law and astronomy at the University of Bologna between 1496 and 1501, and lectured in Rome in 1499 on his astronomical views, although probably not to two thousand. He dedicated *De revolutionibus* (1543) to Paul III.

117. Torrini 1973, Zanfredini 2001c, and Baldini 2002, 312. For more on Ferroni, see chap. 13.
118. The text with notes are found in *La scienza dissimulata* 2005, 107–40.
119. *La scienza dissimulata* 2005, 115.

One interlocutor then added that those were different times; today such freedom of opinion is severely restricted by the laws.[120] This was Ferroni's criticism of the Holy Office prohibition against heliocentrism. And setting the dialogue in a Jesuit boarding school was a means of criticizing Jesuit adherence to the prohibition that prevented Ferroni and all other Jesuit mathematicians from teaching heliocentrism as physical reality.

In the course of the dialogue the two interlocutors presented an accurate account of the cosmology of Copernicus. By contrast, the arguments presented against Copernicus were scriptural and miraculous. For example, the interlocutors referred to Isaiah commanding the sun to back up, which caused a shadow to move ten steps on the stairs of a temple (Is 38:8), as evidence that the sun moved around the earth.[121] Readers of the dialogue might not have judged such arguments as convincing in the light of the knowledge of the heavens available in 1680.

In short, the mathematics instruction at the Jesuit school was excellent. But is not likely that Ferroni or any other Jesuit posted mathematical conclusions in the courtyard of the university building. That would have been a provocative act. It is more likely that students, proud of their accomplishments, did so while Father Ferroni and other Jesuits said nothing. In any case, posting conclusions told the mathematically literate that the Jesuit school was teaching up-to-date mathematics and astronomy. It invited comparison with the university.

The university also strongly objected, once again, to the Jesuit cases of conscience lecture. Obviously the university professorship of cases of conscience begun in 1637 had not attracted very many clergymen. Instead, they continued to attend the cases course sponsored by the archdiocese and delivered by a Jesuit who lectured in the cathedral of San Petronius across the piazza from the university building. The current Jesuit lecturer was Francesco Adorni (d. 1688 in Bologna), who had been teaching cases of conscience under license of the archdiocese since 1650.[122] He also advised the archdiocese and served on the committee that examined priesthood candidates on their knowledge of the rules of confession, penances, and restitution.

In 1670 Adorni requested permission to move his lectures to the Jesuit college, and the archbishop agreed. The university perceived this as another example of the Jesuit school teaching external students, which was

---

120. "Ma ora non corrono più quei tempi; anzi la libertà di si fattamente opinare viene oggi sotto severe leggi ristretta." *La scienza dissimulata* 2005, 115–16.

121. *La scienza dissimulata* 2005, 112–37.

122. On Adorni, see Fabrini 1941, 49; and Sommervogel 1960, 1:55–56.

true, and in contravention of Urban VIII's brief, also true. The Assunteria di Studio took up the cause of the university, arguing that the archbishop should deputize a professor of theology from the university to teach cases. Adorni declared that canon law permitted the archbishop to appoint anyone he chose. And since he had been chosen, he might teach where he wished.[123] The university responded by increasing the number of university professorships of cases to two in 1670, three in 1671, and four in 1674.[124] It is not likely that they had much success attracting students, because Adorni lectured to 80 to 90 secular priests in 1672.[125]

The protests of parts of the university and the Assunteria di Studio persuaded the legate to try again. On May 6, 1672, Cardinal Pallavicino issued another edict. In it he noted that the Jesuits were teaching university courses and posting mathematical conclusions, contrary to the brief of Urban VIII. He reiterated that neither the Jesuits nor any other religious order might teach publicly or privately any courses taught by university professors, and he forbade the Jesuits from posting notices of such courses or conclusions in the university building.[126]

The Jesuits fought back by taking the brief of Urban VIII literally. On May 8, two days after the edict of Cardinal Legate Pallavicino, the Jesuits closed the two highest classes in their lower school, rhetoric and humanities. Since the university also taught the humanities and rhetoric, the Jesuits were making the point that they were not permitted to teach these courses if Urban VIII's brief was strictly observed.[127] The closing meant that there were no classes for about a hundred students. Although some were noble and citizen boarders, the majority were day students, many of them sons of Bologna's leading families. The Jesuits reopened their rhetoric and humanities classes on May 9 and closed them again two days later, followed by another opening.[128] The closures and openings reminded parents and the commune of the importance of the Jesuit school.

Commune and Jesuits were at an impasse. Something had to be done and, once again, Rome decided. There the climate of opinion had changed,

123. Fabrini 1941, 48–50, 62–64, 72–75, in particular Adorni's letter which is quoted at length on 72–73.

124. For the details, see chap. 15, "Cases of Conscience."

125. ARSI, Veneta 106 II, f. 234v, annual report for Bologna of 1672.

126. Fabrini 1941, 57–59.

127. In the academic year 1671–1672, there were three ordinary professors of the humanities (Ad lecturam Humanarum litterarum) teaching at the University of Bologna. It was the same in the academic year 1672–1673. While there were no rhetoric professors, rhetoric based on the classics was a key part of humanities instruction. Dallari 1888–1924, 3:56, 58, 62–63.

128. Fabrini 1941, 59.

and Ambassador Camillo Paleotti faced an uphill struggle. In July 1672 he made the case to Pope Clement X and Cardinal Paluzzo Altieri that the Jesuits had damaged the university in every town in which they were permitted to teach, and that this was happening in Bologna. But now pope and cardinal were skeptical; they did not see how the Jesuits teaching a few boarding school students could harm the University of Bologna. In early August the ambassador warned the Assunteria di Studio that Roman opinion favored the Jesuits, and that the Assunti should drop the issue and wait for a more propitious time. On August 8, 1672, he reported that the issue had been referred to a commission of cardinals including Altieri, Gaspare Carpegna, and Carlo Carafa, all firm friends of the Jesuits in his view, plus possibly a fourth cardinal, Pietro Vidoni senior.[129]

Paleotti had read the situation correctly: the pope and several of the cardinals looked benevolently on the Jesuits. Clement X had studied at the Roman College and as pope regularly sent money to Jesuit colleges across Europe.[130] As mentioned earlier, Cardinal Carlo Carafa was a friend of the Jesuits. Gaspare Carpegna (1625–1714, cardinal from 1670) was a curial cardinal who held many offices in Rome.[131] His views on the Jesuits are unknown except for the comment of the ambassador. Pietro Vidoni (1610–1680, cardinal from 1658) had been legate of Bologna from 1662 to 1665.[132] Although his views on the Jesuits are unknown, he was familiar with the situation in Bologna. Most important, Cardinal Altieri had changed his mind.

The decision came quickly. On August 17, 1672, Jesuit General Giovanni Paolo Oliva wrote to the provincial superior of the Province of Venice to report a near-complete victory. Cardinal Altieri had authorized the Jesuits to teach "le scienze superiori" (higher studies) to the students in the Jesuit-run boarding schools, although they were forbidden to hold solemn public disputations. The Jesuit lectureship on cases of conscience would continue as before, with all external students welcome to attend. Where Adorni lectured was up to the archbishop, which meant that he would lecture in the Jesuit college. The Jesuits might hold public disputations but without ceremony, an undefined restriction. General Oliva mentioned that Cardinal Altieri had also written a letter in support of the Jesuits to Cardinal Leg-

---

129. Fabrini 1941, 67–71.

130. Pastor 1891–1953, 31:449; Villoslada 1954, 288–89; Osbat 1982, 294; and O'Neill and Viscardi 2001b, 2988.

131. Romeo 1977.

132. Pastor 1891–1953, 31:131, 134, 433, 435; *Legati e governatori* 1994, 156; and The Cardinals of the Roman Church, www2.fiu.edu/~mirandas/bios1660.html#Vidoni.

ate Pallavicino. Oliva closed by cautioning the Jesuits of Bologna to avoid expressing satisfaction about their triumph.[133] Thus the papacy confirmed the authority of the Jesuits to teach upper level classes in theology, cases of conscience, and philosophy to their own members and students from their boarding schools.

The subjects now included law, although the Jesuit would not do the teaching. In 1649 the Senate had ruled that a law professor could not teach *Institutes* to noble boarders. However, some parents still wanted this, so the Jesuits tried again in 1670. They asked that a law professor be permitted to come to the St. Francis Xavier Noble School to teach law in a small class separate from the rest of the courses. They pointed out that some boarders were already attending law lectures at the university. The Assunteria di Studio and opponents of the Jesuits objected. The issue went back and forth between Bologna and Rome for two years.[134]

Then on November 8, 1672, the Bolognese Senate said yes. It also ruled that the Jesuit students might hold legal disputations in their boarding schools. And the students might print the conclusions of the disputations in a simple, unadorned form, without title, heraldic device, or ornaments, so long as they included the name and title of the university professor who assisted in the disputations. The students were not permitted to post the conclusions throughout the city, but they might post them in the university building. The Senate also noted that the Jesuits had agreed that any of their students interested in law were obligated to attend law lectures at the university.[135] With the Senate's approval, the Jesuits invited law professors to teach law to the noble boarders at the St. Francis Xavier school.[136]

The episode revealed that some students from the Jesuit boarding schools were attending university lectures, a fact that the angry complainants had not mentioned. Of course, it made perfect sense for older boarders interested in the law to attend university law lectures. It also showed that Jesuit upper schools imitated universities, as critics charged. Although the Jesuits did not teach law themselves, they arranged for legal instruction. The law professors who came to teach received payment from the students, which demonstrated that some university professors would cooperate with the Jesuit school when it was in their interest.

133. Letter of General Giovanni Paolo Oliva to Domenico Brunacci, August 17, 1672, Rome, in Fabrini 1941, 72.

134. Fabrini 1941, 50–54.

135. Fabrini 1941, 75–76.

136. Brizzi 1976, 119n50. For some of the professors who came and the legal texts studied, see 233–34.

On April 10, 1673, Cardinal Legate Pallavicino finally issued a decree stating what the cardinals in Rome had decided in August 1672. Although couched in cautious terms, it rendered Urban VIII's brief a dead letter. Despite its prohibitions, the Jesuits were permitted to teach philosophy to the students of their boarding schools and cases of conscience to clergymen who wished to come.[137]

The Jesuit school expanded. In 1696 it offered 14 classes taught by Jesuits: two in scholastic theology; one each in scripture, cases of conscience, metaphysics, natural philosophy, logic, mathematics, Hebrew, Greek, rhetoric, humanities, and two in grammar. There may also have been one or two classes for beginners taught by secular priests. There were at least 75 Jesuits in the Santa Lucia College, either 32 or 40 of them Jesuit scholastics. The ultimate gift of Alberto Serpa Angelelli provided the endowment that paid their living expenses. In addition, there were 29 Jesuits, 16 of them novices, in the novice house on the other side of the city, and a handful of Jesuits lived in the two boarding schools.[138] The St. Francis Xavier School for Nobles had 126 boarders in 1699. The number of boarders in the Blessed Luigi Gonzaga School for Citizens at this date is unknown, but may have been 80 to 100.

The Bologna school continued to operate at a high level. In 1746 there were at least 13 courses taught by Jesuits: two for scholastic theology, two grammar classes, and one each for moral theology, scripture, metaphysics, natural philosophy, logic, canon law (*canones*), mathematics, rhetoric, and humanities. The major innovation was the class in canon law, an eighteenth-century development discussed in chapter 11. There were more than 80 Jesuits at the college of Santa Lucia including 30 philosophy scholastics and 10 theology scholastics. In addition to studying, two theology scholastics served as tutors at the St. Francis Xavier School for Nobles and another two at the St. Luigi Gonzaga School for Citizens (he was canonized in 1726). The former had 57 boarders in 1746, while the number at the School for Citizens is unknown.[139] Additional Jesuits lived in the novice house.[140]

The Santa Lucia college and school remained strong in 1770 on the eve

137. Pallavicino's decree of April 10, 1673, Bologna, is printed in Fabrini 1941, 76–77n2. There is a handwritten copy of the degree plus an anonymous and undated interpretation of the decree that argues that the brief of Urban VIII was not meant to bar the Jesuits from teaching cases of conscience and philosophy, in BAB, Ms. Gozzadini 105, no. 27, ff. 275r–76v.

138. ARSI, Veneta 49, ff. 107r, 108r, May 15, 1696. Triennial catalogues do not always list beginner classes taught by non-Jesuits.

139. Brizzi 1976, 136.

140. ARSI, Veneta 59, ff. 316r, 317r, 318r, 319r. There is no information on school enrollment.

of the suppression. Again there were over 80 Jesuits, 42 of them scholastics, at the college, plus another four Jesuits at the St. Francis Xavier School for Nobles, six Jesuits at the St. Luigi Gonzaga School for Citizens, and 43 Jesuits at the novice house, a total of more than 133. The Santa Lucia school had 12 classes taught by Jesuits: two in scholastic theology, two in grammar, and one each in moral theology, scripture, metaphysics, natural philosophy, logic, mathematics, rhetoric, and humanities. However, there were only 43 boarders at the St. Francis Xavier School for Nobles and 36 boarders at the St. Luigi Gonzaga School for Citizens.[141] Enrollments in all the Italian Jesuit boarding schools were in decline at this time.[142]

When the Society of Jesus was suppressed in 1773, the church, college, and classrooms of Santa Lucia were given to the Barnabites who continued the school. The French occupation forced other dispositions, because the French suppressed all religious orders in 1810. Although the Society of Jesus was reconstituted in 1814, the buildings were not returned to the Society. Instead, in 1882 the college of Santa Lucia became the Liceo Classico Statale "Luigi Galvani," the most prestigious university preparatory school in the city. It continues to teach in the same location today. The large church of Santa Lucia was deconsecrated, served as a military depot, then became a gymnasium for the Liceo students. It was restored between 1987 and 1989 to become the Aula Magna of the University of Bologna. Most of the rest of the buildings of the Jesuit urban island have undergone such extensive alterations over time that they are unrecognizable today.[143]

Conclusion

Francis Xavier was the first Jesuit to come to Bologna, and the Jesuits began to teach in 1551. They reached out to university students and professors, and relations were friendly for many years. Then in the 1630s the Province of Venice needed a new upper school in which to teach its scholastics, and chose Bologna. The prospect of the Jesuits teaching philosophy and theology alarmed the university, and various groups protested what they saw as unlawful competition. Colleges of doctors led the way, because they increasingly determined university policy in the seventeenth century.[144] A compromise was reached in 1636. The Bologna Jesuits were permitted to

141. ARSI, Veneta 62, ff. 293r, 294r, 295r, 296r. Brizzi 1976, 137, using a different source, gives the number of boarders at the St. Francis Xavier Noble School as 57 in 1770.

142. Brizzi 1976, 31–36, 131–37, esp. 136–37 for the St. Francis Xavier School for Nobles.

143. See the articles, diagrams, and illustrations in *Dall'isola alla città* 1988.

144. Lupi 2005, 80–84; Brizzi 2008, 41–42.

teach theology and philosophy, but only to their own members. However, the Jesuits began to teach logic to a handful of noble boarding students with the permission of the cardinal legate. Elements of the university protested. The commune took up their cause and obtained a brief from Urban VIII in 1641 that forbade the Jesuits from teaching any discipline that the university taught.

The draconian brief of 1641 was not fully implemented. The growth of the Jesuit school and lack of strict enforcement of the restrictions caused the university and the city government to renew their denunciations in 1670. But now legates and Vatican cardinals generally supported the Jesuits. Exceptions were carved out. The Jesuits were allowed to teach upper level courses, plus mathematics and law, to students from the two boarding schools. Their right to teach cases of conscience to anyone who came was affirmed. These were small victories. The Jesuits were still not permitted to teach theology and philosophy to all, as they did in most cities with universities. But other universities were not Bologna. Still, the enrollment numbers demonstrate that the Bolognese Jesuit school expanded in the eighteenth century despite the restrictions.

There were similarities and differences in the campaigns against the Jesuits in Bologna and Padua. Professors and students of the University of Bologna and their supporters voiced some, but not all, of the arguments that opponents used against the Jesuits at Padua. They had less success, because Bologna was different from Padua. The University of Padua was located in the independent Republic of Venice, many leaders of which embraced an anti-Jesuit ideology. Bologna had neither political independence nor a foreign policy. So opponents of the Jesuits couched their arguments in legal terms, that the university had the exclusive right to teach philosophy and theology. The Jesuits were not able to teach theology and philosophy to all students in either Bologna or Padua. The two premier universities of Italy limited the competition from the Jesuits.

II

THE BATTLE OVER CANON LAW

IN ROME

The University of Rome faced the Roman College (Collegio Romano), the largest and most important Jesuit school in Italy. Because the Roman College met their needs so well, the Jesuits had no interest in teaching at the University of Rome, and the university had no hope of shutting down the Roman College. But when the Roman College began to teach canon law, the university protested. The dispute uncovered a major educational departure from the Constitutions written by Ignatius Loyola.

The Roman College and the University of Rome

Founded in 1551, the Roman College had some of the ablest Jesuit scholars as teachers, including Robert Bellarmine, Christoph Clavius, and Francisco Suárez. It served several constituencies besides the Jesuits themselves.[1] It taught Latin and Greek grammar, humanities, and rhetoric to a very large number of boys from the upper, middle, and lower ranks of Roman society, including future cardinals and popes. The Roman College provided instruction in logic, natural philosophy, and metaphysics, mathematics, and moral philosophy to youths aged 16 to 19 intending to go on to a university. It educated lay youths and future clergymen who lived in the student residences supervised by the Jesuits: the German and Hungarian College, the Greek College, the Hibernian College, the English College, the College of the Scots, and the Maronite College. Present and future secular clergymen attended the theology, scripture, and Hebrew classes. So did youths and young men from the Roman seminary, which trained priests for the archdiocese of Rome. The cases of conscience classes were primarily

1. Villoslada 1954 is the best study of the Roman College.

319

intended for parish priests. Only a limited number of members of the medieval mendicant orders went to the Roman College, because they studied in the monastic studia of their own orders and at the University of Rome.

The Roman College building, erected in the center of Rome in 1584, was the largest educational building in Italy. It provided classrooms, a library, and modest living accommodations for many Jesuits. It symbolized the commanding position of the Collegio Romano in Roman education. So did the size of its enrollment, an estimated 2,000 students in 23 classes in 1600.[2] In the academic year 1696–1697 the upper school of the Roman College offered 17 daily classes taught by 14 Jesuits: 3 taught scholastic theology, 2 taught cases of conscience (on different topics), and single Jesuits taught controversial theology, scripture, Hebrew, metaphysics, natural philosophy, logic, mathematics, moral philosophy, and canon law.[3] The classes in metaphysics, natural philosophy, and logic met twice daily; all the other classes of the upper school met once daily. Hence, there were 17 daily classes devoted to different subject matter, almost always with a different group of students. Given the large size of Jesuit classes, it is likely that the Roman College upper school had 1,000 to 1,100 students in the academic year 1696–1697.[4]

The lower school of the Roman College had 12 Jesuit teachers who taught 2 rhetoric classes, 2 humanities classes, and 7 grammar classes, all of which met in both the morning and the afternoon for a total of about five hours a day, and a Greek teacher who probably taught two or three hour-long Greek classes for students of different levels of skill.[5] Because the lower school curriculum was rigidly progressive, all classes had a different group of students. That is, a student had to satisfy the requirements of the lowest grammar class in order to advance to the middle grammar class, he had to satisfy the requirements of the middle grammar class to advance

2. For the number of classes, see ARSI, Roma 54, f. 50v. Lukács 1960–1961, part 2, 48, concurs. The enrollment estimate comes from Di Simone 1982, 36; and is repeated by Colpo 2001, 849. Although Di Simone provides no evidence, it seems a reasonable estimate.

3. The evidence for 17 classes and 14 Jesuit teachers in the upper school comes from ARSI, Roma 66, f. 284r (1696); and ASR, Università 195, f. 23, the Roman College roll for the academic year 1696–1697. This is a large printed sheet of paper listing the courses offered, the texts to be taught, the hours at which they would meet, but not the names of the Jesuit teachers. Like Italian universities, the Roman College printed annual rolls and posted them throughout the city. But I have located only single copies of four rolls, for the academic years 1696–1697, 1697–1698, 1698–1699, and 1699–1700. ASR, Archivio dell'Università di Roma (hereafter Università) 95, ff. 23, 104, 185, 384.

4. See note 6 on the size of classes.

5. ARSI, Roma 66, f. 284r; and ASR, Università 195, f. 23.

to the upper grammar class, and so on. Individual lower school classes in Jesuit schools normally had enrollments of a hundred and more.[6] Hence, it is very likely that at least 1,300 to 1,400 different students attended lower school classes at the Roman College in the academic year 1696–1697. This conservative estimate suggests that the combined upper and lower school enrollment was at least 2,300 to 2,500 students in 1696. And there were 356 Jesuits living in Rome in 1696, scattered among the Roman College, a novice house, residence colleges, and other institutions.[7]

The University of Rome, called La Sapienza from the 1560s to today, was a much smaller institution. In the academic year 1696–1697, it had 34 professors, which made it a medium-sized Italian university. Of these 34 professors, 10 taught law, 8 taught medicine, 5 taught natural philosophy, 3 taught theology, and one each taught scripture, ecclesiastical history, metaphysics, logic, moral philosophy, mathematics, Arabic, Greek, Hebrew, Chaldean (i.e., Syriac), and a combination of rhetoric and humanities. Twenty-five professors were laymen, while 9 were clergymen from medieval mendicant orders.[8] None was a Jesuit. La Sapienza had about 490 students (250 in law, 140 in medicine, and 100 in other disciplines) in 1628.[9] About 440 students were attending lectures in 1651, which meant the enrollment was somewhat higher, because not all students attend classes regularly, then or now.[10] Like every other Italian university, La Sapienza concentrated on law and medicine. While the Roman College and the University of Rome competed for students in many subjects in the seventeenth century, only the new class in canon law drew ire from the university.

---

6. For example, the Brera Jesuit school in Milan had 1,813 students in 13 classes in 1661, and some classes had 200 and more students. ARSI, Mediolanensis 73, ff. 168r–69v; also Negruzzo 2001, 129.

7. ARSI, Roma 66, ff. 284r–92r.

8. *I maestri di Roma* 1991, 1:493–95.

9. ASR, Università 83, f. 39bis recto. The numbers come at the end of a three-page *relazione* of 1628 discussing the university in some detail. Although the relazione is anonymous, it clearly came from an official of the university, perhaps the beadle.

10. An anonymous document of 1651 (no month or day) named 28 professors and the number of students attending the lectures of each. Attendance ranged from none to 60. The total was 438 to 440. The document looks like a list prepared by the *puntatore*, the official charged with visiting each class daily to make sure that the professor appeared and to count the students. Because the document lacked month or day, and the numbers were rounded by fives (10, 15, 20, etc.), these were average attendance figures rather than attendance on one particular day. Carella 2003, 14–15; and Carella 2007, tavola 2 after p. xvi, which is a photograph of the document. Incidentally, there were 31 professors in 1651, which probably meant that three were not lecturing because of absence, illness, or another reason. *I maestri di Roma* 1991, 1:311–13.

The Jesuits and Canon Law

Ignatius Loyola did not believe that Jesuit schools should teach canon law. Subsequent Jesuits disagreed, and the Society eventually did teach canon law.

The Constitutions, written by Ignatius, barred the Jesuits from teaching canon law, civil law, and medicine.[11] But he relented a little on canon law, because he believed that professors of theology needed to know a little bit about canon law. "Accordingly, there should be diligent treatment by excellent professors of what pertains to scholastic doctrine and Sacred Scripture, as also to that part of positive theology which is conducive to the aforementioned end, without entering into the part of the canons which is directed toward court trials."[12]

This turgid sentence introduced the term positive theology. John Major (or Jean Mair, 1467/69–1550), a Scot who taught theology at the University of Paris for many years, was the first to draw a distinction between positive and scholastic theology that has been followed ever since. Positive theology is the branch of theology that explains Christian doctrine through accumulated knowledge about Christianity.[13] Catholic positive theology relies on scripture; the writings of Church Fathers; decrees of ecumenical councils, popes, and synods; the works of theologians; tradition; history; and canon law to explain God's plan for humans. It might be said that positive theology documents the faith of the Catholic church. Erasmus of Rotterdam was the most famous practitioner of positive theology in the Renaissance because he used scripture and the Church Fathers to teach eloquently what he called "the philosophy of Christ." By contrast, speculative theology seeks to understand the nature of God and his message for humans through philosophical and theoretical investigation, for example, by means of scholastic analysis, at which point it becomes scholastic theology

Positive theology was only a method or tendency for the Jesuits and most other theologians of the era. The Constitutions mentioned it four times, always in passing, while the Ratio Studiorum ignored it.[14] But the Jesuits did use the method and sources of positive theology when needed. For example, Jesuit moral theologians and casuists used papal pronounce-

---

11. "The study of medicine and laws ... will not be treated in the universities of the Society, or at least the Society will not undertake this teaching through its own members." *Constitutions* 1970, part IV, chap. 12, par. 452 (215); and *Constitutions* 1996, par. 452 (180).

12. *Constitutions* 1970, par. 446 (213); *Constitutions* 1996, par. 446 (179).

13. For the Jesuit understanding of positive theology, see the brief comments in *Constitutions* 1970, 188n5; and Wicks 2001b. For a broader discussion, see Congar 1946, cols. 462–72.

14. *Constitutions* 1970, pars. 351, 366, 446, 464 (188, 191, 213, 219); *Constitutions* 1996, pars. 351, 366, 446, 464 (150, 154, 179, 182).

ments, conciliar degrees, and canon law extensively when they discussed justice, sin, usury, and restitution.[15] Nevertheless, the Constitutions prohibited the teaching of canon law *per se*.

After the death of Ignatius, some Jesuits disagreed with the prohibition against teaching canon law as a subject unto itself and hoped that it would be taught. Diego de Ledesma, prefect of studies at the Roman College, was one. While summarizing the curriculum of the Roman College for the academic year 1564–1565, he noted that canon law was not taught. He was not opposed to teaching it, and he opined that canon law was useful and might be taught in the future.[16] But the Collegio Romano did not teach it.

In March 1580 Cardinal Carlo Borromeo, archbishop of Milan, strongly urged the Milanese Jesuits to teach canon law for the convenience of the clergymen who studied at the Jesuit school there. And he recommended a non-Jesuit. Some of the Jesuit scholastics at the Brera school also wanted a course in canon law, but thought that a Jesuit should teach the course. General Mercurian said no, then died. The next general, Claudio Acquaviva, elected February 19, 1581, also said no, on the grounds that this would be a novelty not permitted by the Constitutions. But in a gesture to the imperious Borromeo he authorized Father Francesco Adorno (Genoa 1532–1586 Genoa), who was teaching cases of conscience three times a week in the archiepiscopal palace, to discuss canons when needed to explain cases of conscience material. This did not satisfy Borromeo, but Acquaviva would not budge. Adorno later transferred his teaching to the Jesuit school.[17]

Although the Jesuits did not teach canon law at the Roman College, they arranged for instruction in it for the students of the German and Hungarian College. It annually enrolled at least one hundred young Germans (and Hungarians after 1580), most of them boarders and half to two-thirds of them nobles. After completing their education, they normally returned to central Europe as priests and often became bishops.[18] Instruction in canon law would obviously be useful for these future leaders of the church. Hence Cardinal Giovanni Ludovico Madruzzo (1532–1600), bishop of Trent and one of the cardinal-protectors of the German and Hungarian College, recommended that it provide canon law instruction. In 1586 it hired a secu-

15. See any Jesuit treatise or manual on moral theology or cases of conscience from the sixteenth, seventeenth, and eighteenth centuries.

16. MP 2:532.

17. Letter of Giovanni Battista Peruschi of June 1, 1580, Turin, in ARSI, Italiae 156, f. 105v; Rurale 1992, 157–58 (the best account); and Negruzzo 2001, 79. For Adorno see Scaduto 2001a.

18. Schmidt 1984, 78–86, 112–20. As noted in chap. 1, note 83, the German and Hungarian College in its first years also accepted numerous Italian secular nobles in order to pay the bills. As the finances of the College improved, there were fewer and fewer of them.

lar priest with a doctorate of law from the University of Pisa to lecture on canon law four days a week for about an hour, for which he received 15 scudi per month.[19]

Not everyone approved. In 1616 the Jesuit rector of the German and Hungarian College believed that canon law instruction led the students to think more about winning prelacies than caring for souls. On his recommendation canon law moved to the vacation period, September 1 to early November. After a long hiatus, canon law instruction returned to the regular academic year in 1663 as an hour-long daily lecture taught by a non-Jesuit and accompanied by public disputations, tutorials, and examinations.[20]

Over time the Jesuits arranged for more law instruction, always by non-Jesuits, in the Roman student residences that they governed. Members of the Roman legal community did the teaching, which was broader than a little canon law. At the end of the seventeenth century eight members of the Avvocati Concistoriali, the name of the college of doctors of law of Rome, reported that they had been teaching both canon and civil law at the Roman Seminary and other colleges governed by Jesuits for periods ranging from one to a dozen years. Four of them were professors at La Sapienza.[21]

The Jesuits did the same elsewhere in Italy. Beginning in the second decade of the seventeenth century the Jesuits at the Parma school for nobles arranged for professors from the University of Parma to come to the school to teach law. By 1716 they came daily to teach *Institutes*, plus topics in civil law, canon law, criminal law, and feudal law. Fees from the boarders paid them. The justification offered was that legal studies were necessary for good public and private government, and studying law instilled respect for a regulated life in youths prone to the dangers of too much freedom.[22]

However, the Ratio Studiorum did not permit the Jesuits to teach canon law *per se*. It only allowed a few Jesuit theology students to study canon law. After completing theological study, a few Jesuits of outstanding ability were to be selected for two years of private study of theology. During the two years they were encouraged to range widely in their reading, and might study canons. However, they were told that "in their study of the canons they should leave out the judicial section, and concentrate entirely

19. Villoslada 1954, 244–45; Schmidt 1984, 23n74. Pastor 1891–1953, 19:239, reports that a papal bull by Gregory XIII of 1573 reestablishing the German College with substantial papal financial support expected that it would teach canon law.

20. Villoslada 1954, 245–46.

21. ASR, Università 195, ff. 34r–v (affidavits of the four professors of March 6, 1696), 214v–15r (affidavits of four other members of the Avvocati Concistoriali of January 1, 1699).

22. Capasso 1901, 18, 68–69, 106–7; Turrini 2006, 52, 68n179, 146–48.

on the ecclesiastical material."[23] This reiterated the limitation imposed by Ignatius in the Constitutions. The provision of two years of private theological study also came from the Constitutions.[24] However, it fell into abeyance as four years of classroom theological study became the norm.

Despite the Constitutions and the Ratio Studiorum, northern European Jesuit schools taught canon law. In 1625 the Jesuit University of Dillingen in Bavaria created a professorship of canon law, the first in a Jesuit school in Europe. It appointed the Jesuit Paul Laymann (1574–1635), who had previously published several works of moral theology, to the position. He attracted many students until 1632, when war and the plague closed the university temporarily. Laymann also advised church and state authorities on legal issues surrounding the Thirty Years' War, always adopting a militant Catholic position. His three-volume commentary on the *Decretals* (explained below) was published posthumously.[25] After Laymann's death the canon law professorship at Dillingen languished for a while. But the Jesuits established a professorship at Graz in 1643, while the University of Ingolstadt entrusted the teaching of canon law to the Jesuits in 1675.[26] Another distinguished German Jesuit professor of canon law was Ehrenreich Pirhing (1606–1679), who taught canon law at the University of Dillingen from 1643 to 1646 and 1658 to 1671. He published a five-volume study of the *Decretals* between 1674 and 1678.[27]

By 1696 Jesuit instruction in canon law was widespread in northern Europe. In response to a legal action brought by the Avvocati Concistoriali (see below), the Roman College presented affidavits to the Sacred Roman Rota in July and August 1696 testifying that Jesuit schools and universities in Dillingen, Graz, Ingolstadt, Cologne, Bamberg, Mainz, Passau, Strasbourg, Vilna, and Warsaw had been teaching canon law as an independent lectureship since the 1670s or earlier.[28] This was not all: Jesuit schools in Linz and Trnava (Nagyszombat in Slovakia) were also teaching canon law.[29] And a Jesuit was expected to teach canon law at the proposed civic-Jesuit University of Chambéry. Most important, the Roman College told the Sacred Roman Rota that the Jesuits had been teaching canon law at Genoa for twenty years.[30]

This was true. The Jesuits instituted a professorship of canon law in their school at Genoa in 1669. The impetus came from the city. In 1536, before the Society of Jesus existed, Ansaldo Grimaldi (1471–1539), an immensely

---

23. *Ratio Studiorum* 2005, pars. 16, 456–57 (11, 196; quotation at 196).
24. *Constitutions* 1970, par. 476 (222); *Constitutions* 1996, par. 476 (184).
25. Bireley 1973; and Bireley 2001.   26. Olivares 2001, 1091.
27. Gerlich 2001.   28. ASR, Università 195, ff. 44r–52r.
29. Szilas 2001, 281.
30. ASR, Università 195, f. 44r, August 2, 1696.

wealthy banker and diplomat from one of the four dominant families of Genoa, bequeathed a sum of money for the establishment of four professorships: mathematics, moral philosophy, canon law, and civil law.[31] The ultimate goal was to create a university. Part of the will was implemented in 1650 when the commune provided 100 scudi annually from the Grimaldi bequest to support a Jesuit to teach mathematics in the Jesuit school.[32]

But not until 1669 was Grimaldi's will fully implemented. The Genoese doge brokered an agreement in which the other three professorships were also placed in the Jesuit school. The bequest, invested in shares of the Banco di San Giorgio, provided 300 scudi annually to the Jesuits in support of the professorships. It was agreed that Jesuits would teach moral philosophy, and canon law, while a layman would teach civil law.[33]

The first Jesuit professor of canon law at a Jesuit school in Italy was Father Ippolito Durazzo (Genoa 1628–1675 Genoa), who taught from 1669 to 1672. Francesco Antonio Massola (Lepanto 1626–1706 Genoa) taught canon law from 1673 through 1681. Then came Giovanni Stefano Fieschi, who taught from 1682 at least through 1695, when he became rector of the Genoa college.[34] No Jesuit taught canon law in 1696, but it reappeared in the eighteenth century.[35] The appointment was not controversial, because the city wanted canon law taught, and because Genoa had no university to object.[36] But the Jesuits made no other move to teach canon law in Italy.[37] The unspoken reason was to avoid provoking Italian universities, for whom law was so important.

31. Isnardi 1975, 1:225–27; Monti 1914–1915, 1:88. For the biography of Grimaldi, see Cavanna Ciappina 2002, which mentions the bequest in passing at 477.

32. ARSI, Mediolanensis 80, "Annue memorie del collegio di Genova o siano annali abbozzati da quando principiò nel 1553 per commissione dal P. Pietro Antonio Pallavicino rettore raccolte da Nicolò Gentile nel 1686" and continued by others, ff. 51r, 52r, 125v–26v.

33. ARSI, Mediolanensis 80, ff. 71r (1669), 72v (1670).

34. ARSI, Mediolanensis 80, ff. 72v, 93v, 126r–v, 153r. On Durazzo, see Sommervogel 1960, 3:302. For Massola, who was considered learned in canon and civil law and left some legal *consulte*, see ARSI, Mediolanensis 80, f. 210r; and Sommervogel 1960, 5:708–9. Fieschi, probably from the famous Genoese noble family of that name, is not in Sommervogel.

35. ARSI, Mediolanensis 4, ff. 177r–78r (1696); Mediolanensis 14, ff. 11v–13r (1750); Mediolanensis 18, f. 136r–v (1773).

36. Using Jesuit properties seized by the state, Genoa created a university in 1773. Cosentino 1982, 57; Isnardi 1975, 2:1–17; and Massa 2007, 371–73.

37. Two incidents need to be mentioned. On June 1, 1627, Pope Urban VIII issued a brief authorizing the Jesuits of the Illyrian College of Loreto to teach canon law and other subjects, and to award degrees. Founded in 1581, the college trained Slavic-speaking clergymen to serve Catholics in Dalmatia and the Balkans, especially those living under Ottoman rule. But the Loreto Jesuits did not teach canon law. ARSI, Roma 150 I, f. 16r; and Veneta 125, no foliation or date, a brief summary of the history of the Collegio Illirico in Loreto. Second, in 1558 a Jesuit

The Roman College Teaches
Canon Law

This changed in 1695, as the Collegio Romano established a lectureship in canon law. It provoked strong opposition from the University of Rome.

The roll of the Collegio Romano for the academic year 1696–1697 included the following words: "In the Class of Canon Law: Selected titles from the book of the *Decretals* will be explained. Hour 17."[38] This was in the late morning, the precise time determined by sunset and sunrise. The text was the *Decretals* of Gregory IX, a collection of papal decrees sent to the faculties of law at Bologna and Paris in 1234. Designed to serve as a complete course of instruction in canon law, over time the *Decretals* became the primary pedagogical text for canon law, supplanting Gratian's *Decretum* (ca. 1148), a collection of church laws which was the foundation of a legal code for the church. Practically every Italian university had a *Decretals* professorship filled by one or more professors.

The Jesuits appointed Francesco Antonio Febei (Orvieto 1652–1706 Rome) to the position.[39] He had previously taught mathematics, natural philosophy, and moral theology at the Roman College, then philosophy at Fermo and moral theology at Siena. He then taught canon law at the German and Hungarian College, obviously to a small number of students, for one to three years between 1692 and 1695.[40] Febei was a distinguished canonist who in 1698 published a four-volume compendium of canon law that had seven more printings. He wrote another canon law work which used ancient sources and Roman civil law as well. It appeared posthumously in 1725 and was reprinted four more times in the eighteenth century. Since he

---

at Perugia reportedly was teaching canon law privately at Perugia. Details are unknown, and there is no subsequent information. Scaduto 1974, 377. At this time the Perugia Jesuits were striving to win goodwill.

38. "IN CLASSE JURIS CANONICI. Ex Libris Decretalium Tituli selecti explicabuntur. Hora xvij." ASR, Università 195, f. 23, a printed roll of the Roman College for the academic year 1696–1697 but lacking the names of the Jesuit teachers. Nevertheless, all the sources confirm that the canon law professorship began in November 1695.

39. Villoslada 1954, 246, 325.

40. The sources differ concerning when Febei taught canon law in the German College. Villoslada 1954, 246, states that Febei taught canon law at the German College from 1692 to 1695, while Zanfredini 2001b states that he taught canon law there for only one year, 1693–1694, before teaching moral theology at the Roman College in 1694–1695. Villoslada 1954, 326, confirms this last appointment despite his earlier statement. In addition, a sworn statement of 1698 or 1699 from Jesuit sources states that an unnamed Jesuit, which had to be Febei, taught canon law in the German College from 1693 to 1695. ASR, Università 195, ff. 52v–53r.

LIBRORUM ELENCHUS

IN ROMANO SOC. JESU GYMNASIO EXPLICANDORVM

EX NONIS NOVEMBRIBVS ANNI VERTENTIS

IN MDCXCVII. PROXIME INSEQVENTEM.

Moderatoris ejusdem Gymnasij auctoritate propositus.

IN CLASSE THEOLOGIÆ.

Ex Sacris Litteris.

De Expositione Sacræ Genesis.   hora xxij ÷

HORIS ANTEMERIDIANIS.

In 1. 2. D. Thomæ.

De Vltimo Fine, Beatitudine, & Actibus Humanis. hora xvi.

In 3. Partem.

De Sacrificio Missæ.   hora xvij

POMERIDIANIS HORIS.

In 3. Partem D. Thomæ.   hora xxi ÷

De Divini Verbi Incarnatione.

EX HEBRAICIS.

Tradetur primò Institutio Hebraicæ linguæ Roberti
Card. Bellarmini. Deinde explicabitur aliquis ex
Prophetis Minoribus   hora xxi.
De Controversijs Fidei

IN CLASSE RHETORICÆ.

MATVTINIS HORIS.

M. Tull. Cic. Orario pro lege Manilia multiplici eruditione explanabitur.   hora xv ÷
Diebus Pomeridianæ Vacationis Titi Livii Conc.   hora xv.

A MERIDIE.

Selecta Martialis Epigrammata explicabuntur.   hora xxi.
Die Saturni Horatius de Arte Poetica.   hora xx.
Ex Græcis Orat. SS. PP. Tom.I. & Homeri Odyssea. hora xxii. ÷

IN CLASSE HUMANITATIS.

Elucidabitur M. Tull. Cic. pro Marcello.   hora xvi. ÷
Ars Metrica Inferior.   hora xxij.
Ex Poetis Virgilianæ Aeneidos Lib. VII.   hora xxi. ÷
Ex Græcis Orat. SS. PP. Tom. II.
Jacobi Grethzeri Institut. Gramm. Lib. II.   hora xvi.
Diebus Pomeridianæ Vacationis Senecæ Tragœdiæ. hora xv.
Die Saturni S. . . .

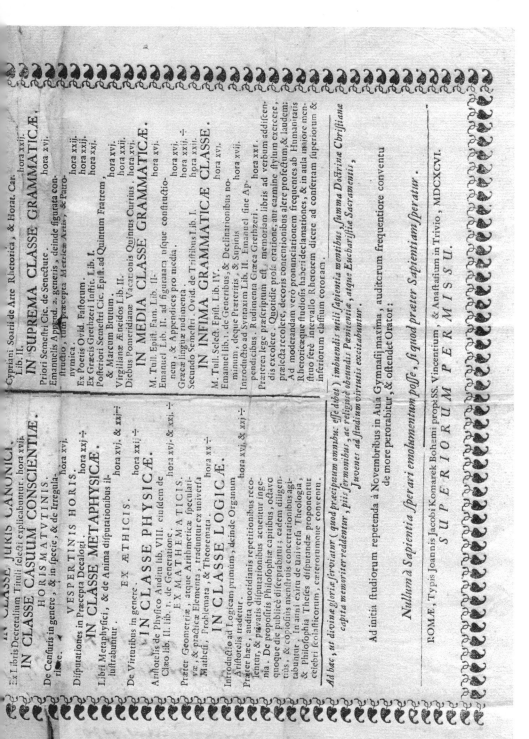

FIGURE 4. Roll of the Roman College, 1696–1697

became a Jesuit novice at the age of fifteen, he must have studied canon law as a Jesuit, but where and how is unknown.[41]

Filippo Maria Renazzi (1742–1808), professor of law at the University of Rome and author of a comprehensive history of the university, offered two possible explanations for the move. Either the Jesuits were profiting from the decay (*decadimento*) of the university or they were responding to the needs of their students. He acknowledged that Febei was learned. As he was also well-practiced in teaching youths, he began to teach canon law through the dictation-and-explanation system used by the Roman College, according to Renazzi. Teaching by dictation was a common criticism leveled against the Jesuits.[42] Renazzi added that it was natural for students who had been formed in piety and instructed in letters by the Jesuits to want to study canon law with them as well. Hence, Febei attracted many students. Renazzi judged the introduction of canon law by the Roman College as very damaging to the university; he then briefly narrated the battle of the Avvocati Concistoriali against it.[43]

Modern scholarship agrees that the University of Rome was not doing well at this time. Legal studies at La Sapienza were rigid, narrowly focused, and tied to the past, while the professors published little.[44] In the academic year 1695–1696 Filippo Canuti, Flaminio Vigoriti, and Diego Aghirre, none of them distinguished, taught canon law at the university.[45] However, neither university decadence nor student need played large roles in the decision of the Jesuits to teach canon law at the Roman College. The major reason was that the leadership of the Society had decided that it was time to give universal approval to the teaching of canon law. Adding it to the curriculum of the Roman College, the flagship school, was a way of doing this.

The Collegio dei Signori Avvocati Concistoriali, the name of the Roman college of doctors of law, believed that the canon law professorship threatened the university and responded. This was not simply one group allied to the university protecting its turf. This was the university acting, because the Avvocati Concistoriali dominated the university. Two committees had traditionally governed the University of Rome, the Riformatori dello Studio who reported to the Senate of Rome, and a congregation of cardinals who reported to the pope. But in 1588 Pope Sixtus V entrusted

41. Sommervogel 1960, 3:574–75; and Zanfredini 2001b.

42. See chap. 14, "Summisti, Compendia, and Quaestiones."

43. Renazzi 1971, 4:26–28.

44. Di Simone 1980, 72–92, esp. 76–77, 84.

45. *I maestri di Roma*, 1:489, 491. On them see Carafa 1971, 2:429–31; Renazzi 1971, 3:187–88; and Di Simone 1980, 89–92, 102, 106–7.

the daily administration of the university to the Avvocati by decreeing that the rector had to come from the ranks of the Avvocati. In the seventeenth century Pope Innocent X (1644–1655) abolished the Riformatori dello Studio, while the congregation of cardinals paid less and less attention to the university. In addition, over the years the Avvocati had built up a network of supporters among its curial patrons and clients.[46] The Jesuits faced a strong adversary.

The Avvocati Concistoriali demanded that the Jesuits stop teaching canon law.[47] It argued that only the University of Rome, a studium generale, had the right to teach canon law in Rome. And it feared that the Jesuits would soon want to award degrees to those who attended their canon law lectures. This would be another violation, because only the university with the assistance of the Avvocati Concistoriali possessed this authority.[48]

There was a financial side as well. Canuti, Vigoriti, and Aghirre, the three canon law professors at the university, stated in March 1696 that they had taught canon and/or civil law in the Roman Seminary and other student colleges governed by the Jesuits for thirteen years, twelve years, and one year respectively.[49] The Jesuits had asked them to do this. Obviously they were paid, although they did not mention this. But now students from the Roman Seminary and other colleges governed by the Jesuits seeking canon law instruction would attend the free lectures of Father Febei at the Roman College. This meant a loss of income for the trio, and other university legists who had taught in the Roman Seminary and elsewhere over the years.

The Jesuits rebutted the charges. They pointed out that Jesuit schools elsewhere taught canon law, and that the papacy had conferred many university privileges on the Roman College, including the right to teach canon law. They argued that the canon law professorship in the Roman College eased the path to the doctorate for clergymen. They could come to

46. For the statutes of the Avvocati Concistoriali, see Adorni 1995 and 2003. For the power of the Avvocati Concistoriali, see Renazzi 1971, 3:11–20, 203–4, 209–13; Di Simone 1980, 65–67; Conte 1992, 195–96; and Voelkel 1992, 327, 338–39.

47. This account of the struggle between the university and the Roman College is based on the documents and secondary sources cited below. There are other accounts of the conflict. The two oldest are Carafa 1971, 1:257–62 (first published in 1751), which includes quotations from the legal decisions; and Renazzi 1971, 4:26–28 (first published in 1806). Villoslada 1954, 246–48, is particularly valuable because it is based on APUG, Ms. 142, a late eighteenth-century history of the Roman College. Examination of Ms. 142 confirms that Villoslada's quotations and references are accurate. See also Di Simone 1980, 48–49; and Lupi 2005, 49–50.

48. See ASR, Università 195, f. 32r–34v, a printed *Summarium* of November 1696; and Di Simone 1980, 48.

49. ASR, Università 195, f. 34r.

the Roman College to study moral theology and stay for canon law. The university would benefit because these well-taught students would then go on to the university to acquire doctorates in law. The Jesuits refused to stop teaching canon law.[50]

The Avvocati Concistoriali took its case to Pope Innocent XII (Antonio Pignatelli, 1615–1700, pope from 1691), who in February 1696 appointed a commission of three cardinals to resolve the issue.[51] What they decided, if anything, is unknown. Then the rector of the university asked the vice-regent of the Apostolic Camera to prohibit the Jesuits from teaching canon law. But the vice-regent, a Dominican Monsignor Sperelli not further identified, ruled in favor of the Jesuits on June 4, 1696.[52] With this approval the Jesuits continued to teach canon law. The 1696–1697 and 1697–1698 rolls of the Collegio Romano listed the canon law professorship.[53] The Avvocati Concistoriali appealed to the Sacred Roman Rota. Various Roman legists wrote briefs against the Jesuits and in defense of the university and the Avvocati Concistoriali.[54] The Jesuits replied with their briefs.[55]

In the winter of 1696–1697, when the controversy was intense and the outcome unclear, the Society as a whole formally added canon law to the list of disciplines that Jesuit schools might teach. In their Fourteenth General Congregation, meeting from November 19, 1696, to January 16, 1697, the delegates decreed "Let the teaching of canon law be undertaken in colleges where it has not yet been begun." The General Congregation offered two reasons for rejecting the prohibition against teaching canon law in the Constitutions. It pointed out that the Constitutions several times recommended the teaching of positive theology "which in great part rests upon the sacred canons." That is, teaching canon law was acceptable because it supported positive theology. Second, the Congregation noted that many colleges al-

50. APUG, Ms. 120, ff. 3r–9v, at f. 9r, an anonymous and untitled statement of the Jesuit position dated 1695.

51. Villoslada 1954, 247.

52. ASR, Università 4, f. 198r, memorandum of Paolo Manfredi. See also Carafa 1971, 1:258; and Lupi 2005, 49–50. Although the Apostolic Camera oversaw papal financial matters, it and its members sometimes acted as judges. Although a copy of Sperelli's decision has not been found, other documents refer to it. See ASUP, Constitutiones et jura, P I VII, f. 143v (Muto's opinion of May 16, 1698, see below), 151v (document of July 3, 1699, in which Sperelli is referred to as "R. P. D. Sperelli Iudicis ab A. C. Deputati." This was not the future Cardinal Sperello Sperelli (1639–1710, cardinal from 1699), who had the reputation of being a friend of the Jesuits, because Cardinal Sperelli was not a Dominican. The Cardinals of the Holy Roman Church, www2.fiu.edu/~mirandas/bios1699.htm#Sperelli.

53. ASR, Università 195, ff. 23, 104. See also Villoslada 1954, 247.

54. ASR, Università 195, ff. 56r–81r, 143r–52v, 236r–45v.

55. ASR, Università 195, ff. 44r–53r, 198r–211v, 332r–41v.

ready taught canon law "with no small enhancement of their literary endeavors." Hence, the General Congregation encouraged provincial superiors to establish canon law professorships in the principal colleges in their provinces. Finally, the Congregation was careful to repeat the prohibition of the Constitutions: they should not teach the parts of canon law useful in litigation.[56] One wonders how such distinctions could be made. Despite these words, the Congregation reversed what Ignatius decreed in the Constitutions.

In the meantime the Sacred Roman Rota considered the appeal of the Avvocati Concistoriali. On May 16, 1698, Monsignor Giovanni Muto, one of the twelve auditors, issued a long opinion. Although he wrote in his own name, he spoke for the Rota. He reviewed the dispute with references to papal pronouncements, ancient Roman law, and modern legal authorities. He emphasized the historical monopoly of the university to teach both laws. He also observed that the Jesuits had occasion to discuss decrees of councils and church canons in their teaching on the Old and New Testaments, scholastic theology, moral theology, cases of conscience, and positive theology. He mentioned that the Constitutions of the Society forbade the teaching of canon law when it dealt with court trials, a point that the Avvocati Concistoriali and legists supporting the university had repeatedly made. He saw this as an impediment. Although Mota did not issue a formal order, he did not endorse a separate professorship of canon law in the Collegio Romano.[57] And the roll of the Roman College for the academic year 1698–1699 did not list a professorship of canon law.[58]

The Jesuits appealed to the pope. They argued that previous popes had granted the superior general the right to interpret the Constitutions, and that this mattered more than the opinion of the auditor of the Sacred Roman Rota. Moreover, the Benedictines, Olivetans, and Theatines taught canon law in their Roman studia, and even held public disputations, the Benedictines with explicit papal approval granted in 1687. Why should the Jesuits not be permitted to do the same, they asked?[59]

---

56. For Matters of Greater Moment 1994, 368, Decree 20. The rector of the Roman College, Angelo Alamanno (1695–1698), and a former rector, Curzio Sesti (1680–1683), were among the 86 participants, 70 from outside of Italy, of the General Congregation. See Villoslada 1954, 322; and For Matters of Greater Moment 1994, 725. What role, if any, they played in the adoption of Decree 20 is unknown.

57. ASUP, Constitutiones et jura, P I VII, ff. 140r–50v, printed document. The archive of the University of Perugia possesses copies of decisions involving the University of Rome and the Roman College, possibly because the Perugia legists acquired them to use in their own dispute with the Jesuits of Perugia. See chap. 12.

58. ASR, Università 195, f. 185.

59. APUG, Ms. 120, no title, f. 1r–v. Although undated, internal evidence demonstrates

The Jesuits also asked for another hearing from the Sacred Roman Rota. In addition, some auditors of the Rota wondered whether the Jesuits might teach in a separate professorship some parts of canon law that did not concern judicial matters.[60] So Muto issued two more opinions. On January 9, 1699, he recognized the exclusive right of the university to teach canon law as such and denied this right to the Roman College.[61] Then on July 3, 1699, he issued a "definitive sentence."[62] Muto again ruled in favor of the university and the Avvocati Concistoriali. The university had the exclusive right to teach canon law as a complete and distinct discipline. Only the university could teach canon law, create professorships of canon law, and name professors who would defend and publish conclusions.[63] The Jesuits did not have the right to establish a professorship of canon law in the Roman College.

However, Muto continued, the Jesuits as teachers of moral theology might teach or lecture on the sacred canons as part of theological instruction. Discussion of canon law had to be incidental, intrinsic to, inseparable with, and conjoined to the teaching of theology. The Jesuits were not permitted to have a "separate and divided chair" of canon law in the Roman College, nor might they teach the part of canon law used in courts in the Christian Republic.[64] The decision applied to the Roman College only; Muto did not

---

that it was written after May 16, 1698, and before January 9, 1699. In 1687 the Avvocati Concistoriali launched a legal action to stop the Benedictines from allegedly teaching law in their monastery of St. Calixtus. Di Simone 1980, 49n118. The Olivetans, founded in 1319, were a small offshoot of the Benedictines, while the Theatines were founded in the sixteenth century.

60. Renazzi 1971, 4:27.

61. ASR, Università 195, ff. 288r–91v, for the printed decision. See also Villoslada 1954, 247; and Di Simone 1980, 49.

62. ASUP, Constitutiones et jura, P I VII, ff. 151r–52v, printed document that begins "Sententia diffinitiva Sacrae Rotae Auditorij coram Illustrissimo, & Reverendissimo D. Muto lata ad favorem Almae Universitatis, & Archigymnasij Sapientiae Urbis." Two more printed copies of Muto's decision can be found in ASR, Università 195, ff. 374r–81v.

63. "Quartò demùm pari nostra sententia dicimus, diffinitivè declaramus, & sententiamus competijsse, & competere eidem Universitati Archigymnasij Studij generalis Urbis, eiusque Collegio DD. Advocatorum Consistorialium, ac pro tempore DD. Rectoribus, & respectivè DD. Lectoribus ius, & facultatem legendi, docendi, explanandi, glossandi, & interpretandi Ius Canonicum, & Pontificum in Universum, eiusque Institutiones, ac omnes Sacros Canones, & Scholas aperiendi, Cathedras erigendi, ac ascendendi in eadem facultate, seù scientia Canonica, eamque profitendi publicè, & ex professo, conclusionesque publicandi, ac defendendi in Urbe privativè quoad alios." ASUP, Constitutiones et jura, P I VII, f. 152r. It is also found in ASR, Università 195, f. 374v.

64. "Tertiò pari nostra sententia dicimus, ac diffinitivè pronunciamus, competere dumtaxàt eidem Collegio Romano Societatis Iesu, eiusque Patribus Magistris, & Praeceptoribus Theologiae Moralis, seù casuum conscientiae ius legendi illam Sacrorum Canonum partem, quae eidem Theologiae inservit, & famulatur complexivè, & incidentèr tantùm, ac inseparabaliter, & coniunctim, atque intrinsecè cum eadem Theologia, ac levitèr inter eiusdem tractatus, non tamèn ex

mention that the Jesuits had "separate and divided" professorships of canon law elsewhere. Giovanni Battista Tolomei (Florence 1653–1726 Rome), rector of the Roman College from 1698 to 1701, formally accepted the decision of Monsignor Muto and the Sacred Roman Rota on July 23, 1699.[65]

It was a major defeat for the Jesuits. Even though they had many professorships of canon law in their colleges and universities in northern Europe, the highest court in the Catholic church did not permit them to teach canon law in the Roman College. Because the Jesuits could not openly defy the Sacred Roman Rota, they engaged in subterfuges. An eighteenth-century manuscript list of Roman College teachers indicated that Febei continued to teach canon law until 1699, when he switched to scholastic theology. That same list states that another Jesuit, Baldassare Montecatini (Lucca 1651–1720 Rome), taught canon law at the Roman College from 1699 to 1701.[66] What was happening?

The roll of 1699–1700 did not list a canon law professorship. It did list a new class in positive and moral theology, an unusual combination, to be taught in hours 16 and 17, with different topics for each hour. At hour 16 the topic was "on contracts in general and in detail." This was a typical civil law topic, marginally appropriate for canon law in a stretch, but not relevant for moral or positive theology. At hour 17 the topic was the sacrament of matrimony.[67] This was a topic appropriate for moral, positive, or scholastic theology, and canon law, if it dealt with the contractual obligations of marriage. Although the roll did not name the teacher or teachers, it is most likely that Montecatini lectured at both hours and taught a great deal of canon law under the guise of positive and moral theology. It is also possible that Febei taught one of the two hours, even though he was also listed as teaching scholastic theology in that year.[68] Whatever the exact arrangement, the Roman College took full advantage and more of Muto's

---

professo, neque in Cathedra divisa, ac separata, neque de per se, neque principalitèr more Canonistarum, sed famulative, & occasionalitèr more Theologorum, ac nunquam attingendo eam partem Canonum, quae foro contentioso, inservit partem iudiciariam respicit, ac regimen civile, seù politicum Christianae Reipublicae concernit." ASUP, Constitutiones et jura P I VII, f. 152r.

65. ASUP, Constitutiones et jura, P I VII, f. 153r–v, printed notice of August 6, 1699. Another copy is found in ASR, Università 195, ff. 382v–83r. Tolomei was a philosopher who attempted to unite speculative philosophy with the new experimental philosophy, and he respected Leibniz. He was made a cardinal in 1712. Korade 2001b.

66. Villoslada 1954, 247–48, 325 (which reproduces the manuscript list of Jesuit professors). For Montecatini, see Sommervogel 1960, 5:1239–40.

67. "IN CLASSE THEOLOGIAE POSITIVAE, ET MORALIS, HORIS MATUTINIS. De Contractibus in communi, & in particulari. hora xvi. De Sacramento Matrimonii. hora xvij." ASR, Università 195, f. 384.

68. See Villoslada 1954, 325.

LIBRORUM ELENCHUS

IN ROMANO SOC. JESU GYMNASIO EXPLICANDOR.
EX NONIS NOVEMBRIBUS ANNI VERTENTIS
IN MDCC. PROXIME INSEQUENTEM.

Moderatoris ejusdem Gymnasii auctoritate propositus.

IN CLASSE THEOLOGIÆ.
Ex Sacris Literis.

De Expositione Sacræ Genesis.   hora xxij. ÷

HORIS ANTEMERIDIANIS.

De Deo Optimo Maximo. *In primam partem D. Thomæ.*   hora xvj.

De Legibus. *In Primam Secundæ.*   hora xvij.

POMERIDIANIS HORIS.

De Justitia, & Jure. *In secundam 2. D. Thomæ.*   hora xxj. ÷

IN CLASSE THEOLOGIÆ POLEMICÆ.

Disceptabitur adversus Anabaptistas, & Sacra-   hora xx. ÷
mentarios.

EX HÆBRAICIS.

Tradetur primò institutio Hebraicæ linguæ Roberti Cardinalis Bellarmini. Deinde explicabitur
Sacra Genesis.   hora xvij.

IN CLASSE RHETORICÆ.
MATUTINIS HORIS.

M. Tull. Cic. Philippica 2. multiplici eruditione
explanabitur.   hora xv. ÷

Diebus pomeridianæ vacationis Senecæ Tragœdiæ.

A MERIDIE.

Virgilii Carmina.   hora xxj.

Die Saturni Martial. Epigr.

Ex Græcis Acta Apostol.   hora xx. ÷

IN CLASSE HUMANITATIS.

Elucidabitur M. Tull. Cic. in Catilinam.   hora xvj. ÷

Ars Metrica interior.   hora xxij.

Ex Poetis Virgilianæ Æneidos. lib. viij.

Ex Græcis explicabitur aliquis ex Prophetis minoribus.

Jacobi Gretzeri instit. Grammat. lib. 2.   hora xvj.

Diebus Pomeridianæ vacationis Ovid. Metamor. hora xvj.

Die Saturni Sallustius, & L. Florus.   hora xvj.

Sacra Genesis. hora xxj.

IN CLASSE THEOLOGIE POSITIVE, ET MORALIS.

HORIS MATUTINIS.

De Contractibus in communi, & in particulari. hora x=j
De Sacramento Matrimonii. hora xvij.

VESPERTINIS HORIS.

De Sacramentis in genere, & in specie. hora xxj.÷

IN CLASSE METAPHYSICE.

Libri Metaphysici, de Anima, & de Ente, disputationibus illustrabuntur. hora xvj. & xxj.÷

EX ETHICIS.

De Prudentia, & aliis Virtutibus. hora xxij.÷

IN CLASSE PHYSICE.

Aristotelis de Physico auditu, lib. viij. Ejusdem de Caelo lib.iij, lib. 1. de Generatione. hora xvj. & xxj.÷

EX MATHEMATICIS.

Praeter Geometriae, atque Arithmeticae speculativae, & practicae Elementa, tradentur ex universa Mathei Problemata, & Theoremata. hora xx.÷

IN CLASSE LOGICE.

Introductio ad Logicam primum, deinde Organum Aristotelis tradetur. hora xvj. & xxj.÷
Praeter haec audita quotidianis repetitionibus recolentur, & privatis disputationibus acuentur ingenia. De propositis Philosophiae capitibus octavo quoque die publice disputabitur, eadem diligentia, & copiositus menstruis concertationibus disputabuntur. In anni exitu de Universa Theologia, & Philosophia Theses disputande proponentur celebri scholasticorum, exterorumque conventu.

Die Saturni Sallustius, & L. Florus.
Senis posterioribus mensibus M. T. C. Pro Sexto Roscio Amer. hora xvj.
Cyprian. Soar. de arte Rettorica, & Horatii Carm. hora xxij.

IN SUPREMA CLASSE GRAMMATICE. hora xvj.

Prima Emanuel. Cic. de Offic. lib. 3.
Emanuelis appendices 2. Generis, deinde figurata construction, tum praecepta Metricae artis, & Patronimica.
Ex Poetis Ovid. de Ponto. hora xxij.
Ex Graecis Gretzeri instit. lib. 1. hora xxij.
Posteriori semestri Cic. de Amicitia. hora xvj.
Virgilianae Aeneidos lib. u. hora xxij.
Diebus pomeridianae vacationis Q. Curtius.

IN MEDIA CLASSE GRAMMATICE. hora xvj.

M.T. Epist. Fam.
Emanuel. lib. 2. ad figuratam usque Constructionem, & Appendices pro Media. hora xvj.
Graecae linguae Rudimenta. hora xxij.÷
Secundo semestri Ovid. de Trist. lib. 1t hora xxij.÷

IN INFIMA GRAMMATICE CLASSE.

M. Tull. Select. Epistolae. hora xvj.
Emanuel. lib. 1. de Generibus, & declinationibus nominum, deque Praeteritis, & Supinis. hora xvij.
Introductio ad Syntaxin lib. 2. Eman. sine Appendicibus. Rudimenta Gretzeri. hora xxj.
Praeterea lege praescriptum est memoriam libris ad verbum ediscendis excolere Quotidie profa, oratione, aut carmine stylum exercere, praelecta recolere, decoris contentionibus alere profectum, & laudem: Ad moderandam vero pronunciationem frequentes ab Humanitatis, Rhetoriceq; studiosis habere declamationes, & in Aula majore menstruo fere intervallo Rhetorem dicere ad confertam superiorum, & inferiorum Classium coronam.

Adhaec, ut Divinae Gloriae serviatur, quod praecipuum omnibusque debet, imbuendis utili Sapientiae mentibus Summa Doctrina Christiana capita memoriter reddantur; piis formularibus, ac religione obeundi poenitentiae, atque Eucharistiae Sacramenti, Jesuumae ad studium Virtutis, excitabantur.
Ad initia studiorum repetenda à Novembribus Kalendis in Aula Gymnasii maxima, & Auditorum frequentiae Conventu, de more perorabitur, & offendet Orator.
Geminum nobis ad literas incliamenium esse, Annum unum, eundemque, Sanctum, & Saecularem.

ROME, Typis Joan. Jacobi Komarek Bohemi, prope SS. Vincentium, & Anastasium in Trivio 1699.. SUPERIORUM PERMISSU.

FIGURE 5. Roll of the Roman College, 1699–1700

concession that the Jesuits might teach some canon law as part of moral and positive theology. It was teaching canon law.

When Clement XI (Gian Francesco Albani, 1649–1721) was elected pope on November 23, 1700, the Jesuits appealed to him. They speculated that the pope might approve the teaching of canon law to students at the Collegio Romano if it was done behind closed doors and without the name, which was what they were doing.[69] The pope's answer, if any, is unknown, In any case, Montecatini taught positive theology, at least nominally, from 1701 to 1706.[70]

Several more Jesuits filled the professorship of positive theology after Montecatini. Then in 1724 Francesco Volumnio Piccolomini (Siena 1682–1740 Rome), who had taught positive theology at the Roman College the previous year, began to teach canon law under its own name. Piccolomini taught canon law until 1731, followed by four other Jesuits who taught canon law continuously until 1773.[71] Since the dispute disappeared from the documents, it has to be concluded that the Avvocati Concistoriali had given up the fight.

The Jesuits also freed themselves from their own constitutional restraint. The Sixteenth General Congregation meeting between November 19, 1730, and February 13, 1731, decreed that Jesuits might teach all parts of canon law when they taught in "public universities." The term meant institutions of higher education open to all students, which would include both Jesuit and non-Jesuit universities. The Congregation explained the change with the argument that the judgment of the father general might overrule the Constitutions and Decree 20 of Congregation 14 on this matter.[72] He did have that power.[73] Thus, the Jesuits eliminated the prohibition imposed by Ignatius Loyola.

This produced a significant increase in the number of Italian Jesuit schools offering canon law classes. Around 1750 Jesuits taught canon law in seven schools or student residences in Italy: the Roman College and the German and Hungarian College in Rome, plus schools in Bologna, Genoa, Milan, Palermo, and Turin.[74] The Jesuit school at Naples taught canon law in 1764.[75]

69. APUG, Ms. 120, f. 2r–v. Although undated, it referred to the beginning of teaching of canon law five years previously. Hence, it was written at the end of 1700 or early 1701.

70. Villoslada 1954, 248, 325.

71. Villoslada 1954, 248–49, 325. On Piccolomini, see Sommervogel 1960, 6:700–701.

72. *For Matters of Greater Moment* 1994, 383, Decree 30.

73. *Constitutions* 1970, pars. 746–47 (314); *Constitutions* 1996, pars, 746–47 (362).

74. ARSI, Roma 105, ff. 155r (Roman College in 1749), 166v (German and Hungarian College in 1749); Veneta 59, f. 316r (Bologna in 1746); Mediolanensis 14, ff. 11v–13r (Genoa in 1750), 16v–18v (Milan in 1750), 27v–29r (Turin in 1750); Sicula 139, f. 23r (Palermo in 1749).

75. ARSI, Neapolitana 97, f. 136r.

By contrast, the Parma Jesuits, who were part of the University of Parma, did not, because they had no authority over the law part of the university. The Italian Jesuits were teaching canon law almost everywhere they wished.

Doctorates at the Roman College and the University of Rome

At the beginning of the dispute over the canon law professorship, the Avvocati Concistoriali argued that the Roman College would want to confer degrees in canon law if permitted to teach it.[76] The Jesuits responded in 1695 with the rhetorical question: would it be such a bad thing if someone wanted a doctorate in canon law alone? The university and the Avvocati Concistoriali would suffer no harm if one student in a thousand wanted a doctorate in canon law alone from the Collegio Romano rather than in both laws or civil law from the university.[77] However, the Roman College had no intention of conferring degrees in canon law, and the Avvocati Concistoriali did not pursue the issue directly.

Instead, the Avvocati strongly urged the college of doctors of medicine and philosophy to challenge the authority of the Jesuits to confer doctorates in philosophy.[78] The college of doctors of medicine and philosophy obediently did so. It conceded the existence of briefs of various popes granting the Jesuits the authority to confer doctorates in philosophy and theology.[79] But it argued that the Jesuits could only confer doctorates on their own members. It also claimed that the Jesuits were obliged to pay doctoral fees to the college for the degrees that the Jesuits conferred. And the college declared that the doctorates conferred by the Jesuits did not have the prestige of "veri e legali" (true and legal) doctorates conferred by a university.[80]

The Jesuits responded that the papal briefs did not impose restrictions on their authority to confer doctorates, and that they did not need to pay the college of doctors of medicine and philosophy anything. They pointed out that they had been conferring doctorates on non-Jesuits for 130 years without complaint. As evidence the Jesuits submitted a list of 99 men who

---

76. Di Simone 1980, 48, makes this point. See also ASR, Università 195, f. 34v, statement barring anyone from obtaining doctorates in civil or canon law except through the Collegio degli Signori Avvocati Concistoriali. It cites various pontifical briefs in support.

77. APUG, Ms. 120, ff. 3r–9v, at 8v–9r, untitled but dated 1695.

78. Di Simone 1980, 51.

79. For a brief account of the decrees of Julius III of 1552, Paul IV of 1556, and Pius V of 1566, see Villoslada 1954, 33–35.

80. ASR, Università 4, ff. 23r–30r, quotation at 24r, statement of Paolo Manfredi (see below), no date, but 1699. See also Di Simone 1980, 49–50.

had received doctorates of philosophy or theology from the Roman College between 1565 and 1633, followed by a list of about 25 men, the majority non-Italians, who received doctorates from the Roman College between 1656 and the end of the 1680s. Almost all were clergymen or became clergymen; many had been students at the Roman Seminary. None was a Jesuit.[81]

Paolo Manfredi, professor of medical theory, presented the case for the university and the college of doctors of medicine and philosophy. Born near Lucca in 1640, he obtained a doctorate of medicine from the University of Rome in 1659 and became an extraordinary professor of medicine in 1663, rising to ordinary professor of surgery and anatomy in 1668, and ordinary professor of medical theory in 1682, which position he held until death in 1716. He wrote several medical works and is remembered for his research on blood transfusion. He successfully injected calf's blood into a man in January 1668, six months after it was first done in Paris.[82] In 1699 he was named *protomedico* for Rome, the chief medical officer of the city. In conjunction with the college of doctors of medicine and philosophy, he oversaw physicians, licensed apothecaries, and made decisions in medical emergencies. In the fall of 1699 he shouldered the task of voicing the opposition of the university and the college of doctors of medicine and philosophy against the Jesuits. The college met at Manfredi's house and at the university to consider the matter.[83] Following the example of the Avvocati Concistoriali, it obtained supporting legal opinions which were submitted to various judicial bodies in Rome in the hope of favorable rulings.[84]

The Avvocati Concistoriali gave Manfredi a copy of the Jesuit Constitutions. He read it closely and concluded that the authority of the Jesuits to confer degrees in philosophy and theology was quite restricted. In his view, the Jesuit colleges were not universities (studia generalia). Hence, the Roman College was obligated to present its lay students to the University of Rome, meaning to the college of doctors of medicine and philosophy, to be examined for the doctorate. If the candidate was successful, the university would confer a doctorate on him. Only when the college of doctors of medicine and philosophy would not admit the candidate to examination or failed him, might the Roman College examine and confer a doctorate on the candidate, in the opinion of Manfredi.[85]

81. ASR, Università 4, ff. 138v–44v, 162v–65v, 168v–69r, 180r–90r, dated 1699 and 1700. See also Di Simone 1980, 50.

82. See *I maestri di Roma* 1991, 2:958–59; Lupi 2005, 51–52n79; and Donato 2007.

83. Lupi 2005, 52–53.

84. ASR, Università 4, ff. 31r–137v. See also Di Simone 1980, 50; and Lupi 2005, 50–51.

85. ASR, Università 4, ff. 23r–30v, undated but 1699.

Manfredi also raised the issue of fees. Every member of the college of doctors of medicine and philosophy contributed 150 scudi, a large sum of money, toward college expenses, such as paying the doctoral expenses for candidates without funds, overseeing the physicians and apothecaries of the city, and providing medicine for the poor. Because the Jesuits conferred doctorates, they should contribute to the college of doctors of medicine and philosophy. The Roman College enjoyed revenues of many thousands of scudi and could therefore afford this, he argued.[86] Thus Paolo Manfredi articulated the arguments of the college of doctors of medicine and philosophy against the Jesuits.

The dispute then became fraternal. Antonio Manfredi, Paolo's older brother, was a Jesuit at the college at Loreto.[87] He responded on behalf of the Society of Jesus. From late spring to at least October 22, 1699, the brothers argued the cases of the organizations to which they belonged and added personal comments.[88] The exchange revealed some of the resentments and connections between the university and the Roman College.

Antonio the Jesuit criticized Paolo the professor for persecuting the Jesuits, who were the scourge of heretics. He accused Paolo of ingratitude, because he had turned against his former teachers at the Roman College. And Paolo's actions had alienated the superior of the Jesuit Province of Rome, who was a protector of the Manfredi family. Antonio feared that Paolo's words would engender ill will against himself from other Jesuits, despite his forty-four years in the Society. Paolo replied in kind. He wrote that the rector of the Roman College was the persecutor of the university, and that the Jesuits were determined to destroy the universities of Rome and Perugia.[89] By refusing to respect papal decrees on the rights of universities the Jesuits were breaking their vow of obedience to the pope. Finally, he declared that he had studied only *grammatica* at the Roman College and had received very few *cortesie* (courtesies) from the teachers.[90]

After this sharp exchange, they remembered that they were brothers and drew back. Antonio the Jesuit suggested that compromises were possible that would recognize the authority of the college of doctors of medicine and philosophy to confer degrees while recognizing that the Roman College also conferred degrees. And he assured Paolo that he had defended

---

86. ASR, Università 4, ff. 25r–v, 30v.

87. He has not been further identified.

88. A long undated memorandum of Paolo and three letters of Antonio (September 20, October 12 and 22, 1699) survive of the exchange. ASR, Università 4, ff. 192r–207v. See also the summaries of Lupi 2005, 52–54; Di Simone 1980, 51–52; Carella 2003, 28–29; and Carella 2007, 31–32.

89. For the simultaneous dispute in Perugia, see chap. 12, "La Sapienza Nuova and the Jesuits."

90. ASR, Università 4, ff. 192r–94v, 204r–6r, quotation at 204r.

him against criticisms from his fellow Jesuits.[91] Paolo the professor may have replied in a similar conciliatory vein. The disagreement disappeared from the records.

The complaints of the university against the Roman College conferring doctorates in philosophy, and the possibility of conferring doctorates in canon law, were much ado about very little. Both laymen and clerics went to universities to obtain doctorates in both laws, not canon law alone, which was considered of little importance.[92] Very few students obtained degrees in canon law only.[93] Even young clerics intended for high ecclesiastical office almost always obtained degrees in both civil and canon law. Even if the Jesuits should manage to persuade the papacy to grant the Roman College authority to confer degrees in canon law, a political impossibility, it would have had a minimal impact on the university. The same was true for philosophy. Universities conferred a very large number of degrees in medicine, a small number in medicine and philosophy, and only a handful in philosophy alone.[94] Medicine was the important discipline, because it led to a lucrative professional career. But the Jesuits never taught nor wished to award degrees in medicine. Thus, although the Collegio Romano conferred a limited number of doctorates in philosophy, this had very little impact on the university and the college of doctors of medicine and philosophy.[95]

Why, then, did the colleges of law and medicine and philosophy spend time and energy attacking the Roman College? Both colleges guarded their

91. ASR, Università 4, f. 196r–v.

92. See Grendler 2002, 443–47, on the decline of canon law.

93. For example, from 1501 through 1796, the University of Bologna awarded 8,648 doctorates in both laws, 569 in canon law only, and 267 in civil law only. Canon law doctorates comprised 6 percent of the total. Guerrini 2005, 32. Another example: from 1541 through 1824 the University of Macerata conferred 3,306 law degrees of which only 49 (1.5 percent) were in canon law only. Serangeli 2003, 8. Data from these universities is used because comparable information for the University of Rome is lacking.

94. For example, from 1541 through 1824 the University of Macerata conferred 748 doctorates in medicine and philosophy, and another 62 doctorates that combined medicine with another arts subject, for a total of 810 degrees in medicine and something else. By contrast, it awarded 18 degrees in philosophy only and 3 in philosophy combined with an arts subject that was not medicine, for a total of 21 philosophy degrees. Hence, the philosophy doctorates were only 2.5 percent of the combined total of medicine and philosophy. Serangeli 2003, 8.

95. The number of doctorates in philosophy the Roman College awarded is unknown. As mentioned above, in response to attacks from the college of doctors of arts and medicine, the Jesuits listed about 125 recipients of doctorates in philosophy and theology, without indicating how many for each discipline, from 1565 through the 1680s, approximately one per year. While this may not have been all, it is not likely that there were many more. Villoslada 1954, 267–72, lists five doctorates conferred on nobles, some of them future cardinals. See also Grendler 2011b.

prerogatives fiercely, and the Avvocati Concistoriali, which dominated the university, wanted the college of doctors of medicine and philosophy to join it. Both were concerned about the decline in university attendance, which had several causes, including competition from Jesuit schools. They resented the Jesuits, who were aggressive, determined, sometimes devious, and usually successful in reaching their educational goals. Last but not least, it was a litigious world to which universities contributed mightily.

By contrast, the college of doctors of theology did not attack the Collegio Romano. It was not necessary, because no Jesuits taught or tried to obtain positions in the University of Rome between 1539 and 1773. Members of the medieval mendicant orders filled all the professorships of theology and related subjects, and all ten or eleven positions in the college of doctors of theology.[96] The Jesuits did not try to join the college of doctors of theology. They had no need of the University of Rome and its college of theologians, because the Roman College taught theology and possessed the authority to confer degrees in theology and philosophy. In these disciplines the Roman College was more important than the university.

Limited Collaboration

Despite the attacks, La Sapienza was willing to collaborate with the Collegio Romano to a limited extent.

Young men seeking medical doctorates in Italian universities usually studied logic and natural philosophy before hearing medical lectures. Because Jesuit upper schools taught logic, natural philosophy, and metaphysics in a three-year sequence, some medical students studied at Jesuit schools before entering a university. This was true in Rome. In 1699 five Roman physicians, who had obtained their medical doctorates between 1652 and 1670, affirmed that they had studied philosophy for three years at the Roman College before studying medicine at La Sapienza.[97] If five physicians could be found to say this at the height of the controversy between the two institutions, there must have been others.

An incident of academic backbiting revealed that professors at the University of Rome were divided on the utility of philosophical studies at the Roman College. In 1651 Giovanni Benedetto Sinibaldi, afternoon ordinary professor of medical practice, in the course of a lecture informed the stu-

---

96. Adorni 1996, 126–27; repeated and supplemented by Carella 2007, 39–44. Because the archive of the college of theologians has not been located, and probably has not survived, it is not possible to provide more information.

97. Carella 2007, 33–35.

dents of another professor of natural philosophy that they had to study philosophy with the Jesuits if they wanted to obtain doctorates of medicine. He
said that "our constitutions" barred doctorates to those who had not studied
philosophy with the Jesuits for three years. "Our constitutions" meant the
constitutions of the college of doctors of medicine and philosophy.[98]

Demetrio Fallirei of Constaninople (1600–1664) was the professor of
natural philosophy whose students were threatened. He was a popular professor with a point of view. In 1647 or 1648, when he was a professor of
Greek at the University of Rome, he petitioned the papacy to be appointed
to a vacant position in natural philosophy. Fallirei argued that the university had few medical students because many poor students could not afford
to spend three years studying philosophy with "the religious," meaning the
Jesuits. Moreover, because their philosophy was directed toward theology,
it was not useful for the study of medicine, a common view of university
philosophers. If given the position, Fallirei promised that he could teach
the necessary philosophy "directed toward medicine" in a year-and-a-
half.[99] He won the position in 1648; from that date through the academic
year 1663–1664 he filled two positions in the university, Greek and natural
philosophy.[100] He attracted more than a hundred students to his philosophy
lectures, according to one report.[101] A detailed list of 1651 put the number
at fifty, which was still the second-highest individual lecture enrollment.[102]
Obviously, his success in attracting students created jealousy and hostility
which found expression in the threat from Sinibaldi. The incident also indicated that Fallirei offered an alternative to an established pattern.

The known evidence does not support Sinibaldi's assertion that medical students were obliged to study first at the Collegio Romano. The 1676
printing of the statutes of the college of doctors of medicine and philoso-

98. "Che non studiate la filosofia delli Gesouiti [sic], le nostre Constitutioni dicono che non
dottoriamo chi non studia la filosofia tre anni dalli Gesouiti." ASR Università 86, f. 196r. It is
quoted in full in Carella 2003, 18; and Carella 2007, xviii, 35–36. On Sinibaldi see *I maestri di
Roma* 1991, 1:309, 312; 2:921; and Carella 2007, 36.

99. "Come d'alcun'anni in qua sono mancati li scolari della medicina in Sapienza perche
essendo poveri non possono spendere tre anni nello studio della filosofia de' religiosi la quale
anco essendo diretta alla theologia non gli giova per lo studio della medicina; però essendo la
professione del oratore di leggere la filosofia in un anno e mezzo diretta alla medicina." Quoted
by Carella 2003, 19–20; and Carella 2007, 29, and Tavola 1 after p. xvi, which is a photograph
of the document. For more on Fallirei, see Carella 2007, note 1 on p. xvii, 75–81, 84–95, 147–48.

100. *I maestri di Roma* 1991, 2:887.

101. Carella 2003, 19n44; Carella 2007, xviii–xix.

102. Carella 2003, 12–13; and Carella 2007, Tavola 2 after p. xvi is a photograph of the document. It does not indicate if 50 students attended his natural philosophy lectures (most likely),
his Greek lectures, or both.

phy required degree candidates to learn logic and natural philosophy, but did not indicate where or how.[103] Instead, it was simply common practice for future physicians to study logic and natural philosophy at the Roman College. And Sinibaldi used this to attack a colleague.

In another area of potential conflict the university tacitly accepted the existence of the Collegio Romano. Although the university objected to the fact that the Roman College conferred doctorates, it did not bar recipients from filling university professorships. At least two men obtained doctorates at the Roman College and then became professors at the University of Rome. Pomponio Ugonio of Rome (d. 1614), a student at the Roman Seminary, studied humanities, philosophy, and theology at the Roman College, and then took his doctorate there in 1565. He was appointed professor of rhetoric at the University of Rome in 1586 and held the position until death. Although a famous orator, he is remembered today for his scholarship on early Christian Rome.[104] Ippolito Strada (d. ca. 1623), a Roman layman, obtained a doctorate (whether in philosophy or theology is unknown) at the Roman College in 1606, and taught moral philosophy at the University of Rome from 1617 through 1622. He edited a compendium written by a Jesuit on the *Summa Theologica* of Thomas Aquinas.[105]

Other professors studied in the upper school of the Roman College without taking degrees there. Luca Valerio (1552–1618), remembered for his geometry studies, was a student of Christoph Clavius and may have taken other classes at the Roman College. Valerio taught Greek and mathematics at the University of Rome from 1600 to 1603, then mathematics and moral philosophy from 1603 to 1617.[106] Giuseppe Carpani of Rome, who taught civil law at the University of Rome from 1641 to 1678 and wrote several works, studied grammar, humanities, rhetoric, logic, natural philosophy, and metaphysics (the complete Jesuit curriculum up to theology) at the Roman College.[107] The Englishman Guglielmo Arezzo of Lancaster

103. Carella 2003, 18.

104. "Poiche dopò haver studiato le lettere humane, filosofia, e teologia nel seminario, et addottoratosi in queste scienze fù prima provisto d'un chiericato del capitolo di San Pietro." ASR, Università 4, ff. 162r, 164r–v (quotation). Whether his doctorate was in philosophy or theology, or whether he took both, is unknown. For his university career see *I maestri di Roma* 1991, 2:967; and Lines 2005, 236, 238–39. See also Renazzi 1971, 3:45–46. For his importance as a sacred orator and the influence of Jesuit rhetoric on him, see McGinness 1995a, 601–4; and McGinness 1995b, index.

105. ASR, Università 4, f. 163r. For his university career, see Carella 2007, 161; *I maestri di Roma* 1991, 1:187, 191, 193, 197n7, which indicates that he began teaching at the University of Rome in 1617, rather than 1619, as Carella has it; and Lines 2005, 243.

106. Strøholm 1976; *I maestri di Roma* 1991, 2:941–42; and Carella 2007, 165–66.

107. *I maestri di Roma* 1991, 2:931; Carella 2007, 18–19.

(1597–1660) studied philosophy and theology at the Roman College for at least a year when he was eighteen, and later taught natural philosophy at La Sapienza from 1643 to 1660.[108] Undoubtedly other professors at La Sapienza also studied at the Collegio Romano, especially in its lower school.

Conclusion

The Italian Jesuits wanted to teach canon law. However, the Jesuit Constitutions, written by Ignatius Loyola, barred them from doing so except as a small part of positive theology. Some Jesuits disagreed with the prohibition and made changes after the death of Loyola. When students at some Jesuit student residences in Rome wanted legal instruction, non-Jesuits were invited to come and teach a little canon and civil law. In northern Europe Jesuits began to teach canon law in their own schools in the early seventeenth century. Italian Jesuits hung back because they anticipated strong opposition from universities. Only the Jesuit school in Genoa, a city without a university, taught canon law.

Then in 1695 the Roman College began to teach canon law. The Avvocati Concistoriali of the University of Rome objected. In the next thirty years the Roman College lost the legal battle but won the war through persistence and subterfuge and taught canon law. The Society also revoked the prohibition against teaching canon law of the Constitutions. Following the lead of the Roman College, other major Jesuit schools in Italy taught canon law in the eighteenth century. This was direct but limited competition with Italian universities, because civil law was far more important than canon law, and the Jesuits did not teach civil law.

In addition, the college of doctors of medicine and philosophy of Rome argued unsuccessfully that the Jesuits should not award degrees in philosophy. Despite their differences, the university and the Roman College coexisted in other areas. Medical students often studied philosophy in the Roman College. And a doctorate from the Roman College did not bar a man from a university professorship.

The results of the conflicts between the Roman College and the University of Rome reflected their relative strength. The Collegio Romano had many more students and a more distinguished and productive group of scholars in philosophy and theology than La Sapienza. On the other hand, the university had allies in the most important papal court. The persistent Jesuits eventually got their way, because the Roman College was too strong to be denied.

108. *I maestri di Roma* 1991, 2:905–6; Carella 2007, 138–40.

12

THE JESUITS
AND THE UNIVERSITY
OF PERUGIA

There were three interactions between the Jesuits and the University of Perugia. In 1555 a young Jesuit was invited to teach humanities in the university. In 1680 a visiting Jesuit criticized the inadequacies of the University of Perugia and recommended that the Jesuits should be invited into the university to improve it. In the 1690s the governors of the most important university student residence proposed that the Jesuits should convert it into a Jesuit boarding school. This sparked strong opposition from the powerful college of doctors of law.

The Jesuits and the University
in the 1550s and 1560s

Strong ecclesiastical support brought the Jesuits to Perugia. Pope Julius III invited Laínez to preach in Perugia during Lent in 1552, which he did to acclaim. The bishop then acted. This was Cardinal Fulvio Della Cornia (or Corgna) of Perugia (1517–1583, cardinal from 1551), nephew of Julius III and bishop of Perugia from 1550 to 1553 and 1564 to 1574. He persuaded Loyola to send ten Jesuits to Perugia in June 1552 to found a college. Ignatius may have agreed because he liked to found colleges in towns with universities, and Cardinal Della Cornia provided financial and political support. In October 1552 the Jesuits inaugurated a school of three classes which soon had 150 students.[1] Cardinal Della Cornia continued his strong support even

---

1. For the founding and early years of the Jesuit college and school at Perugia, see *Year by Year* 2004, 199–202; Tacchi Venturi 1951b, 447–56; Scaduto 1974, 376–83; and Scaduto 1992, 199–204. For Della Cornia, see Fosi Polverini 1988, esp. 769–70.

when he was no longer bishop or living in Perugia, and Ippolito Della Cornia, a young relative who was bishop of Perugia from 1553 until his death in 1564, continued the family's support of the Jesuits.

As was often the case, the teachers of the city lost students to the free classes of the Jesuits. So they criticized the learning and pedagogy of the Jesuits and challenged them to demonstrate their skills. A public oration in a church was arranged. The Jesuit who orated was Émond Auger (Alleman, France 1530–1591 Como, Italy), one of the ablest humanities scholars in the early Society. He spoke brilliantly in the presence of leading citizens, scholars, and, above all, most of the professors of the university. Other Jesuits and their students also did well in public performances, which boosted the reputation of the Jesuit school.[2] In 1556 the school had four classes with an enrollment of 170 students.[3] And from 1557 through 1564 the Perugia Jesuit school offered four or five classes, typically rhetoric, humanities, two levels of Latin grammar, and/or a class for beginners, with total enrollments that fluctuated between 125 and 200 students.[4]

Then the Jesuits were suddenly offered a university professorship. A humanities vacancy occurred in 1555. Marcantonio Oradini, who taught canon law in the university while simultaneously serving as vicar to the Bishop Ippolito Della Cornia, and other Perugians recommended Giovanni Antonio Viperano, then teaching in the Jesuit school, for the position.[5]

Viperano (Messina ca. 1535–1610 Bari) entered the Society of Jesus at Messina in 1550.[6] He immediately demonstrated extraordinary scholarly skills in the humanities. He taught at Gubbio in 1553 at the age of eighteen, and was sent to Perugia in 1554 where he taught rhetoric and Greek, and generated excitement beyond the classroom. His combination of youth, erudition, and oratorical prowess made him a local sensation, and won him the recommendation. The rector of the Perugia college asked Loyola if Viperano might fill the vacancy at the University of Perugia.[7]

The question of whether a single Jesuit should teach in a university without an institutional role for the Society was a complex one for Ignatius, and his responses depended on the Constitutions, priorities, and pragmatism. Loyola eagerly sent individual Jesuits to teach in non-Jesuit uni-

---

2. Tacchi Venturi 1951b, 451–52; and *Year by Year* 2004, 201.

3. Lukács 1960–1961, part 1, 242.

4. Scaduto 1974, 377–78, esp. n2.

5. Tacchi Venturi 1951b, 453–55; and Springhetti 1961, 105. For Oradini, see Ermini 1971, 1:548.

6. For his biography and scholarship, see Springhetti 1961; Scaduto 1968, 155; Zanfredini 2001g; and *Maestri insegnamenti* 2009, 54, 67 scheda 8.7.

7. Tacchi Venturi 1951b, 453–54; Springhetti 1961, 105–6.

versities in lands where Catholicism was under attack. For example, in 1549 he dispatched Claude Jay, Alfonso Salmerón, and Peter Canisius to teach theology at the University of Ingolstadt.[8] And in 1554 he permitted Peter Canisius and another Jesuit to accept professorships of theology at the University of Vienna.[9]

But this was Italy, which was not threatened by Protestantism. In the peninsula he wanted to establish Jesuit universities, or at least a Jesuit-civic university in which the Society would have a large governance and teaching role, as he was trying to do at Messina. Hence, Ignatius had denied permission for individual Jesuits to teach in Italian civic universities. In 1553 the Society was invited to provide two Jesuits to teach scripture and the *Sentences* of Peter Lombard in the University of Naples.[10] In 1554 Naples wanted Alfonso Salmerón to teach theology. At about the same time Cardinal Marcello Cervini (1501–1555), briefly Pope Marcellus II in 1555 and a strong friend of the Jesuits, wanted a Jesuit to teach theology at the University of Rome. In all three cases, Ignatius said no. In the last two, Ignatius wrote that a university position was not compatible with the Constitutions, which forbade members of the Society from accepting payment for any of their ministries, including teaching.[11]

This time Ignatius said yes.[12] The Constitutions did allow a Jesuit to teach the humanities in a university if the appointment was temporary and necessary, and Perugia fit those requirements.[13] The appointment was in the humanities, a lower school class, rather than theology. Powerful friends of the Jesuits wanted Viperano to teach in the university, and the Perugia college needed the money. Viperano was appointed extraordinary professor of rhetoric and Greek in 1555, while he also continued to teach in the Jesuit school.[14] (Extraordinary professors were lower in rank and salary than or-

8. See chap. 15, "Quick Doctorates for the First Jesuits."

9. *Year by Year* 2005, 338.

10. Letter of Salmerón to Polanco of September 30, 1553, Naples, in Salmerón 1971–1972, 1:110; and Bangert 1985, 409n194.

11. Letter of Polanco for Ignatius to Juan Fonseca, November 3, 1554, Rome, in *Ignatii Epistolae* 1964–1968, 7:729–30; and Bangert 1985, 219, 409.

12. Letter of Polanco to Everard Mercurian, October 2, 1555, Rome, in *Ignatii Epistolae* 1964–1968, 9:681; and letter of Polanco for Ignatius to Mercurian, May 16, 1556, *Ignatii Epistolae* 1964–968, 11:396–97.

13. "No member of the Society will give lectures publicly [meaning in a university] without the approbation and permission of the provincial superior, except in the lower classes or for a time because of some necessity. But those who have the talent, especially those who have finished their studies, could be employed in lecturing if matters of greater importance do not require something else." *Constitutions* 1996, par. 371 (156); and *Constitutions* 1970, par. 371 (193).

14. Tacchi Venturi 1951b, 453–54; Springhetti 1961, 105–6; Scaduto 1974, 377.

dinary professors but otherwise the same at Perugia.) For his teaching the Jesuit college received 100 gold scudi per annum, not as a stipend for teaching but as alms. The amount did not vary in subsequent years.[15]

Viperano exceeded expectations. The papal governor of Perugia, who fancied himself an orator, asked Viperano to deliver a trial oration in early November at the beginning of the academic year. Viperano did so to much praise from professors and others. His lectures attracted attendance of about a hundred including the nephews of a pope and a cardinal and other young nobles. He composed pieces for, and orated on, special occasions.[16] Cardinal Fulvio Della Cornia wanted him to give private instruction to his nephew, another sign of favor, but Ignatius said no, because Viperano needed to rest.[17]

Viperano taught rhetoric and Greek at the University of Perugia from November 1555 through the beginning of the academic year 1559–1560. Then in January 1560, with his health deteriorating, the Society sent him to Messina to recuperate. Lelio Bisciola of Modena (1542–1629 Milan), another reputedly brilliant young Jesuit, substituted for Viperano at the university and the Jesuit college for the academic year 1560–1561 and possibly the next academic year.[18] Viperano returned to teach in the university in 1562 and stayed through 1564. In frail health and no longer happy as a Jesuit, Viperano left Perugia and moved to Spain in 1565 or 1566. He was dismissed from the Society in 1568, probably with his consent. In Spain he was ordained a priest, became a court chaplain and royal historian, and wrote many works, some of which had originated in his teaching and oratory at Perugia. Thanks to the influence of Philip II, in 1588 he became bishop of Giovinazza (near Bari) where he spent the rest of his days.[19]

Viperano's popularity inevitably kindled resentment from members of the university community. On the Feast of the Ascension (May 14) in 1556 Viperano recited a Latin discourse. A professor asked for a copy, received it, and declared that it contained errors. Viperano wrote to ask what were the errors, but received no response. Then a more important figure, Cristoforo Sasso (1501–1574), a native of Perugia and humanities professor since 1541 or earlier, added his criticism.[20] He accused Viperano of undermining his own

15. MP 3:10; Scaduto 1992, 199.

16. Tacchi Venturi 1951b, 453–54; Springhetti 1961, 106.

17. Letter of Polanco for Ignatius of May 16, 1556, in *Ignatii Epiistolae* 1964–1968, 11:396–97; and Springhetti 1961, 105–7.

18. Scaduto 1964, 355; Scaduto 1974, 377n2. On Bisciola, see Scaduto 1968, 16.

19. Scaduto 1974, 379–81; Zanfredini 2001g.

20. Springhetti 1961, 109. On Sasso, a prominent figure in the intellectual life of the university and community, see Ermini 1971, 1:612; and MP 3:278n3, for his life dates. Springhetti

teaching by lecturing at the same hour. Sasso made this charge even though Viperano was lecturing on an astronomical text, *De sphaera* of Johannes de Sacrobosco, instead of a humanities text. Some students took the side of Viperano by making rude gestures to Sasso and his colleague for failing to produce a list of Viperano's alleged errors.[21]

Another episode followed. Temporarily abandoning his strong support of the Jesuits, Bishop Ippolito Della Cornia in March 1558 complained to the rector of the Jesuit college that Jesuit teachers were not using the Latin grammar manual of Cristoforo Sasso. Instead, they were using that of Ioannes Despauterius. The bishop pointed out that Jesuit schools were free to choose any grammar manual, which was true at that time, and he wanted the local Jesuits to use Sasso's manual. He had told young people that they should attend the Jesuit school; in return, he expected the Jesuits to use Sasso's grammar.[22] It was not unusual for students and parents to criticize the grammar manuals used by Italian Jesuit schools and to want the Jesuits to use another one. However, in this case the bishop was supporting a local university professor, and he may have been tacitly criticizing Viperano, who had praised the grammar of Despauterius.[23] Although this was a small irritant, it showed some hostility toward the Jesuits and possibly Viperano.

The criticisms were symptoms, not the cause of discontent. The bishop and university professors knew that Cardinal Della Cornia and other supporters of the Jesuits wanted to insert the Jesuits more deeply into the university. In 1556 they urged the dismissal of all current humanities professors in favor of the Jesuits. In practical terms, this would have meant replacing only one or two incumbents. It did not happen. When another professor died in early 1558, it was proposed, with the enthusiastic support of Oradini, to transform Viperano's position into an ordinary professorship. But the cautious Laínez, now vicar general of the Society, said no, on the grounds that it might provoke controversy, because there were other candidates.[24]

In this case Laínez evoked a principle that the Society soon adopted. At the First General Congregation of the Jesuits meeting between June 19 and September 10, 1558, the question was raised, "Should Ours (Jesuits) be allowed to occupy public chairs in universities and elsewhere, with the usual struggle for votes and rivalry?" The Congregation decreed: "It seemed bet-

---

believes that the first critic was Orazio Cardoneto (d. 1588), a pupil of Sasso who began teaching in the university before 1561. On Cardoneto, see Ermini 1971, 1:568, 612.

21. Springhetti 1961, 109–10.

22. Letter of Giovanni Niccolò Notari to Laínez of March 21, 1558, Perugia, in MP 3:278–81.

23. MP 3:279n4.

24. Scaduto 1964, 355.

ter that they should not be allowed to do so. Nevertheless, if chairs of this sort should be offered, unsolicited, by universities or their rectors, and the lectures do not entail a stipend, and no competitor presents himself as objecting to it, such chairs could be accepted." It added that the superior general should always be consulted.[25]

After Viperano left Perugia, the Society returned to the issue of university teaching and its remuneration. The Second General Congregation meeting, held from June 21 to September 3, 1565, expressly forbade the Perugia arrangement. Decree 24 after the election stated: "A public lecture on humane letters, involving a stipend, is abandoned." The explanation clarified that the Perugia professorship was meant. "On occasion the city of Perugia made use of the services of one of Ours in a public lecture in humane letters. In place of the stipend that the city usually gave to those who present such lectures, the city gave to our college at Perugia one hundred gold pieces each year, not as a stipend, but only as alms. The question was raised whether in the future these transactions were to be allowed under whatever title or mode. It appeared proper in the Lord that in the future neither the task of delivering this kind of lecture nor the reception of the hundred gold pieces was to be permitted."[26]

The decree was a backlash against the unwritten policy that the Jesuits were adopting. It hearkened back to a stricter interpretation of poverty that Ignatius himself had originally preferred. This had given way in the face of the reality that the Society needed substantial financial support for its worldly ministries, especially the schools.[27] The decree was an expression of disapproval and nostalgia against the path on which the leadership had embarked: the Society would accept financial support from governments for its teaching so long as the payments went to the colleges as alms to be used in support of the college and all its ministries.

The Jesuits ignored the decree in Perugia, as they did elsewhere. They continued to fill a humanities position at the University of Perugia for two or three more academic years, because Cardinal Della Cornia wanted it, and the college was grateful to him. The cardinal had a native son in mind as the next Jesuit lecturer in the university. This was Paolo Comitoli (Perugia 1545–1626 Perugia), the same man who wrote a sharp rebuttal to Cre-

25. *For Matters of Greater Moment* 1994, 98–99, Decree 118 after the election. Decrees enacted by the first four general congregations (1558 through 1581) are designated as "before the election" and "after the election." Some business, typically decisions on the admittance of delegates and election rules, was transacted before the election of a new general. Hence, they were decrees before the election. Then a new general was elected. Decisions made after the election were described as decrees after the election. Subsequent general congregations dropped the distinction.

26. *For Matters of Greater Moment* 1994, 119. For the Latin, see MP 3:10.

27. O'Malley 1993, 348–51.

monini at Padua in 1592 and against Venice in 1606. Comitoli came from a prominent Perugia family, entered the Society at Perugia in 1558, then studied at the Collegio Romano where he demonstrated considerable skill in Greek. The cardinal wanted him to return to Perugia to teach in the university. Aware of the decision of the Second General Congregation, he increased the food supplies that he furnished the college and sought a roundabout way for the Jesuits to receive 100 gold scudi from the city as alms. He also contributed substantially to the construction of the Jesuit church in Perugia, which opened in 1571.[28]

Cardinal Della Cornia was too important to be denied. Comitoli was appointed to teach Greek in the University of Perugia in the autumn of 1565. Listed as teaching gratuitously, he delivered his inaugural oration and taught all year. He continued to teach in the university through the academic year 1566–1567, and possibly 1567–1568, after which he was sent to the Collegio Romano to teach rhetoric.[29]

That was the end. No other Jesuits taught in the University of Perugia in the sixteenth century, and the Jesuit school reduced the number of its classes from four to three for financial and personnel reasons.[30] The Perugia Jesuit school offered only three lower school classes in the 1570s even though the number of Jesuits rose to 18. Nevertheless, the Perugia Jesuits were happy to report in 1576 that five professors of the university and eight dottori were enrolled in one of their Marian congregations.[31] They did not expand their school for another forty years, although the enrollment increased to 210 students in 1612.[32] Finally in 1615 the Jesuit school added a philosophy class.[33]

Thus, three consecutive Jesuits filled a professorship of rhetoric and Greek, or Greek alone, at the University of Perugia from 1555 through 1567 or 1568. This was the same as at Macerata, where two Jesuits taught humanities courses in the university for two academic years, 1561–1563. But there was opposition in Perugia, and some Jesuits believed that such appointments were contrary to the Jesuit way of proceeding. The leadership

28. Scaduto 1992, 199–202; and Donnelly 2001c.

29. Scaduto 1992, 199–202. For Comitoli, see Donnelly 2001c. Ermini 1971, the fundamental history of the University of Perugia, does not mention the three Jesuits who taught in the university.

30. Scaduto 1992, 202–3.

31. Lukács 1960–1961, part 2, 48 (1574); ARSI, Roma 126b I, ff. 77r (January 1575), 101r–v (1576); and Roma 126 I, f. 211r (1579).

32. Lukács 1960–1961, part 2, 48 (1600); ARSI, Roma 130 II, f. 317r (1612).

33. ARSI, Roma 126 I, f. 101v. Although only one grammar teacher is listed, there must have been three lower school classes.

was not ready for individual Jesuits to teach in civic universities on a long-term basis, so the Jesuits relinquished the Perugia professorship

Jesuit Criticism of the University

The possibility of the Jesuits entering the University of Perugia rose again. On March 9, 1680, the papal governor of Perugia wrote a letter to Cardinal Alderano Cibo, secretary of state to Pope Innocent XI (Benedetto Odescalchi of Como, 1611–1689, elected in 1676), deploring the scandalous behavior of students at the University of Perugia. He particularly criticized students living in student residences for consorting with the wrong kind of women.[34] There was nothing new about the complaint: civic and religious authorities had been criticizing students for going to prostitutes for centuries. However, the papacy decided to look into the matter. It commissioned a Jesuit, Father Filippo Poggi (Lucca 1622–1689 Fano), a well-known preacher and puritanical scold, who preached in Perugia at some point during 1680, to report what he saw.[35]

Poggi delivered his judgment in a memorandum. He began by criticizing the immodest dress of Perugian women in church. He chastised nuns for spending too much money from outside sources on religious services. And he censured the unbridled luxury that, in his view, threatened to ruin the great families of the city. He next turned to the university.

In addition, the public university of the city of Perugia, once one of the most celebrated universities of Europe for the excellence of its professors and the great number of students that enrolled, is reduced to such a state that there cannot be a more wretched body of professors nor a greater shortage of students. It needs reform. One of the best ways would be to bring in the Jesuit Fathers, as has been done at Fermo and Macerata. Through their competition and learning they would produce a great benefit to the public and would also be useful to the treasury, because with little or nothing in salary they could save many hundreds of scudi and renew fervor. With their instruction [they could] attract foreigners even from far away, as happens elsewhere. Moreover,

34. Lupi 2005, 38–40, provides a good brief account of the episode of 1680. See also Scalvanti 1910, 65–66; and Ermini 1971, 1:214–15.

35. On Poggi, see Sommervogel 1960, 6:917; and Lupi 2005, 37n48. The exact dates of Poggi's visit and preaching in Perugia are unknown. It might have been in Lent (March 6 to April 21), it might have been later in the year. In any case, he had been commissioned by the pope to inspect, and Bishop Luca Alberto Patrizi accompanied him on his visit to La Sapienza Nuova: "... che però quando il P. Poggi si contentasse essere con esso me alla visita della Sapienza Vecchia, dove io posso condurlo con l'autorità propria, et alla visita della Sapienza Nova si interponesse la commissione della Santità Sua." Patrizi, "Informazione data da Monsignore Vescovo sopra il Memoriale del P. Poggi 9 novembre 1680," in ASUP, Constitutiones et jura, P I VII, f. 24v.

there are in this city two university student residences [*Sapienze*] that could maintain about fifty students each because of the large incomes they have. But they are reduced to a very low number of students. It is proposed to Your Lordship that you should press for some reforms there and a visit in order to uncover the reason for the fault and to give them some instructional method and better management.[36]

One wonders if Poggi was promoting the wishes of the Perugia Jesuits. So far as is known, he had not previously visited Perugia and had no direct knowledge of universities. It was possible that the Perugia Jesuits and/or their lay supporters in the town primed him.

The papacy asked the bishop of Perugia to respond to Poggi's report. The pope looked to the bishop because Urban VIII in a brief of 1625 had given the bishop greater authority than bishop-chancellors of other universities enjoyed. Hence, in addition to conferring degrees, he participated in the selection of professors and determination of salaries in conjunction with colleges of doctors and the Savi dello Studio, the city magistracy that oversaw the university. And he had responsibility for maintaining Catholic orthodoxy in the university.[37] The bishop was Luca Alberto Patrizi (1633–1701), a native of Perugia who obtained a doctorate in both laws from the University of Perugia and taught civil law there from 1654 to 1666. He then moved to Rome, became a priest in May 1669, and was named archbishop of Perugia in June 1669, a position he held until death.[38]

Patrizi was angry. He saw Poggi's words as an unjustified indictment of the people of Perugia, the university, and himself. He vigorously rebutted Poggi on November 9, 1680.[39] He began by defending the clergy and

---

36. "Inoltre lo Studio publico di detta Città di Perugia, che per l'eccellenza de Maestri, e per la moltiplicità de scolari, che vi concorrevano, era uno de più celebri Studij d'Europa, è ridotto a tal stato, che non può essere più meschino de Maestri, ne' più scarso de' scolari. Haveria bisogno di riforma, una delle quali sarebbe ottima il ponervi i PP. Giesuiti, come hanno fatto Fermo, e Macerata, i quali con l'emulatione, e discipline farebbero un gran pro[fitto] al publico, et utile insieme alla Camera, mentre con poco o' niente di stipendio potriano far' avanzare molte centinaia di scudi, e rimettere in piedi il fervore, et allettare con la disciplina loro li forastieri anche di lontano, come succede altrove. Vi sono parimente in detta città due Sapienze, che possono mantenere quasi cinquanta studenti per ciascheduna per le grosse entrate che hanno, e pure sono ridotte a pochissimo numero de studenti: Si propone a V[ostra] S[ignoria] che vi vorria qualche riforma e visita per rintracciare le cagione del difetto, e dargli qualche metodo di disciplina, e migliore economia." ASUP, Constitutiones et jura, P I VII, f. 21r–v. The same is found in BAP, Ms. 82, f. 170r–v. Both are copies lacking date, signature, and the customary salutation and closure.

37. Ermini 1971, 1:209–14; Lupi 2005, 39–40; and Lupi 2014, 188–89.

38. Ermini 1971, 1:538n168, 543; Lupi 2005, 40, 108; and *Hierarchia Catholica* 1913–1978, 5:311.

39. "Informazione data da Monsignore Vescovo sopra il Memoriale del P. Poggi, 9 novembre 1680." ASUP, Constitutiones et jura, P I VII, ff. 22r–24v. For very brief summaries see Scalvanti 1910, 65–66; Ermini 1971, 1:214–15; and Lupi 2005, 40–41.

women of Perugia and by criticizing Poggi's preaching. Even before Poggi arrived, the women had been dressing more modestly in response to the admonitions of the confessors of the city. By contrast, Father Poggi's violent words and intemperate zeal "si raffredò lo spirito" (had chilled the spirit) and provoked derisive comments from the women who heard him. He had even criticized the uncovered arms of a woman who was bringing alms to church. Bishop Patrizi reassured the papacy that he had issued decrees ordering nuns to spend less on divine services. He agreed that the excessive amount of money that great families spent on dowries, dress, jewelry, servants, and carriages threatened to ruin them. But he pointed out that numerous papal decrees had not curbed their spending.[40]

Bishop Patrizi devoted most of his response to defending the university. He saw Poggi's words as a threat that the Jesuits would be given control of the university. Patrizi began by noting that the citizens of Perugia had founded the university nearly four hundred years ago (in 1308) and had supported it ever since. At present it has fifty-two good professors, all Perugians, he wrote. And if any of them are incapable, the authorities have the power to dismiss them. Patrizi agreed that enrollment had declined. But this had also happened to other universities that had to compete with boarding schools, colleges, and student residences (Sapienze). Therefore, it would be unjust to give the university to the Jesuits.[41]

The last part was direct criticism of the Jesuits, because boarding schools mostly meant Jesuit boarding schools for youths of noble blood, while colleges referred to Jesuit colleges, and they almost always included a school.[42] In other words, Bishop Patrizi wrote that since competition from Jesuit schools had caused the decline in university enrollments, it would be unjust to reward the Jesuits with university positions.

Patrizi next made a plea on behalf of the town, students, and professors of Perugia. Giving the university to the Jesuits would deprive the town

40. ASUP, Constitutiones et jura, P I VII, f. 22r–v (quotation at 22r).

41. "Nè deve apportar maraviglia, che siano diminuiti i scolari, se si considera che non è quasi città dove non siano aperti, ò non s'aprarno del continuo studij publici, ò privati e dove non siano seminarij, collegij, e Sapienze, e per quello si sente anco nell'altre università si è diminuito il concorso, che perciò non pare esservi giusta causa di levare detto Studio alli dottori, e darlo alli Giesuiti." ASUP, Constitutiones et jura, P I VII, f. 23r–v.

42. In the quotation in the previous note, *seminario* (and the Latin *seminarium*) meant a boarding school for lay boys or youths, usually of noble blood. It did not mean a school or residence educating candidates for the priesthood. For example, the Ratio Studiorum referred to "convictorum et alumnorum seminariis" (seminaries of boarders and lay students). *Ratio Studiorum* 2005, par. 8 (8). Recognizing this, Brizzi defines "seminarium" and "seminarium laicorum" as a Jesuit boarding school for lay youths of noble blood. Brizzi 1976, 21. The subtitle of his book is *I seminaria nobilium nell'Italia centro-settentrionale.*

of its greatest asset. If the Jesuits took over the university, the young men of Perugia who wanted to study law and medicine would have to go elsewhere at considerable cost, because the Jesuits did not teach those subjects. Professors would no longer have positions and salaries, thus ruining families that depended on the small salaries (no more than 100 scudi even for those who had taught for thirty years, according to Patrizi) that professors earned. Should the papacy decide to give the university to the Jesuits, Patrizi predicted that members of the university and the city would throw themselves at the feet of the pope begging him not to do it.[43]

Patrizi exaggerated the projected dire consequences. Students from Perugia would still be able to study law and medicine at the university, because the Jesuits would not eliminate these disciplines. The only professors who would be replaced by Jesuits would be theologians, some philosophers, the mathematician, and humanists, a minority of the professoriate. And because all the professors were local men, their families would not be ruined. At this time, almost all lay professors in Italian universities came from prominent local families which did not rely exclusively on professorial stipends for their well-being.

Bishop Patrizi continued. The Perugia Jesuits have their own school where they teach grammar, rhetoric, logic, philosophy, and theology, and used to teach mathematics. He chided the Jesuits for dropping their mathematics class, because the only other one in the city was the university mathematics class. He noted that the Jesuits at the Collegio Romano, Fermo, and Macerata taught a range of courses, and he invited the Perugia Jesuits to expand their school. This would benefit Perugia without harming the university. Patrizi finished with brief comments on the two student residences, the Sapienza Vecchia and the Sapienza Nuova, both of which housed foreign (non-Perugian) university students. He declared that they were well run. Patrizi concluded with a dig at Poggi. He noted that Poggi had seemed satisfied with the governance of the student residences when he and the bishop had toured the Sapienza Nuova during his visit to Perugia. Then he expressed a different view in his memorandum.[44]

A Jesuit move into the university was feasible because the Perugia Jesuits had more resources than in the past. In 1651 there were still only 15 Jesuits at Perugia, and their school offered only four classes: philosophy (probably logic, natural philosophy, and metaphysics taught in a three-year rotation), humanities, and two grammar classes.[45] In 1661, by contrast, they

43. ASUP, Constitutiones et jura, P I VII, f. 23v.
44. ASUP, Constitutiones et jura, P I VII, ff. 23v–24v.
45. ARSI, Roma 59, f. 266r.

taught eight classes: scholastic theology, cases of conscience, metaphysics, natural philosophy, logic, a combination of rhetoric and humanities, and two grammar classes. The college housed 21 Jesuits. The expansion had come about because the college had received a donation that supported the three philosophy classes.[46] And, as the Jesuits often did in such circumstances, they had also added classes in scholastic theology and cases of conscience. From 1661 through the end of the century, the Jesuits offered the same eight classes. The number of Jesuits at Perugia varied from 21 to 24, once reaching 27, when 6 scholastics were there as well.[47] Thus, the Perugia Jesuits had the personnel to fill positions in theology, philosophy, and the humanities in the university without adding more staff, so long as the Jesuit classes might serve both Jesuit and university students. Only mathematics was lacking, as Bishop Patrizi pointed out.

Nothing happened. Perugia did not follow the example of Fermo and Macerata and appoint Jesuits to the university. Bishop Patrizi's strong defense of the university made it clear that the city did not want that. But the idea that the Jesuits should have a place in the University of Perugia had been raised.

La Sapienza Nuova and the Jesuits

A few years later some Perugians wanted to insert the Jesuits into the university by giving them direction of a university student residence. They believed that this would aid the university and benefit Perugian youths. Others opposed the idea, and an intense dispute followed because the student residence was considered a key part of the university.[48] The arguments advanced also revealed violence at the University of Perugia and suspicion of the motives of the Jesuits.

Perugia had two endowed residences offering room and board at low cost to non-Perugian university students. The more important was the Collegio di San Girolamo, universally called La Sapienza Nuova because it was founded some sixty-five years after the other residence. La Sapienza Nuova had deep local roots. Benedetto Guidalotti (1389–1429), a Perugian

46. ARSI, Roma 61, f. 133r. The donation came from one "P. Ant. M. Guaggi nostr. Soc." who has not been identified. ARSI, Roma 109, f. 228v (1773). There are many references to the donation in the triennial catalogues from 1661 through 1773.

47. ARSI, Roma 61, f. 268r (1665, 27 Jesuits including 6 scholastics); Roma 62, ff. 110r (1669), 310r (1672); Roma 63, f. 181r (1675); Roma 64, ff. 138r (1678), 276r (1681); Roma 66, f. 307r (1696).

48. See Ermini 1971, 1: 412; and especially Lupi 2005, 41–43, for brief accounts of the events of 1691 to 1699.

who obtained a law degree at the University of Perugia and taught there before becoming a bishop, made arrangements to leave money for the creation of a residence for poor foreign students. Pope Martin V (Colonna 1368–1431, pope from 1417), also a student at the university, accepted his proposal in 1425 and directed some benefice income to the project. Perugian civic and ecclesiastical organizations lent support. In 1443 La Sapienza Nuova opened its doors to 40 university students who came from at least 30 miles beyond Perugia. They might live and board in La Sapienza Nuova for 7 years for a fee of 40 florins for the entire period. Although the fee increased over the years, it was still only 100 scudi in 1635, making it a significant bargain.[49]

Originally located next to the university building, La Sapienza Nuova moved to a larger home in the sixteenth century. It had a library and some in-house law instruction. Reforms of 1596 established a minimum entry age of 18 and decreed that there should be four students each from Germany, France, and Spain. They were given preference over Italians. No more than four students might study medicine, which meant that about ninety percent studied law. In 1635 the number of students was reduced to 22, then raised to 25 in 1639, with a maximum of three students from one region. At least four students had to be ultramontanes.[50]

Ecclesiastical, merchant, and legal groups and individuals shared governance of La Sapienza Nuova, a feature that played a major role in the dispute. The prior of the cloister of the cathedral and the consuls of the college of the Mercanzia were the early governors and continued to play prominent roles. New constitutions promulgated by Pius IV in 1564 decreed that the rector of the Sapienza Nuova, the man who presided over the residence, made decisions about students, staff, and budget, and received a salary, had to come from the membership of the college of doctors of law. This inserted the college into the governing mix.[51]

But La Sapienza was not doing well. Hence, in or about 1690 the prior of the cloister and the consuls of the college of the Mercanzia resolved that it should become a combination Jesuit boarding school and university student residence. The office of rector would be eliminated, meaning the exclusion of the college of doctors of law from governance, and direction given to the Jesuits. They would teach theology, philosophy, humanities, and grammar, classes already available in the Perugia Jesuit school, to the

49. Il fondo archivistico della Sapienza 2006, 23–29.
50. Il fondo archivistico della Sapienza 2006, 29–30.
51. Il fondo archivistico della Sapienza 2006, 28–29.

students. One or two professors of law would come to deliver law lectures as needed. The school would also teach "knightly arts, that is, fencing, dancing, and horsemanship as was done in the schools of Siena and Parma."[52] The reference was to the Jesuit noble boarding schools at Parma and Siena. The age of admission and length of residence would be drastically changed. Admission would be limited to boys younger than twelve so that they might be guided at a tender age. Because no upper age limit was proposed, they would be permitted to continue to live in La Sapienza Nuova while studying at the university. And Perugian boys would be accepted, a major change. Each student from Perugia would be obligated to pay 3 scudi per month, while foreigners would have to pay 6 scudi per month. In short, La Sapienza would become a Jesuit boarding school with three modifications. Noble birth would not be required, Perugian boys would pay lower fees than outsiders, and the boarders might continue their studies into the university.

Papal approval was needed. Not only did the papacy rule Perugia, but it had helped create La Sapienza Nuova. Later popes had granted tax exemptions and approved the first constitution and subsequent revisions.[53] Hence, the prior of the cloister and the consuls of the Mercanzia who made the proposal, and the college of doctors of law who opposed it, bombarded the papacy with claims and counter claims, sent delegations to Rome, and sought help from anyone who might move the papacy. But the Jesuits took no public role. If they advised the prior and consuls of the Mercanzia behind the scenes, neither side mentioned it.

On March 20, 1692, five Perugians went to Rome to tell the pope that students at the Sapienza Nuova lived in peril of their lives because of the brawling of undisciplined students.[54] On April 1, 1692, the prior of the cathedral cloister and the consuls of the college of merchants sent a long memorandum to the pope. They began by noting that the disorders in the Sapienza Nuova had produced acute violence, even homicides. Fathers had stopped sending their sons to the University of Perugia, and La Sapienza Nuova had only four or six students.[55] In order to overcome these

52. "In cui non solo dovranno insegnarsi le scienze, ma anco l'arti cavalleresche, cioè scherma, ballo, cavallerizza come si pratica nel collegio di Siena, e di Parma." BAP, Ms. 82, f. 167, undated and untitled document that is one of a group of copies of documents with the general title of "Notizia sopra la controversia tra li dottori legisti, et i superiori della Sapienza Nuova per motivo, che questi ideavano di dare il d[ett]o Collegio a PP. Gesuiti per erigervi un seminario" (f. 165).

53. *Il fondo archivistico della Sapienza* 2006, 23–32, esp. 26–30.

54. ASUP, Constitutiones et jura, P I VII, f. 55r.

55. "Memoriale dato a N[ostro] S[ignore] dalli Superiori della Sapienza Nova," in ASUP, Constitutiones et jura, P I VII, ff. 48v–49r.

problems, it should become a boarding school with the same constitution and rules as schools in Rome, Siena, Parma, and other major cities. Under new direction La Sapienza would have much better order and discipline. It would attract the foreign students who had always come. Indeed, enrollment would be higher than in the past, because students would seize the opportunity to acquire knowledge and knightly virtue (*virtù cavalleresca*). The site and house were large enough. La Sapienza Nuova had sufficient income from its properties to maintain a suitable number of students plus the servants or lay brothers that the religious order would introduce.[56]

In the rest of their memorandum to the pope the prior and the consuls dismissed the objections of the college of doctors of law by asserting that they, not the college, had the authority to govern La Sapienza Nuova, and that there was no legal impediment barring them from awarding direction to a religious order or non-Perugians. They also extended an olive branch to the legists for the loss of the rectorship. They assured the college that it might name two of their number, presumably university professors, to teach *Institutes* and other legal texts in La Sapienza Nuova. They would receive the same stipends that the two legists now teaching there received.[57]

Pope Innocent XII ordered his secretary of state, Cardinal Fabrizio Spada (1643–1717, cardinal from 1675), a veteran diplomat and curialist, to write to Bishop Luca Alberto Patrizi for his opinion.[58] Patrizi replied by outlining the history of La Sapienza Nuova. He described what the prior and consuls wanted to do, and noted that the college of doctors of law was opposed. But he did not take a public position, probably because two local groups were locked in combat. His phrase "fleeing the uncertainty of new things" may have expressed his unspoken opinion.[59]

The college of doctors of law countered with the argument that the prior of the cathedral cloister and the consuls of the Mercanzia did not have the right to change the management of La Sapienza Nuova. More provoc-

---

56. "Di beni stabili sufficienti al mantemento di congruro numero di scolari, di serventi, che da religiosi vi s'introduranno." In "Memoriale ... dalli Superiori della Sapienza Nova," in ASUP, Constitutiones et jura, P I VII, f. 49r–v (quotation at 49v). "Serventi" means both "servants" and "lay brothers." Although the prior of the cloister and the consuls of the Mercanzia intended to give direction to the Jesuits, they did not name the Society in this memorandum.

57. "Memoriale ... dalli Superiori della Sapienza Nova," in ASUP, Constitutiones et jura, P I VII, f. 49.

58. Letter of Cardinal Spada to Bishop Patrizi, April 1, 1692, Rome, in BAP, Ms. 82, f. 170. For Spada, see The Cardinals of the Roman Church, ww2.fiu.edu/~mirandas/bios1675. html#Spada. Spada had a doctorate in both laws, from either the University of Perugia or the University of Rome.

59. "Sfuggendo l'incertezza delle novità." BAP, Ms. 82, ff. 172–75, quotation at 175.

ative were their arguments concerning the Jesuits. They charged that the Jesuits had hoodwinked the prior and consuls. In their view, the Jesuits were scheming to get control of the Sapienza Nuova in order to insert themselves into the affairs of the university, as they always tried to do.[60] According to the legists, in 1691 the Perugian Jesuits through their Congregation of the Penitents had persuaded heads of families, especially those with many children, that there was a better and less expensive way of educating their sons than sending them to out-of-town schools. The Jesuits told receptive ears that if they were given the direction and revenues of both university student residences they would teach better than the professors of the university. They would create a new and successful school, like those in Siena and Rome, which would flourish even with small revenues and no princely patron. Convinced by these arguments, the prior and consuls had gone to the Jesuit general Tirso González with the proposal that the Jesuits should assume direction of the Sapienza Nuova, and the general had agreed.[61]

The college of doctors of law rejected the view that student violence justified a management change. It used the tactic, beloved by lawyers, of demanding sworn statements that students at the Sapienza Nuova were involved in fights in order to diminish the brawling and violence argument. The doctors of law pointed out, correctly, that university students had always fought. Scandals and disorders—the college avoided writing "violence"—were common when students of different blood, homelands, and inclinations were thrown together. A certain amount of disorder should be tolerated. Rigorous rules would drive away foreign students.[62]

Although the college minimized student violence in Perugia, others

---

60. "E stata sempre mira de Padri della Compagnia di Giesu di volere introdersi [sic] agli affari delle publiche universali accademie." ASUP, Constitutiones et jura, P I VII, f. 48r, no date but written in 1698 or later because it refers to a legal decision of 1698. This is the first section of a group of documents (ff. 48r–56v) entitled "Informatione del successo tra li Signori Nobili della Mercanzia, e Signori Dottori del Collegio de' Legisti sopra il governo del Collegio della Sapienza Nova 1691 e 1692," which are mostly copies of documents coming from the college of doctors of law.

61. ASUP, Constitutiones et jura, P I VII, f. 48r–v. Despite this accusation, the general's role is unknown.

62. "Risposta informativa al memoriale dato da SS.ri Superiori della Sapienza Nuova a N. Sig.e Innocenzio XII sopra la rinovazione di d.ta Sapienza." ASUP, Constitutiones et jura, P I VII, ff. 61v–62v. The entire "Risposta informativa" is ff. 58r–75v. It is a copy of a long document detailing the many objections of the college of doctors of law to the proposal to give direction of La Sapienza Nuova to the Jesuits. It has thirteen sections and is festooned with legal citations, Latin phrases, and references to papal briefs and the constitutions of La Sapienza Nuova. Although lacking a date, it was probably written in 1692. There is another copy in BAP, Ms. 82, ff. 180–205. Only some of the many arguments presented by the college are mentioned here.

cited frightening examples. In 1698 a Jesuit Father Rivoli, who taught philosophy at the Perugia school, wrote to the pope on behalf of a noble boy, Pompeo Giustiniani of Genoa. The ten-year-old boy had been sent to Perugia to take advantage of the legacy of Cardinal Benedetto Giustiniani of Genoa (1554–1621, cardinal from 1586), a very wealthy papal administrator and art collector, who had studied law at Perugia. In 1619 Cardinal Giustiniani created a fund enabling two members of the Giustiniani family to spend eight years studying in Perugia, three years studying grammar and humanities, and five years studying law at the university, culminating in a degree in both laws.[63] However, the boy had found the students in Perugia to be very dissolute. When he learned that two Giustiniani youths who had come to Perugia in the past had been killed, he feared for his life. So Father Rivoli asked the pope to allow the boy to move to the Roman seminary, which the Jesuits directed, while still allowing him to receive the income of the legacy. Rivoli said that another Giustiniani youth, who had left Perugia for the same reason, had been permitted to do this.[64]

The college of doctors of law found someone to rebut Father Rivoli. This person, who claimed to have lived in the Sapienza Nuova, wrote that Pompeo Giustiniani, who was still in Perugia, was under the caring custody of a good priest from another religious order, and that the boy's comrades were sons of well-regarded nobles. He dismissed the fears of the boy. He had not seen any dissolute students in the Sapienza Nuova. As for the two members of the Giustiniani family allegedly killed, one was an adult, and his death had been an unfortunate accident. There were only stories about the other, although a Giustiniani had killed a Perugian. But why would a boy of ten years fear for his life? Finally, the author wrote that "last year" Father Rivoli tried to introduce the teaching of canon law in the Jesuit school in Perugia in order to attract students from the university.[65] Obviously, the Perugia college of doctors of law was aware of the canon law battle in Rome.

The doctors of law argued that the Jesuits would be unable to improve

---

63. Scalvanti 1910, 66–67. For Cardinal Giustiniani, see Feci and Bortolotti 2001 and *Le istruzioni generali di Paolo V* 2003, 2:1, 240, and 240n2; although neither mentions this bequest.

64. "Accresca il timore il caso lacrimevole di due giovenetti della stessa familia Giustiniani, i quali sono nella città medesima dove s'erano portati a studio furono successivamente in diversi tempi uccisi," in "Memoriale presentata alla Santità N. S. Papa Innocenzio XII dal Padre Rivoli Gesuita in nome del nobile Pompeo Giustiniani per avere facoltà di potere trasferirsi da Perugia a Roma a proseguire li suoi studij," in BAP, Ms. 82, f. 213. No date but written in 1698. There is a reference to an earlier Giustiniani youth who left Perugia in ASUP, Constitutiones et jura, P I VII, f. 48r. Father Rivoli has not been further identified.

65. BAP, Ms. 82, ff. 214–15. Copy of a letter lacking name and date.

the behavior or academic performance of the students because they would not be introducing any new practices. The Sapienza Nuova already had a chaplain, and its residents listened to spiritual reading during meals. The students already participated in disputations and academic competitions. La Sapienza Nuova under Jesuit direction would not compete successfully for students with other boarding schools, such as those at Siena, Rome, and Parma. Siena, in particular, would offer formidable competition because students went to Siena in order to learn the purest Tuscan.[66]

The legists did not believe that La Sapienza Nuova under the direction of the Jesuits would attract more university students because the Jesuits lacked the right expertise. The doctors of law conceded that the Jesuits taught sacred and moral disciplines well. But university students, especially foreigners from Germany, could study philosophy and theology at home. They came to Perugia to study law in the university where the famous Bartolo da Sassaferrato and Baldo degli Ubaldi had lectured.[67] Given the numerous German students who came to Perugia over the centuries and the prestige of the Italian legal tradition, this argument may have been persuasive.

The college of doctors of law did not want La Sapienza Nuova to teach riding, fencing, and dancing. The founder, the constitutions, and many papal briefs had charged it with teaching learned sciences, not "essercitij leggiadri" (light exercises). And where would the money come to pay a fencing master, a dancing master, a riding instructor, to maintain horses, and to pay the salaries of the additional personnel needed? To the response that wealthy boarding students would pay for the extra services, the college objected that Bishop Guidalotti and Pope Martin V had wanted the Sapienza Nuova to be a residence for poor students. If the prior, consuls, and Jesuits wanted a different kind of boarding school, they should create a new school.[68] Next came a long discussion of finances.[69] The doctors of law concluded with an appeal to the papacy on behalf of the city and citizens of Perugia not to authorize changes in La Sapienza Nuova, because this would anger all the professors of the university, legists, philosophers, medical scholars, and theologians alike.[70] However, the professors at the university were not angry enough to take a stand. Instead, they asked Cardinal Spada to settle the issue.[71]

66. ASUP, Constitutiones et jura, P I VII, ff. 63v–64r. This is a view that some Italians still hold today.

67. ASUP, Constitutiones et jura, P I VII, f. 65r–v.

68. ASUP, Constitutiones et jura, P I VII, f. 66r.

69. ASUP, Constitutiones et jura, P I VII, ff. 67r–69r.

70. ASUP, Constitutiones et jura, P I VII, ff. 74v–75r.

71. BAP, Ms. 82, f. 206, no date.

Both sides sent deputations to Rome where they searched for allies.[72] The college of doctors of law won over the French, Spanish, and imperial ambassadors to the papacy. All three were concerned that students from their lands would lose their inexpensive places in a Sapienza Nuova governed by the Jesuits, and went to the pope. Cardinal Spada told the papal governor of Perugia that the pope did not want any innovation that would damage the interests of Spanish students.[73] This was an order favoring the status quo, and a victory for the college of doctors of law. The Jesuits were not given direction of La Sapienza Nuova.

The dispute petered to an end in or about 1699.[74] La Sapienza Nuova remained under the joint control of the three parties despite their differences. Nevertheless, the prior and consuls of the Mercanzia eventually achieved some of their goals. In 1732 La Sapienza Nuova opened its doors to Perugians, it reserved fewer places for foreign students, and it lowered the age of admission to sixteen. In 1806 the age of admission was lowered again to ten to twelve, and students might stay to the ages of twenty or twenty-two. La Sapienza Nuova became a boarding school for both university and pre-university students, Perugians and foreigners.[75]

Without La Sapienza Nuova, the Perugian Jesuits continued as before. In the eighteenth century the school offered eight classes: scholastic theology, cases of conscience, metaphysics, natural philosophy, logic, rhetoric, humanities, and grammar. The number of Jesuits at Perugia was twenty-one or twenty-two.[76] They never taught in, or had any association with, the University of Perugia.

Conclusion

The three interactions between the Jesuits and the University of Perugia were quite different. In 1555 a wave of praise and a powerful local ecclesias-

---

72. ASUP, Constitutiones et jura, P I VII, f. 48r–v.

73. ASUP, Constitutiones et jura, P I VII, f. 72v; and Lupi 2005, 42–43. Another reason was that the papacy did not want to alienate any of the three powers during the crisis of the Spanish succession. King Charles II Habsburg (1661–1700, r. from 1665) was mentally deficient, sickly, and childless. Who would inherit his throne? Would the Spanish Empire, which ruled much of Italy, be divided when he died? The papacy and other states were engaged in intense diplomacy in an effort to find a peaceful solution. Pastor 1891–1953, 32:686–88. Diplomacy did not solve the issue and the War of the Spanish Succession erupted in 1700.

74. Lupi 2005, 43.

75. *Il fondo archivistico della Sapienza* 2006, 31, 193–94.

76. ARSI, Roma 71, ff. 154r (1730), 324r (1734); Roma 72, f. 160r (1737); Roma 73 ff. 153r (1743), 329r (1746); Roma 74, f. 167r (1749); Roma 75, ff. 165r (1758), 342r (1761); Roma 77, f. 319r (1770); Roma 109, f. 228v (1773).

tic swept a young Jesuit into a university professorship. Ignatius approved because Viperano's appointment strengthened the Jesuit position in the city. Three Jesuits filled the humanities professorship for ten or eleven years until 1567 or 1568. However, this was an anomaly for the Italian Jesuits. At this time the leadership preferred that the Society fill more positions and dominate or share the governance in any university that they joined.

In 1680 a Jesuit commissioned by the papacy to examine the University of Perugia judged that it had declined greatly in enrollment and in quality of instruction. He recommended that the Jesuits should be invited to teach in it, and that the two student residences for foreign students needed new management and rules. The bishop of Perugia rejected both ideas.

Part of the 1680 recommendation was revived around 1690. Dismayed by low attendance and violence in a university student residence, two of the three local bodies that governed La Sapienza Nuova wanted change. They admired the Jesuits as educators and looked to them for help. They wanted to transform La Sapienza Nuova into a combination university student residence and Jesuit boarding school, with the latter model dominating, so they decided to invite the Jesuits to take control. But the college of doctors of law strongly objected. The papacy, the final arbiter, did not support the Jesuits because international political considerations mattered more than one more Jesuit boarding school. Since a simultaneous effort to give the Jesuits control over a student residence in Fermo failed in the same years, the message was clear. Whatever problems a university might have, local governance would continue.

13

JESUIT MATHEMATICIANS
IN THE UNIVERSITIES OF FERRARA,
PAVIA, AND SIENA

By the late seventeenth century the Society had quietly changed its mind about individual Jesuits teaching in civic universities. It decided that single Jesuits might accept professorships even though the Society would have no other role in a university. And some civic universities now welcomed individual Jesuits who became mathematics professors in three universities with strong traditions of civil governance. This happened because lay and ecclesiastical authorities wanted to add distinguished scholars and their expertise, especially in hydraulics, to the university and the city. The mathematics professorships led to a few more Jesuits teaching in universities, always as individuals. The rest of the professoriate and their allies sometimes objected, but they could not stop the appointments.

The Jesuit School in Ferrara

When the last duke of the direct line of the Este family died without an heir in 1597, the Duchy of Ferrara devolved to the papacy because the Este had ruled as papal vicars. Pope Clement VIII took formal possession in the summer of 1598. Cardinal legates then ruled the city and duchy on behalf of the papacy. The papacy left in place the city government whose major organ was the council of one hundred dominated by the local nobility. Although it had considerable local authority, the cardinal legate made the most important decisions.

Because of the political uncertainty and change of rulers the university declined to a handful of professors between 1596 and 1602.[1] Clement VIII

---

1. *I maestri di Ferrara* 1991, 49.

revived it in June and August 1602. He confirmed and expanded the university's privileges, which included many tax breaks and benefits to professors and students. He put the university on a sound financial basis by instituting a salt tax whose income went to the university, and he reorganized its governance. The council of one hundred granted authority over the university to its nine-member executive body, called Savi. They were joined by two Riformatori dello Studio, who were professors of noble rank, one from law, the other from arts and medicine, chosen by the professoriate. These eleven men constituted a Congregazione dello Studio which oversaw the university. After Clement VIII's restoration, the university resumed its position as a second-tier Italian university in which medicine played a prominent role.[2] On the other hand, local men of noble rank and little scholarly distinction filled most faculty positions in the seventeenth and eighteenth centuries.

The Jesuits founded a college and a school in Ferrara in 1551. Growth was slow because of personnel and political difficulties as well as a natural disaster. In 1556 there were a dozen Jesuits in Ferrara and the school offered three lower school classes which enrolled about 90 students.[3] In August 1569, there were eighteen Jesuits in Ferrara, one of whom was a German who heard the confessions of Duchess Barbara Habsburg Este (1539–1572, married 1565), and a school with two classes: grammar and humanities. But then an earthquake devastated Ferrara on the night of November 16–17, 1570.[4] The college was forced to close its school in 1572; in 1579 the college could offer only a twice-weekly cases of conscience lecture.[5] But the Jesuits recovered. In 1600 there were twenty Jesuits in the college and the school offered classes in rhetoric, upper grammar, and lower grammar.[6]

In 1609 the university appointed the Jesuit Silvestro Muzio (Macerata 1572–1647 Ferrara) to teach humanities in the university. The appointment was made because the university was short of humanists; except for a Greek who taught Greek, the university had lacked a humanist since 1596.[7] It went

2. Visconti 1950, 74–75; Fiocca and Pepe 1985, 127; *I maestri di Ferrara* 1991, 49–50; Gardi 1995, 311–13. For the history of the University of Ferrara as a whole, Borsetti 1735 remains useful. Recent scholarship includes *La rinascita del sapere* 1991; Grendler 2002, 199–206, and index; and the studies in *Annali di Storia delle Università italiane* 8 (2004).

3. Lukács 1960–1961, part 1, 242.

4. For a visitation report of August 19, 1569, see ARSI, Veneta 94, f. 47r–v. For the larger story, see Tacchi Venturi 1951b, 393–99; Scaduto 1974, 406–15; Angelozzi 1991, 355–57; Scaduto 1992, 298–305, 350–53.

5. ARSI, Veneta 105 I, f. 60r; and Grendler 2004a, 495–96.

6. ARSI, Veneta 37, f. 254r–v.

7. Chiellini 1991, 238; *I maestri di Ferrara* 1991, 40–52, 162, 187.

to Muzio because the cardinal legate had a high opinion of the Jesuits. This was Orazio Spinola (1564–1616, cardinal from 1606), from a famous Genoese noble family. He studied in Jesuit schools in Genoa and Rome, and undoubtedly remembered them fondly.[8] Muzio was the sole Latin humanities professor until 1611 when another humanist, a layman, joined the university. He continued to teach at the University of Ferrara through the academic year 1617–1618.[9] Muzio's appointment was similar to those at the universities of Macerata and Perugia, where Jesuits filled humanistic professorships for a few years.

Although Muzio stopped teaching in the university in 1618, he continued to exert some influence. He was the confessor of the next cardinal legate, Giacomo Serra (1570–1623, cardinal from 1611), legate from 1615 to 1623.[10] Serra also favored the Jesuits. In 1616 he created a small boarding school for noble youths in Ferrara and gave direction of it to the Jesuits. To cover its initial expenses he took 400 scudi from the income designated for the university and applied it to the boarding school. However, the school failed after a few years, as did two subsequent attempts in the seventeenth and eighteenth centuries.[11]

The Jesuit school grew and then retrenched in the seventeenth century. In the academic year 1621–1622 it had five classes: cases of conscience, rhetoric, humanities, upper grammar, and lower grammar, with a total enrollment of 219.[12] Not until 1637 did the Ferrara school inaugurate the philosophical cycle of logic, natural philosophy, and metaphysics.[13] In 1642 the Ferrara school taught six classes: cases of conscience, philosophy, rhetoric, humanities, upper grammar, and lower grammar.[14] However, in 1649 the Ferrara school dropped the philosophical cycle and reverted to teaching only the lower school curriculum plus cases.[15] It is likely that the Ferrara Jesuits did this and refrained from teaching scholastic theology in order to avoid conflict with the university. In 1660 the Ferrara school offered cases of conscience and six lower school classes, two of them on the rudiments of

8. Spinola became vice-legate of Ferrara in 1605 and legate in 1606, and served until December 1615. *Le istruzioni generali di Paolo V* 2003, 1:489–90n30.

9. Borsetti 1735, 2:227–28; Sommervogel 1960, 5:1483; Chiellini 1991, 238; *I maestri di Ferrara* 1991, 52–56, 175, 254; and Baldini 2000, 197, 209. Muzio's only known publication was a book of epigrams.

10. *Le istruzioni generali di Paolo V* 2003, 1:222–24, 490n30.

11. Angelozzi 1991, 361–64.   12. ARSI, Veneta 39 I, f. 58r.

13. Baldini 1992, 414 and 445n43.

14. ARSI, Veneta 39 II, f. 462r. The number and distribution of classes were the same in 1646, at which time the total enrollment was 298 students. ARSI, Veneta 125, f. 10v.

15. Baldini 1992, 416.

Latin grammar taught by secular priests hired and paid by the Jesuits. The total enrollment was 326 students.[16]

The Jesuits, their school, and students suffered some harassment and vandalism. In 1662 the cardinal legate issued a proclamation threatening punishment for anyone who molested students at the Jesuit school by writing on its walls, breaking windows, throwing mud at the school building or the Jesuit residence, or posting pasquinades and libelous placards against any Jesuit priest, teacher, or student.[17]

Managing the Waters: Jesuit Mathematicians in the University of Ferrara

In 1675 a Jesuit was given the professorship of mathematics in the University of Ferrara. Jesuits then filled the mathematics position with one interruption until 1771.

On October 31, 1675, cardinal legate Sigismondo Chigi (1649–1678, cardinal from 1667) issued an edict ordering the establishment of a "lettura privata" (private lectureship) of mathematics in the Jesuit college.[18] Its purpose was to train local men in "regolamenti di acque, costruzioni di Arginature" (the management of waters and construction of dikes) for the benefit of the city. The lecturer was expected to teach daily from November until the end of July, a month longer than the customary university year. He would receive 100 scudi annually, the money coming from a higher tax on guns. The cardinal legate would choose the lecturer from a list prepared by the city magistracy that oversaw the university. Most significant, the lectureship would be located in the Jesuit college.[19] That made it obvious that it would go to a Jesuit. Chigi chose the able Jesuit mathematician Francesco Lana Terzi (Brescia 1631–1687 Brescia).[20] And in a surprise development, Lana Terzi immediately became the professor of mathematics at the University of Ferrara.[21]

16. ARSI, Veneta 97 I, f. 142v (September 15, 1660). See also Angelozzi 1991, 360.

17. Angelozzi 1991, 360–61.

18. For Chigi's biography see Pastor 1891–1953, 31:322, 344; and Chigi, Sigismondo, in The Cardinals of the Holy Roman Church, www2.fiu.edu/~mirandas/bios1667-ii.htm#Chigi.

19. The edict and Clement IX's letter of confirmation of December 16, 1676, are found in Borsetti 1735, 1:308–13 (quotation at 310). See also Visconti 1950, 92–93; Fiocca and Pepe 1985, 137; and Fiocca 1991, 367–69.

20. For biographical and bibliographical information see Sommervogel 1960, 4:1441–45; Fiocca and Pepe 1985, 144–45, 164–65; Zanfredini 2001d; Baldini 2002, 312n201; and Fiocca 2011, 302–5.

21. Borsetti 1735, 1:308, 2:253; *I maestri di Ferrara* 1991, 76.

The appointment was made because the Duchy of Ferrara had several pressing water issues, beginning with the Po River. It was both a major commercial artery and the border between the Republic of Venice and the Duchy of Ferrara, and after 1598, the papal state. It regularly overflowed its banks and subdivided into several channels as it approached the Adriatic Sea. The Po delta was shifting north, thus threatening to fill with silt the shallow Venetian lagoon near Chioggia.

The Venetian Republic had taken unilateral action to prevent this. Between 1600 and 1604 it created the *Taglio di Po* (Po cutoff), a 7,000 meter waterway that diverted the main channel of the Po River southeast to link with another channel. The Taglio di Po saved the Chioggia lagoon, but it poured water into the Duchy of Ferrara, flooding farmland and creating more marshes. The Taglio di Po was not the last act, as both the Republic of Venice on one side, and the papacy and the Duchy of Ferrara on the other, tried to manage the Po, each to its advantage, for another century.

The second problem was the Reno River, which marked much of the boundary between the Duchy of Ferrara and the Romagna. It also flooded and needed embankments. Third, the Ferrara plain southeast of the city and the extensive Comácchio marshes near the Adriatic Sea (south of Ferrara and north of Ravenna) were low, water-soaked areas. Here the need was land reclamation. As was the norm in Italian water management issues, then and now, there were many plans, endless disagreements, and little action.

The 1675 appointment to the University of Ferrara was not a complete surprise, as Jesuit mathematicians had counseled Ferrara and the papacy in the past. In late 1598, before the Venetian Po cutoff project began, Pope Clement VIII consulted several water management experts, including two Jesuits, about Ferrara's issues; these discussions continued through 1608 and probably beyond.[22] In 1624 the city of Ferrara asked the superior general of the Jesuits, Muzio Vitelleschi, to lend them the services of Father Niccolò Cabeo (Ferrara 1586–1650 Genoa) to help on water issues.[23] The perennially cautious Vitelleschi turned down the request. If Cabeo helped Ferrara and the papacy manage the waters, this might create ill will against the Society, he wrote. Past experience had demonstrated that when Jesuits became involved in controversial matters in which it was impossible to satisfy all parties, the result was anger against the Society.[24] Vitelleschi may have had in mind difficulties with the Venetian government.

22. Baldini 2000, 111–28.
23. For Cabeo see Sommervogel 1960, 2:483; Ingegno 1972; Bedini and Mellinato 2001; Baldini 2002, 296n52; Fiocca 2002a, 344–46; Fiocca 2002b, 340–41; and *Giambattista Riccioli* 2002, index.
24. Fiocca 2002a, 344–45; and Fiocca 2002b, 340–41.

The general was ignored. Cabeo taught logic at the Ferrara Jesuit college in the academic year 1622–1623.[25] Most important, he prepared a memorandum on the Po and Reno rivers which he presented to the city of Ferrara in 1624. Cabeo spent the years 1627 to 1630 and 1632 to 1639 teaching cases of conscience in Ferrara, while dispensing advice and writing about flood control. In July 1634 he participated in a water management meeting there.[26] Thus, although the Jesuit school in Ferrara did not offer a mathematics class, the highly skilled Cabeo was advising the city on water issues.

Lana Terzi was the sole professor of mathematics at the University of Ferrara in 1675. He replaced Gaspare Carra (d. 1684) who had taught mathematics at the university the previous year. A generalist with no particular expertise in mathematics, Carra taught medical theory, natural philosophy, logic, surgery, moral/political philosophy, metaphysics, and mathematics over the years, and published nothing.[27] He typified mathematical instruction at the University of Ferrara.[28] Lana Terzi was a major improvement, and the appointment benefited both sides. The city, legate, and papacy had a skilled mathematician to train hydraulics engineers and give advice on taming the waters. The Society acquired a professorship in a civic university, more income, increased visibility, and much goodwill.

A decree of March 4, 1679, from the Magistrato dei Savi, the executive organ of the council of one hundred, added further requirements. The mathematics lecturer should concentrate on the first six books of Euclid, and he should lecture in Italian. Anyone who wished to take the examination in order to earn accreditation as an expert in hydraulics had to attend his lectures.[29] If this decree was implemented as written, the Jesuit mathematician delivered two lectures daily, one in Latin for university and Jesuit students, and the other in Italian for men without Latin seeking accreditation. However, given that diagrams, equations, and theorems were the essential components of mathematics instruction, and that the number of students was undoubtedly small, the Jesuit lecturer may have used a combination of Latin and Italian according to the skills of the students. In that case, a single daily lecture for all students might have sufficed.

Once established in the university, the Jesuit mathematicians stayed.

25. Baldini 1992, 415 and 455n29.

26. Fiocca 2002a, 345–49; Fiocca 2002b, 340–54; Fiocca 2011, 296–98.

27. Fiocca and Pepe 1985, 161; I maestri di Ferrara 1991, 72–78, 210.

28. See the rolls for 1672 to 1674 in I maestri di Ferrara 1991, 74–75. Girolamo Brasovola (1628–1705) taught mathematics from 1659 to 1672. He was another generalist who taught medical theory, mathematics, moral and political philosophy, and logic at Ferrara. Fiocca and Pepe 1985, 161, 164; I maestri di Ferrara 1991, 68–81, 203.

29. Borsetti 1735, 1:312–13; Fiocca and Pepe 1985, 138.

Lana Terzi held the position from 1675 to 1679. After a hiatus of a year, Agostino Fabri or Fabbri (d. 1730), a layman, taught for eight years, 1680 to 1688, then departed in order to direct the construction of embankments to protect Cremona against the Po.[30] From 1688 to 1771 four more Jesuits filled the mathematics professorship. Giovanni Magrini (or Macrini, Imola 1632–1698 Ferrara), taught from 1688 to 1697. Ippolito Palmieri (Ferrara 1658–1734 Ferrara) filled the professorship from 1698 to 1734. Ippolito Sivieri (Ferrara 1697–1780 Ferrara) taught from 1735 to 1760, and Girolamo Prandini (Mirandola 1724–after 1771) taught from 1760 to 1771.[31] They taught at the Jesuit college rather than in the university building.[32]

The Jesuit professors of mathematics taught a three-year cycle of texts and techniques mandated by university statutes and tradition. This was typical of Italian universities. In the first year the mathematician was expected to teach Euclid's *Elements*, with a focus on the first six books covering principles, theorems, triangles, and more. In the second he taught the theory of planets, that is, the motions of celestial bodies. It was Ptolemaic astronomy based on several traditional texts including an anonymous *Theorica Planetarum* from the thirteenth century, the *Theoricae novae planetarum* of George Puerbach (1423–1461), and the *Epitome* of the *Almagest* of Ptolemy of Egypt (ca. 100–170 A.D.) of Regiomontanus (Johannes Müller of Königsberg, 1436–1476). In the third year he was required to lecture on the *De sphaera* of Johannes de Sacrobosco, usually published with newer and better astronomical tables.[33] The goal was to teach the students to deal with calendar issues. Although the texts were traditional, commentaries by recent mathematicians were as important as the texts themselves. The three-year cycle also left a good deal of time for other topics, such as hydraulics.

Jesuit mathematicians moved easily into the University of Ferrara because the university curriculum was simply an expanded version of what Jesuits taught in their own schools.[34] According to the Ratio Studiorum, a Jesuit mathematician should teach the *Elements* of Euclid, "something about

30. Borsetti 1735, 1:318, 2:254, 255; Fiocca and Pepe 1985, 145, 159, 164; *I maestri di Ferrara* 1991, 77–80, 219.

31. Borsetti 1735, 2:261, 266, 274; *I maestri di Ferrara* 1991, 243, 257, 265. For biographical and bibliographical information on Magrini, see Sommervogel 1960, 5:266, 9:626, and Baldini 2002, 301n106; for Palmieri, see Sommervogel 1960, 6:156, and Baldini 2002, 313n211; for Sivieri, see Sommervogel 1960, 7:1264, 12:1225, and Baldini 2002, 315n215; for Prandini, see Baldini 2002, 308n182.

32. Fiocca and Pepe 1985, 138.

33. Fiocca and Pepe 1985, 139–43, 158–60. All of this was standard mathematical fare in Italian universites. See Grendler 2002, 408–29.

34. For example, see what the Jesuit mathematician taught at the civic-Jesuit University of Mantua from 1625 through 1629. Grendler 2009b, 200–201.

geography or the *Sphere*" (of Sacrobosco), or about those things that are usually of interest," in a one-year course.[35] "Things ... of interest" opened up many possibilities including hydraulics. The Jesuits initially had no expertise in hydraulics, but over time a group of talented Jesuit mathematicians in the Province of Venice, to which the Ferrara college belonged, developed considerable expertise and taught it.[36] And from 1653 to 1655 a Jesuit taught hydraulics in the Roman College.[37]

Only in one area might critics have faulted Jesuit professors of mathematics: they did not teach heliocentrism as physical reality, although some used the book of Copernicus as a useful mathematical fiction that could explain phenomena. What Jesuit mathematicians privately thought about heliocentrism is often difficult to determine.[38] On the other hand, not all lay university mathematicians and astronomers accepted and taught heliocentrism either. Jesuit mathematicians did not teach astrology or cast horoscopes. Neither did most non-Jesuit professors of mathematics in the seventeenth and eighteenth centuries, because they had abandoned these offshoots of astronomy.

As expected, the Jesuits who taught at the University of Ferrara studied water management issues and advised the legate and city. They also engaged in many other scientific and mathematical projects. Lana Terzi, possibly the most distinguished and versatile, conducted experiments in an effort to disprove Galileo Galilei's gravity theory. He was a member of the Royal Society of London, and he created a design for a flying boat. Magrini advised Ferrara on water issues, and the duke of Parma on building levees to hold back the Po River at Piacenza. The Ferrara city government charged Ippolito Sivieri with the maintenance and accuracy of the clock in the ducal palace. He also wrote about navigation, aqueducts, and water management, and worked on the port canal at Fano in the papal state.[39]

The teaching staff of the university opposed the conferral of the math-

---

35. *Ratio Studiorum* 2005, par. 239 (109).

36. For Jesuit scientific studies in the province of Venice, see Baldini 1992, 347–465; Baldini 2000, 171–211; and Baldini 2002, each with much more bibliography. On Jesuit science as a whole before 1773, start with the survey of Udias 2015, chaps. 1–5.

37. This was Paolo Casati (Piacenza 1617–1707 Parma) who taught hydraulics at the Roman College from 1653 to 1655. He published a book on hydrostatics in 1695. Sommervogel 1960, 2:799–803, 9:2; De Ferrari 1978; Colpo and Martínez de la Escalera 2001; Fiocca 2002a, 349; Gavagna 2002; and Gavagna 2011.

38. For example, see Casanovas 2002 and Dinis 2002 on the views of Giambattista Riccioli (Ferrara 1598–1671 Bologna), one of the ablest Jesuit scientists of the century.

39. Fiocca and Pepe 1985, 143–47, 164–65, 167; Fiocca 1991, 369–71; Fiocca 2002a; and Fiocca 2004, 109–13. Little is known about Prandini.

ematics professorship on the Jesuits. Speaking for them, the Riformatori dello Studio objected on the grounds that once the Jesuits gained entry into the university they would want more. The cardinal legate dismissed their complaint. The issue arose again a few years later. The Jesuit school added a teacher of scholastic theology in 1694 and asked that he be given a university professorship. Again the professors objected and this time the cardinal legate heard them. The Jesuit theologian did not become a university professor.[40]

More pointed opposition to the Jesuit mathematics professorship appeared in the early 1730s. An anonymous petitioner wanted the Jesuits dismissed from the mathematics professorship and replaced with a famous (but unnamed) mathematician who would be a better scholar and would defend the interests of the city more forcefully. The petitioner faulted the Jesuit mathematicians. First, they were not very learned and did not teach very well. They did not train excellent students for fear that a student might supplant them. They feared that a really excellent local student would win the support of his fellow citizens who would appoint him to replace the Jesuit mathematician. Second, the Jesuit mathematicians were members of a religious order whose superiors were in Rome. Consequently, they were either indifferent to Ferrara's interests or hesitated to represent them forcefully to her adversaries. The petitioner probably meant that a Jesuit would not defend Ferrara strongly enough in water management disputes with other states. A secular person would do better, the petitioner argued, because his contract to teach would be limited. Because most Italian university contracts were annual or biannual, he meant that a lay professor would represent the city forcefully in order to hold on to his job. The petition concluded: when Ippolito Palmieri dies, the city should take the 100 scudi paid for his teaching, add another 200 scudi, and hire a famous mathematician for the university.[41]

The fundamental objection was the familiar one that the Jesuits were foreigners who were not sufficiently loyal to the city. Although Palmieri was born and raised in Ferrara, the petitioner viewed him as a foreigner who would not defend Ferrara interests strongly because he was a Jesuit. The petition had no effect. Jesuit mathematicians continued to fill the professorship of mathematics until 1771.

The Jesuit college and school at Ferrara expanded. In 1746 there were 33 Jesuits in residence, and the school taught eight classes: scholastic theology,

40. Angelozzi 1991, 358–59.
41. Pepe 1995, 66–67, 72–74; and Fiocca 2004, 113. Because Palmieri died in 1734, it is assumed that the petition comes from the early 1730s.

cases of conscience, philosophy, mathematics, rhetoric, humanities, upper grammar, and lower grammar.[42] Ippolito Sivieri either lectured to university and Jesuit students separately or in a single class open to both.

Pope Clement XIV (Ganganelli 1705–1774, pope from 1769) was persuaded by some local men that the University of Ferrara had declined. So in 1771 he charged the president of the university, a papal appointee, with reforming the institution. This was Monsignor Giovanni Maria Riminaldi (1718–1789, cardinal from 1785), a veteran curialist from a Ferrara noble family. He immediately dismissed the Jesuit professor of mathematics and replaced him with a young layman. Over the next decade he imposed major changes in the curriculum, governance, and organization of the university.[43] Given the disaster of 1773, the loss of the Ferrara professorship did not loom large in Jesuit eyes.

Five Jesuits filled the professorship of mathematics from 1675 to 1771 with the exception of a nine-year gap. The city and the papal legate appointed them because they valued their expertise in hydraulics. The Jesuits did not disappoint. They were better mathematicians than their lay predecessors. They taught hydraulics, advised the city on water management, and developed other scientific and technological projects. But their success did not lead to more Jesuits in the university, and lay professors opposed the Jesuit mathematicians, because they wanted local men to fill the positions. They saw the Jesuits as outsiders who did not have the best interests of Ferrara at heart, even though two of the five Jesuit mathematicians were born and raised in Ferrara.

The University of Pavia

The Jesuits came to Pavia late and the growth of their school was slow. Nevertheless, a handful of Jesuits taught in the University of Pavia in the eighteenth century.

The Barnabites and Somaschans arrived in Pavia before the Jesuits and had larger presences in the city for a long time. The Barnabites (Clerics Regular of St. Paul), founded in nearby Milan in 1530 (papal approval 1533), arrived in Pavia in 1557 and established a school for their own members. They created a congregation of lay people to teach Christian doctrine and another for nobles that enrolled the most important men of the city. One of

42. ARSI, Veneta 59, f. 330r.
43. Visconti 1950, 114–41; Fiocca and Pepe 1985, 147–48; Fiocca 2004, 114–15. For Riminaldi see The Cardinals of the Holy Roman Church, www2.fiu.edu/~mirandas/bios/1785.html#Riminaldi.

the original band of Barnabites in Pavia was the charismatic St. Alessandro Sauli (1534–1592, canonized in 1904), who won much favorable attention for the Barnabites from the university community during his decade in Pavia, 1557 to 1567. Among his accomplishments was the foundation of an academy in which university students met to study theological and philosophical texts, to dispute, and to lecture.[44] The Somaschans (Clerics Regular of Somascha, a small town near Bergamo), founded in 1534, established a school in Pavia in 1567 in which they taught theology, philosophy, and rhetoric, and added a boarding school for boys in 1601. They also taught the students of the episcopal seminary, for which they received payment.[45]

The Jesuits came later. A handful of Jesuits established a house in Pavia in 1601. A house, also called residence, was an initial Jesuit establishment that might become a college.[46] The Pavia Jesuits opened a school with two classes, grammar and rhetoric, in 1615. They added a boarding school for noble boys between ten and fifteen years of age in the academic year 1616–1617, but it lasted only a few years. In 1617 the Jesuits still numbered only eight and faced significant obstacles. The church, which was not for their exclusive use, was small, uncomfortable, and ugly; the contiguous building in which they lived and taught was old and needed extensive repairs. The location was worse. Building and church were on the Strada Nuova, the main north-south artery of the city, and across the street from the arcade leading into the medical lecture rooms of the large university building. University students regularly harassed those who came to the Jesuit school.[47] By contrast, both the Barnabites and Somaschans had their own churches and buildings in quiet parts of the city. The Jesuits searched for decades for a better church, building, and location.

They persevered. In 1631 the superior general of the Jesuits elevated the Pavia house to a college.[48] A college had to have a suitable building in which the Jesuits could live, and teach if necessary, a church owned by the

---

44. For the Barnabites at Pavia and Sauli, see Premoli 1913, 153–64, 173–74, 208–10; Bascapé 1931, 85–101; Boffito 1960; Negruzzo 1995a, 80–88; Negruzzo 1995b, 125–32; and Negruzzo 2001, 212–27.

45. Negruzzo 1995a, 63–80; and Negruzzo 2001, 185–212.

46. That was the de facto meaning of house or residence at this time. Ignatius Loyola originally viewed houses as places without a fixed income in which Jesuits lived and begged for their needs and thereby attained a higher degree of spiritual perfection. Over time he and his successors emphasized colleges with schools, and house took on a new meaning. I am grateful to John O'Malley for this information.

47. For the early history of the college at Pavia see Fantini 1989, 329–37; and Negruzzo 1995a, 88–98; and Negruzzo 2001, 227–30.

48. Fantini 1989, 335.

Jesuits or set aside for their exclusive use, and secure financial support, preferably an endowment.[49]

But the college's financial support was not secure. The bishop, who had provided financial and other support since 1617, died in 1637, and his successor did not help. Reduced income forced the Jesuits to close their school around 1640—which galvanized supporters into action. A large donation enabled the school to reopen in 1646, while leading citizens urged the city government to help. In 1647 the city and the Jesuits made a long-term agreement. The city would provide funding to support a school of four classes: rhetoric, humanities, upper grammar, and lower grammar.[50] The Jesuit school had three classes in 1649 and reached the required four in 1655.[51] In 1661 the Jesuit school of four classes had an enrollment of 145, a modest figure by Jesuit standards.[52] The Jesuit contingent remained quite small at nine in 1649. By contrast, in 1650 there were twenty-six Somaschans in Pavia, and probably more Barnabites than Jesuits.[53]

The Jesuits finally secured a church and building in a good part of town. In 1668 the papacy suppressed the Lombardy congregation of the Hieronymites (Hermits of St. Jerome) because of declining membership. In 1670 the pope transferred to the Jesuits their handsome church and convent located in a neighborhood dotted with noble and merchant residences far from the Strada Nuova. The Jesuits were also given the charge of teaching the students at the episcopal seminary, previously entrusted to the Somaschans, for which they received 200 lire annually. The new location made a big difference. The school grew to six classes with a total enrollment of 370 students in 1695: cases of conscience 30, philosophy 40, rhetoric 50, humanities 70, upper grammar 120, and lower grammar 60. The Jesuit contingent rose to twelve or thirteen in the early eighteenth century.[54] After nearly a century of struggle the Pavia Jesuits had a small but stable college and a school with good enrollment.

This did not mean acceptance by the University of Pavia (founded in

---

49. See *For Matters of Greater Moment* 1994, 86–87, Congregation 1 (1558), Decree 73 after the election. However, the decree also states that each Jesuit college had to have fourteen Jesuits, a provision often ignored.

50. Fantini 1989, 337–38; Negruzzo 2001, 231.

51. ARSI, Mediolanensis 2, f. 120v (1649); Fantini 1989, 338 (1655).

52. ARSI, Mediolanensis 73, f. 170r (1661); and Negruzzo 2001, 232, with the same information.

53. Negruzzo 2001, 199, 221–23.

54. Fantini 1989, 338–39. See also ARSI Mediolanensis 4, f. 174r, which lists eleven Jesuits at Pavia in 1696, and a school of five classes: cases of conscience, philosophy, rhetoric, humanities and grammar. There may also have been a lower grammar class taught by a non-Jesuit.

1361) which initially turned a cold shoulder to all three Catholic Reform orders.[55] Like most Italian universities, Pavia became very provincial in the seventeenth century. Laymen from Pavia, Milan, and the rest of Lombardy, plus a limited number of medieval order clergymen, filled the professorships. Nevertheless, coldness toward the Catholic Reform orders began to change. The Senate of Milan, which governed the University of Pavia, appointed a Somaschan to teach philosophy in 1689, and another one to teach Greek and Latin rhetoric in 1692.[56]

Then on January 24, 1699, the Senate of Milan appointed the Jesuit Girolamo Saccheri (San Remo 1667–1733 Milan) to fill the mathematics professorship at the University of Pavia.[57] Saccheri was a distinguished scholar and the friend of prominent Milanese senators. He had studied philosophy, mathematics, and theology at the Jesuit Brera school in Milan, at which time he published a book (1693) that solved a number of geometry problems.[58] His mathematics teacher at the Brera school was Father Tommaso Ceva (Milan 1648–1737 Milan). From a wealthy Milanese family, Ceva taught mathematics and rhetoric at the Brera school for thirty-eight years while publishing many works of mathematics and religious poetry. Tommaso Ceva introduced Saccheri to his brother Giovanni (Milan 1647–1734 Mantua), a layman. Giovanni Ceva studied at the University of Pisa where he came under the influence of the works of Galileo Galilei. Beginning about 1686 he served the duke of Mantua as mathematician, hydraulics engineer, and monetary expert, and published several works on geometry and water flow control.[59]

Saccheri's accomplishments and association with Tommaso and Giovanni Ceva gained him entry into an academy of Milanese noblemen with mathematical and scientific interests. There he became a close friend of two prominent Milanese senators, Filippo Archinto (1644–1712) and his son Carlo (1670–1732).[60] Father and son had prior associations with the Jesuits: Carlo had studied with Tommaso Ceva at the Brera school and then at the Jesuit-dominated University of Ingolstadt.

Saccheri's accomplishments and a series of fortuitous events brought him into the University of Pavia. He began to teach philosophy at the Jesuit

55. For the University of Pavia see Grendler 2002, 82–93, with additional bibliography.

56. *Memorie di Pavia* 1970, part 1, 181.

57. Baldini 1982b, 876–77n18. *Memorie di Pavia* 1970, part 1, 151, gives the beginning of his teaching as 1697, which is incorrect.

58. For short biographies of Saccheri with much bibliography, see Sommervogel 1960, 7:760–62; Struik 1981; Fantini 1989, 345n62; Corradino 2001; and Capelo 2002, 125–31.

59. For Giovanni Ceva, see U. Baldini 1980 and Oettel 1981a; for Tommaso Ceva, see Gronda 1980, Oettel 1981b, and Guidetti 2001.

60. See Raponi 1961a; Raponi 1961b; and Baldini 1982a, 510–12.

school in Turin, also part of the Jesuit Province of Milan, in 1694. There he wrote *Logica demonstrativa* (published in 1697 with a dedication to Carlo Archinto), a book that was far ahead of its time.[61] In 1697 the professor of mathematics at the University of Pavia died. In that same year the Jesuits moved Saccheri from Turin to Pavia to teach philosophy. Then on January 24, 1699, the Senate of Milan appointed Saccheri professor of mathematics.[62] The sequence of events fitted together neatly enough to suggest some planning. When the incumbent mathematician died, perhaps the Archintos decided to try to appoint Saccheri in his place. The Jesuit provincial superior, who also lived in Milan, helped by transferring Saccheri from Turin, a major Jesuit college and school, to Pavia, a small college and school. And there is little doubt that Filippo and Carlo Archinto, both influential members of the Senate, persuaded it to appoint Saccheri to the University of Pavia.[63]

Saccheri taught mathematics at the University of Pavia from 1699 until his death. He was accomplished in hydraulics, arithmetic, algebra, geometry, and mechanics. He published a book on Aristotelian statics in 1708 and a study on non-Euclidian geometry that anticipated future developments in 1733. In addition to his lectures, Saccheri led wide-ranging seminars. He represented the city of Pavia in a meeting to discuss a hydraulics project involving the Po River. He also taught scholastic theology in the Jesuit college part of the time.[64]

As at Ferrara, after the first appointment the Jesuits dominated the mathematics professorship. When Saccheri became ill and died on October 25, 1733, the Senate appointed Father Giulio Brusatti (Novara 1692–1743 Pavia), extraordinary professor of logic for the academic year 1732–1733, then professor of mathematics in 1733. He filled the position until his death. Because few of his papers have survived, very little is known about his skills. He did make long trips to France, England, and Holland, possibly to visit other mathematicians.[65] Giovanni Antonio Lecchi (Milan 1702–1776

61. There are three recent (1980, 2011, and 2012) editions, two of them with Italian translations.

62. In 1541 Charles V promulgated the *Constitutiones Domini Mediolanensis* which proclaimed that the Senate of Milan, dominated by nobles, was the highest administrative and jurisdictional organ of the state, and that it had exclusive and total authority over the University of Pavia. Spanish governors of Milan more than once tried to remove the university from the Senate's control, but without success. Zorzoli 1995, 441, 446–48; and Negruzzo 2003, 53–54, 64.

63. That the Archintos exercised their influence in the Senate is the surmise of Baldini 1982a, 510n10, with which I concur. The rest is my conjecture.

64. See the references in note 58 plus Baldini 1982b, 875–78. His *Euclides vindicatus* (1733) has been reprinted in modern Latin editions with Italian and English translations.

65. *Memorie di Pavia* 1970, part 1, 151, 183; Fantini 1989, 345n62; Baldini 1982a, 512; Baldini 1982b, 878.

Milan), a Jesuit known for his publications in hydrostatics, may have substituted for him in the academic year 1734–1735.[66] After Brusati's death, an Olivetan (Benedictine Congregation of Our Lady of Mount Olivet) held the professorship of mathematics until 1758, after which it remained vacant until 1764. In that year Ruđer Josip Bošković (Ruggero Giuseppe Boscovich in Italian, Dubrovnik 1711–1787 Milan), the most famous Jesuit mathematician and polymath of the century, was appointed to the professorship of mathematics. He held it until 1768, although he was often absent.[67] After the suppression of the Society and reorganization of the university, a former Jesuit held the mathematics professorship, renamed geometry and general physics, from 1773 to 1778.[68]

The breakthrough in mathematics opened the door for three more Jesuits to fill professorships in other disciplines in the eighteenth century. In or about 1704 Francesco Gambarana (Pavia 1669–1739 Pavia) began to guide groups of university students through the Spiritual Exercises in three-day retreats held in a *villetta* (little villa) in or near the walls of the city. He also served as rector of the Pavia college from 1713 to 1716. The Milanese Senate appointed him professor of Greek and Latin oratory in 1706, a position that he held until 1726. The Pavian Jesuits believed that the Senate appointed Gambarana in the expectation that he would teach piety as well as Greek and Latin.[69]

Gambarana was succeeded by another Jesuit, Luigi Rovarino (Pavia 1694–1769 Pavia), who held the professorship of Latin and Greek oratory from 1726 to 1768.[70] Francesco Bazzetta (Milan 1709–after 1773) came to the Jesuit college in 1741 and for many years was the moderator of the Jesuit congregation of nobles and won the friendship of local notables. In 1751 the

66. Lecchi taught mathematics at the Brera school from 1738 to 1760, then mathematics and hydraulics from 1760 to 1773. He wrote many works on hydraulic engineering, advised on Po and Reno River projects, and was named imperial mathematician by the Austrian government in 1759, for which he received an annual pension of 300 florins. Sommervogel 1960, 4:1633–38; Fantini 1989, 345n62; Zanfredini 2001e; and Brambilla 2005.

67. *Memorie di Pavia* 1970, part 1, 441, 447–48, and part 3, 45–59; Casini 1971; Marković 1981; and Strilič 2001. There is an enormous bibliography on his scientific works.

68. This was Francesco Luino or Luini (Luino near Milan 1740–1792 Milan or Mantua). *Memorie di Pavia* 1970, part 1, 441; and especially Baldini 2006a. As a Jesuit he both studied and taught mathematics at the Brera college in Milan before the suppression and the appointment to the University of Pavia. However, the Milanese government removed him from his professorship because of an accusation of materialism. Luino published several mathematical works.

69. *Memorie di Pavia* 1970, part 1, 182; Fantini 1989, 345n62, 346n65, 347–48, who states that he began teaching rhetoric at the university in 1704. See also ARSI, Mediolanensis 78, f. 76v, annual letter of 1710.

70. *Memorie di Pavia* 1970, part 1, 183; Fantini 1989, 345n62.

Milanese Senate appointed him professor of scholastic theology, a position he held until the suppression. From 1767 to 1771 he served on a committee of eight professors charged with ruling the university while the Austrian government discussed its restructuring. Both Rovarino and Bazzetta also led university students through the Spiritual Exercises.[71]

After the difficulties of the seventeenth century, the Jesuit school in Pavia flourished in the eighteenth. In 1770 it offered six classes with a total enrollment of 419 students: scholastic theology 15, cases of conscience 50, philosophy 70, rhetoric 70, humanities 84, and upper grammar 130. Although the Jesuits had no boarding school in Pavia, slightly more than half of their students came from outside Pavia, mostly from Lombardy.[72]

Even though Jesuits now taught at the University of Pavia, or perhaps for that reason, university students and Jesuit students still fought on the Strada Nuova.[73] In an incident of 1730, forty students of the Jesuit school entered the university classroom of Father Rovarino, where they scuffled with university students. This may have been retaliation for something that happened earlier.[74] But now the Jesuit students had the numerical advantage; there were two to three times as many of them as there were university students (see below).

The last appointment of a Jesuit (Boscovich in 1764) came just before the Senate of Milan lost control of the university. In the 1750s and 1760s Austria, which had taken control of Lombardy in the early eighteenth century, made it clear that it wanted Enlightenment-style changes at the University of Pavia. It charged the Senate of Milan and the university with drafting them. But Vienna decided that the Senate's reform proposals were not drastic enough. So it ended the Senate's governance of the university on November 24, 1765, and assumed direct control. It then appointed individuals and committees, some of them hostile to the Jesuits, to draft more radical proposals. Vienna approved a plan for the reform of the university in October 1771 and it was implemented by October 1773, a few months after the suppression of the Society of Jesus. More far-reaching reforms were imposed in the 1780s and 1790s.[75]

Seven Jesuits taught at the University of Pavia between 1699 and 1771, most of the time a mathematician and a humanist. This was a small number

---

71. *Memorie di Pavia* 1970, part 1, 17, 197; Fantini 1989, 345n62, 347–48; Zorzoli 1995, 463n186.

72. Fantini 1989, 349–53; Negruzzo 2001, 234, also gives the class sizes.

73. Zorzoli 1986, 65–66; Negruzzo 2001, 235–36.

74. Negruzzo 2001, 235–36, March 1, 1730. See also Fantini 1989, 333.

75. Vaccari 1957, 147–76; Guderzo 1982; Bernuzzi 1982; and Zorzoli 1995, 454–81.

in an average annual faculty complement of thirty professors.[76] The Jesuits had the same measure of success in entering the university as the Somaschans (six of whom taught in the university between 1689 and 1796) and more than the Barnabites (two between 1720 and 1762).[77]

Jesuit professors were given professorships at the University of Pavia for several reasons. Most important, the mathematicians were highly competent scholars. They also benefited from the friendship of Milanese senators with whom they shared an interest in mathematics and science. A related reason was that the Jesuits came from the same towns and stratum of society as senators and lay professors. About three-fourths of the professors at the University of Pavia came from Pavia, Milan, and the rest of Lombardy, usually from prominent families.[78] So did Jesuit professors: four of the seven were born in Pavia or Milan, sometimes into well-known families, and a fifth came from nearby Novara.[79] Francesco Gambarana, a count before he became a Jesuit, was a member of a Pavian patrician family that produced six men who taught law in the university between 1464 and 1763.[80] Francesco followed the family tradition, but as a Jesuit teaching the humanities. It was difficult to argue that Jesuits born in Pavia or Milan, who studied at the Jesuit school in Milan, taught in Jesuit schools in Pavia or elsewhere in the Jesuit Province of Milan, and enjoyed the friendship of Milanese senators, were outsiders not sufficiently loyal to the university and town. Finally, the Society made no demands on the University of Pavia. They were content that one or two of them should teach there.

But the Jesuits entered a much diminished university. The most obvious sign was enrollment. The University of Pavia had an estimated 600 to 700 students, about one-quarter of them non-Italians, in the fifteenth century. After the closures of the first half of the sixteenth century, enrollment rebounded to about 500 by the end of the century.[81] The next two centuries saw a huge decline. There were only about a hundred students in atten-

---

76. In 1700 there were 27 professors (9 law, 8 medicine, 1 mathematics, 6 philosophy and humanities, and 3 theology). *Memorie di Pavia* 1970, part 1, 94–95, 139–42, 151, 180–81, 195. In 1730 there were 31 professors (12 law, 6 medicine, 1 mathematics, 9 philosophy and humanities, and 3 theology). *Memorie di Pavia* 1970, part 1, 94–97, 143–44, 151, 182–83, 196.

77. *Memorie di Pavia* 1970, part 1, 153, 181–82, 196, 461, 465–68; and Negruzzo 2001, 211–12.

78. In the seventeenth century and the first half of the eighteenth, about half of the law professors were born in Pavia, and another quarter in the rest of Lombardy. Zorzoli 1986, 187–88. The fractions were about the same for the rest of the professoriate, as *Memorie di Pavia* 1970, part 1, demonstrates.

79. The exceptions were Saccheri, born in San Remo, and Boscovich.

80. *Memorie di Pavia* 1970, part 1, 56, 72, 79, 83, 91, 97; and Zorzoli 1986, 281.

81. Grendler 2002, 88, 93, 515. For the closures because of war, see Grendler 2011a, 24–30.

dance in 1715, and only 153 in 1766. About sixty percent came from Lombardy, some came from elsewhere in Italy and Sardinia, and a handful from the rest of Europe.[82]

A major reason for the drastic decline was that other institutions in Lombardy offered both degrees and instruction in law and medicine. Several local professional colleges of legists and physicians in Lombardy had the authority to confer degrees and offered limited instruction.[83] The same was true in other north Italian states.[84] The Jesuits were part of this network of institutions that undermined the University of Pavia. For example, in 1584 the college of physicians of Milan decreed that candidates for doctorates of medicine might count three years of philosophical studies at the Milan Jesuit school toward the seven years of philosophy and medicine courses required for the doctorate.[85] Of course, the candidate for a law degree who attended a course or two in *Institutes* offered by the professional college in a town in Lombardy could not hear multiple lectures in civil law, canon law, penal law, feudal law, and humanistic jurisprudence offered by the University of Pavia. The aspiring physician who attended Jesuit philosophy classes and heard one medical lecturer in his home town, then accompanied a local physician on his rounds, was not so well educated as the student who attended lectures on medical theory, practical medicine, clinical medicine, anatomy, surgery, and medical botany offered by the University of Pavia. But they could obtain doctorates without leaving home and at much less expense.

The University of Siena

The Jesuits came to Siena at a very difficult time for the city. Although an independent republic for centuries, Siena had been forced to accept a garrison of Spanish troops in 1530 during the Italian wars. When the brave Sienese drove them out in 1552, the Spanish responded with a siege that starved the city into surrender in 1555. Siena was now part of the Spanish Empire, and the people of the city were dispirited, diseased, poor, and hungry. The Spanish governor of the city, Cardinal Francisco de Mendoza y Bobadilla (1508–1566, cardinal from 1544), a longtime friend of Ignatius, asked him to establish a college for the spiritual consolation of the city. Although the Sienese were unable to offer much financial support, and Ignatius had declined many requests that offered better prospects, he agreed.

82. Zorzoli 1986, 73–74; repeated in Zorzoli 1995, 438–39.
83. Zorzoli 1986, 262–64; repeated in Zorzoli 1995, 453. See also Grendler 2002, 484–86.
84. Penuti 1998.
85. Rurale 1992, 145–46.

Four Jesuits arrived in April 1556. By June they had 50 students in a school located in rented quarters.[86]

The Jesuits had to deal with difficult and changing circumstances. Cardinal Mendoza y Bobadilla welcomed them, but offered little financial support and left in 1557. The Sienese were too poor to provide much aid and may not have been eager to assist a religious order brought into the city by a Spanish governor and led by a Spaniard. In July 1557 Spain sold Siena to Duke Cosimo I de' Medici, ruler of Florence from 1537 to 1574. Now the Jesuits had to beg financial aid from a reluctant Cosimo I and his mercurial consort, Eleonora of Toledo. The couple eventually provided limited help. Led by able and determined rectors, the college, named San Vigilio for its church, and school grew to eight Jesuits and 120 students in 1557, and ten Jesuits in 1563.[87]

The University of Siena suffered alongside the city. Founded in 1246 and with a strong reputation in law that attracted many German students, the university had about forty professors in the 1530s and 1540s. It stopped teaching during the siege and was very weak afterward. Although the Sienese were keen to restore the university to its former glory, Cosimo I blocked their efforts. He made Pisa the major university in Tuscany and limited Siena to the status of a small provincial institution. In the academic year 1563–1564 Siena had only fourteen ill-paid professors, plus a handful of unpaid lecturers in logic and *Institutes*.[88]

In November 1560 the professors and students of the impoverished university invited one of the Sienese Jesuits, Giovanni Maggiori (Locarno ca. 1536–1575 Rome), to teach a course on Aristotle's *Rhetoric*. General Laínez agreed. Maggiori began the course but then Pedro Ribadeneira, superior of the Province of Tuscany, ordered him to stop.[89] Ribadeneira feared that the university course would undermine the rhetoric course at the Jesuit college, probably also taught by Maggiori.[90] Another request had the same re-

86. Letters of Ignatius, written by Polanco, to Alfonso Salmerón and Cardinal Mendoza y Bobadilla, of March 16 and 17, 1556, Rome, in *Ignatius Epistolae* 1964–1968, 11:139, 143; Scaduto 1964, 227, 249; and Scaduto 1974, 371, 723.

87. Scaduto 1964, 249n16, 338, 580–81, 583; Scaduto 1974, 371–72.

88. Grendler 2002, 50–52, with further bibliography.

89. The Province of Tuscany was a short-term arrangement. Created in December 1560, it included Liguria, the Marches, and Tuscany, but not Rome and Lazio. In 1567 the Society divided Italy into four provinces: Rome, Lombardy, Naples, and Sicily. The new Province of Rome included the papal state and Tuscany. Scaduto 1964, 251. In 1568 the Province of Lombardy was divided into the provinces of Venice and Milan. The five- province organization did not change until the suppression, except when the Province of Sicily was divided into two from 1626 to 1633.

90. Scaduto 1968, 89; Scaduto 1964, 355–56, which refers to it as a course in Greek; and

sult. In the autumn of 1562 Giorgio Mercato (Palermo 1538–1583 Siracusa) was invited to teach at the university. This time Francisco de Borja, acting superior general of the Jesuits while Laínez was at the Council of Trent, said no.[91] Ribadeneira and Borja may have agreed with the First and Second General Congregations that Jesuits should not fill university professorships.[92] There were no more requests for Jesuit professors because Cosimo I's successors permitted the University of Siena to regain its former size and importance.[93]

Despite its difficult start, the Jesuit college at Siena became the largest and most important in Tuscany. It had 16 Jesuits and a school of two classes enrolling 70 students in 1574.[94] In 1600 it had grown to 27 Jesuits who taught four classes: cases of conscience, humanities, and two grammar classes. Its annual income was 1,250 florins.[95] In 1610 the Jesuits inaugurated thrice weekly lectures in cases of conscience and were very pleased that it attracted law students, merchants, and clergymen.[96] In 1649 the number of Jesuits had declined to 20. But the school now offered six classes: scholastic theology, philosophy, cases of consciences, humanities, and two grammar classes. Its annual income was 1,744 florins.[97]

The creation of a noble boarding school greatly increased the importance of the Jesuits in the eyes of the city, the university, the ruler, and the rest of Italy. Celso Tolomei (1572–1634), a Sienese noble, left a large bequest to establish a boarding school for Sienese noble boys. He entrusted the Monte dei Paschi bank with managing the funds, which it did under the supervision of the Balìa, the supreme city magistracy, until the bequest had increased enough to support a school. Thanks in part to additional funding from Grand Duke Cosimo III (1642–1723, r. from 1670), the legacy reached the needed sum. The Collegio Tolomei, as it was named, opened its doors on November 25, 1676. Ten noble boys from Siena, Florence, Lucca, Fermo, and Genoa enrolled.[98]

Scaduto 1974, 372–73. The different views of Laínez and Ribadeneira demonstrate, once again, that at this time the Italian Jesuits were divided on whether individual Jesuits should teach in civic universities. It is also interesting that Laínez did not overrule Ribadeneira, who was a highly respected figure in the Society despite his youth.

91. Scaduto 1964, 356; Scaduto 1968, 98.

92. See chap. 12, "The Jesuits and the University in the 1550s and 1560s."

93. Grendler 2002, 52–55, with additional bibliography.

94. ARSI, Roma 126b I, f. 79v; repeated in Grendler 2004a, 488.

95. ARSI, Roma 54, f. 27r; and Lukács 1960–1961, part 2, 106.

96. ARSI, Roma 130 I, f. 90r.

97. ARSI, Roma 59, f. 85r.

98. Gigli 1723, 450–52; Pendola 1852, 7–9, and appendix p. iii; Catoni 1991, 56; Catoni 1996, 81–84; *L'istituto di Celso Tolomei* 2000, 163; and P. Turrini 2000, 17–19.

The rules of the Collegio Tolomei closely followed Tolomei's instructions. The Jesuits exercised academic, spiritual, and supervisory direction. The boarders had to be at least twelve years of age, to have some knowledge of Latin upon entry, and were charged 2 scudi a month, later increased. Tolomei family members were given first preference in admissions, followed by Sienese noble boys, then non-Sienese noble boys, who were charged 4 scudi. Siblings and family members of current boarders also received preference. The students attended academic classes at the Jesuit school at San Vigilio, located practically across the street from the Collegio Tolomei, while additional teachers for riding, drawing, military and civil architecture, dancing, music, and fencing were hired. The legacy provided 500 scudi annually to support the Jesuits who lived at the Collegio Tolomei, and it paid the salaries of the non-Jesuit teachers.[99]

In 1688 Grand Duke Cosimo III ordered that 100 scudi previously assigned to the first ordinary afternoon professorship of the university be diverted to law instruction at the Collegio Tolomei. The Jesuit rector was authorized to choose two doctors of law not teaching at the university to receive 50 scudi each for teaching civil and canon law to the boarders.[100] Grand Duke Cosimo III encouraged Italian and foreign nobles to send their sons to the Collegio Tolomei, and they did. It quickly became one of the three or four most important Jesuit boarding schools in Italy. Enrollment rose to a hundred in 1681, and remained at this level or higher until the 1740s, when it began to decline.[101] Collaboration between donor, city, religious order, and ruler produced a successful noble school.

The Sienese Jesuit community expanded to meet its greater responsibilities. In 1696 there were 33 Jesuits in Siena, 19 in the San Vigilio college and 14 in the Collegio Tolomei. The school offered eight classes: scholastic theology, cases of conscience, metaphysics, natural philosophy, logic, rhetoric, and two grammar classes; sometimes a humanities class replaced the upper grammar class. In addition, a Jesuit priest who lived at the Collegio Tolomei was described as teaching various subjects. This may have been Giuseppi Ferroni, professor of mathematics at the University of Siena (see below), who sometimes taught mathematics and possibly other subjects informally at the college. The Collegio Tolomei had 95 boarders in 1696; nine Jesuit priests, who also had other duties, oversaw their dormitories. Twenty-four servants who lived in the college building and other servants

---

99. See the references in note 101.   100. Catoni 1991, 56.

101. Gigli 1723, 451–54; Pendola 1852, 9–15, and appendix listing the boarders to 1852; Brizzi 1976, 32–33, 65; Catoni 1991, 56; Catoni 1996; *L'istituto di Celso Tolomei* 2000, 163–90, which repeats the list of boarders found in Pendola 1852, appendix; and P. Turrini 2000, 19–32.

who lived outside tended to the physical needs of the noble boarders. The college at San Vigilio enjoyed annual income of 1,800 florins. The Collegio Tolomei had several sources of income: payments from the boarders which rose and fell with their number, 500 scudi from the Tolomei bequest, a gift of 1,000 florins from Grand Duke Cosimo III, and more.[102]

Members of the university did not like the fact that the Jesuit school taught logic, natural philosophy, and metaphysics, or the favors shown the Collegio Tolomei. On November 13, 1697, the university decreed that in the future anyone who wanted a doctorate from the university, and who expected to be appointed to a professorship thereafter, had to study philosophy at the University of Siena for five years.[103] This was a direct attack on the Jesuit school. The Jesuit rector at San Vigilio wrote that the decree would empty the Jesuit philosophy classes. He attributed the university's action to the fact that the Jesuit classes attracted more students than the university philosophy classes.[104]

Grand Duke Cosimo III came to the rescue. On December 18, 1697, he issued a counter decree: students attending Jesuit philosophy classes would be exempt from the university decree. They would receive all privileges as if they had attended the university lectures. The Jesuit superior for the province of Rome recommended that the general should write a letter of gratitude to Grand Duke Cosimo III and his brother, Cardinal Francesco Maria de' Medici (1660–1711, cardinal from 1686).[105]

The city, possibly under pressure from Cosimo III, went further. On September 12, 1698, the Balìa ruled that Jesuits teaching philosophy at their school might assist in university disputations. And they might participate and vote in the examination of candidates for the doctorate of philosophy, if they were members of the college of doctors of philosophy.[106] Since the permission was meaningless if the Jesuit philosophers were not enrolled in the college, they must have been. The Siena permission was extraordinary and unique in Italy. Jesuits who taught philosophy in the civic-Jesuit uni-

---

102. ARSI, Roma 66, ff. 313r, 314r. The information on income is brief and undoubtedly incomplete.

103. ARSI, Roma 118, f. 303r, "Informatione" for the superior general from Giovanni Vincenzo Imperiale, the provincial superior for the Province of Rome, no date but written at the end of December 1697 or early January 1698. Imperiale was an important Jesuit administrator who attended two general congregations and was elected the assistant for Italy in 1706. *For Matters of Greater Moment* 1994, 274, 725–26.

104. ARSI, Roma 118, f. 303r.   105. ARSI, Roma 118, f. 303r–v.

106. Catoni 1991, 56. Although the document quoted by Catoni refers to the "collegio dei filosofi," this had to be the college of doctors of medicine and philosophy, because Italian universities did not have colleges of doctors of philosophy only.

versities of Parma, Mantua, and Fermo had the right to examine doctoral candidates in philosophy, as did the Jesuits teaching in the civic University of Macerata. But no Jesuits taught in the University of Siena at this time.

A Mathematician and a Geographer in the University of Siena

One Jesuit took advantage of the expanded Jesuit presence in Siena and the influence of the Medici court in order to obtain a professorship at the University of Siena. This was Francesco Ferroni, who was then teaching at the Bologna school (see chapter 10, "A Limited Jesuit Victory"). In June 1683 Ferroni wrote a letter to his former teacher and friend, Vincenzo Viviani, who had influence at the Florentine court. Having taught mathematics for twenty-five years in distant places, Ferroni now wished to return to his native Tuscany (he was born in Pistoia). He asked Viviani to help him get the professorship of mathematics at the University of Siena. Lorenzo Magalotti (1637–1712), another Florentine diplomat and intellectual with scientific interests and influence at the court, recommended to Francesco Maria de' Medici, governor of Siena from March 1683 until late 1686, this be done. His patrons delivered. Ferroni was appointed professor of mathematics at the university beginning in the fall of 1686 at an annual salary of 82 scudi, which went to the Jesuit college.[107] Whether his Jesuit superiors encouraged the unhappy Ferroni to seek the position is unknown. They did permit him to accept it.

Ferroni commented on the reaction to his appointment in a letter of September 1686. He noted that everyone was happy that he was coming to Siena except for a few malcontents who complained that the Jesuits wanted to enter the university in order to take over the teaching. But Ferroni had spoken with unidentified "heads" of the university and convinced them that the professorship was not for the Jesuits. Instead, the grand duke had given it to Ferroni personally, not as a member of a religious order.[108] Nevertheless, the complaint showed that university professors and possibly others in Siena feared a Jesuit presence in the university.

107. For the letters, see Torrini 1973, 414–15; for the appointment see ASUS, XX.A.5, Luigi De Angelis, "Notizi relative all'Università di Siena e catalogo dei suoi Professori dal 1246 fino al presente [1809]," roll of 1686. I am grateful to Dr. Alessandro Leoncini, archivist of ASUS, for this information.

108. "Universalmente è stata gradita in Siena questa mia venuta, ma alcuni pochi interessati e malevoli si sono adombrati, che i Gesuiti voglino entrare in studio a prender loro le Catedre. Ma io in visitare i capi del Studio li trarrò da quest'inganno, mostrando loro, che questa Catedra non è stata data alla Religione, ma il S(erenissi)mo Granduca l'ha data personalmente a me solo." Letter to Antonio Magliabecchi of September 5, 1686, quoted in Torrini 1973, 415.

Ferroni began teaching at the university in November 1686. He also taught informally, that is, without the class being listed.[109] In the morning he taught astronomical calculations and how to construct sundials at the Jesuit school. In the afternoon he taught astronomy and physics, including meteors and comets, at the university. Then his students followed him to the Jesuit school where he dictated and explained how to use an altimeter and measure fields.[110] In short, Ferroni offered a great deal of mathematical instruction through university lectures and informal instruction at the Jesuit school.

But the tepid response disheartened him. In the first five years of his appointment his students numbered only six to fifteen. He lamented that the Sienese would rather learn to ride well than study mathematics. It was the same in the local scientific academy. Its leader and members pursued Lullism, curiosities, Hermeticism, and even controversies with Protestants, rather than the practical mathematics that Ferroni favored. When Viviani encouraged him to publish, he responded that the Jesuit censors in Rome would not permit his works to be printed because they were committed to an Aristotelian approach to physical reality instead of the "wisdom of our admirable and common master Galileo."[111] Nevertheless, Ferroni taught mathematics at the University of Siena and in the Jesuit school until he died on January 15, 1709. Although he published nothing while at Siena, he left a number of manuscripts.[112]

Although Ferroni's university appointment was personal, it led to a subsequent Jesuit mathematics appointment, just as it did at Ferrara and Pavia. In 1723 Stefano Antonio Desideri at the Jesuit college at San Vigilio was appointed to teach mathematics at the University of Siena at a salary of 77 scudi.[113] He was still teaching mathematics there in the late 1740s, but not in 1750.[114]

109. For example, the roll of the Jesuit school for the academic year 1702–1703 did not list a mathematics class. See the illustration in Catoni 1991, 55. Moreover, the Jesuit triennial catalogue of 1696 did not mention a mathematics class in the school. ARSI, Roma 66, ff. 313r, 314r.

110. Torrini, 1973, 418 (including n37).

111. "Si che non è possibile co' nostri revisori incontrarla, che quando questa pur mi passassero, mi cancellarebbero la prima propositione che è de elementis in genere, dove con molte e' sensate sperienze si prova per vera la dottrina del nostro ammirabile e comune maestro il Galileo." Letter to Vivarini of May 12, 1692, Siena, quoted in Torrini 1973, 420. Elsewhere in the letter Ferroni ridiculed Aristotelianism.

112. Sommervogel 1960, 3:696; Torrini 1973, 417, 419, 421; Baldini 2000, 60n27, 223, 227–28, 233–34; and Franci 2006, 196.

113. ASUS, XX.A.5, De Angelis, "Notizie ... e catalogo dei suoi Professori," roll of 1723. See also ASUS, Indici dei motupropri, rescritti ed ordini riguardanti persone o cose, 1560–1866, Indice I.71, lettera D, n. 61, for his appointment notice. I am grateful to Dr. Alessandro Leoncini for these references.

114. ARSI, Roma 105, ff. 31v (1746), 80v (1747), 132r (1748), 183r–v (1749), 235r (1750). I have

The final Jesuit to teach in the University of Siena was a geographer, a surprising development. In the academic year 1702–1703 the Jesuit school at San Vigilio taught a class in geography, the content of which was described as "De Germani inferiori, seu de Belgio," that is, the study of Lower Germany or Belgium.[115] It was probably added for the benefit of the noble boarders at the Collegio Tolomei, because major Italian Jesuit noble schools commonly taught geography. Jesuit geography began as the study of the ancient world, then added modern states. It had military utility when instruction in map-reading and the positioning of military fortifications was included.[116] But Italian universities normally did not teach geography. Nevertheless, Giorgio Zambelli, a Jesuit from the Collegio Tolomei, was appointed to teach geography at the University of Siena for the academic year 1726–1727. He reappeared as a professor of geography at the university in 1743 at a salary of 47 scudi. He held the professorship through 1749, and probably until 1764, when he asked for a pension.[117]

In 1560 and 1562, when the University of Siena was struggling, two Jesuits were offered professorships. They did not teach in the university because Jesuit superiors forbade them. Over time the Siena Jesuits prospered and opened a noble boarding school. Then in 1686 a Jesuit mathematician obtained the professorship of mathematics at the university through the influence of his friends at the Florentine court. Another mathematician and a geographer also taught in the University of Siena in the eighteenth century. In addition, the philosophy teachers at the Jesuit school were permitted to participate in university disputations and the examination of degree candidates. Members of the university were unhappy at the favor shown the Jesuits, but could do nothing, because the Medici government, especially Grand Duke Cosimo III, strongly supported the Siena Jesuits.

---

been unable to find any additional information on Desideri, not even in Sommervogel 1960, which means that he published nothing that has come to light.

115. See the illustration in Catoni 1991, 55.

116. Brizzi 1976, 242, 244–47. On Jesuit research and teaching in military architecture, see De Lucca 2012.

117. ASUS, XX.A.5, De Angelis, "Notizie ... e catalogo dei suoi Professori," roll of 1743; and Indici dei motupropri, Indice 1.71, lettera Z n. 4. See also ARSI, Roma 105, ff. 32v (1746), 81v (1747), 133r (1748), 184r (1749), 236r (1749); and Roma 74, ff. 174r (1749), 353r (1749). Whether Zambelli also taught geography in the Jesuit school or at the Collegio Tolomei is unknown. No additional information on Zambelli has come to light.

Conclusion

A small number of individual Jesuits became professors in civic universities. Between 1675 and 1699 they secured mathematics professorships at Ferrara, Pavia, and Siena. Jesuits were appointed because they were able scholars whose expertise was needed. Friendship and shared interests with the powerful also helped. The friendships developed because by the late seventeenth century many Jesuits came from the same towns and social class as local notables. For those who ruled universities, appointing Jesuits to teach mathematics provoked limited controversy because mathematics was not nearly so important or visible as law, medicine, and philosophy. Mathematics was also a minor discipline in the Jesuit curriculum. Jesuits continued to fill the mathematics professorships at these universities most of the time until the suppression. A tiny number of Jesuits in other fields followed the mathematician into the universities of Ferrara, Pavia, and Siena.

The professorships were individual and personal. In the sixteenth century the leaders of the Society were not sure that single appointments to civic universities were a good idea. But they had quietly changed their minds over time. Recognizing the reality of the university environment, the Society did not make additional demands on the three universities. They still wanted to improve the moral and spiritual lives of students and tried to do so by guiding willing students through the Spiritual Exercises. Although only a handful of Jesuits became professors, university hostility did not cease. But papal legates, Milanese senators, and Grand Duke Cosimo III overrode the opposition. In the end the Jesuits secured a few professorships in three civic universities as a result of local circumstances.

14

PHILOSOPHICAL

AND PEDAGOGICAL

DIFFERENCES

Italian university professors taught secular Aristotelianism and charged that the Jesuits taught philosophy badly because they did not concentrate on the words of Aristotle. The Jesuits embraced Christian Aristotelianism and accused university philosophers of teaching atheism. University philosophers argued that Jesuit professors lacked originality because they taught from summaries and each other's lecture notes. The Jesuits wanted uniformity in philosophical instruction and believed that they taught an integrated understanding of Aristotle. Behind the polemics were significant philosophical and pedagogical differences.

The Jesuits Teach Philosophy Badly

Italian professors accused the Jesuits of teaching Aristotle badly in several ways. They did not teach directly from the texts of Aristotle but from summaries. They did not use the most important commentaries. Their pedagogical order was mixed up. And they directed their teaching to the wrong goal.

The most detailed and substantive statement came from an anonymous writer in Turin in 1593, possibly a professor of natural philosophy at the university.[1] The writer contrasted the good philosophical teaching of distinguished Italian university professors with what he viewed as poor, confusing, and wrongly focused Jesuit philosophy instruction. He charged that the Jesuits rejected the modern philosophy of Italian universities in favor of outdated content and method. In his opinion, the Society had turned its back on the best university philosophical practice.

1. AST, Istruzione Pubblica, Regia Università, Mazzo 1, no. 72, "Raggioni 1593."

393

The Turin critic began by naming six distinguished professors of philosophy who, he asserted, had chased from the world the old, sophistic, and barbarous way of philosophizing that the Jesuits used. They had replaced the old with the truth of the ancient Greek commentators on Aristotle.[2] The commentators were Ammonius (ca. 517–526), Simplicius (ca. 500–after 533), Themistius (ca. 317–ca. 388), and especially Alexander of Aphrodisias (fl. second or third century A.D.). Most of their works had only become available at the end of the fifteenth century and the beginning of the sixteenth.

The six professors who used ancient Greek commentaries and taught philosophy rightly were well-known Renaissance philosophers still much studied by historians today. The first was Angelo Poliziano (1454–1494), a pioneer in humanist textual criticism who taught at the University of Pisa, temporarily located in Florence. The second was Niccolò Leonico Tomeo (1456–1531) who had taught at the University of Padua. Tomeo translated several works of Aristotle, taught Aristotle from the Greek text, used ancient Greek commentators, and taught Plato.[3] Next came Simone Porzio (1496–1554) who taught natural philosophy at the universities of Pisa and Naples. A versatile and original thinker, he wrote commentaries on several of Aristotle's works in which he demonstrated his philological skills and knowledge of the Greek commentators.[4]

Then came "Il Maggio." This may have been Vincenzo Maggi (1498–1564) who taught natural philosophy at the universities of Padua and Ferrara and employed ancient Greek commentators in his commentaries on several works of Aristotle, especially the *Poetics*.[5] Or it was Lucillo Filalteo Maggi (ca. 1510–1578) who taught philosophy at the University of Pavia from 1553 to 1568 and medicine at the University of Turin from 1572 until his death. He translated from Greek to Latin Simplicius' commentary on Aristotle's *Physics* and Alexander of Aphrodisias' commentary on Aristotle's *De sensibus*, and wrote commentaries on *De caelo* and *De anima*.[6] Next

---

2. "Di più essendosi affaticati Angelo Politiano, Nicolao Leonico, Simone Portio, il Maggio, il Genova, il Vicomercato [sic], et altri segnalati lettori di filosofia di cacciare dal mondo con la verità de gli interpreti greci, Amonio, Simplicio, Temistio, Alesandro, et altri, la sofistica et barbara maniera di filosofare i gli [= degli] Gesuitti." AST, Istruzione Pubblica: Regia Università, Mazzo 1, no. 7.2, "Raggioni 1593," no pag.

3. For Poliziano, see Grafton 1983, 9–44, 231–44; and D'Amico 1988, 21–27, 215–17; for Tomeo, see Lohr 1988a, 452–54; Grendler 2002, 151, 273–74, 297–98. Here and in the following notes concerning other professors, only one or two sources, each with much additional bibliography, will be given.

4. Lohr 1988a, 364–67; and Del Soldato 2010.

5. Lohr 1988a, 232–34; and Selmi 2007.

6. *Memorie di Pavia* 1970, part 1, 172; Chiaudano 1972b, 106–14; and Lohr 1988a, 328.

came Marc'Antonio Genua de' Passeri (1490/91–1563), who taught natural philosophy at the University of Padua from 1517 until his death. He relied heavily on the commentary of Simplicius in his analysis of Aristotle's *De anima*, and was immensely popular with students and Venetian nobles.[7] The last was Francesco Vimercato of Milan (1512–after 1571), who taught at Paris and the universities of Mondovì and Turin. He wrote commentaries on many works of Aristotle using the ancient Greeks.[8] The Turin critic did not mention a very important piece of supplementary information. Porzio, Vincenzo Maggi, Genua de' Passeri, and possibly Vimercato followed Averroes and Pomponazzi in denying that philosophy could demonstrate the immortality of the human soul.

The Turin critic next charged that the Jesuits borrowed from outdated authors. He stated that an unnamed Jesuit had taken his *recitatione* from the opinions of others. His point was that the Jesuit had delivered a "recitation," something he had learned and/or memorized, instead of presenting his own ideas in his lecture. He had borrowed some material from the books of "Boccaferro professor at Bologna" and most of the rest from the books of "Dominico." Although no one would teach from these books anymore, their reprinting had revealed the theft.[9] The first was Ludovico Boccadiffero (1482–1545), a well-known philosopher of Averroist orientation who commented on Aristotle and taught natural philosophy at the University of Bologna for twenty-seven years.[10] The other was Domingo de Soto, OP (1494/95–1560), a very influential Spanish logician, philosopher, and theologian who taught at the universities of Alcalá de Henares and Salamanca, and whose works were often reprinted. While his books on Aristotle's *Physics* innovated, his logical works marked only a transition between medieval and Renaissance logic.[11]

The Turin critic continued. There were three different ways of teaching Aristotle. One could teach from the text only, like a grammarian, a method that was poor and lacked substance. One could teach Aristotle by ignoring the text completely and just teaching the questions (quaestiones), a method that was too sophistical and barbarous, words implying a medieval scholas-

---

7. Lohr 1988a, 198–204; Kessler 1988, 523–27.

8. Gilbert 1965; Chiaudano 1972b, 91, 96; and Lohr 1988a, 479–81.

9. "Altretanto si affaticano per rimeterla onde i libri d'uno di luoro levata la recitatione dalle opinioni di diversi, la quale egli há trasportato da' i libri del Boccaferro lettore in Bologna, sono per il resto per la magior parte levati da libri di Dominico, sono stimandosi forse, che quei libri mai piu niuno leggerebbe, má altri facendo[li] dopo ristampare, il sono ha palesato il furto." AST, Istruzione Pubblica, Regia Università, Mazza 1, no. 7.2, "Raggioni 1593," no pag.

10. Rotondò 1969; and Lohr 1988a, 57–65.

11. CHRP 1988, index; Lohr 1988a, 430–31; and Wallace 1999a.

tic approach. Quaestiones were traditional disputed points in the text that the teacher tried to resolve logically with the aid of other texts of Aristotle, commentaries, and/or his own cleverness.[12] Or one could lecture using the text of Aristotle with digressions on the questions in their place, which method the Greeks and Averroes followed. But the Jesuits clung to the second method that focused on questions.[13]

Other critics agreed that good university philosophy instruction consisted of close textual analysis, using the best commentaries and discussing disputed points, without using a compendium or dictating. In 1596 the Senate of Messina and the Society were negotiating the terms for Jesuit participation in the proposed civic-Jesuit University of Messina (see chapter 3). The Senate indicated that it expected the Jesuits to teach philosophy exactly as it was taught in Italian universities. They meant that the lecturer must declare the text of Aristotle word for word along with explanations from the weightiest authors and ancient commentaries, but not from a compendium. After the exposition, the teacher must discuss the customary questions rising from the text, as was done in all universities. Professors must not dictate. The Senate affirmed that this form of teaching was necessary because the instruction must be useful to students going on to study theology, as well as those intending to study medicine.[14]

The Turin critic also argued that the Jesuits taught logic and philosophy in poor order because they oriented philosophy toward theology. He gave examples. The Jesuits began the predicaments (categories, i.e., Aristotle's *Categories*, the first of his six books on logic) by examining the predicates *utrum Deus sit* (whether God exists) and *utrum sit Infinitus* (whether he is infinite). But they omitted other good things proper to philosophy and pertaining to medicine, which was just the opposite of what the universities

12. Baldini 1999, 251, offers this definition: "problem points identified from the exegesis of Aristotelian texts, each with an old tradition."

13. "Et di piu tre sono i modi con i quali fino qui sie leto la filosofia, uno tropo digiuno et povero, legendo il testo solo di Aristo[ti]le, come farebbe un grammatico: un troppo sofistico et barbaro, lasciando il testo d'Aristotile affatto, má sempre trattando quistioni, et uno di mezo legendo il testo d'Aristotile e digredendo nelle questioni a suo luogho, il qual modo tengono i greci et Averroe, [ma] questi Rev.di padri si sono apigliati al modo secondo quistionoso." AST, Istruzione Pubblica, Regia Università, Mazzo 1, no. 7.2, "Raggioni 1593," no pag.

14. "4. Nella filosofia si dichiari il testo d'Aristotele de verbo ad verbum, coll'espositioni delli più gravi auttori et antichi commentatori sopra il medesimo testo et non per compendio, quale tosto poi finito di dichiararsi, si proponghino questioni solite dichiararsi sopra lo medesimo testo come s'usa in tutti li Studii publici et questo perché la lettura predetta giovi cossì a quelli che vorranno passari alla teologia come agl'altri che li piacerà attender alla medicina. 5. Che tutti li lettori legghino senza dettare." ARSI, Sicula 197 I, f. 135v, as printed in Novarese 1994, 441.

expected. It was much better to know how to reason about things, as someone who has studied philosophy in academies and universities can do. But one did not learn this from the Jesuits.[15] Perhaps this was the reason that the University of Paris decreed that it would not confer the doctorate on anyone who had studied philosophy with the Jesuits, the Turin critic opined.[16]

The reference to Paris was a polemical aside, and the Turin critic had most of the story wrong. It was true that in 1573 the University of Paris refused to confer licentiates and doctorates on students who had studied at the Jesuit college in Paris, and in 1574 the Faculty of Arts of the university would not grant any academic privileges to students at the Jesuit college there.[17] But it was not because of the content of Jesuit philosophy instruction. Instead, these were two of many actions that the university, the Parlement of Paris, the bishop of Paris, and other opponents took in their efforts to prevent the Jesuit college in Paris from becoming a constituent part of the University of Paris.

The story was long and complex. After years of struggle, the Jesuit college in Paris established itself and began teaching in 1564. The Jesuits immediately asked that it be incorporated into the university alongside the approximately forty existing secular colleges (i.e., colleges not affiliated with medieval mendicant orders) that taught the humanities and philosophy. The university said no. Although the university traditionally kept religious orders at arm's length, this was not the primary reason for denying the Jesuit request. It was because the university, and the ecclesiastical and legal powers behind it, saw the Jesuits as agents of the papacy determined to undermine the Gallican church. Among much else, the Jesuits supported the decrees of the Council of Trent, which the French church rejected. Another reason was that university theologians did not like the competition coming from the Jesuits, especially Juan Maldonado (1533–1583), who began teaching theology at the Jesuit college in 1565 and quickly attracted hun-

15. "Insegnano anco la filosofia con ordine non poco buono a mio parere applicandola totalmente alla teologia: onde há principio di predicamenti comminciando ad essaminano la disputa utrum Deus sit in predicamento et utrum sit infinitus, tralasciano intanto altre belle cose proprie della filosofia et quelle che apertengono alla medicina, alle quali al opposto nelle publice [sic] scuole piu si attende. Et percio molto meglio, et con maniera piu bella sapra raggionare delle cose, chi havera imparato la filosofia nelle academie et studij, che non fara chi l'havra imparata da questi padri." AST, Istruzione Pubblica, Regia Università, Mazza 1, no. 7.2, "Raggioni 1593," no pag.

16. "Et questa forse é la cagione, e há mosso la università di Parigi a fare l'ordine che non si dia in essa il grado del dottorato a' chi havra studiato filosofia sotto ad essi Rv.di Padri Giesuuiti." AST, Istruzione Pubblica, Regia Università, Mazzo 1, no. 7.2, "Raggioni 1593," no pag.

17. Piaget 1893, 91–92; Delattre 1955, col. 1115; Lécrivain 2004, 310–11, for this and the following paragraph.

dreds of students. Besides the decrees of 1573 and 1574, the enemies of the Jesuits employed legal actions and other maneuvers against them.

Nevertheless, during the last stages of the French Wars of Religion the university, the Catholic League, and the Jesuits made common cause against Henry of Navarre. At this time the prohibition against granting licentiates and doctorates to students from the Jesuit college was not enforced. Hence, in 1593 the Faculty of Theology of the University of Paris included more than a few former students of the Jesuit college who had obtained their doctorates in theology from that same faculty.[18] This was a brief truce in the long war waged by the University of Paris, the Parlement of Paris, and other entities against the Jesuit college. The attacks on the Jesuits in Paris resumed in 1594.

The Turin critic then returned to his major charge, that the Jesuits taught philosophy badly. He offered additional evidence. He pointed out that Porphyry, in the preface of his *Isagoge* (*Introduction*) to the study of Aristotle's logic, explained that he had omitted three disputation questions of Aristotle because they were not suitable for the intelligence of someone just beginning to study philosophy.[19] But these fathers tangled up their teaching by beginning with ideas and the universal, which was appropriate for metaphysics, the last part of philosophy (Aristotle discussed ideas and the universal in *Metaphysics* book 7). Following Porphyry, the Jesuits did not discuss the long tracts at the beginning of the logic of Aristotle. They did worse by discussing *ens rationis* in a sophistical and boring way, although this could be truthfully explained to youths in a few words, the Turin critic concluded.[20]

It was true that the Jesuits, like many university professors, used Porphyry's *Introduction* to help explain Aristotle's logic.[21] They continued to do

18. Piaget 1893, 91–100, 156–276, esp. 156–57; and Delattre 1955, cols. 1111–19, 1129–36, 1180–81.

19. The passage to which the Turin critic referred reads as follows: "For example, about genera and species—whether they subsist, whether they actually depend on bare thoughts alone, whether if they actually subsist they are bodies or incorporeal and whether they are separable or are in perceptible items and subsist about them—these matters I shall decline to discuss, such a subject being very deep and demanding another and a larger investigation." Porphyry 2003, 3.

20. "Confermasi anco che essi insegnano la filosofia con ordine non buono che Porfirio nel proemio de predicabili propone di voler translaciare tre dispute, le quali non si confanno co' l'ingeg[n]io di chi comincia ad attendere alla filosofia, et questi padri commiciano ad intricar luoro in esse, commiciando a trattare la disputa delle Idee et dello universale, che piu tosto si confa' con la metafisica ultima parte della filosofia—traslascio di dire quanti longhi trattati faciano a principio della logica, di quello ens rationis, con modo sofistico et noiosso, over bastarebbe in poche parole chiare dare ad intendere la verita schietta a' giovani." AST, Istruzione Pubblica, Regia Università, Mazzo 1, no. 7.2, "Raggioni 1593," no pag.

21. For example, in response to the first draft of the Ratio Studiorum of 1586, which

so in the seventeenth century even though the Ratio Studiorum of 1599 recommended that they use the logic manuals of the Jesuits Francisco de Toledo (1532–1596) and Pedro da Fonseca (1528–1599).[22] And metaphysics was very important in Jesuit philosophical studies, because it was the gateway to theology.

The mention of ens rationis (being of reason or mind-dependent being) referred to a new development, a hot topic, in which Jesuit philosophers had taken the lead. Francisco de Toledo in his commentary on Aristotle's *Physics* (1575), Fonseca with his extensive commentary on the *Metaphysics* (1577 and 1589), and Benito Perera in a work published in 1576 discussed ens rationis. Francisco Suárez (1548–1617) then made the exploration of ens rationis a major philosophical issue throughout Europe with the publication of his very influential *Disputationes metaphysicae* (1597). All of the above except Fonseca taught at the Collegio Romano for significant periods of time, which undoubtedly increased their influence on Italian Jesuits. As part of their larger discussions of being and infinity, and whether philosophy could demonstrate the existence of God as an infinite being, these Jesuit philosophers made subtle distinctions between real being (God as infinite being and some finite forms of being) and beings of reason (*entia rationis*), which were conceptions of the mind. For example, time in some ways was a being (conception) of reason. The details of their complex and subtle discussions, which even today attract the attention of philosophers, cannot be followed here.[23] The Turin critic did not necessarily reject ens rationis. He judged that the Jesuits taught it in a sophistical, boring, and unnecessarily complex way.

The critics of the Jesuits believed that university professors taught Aristotle the right way, which was a close analysis of the text with the aid of ancient Greek commentators. They concluded that the Jesuits taught Aristotle the wrong way, because they did not pay enough attention to the text, they followed outdated approaches, they made logic subservient to metaphysics, and they needlessly complicated matters.

---

dismissed Porphyry as an impious man and the *Isagoge* as of little merit to Christians, the Jesuits of the Province of Milan objected, noting that the *Isagoge* was a common text in all the universities and was taught by all the doctors. MP 6:263. See also ibid., 6:261, 265, and 5:100, for the harsh words of the 1586 Ratio Studiorum. There are many references to the teaching of Porphyry by the Jesuits earlier in the sixteenth century in MP, vols. 1–4, index.

22. *Ratio Studiorum* 2005, par. 215 (101).

23. Lohr 1988b, 611–17; Leijenhorst 2002, index; Pereira 2007, 106–18, and index; Shields 2012; and Edwards 2013, 22–32.

University Secular Aristotelianism

Behind these pedagogical complaints was the major issue. Italian university universities taught secular Aristotelianism and the Jesuits taught Christian Aristotelianism.[24] The flashpoint was whether Aristotelian philosophy could demonstrate, that is, prove philosophically, that the human soul was immortal.

With the major exception of Averroes (Ibn Rushd, 1126–1198), most medieval philosophers argued that Aristotelian philosophy could demonstrate the immortality of the individual human intellective soul. This was the view of Thomas Aquinas and his very numerous followers, especially in northern Europe. Italian university philosophers in the late Middle Ages did not dissent very much from this view. However, they approached the intellective soul from a somewhat different perspective than northern European and Spanish philosophers. They paid closer attention to what Aristotle wrote about the body and sensation (sense experience) in their study of the human soul and how the intellect knows, because medicine was a major subject in Italian universities. Moreover, they tended to see their discipline as separate and detached from theology, partly because, unlike their counterparts in northern European universities, theology had a very small presence in Italian universities. There was no theologian in the next lecture hall.

Italian university professors of logic and natural philosophy, almost all of them laymen, and members of religious orders, approached the teaching of Aristotle's books with different aims. For lay university professors Aristotelian logic and natural philosophy led to medicine, to the study of scientific method, or became ends in themselves. For members of religious orders metaphysics (the science of being) was an essential part of the path to theology and worthy of a year's study. By contrast, very few Italian universities had professorships of metaphysics before 1500, and only the largest universities had them in the sixteenth century. Those who filled the positions were friars who came from the local medieval mendicant monasteries. University professors of philosophy held metaphysicians in low regard when they noticed them at all.[25]

Both lay university and religious order philosophers were scholastic Aristotelians, which meant that they systematized Aristotle. Scholastic philosophers presupposed that Aristotle's works were part of a seamless whole, that all the parts fitted together. Logical categories, which came from Ar-

---

24. Kristeller 1964, 74, used the term "secular Aristotelianism," while Baldini 1999, 260, refers to "lay Aristotelianism." The meaning of Christian Aristotelianism will become evident.

25. See Grendler 2002, 387–89, for some examples.

istotle's first book on logic, could be and should be used to organize other parts of Aristotelian philosophy, such as the study of substance and being. Neither medieval nor Renaissance scholastics saw or accepted that Aristotle might contradict himself or change his mind, and only gradually did they realize that he was simply wrong on some points.[26] The fact that both Italian university and Jesuit philosophers were systematizing scholastics made it inevitable that they would disagree, and that it would be very difficult to reconcile differences.

Aristotelianism entered a new era in the sixteenth century. Some university philosophers learned Greek and preferred to read the ancient works in the original language. They criticized medieval Latin translations and commentaries. Between 1495 and 1540, the books of Aristotle and practically all surviving Greek commentaries on Aristotle, plus other ancient works, were printed in Greek and translated into Latin, often for the first time. Works previously available in Latin translation were sometimes translated anew by scholars with a better command of Greek and a broader knowledge of Greek philosophy. University philosophers now studied Aristotle with the assistance of ancient Greek commentaries.[27] And they became more adventurous. They were more open to other influences than their medieval predecessors, and they introduced greater diversity into their treatises. They looked at Plato and the ancient Neo-Platonists and sometimes sought to reconcile Aristotle and Plato. All of this produced what a modern scholar called "eclectic Aristotelianisms."[28]

Fresh scholarly interpretations of the inanimate world, scientific method, human cognition, and the human intellective soul, always within the Aristotelian framework, appeared. The last topic attracted the most attention. Many Italian university philosophers adopted the approach of secular Aristotelianism, whose chief tendency was to deny or doubt that Aristotelian philosophy could demonstrate the immortality of the human soul and to separate philosophy from theology.

Pietro Pomponazzi (1462–1525), especially in his *Tractatus de immortalitate animae* (1516), played a key role. He argued that the human intellective soul could not function, that is, could not know, without *phantasmata* (phantasms or mental images) which were dependent on sense experience, an operation of the body. The soul and the body were indissolubly united. Hence, the individual intellective soul was essentially material and mortal.

26. Pasnau 2012, 673–74, makes these points.

27. This is a well-known story. See Grendler 2002, 271–79, for an account and more bibliography.

28. Schmitt 1983, 99–103.

This was the only possible truth that philosophy based on Aristotle could reach in his view. Pomponazzi then drew the stark religious and moral consequences of the soul's mortality. However, he concluded *De immortalitate animae* by stating that faith, whose evidence was revelation and canonical scripture, proved that the soul was immortal. In short, Pomponazzi asserted in the strongest possible terms that philosophy and theology must reach different conclusions because they were separate disciplines, with different proof systems.

After Pomponazzi there were almost as many positions, with innumerable intricacies and nuances, concerning whether or not Aristotelian philosophy could demonstrate the soul's immortality, as there were university philosophers eager to put pen to paper. Some argued that the human soul was in some ways mortal and in other ways immortal. In general, the majority of Italian university philosophers, and especially the best known figures, separated philosophy from theology to some degree. They denied that Aristotelian philosophy by itself could demonstrate fundamental Christian beliefs. However, like Pomponazzi, they often concluded that other evidence, including faith, proved that the human soul was immortal and supported other Christian beliefs.[29]

Jesuit Christian Aristotelianism

Italian university secular Aristotelianism presented a challenge to the Jesuits. They knew through faith and scripture that the human soul was immortal, and that the world had an infinite creator. Moreover, the first Jesuits were the philosophical products of northern European Christian Aristotelianism. Although not a philosopher himself, Ignatius endorsed scholasticism and Thomism. In so doing, he determined that the Jesuits would follow late medieval university philosophical traditions. The Jesuits would assert that Aristotelian metaphysical principles could be and should be used to confirm theological truths.[30] Other factors, including how much respect should be paid to the ancient Greek commentators, and the desire of the Jesuits for philosophical uniformity, also divided the Jesuits from Italian university philosophers. The Jesuits needed to assert and defend a Christian Aristotelianism while simultaneously demonstrating that they were just as knowl-

29. Di Napoli 1963 remains the basic source.

30. Lohr 1976, 205, 211, puts it as follows. The Jesuits and other religious orders saw the effort to "maintain the Scholastic Aristotle in the service of Catholic theology" as "a mission, the sense of trying to preserve a heritage." They wanted to consolidate the inheritance of scholasticism while preserving "sound, Catholic doctrine."

edgeable and skilled in understanding and teaching Aristotle as Italian professors.

The papacy imposed a further duty. The papal bull *Apostolici regiminis* of 1513 condemned the view that the human soul was mortal and two other Averroist positions, the universal intellect in which man participated only during the life of his body, and the eternity of the world. It obliged teachers of philosophy in universities and elsewhere "to clarify for their listeners the truth of the Christian religion, to teach it by convincing arguments so far as this is possible, and to apply themselves to the full extent of their energies to refuting and disposing of the philosophers' opposing arguments."[31] However, it did not declare the immortality of the human soul an article of Catholic faith, and it left some latitude ("so far as this is possible") to philosophers.

Of course the Jesuits would clarify the truths of the Christian religion and refute wrong philosophical arguments. And they would teach a true Aristotle who was in harmony with Christianity. But how to do it? The initial response of the Jesuits in the 1560s was to adopt a conservative and restrictive approach. They strongly rejected the positions of Italian university secular Aristotelians, plus Averroes and the Greek commentators who helped them reach those positions. They adopted guidelines informing Jesuit philosophers what they should and should not teach on disputed points of Aristotle. Two Jesuits at the Collegio Romano were primarily responsible for this approach.

The first was Diego de Ledesma (1519–1575). Born in Cuéllar in what is now the autonomous community of Castile and León, Ledesma studied humanities, philosophy, and theology at the universities of Alcalá de Henares, Paris (five years), and Louvain, and probably taught at the latter two.[32] It is likely that he obtained one or more degrees in these institutions, but information is lacking. He became a Jesuit at Louvain in 1556. Recognizing his ability, his superiors brought him to Rome where he was ordained a priest in 1557. In that same year Ledesma began teaching scholastic theology at the Roman College, and in 1562 became prefect of studies. After a year's absence in 1566, he returned and began to teach controversial theology in 1569. He was again prefect of studies from 1569, or 1571, until his death. He wrote several treatises on Jesuit education that molded the Jesuit curriculum and pedagogy and influenced the Ratio Studiorum. Ledesma

31. *Decrees* 1990, 1:605–6*. There is considerable scholarship on this bull, of which Minnich 1986; Constant 2002; and Sander 2014a, 39–46, are particularly useful.

32. For Ledesma's biography, see Lukács 2001c; and Belmonte 2006, 46–59, 83–138, and 164–65.

was the product of northern European Christian Aristotelianism, and he had no personal knowledge of Italian universities. These factors influenced his views.

The second was an Italian who had studied philosophy at the University of Padua and did not like what he found there. This was Achille Gagliardi, who later played controversial roles in the disputes at Turin and Venice. Gagliardi attended the University of Padua for an unknown number of years around 1557. He studied philosophy with Marc'Antonio Genua de' Passeri who followed Simplicius and saw much agreement between Aristotle and Plato. As noted in the biography in the appendix, Gagliardi entered the Society of Jesus in Rome in 1559 and taught at the Roman College from 1562 through 1567.[33]

In 1564 and 1565, probably on request from general Laínez, Ledesma solicited the opinions of the teachers at the Collegio Romano about how and what they should teach. Ledesma compiled and condensed the responses, scrupulously indicating who presented each comment, in his report to general Borja, who replaced Laínez on July 2, 1565.[34] Almost all the comments on philosophy came from Ledesma and Gagliardi. They were in agreement: Jesuit philosophers should hold and teach views and interpretations that differed from Italian university secular Aristotelians.

Ledesma and Gagliardi wanted careful, conservative, and nearly uniform philosophy instruction. Jesuits teachers should teach the same learning (*doctrina*) in so far as possible. They should not introduce new interpretations or views (*opiniones*) contrary to common views or Aristotle without first consulting the traditional sources and a superior. New interpretations should accommodate accepted common views. Jesuit philosophers should praise Albert the Great, Thomas Aquinas, and other pious Christian authors. They should not praise Averroes or other impious authors. Jesuits should not show themselves to be Averroists or follow the Greek faction (*factio*), or the Arab party, against the Latins or theologians. Ledesma and Gagliardi agreed that philosophy should serve theology. And that meant that all Jesuit professors should defend the immortality of the soul according to Aristotle.[35]

Gagliardi added some comments that reflected his experience at the University of Padua and what he heard in the lectures of Genua de' Passeri.

33. G. Brunelli 1998, 258–59.

34. Ledesma, "Relatio de professorum consultationibus circa Collegii Romani studia," in MP 2:464–81. The philosophy material has a subtitle, "Opiniones magistrum et doctrinae quae et qualis esse debeat," and is found on 477–79. For more on this document and the circumstances, see Lohr 1976, 212–13; Sander 2014a, 48–49; and Sander 2014b.

35. MP 2:477–78. See Bartlett 1984, 79–80, for a brief English summary.

He did not want Jesuit teachers to interpret the deviations (*digressiones*) of Averroes, Simplicius, and others; they should just describe their positions with indifference. And Jesuit teachers should avoid two pitfalls. The first was excessive liberty that weakened the faith, which Gagliardi believed happened in Italian universities. Second, Jesuit teachers should avoid following one author too much, because this would earn hatred and scorn in Italy.[36] On the other hand, in matters not involving the faith, Jesuit teachers were not obligated to teach identically. Doing so would also earn derision in Italy and impede good learning.[37]

Ledesma wrote two more reports in 1564 for General Laínez about the Collegio Romano in which he again stated that Jesuit philosophers should follow Aquinas and Aristotle. They should defend philosophically the human immortal soul and other positions, they should not introduce novel views, and they should avoid Averroes and the Greeks.[38] Some of the prohibitions and warnings were aimed at a fellow Jesuit at the Collegio Romano, Benito Perera or Pererius (1535–1610), whom Ledesma and Gagliardi believed was teaching erroneous views to his students.[39] Perera taught logic, natural philosophy, and metaphysics at the Roman College from 1557 through 1567, and was a popular teacher. He was the odd man out, because he denied that Aristotelian philosophy could demonstrate the immortality of the human soul, and he made considerable use of the works of Averroes and the Greek commentators.[40]

The reports of Ledesma persuaded General Borja to act. In November 1565 he promulgated a list of five disciplinary commands and sixteen philosophical and theological principles that Jesuit teachers must uphold and teach.[41] Most of them repeated what Ledesma advocated in his reports.

---

36. "9. In docenda philosophia duplex abusus vitetur: primus, nimiae libertatis, quae quidem nocet fidei, ut experientia ostendit in accademiis Italiae; secundus, esse adstrictos unius tantum aut alterius authoris doctrinae; nam hoc efficit in Italia odiosos et contemptibiles. Achi." MP 2:478. "Accademiis" usually meant universities in sixteenth-century Italy. "Achi" referred to Achille Gagliardi. See Ledesma's key on 465 and Lukács' identifications in the notes on 465–66.

37. MP 2:478–79; Bartlett 1984, 80–81.

38. MP 2:487–88, esp. 496–502; Bartlett 1984, 81–85; and Sander 2014b, 38–39.

39. See the section entitled "Hac propositiones affirmantur ab eo secundum veritatem in scriptis sui discipuli" in MP 2:502–3. The unnamed teacher to which Ledesma referred was Perera. See also Sander 2014b, 38–40.

40. For Perera's biography, see Villoslada 1954, index; and Sola 2001. For his philosophy see Blum 2012, 139–82; the articles in *Benet Perera* 2014; and Casalini 2014 and 2015.

41. They are printed in MP 3:382–85, on the basis of eight manuscripts. A later manuscript added another principle. Bartlett 1984, 88–90, provides English translations. See also Lohr 1976, 213; Martin 2014, 88–92; especially Sander 2014a, 49–50; Sander 2014b, 38–39; and Casalini 2015, 224–28.

The first of the five disciplinary commands ordered Jesuits not to teach or defend anything against the faith or that would detract from or diminish it. The next three ordered Jesuits not to teach or defend any propositions contrary to accepted opinions of philosophers and theologians, or not commonly held by them, or new opinions, without consulting a Jesuit superior. Then came sixteen specific principles (*opiniones*). They included the affirmation that God was infinitely powerful and a free agent, and that the human rational soul was immortal according to Aristotle and true philosophy.[42] Another principle was that there was not a single rational soul for all mankind (the universal agent intellect argument of Averroes), but an individual rational soul for each human being, according to Aristotle and true philosophy.[43] Several other principles were Aristotelian philosophical concepts whose pro- or anti-Christian meaning and significance depended on how they were interpreted and used. But that was the point: the philosophical principles that Jesuit philosophers and theologians were commanded to hold and teach fused Aristotelian philosophy and Christian theology into a unity. General Borja decreed that a Jesuit could not deviate from Aristotelianism interpreted in a Christian way without deviating from Catholic Christianity.

That was the position of the Jesuit leadership at this time. The Third General Congregation of 1573 reinforced it by decreeing that "irreligious interpreters of Aristotle should be read with caution by teachers" and that teachers should "so interpret philosophy that it subserves and becomes the handmaiden to the true scholastic theology." It also told teachers that they should vigorously rebut writings opposed to Christian truth.[44] And in 1574 Ledesma wrote another long and strong letter to Everard Mercurian, the new superior general as of April 23, 1573. He hammered away at the same points as before. Jesuits should follow Aquinas and Aristotle; they should avoid Averroes, the Greeks, and the Arabs. All Jesuits should teach the same material; and philosophical freedom was dangerous to the Society and God's church. He cited *Apostolici regiminis*, the Jesuit Constitutions, the decrees of Borja, and the Council of Chalcedon (451) in support of his

---

42. "7. Anima intellectiva est immortalis secundum Aristotelem et veram philosophiam." MP 3:384. The term "true philosophy" appeared six times in Borja's principles and was used by other Jesuits, such as Francisco de Toledo, in the 1560s and 1570s, without definition. It meant what human reason with the aid of faith and/or Christian revelation knows is true. True philosophy rejected the so-called double truth, because truth cannot contradict itself. Hence, both Aristotle properly understood and true philosophy led to truth, which was one.

43. MP 3:384.

44. For *Matters of Greater Moment* 1994, 149, Decree 47 after the election.

views.[45] And the very influential Francisco de Toledo, who taught philosophy (1559–1562) and theology (1562–1569) at the Collegio Romano, reiterated the position of Ledesma, Gagliardi, and Borja, and attacked Pomponazzi, in his 1574 commentary on De Anima.[46]

Nevertheless, differences remained in the Roman College. Perera ascended to a professorship of scholastic theology (1567 to 1570) and of scripture, beginning in 1576, without changing his views. So the conservatives attacked him directly. Achille Gagliardi returned to the Collegio Romano as prefect of studies and professor of scholastic theology in 1576. In 1578 Gagliardi, two other Jesuit teachers at the Collegio Romano, and Benedetto Palmio, superior of the Italian assistancy at that time, denounced Perera to Pope Gregory XIII. Of course, their action also implied that General Mercurian was not exercising proper oversight over the Roman College. The denunciation irritated the pope, who turned the matter over to Mercurian, who supported Perera and exiled Gagliardi to Padua in 1579.[47] Perera continued to teach scripture until 1597, plus scholastic theology from 1583 to 1586. Although he no longer taught philosophy, he continued to favor a broad approach that included using Averroes and the Greek commentators.

This was not the norm. The dominant Jesuit position in Italy through the 1570s, 1580s, and 1590s was strong hostility toward university secular Aristotelianism, which they usually called Averroism. For example, in 1586 or 1587 the Province of Venice argued that the works of Averroes should not be taught because they destroyed truth and troubled souls.[48] They had in mind what they believed was being taught at the University of Padua. In 1585 Jesuits teaching philosophy at the Roman College feared that teaching Averroes would lead to atheism. And the 1586 draft of the Ratio Studiorum warned against the Averroists.[49]

In 1592 four of the five Jesuits responding to the attacks from the University of Padua and Cremonini reiterated the position of Ledesma and Achille Gagliardi. For example, Paolo Comitoli admonished Cremonini not to learn from Simplicius, Alexander of Aphrodisias, and Averroes, but to teach pure doctrine, as three medieval popes and Charlemagne com-

45. MP 4:196–204; Bartlett 1984, 96–99; and especially Sander 2014a, 51–55. The Council of Chalcedon offered a strong confession of Christian belief and a series of disciplinary decrees for the clergy.

46. Sander 2014a, 56–59; Donnelly 2001h.

47. Villoslada 1954, 78–79; Lohr 1976, 214; G. Brunelli 1998, 259–60; and Mucci 2001.

48. MP 6:267. The text lacks a date. Because it was a comment on the draft Ratio Studiorum of 1586, it probably was written in 1586 or 1587.

49. MP 6:39 (1585); MP 5:100–101 (1586).

manded.[50] Four of the responding Jesuits invoked *Apostolici regiminis* and its command that professors of philosophy were obliged to confute the doctrines of philosophers who taught against Catholic truth.[51] On the other hand, the fifth Jesuit, Benedetto Palmio, who had denounced Perera, had changed his view somewhat. He believed that Jesuit professors could meet the secular Aristotelians on their own ground. He argued that the Padua Jesuits did just as good a job of teaching Aristotle as University of Padua professors because they interpreted the same Aristotelian texts and they dealt with the same difficulties and questions. The Jesuits used the same ancient and modern Latin, Greek, and Arabic commentators on Aristotle, and they used the same books as university professors, he wrote.[52]

Ironically, the Italian Jesuits may have been more faithful Aristotelians than their critics, because they were less eclectic. They did not make as much use of non-Aristotelian sources, whether ancient Greek commentaries or other authors and works. But fidelity to Aristotle did not make either the Jesuits, or Italian university Aristotelians who rejected mathematical physics, very modern. Both clung to Aristotle in the face of mounting contrary evidence.[53]

The Jesuit leadership slightly softened its stance against secular Aristotelianism as the century came to a close. In 1582 General Acquaviva abolished Borja's 1565 decree, which had not been universally obeyed. Other small actions followed. At the same time, a younger group of Jesuit philosophers and theologians, notably Francisco Suárez, responded philosophically to Averroes and Italian secular Aristotelianism. He and other Jesuits of his generation were more welcoming to non-Aristotelian sources.[54]

The Ratio Studiorum of 1599 presented an uneasy compromise. It told professors of philosophy that they should not depart from Aristotle unless "he contradicts orthodox belief," at which point the teacher should refute him or any other philosopher who opposed the faith, as *Apostolici regimi-*

---

50. "Impara, impara Cremonino non da Simplicio, non da Alessandro Afrodiseo, non da Averroé." Sangalli 2001, 101–2. Possevino also referred to Averroists and followers of Alexander of Aphrodisias in his response to Cremonini. Sangalli 2001, 171.

51. Sangalli 2001, 87 (Ludovico Gagliardi); 97 (Comitoli); 118–19, 125 (Bonaccorsi); 163, 167, 170 (Possevino).

52. "Ci pareva esser certi di servire nelle stesse lettioni nostre a' publici lettori, poiché si leggevano li stessi autori, s'interpretavano li stessi testi di Aristotele con diligenza ad uno ad uno, si trattavano le stesse difficoltà et questioni, et si adopravano li stessi commentatori et interpreti così latini come greci et arabi, moderni et antichi, et in somma si adopravano li stessi libri che adoprano i lettori, et gli scolari di essa Università." Sangalli 2001, 149 (Palmio).

53. Baldini 1999 provides an excellent account of Jesuit philosophy; see 261 for the opposition to mathematical physics by Cremonini and secular Aristotelians generally.

54. Lohr 1976, 217–20.

nis ordered. The Ratio Studiorum went on to say that a Jesuit philosophy teacher should only very selectively "read or present in class interpreters of Aristotle who do not serve Christianity well." He "should not make Averroes' digressions the subject of some separate extended treatment," a statement that echoed Ledesma and Borja's decree. And he "should not commit himself . . . to any sectarian school of thought like that of the Averroists, of the Alexandrians, and the like, and he should not gloss over the errors of Averroes or Alexander [of Aphrodisias] or the rest, but he should diminish their authority all the more pointedly because of those errors."[55] On the other hand, the general condemnations of the Greeks and Arabs were gone. Jesuit professors of philosophy could engage philosophers of different views, albeit very cautiously. And they did not have to ask permission before doing so. It recognized that Aristotle could be wrong and expressed limited confidence that Jesuit philosophers might engage and refute philosophical texts that differed from Christian Aristotelianism.[56] But this was still very far from the secular Aristotelianism that the Turin critic endorsed in 1593.

Even though the Jesuit leadership under General Acquaviva and the Ratio Studiorum of 1599 offered a slightly more measured response to secular Aristotelianism, prominent Italian Jesuits continued to criticize university professors for teaching atheism or denying the immortality of the human soul. They were one and the same to many Jesuits. In 1572 Michele Lauretano at the German College in Rome charged that students learned atheism at Italian universities.[57] In 1592 Bonaccorsi complained that four philosophers who had taught at the University of Padua over the years (Pomponazzi, Genua de' Passeri, Marcantonio Zimara di Galatina [ca. 1475–1532], and an unidentified fourth) had defended the mortality of the soul and the eternity of the world according to Aristotle.[58] Bonaccorsi had also heard that Cremonini boasted that he wished to teach and defend publicly (meaning in his lectures or in a disputation) the mortality of the soul according to Aristotle.

Antonio Possevino was especially hostile to the secular Aristotelianism taught by Italian university professors. He first encountered it in university

55. *Ratio Studiorum* 2005, pars. 208–11 (99–100, quotations at both pages).
56. Lohr 1976, 218, makes this point well: "the new confidence of the professors of the Roman College in their ability to meet the difficulties posed by Italian secular Aristotelianism."
57. MP 2:996–97.
58. Sangalli 2001, 125 and 125n84. Zimara studied under Agostino Nifo and Pomponazzi at the University of Padua, then taught logic (1501–5) and natural philosophy (1505–9) there, moved to other universities, and returned to Padua to teach philosophy from 1525 to 1528. CHRP 1988, 841. For Genua de' Passeri see note 7 above.

lectures at Ferrara and Padua. Before he became a Jesuit Possevino served as a tutor and guide to two Gonzaga princelings. He accompanied them to the University of Ferrara in 1556 and then to the University of Padua for a few months of study in early 1557, followed by a short repeat visit in 1558, and another from April to September in 1559. Alongside his charges he heard Vincenzo Maggi, ordinary professor of natural philosophy from 1543 to 1564, lecture at Ferrara.[59] At Padua he heard Giovanni Giacomo Pavesio (Calaber, d. 1566) lecture on the *Physics* of Aristotle, Genua de' Passeri lecture on *De anima* and *De caelo* of Aristotle, as well as various unnamed professors.[60]

The secular Aristotelian views of Maggi and Genua de' Passeri have been mentioned. Although Pavesio's works have attracted very little attention from scholars, the name of Averroes was prominent in his published and unpublished works.[61] Possevino so abhorred the opinions of Pavesio that he could not bear to hear them. He concluded that Pavesio, Genua de' Passeri, and other professors at Padua were little more than Averroists. When he listened to them, he felt that he was losing God's light and beginning to believe in the universal intellect of Averroes.[62] Throughout his long career as a Jesuit Possevino was convinced that Italian university philosophers taught an Averroist version of Aristotle that was a veiled form of atheism or, at the minimum, led directly to it. In 1606 he again wrote that the philosophers at the University of Padua taught an atheistic form of Aristotelianism.[63]

The issue of immortality preyed on the minds of princes and parents. When Duke Emanuele Filiberto and noble parents in Turin expressed fear about "secular philosophy tending toward atheism," Achille Gagliardi assured him that the Jesuits would introduce Christian philosophy into the University of Turin. When princes and parents did not raise the issue, the Jesuits did. Possevino warned Duke Ranuccio I of Parma that lay profes-

59. *I maestri di Ferrara* 1991, 27–37, 242.

60. On December 8, 1604, Possevino wrote in his own hand an account of his life for another Jesuit. It is published with an introduction and notes in Castellani 1945. See esp. 107–8, 114–15.

61. Lohr 1988a, 302–4. Born in Calabria, Pavesio taught medicine at the University of Naples, was second-position extraordinary professor of natural philosophy at the University of Padua from 1550 to 1560, and was ordinary professor of natural philosophy at the University of Rome in the academic years 1561–1562 and 1563–1564. Other Roman rolls from the 1560s are missing. Facciolati 1978, part 3, 288; Tomasini 1986, 320; and *I maestri di Roma* 1991, 1:33, 35. See Lohr 1988a, 302–4, for a list of his works and more bibliography.

62. "Che co' studi della filosofia insegnata in quel modo, che in Padova dal Genova, dal Calabrese, et da altri si faceva, [i quali per lo più erano meri Averroisti], sí sentiva a poco a poco a perder'il lume di Dio, et a credere dell'anima intellettiva ciò che insegna Averroe. In questo ragionamento, perciochè ancor io, il quale haveva udito tutta la fisica dal Calabrese, et i libri dell'anima, et de cielo dal Genova, et abhorriva dall'opinioni del Calabrese, sì che più non volsi udirlo." Possevino as quoted in Castellani 1945, 115. Piaia 1973, 139–40, also quotes this passage.

63. Piaia 1973.

sors of philosophy were likely to teach that the soul was mortal. This issue made the gap between university secular Aristotelianism and Jesuit Christian Aristotelianism unbridgeable.

Summisti, Compendia, and Quaestiones

Critics accused the Jesuits of not teaching directly from the texts of Aristotle. They lacked originality because they dictated from textbooks or notes from other scholars. And they devoted too much time to quaestiones, traditional key passages in the text on which important meaning hinged. All the accusations were true. But the Jesuits had reasons for their actions, and they were not alone.

In 1593 the Turin critic charged that all the writings that the Jesuit fathers dictated to their own students had the same meaning. Hence, when students proposed conclusions for disputations, they were interchangeable with minor variations. A new conclusion was never welcomed.[64] In addition, in December 1591 the leader of the student arts organization at the University of Padua claimed that the Jesuits taught logic and philosophy by means of modern *summisti* (summaries) without lecturing from the text of Aristotle. Students could not become good philosophers without studying Aristotle directly, he asserted.[65] And Cremonini in his oration to the Venetian Senate asserted that Jesuit teachers read from sheets of paper containing "antidottrina" (anti-knowledge), meaning borrowed knowledge. When they taught from notes based on the work of other scholars, they made mistakes or produced secondhand knowledge.[66] Cremonini also claimed that the riformatori of the universities of Pavia, Padua, Ferrara, Bologna, and Pisa had repeatedly ordered professors not to dictate their lectures.[67] But the Jesuits did nothing but dictate.

64. "Et gli scritti che i padri Giesuuiti [sic] dettano, a' scolari luoro sono, quanto al senso, tutti similli: onde quando gli scolari propongono conclusioni da disputare, tutti propongono le medesime, paucis mutatis, ne mai è chi propongono un nuovo beltr[–illegible–]to." AST, Istruzione Pubblica, Regia Università, Mazzo 1, no. 7.2, "Raggioni 1593," no pag. The last word, obscured by an ink blot, is probably "beltrovato."

65. "Leggendo come fanno la logica, et filosofia senza però legger il testo d'Aristotile, ma solamente alcuni moderni Summisti non approvati dalle Università de' studi generali con danno delli scolari che non possono riuscir boni filosofi senza studiar Aristotile." Letter of the Venetian governors (names not given) of Padua to the Venetian Senate, December 5, 1591, printed in Favaro 1877–1878, 487–88.

66. Cremonini 1998, 66.

67. It was true that universities issued decrees banning the dictation of lectures. However, I did not compile a list during research for this book or Grendler 2002. Of course, frequent prohibitions meant that the practice was widespread.

One Jesuit turned Cremonini's accusation that Jesuit teachers relied on the scholarship of others against him. In 1592 Bonaccorsi asked rhetorically if Cremonini never relied on the works of others and taught only his own ideas? He offered mock praise to Cremonini as a miraculous scholar who held all the learning of the ages in his head. Bonaccorsi believed that a teacher should avail himself of the wisdom of distinguished scholars of the past.[68]

Nevertheless, the accusations were significant. And Jesuit teachers did use the notes of others, read from sheets of paper, dictate, and rely on summisti. The first two were embedded in Jesuit pedagogy. Influenced by the practices of the Paris colleges, Ignatius recommended in the Constitutions that Jesuit students should take careful notes in class. Polanco and Ledesma developed notetaking practices further and made them an important part of Jesuit pedagogy. Students in the philosophy and theology courses were advised to bring loose sheets of paper to the lectures in order to take detailed notes. They were expected to fill in the gaps in their notes during repetitions (recapitulation and review exercises) to produce notebooks that would be useful for disputations and compositions.[69] At the end of the year a Jesuit student was expected to have a detailed set of lecture notes that could be used for his own lectures, made available to other students, or to circulate beyond Jesuit circles.[70]

Although many Jesuits disapproved, Jesuits used dictation when teaching philosophy because it was an effective way of instructing less able students. An official Jesuit visitor to the Collegio Romano in 1578 discovered that teachers used dictation to teach philosophy. But he did not dare to speak against it because it was widely used and the students much appreciated it. He conceded that dictation helped mediocre students.[71] It was the same in Jesuit schools across Europe in the 1570s, 1580s, and 1590s. Many Jesuits complained that Jesuit teachers used dictation too much, and some wanted to prohibit it completely. But because it helped weak students, it was permitted.[72] The Ratio Studiorum of 1599 cautiously permitted dictation in the upper school.[73]

68. Sangalli 2001, 125. 69. Nelles 2007, esp. 88–95.

70. Hellyer 2005, 75; and Nelles 2007, esp. 102–4.

71. "Del studio della filosofia non so dir altro senon che il modo di leggere, qual'è dettando, mi dispiace et tanto scrivere. Ma vedo questo modo tanto introdotto e tanto grato alli scolari, che non hebbi ardire di parlare di mutarlo. Saria anche bene servare una mediocrita." MP 4:323. The visitor was Father Sebastião Morais (Morales), ca. 1535–1588, a Portuguese Jesuit who later was provincial superior of the Province of Portugal and a bishop. Ruiz de Medina 2001.

72. MP 4:225, 232, 239–40, 254, 282, 323, 433, 673–74, 679; 6:171–72, 230, 272, 274, 291; 7:236, 301, 337, 369, 587. See also Nelles 2007, 88.

73. *Ratio Studiorum* 2005, pars. 137–38, 215 (51, 101). Dictation was an essential part of teaching in the lower school and never questioned.

The Italian Jesuits were well acquainted with summisti (*summulae* in Latin).[74] They were of two minds. The Province of Milan did not like summulae and in 1586 recommended that its teachers should be forbidden to dictate from them.[75] On the other hand, the Jesuits at the Roman College discussed at length in the 1580s whether they should create a comprehensive theology textbook. Although they believed that it would have many pedagogical benefits, including uniformity and freeing teachers and students for other academic exercises such as disputing, they decided not to do it.[76] The Ratio Studiorum did not mention comprehensive works in philosophy or theology.

Nevertheless, manuscript summaries compiled by students or prepared by professors circulated and were used. Hence, the criticism was accurate. A Jesuit teacher who used summaries or lecture notes from a course that he had previously attended in a major Jesuit school was not creating original knowledge unless he added new material from his own research. And summaries and lecture notes were probably not so tightly bound to Aristotle's exact words as were traditional paraphrase-commentary lectures.

But pedagogical preferences were changing. The 1590s marked the beginning of the age of Aristotelian philosophical textbooks of which the Jesuit Coimbra Commentaries were famous examples.[77] They originated as dictations to students, not intended for publication, by the Jesuits at the University of Coimbra. When some of the material appeared in unauthorized printed editions, General Acquaviva commissioned Pedro da Fonseca with revising and preparing them for publication. Although called commentaries, they were eight well-organized presentations of Aristotle's major works beginning with the volume on the *Physics* in 1592 and concluding with a volume on Aristotle's dialectic in 1606.[78] Many more editions followed, sometimes with Aristotle's Greek text included. They were widely used across Europe until about 1650 when their popularity waned. Cremonini and the Turin critic were railing against an emerging and popular method for teaching Aristotle.

In the early seventeenth century the Jesuits accepted textbooks and course summaries because the leadership wanted greater philosophical and theological uniformity. The introduction of internal prepublication cen-

---

74. MP 6:260–61, 263, 267, always in 1586. The comments about *summulae* came from the provinces of Rome, Naples, Milan, and Venice in the course of evaluating the trial Ratio Studiorum of 1586.

75. MP 6:263 under points 6 and 18.

76. MP 6:34–36, 42; and Hellyer 2005, 25–27.

77. Schmitt 1988.

78. Casalini 2012, is a good study of their development.

sorship procedures, albeit with loopholes, in 1601 signaled a preference for greater unanimity and less tolerance for divergent views.[79] Then in 1611 General Acquaviva wrote to the superiors of all provinces to impress on them the necessity of "soliditas et uniformitas doctrinae" (solidity and uniformity in knowledge) by which he primarily meant greater allegiance to Aquinas.[80] He followed this with an ordinance of 1613 directed to all provincial superiors concerning both theology and philosophy. Acquaviva reaffirmed that philosophy served theology, and that Jesuits should follow Aristotle so long as he did not differ from the Catholic faith. He warned against adding new philosophical ideas or introducing obscure authors and pertinacious opinions into Jesuit philosophy teaching. He reminded prefects of studies of their duty to visit classrooms regularly, to question students, and to read the notes of students, all of which the Ratio Studiorum had commanded. Acquaviva did not condemn any author or idea, or promulgate new rules. Rather, he ordered provincial superiors to enforce the existing ones.[81]

In this atmosphere, Jesuit philosophical compendia began to appear in print. Compendia were well-organized and quite thorough summaries of the year's work in logic, natural philosophy, or metaphysics, or all three, that made extensive use of questions, assertions, objections, and responses. Although they had some characteristics of commentaries, they were not word-for-word explications of the text, but taught at a slight distance from the text. Their goal was to impart of body of organized knowledge, with an emphasis on organization. An example was the *Cursus philosophicus* of Rodrigo de Arriaga (1592–1667), first published in 1632. It claimed to explain philosophy as it was actually taught in Jesuit schools.[82] Such works provided the solidity and uniformity of philosophical instruction that General Acquaviva sought.

Critics also charged that Jesuit teachers devoted too much attention to quaestiones. This was another pedagogical issue that the Jesuits debated among themselves. In 1583 a Jesuit visitor sent to evaluate Jesuit teaching at the University of Vienna reported that the teacher in the logic class had hardly lectured on a line of Aristotle during the year.[83] The implication was that he devoted too much time to quaestiones. The Ratio Studiorum

79. Baldini 1992, 75–119.

80. MP 7:657–59.

81. MP 7:660–64, for philosophy see section 6 at 662–63. For an English translation see *Jesuit Pedagogy* 2016, 233–38. See also Hellyer 2005, 33–35; *Ratio Studiorum* 2005, par. 115 (43).

82. Hellyer 2005, 74–75. On Arriaga see Baciero 2001.

83. MP 7:445; Hellyer 2005, 77, first noted this passage.

of 1599 tried to strike a balance between Aristotle's text and quaestiones. It told Jesuit teachers to "devote no less effort to it [the text of Aristotle] than to the questions." It also told teachers which parts of Aristotle's books should be discussed and sometimes the order of presentation. It told them to use quaestiones extensively and to pay particular attention to famous passages often mentioned in disputations. Teachers should tell students which interpretations were preferred because of the weight of the argument, "the meaning of the Greek expression," or "the authority of famous interpreters."[84] In practice, Jesuit philosophy teachers tended to provide literal explanations of the text which served as connectives between quaestiones on which they focused.[85]

Jesuit Criticism of University Pedagogy

The Jesuits defended their teaching and criticized university pedagogy. For example, in 1592 Possevino charged that university professors did not offer a thorough and integrated understanding of Aristotelian texts or Aristotelian philosophy as a whole. They jumped about, teaching passages here and there, skipping over half of it, leaving so many gaps that students could not understand the "method and marrow" of Aristotle. Nevertheless these same professors conferred doctorates on students who did not understand the whole of philosophy.[86]

Cremonini charged that Jesuit teachers were young, inexperienced, unproven, and barely more than students themselves.[87] The Jesuits disputed this vigorously. They acknowledged that some Jesuit teachers were young. But a keen intellect and good preparation, not a long beard, produced the wisdom to teach well, they contended. And Jesuit teachers were well prepared because they had studied for ten years or more, including three years of philosophy and four years of theology. Thanks to intense study a Jesuit learned more in ten years than others did in twenty or thirty.[88] The unspoken comparison was with young men who studied at a university for about

84. *Ratio Studiorum* 2005, pars. 215–29 (102–6, quotations at 104 and 105).

85. "The *quaestiones* were the true course programme, while the literal explanations were only the link between them." Baldini 1999, 251.

86. "Anzi a punto sarebbe volto et salto il non farne tante, percioché il non leggere pezzi di Aristotele, et lasciarne buona parte di mezo, et fare tante parentesi in sì breve periodo de' tempi ne' quali i scolari vi vogliano o possano attendere, et nondimeno il dottorare per filosofi quei che non hanno udita intiera filosofia, né per conseguente hanno potuto comprendere la metodo et midolla." Sangalli 2001, 174.

87. Cremonini 1998, 66.

88. Sangalli 2001, 124–25 (Bonaccorsi), 149–50 (Palmio), 173–74 (Possevino).

five years, acquired a doctorate, and began university lecturing by the age of twenty-five, a common pattern. Jesuits, by contrast, did not normally begin teaching philosophy until their early thirties.

The Jesuits argued that their schools prepared students well for university studies. Hostile professors agreed. In 1594 the city council of Padua drafted a long memorandum extolling the benefits of Jesuit schooling as part of its effort to persuade the Venetian Senate to permit the Padua school to reopen its doors to non-Jesuit students. Thirty-three professors (of about fifty) at the University of Padua signed a statement affirming that a reopened Jesuit school would be useful for preparing students for university courses.[89] The Jesuits underscored this point.[90] Although university professors did not want Jesuits teaching at the university, they were quite willing for them to prepare students for university studies.

The Jesuits claimed that they offered much more philosophy instruction than did university professors. In 1592 two Jesuits argued that a Jesuit teacher delivered three hundred or more lectures in the Jesuit academic year, while a University of Padua professor delivered only sixty or seventy lectures in the university academic year.[91] A 1594 memorandum from the city council of Padua elaborated. It stated that before the Jesuit school was closed to external students, the logic teacher there lectured twice a day for 160 days, thus delivering a total of 320 lectures in an academic year. The philosophy teacher did the same.[92]

The claims were true. Jesuit logic, natural philosophy, and metaphysics teachers commonly, although not universally, lectured twice a day.[93] And the Jesuit academic year was much longer than the Italian university academic year. Upper school classes in Jesuit schools in Italy began in early November and lasted through the end of August. By contrast, although the

89. "Anche l'università giunge ad ammettere l'utilità di avere una struttura ben organizzata che prepari gli studenti a frequentare i corsi dello Studio pubblico." As quoted in Sangalli 1999, 288–89.

90. Sangalli 2001, 144–46, 149 (Palmio).

91. Sangalli 2001, 124 (Bonaccosi), 134 (Palmio).

92. "Quelli di logica et filosofia due per uno al giorno. I giorni dell'anno che si leggevano in dette letture maggiori erano da cento et sessanta et così le lettioni di logica et filosofia, per essere due al giorno, venivano ad essere trecento e venti." Quoted in Sangalli 1999, 290–91. It is likely that the Padua Jesuits helped prepare the memorandum.

93. Two examples. One Jesuit who taught logic, natural philosophy, and metaphysics successively at the Collegio Romano from November 1589 through early September 1592, delivered 1,100 lectures, an average of 367 per academic year. Wallace 2006, 318–19. And the 1624–1625 roll of the Jesuit upper school at Mantua shows that the rhetoric teacher, the logic teacher, and a third Jesuit who taught a combination of natural philosophy and metaphysics all lectured twice a day. Grendler 2009b, 81.

University of Padua calendar mandated about 135 ordinary lectures in an academic year (early November to early June), unauthorized holidays, professorial absenteeism, and student disturbances had reduced the number to sixty to seventy in the early seventeenth century. It was the same at other universities.[94] Finally, the full Jesuit philosophy course consisted of three successive year-long courses in logic, natural philosophy, and metaphysics. If a student did all three, he learned a great deal of Aristotelian philosophy, in most cases considerably more than students in Italian universities.

A very effective Jesuit response to criticism was that they provided a peaceful and morally good environment conducive to learning and free of the violence and immorality found in universities. They claimed that university lectures were interrupted by shouts, whistling, and fighting in the student benches; this produced so much noise that nine out of ten sentences of professors could not be heard. By contrast, students in Jesuit schools were not permitted to bring knives into classes, and no student at the Jesuit school at Padua had ever been wounded or killed.[95] The Jesuits did not exaggerate: chronic fighting among university students produced wounds and deaths.[96] And no incident of this kind in a Jesuit school has come to light.

Conclusion

University professors taught secular Aristotelianism, while the Jesuits taught Christian Aristotelianism. Of course, there was a great deal of agreement despite polemical statements. And both university philosophers and Jesuits argued vigorously among themselves. Nevertheless, the differences were real. Philosophers in civic universities embraced the Greek commentators much more enthusiastically than did Jesuit philosophers. Some lay professors used Averroes extensively, while Jesuit philosophers were told to reject his works or treat them with extreme caution. *Apostolici regiminis* and the Jesuit leadership pressed Jesuit philosophers to point out and correct doctrinal error. It was not likely that many university professors did this. Most important, some prominent university professors argued that Aristotelian philosophy could not demonstrate the immortality of the human intellective soul. Influential Italian Jesuits saw this as veiled atheism or philosophizing that led to atheism.

94. Grendler 2002, 495–96.

95. Sangalli 2001, 88–89 (Ludovico Gagliardi), 124, 126 (Bonaccorsi), 157 (Palmio), 171 (Possevino).

96. For three recent studies see Grendler 2002, 500–505; Grendler 2009a, 301–6, 316–18; and Carlsmith 2012.

University professors and the Jesuits embraced different pedagogical methods. The Jesuits used dictation, summaries, compendia, notes from the lectures of more learned Jesuits, and a focus on the major points of Aristotle. Jesuit professors sacrificed some direct contact with the texts of Aristotle in favor of an integrated and comprehensive approach. The Society wanted considerable, but not total, uniformity of instruction. University professors preferred the paraphrase-commentary, which was a close analysis of Aristotle's words. Their ideal philosopher was the learned individual who offered his own original insight into Aristotle. That was the path toward recognition. Given the differences in their interpretation of Aristotle and pedagogy, it was inevitable that university professors and Jesuits would disagree sharply.

15

THE JESUIT CONTRIBUTION TO
THEOLOGICAL EDUCATION

The Jesuits made major contributions and innovations to Italian theological education. They taught cases of conscience. They provided many classes in theology, always gratis. They decided that four years of theological study was enough. After obtaining many quick doctorates in their first years, the Italian Jesuits practically eliminated doctorates of theology for themselves but awarded a limited number to non-Jesuits. They made these changes in civic-Jesuit universities and in their own schools. But universities lacking Jesuits almost completely ignored what the Jesuits did.

Cases of Conscience

The most important curricular innovation of the Jesuits was the introduction of cases of conscience. Sometimes called casuistry, cases of conscience is a branch of moral theology. Catholic moral theology is predicated on the supposition that human beings are free to make informed moral choices. Hence, moral theology is the analysis of the principles of good and evil that influence choices. Moral theology examines conscience, love, responsibility, law, and man's ultimate happiness. The second part of Aquinas' *Summa Theologica* was a fundamental source for the study of moral theology for the Jesuits and others in the sixteenth century.[1]

Cases of conscience is the application of the principles of moral theology to individual human actions, especially sins. Moral theology is theoretical; cases of conscience is practical. The goal of cases of conscience instruction was to provide guidance to confessors who had to judge the sinfulness or licitness of human actions as revealed in the confessional or

---

1. See Lisson, Moore, and Bretske 2001 for a good introduction to Jesuit moral theology.

elsewhere. Lectures in cases of conscience helped a confessor to understand different kinds of sins, under what conditions he might grant absolution to the sinner, what penances he should impose, and which sins and sinners had to be referred to higher ecclesiastical authority for resolution.[2] The most important works of cases of conscience were manuals for confessors. Their contents included limited analysis of moral principles, followed by many pages on the Ten Commandments, church laws, definitions of sins, and what penances confessors should impose.[3] Cases of conscience had a juridical caste in the sixteenth, seventeenth, and eighteenth centuries.

The Jesuits mostly taught cases of conscience. Jesuit pedagogical documents listed many courses in cases of conscience and very few courses in moral theology. The Ratio Studiorum of 1599 referred frequently to cases or cases of conscience but never used the term moral theology, because it saw the latter as part of scholastic theology.[4] However, less formal Jesuit documents, such as the triennial reports on the activities of colleges and schools and letters, used moral theology and cases of conscience interchangeably, especially in the seventeenth and eighteenth centuries. In what follows, the terms found in the documents will be given. Otherwise, "cases of conscience" or "cases" will be preferred, because this was what the Jesuits almost always taught.

Although the study of cases of conscience originated in the Middle Ages, it only became a significant part of the training of priests in the sixteenth and seventeenth centuries. The Jesuits were important in this development because they taught cases from their earliest years. In 1546 Paschase Broët, one of the first ten Jesuits, lectured on cases of conscience to diocesan priests in Faenza.[5] Jerónimo Nadal lectured on cases of conscience on religious holidays at the Jesuit church in Messina in 1548.[6] The rector of the Roman College taught cases of conscience on feast days, Sundays, and/or the non-teaching day (normally Thursday) in 1553. Cases became a permanent part of its curriculum, usually with two teachers, in 1573.[7] Parish priests and curates flocked to the cases lectures, which attracted 300 listeners in 1576.[8]

---

2. On Jesuit cases of conscience, start with Angelozzi 1981; O'Malley 1993, 144–47; and Moore 2001a and 2001b, each with additional bibliography.

3. Turrini 1991, offers a comprehensive census and study of manuals for confessors by Jesuits and others in Italy from the origins of printing to 1650.

4. The closest it came was "rerum moralium principiis" (principles of moral issues). *Ratio Studiorum* 2005, pars. 185, 191, C45, C78, C97, C129 (65, 67, 77, 82, 86, 94; quotation at 67).

5. O'Malley 1993, 145.   6. Moore 2001a, 691–92.

7. Villoslada 1954, 30, 71, 90, 325–26.

8. ARSI, Roma 126b I, f. 96v, annual letter of 1576 of Benedetto Giustiniani.

The Council of Trent created demand. Its decrees on penance of Session 14 (November 25, 1551) affirmed the role of priests in judging and absolving sins, and determining penances.[9] Session 23 (July 15, 1563) emphasized that priests should be trained in administering the sacraments, "especially things that seem adapted to the hearing of confessions."[10] It decreed that candidates for the priesthood had to be approved by the bishop, and recommended that bishops examine them before ordination. Conscientious bishops began to examine priesthood candidates, which obliged candidates to learn something about penitential matters.

But how and where would they learn? Italian universities did not teach cases of conscience. Medieval mendicant religious orders did in some of their convent studia, but secular priests did not always have access to them. Few dioceses had seminaries and they did not teach much. To fill the gap some bishops appointed clergymen to instruct parish priests on cases of conscience in the cathedral church or episcopal palace. The Society saw the need and made cases of conscience a feature of Jesuit education. In 1696, for example, 57 percent (68 of 119) of the Jesuit schools in Italy had teachers of cases of conscience.[11] A small Jesuit school might offer two or three classes in grammar and humanities plus cases. Other religious orders in Italy, notably the Dominicans, also taught cases, and some of their members published important works. But the Jesuits led the way.

The cases of conscience lectureship was separate from the tightly connected Jesuit curriculum of Latin grammar, humanities, rhetoric, logic, natural philosophy, metaphysics, and theology. In a handful of major Jesuit schools, including the Roman College, the cases class met five days a week. Everywhere else it met one to three times per week. Cases were taught in the vernacular, and auditors did not have to attend other Jesuit courses to prepare for them. The teachers whom the Jesuits chose to teach cases reflected the separate and lower status of the course. Although some well-known Jesuits taught cases of conscience at some point in their careers, most teachers were chosen because their superiors judged them to lack the academic ability to teach philosophy or scholastic theology.[12]

9. *Canons* 1978, session 14, chaps. 2, 5, 7, 8 (90, 92, 96, 98).

10. *Canons* 1978, session 23, chaps. 7, 15, 18 (169, 173, 176, quotation at 176). See also Turrini 1990, 224.

11. This information comes from a survey of all Jesuit schools in Italy and the classes that they offered in 1696 from ARSI, Roma 66, Veneta 49, Mediolanensis 4, Neapolitana 88, and Sicula 91 III.

12. The Ratio Studiorum made this clear. "Who should be chosen for case studies [casibus], who for philosophy? If any have been found unsuited for philosophy in the earlier examination, they should be sent to case studies." "Or they are below the average, and all of these ought to

When the Jesuits entered universities they brought cases of conscience lectures with them. The new civic-Jesuit universities of Parma and Mantua included professorships of cases, sometimes called moral theology at Parma, taught by Jesuits. The Jesuits at the small civic-Jesuit University of Fermo did not teach cases as a university position, but did teach it in their own school. Despite its separate and lower status, the cases of conscience lectureship was a major Jesuit innovation that expanded the theology curriculum and improved clerical education.

Italian civic universities did not follow the example of the Jesuits. No Italian university had a professorship of cases of conscience (or moral theology) before the Society of Jesus came into existence in 1540, and they did little or no teaching of it later. Four civic universities completely ignored cases of conscience. The University of Padua never taught cases of conscience or moral theology in the sixteenth, seventeenth, or eighteenth centuries.[13] The University of Turin did not teach cases or moral theology through 1690 and probably not after.[14] The University of Macerata did not teach cases or moral theology.[15] And the University of Perugia never taught cases or moral theology.[16]

Five civic universities did eventually teach cases of conscience or moral theology, but only slowly, reluctantly, fitfully, and mostly in the eighteenth century. A prominent local parish priest taught moral theology at the University of Pavia for a few years in the 1620s, and a Dominican taught moral theology from 1732 until his death in 1755.[17] That was all. The University of Ferrara taught moral theology for two academic years, 1592–1593 and 1611–1612. Then in the first thirty years of the eighteenth century the university added several new positions in religious studies including moral theology in the academic year 1723–1724. But no stipend was attached to the position. The unpaid and unimportant moral theology position lasted

be assigned to case studies." "For if they are average in humanistic literary studies, and they are endowed with no other talent, then they will be sent to the course in case studies as well." *Ratio Studiorum* 2005, pars. 27–29 (quotations at 15–16).

13. For a complete list of the professorships and their occupants at the University of Padua to 1757, see Facciolati 1978. A document of August 29, 1771, listing the professorships at that time does not include moral theology, which also suggests that the subject was not taught between 1757 and 1771 either. Del Negro 2002, 302.

14. For lists of the professors from 1566 to 1690, see Chiaudano 1972a, Chiaudano 1972b, Dellacorno 1972, and Fisicaro Vercelli 1972. Information on the eighteenth century is lacking.

15. Although rolls for the seventeenth and eighteenth century are missing, Serangeli, Ramadù-Mariani, and Zambuto 2006 prints statutes which occasionally list parts of rolls, while Serangeli 2010 lists all the professors between 1540 and 1824 so far discovered.

16. Ermini 1971, 1:239–41, 619–23.

17. *Memorie di Pavia* part 1, 1970, 193, 197; and Negruzzo 1995b, 148.

until 1771.[18] The University of Messina had an extraordinary and holiday professorship, with lectures on Thursdays and holidays, of cases of conscience for at least some years in the first half of the seventeenth century.[19]

The University of Catania had no professorship of moral theology until an unpaid position was created in 1739 during a period of changes imposed on the university by new overseers. In or about 1746 the professor of moral theology began to receive a low salary, and the position continued through 1773. A series of clergymen, but never a Jesuit, filled the position.[20] The University of Naples did not teach moral theology in the sixteenth and seventeenth centuries. In 1703 a new Spanish viceroy with strong ideas about university education added some new positions, including moral theology, to the university. But it lasted only four academic years, because Austria seized the Kingdom of Naples from Spain in 1707, and the new government restored the previous curriculum.[21]

The University of Pisa created a professorship in cases of conscience in 1622 which lasted through the academic year 1628–1629.[22] After a hiatus of seven years, the university created a professorship of moral theology in 1636 that lasted until 1807.[23] Because the Jesuits never had a college or school in Pisa, they were not available to teach in the university.

The University of Rome taught moral theology about one-quarter of the time between 1600 and 1773, but never appointed a Jesuit. It introduced an ordinary professorship of moral theology (Sacra Theologia moralis: de sacramentis) in 1642, filled by a Friar Minor Conventual, which lasted for three years. The position reappeared in the academic year 1649–1650 (In sacra Theologia morali: de immunitat. ecclesiast.) again filled by a Friar Minor Conventual, which continued to 1658. In that year Pope Alexander VII eliminated the moral theology position in favor of a new position entitled "In Controversiis dogmaticis," which meant defending Catholic doctrine against attacks.[24] After an absence of ninety-three years, moral theology reappeared in the academic year 1751–1752. Several Carmelites filled the position from 1751 to 1787.[25]

18. Dal Nero 1991, 258; and *I maestri di Ferrara* 1991, 174.

19. Novarese 1994, 232–33, 530–31, 552. Unfortunately, faculty rolls have not survived, and the Spanish government closed the University of Messina after the uprising of 1674.

20. Paladino 1934, 227–41.

21. Cortese 1924, 67–71, 101–4, 128–29, 142–45, 156–57.

22. Barsanti 1993, 529, 542.

23. Barsanti 1993, 505–42; and Barsanti 2000, 272–339, 341.

24. Carafa 1971, 1:284; and *I maestri di Roma* 1991, 1:276, 280, 284, 307, 336, 338–39, 346, 350.

25. *I maestri di Roma* 1991, 2:867, 872, 910, 918, 966, for individual teachers and the summary on 1114–15. See the annual rolls for further information.

The University of Bologna devoted the most attention to cases of conscience and moral theology. But the reason was to thwart the Jesuits. As described in chapter 10, the university inaugurated a professorship of cases of conscience in 1637, appointing a secular priest, in order to compete with the Jesuit lectures. The university went further in 1670. At that time a popular Jesuit was teaching cases under license of the archbishop in the cathedral of St. Petronius, plus advising the archdiocese on casuistry issues. The archbishop then authorized the Jesuit to move his lectures, which attracted eighty to ninety attendees, to the Jesuit college. Concerned that his popularity would attract clergymen to other courses in the Jesuit school, the university doubled, tripled, and quadrupled the number of its cases of conscience lecturers: two in 1670, three in 1671, and four in 1674. One of the cases lectureships was renamed moral theology in 1695.[26] The university increasingly used the name "moral theology," and it sometimes combined the two names, for example, "Theol. Moralis legant de casibus conscientiae."[27] In the eighteenth century the number of cases of conscience and moral theology professors at the university remained high: two, three, or four in the first third of the century, rising to five in 1745, six in 1755, then falling to four or five in the last half of the century. Barnabites, Benedictines, Carmelites, Dominicans, Franciscans, canons from the cathedral, and secular priests taught cases of conscience and/or moral theology at the university.[28] But no Jesuit ever filled that position or any other in the University of Bologna.

Multiple teachers did not mean that the University of Bologna or the city saw teaching cases of conscience or moral theology as a priority. Nor did it mean that the university offered a great deal more instruction than before. The growth in the number of professorships of cases of conscience was part of a large increase in the total number of professors in all disciplines at the University of Bologna in the seventeenth and eighteenth centuries. For example, in the academic year 1736–1737, there were 81 professors in theology, medicine, philosophy, mathematics, and the humanities, twice the number in the 1550s. Seventeen of the 81 taught religious subjects: eight scholastic theologians, three controversial theologians, two scripture lecturers, and one each for moral theology, cases of conscience, ecclesiastical history, and the study of church councils.[29]

26. Dallari 1888–1924, 3.1:172.
27. Dallari 1888–1924, vols. 2 and 3, part 1. See 3.1:305 for the quoted title.
28. Dallari 1888–1924, vol. 3, parts 1 and 2. Turrini 1990, provides an excellent overview and a convenient list of all the cases of conscience and moral theology professors and the years that they taught at 235–36.
29. Dallari 1888–1924, 3.1:354–56. For the 1550s see Grendler 2002, 9.

Two developments produced the expansion. First was the growth in the number of clergymen in Bologna and across Italy in the seventeenth and eighteenth centuries. Because the Council of Trent and bishops insisted that clergymen, especially secular priests, had to be better educated if they wished to hear confessions and hold benefices, more clergymen attended universities than in the sixteenth century. This justified the creation of new religious studies positions.[30] Second, and much more important, in order to encourage Bolognese men to study, the city government rewarded Bolognese citizens who obtained doctorates with university professorships at low salaries. But it is very unlikely that all seventeen men who taught religious subjects in the academic year 1736–1737 attracted students. And if they did not attract students, they did not teach. The majority of these professorships were nominal positions.[31]

Theology outside the University

The Jesuits also added greatly to the quantity of theological instruction available in Italy. In 1594 Antonio Possevino wrote that, because of poverty, not everyone who wished to become a clergyman was able or accustomed to study at a university. And, of course, the lectures were in Latin which not all clergymen understood very well. He opined that university lectures were not necessary for everyone, and that there should be free instruction.[32]

The first Jesuits recognized this long before 1594 and offered theological instruction in a handful of their schools from the beginning, albeit mostly for their own members. In 1600 five Jesuit schools in the Italian peninsula and Sicily offered two or more courses in scholastic theology, cases of conscience, and/or scripture, while another eleven Jesuit schools offered a course in cases of conscience.[33] All courses were gratis. The number grew. In 1696 twenty-seven Italian Jesuit schools offered two or more classes in scholastic theology, cases, and scripture, while another forty-four Jesuit schools offered a single course in cases of conscience.[34] By contrast, Italy

---

30. Turrini 1990, 228–30.   31. Simeoni 1987, 92–100.

32. "Or questo numero di gente, la quale ha a clericarsi non può né suole tutto andar allo Studio publico, ma per la povertà et perché quelle maggiori letture non sono a tutti necessarie per questo effetto, hanno bisogno apunto che loro insegni gratis." Letter of Possevino of July 31, 1594, quoted in Sangalli 1999, 298.

33. ARSI, Roma 54, Veneta 37, Mediolanensis 47, Neapolitana 80, Sicula 60; and Lukács 1960–1961, part 2, 48–51.

34. ARSI, Roma 66; Veneta 49 ff. 106r–30r et passim; Mediolanensis 4; Neapolitana 88, ff. 179r–235r; and Sicula 91 III.

had only seventeen universities teaching theology, almost always without cases of conscience, at the end of the seventeenth century. The number of non-Jesuit clergymen who studied theology for periods of time ranging from a year of lectures in cases of conscience to four years of scholastic theology in Italian Jesuit schools from the middle of the sixteenth century to the suppression of 1773 is impossible to quantify but was enormous.

Quick Doctorates for the First Jesuits

The attitude of the Jesuits toward the doctorate of theology evolved. In the first twenty-five years of the Society the Jesuits acquired numerous quick and easy Italian doctorates of theology so that they might teach theology in northern European universities. This action was a response to an immediate need and a reaction against the degree requirements of the University of Paris.

The long road to the Paris doctorate of theology had six stages.[35] The candidate began attending theology lectures after securing the licentiate of arts or master of arts. He was required to hear four years of lectures delivered by advanced theology students on the Bible and six years on the *Sentences* of Peter Lombard, although they might be heard concurrently. In so doing he acquired ten credits. The student next became a *cursor* or a *biblicus ordinarius* if he belonged to a religious order. A cursor had to be at least twenty-five years of age. He then lectured on the Bible for three years and participated in a disputation. If he was judged to have performed satisfactorily, he became a *baccalarius Sententiarius* (bachelor of the *Sentences*), which meant that he lectured on the *Sentences* for one year. If judged satisfactory, he became a *baccalarius formatus* (formed bachelor) and participated in three disputations over the next three or four years.

When he had successfully concluded the three disputations, a committee of the Faculty of Theology decided if he was ready to receive the licentiate of theology, the fifth stage. The candidate had to be thirty-five years of age, legitimately born, and in good health. He then received the *licentia docendi*, the authorization to teach theology anywhere. The final step was the doctorate of theology, which required two more solemn disputations. Overall, a doctorate of theology from the Faculty of Theology of the University of Paris required twelve to fifteen years of residence, attending lectures, disputing, lecturing, and examinations. This was two to three times as many years as for a doctorate in canon law, civil law (which Paris did not

---

35. This and the following paragraph summarize Farge 1985, 16–28; and Farge 1996b, 88.

confer), or medicine. A doctorate of theology took just as long elsewhere, because Catholic faculties of theology across Europe modeled their curricula and degree requirements on those of Paris.

While all the early Jesuits studied theology at Paris, none advanced beyond the first stage of attending theology lectures, and only Jerónimo Nadal obtained a doctorate. But he did not do it in Paris and he leaped over the requirements. In the fall of 1536 Nadal left Paris for Avignon, a papal territory with an international population including a small Mallorcan contingent. Nadal may have studied theology at the University of Avignon. In any case, he received the doctorate of theology there on May 11, 1538. The only information about it comes from a brief notice in an archive stating that he received the degree from Pietro da Forlì, a professor of civil law not further identified.[36]

Professors of civil law do not teach theology then or now. But in the Renaissance they often held the title of count palatine with the power of conferring doctoral degrees in any discipline. Pietro da Forlì was probably a count palatine who used his authority to confer a doctorate on Nadal.[37] The office and name originated in the Lombard kingdom of northern Italy (ca. 575–774). It meant that a pope or emperor empowered a man to exercise authority on his behalf to perform certain legal actions including conferring doctorates. Once count palatine authority was secured, all males in the direct legitimate line of a count palatine inherited it in perpetuity. In the sixteenth century all university towns had a number of counts palatine, some of them professors, others not. Many students turned to counts palatine for their doctorates because the process was simple and the expenses much lower than a doctorate conferred by a college of doctors and the university chancellor. A count palatine examined the candidate to determine if he merited the doctorate, or he entrusted this task to a committee of his choosing. In either case, the count palatine made the decision and conferred the doctorate. Count palatine doctorates were quick, cheap, and numerous. Whether they were less respected than doctorates conferred by colleges of doctors at universities is difficult to determine.[38] Nadal had studied theol-

36. "Maius [1538] ... Natalis, doctor theologiae. Die xi dominus Hieronymus Natalis, presbyter hispanus, maioricensis diocesis, accepit gradum doctoratus in theologia sub domino de Forlivio." Codina Mir, 1967, 250–51 (quotation at 250). See also Bangert and McCoog 1992, 11.

37. That Nadal's degree was a count palatine doctorate is the overwhelming possibility. There are many examples of professors with count palatine authority conferring doctorates on candidates in disciplines outside of their own expertise, as well as counts palatine without degrees conferring degrees. Martellozzo Forin 1999; and Grendler 2002, 184–85.

38. See Grendler 2002, 183–86, for further explanation and bibliography on count palatine doctorates.

ogy possibly for two or three years in Paris and eighteen months at most at Avignon but had not satisfied the lengthy requirements of faculties of theology. Nevertheless, he was Doctor Nadal.

Although Nadal obtained a doctorate of theology at Avignon, Italy was the land of quick and easy doctorates from a count palatine or by examination, which was just as fast. Ignatius took advantage of Italian practices when Jesuits needed theology doctorates in a hurry. He arranged for three first Jesuits to obtain Italian doctorates in theology without spending years in residence, hearing lectures, disputing, or lecturing.

In 1549 Wilhelm IV Wittelsbach (1493–1550, r. from 1508), duke of Bavaria, wanted some Jesuits to teach theology at the University of Ingolstadt, a small university founded in 1472. Because of deaths it had only one theologian and a dozen theology students. Ignatius saw this as an opportunity to help beleaguered Bavarian Catholicism by providing good theological instruction to future clergymen. He also hoped that the Jesuits would be able to found a college in Ingolstadt. Ignatius decided to send three Jesuits, Claude Jay, Alfonso Salmerón, and Peter Canisius to teach theology at the University of Ingolstadt.[39]

Ignatius knew that professors of theology were expected to possess doctorates. However, none of the three had any degrees in theology, let alone doctorates. They had studied theology in a university for only about one to three years each.[40] So Ignatius arranged for Canisius, Jay, and Salmerón to acquire doctorates by examination. He spoke to Cardinal Marcello Cervini (the future Pope Marcellus II), who wrote to Cardinal Giovanni Maria Ciocchi Del Monte, the legate for Bologna who became Pope Julius III in 1550. Ignatius then ordered Jay who was in Ferrara, Salmerón in Verona, and Canisius in Messina to proceed immediately to Bologna. They arrived at different dates in September. Del Monte arranged for the three Jesuits to be examined for doctorates. On October 2, 1549, the Dominican deacon of the Faculty of Theology of the University of Bologna, the regent master of the Dominican monastery in Bologna, and a Dominican bishop examined Jay, Salmerón, and Canisius. The Faculty of Theology then voted unanimously to confer doctorates on the trio. Cardinal Del Monte conferred the degrees on behalf of the Faculty of Theology on October 4, 1549.[41]

39. Bangert 1986, 108–9; Brodrick 1998, 123–24.

40. Canisius studied theology at the University of Cologne from 1540 to 1543, whether by hearing lectures, private study, or both is unknown. Brodrick 1998, 28. For the theological studies of Jay and Salmerón, see chap. 1.

41. Letters of Ignatius and Polanco to Salmerón, Jay, and Canisius, August 10 to September 24, 1549, in *Ignatii Epistolae* 1964–1968, 2:509–10, 517, 539; Canisius 1896–1923, 1:685–86;

The three Dominicans who examined the Jesuits came from the Faculty of Theology of the University of Bologna, but had no connection with the university. Indeed, the University of Bologna did not teach any theology between 1539 and 1566.[42] Unlike Paris and the rest of Europe, an Italian faculty of theology was not a teaching faculty of professors, students, and lectures inside a university. In Italy faculty of theology meant everyone teaching, studying, or with doctorates in theology in a town that hosted a university. Although it carried the name of a university, the faculty of theology was only a loose confederation of the medieval mendicant order studia and their teachers and students. The members of the faculty of theology taught in their respective monastic studia, they elected a deacon as leader, and some of them possessing doctorates of theology examined candidates for degrees.[43] The Faculty of Theology of the University of Bologna was completely separate from the civic university that taught law, medicine, philosophy, and the humanities. This was the case throughout Italy; indeed, a few Italian towns had faculties of theology but no university.

The three Jesuits, especially Salmerón, were learned men. But they did not fulfill the requirements of the Faculty of Theology of Bologna for doctorates of theology, which echoed those of Paris. The Bologna statutes required the candidate to obtain a master of arts, then to devote twelve to sixteen years to study, attending lectures, disputing, lecturing, preaching, and being examined.[44] But the Faculty of Theology could waive its own requirements, which it did for the three Jesuits. And it decided that the Jesuits were sufficiently learned to receive the degrees.

Degrees by examination were not as frequently awarded as count palatine degrees in Italy, but they were common. The most famous Italian doctorate by examination was Erasmus of Rotterdam's doctorate of theology from the Faculty of Theology of the University of Turin of September 4, 1506. Erasmus came to Turin, spent about two weeks in the city, passed an examination, was awarded the degree, and left, never to return.[45] The three Jesuits did the same.

Canisius, Jay, and Salmerón arrived in Ingolstadt on November 13, 1549, and immediately began to teach. But they were unable to establish a

Salmerón 1971–1972, 1:84–86; Bangert 1986, 109–10; Brodrick 1998, 126–27; *Year by Year* 2004, 111–12.

42. Dallari 1888–1924, 2:90–167, for the annual rolls from 1539 through 1566.

43. Grendler 2002, 357–60, with additional bibliography.

44. The statutes are found in Ehrle 1932. See also Grendler 1998, 45–47; and Grendler 2002, 360–62.

45. Grendler 1998, which lists some other degrees by examination on 52–54.

Jesuit college and left for the more promising University of Vienna in 1552. The Jesuits did establish a college in Ingolstadt in 1556, after which they eventually won two theology professorships and controlled philosophy instruction in the university.[46]

More quick and easy doctorates by examination followed. In March 1558 Derick (better known as Theodoric in English) Canisius (Nijwegen 1532–1606 Ingolstadt), younger half-brother of Peter, also received a doctorate of theology at Bologna. Because there is no evidence of university theological study in his biography, and he was scheduled to teach logic at the Roman College in the academic year 1557–1558, this must have been another doctorate by examination.[47] Theodoric Canisius immediately became a professor of theology at the University of Vienna and later was chancellor of the Jesuit University of Dillingen. The tiny Jesuit school at Gandía founded by Francisco de Borja in 1545, which had a university charter, awarded doctorates of theology to Borja, three other Spanish Jesuits, and a French Jesuit in 1550.[48]

When the Jesuits received from the papacy authorization for their schools to confer degrees in theology and philosophy after a rigorous public examination, this provided another way to confer doctorates on short notice to members of the Society.[49] When the first papal permission was granted in 1552, Nadal drafted a plan for Jesuit universities in 1552 that insisted that candidates had to go through the lengthy process of obtaining bachelor, master, licentiate, and doctorate of theology, the traditional requirements that he skipped over.[50]

The Jesuits did not follow Nadal's plan or the Paris procedures. Instead, schools of the Society conferred degrees on Jesuits without insisting that they devote a decade or more to studying theology. From 1555 through 1564, Jesuit schools conferred doctorates of theology on at least 27 Jesuits. The Roman College conferred the majority of them, while Jesuit universi-

---

46. Brodrick 1998, 128–67; Hengst 1981, 88–94; and Mobley 2004.

47. Derry 1913; letters of Laínez of March 12 and 26, 1558, in *Lainii Epistolae* 1912–1917, 3:189, 211; Scaduto 1968, 25–26; Lukács 1970, 363; MP 2:423; and Haub 2004, 149–50, 156–57, 162–65. The degree and details have not come to light.

48. Letter of Laínez to Jean Couvillon of August 6, 1558, in *Lainii Epistolae* 1912–1917, 3:435 and n2; Scaduto 1968, 38 (Couvillon), 109 (Andrés de Oviedo); and Scaduto 1992, 24.

49. The papal bulls and decrees are found in *Institutum Societatis Iesu* 1892, 28–31 (*si praevio rigoroso et publico examine* on 29) in 1552, 34–37 (1556), 44–46 (1561), 76–77 (1571), and 595–97 (1578). See also Scaduto 1964, 207–10.

50. See the section on degrees in his "De studii generalis dispositione et ordine" of 1552 in MP 1:161–62. See also the very lengthy procedures for theology degrees prescribed for the Roman College in 1572 in MP 2:272–87. Villoslada 1954, 91–96, summarizes the latter.

ties in northern Europe conferred the rest. Nineteen doctorates were conferred on northern European Jesuits, men from lands that are now Austria, Belgium, the Czech Republic, France, Germany, Hungary, the Netherlands, Poland, and Scotland. Five doctorates were conferred on Spanish and Portuguese Jesuits, and only three on Italian Jesuits. It was obvious from their biographies that none of them had studied theology for more than a few years. Almost without exception the Jesuits who received doctorates from the Roman College returned to their native lands where many taught theology.[51]

The reason that the Jesuits rushed to confer so many doctorates of theology was that the Society desperately needed teachers for its schools and universities in northern and central Europe.[52] Jesuits in northern Europe sent letter after letter begging for teachers for all subjects but especially theology. The Roman leadership agreed that this was a high priority. Polanco, writing for Laínez, declared in 1557 that there is no place where a talent for teaching theology can be more useful and necessary and "better serve Our Lord" than in Germany. There is such a scarcity and extreme need for learned Catholic professors of theology, he wrote.[53] Hence, generals Loyola and Laínez did their best to supply theologians for their schools and universities in northern Europe.

Trier offers an example. The University of Trier, founded in 1473, was nearly moribund in the 1550s. To bring it back to life the prince-archbishop

51. This analysis is primarily based on a study of the capsule biographical data for approximately 1,750 Jesuits in the Society between 1540 and 1565 presented in Scaduto 1968. Although there were about 2,800 Jesuits at the death of Laínez in January 1565, the missing 1,000 included many temporal coadjutors, who did not study, and Jesuit scholastics. In other words, Scaduto included a very large proportion of the priests. Moreover, despite the title of the book, it includes Jesuits from everywhere; few Jesuits of significance are omitted. Approximately 1,000 (of the 1,750) were Italians, the high number the result of the fact that the greatest number of new Jesuits were Italians in the 1550s and 1560s, and because men from other countries often came to Italy to join the Jesuits and spent years in Italy before returning home. Scaduto 1968, viii–x, xvii. It is remarkable that only 41 of the 1,750 Jesuits obtained doctorates (always in theology) as Jesuits between 1549 and 1575. (Scaduto lists 40; in a minor slip he omits to mention that Claude Jay had a doctorate.) The Jesuits with doctorates were 27 northern Europeans, 9 Spaniards, and 5 Italians. For additional information on some Jesuits who acquired doctorates, all listed in Scaduto 1968, see *Lainii Epistolae* 1912–1917, 3:189, 197, 211, 435; Tacchi Venturi 1931, 74–75; Polanco 1969, 2:582, 584, 605; and Lukács 1970.

52. There are many letters making this point in *Lainii Epistolae* 1912–1917.

53. "Che in verità li dico, che non reputiamo in tutta Alemagna essere loco alcuno, dove più sia servito Dio N. S. del talento de leggere theologia; et pur se in alcuna natione fosse utile et necessario tale essercitio, teniamo sia Alemagna, dove c'è tanta charestia, anzi bisogno quasi estremo, de cattholici et dotti professori di theologia." Letter of Polanco for Laínez to Joannes Couvillon, Rome, June 17, 1557, in *Lainii Epistolae* 1912–1917, 2:271.

of Trier invited the Jesuits into the university to teach, giving them a university hostel as a residence. The Jesuit school became one of the two colleges comprising the university, and the Jesuits began teaching in the university on or about February 4, 1561. They scrambled to fulfill their teaching commitments, with the result that some Jesuits lectured two or three times a day.[54] And Jesuit professors needed credentials. Everard Mercurian, at that time the provincial superior of the Province of Lower (Northern) Germany and Belgium, explained how these were provided in a letter of April 1561.

A Jesuit named Maximilien de La Chapelle, more often called Maximilian Capella in the documents (Lille 1521–1593), arrived to teach theology at the University of Trier in or about April 1561. He had studied theology at Alcalá de Henares in 1546, and had lectured on theology to Jesuit students at Salamanca in 1553, although not as a university appointee. He may have taught philosophy in the Jesuit school at Coimbra in 1556.[55] But he had no degrees in theology. So, two local Jesuits examined him secretly and had him dispute and lecture, always "rigorously." The Jesuit school at Trier then conferred bachelor and licentiate of theology degrees on him without "exterior solemnities." They used the authority given to the Society and "ordinary" authority, because one of the Jesuits who examined de La Chapelle was deacon of the Faculty of Theology. Thus credentialed, de La Chapelle began teaching theology in the university to the satisfaction of his students. One day they will make him a doctor in the university, Mercurian concluded.[56] Indeed, the University of Trier conferred a doctorate

---

54. Establishing themselves in the University of Trier was a priority of the Jesuits. See the letters of Everard Mercurian to Laínez of December 17, 1560; March 7, 1561; and April 16, 1561; and the letter of Anton Vinck to Laínez of April 27, 1561, among others, in *Lainii Epistolae* 1912–1917, 5:335–39, 414–23, 480–82, 497–99. See also Hengst 1981, 110–16; and Pillat 2004, 90–91.

55. For his life dates see MP 4:507n2, and 6:8*n3. For the rest of what is known about him before 1561, see *Epistolae Mixtae* 1898–1901, 5:29n2, 97, 645.

56. "Il P. Maximiliano è arrivato lì a Trevere, et perchè non era graduato ne la theologia, la quale bisognava insegnasse presto, nè pareva conveniente lo fecesse sanza grado, il quale non poteva havere commodamente così in prescia, parve al P. Anthonio et al P. Hermanno l'essaminassero secretamente, et lo fecereo leggere et disputare anche rigorosamente, et poi lo fecero baccheliero et in fine licentiato sanza solennità esteriore, usando parte l'authorità concessa a la Compagnia, et parte ordinaria, per essere il P.Anthonio decano de la facultà di theologia; et poi li fecero tenere positioni publicamente ne la schola, come licentiato futuro professore, con solennità in presentia di molti, et si fece con sodisfattione de gl'auditori. Poi lo vorrebbono fare dottore qualche dì in quella università." Letter of Everard Mercurian to Laínez of April 16, 1561, Cologne, in *Lainii Epistolae* 1912–1917, 5:481. "P. Anthonio" was Anton Vinck or Winck (Boutersem, Belgium 1519–1576 Bologna), the rector of the Jesuit college in Trier and an important Jesuit in Germany for many years. "P. Hermanno" was Hermann Thireus (Dorkens) (Cologne 1531–1591 Mainz), who received a doctorate of theology from the Roman College in 1556. Scaduto 1968, 145.

of theology on de La Chapelle on September 29, 1561.[57] He subsequently had a distinguished career as a Jesuit.[58] Loyola, Laínez, and provincial superiors found the men, arranged to give them doctorates, and sent them north to teach. It was educational opportunism in order to save souls.

Four Years of Theology

A number of Jesuits successfully taught theology in the 1550s, and 1560s even though they had only limited theological study and quick doctorates. This persuaded the leadership that their young men did not need ten to fifteen years of study and three degrees to be competent theologians. They decided that four years of theology was enough.

In the Constitutions Ignatius several times stated that Jesuits and non-Jesuit students alike should study theology for only four years.[59] In reality, the desperate need for teachers in the early decades of the Society often caused the leadership in Rome to send out Jesuits before they had completed the four years.[60]

Nevertheless, four years of theological study became the norm. In 1599 the Ratio Studiorum mandated that Jesuits would study scholastic theology under the direction of two Jesuit professors for a period of four years.[61] During that time the students were also expected to attend two years of daily lectures in moral theology and scripture, the last only forty-five minutes in length. If the scripture professor could teach Hebrew, they should study Hebrew as well.[62] However, only Jesuit schools in Rome, Milan, Naples, Parma, and Palermo offered lectures in scripture most of the time, and Hebrew very rarely, during the seventeenth and eighteenth centuries.

At the end of four years of theological study, provincial superiors might award some outstanding students an additional two years to review what they had learned and to engage in private study.[63] Those chosen were in-

---

57. Hengst 1981, 111n10.

58. *Epistolae Mixtae* 1898–1901, 5:97; Polanco 1969, 2:659, 667; MP 3:147; vol. 6:8*; McCoog 2004, 655; Giard 2012, 97, 99, 101.

59. *Constitutions* 1970, pars. 418, 474, 476, 518–19 (205, 221–22, 236); *Constitutions* 1996, pars. 418, 474, 476, 518–19 (172, 184, 198). At one point (par. 476) the *Constitutions* mentions two years of review study, which the Ratio Studiorum clarified.

60. For example, see the letter of Jerónimo Doménech, provincial superior of Sicily, of February 1, 1575, Palermo, in ARSI, Italiae 146, f. 97r.

61. "He [the provincial superior] should see to it that the theological course is completed in a four-year period, in accordance with the *Constitutions*." *Ratio Studiorum* 2005, par. 15 (10).

62. *Ratio Studiorum* 2005, pars. 12–13, 18 (9–10, 12).

63. *Ratio Studiorum* 2005, par. 6 (12).

tended to become the Society's leading theological scholars and teachers. At the same time, the Ratio Studiorum did not mandate four years of theological study for all Jesuit priests. Some would study for three years, others for two years; the decision was to be made by Jesuit superiors. They were destined for lower status and lesser intellectual ministries in the Society. Nevertheless, most Italian Jesuits studied theology for four years in the seventeenth and eighteenth centuries.[64] They might end with Special or General Acts, which were public disputations in which the student defended theses in a formal setting.[65] Since acts were not degrees, Jesuits did not conclude their theological study with degrees.

Thus, the Jesuits settled on a short and flexible path to theological competence. Four years was ideal for the Jesuits because it enabled them to move quickly to their ministries in the world. It also worked well for members of the secular clergy who lacked access to universities or monastic studia and did not need a decade or more of theological study to perform their duties. Four years of theological study was a major Jesuit innovation that has not been noticed.

The Italian Jesuits Do Not Want Doctorates

The Jesuits took another step that separated them from Italian university practice by deciding that their members did not need or want doctorates in theology. After the rush to confer doctorates on their own members in the 1550s and 1560s, the Jesuits de-emphasized degrees. Italian Jesuits did not confer degrees on themselves and conferred only a limited number on non-Jesuits who studied in their schools. They emphasized the study rather than the degree.

Again Ignatius pointed the way in the Constitutions: it had very few ref-

---

64. Here is a samping of Italian Jesuits who studied for four years. Girolamo Andreucci (1684–1771) studied theology 1711–1715; Carlo d'Aquino (1654–1737) studied theology 1679–1683; Tommaso Auriemma (1614–1671) studied theology 1639–1643; Giovanni Andrea Avogardro (1735–1815) studied theology 1763–1767; Giovanni Maria Baldigini (1652–1707) studied theology 1680–1684; Giuliano Baldinotti (ca. 1591–1631) studied theology 1618–1622; Domenico De Marini (1627–1691) studied theology 1651–1655; Ardelio Della Bella (1655–1737) studied theology 1684–1688; Giovanni Battista Di Francisci (1699–1757) studied theology 1724–1728; Filippo Febei (1652–1706) studied theology 1678–1682; and Giuseppe Ferroni (1628–1709) studied theology 1651–1655. See DHCJ 1:165–66, 210–11, 271, 307, 328–29; 2:1057–58, 1077–78, 1111, 1384–85, 1411. Non-Italian Jesuits also normally studied theology for four years. A few Jesuits studied theology for three years: Stanislao Bardetti (1688–1767) studied theology 1716–1719, and Camillo Costanzo (1571–1622) began to study theology in 1600 and left for India in 1603. DHCJ 1:345–46; 2:981.

65. *Ratio Studiorum* 2005, pars. 16, 18, 29–31, 105–7, 110 (11, 16–17, 40–42).

erences to academic degrees.[66] Most tellingly, the Constitutions did not include any discussion about the conferral of degrees. This was a significant omission because the Constitutions discussed other aspects of Jesuit universities, and because the Society was trying to found a university at Messina when he wrote the section on universities. Ignatius was noticeably unenthusiastic, almost disapproving, about academic degrees for Jesuits. In his longest comment Ignatius stated that candidates for degrees should be examined carefully. He then immediately warned Jesuits against treating degree holders with too much deference: no Jesuit should be honored above his fellows because he had a degree.[67] Ignatius may have had in mind the Order of Preachers, because Dominicans who possessed degrees or taught received many privileges. They did not have to attend choir or read during refectory meals. They were dispensed from fasts and abstinences in order to have the strength to teach. They were given positions of honor in community functions.[68] The privileges provoked resentment, and Ignatius wanted to avoid this.

After the flurry of doctorates by examination, the Italian Jesuits reverted to Loyola's lack of enthusiasm. In 1573 a congregation of the Province of Lombardy discussed whether Jesuits should accept doctorates and master's degrees. And if degrees were deemed useful, the congregation wondered if they might be conferred in a way that would discourage ambitious persons from seeking them. The majority of the delegates responded that one way to accomplish the latter was to forbid Jesuits from using the title doctor or master, and that the provincial superior should enforce such a rule. The congregation further decided that if the doctoral degree was to be conferred on a Jesuit, the Society should do it.[69] It did not want Jesuits to pursue doctorates elsewhere.

General Everard Mercurian (1573–1580) also de-emphasized degrees, especially the doctorate, among Jesuits. In a directive concerning Jesuits schools sent to provincial superiors he wrote that while the Constitutions permitted Jesuits to receive doctorates and master's degrees, the recipients should not use the title, nor be addressed as doctor or master. Moreover, degrees should be conferred on Jesuits "rarissime" (very rarely) lest they be held in low regard.[70] His position had changed greatly since 1561.

---

66. *Constitutions* 1970, pars. 368, 390, 478, 490, 499 (192, 198, 222, 225, 227); *Constitutions* 1996, 156, 164, 185, 187–88.

67. *Constitutions* 1970, pars. 390, 478 (198, 222); *Constitutions* 1996, pars. 390, 478 (164, 185).

68. Hinnebusch 1973, 56–57.

69. MP 4:222–23.

70. MP 4:22 (instruction to provincial superiors of 1578–1580), 596 (letter of Mercurian to provincial superiors of August 6, 1575).

Another reason why the Italian Jesuits hesitated to use their authority to award degrees was that they did not want to anger universities. In 1570 the Jesuit superior of the Province of Sicily reported that he had received requests for the Jesuit schools in Sicily to award doctorates, especially on Jesuits. But he did not think this was a good idea, because it would anger the city and University of Catania, which claimed to be the only institution in Sicily empowered to confer degrees. In 1571 the new provincial of Sicily was a little more optimistic. He wrote that when a civic-Jesuit university was established in Messina, it might cautiously begin conferring doctorates, first on Jesuits, then on non-Jesuits.[71] However, the Jesuits were not included in the University of Messina when it was eventually established, and the Sicilian Jesuits did not confer doctorates.

The Italian Jesuits held to this position. The 1586 and 1591 trial versions of the Ratio Studiorum included procedures for awarding bachelor, master, and doctoral degrees in philosophy and theology.[72] The provinces then commented. The Province of Naples wrote in 1586 that the licentiate was not used in Italy, nor was it likely to be introduced. Further, if the doctorate had to be conferred, it should be done after public acts and as simply as possible by omitting the biretta, ring, lecture, and oration.[73] The Italian assistancy reported in 1594 that it was not the practice of the Italian Jesuits to promote "ours" to academic degrees. When in extraordinary circumstances a promotion was necessary, it was done in the simplest manner.[74]

By contrast, some Jesuit schools in lands where there were Jesuit collegiate universities regularly awarded degrees. The Jesuit University of Évora in Portugal in 1579 reported that it conferred degrees on members of the Society and non-Jesuits alike.[75] Jesuit schools and universities in Austria, France, Germany, and Poland also reported that they conferred bachelor, master, and doctoral degrees.[76] The Province of Aquitaine (southwestern

71. Novarese 1994, 92–93. The first provincial was Juan de Montoya (Miralrío, Guadalajara 1527–1592 Potosí, Bolivia), provincial of Sicily from 1569 to 1571. Baptista 2001. The second was Juan Jerónimo Doménech, provincial from 1571 to 1576. Medina 2001, 1135.

72. MP 5:80–85, 232–33.

73. MP 6:430 (1586). In doctoral ceremonies, the chief promoter of the candidate delivered an exhortatory oration praising the learning of the candidate. Next, the candidate received a ring symbolizing marriage between the new doctor and his discipline, and the three-cornered hat of the scholar that he was now entitled to wear. Finally, the new doctor delivered a short lecture. Grendler 2002, 177–78; and Grendler 2011b, 90.

74. "Visum est provincialibus, non esse introducendum in Italia usum promovendi nostros ordinarie ad gradus. Quod, si necesse sit aliquem extraordinarie promovere, id fiat simplissimo modo, ut hactenus fieri consuevit." MP 7:134.

75. MP 4:779–80.

76. MP 6:191–92 (Rhine Province, i.e., northwestern Germany and Netherlands, 1586),

France) offered a reason: it did not like to award doctorates to Jesuits because then all the teachers, whether worthy or not, would want them, and those denied would become angry. However, there were some provinces in which Jesuits could not teach in universities without doctorates. In such circumstances it recommended that the general should give permission for individual Jesuits to receive the doctorate.[77]

The Jesuits at Coimbra, a collegiate university in which the Jesuits had a prominent role, followed a similar policy. They conferred master of arts degrees on Jesuits who taught the humanities and philosophy so that they would have standing in the university. But they seldom conferred or held doctorates. When King Philip II in 1597 ordered the university to appoint Francisco Suárez to the first-position professorship of theology at the university, some professors objected that he lacked a doctorate. So the Jesuit school of Évora immediately conferred a doctorate of theology on him. In 1603 the Province of Portugal decided that degrees would be conferred on Jesuits only when they were very worthy and were needed to carry on their ministries, which was the case with Suárez.[78]

The Ratio Studiorum of 1599 forged a compromise that grudgingly permitted doctorates. It strongly emphasized that at the conclusion of theological studies both Jesuits and non-Jesuit students would engage in Special Acts and General Acts (*acta generales*). These were formal disputations covering all of theology; the former lasted two and one-half hours and the latter four or five hours.[79] They were intended to provide a climax and conclusion to the candidate's study without conferring a degree. The Ratio Studiorum then added, "Where it is the local custom, some of these [students who participated in General Acts] can be promoted to the rank of doctor or master, with the permission of the general."[80] Thus, the Ratio Studiorum made its preference clear but allowed for exceptions. In short, Italian Jesuits did not confer degrees, while Jesuits elsewhere in Europe, where the Society had considerable success in founding universities or entering existing ones, did.

Very few Italian Jesuits possessed doctorates in the seventeenth and eighteenth centuries. For example, in 1649 only 19 Jesuits of the 618 in the Province of Rome possessed doctorates.[81] Only 16 Jesuits of the 574 in the

---

442 (Dillingen, 1586), 461 (Province of Upper Germany, 1586), 487–88, 491 (Rhine Province, 1586), 496 (Province of France, 1586), 504 (Lyon, 1586), 510 (Province of Poland, 1586); MP 7:310 (Tournon, 1584), 454 (Trier, 1585). None of these reports made a distinction between Jesuits and external students.

77. MP 7:323–24, in 1587.   78. Brockey 2014, 59–61, 451–52.

79. *Ratio Studiorum* 2005, pars. 105–13 (40–42).

80. *Ratio Studiorum* 2005, pars. 16–17 (11–12, quotation at 11).

81. ARSI, Roma 59, ff. 13v–64r. Every three years (four years in the eighteenth century) all

Province of Naples had doctorates in 1649.[82] And only 9 of the 715 Jesuits in the Province of Sicily were doctors in 1649.[83] Twenty-five of these 49 doctorates held by Jesuits were in law, the rest were in philosophy, theology and philosophy, theology, and one in medicine. While the documents do not indicate when and where the doctorates were acquired, all or nearly all had to have been earned before the holders entered the Society. These were men in their twenties or beyond who joined the Society after doing other things in their lives, including acquiring doctorates.

Because Italian Jesuits lacked doctorates, the Society very occasionally had to award one in a hurry. As noted in chapter 3, when the University of Messina decided to appoint a Jesuit to a theology professorship in 1660, the Jesuit school immediately conferred a doctorate on him. During the planning for the University of Chambéry the Jesuit rector demanded that the Jesuits who would be teaching at the university be awarded doctorates. On the other hand the issue did not arise for the Jesuits who taught at the civic-Jesuit universities of Parma, Mantua, and Fermo, and the individual Jesuits who taught at the universities of Macerata, Perugia, Ferrara, Pavia, and Siena.

Major Italian Jesuit schools conferred a limited number of doctorates of philosophy or theology, almost always on non-Jesuit clergymen. In 1584 the Brera college in Milan reported that it conferred doctorates on a few of the best students of the many who finished the philosophy curriculum, to the general satisfaction and joy of the city.[84] It may have done this to satisfy Cardinal Carlo Borromeo, who was pressuring the Milanese Jesuits to confer doctorates.[85] And as noted in chapter 11, the Roman College awarded about 124 doctorates in philosophy or theology in about 90 years between 1565 and 1633, and 1656 through the 1680s, some of them to future cardi-

---

college rectors were required to report about the personnel and activities of their colleges. This information went to the provincial superior and to Rome, where it was summarized in three catalogues of the province. The first catalogue listed all the Jesuits in the province and personal information: date of birth, date of entry into the Society, status (priest, scholastic, or temporal coadjutor), dates of profession of the first three vows and fourth vow; date of ordination; and brief mention of education and ministries in the Society. If a Jesuit possessed an advanced degree, it was noted.

82. ARSI, Neapolitana 83, ff. 118r–50v.

83. ARSI, Sicula 66, ff. 14v–82r. Reading the first catalogues for all five Italian provinces in the years 1579 and 1580, 1600, 1696, 1749, and 1767 through 1773 when the records were less complete, yielded the same results.

84. "Li gradi del dottorato dati a pochi fra molti che hanno finito il studio della filosofia, ma degli migliori con sodisfatt[ion]e et allegrezza della città." ARSI, Mediolanensis 76 I, f. 81v.

85. Figini 1938, 1015–18; and Rurale 1992, 144–45.

nals.[86] This was an average of 1.4 per year, a tiny number by Italian university standards. However, the Brera school and the Roman College were exceptions. So far as can be determined, the vast majority of Italian Jesuit schools never conferred any doctorates.

By contrast, some faculties of theology in university towns awarded ten to twenty doctorates of theology annually.[87] The reason was that Italian clergymen needed doctorates of theology in order to hold benefices or to climb the ladder of ecclesiastical preferment. So they studied theology at universities and obtained doctorates. University faculties of theology facilitated this by easing requirements, allowing shortcuts, and awarding far more doctorates of theology than earlier.[88] Theology was not exceptional: Italian universities debased the doctorate in all disciplines in the seventeenth and eighteenth centuries.

Thus, from the late sixteenth century until 1773, Italy had two roads toward theological expertise. There was the traditional path through a university or monastic studium and faculty of theology that culminated in a doctorate of theology. Clergymen who needed doctorates followed it. And there was the Jesuit route of four years of intense study but no degree.

Conclusion

The Jesuits developed a fresh approach to theological education. They made cases of conscience a major part of their teaching. They offered much free theological instruction. They organized a theological curriculum of only four years. And they approached the doctorate of theology pragmatically. In the 1550s and 1560s the Society obtained or conferred quick doctorates on their members so that they might teach theology in northern Europe. But then they decided that Jesuits did not need doctorates to be competent theologians. The decision to award degrees rarely was a major departure from the practice of Italian faculties of theology and universities, which had the welcome effect of lessening conflict with them. Italian faculties of theology and universities paid little attention to Jesuit contributions and innovations. Hence, civic universities and the Jesuits went separate ways.

86. ASR, Università 4, ff. 138v–44v, 162v–65v, 168v–69r, 180r–90r. See also Villoslada 1954, 267–73; and Grendler 2011b.

87. Grendler 2002, 364–65.

88. Grendler 2002, 116, 364–65.

CONCLUSION

The story of the Society of Jesus and Italian universities had many twists and turns. The Jesuits initially believed that their recruits could be educated in Italian universities. However, they were disappointed with what they saw as the latter's pedagogical deficiencies and immoral culture. Hence, when the Senate of Messina proposed the creation of a new university in which the Jesuits would have a major role, Ignatius Loyola seized the opportunity. It was a bold decision. Neither the medieval mendicant orders nor other new religious orders of the Catholic Reformation tried to found universities in Italy.

In 1548 the Jesuits and the city of Messina began to erect the new university. But the Jesuits wanted a collegiate theology, arts, and humanities university ruled by the Society, while the city leaders wanted an Italian law and medicine university ruled by the city. After a half century of negotiation and acrimony, the city founded the University of Messina without the Jesuits. When plague forced the Messina Jesuit school to move to Catania, the city council voted to provide a subsidy to the Jesuits to teach theology, philosophy, and humanities classes that would compete with the University of Catania. But the Jesuit general rejected the offer.

In 1572 Duke Emanuele Filiberto Savoia and the rector of the Jesuit college in Turin concocted a scheme to insert nine Jesuit professors into the University of Turin. Strong opposition from the university and the town blocked the plan. By contrast, the Jesuits never attempted to enter the University of Padua. However, professors, students, and Venetian senators saw the thriving Jesuit school at Padua as a threat to the university and forbade it from enrolling non-Jesuit students in 1591. A few years later the Jesuits were expelled from the entire Republic of Venice. After their return in 1657 the Jesuit school in Padua was careful not to teach courses that would compete with university offerings.

The Jesuits succeeded when they cooperated with rulers to create new civic-Jesuit universities. Duke Ranuccio I Farnese and the Jesuits together created the civic-Jesuit University of Parma in 1601. The duke appointed the professors of law and medicine, while the Society provided Jesuits to teach theology, philosophy, mathematics, and humanities. With Parma the Jesuits accepted the lesser but still substantial role of teaching some disciplines in a law and medicine university. It was the same at Mantua, where Duke Ferdinando Gonzaga and the Jesuits created the new civic-Jesuit Peaceful University of Mantua in 1625. But it did not survive war, plague, and the sack of Mantua in 1630. In 1609 the archbishop and the city council brought the Jesuits into the new, small, and weak University of Fermo. In like manner Jesuits taught philosophy and theology in the small University of Macerata by means of a series of renewable contracts.

Two failures followed. In the 1630s the cardinal archbishop of Palermo thwarted an attempt by the Jesuits and the city council to found a civic-Jesuit university. From 1679 through 1681 the regent of the Duchy of Piedmont-Savoy tried to establish a civic-Jesuit university in Chambéry for the benefit of the French-speaking subjects of the duchy. But a philo-Jansenist bishop who hated the Jesuits defeated the attempt.

The Jesuits never tried to become professors in the universities of Bologna, Rome, and Perugia. Nevertheless, all three saw the Society as a hostile rival. The University of Bologna judged the Jesuits to be illegitimate competitors. Hence, the university, the city, and the papacy collaborated to limit enrollment in the Jesuit school. In Rome the Roman College began to teach canon law. The law professors of the University of Rome won legal rulings to stop them, but the Jesuits prevailed over time. At Perugia the university, city, and bishop became angry at criticism of the university by a Jesuit visitor. So they rejected a plan to give the Jesuits direction of a university student residence. On the other hand, between 1675 and 1773 the universities of Ferrara, Pavia, and Siena appointed individual Jesuits to professorships of mathematics because they valued their expertise.

If Jesuit success can be defined as obtaining at least three or four positions in philosophy and theology, then the Jesuits succeeded in only four of the sixteen universities with which they interacted: the civic-Jesuit universities of Parma, Mantua (for four years only), Fermo, and Macerata. In addition, they filled the single mathematics professorship in three other universities for nearly a century, plus a very occasional position in other disciplines. The Society had more disappointments than successes.

Although each attempt was unique, some common themes emerged. The strong civic tradition of Italian universities was the most important obstacle to the Jesuits. Civil governments, whether communes or princes, founded universities, governed them, and paid the bills. They did not want to share governance with a religious order. Universities were also civic because civil law and medicine were the most important subjects. And local laymen filled the vast majority of the professorships and did not want to lose them. Their relatives and friends who dominated local governments supported them.

The first Jesuits were committed to the collegiate university model found in northern Europe and Spain because they had studied in the collegiate universities of Paris and Spain, where theology, philosophy, and the humanities dominated. The collegiate university model served the Jesuits well elsewhere in Europe. But it was unacceptable in Italy.

Strong differences in the teaching of philosophy also divided the Jesuits and Italian universities. University philosophers taught secular Aristotelianism, while the Jesuits taught Christian Aristotelianism. Lay professors charged that the Jesuits taught philosophy badly. The Jesuits replied that university professors taught philosophical atheism. In addition, civic universities viewed logic and natural philosophy as preparation for the study of medicine. The Jesuits taught logic, natural philosophy, and metaphysics as preparation for theology. The polemics overshadowed the fact that both university philosophers and the Jesuits followed Aristotle. In theology the Jesuits introduced cases of conscience, shortened the theological curriculum to four years, and seldom conferred the doctorate of theology. Civic universities ignored these innovations.

Dynamic individual Jesuits took the lead in the first decades. From the death of Ignatius Loyola in 1556 to the end of the generalate of Claudio Acquaviva in 1615, Achille Gagliardi, Benedetto Palmio, Juan de Polanco, and Antonio Possevino forged connections with rulers and only later reported to the general in Rome. They assumed a mandate and considerable freedom of action to advance Jesuit higher education as they saw fit, with good results or until a defeat caught them up short.

After the failures at Messina and Turin and the disaster at Padua, the Jesuits changed tactics and goals. They collaborated with princes and city governments to create the civic-Jesuit university. This was new to Italy. The prince and/or the city council provided the funds and appointed the professors of law and medicine. The Jesuits taught theology and philosophy, and sometimes mathematics and the humanities as well. The Society had no role in the governance of the university beyond the classes that they taught and participation in the examination of candidates for degrees in subjects that they taught. The Jesuits accepted this secondary position in order to teach in Italian universities.

The Jesuits had greater success with princely families than with city councils. The reason was pragmatic: princely families were better able to provide the long-term support that Jesuit colleges and schools needed. The operative word was family, including consorts. A good relationship with a dynasty guaranteed support for multiple generations. Even though the son, grandson, or great-grandson, and their consorts might be less attached to the Jesuits than the prince and consort who first welcomed the Society, family tradition and expectations obliged them to continue to support the Jesuits. The Farnese and Gonzaga dynasties were examples. On the other hand, the Jesuits suffered when princes made disastrous political decisions.

Jesuit relations with city councils were more difficult, because local elites who dominated city governments were often divided or fickle. The Jesuits might win support from a majority of the council members, only to be rejected by a new group of councillors. And city councils stoutly defended special interests.

When universities protested against Jesuit competition, they used legal language and historical precedents, however dubious, to argue that only universities had the right to teach certain subjects. Universities took the Jesuits to court several times. In the most important case, Urban VIII took the side of the University of Bologna against the Jesuits. And the Sacred Roman Rota ruled against the Jesuits when they wanted to teach canon law at the Roman College. Although opponents of the Jesuits sometimes accused the Jesuits of being agents of the pope, the Society did not receive much support from the papacy in university matters.

The accusation that the Jesuits were outsiders surfaced regularly. And they were outsiders in the sixteenth century. Hence, a faction of the Venetian nobility nursed an ideological hatred of the Jesuits as alleged agents of Spain. Although the Venetian position was extreme, the Jesuits were not "our religious" to many in Italy. This changed over time. In the seventeenth and eighteenth centuries more and more Jesuits were men from the local community or neighboring towns. After philosophical and theological studies, they returned to the Jesuit college of their birthplace or a nearby one. This helped to win acceptance.

Sometimes Jesuit educational expansion was the result of an internal dynamic, the need to provide philosophical and theological education for their own members. After the first decades, each province was expected to provide all levels of education for its members. Hence, if the province lacked an upper school teaching philosophy and theology, one had to be developed. This led to the expansion of the Jesuit schools in Padua and Bologna, which generated opposition. On the other hand, although opponents did not want the Jesuits to teach in the city's university, they acknowledged that the Jesuit pre-university schools prepared students well.

Jesuit education ended when the Society was suppressed. There was no tsunami of anti-Jesuit public opinion in Italy. It came from outside. The first suppression occurred in Portugal in 1759 and the second in Spain in 1768. When Spain suppressed the Jesuits, the Society had to leave Sicily and the Kingdom of Naples. The Duchy of Parma, ruled by a cadet branch of the Spanish Bourbons, followed the lead of Spain and evicted the Jesuits. And the Habsburgs of Vienna moved against the Jesuits in Lombardy. Pope Clement XIV succumbed to relentless pressure from the rulers of Spain, Portugal, France, and the Austrian Empire, and suppressed the Jesuits universally in July 1773. Jesuit schools were closed and the Society's properties seized. Some Jesuit schools were reopened as state schools and a few former Jesuits appointed to teach in them. But the majority of the school buildings were turned to other uses. When the French occupation and Napoleonic period ended, the Society of Jesus was reconstituted in 1814. But the new Society did not try to found universities in Italy. Jesuit higher education made a new start in the former mission lands far from Europe.

The mostly failed efforts of the Jesuits and civic authorities to work together prompt reflection. Church and state found it difficult to collaborate in higher education. It might have been anticipated that in a land saturated with Catholicism, and an era that many historians call the Catholic Reformation or Counter Reformation, a very learned religious order and civic authorities would work together. It did not happen, because Italian civil authorities seldom wanted the Jesuits in universities. Perhaps the traditional view that the church played an outsize role in Italian life from the middle of the sixteenth century until the late eighteenth century needs to be reexamined.

One wonders if more Jesuits teaching in Italian universities might have had reciprocal benefits. Perhaps lay professors and Jesuits would have learned from each other. Could they have emerged from the trench war between secular Aristotelianism and Christian Aristotelianism and embraced the new sciences more quickly?

The divergent natures of universities and the Society of Jesus made cooperation difficult. Universities are very stable institutions that resist change, which is their great strength and a weakness. The Society of Jesus was an innovative and fiercely independent order with its own "way of proceeding." It did not easily accept any direction except its own, at times not even from the pope. When the Jesuits sought to change Italian universities, the latter stood their ground and fought them off.

Finally, there is the long historical perspective. The battles between civil authorities and Jesuits in Italy between 1548 and 1773 were not the only clashes in the long history of the interactions of princes, priests, and professors. In 1277 the bishop of Paris condemned secular Aristotelian propositions taught at the University of Paris. French monarchs sought to impose their will on the University of Paris several times in the fifteenth and sixteenth centuries and met resistance. German Protestant princes and reformers united to create new universities to educate pastors and lay professionals in the new religion. But when prince and theologians differed on the preferred form of Protestantism, the prince dismissed obstinate professors and brought in malleable ones. Many other disputes followed.

There were very few church-university clashes in nineteenth-century Europe because civil governments almost completely eliminated religious universities. The dominant ideology was aggressive statism: civil governments ruled universities that supported the state. In this environment the Jesuits did not resume their efforts to create universities or to teach in civil universities. There are no Jesuit or civic-Jesuit universities in Italy today. The Society does play a key role in the Pontifical Gregorian University in Rome, because the rector and other officers are Jesuits chosen by the Society and appointed by the pope. It confers degrees in theology, canon law, philosophy, and "the History and the Cultural Goods of the Church" on the basis of papal authority.[1] But it lacks civil standing.

English- and French-speaking North America took a different path by creating distinct state universities and religious universities. State governments in the United States founded and today govern universities from which religious institutions are excluded. They have adopted the Italian civic university model of long ago. In addition, a few wealthy individuals have created private universities, which lay trustees govern. Again religious organizations play no role. Canadian universities are civil institutions governed by provincial governments. They sometimes include a religiously affiliated college with limited and diminishing self-rule. But that is all.

On the other hand, Roman Catholic dioceses and religious orders including the Jesuits, and Protestant churches and groups affiliated with them, have created numerous American universities and colleges. They owe their existence to religious impulses, and religious organizations govern them today, usually with lay participation. In short, English- and French-speaking North American civil authorities and religious entities do not collaborate in the creation and governance of universities. They avoid the battles of the past. But there are other conflicts. Civil governments

1. See the "Statuta generalia Pontificiae Universitatis Gregorianae" of January 17, 2008, the "Regolamento generale dell'Università" of January 16, 2008, and the "Mission Statement" of November 27, 2009, of the Pontifical Gregorian University, www.unigre.it/home_page_en.php.

sometimes impose mandates that state universities resist. And churches and other religious organizations may demand conformity in belief and teaching that faculty and students find oppressive.

It has always been difficult to reconcile religious aims and civil goals in universities. The encounters between the Jesuits and Italian universities are an instructive part of a long and continuing story.

FOUR JESUIT

BIOGRAPHIES AND THE

SUPERIOR GENERALS

Four Jesuits appear in several chapters because they played major roles in multiple attempts to establish Jesuit universities or enter civic universities, or by criticizing the latter. Short biographies of them are presented here. In addition, a list of the eighteen men who served as superior generals of the Society of Jesus from 1541 to 1773 is given.

Achille Gagliardi

Achille Gagliardi was born into a wealthy Padua family at the end of 1537 or the beginning of 1538. After his father died when he was a child, he was entrusted to the care of able teachers. Around 1551 he began to attend lectures at the University of Padua, and in or about 1557 became friendly with Antonio Possevino, who was temporarily at the university. In 1557, Gagliardi, his two younger brothers (Leonetto 1540–1564, and Ludovico 1543–1608), and Possevino were inspired by the preaching of Benedetto Palmio, then at the Jesuit college in Padua. The three brothers decided to become Jesuits. When their mother died in 1558, they gave their properties, valued at 10,000 ducats, to the Society despite legal challenges from relatives. The three Gagliardi brothers and Possevino went to Rome where they became Jesuit novices in September 1559.

Gagliardi studied theology at the Roman College. He then taught moral philosophy in the academic year 1562–1563, logic in 1563–1564, natural philosophy in 1564–1565, metaphysics in 1565–1566, and scholastic theology in 1566–1567 there. In 1564 and 1565 he believed that Jesuits should teach uniform Christian philosophical views and avoid novel opinions (chapter 14). Gagliardi was ordained a priest in January 1563 and obtained a doctorate of theology from the Roman College in 1568. He became rector of the Turin college in March 1568.

In 1572 Gagliardi and Duke Emanuele Filiberto Savoia failed to insert Jesuit professors into the University of Turin (chapter 4). Gagliardi was brought back to Rome in the autumn of 1575. He was appointed prefect of studies and professor of scholastic theology at the Roman College in 1576. On July 6, 1578, Gagliardi, Benedetto Palmio, and two other Jesuits went to Pope Gregory XIII to denounce another Jesuit, Benito Perera, for his use of Averroes (chapter 14). The pope referred the matter to General Mercurian, who exiled Gagliardi to Padua in October 1579. Cardinal Carlo Borromeo, archbishop of Milan, then requested his services, so Gagliardi moved to the Jesuit college in Milan. In 1581 Gagliardi was a delegate to the Fourth General Congregation that elected Claudio Acquaviva general. The Congregation appointed Gagliardi to a committee to prepare a Ratio Studiorum for the Society, the first of several such committees. However, Gagliardi did not play any role in its preparation, but spent the years 1580 to 1594 in Milan. From 1580 to 1584 he was a preacher and confessor at the Jesuit college. On behalf of Borromeo he preached and made a pastoral visit to a remote region of Lombardy bordering on Protestant Switzerland. On commission from Borromeo, Gagliardi published *Catechismo della fede catholica* in 1584. In that same year he became rector of the Jesuit professed house in Milan. He angered the Venetian government by trying to play a role in Venetian diplomacy in 1593 and 1594 (chapter 5).

In Milan Gagliardi became confessor and spiritual advisor to Isabella Cristina Berinzaga (ca. 1551–1624), a devout Milanese woman of mystical and ascetic spiritual tendencies. Gagliardi gave her the Spiritual Exercises, assigned themes for meditation, and encouraged her to write about her spiritual experiences. Gagliardi observed, verified, and organized her experiences into a book, *Il breve compendio intorno alla perfezione cristiana*, that circulated in manuscript. Gagliardi also wrote several meditational works that were not published until the eighteenth and nineteenth centuries, or remain in manuscript.

Some Jesuits attacked the spiritual message that Berinzaga and Gagliardi were promoting, not least because the pair argued that the Society had abandoned the spirit of Ignatius and needed renewal. Reforming the Society was a preoccupation of Gagliardi and sixty to one hundred other Jesuits, usually called *zelanti* or *zelatori*, in the 1580s and 1590s. Their views, writings, and actions threatened to overturn the leadership and change the Constitutions of the Society.

The zealots believed that the general had too much authority. His term of office should consist of a fixed number of years, general congregations should meet every few years, provinces should have more independence, and the Spanish assistancy should be semi-autonomous. Some reformers wanted the Jesuits to pray in common. Thus, while invoking the charism of Loyola, they wanted the Jesuits to be more like traditional monastic orders, a path that Ignatius and the other first Jesuits had decisively rejected. Agitation of the reformers moved Pope Clement VIII to order the Jesuits to hold a general congregation (November 1593 through January 1594) even though General Acquaviva was alive. It reaffirmed the authority of the general, and the rules and the organization of the Society. Clement VIII allegedly quipped that the Jesuits intended to convict their general, but instead had canonized him. Although the zealots continued to complain, the reform movement lost strength. With his authority affirmed, Acquaviva moved Gagliardi to Cremona in December 1594, to Brescia in October 1595, and named him rector of the college of Brescia in 1596. Gagliardi continued to argue for closer adherence to the spirit of Ignatius as he saw it and greater democratization of the Society.

But Gagliardi's reputation in the order suffered a blow in 1601. Acquaviva spoke to Pope Clement VIII about Berinzaga and Gagliardi, and the pope ordered Cardinal Robert Bellarmine to investigate. Bellarmine examined their works and found many new spiritual doctrines that in his judgement threatened the Catholic faith. The Society ordered Berinzaga and Gagliardi to cease all communication and imposed retraction and silence on Gagliardi. Both accepted the judgment. Nevertheless, *Il breve compendio* was published in Brescia in 1611. Often reprinted and translated into five languages, it became an influential work of Catholic quietist spirituality.

Gagliardi returned to Venice in 1600 or 1601 as rector of the professed house there. He accused Paolo Sarpi of heresy, which had no effect. He tried to create an academy of Venetian nobles dedicated to Plato to counter the secular Aristotelianism taught at the University of Padua. In February 1604 he was named rector of the Jesuit college in Bologna, a position that he had to relinquish for health reasons. Acquaviva then again made him rector of the small college at Brescia. In June 1606 the Jesuits were expelled from Venice. Now seriously ill, Gagliardi was sent to Mantua and then to Modena where he died on July 6, 1607.

Achille Gagliardi was an able, zealous, and controversial Jesuit who criticized his superiors. His attempt to insert Jesuits into the University of Turin and his condemnation of secular Aristotelianism were consistent with the rest of his actions and views.

Select Bibliography

The two basic biographies are G. Brunelli 1998 and Mucci 2001, each with additional bibliography. Neither mentions the attempt to insert Jesuits into the University of Turin. See also Scaduto 1964, 290–92; Scaduto 1974, 277, 284, 420; and Scaduto 1992, 329–30, and the index. For a list of Gagliardi's publications, see Sommervogel 1960, 3:1095–99. For further information on his association with Berinzaga, *Il breve compendio*, and its influence, see Cozzi 1967 and Iparraguirre and Derville 1967. For Gagliardi's involvement in Venetian diplomacy, see Cozzi 1963. For his participation in the Jesuit reform movement see Echarte 2001 and Catto 2009, 81–100.

Benedetto Palmio

Benedetto Palmio was born into a Parma noble family on July 11, 1523. He was the younger brother of Francesco Palmio (1518–1585) who became a Jesuit in 1552. The preaching of Diego Laínez in Parma in 1540 inspired Benedetto to consider becoming a priest and a Jesuit. His vocation matured under the influence of Juan Jerónimo Doménech when Palmio was a student at the University of Bologna. Whether he obtained a degree at Bologna is unknown. Palmio became a Jesuit novice in 1546 in Rome, where he came under the spiritual direction of Ignatius Loyola.

Palmio was one of the ten Jesuits sent to Messina in 1548 where he taught Latin grammar and rhetoric for three years (chapter 2). He then preached in Messina and Palermo from 1551 to 1553. He returned to Rome where he was ordained a priest in 1553 and studied philosophy (1555–1557) and theology (1557–1559) at the Roman College. Highly praised for his preaching, he was sent to Padua in 1557 to preach and to oversee the Jesuit colleges at Padua and Venice. He judged the University of Padua to be a depraved university full of heretics and did not want young Jesuits to associate with university students. He planned to denounce heretics in his sermons, but Laínez urged him to exhort rather than denounce (chapter 1).

Palmio was provincial superior of the Province of Lombardy from 1559 to 1565. Invited to preach at the cathedral of Milan in 1563 by Cardinal Borromeo, he helped to establish the Jesuit college there in 1564 and stayed until 1566. He was assistant for Italy from 1565 to 1581. He wanted large colleges and favored suppressing small ones. For example, he decided that the struggling Jesuit college at Venice should become a professed house. As assistant he lived in Rome when not touring Jesuit colleges. Palmio was a delegate to the second (1565), third (1573), fourth (1581), and fifth (1593–1594) general congregations. In 1578 he joined Achille Gagliardi and two other Jesuits in criticizing Benito Perera for his alleged Averroist teaching and General Mercurian's inadequate oversight, but suffered no known negative consequences (chapter 14). Palmio was one of the two Jesuits whom Cardinal Borromeo favored for general in 1581, but Acquaviva was elected.

After the Province of Lombardy was divided into two in 1578, Palmio served as a visitor to the new Province of Venice from 1581 to 1583. He then moved to the Ferrara college where he lived for the rest of his life except when on special assignment. In February 1592 General Acquaviva sent him to Padua to see what he could do to improve relations with the Venetian government, at which time he wrote a defense of the Jesuit school in Padua (chapters 5 and 14). In 1597 he began the negotiations to create a civic-Jesuit University of Parma (chapter 6). Palmio died in Ferrara on November 14, 1598.

Palmio objected to the fact that Spanish Jesuits, including those of Jewish ancestry, filled most of the leadership roles of the Society, including superior generals of Italian provinces, in the 1560s and 1570s. When General Borja died, Palmio went to Pope Gregory XIII in 1573 to argue that the next general should not be a Spaniard. His objections hardened into a vehement criticism of practically all Spanish Jesuits of Jewish lineage. Between 1584 and 1589 Palmio wrote a long and detailed denunciation of numerous Jesuits of Jewish ancestry and the alleged damage that they had done to the Society. He excepted only Laínez, whose preaching had inspired him to become a Jesuit. Although many Jesuits comprised the anti-converso lobby, Palmio's voice was possibly the shrillest. In 1593 the Society barred entry into the Society of men of Jewish ancestry and ordered the dismissal of Jesuits discovered to be of converso lineage, however distant. Although there was little investigation into the pasts of Jesuits of suspected New Christian lineage and few if any dismissals, some Jesuits of converso ancestry left the Society, and those who remained lived under a cloud.

Palmio was an esteemed preacher and determined opponent of heretics, secular Aristotelian philosophers, and converso Jesuits. That several generals appointed him to important positions and entrusted him with complex tasks argues that they saw him as an effective leader.

Select Bibliography

Scaduto 1984 and Zanfredini 2001f are good short biographies. See also Sommervogel 1960, 6:156–57. For Palmio in Messina, see *Year by Year* 2004, 72, 76, 91, 259, 280, 409. For his role in establishing the college at Milan, see Rurale 1992. For his attack against Jesuits of Jewish ancestry, see Maryks

2010, 128–43, 219–56. For the text of his "Apologia" for the Padua school, see Sangalli 2001, 129–59. For his involvement in the affairs of the Jesuits in Padua and Venice, see the index of Sangalli 1999.

Juan Alfonso de Polanco

Juan Alfonso de Polanco was born on December 24, 1517, in Burgos, Old Castile, the son of a wealthy merchant. He studied Latin and philosophy at the University of Paris from 1530 to 1538, and emerged with licentiate of arts and master of arts degrees in 1538 (chapter 1). His family then secured for him an appointment as apostolic notary in Rome where he met Ignatius Loyola, who gave him the Spiritual Exercises. He entered the Society of Jesus in 1541. In April 1542 Loyola sent Polanco to the University of Padua to study theology. But Polanco found the theology lectures unsatisfactory; hence, he studied theology privately for four years (chapter 1). From September 1546 onward he preached and engaged in other ministries in Bologna, Florence, Pisa, and Pistoia.

In March 1547 Loyola chose Polanco as his secretary. From that date until 1573 Polanco served as secretary to generals Loyola, Laínez, and Borja. He wrote many thousands of letters in Spanish, Italian, and Latin. Generals either signed the letters or Polanco conveyed their instructions under his own name. He also wrote many other documents and letters concerning the Society. Historians agree that Polanco gave Loyola substantial assistance in the preparation and writing of the Constitutions. He accompanied Laínez to the Colloquy of Poissy (1561) and the Council of Trent (1563), and Borja on a trip to Spain, Portugal, and France (1571–1572). He served as vicar general of the Society for short periods of time when Loyola died in 1556 and Borja died in 1572.

It was widely anticipated that Polanco would be elected general in 1573, but Gregory XIII ordered the Society not to choose another Spaniard. In addition, some Portuguese and Spanish Jesuits objected to Polanco because of his Jewish ancestry. Everard Mercurian, the new general, dismissed Pontano as secretary as part of a removal of Jesuits of converso ancestry from leadership positions in Rome. No longer secretary, Polanco in 1573 and 1574 wrote *Vitae Ignatii Loyolae et rerum Societatis Jesu historia* (usually called *Chronicon*) in six volumes, a very detailed history of the Society from its origins to the death of Loyola in 1556. It is indispensable to historians.

In late February 1575 Mercurian sent Polanco to Sicily as a visitor with wide powers. When the plague struck Messina, Polanco moved the Messina Jesuits to Catania. He wanted to make the Catania school the major

Jesuit school in Sicily, possibly with the idea of raising it to a Jesuit university. Mercurian vetoed the plan. Polanco strongly dissented, so Mercurian relieved Polanco of his duties as visitor in April 1576, and recalled him to Rome (chapter 3). Now gravely ill with malaria, Polanco slowly made his way back to Rome where he died on December 20, 1576.

Polanco's letters, other writings, and his actions show an incisive mind and a preference for pragmatic action. Polanco and Jerónimo Nadal were the two most important early Jesuits who assisted Ignatius in the task of transforming a small band of followers into a large and a dynamic religious order.

Select Bibliography

García de Castro Valdés 2012 is a full biography, while Ruiz Jurado 1986 and Dalmases 2001f are good short biographies. See Sommervogel 1960, 6:939–47, for a list of his works. See Martini 1952, for Polanco's theological studies. The most important sources for Polanco are the volumes of the published correspondence of Loyola, Laínez, and Borja; and *Polanci Complementa* 1969. For Polanco's role in the Society in Italy, see Tacchi Venturi 1931, 1951a, and 1951b; and Scaduto 1964, 1974, and 1992. O'Malley 1993 assesses his importance to the Society as a whole.

Antonio Possevino

Antonio Possevino, the son of a goldsmith, was born in Mantua on July 12, 1533, and obtained a good humanistic education in Mantua and Rome. While studying in Rome he attended the Jesuit church and felt the stir of a vocation. Instead, he became a secretary to Cardinal Ercole Gonzaga in Mantua, de facto ruler of the Duchy of Mantua for an underage duke. Possevino's chief duty was to tutor two Gonzaga nephews destined for high ecclesiastical office. When they reached their late teens, he escorted them on a study tour that took them to the universities of Ferrara and Padua, plus the cities of Rome and Naples, from 1557 through 1559. In Padua Possevino heard Benedetto Palmio preach and became friendly with the Gagliardi brothers. He became a Jesuit novice in Rome on September 29, 1559.

Possevino began to study theology at the Roman College. But after two months General Laínez sent him to Duke Emanuele Filiberto Savoia to try to persuade the duke to support the establishment of Jesuit colleges in Piedmont-Savoy and to assist him in suppressing heresy (chapter 4). Possevino believed that education and persuasion were more effective than persecution, and in time the duke agreed. Possevino was ordained a priest on April 6, 1561. He then spent the years from early 1562 to the beginning of 1573 in France working to establish Jesuit colleges, serving as college rector, and preaching. He was a delegate to the Third General Congregation (1573) and then was secretary to General Mercurian from 1573 to 1577. When King John III Vasa of Sweden signaled that he wished to become a Catholic, Pope Gregory XIII appointed him special legate to Sweden. Possevino spent the years from 1578 through 1586 as a papal diplomat traveling between Rome and Sweden, Poland, Russia, Transylvania, and Germany. He sought to persuade rulers to restore Catholicism and to bring the Eastern church to unity with Rome. He brokered peace agreements and helped establish Jesuit colleges in northern Europe and seminaries to train clergymen who would return to their Protestant homelands. In the end John III Vasa did not become a Catholic. Historians differ on the responsibility of the king, the pope, and Possevino, and whether there ever was a real chance of it happening. In 1583 or early 1584, between diplomatic missions, Possevino successfully negotiated with Duke Guglielmo Gonzaga to found a Jesuit college and school in Mantua.

Possevino returned to Italy in 1587 and lived in the college of Padua from 1587 to 1591, with visits to Venice. He may have taught theology for a short time in the Padua Jesuit school. He then moved to Rome where he pursued his scholarship and wrote voluminously. In the early months of 1592 he wrote an *Apologia* against Cesare Cremonini and the closing of the Padua school (chapters 5 and 14). The Jesuit leadership continued to send him to northern Italy and France to resolve difficulties in Jesuit colleges and to participate in provincial congregations. He delivered a funeral oration for Duchess Eleonora Gonzaga in Mantua in 1594. In 1599 Possevino negotiated an agreement with Duke Ranuccio I to found the University of Parma (chapter 6). When Pope Paul V placed Venice under interdict in 1606, Possevino wrote against Venice. He spent his last years in northern Italy, preaching in Mantua and Bologna, working to reform the dioceses of Mantua and Monferrato, striving to improve Jesuit colleges, and writing. Possevino died in Ferrara on February 26, 1611.

Possevino wrote nearly forty works, of which *Biblioteca selecta y Apparatus sacer ad scriptores veteris et novi Testamenti* (1593) may be the most important. The first part of this work discusses the methods and authors for studying various disciplines, while the second part offers a comprehensive Catholic bibliography. Between 1576 and 1603 Possevino wrote four memorials and delivered two speeches praising the contributions of Jesuits of new Christian descent and opposing the discrimination decree of 1593. Historians are divided over whether Possevino came from a converso family.

Possevino was an extraordinarily energetic and learned man who used diplomacy, scholarship, and forceful rhetoric to advance Catholicism. He was a zealous opponent of heresy and philosophical atheism. Within the limits imposed by the pope and kings, he was an able diplomat. He fought valiantly against the Society's discrimination against Jesuits of Jewish lineage. Whenever Italian Jesuits needed a skilled negotiator or an eloquent pen, Possevino delivered.

Select Bibliography

There is no full biography of Possevino, for the obvious reason that it would be a daunting task. Scaduto 2001d is a good short biography. Sommervogel 1960, 6:1061–93, lists his publications. See Castellani 1945 for his entry into the Society. The rest of this bibliography concentrates on his Italian career. See Scaduto 1959 for his activities in Piedmont-Savoy. For his career as secretary to Mercurian and a summary of his Swedish mission, see Donnelly 2004a. For his actions in Mantua, see Grendler 2009b, 29–30, 33, 39. For the text of his response to Cremonini, see Sangalli 1999, 161–75. For his defense of new Christian Jesuits, see Donnelly 1986; Cohen 2004; Maryks 2010, 159–82, and the index; and Colombo 2014.

Jesuit Superior Generals 1541 to 1773

In what follows, the place of death was always Rome.

Ignatius Loyola. Born Loyola, Spain, probably in 1491, general April 19, 1541, died July 31, 1556.

Diego Laínez. Born Almazán (Soria), Spain in 1512, vicar general August 4, 1556, general July 2, 1558, died January 19, 1565.

Francisco de Borja. Born Gandía, Spain, October 28, 1510, general July 2, 1565, died October 1, 1572.

Everard Mercurian. Born Marcourt, Luxembourg, in 1514, general April 23, 1573, died August 1, 1580.

Claudio Acquaviva. Born Atri (Teramo), Italy, September 14, 1543, general February 19, 1581, died January 31, 1615.

Muzio Vitelleschi. Born Rome, December 2, 1563, general November 15, 1615, died February 9, 1645.

Vincenzo Carafa (or Carrafa). Born Andria (Bari), Italy, May 9, 1585, general January 7, 1646, died June 8, 1649.

Francesco Piccolomini. Born Siena, October 12, 1582, general December 21, 1649, died June 17, 1651.

Luigi Gottifredi. Born Rome, May 3, 1595, general January 21, 1652, died March 12, 1652.

Goswin Nickel. Born Koslar (Westphalia), Germany, May 1, 1584, general March 17, 1652, suffered stroke November 26, 1660, replaced by temporary vicar general on April 1, 1661, died July 31, 1664.

Giovanni Paolo Oliva. Born Genoa, October 4, 1600, vicar general June 7, 1661, general July 31, 1664, died November 26, 1681.

Charles de Noyelle. Born Brussels, Belgium, August 27, 1615, general July 5, 1682, died December 12, 1686.

Tirso González. Born Argana (León), Spain, January 18, 1624, general July 6, 1687, died October 17, 1705.

Michelangelo Tamburini. Born Montese (Modena), Italy, December 6, 1647, general January 31, 1706, died February 28, 1730.

František Retz. Born Prague, Bohemia, September 13, 1673, general November 30, 1730, died November 19, 1750.

Ignazio Visconti. Born Milan, July 31, 1682, general July 4, 1751, died May 4, 1755.

Luigi Centurione. Born Genoa, August 29, 1686, general November 30, 1755, died October 2, 1757.

Lorenzo Ricci. Born Florence, Italy, August 1, 1703, general May 21, 1758, suppression of the Society in August 16, 1773, died November 24, 1775.

Select Bibliography

Various authors, "Generales de la CJ," in DHCJ 2:1595–1657.

REFERENCES

Archival Sources

Bologna, Archivio di Stato
    Assunteria di Studio
Macerata, Archivio di Stato
    Archivio Priorale del Comune di Macerata
Mantua, Archivio di Stato
    Archivio Gonzaga
Padua, Archivio Antico dell'Università di Padova
    Inventario 1320
Parma, Archivio di Stato
    Archivio del Comune di Parma, Studio
    Istruzione pubblica farnesiana
Perugia, Archivio Storico dell'Università di Perugia
    Constitutiones et jura
Rome, Archivio Pontificia Università Gregoriana
    Manuscript 120, documents concerning the teaching of canon law in the
        Roman College ca. 1695 to 1701
    Manuscript 142, anonymous history of the Roman College
Rome, Archivio di Stato
    Archivio dell'Università di Roma (abbreviated as Università)
Rome, Archivium Romanum Societatis Iesu
    Italiae (Epistolae Italiae)
    Lugduni
    Mediolanensis
    Neapolitana
    Roma
    Sicula
    Veneta
Siena, Archivio Storico dell'Università di Siena
    XX.A.5 Luigi De Angelis, "Notizie relative all'Università di Siena e catalogo
        dei professori dal 1246 fino al presente [1809]
    Indici dei motupropri, rescritti ed ordini riguardanti persone e cose, 1560–1866
Torino, Archivio di Stato
    Istruzione pubblica, Regia Università di Torino
Torino, Archivio Storico della Città di Torino
    Carte sciolte

Manuscripts

Bologna, Biblioteca Archiginnasio
    Gozzadini 105: manuscripts and printed sources concerning the
        University of Bologna

Parma, Biblioteca Palatina
  Parmense 561: material concerning the Collegio de' Nobili di Parma written
    by multiple Jesuits
  Smeraldi, "De' principii," 1670: "De' principii e progressi del collegio de' nobili
    di Parma eretto dal serenissimo duca Ranuccio l'anno MDCI. Racconto
    disteso dal p. Oratio Smeraldi della Compagnia di Gesù. 1670"; part of
    Parmense 561 (63–250)
Perugia, Biblioteca Augusta
  Ms. 82

Printed Primary Sources including
Summaries of Documents

Aristotle. 1941. *The Basic Works of Aristotle.* Edited by Richard McKeon. New York.

Bencini, Serenella. 1970–1971. "La lettura del Cremonini e le apologie inedite dei Gesuiti intorno alla controversia del 1591." Tesi di laurea. Università degli Studi di Padova, Facoltà di Magistero.

Bobadilla. 1970. *Bobadillae Monumenta. Nicolai Alphonsi de Bobadilla sacerdotis e Societate Jesu gesta et scripta.* Madrid, 1913; reprinted in Rome.

Canisius, Peter. 1896–1923. *Beati Petri Canisii, Societatis Iesu, Epistulae et Acta.* 8 vols. Freiburg im Breisgau.

Canons. 1978. *Canons and Decrees of the Council of Trent.* Translated by H. J. Schroeder. Rockford, Ill.

I Capitoli dello Studio di Messina. 1990. *I Capitoli dello Studio della Nobile Città di Messina.* Edited by Daniela Novarese. Messina.

Carra, Gilberto, Luciano Fornari, and Attilio Zanca. 2004. *Gli statuti del Collegio dei medici di Mantova 1313–1559.* Mantua.

Constitutions. 1970. Ignatius of Loyola, *The Constitutions of the Society of Jesus.* Translated by George E. Ganss, SJ. St. Louis, Mo.

Constitutions. 1996. *The Constitutions of the Society of Jesus and Their Complementary Norms.* A Complete English Translation of the Official Latin Texts. St. Louis, Mo.

Cremonini, Cesare. 1998. *Le orazioni.* Edited by Antonino Poppi. Padua.

CWE. 1974–. Desiderius Erasmus. *Collected Works of Erasmus.* Toronto.

Dallari, Umberto. 1888–1924. *I rotuli dei lettori legisti e artisti dello Studio Bolognese dal 1384 al 1799.* 4 vols. Bologna.

Decrees. 1990. *Decrees of the Ecumenical Councils.* Edited by Norman P. Tanner, SJ. 2 vols. London and Washington, D.C.

Ehrle, Francesco. 1932. *I più antichi statuti della facoltà teologica dell'Università di Bologna.* Bologna.

Epistolae mixtae. 1898–1901. *Epistolae mixtae ex variis Europae locis ab anno 1537–1556 scriptae nunc primum a patribus Societatis Jesu in lucem editae.* 5 vols. Madrid.

Fabrini, Natale. 1946b. *Un documento bolognese inedito su le scuole dei Gesuiti.* Rome.

Favaro, Antonio. 1877–1878. "Lo Studio di Padova e la Compagnia di Gesù sul finire del secolo decimosesto. Narrazione documentata." *Atti del Reale Istituto Veneto di scienze, lettere ed arti,* Serie 5, tomo 4, 401–535.

Fontes narrativi. 1943–1960. *Fontes narrativi de S. Ignatio de Loyola et de Societatis Iesu initiis.* 4 vols. Rome.

For Matters of Greater Moment. 1994. *For Matters of Greater Moment. The First Thirty*

Jesuit General Congregations. Edited and translated by John W. Padberg, SJ, Martin D. O'Keefe, SJ, and John L. McCarthy, SJ. St. Louis, Mo.

Gigli, Girolamo. 1723. *Diario sanese. In cui si veggono alla giornata tutti gli Avvenimenti più ragguardevoli spettanti sì allo spirituale, sì al temporale della Città, e Stato di Siena.* In Lucca, Per Leonardo Venturini.

Giraldi Cinzio, Giovanni Battista. 1996. *Carteggio.* Edited by Susanna Villari. Messina.

Gorzoni, Giuseppe. 1997. *Istoria del Collegio di Mantova della Compagnia di Gesù scritta dal padre Giuseppe Gorzoni. Parte prima.* Edited by Antonella Bilotto and Flavio Rurale. Mantua.

Guerrini, Maria Teresa. 2005. *"Qui volueri in iure promoveri ..." I dottori in diritto nello Studio di Bologna (1501–1796).* Bologna.

Ignatii Epistolae. 1964–1968. *Sancti Ignatii de Loyola Epistolae et Instructiones.* 12 vols. Madrid, 1903–1911; reprinted in Rome.

Ignatius of Loyola. 1974. *The Autobiography of St Ignatius Loyola with Related Documents.* Edited by John C. Olin, translated by Joseph F. O'Callaghan. New York.

———. 1991. *The Spiritual Exercises and Selected Works.* Edited by George E. Ganss et al. New York.

Index. 2002. *Index librorum prohibitorum 1600–1966.* Edited by J. M. DeBujanda and Marcella Richter. Index des livres interdits 11. Sherbrooke, Montréal, and Genève.

Institutum Societatis Iesu. 1892. *Institutum Societatis Iesu,* vol. 1: *Bullarum et Compendium Privilegiorum.* Florence.

Le istruzioni generali di Paolo V. 2003. *Le istruzioni generali di Paolo V ai diplomatici pontifici 1605–1621.* Edited by Silvano Giordano. 3 vols. Tübingen.

Jesuit Pedagogy. 2016. *Jesuit Pedagogy, 1540–1616. A Reader.* Edited by Cristiano Casalini and Claude Pavur, SJ. Chestnut Hill, Mass.

Jesuit Writings. 2006. *Jesuit Writings of the Early Modern Period, 1540–1640.* Edited and Translated by John Patrick Donnelly, SJ. Indianapolis and Cambridge.

Lainii Epistolae. 1912–1917. *Lainii Monumenta Epistolae et acta Patris Jacobi Lainii secundi praepositi generalis Societatis Iesu.* 8 vols. Madrid.

Le Camus, Etienne. 1892. *Lettres du Cardinal Le Camus évêque et prince de Grenoble (1632–1707).* Edited by P. Ingold. Paris.

———. 1933. *Lettres inédites du Cardinal Le Camus évêque et prince de Grenoble (1632–1707).* Edited by Claude Faure. Paris.

Le lauree dello Studio senese. 1998. *Le lauree dello Studio senese nel XVI secolo. Regesti degli atti dal 1573 al 1579.* Edited by Giovanni Minnucci e Paola Giovanna Morelli and Silvio Pucci. Siena.

Litterae quadrimestres. 1932. *Litterae quadrimestres ex universis, praeter Indiam et Brasiliam locis in quibus aliqui de Societate versabantur Romam missae,* vol. 7: *(1561–1562).* Rome.

I maestri di Ferrara. 1991. *I maestri di medicina ed arti dell'Università di Ferrara 1391–1950.* Edited by Francesco Raspadori. Florence.

I maestri di Roma. 1991. *I maestri della Sapienza di Roma dal 1514 al 1787: I rotuli e altre fonti.* Edited by Emanuele Conte. Fonti per la storia d'Italia 116. 2 vols. Rome.

Marti, Berthe M. 1966. *The Spanish College at Bologna in the Fourteenth Century. Edition and Translation of Its Statutes, with Introduction and Notes.* Philadelphia.

Memorie di Pavia. 1970. *Memorie e documenti per la storia dell'Università di Pavia e degli uomini più illustri che v'insegnarono.* 3 parts. Pavia, 1877–78; reprinted in Bologna.

MP. 1965–1992. *Monumenta paedagogica Societatis Iesu*. Edited by Ladislaus Lukács. 7 vols. Rome.

Nadal, Jerónimo. 1898–1962. *Epistolae P. Hieronymi Nadal Societatis Iesu ab anno 1546 ad 1577 (et alia scripta)*. 5 vols. Madrid.

———. 1976. *Scholia in Constitutiones S. I.* Edited by Manuel Ruiz Jurado. Granada.

Nunziature di Savoia. 1960. *Nunziature di Savoia*, vol. 1: *(15 ottobre 1560–29 giugno 1573)*. Edited by Fausto Fonzi. Rome.

Ordinationi. 1641. *Ordinationi fatte, et stabilite per conservare la dignità, e riputatione dello Studio di Bologna publicate in Bologna alli 12 di luglio 1641*. In Bologna, per l'Herede del Benacci Stampatore Camerale. Part of BAB, Ms. Gozzadini 105, no. 4.

Piana, Celestino. 1963. *Ricerche su le Università di Bologna e di Parma nel secolo XV*. Florence.

———. 1966. *Nuove ricerche su le Università di Bologna e Parma*. Florence.

Pirri, Pietro. 1959. *L'interdetto di Venezia del 1606 e i gesuiti. Silloge di documenti con introduzione*. Rome.

Polanci Complementa. 1969. *Polanci Complementa. Epistolae et Commentaria P. Ioannis Alphonsi de Polanco*. 2 vols. Madrid, 1916; reprinted in Rome.

Porphyry. 2003. *Porphyry Introduction*. Translated, with a commentary, by Jonathan Barnes. Oxford.

Ratio Studiorum. 2005. *The Ratio Studiorum. The Official Plan for Jesuit Education*. Translated by Claude Pavur, SJ. St. Louis, Mo.

Salmerón, Alfonso. 1971–1972. *Epistolae P. Alphonsi Salmeronis Societatis Iesu*, vol. 1: *1536–1565*, vol. 2: *1565–1585*. Madrid, 1906–1907, reprinted in Rome.

Sanctiones. 2001. *Sanctiones, ac Privilegia Parmensis Gymnasii. Nuperrimè instaurati*. Parmae. Ex Officina Erasmi Viothi. 1601; photographic reprint with introduction by Sergio Di Noto Marella. Parma.

Sarpi. 1765. *Opera di F. Paolo Sarpi*. Vol. 6. Helmstadt.

———. 1969. *Paolo Sarpi, Opere*. Edited by Gaetano and Luisa Cozzi. Milan and Naples.

La scienza dissimulata. 2005. *La scienza dissimulata nel Seicento*. Edited by Emanuele Zinato. Naples.

Serangeli, Sandro. 2003. *I laureati dell'antica Università di Macerata (1541–1824)*. Turin.

———. 2010. *I docenti dell'antica Università di Macerata (1540–1824)*. Turin.

Serangeli, Sandro, Lorella Ramadù-Mariani, and Raffaella Zambuto. 2006. *Gli statuta dell'antica università di Macerata (1540–1824)*. Turin.

Storici e politici veneti. 1982. *Storici e politici del Cinquecento e del Seicento*. Edited by Gino Benzoni and Tiziano Zanato. Milan and Naples.

Studium maceratense 1541 al 1551. 1998. *Atti dello Studium generale maceratense dal 1541 al 1551*. Edited by Sandro Serangeli. Turin.

Studium maceratense 1551 al 1579. 1999. *Atti dello Studium generale maceratense dal 1551 al 1579*. Edited by Sandro Serangeli. Turin.

Tropea, Giacomo. 1900. "Contributo alla storia della Università di Messina." In *CCCL anniversario della Università di Messina (contributo storico)*, part 1, 37–122. Messina.

Year by Year. 2004. *Year by Year with the Early Jesuits (1537–1556)*. Selections from the *Chronicon* of Juan de Polanco, SJ. Translated by John Patrick Donnelly, SJ. St. Louis, Mo.

Printed Secondary Sources

Adorni, Bruno. 1978. "Parma rinascimentale e barocca. Dalla dominazione sforzesca alla venuta dei Borboni." In *Parma la città storica*, edited by Vincenzo Banzola, 149–202. Parma.

Adorni, Giuliana. 1995. "Statuti del Collegio degli Avvocati Concistoriali e Statuti dello Studio Romano." *Rivista internazionale di diritto comune* 5: 293–355.

———. 1996. "L'Università di Roma e i suoi archivi." In *La storia delle università italiane: Archivi, fonti, indirizzi di ricerca*, Atti del Convegno, Padova 27–29 ottobre 1994, 109–31. Trieste.

———. 2003. "Per il Settimo Centenario: i nuovi statuti del Collegio degli Avvocati Concistoriali e dell'Università di Roma (9 settembre 1597–14 aprile 1606?)." *Rivista internazionale di diritto comune* 14: 227–54.

Adversi, Aldo. 1974a. "Accademie ed altre associazioni e isitituzioni culturali." In *Storia di Macerata*, 4:121–74.

———. 1974b. "Le scuole." In *Storia di Macerata*, 4:1–74.

Affò, Ireneo. 1969. *Memorie degli scrittori e letterati parmigiani*. Vol. 5. Parma, 1797; reprinted in Bologna.

Aguilera, Emmanuel. 1737–1740. *Provinciae Siculae Societatis Jesu ortus et res gestae*. 2 vols. Palermo.

Aixalá, Jerome, and Estanislao Olivares. 2001. "Gobierno Local." DHCJ 2:1758–62.

Andretta, Stefano, and Clare Robertson. 1995. "Farnese, Alessandro (cardinale)." DBI 45:52–70.

Angelozzi, Giancarlo. 1981. "L'insegnamento dei casi di coscienza nella pratica educativa della Compagnia di Gesù." In *La "Ratio Studiorum": Modelli culturali e pratiche educative dei Gesuiti in Italia tra Cinque e Seicento*, edited by Gian Paolo Brizzi, 121–62. Rome.

———. 1988. "Collegi, Congregazioni, Missioni popolari: un progetto di disciplinamento sociale." In *Dall'isola alla città*, 125–30.

———. 1991. "Le scuole dei Gesuiti e il convitto Penna." In *La rinascita del sapere. Libri e maestri dello studio ferrarese*, edited by Patrizia Castelli, 355–66. Venice.

Angelozzi, Giancarlo, and Alberto Preti. 1988. "Le scuole di via Castiglione: dai Gesuiti al liceo statale." In *Dall'isola alla città*, 131–44.

Annali di Storia delle Università italiane 8 (2004). Bologna.

Aricò, Denise. 2002. "Politica e istruzione alla corte di Ranuccio Farnese: i gesuiti Mario Bettini e Jean Verviers." In *Gesuiti e università*, 213–42.

Arrigoni Bertini, Maria Giovanna. 2002. "Giovanni Federico Cusani e la costruzione del Collegio di s. Rocco in Parma." In *Gesuiti e università*, 267–81.

Baciero, Carlos. 2001. "Arriaga, Rodrigo de." DHCJ 1:243–44.

Baldini, A. Enzo. 1980. "Per la biografia di Francesco Piccolomini." *Rinascimento* 20: 389–420.

Baldini, Ugo. 1980. "Ceva, Giovanni." DBI 24:316–19.

———. 1982a. "L'attività scientifica nelle accademie lombarde del Settecento." In *Economia, istituzioni, cultura in Lombardia*, 2:503–32.

———. 1982b. "L'insegnamento fisico-matematico a Pavia alle soglie dell'età teresiana," In *Economia, istituzioni, cultura in Lombardia*, 3:863–86.

———. 1992. *Legem Impone Subactis. Studi su filosofia e scienza dei gesuiti in Italia 1540–1632*. Rome.

———. 1994. "La tradizione scientifica dell'antica Provincia Veneta della Compagnia di Gesù. Caratteri distintivi e sviluppi (1546–1606)." In *I gesuiti e Venezia*, 531–82.

———. 1999. "The Development of Jesuit 'physics' in Italy, 1550–1700: a structural approach." In *Philosophy in the Sixteenth and Seventeenth Centuries. Conversations with Aristotle*, edited by Constance Blackwell and Sachiko Kusukara, 248–79. Aldershot.

———. 2000. *Saggi sulla cultura della Compagnia di Gesù (secoli XVI–XVIII)*. Padua.

———. 2001. "Il pubblico della scienza nei permessi di lettura di libri proibiti delle Congregazioni del Sant'Ufficio e dell'Indice (secolo XVI): verso una tipologia professionale e disciplinare." In *Censura ecclesiastica e cultura politica in Italia tra Cinquecento e Seicento*: VI giornata Luigi Firpo, Atti del Convegno 5 marzo 1999, edited by Cristina Stango, 171–201. Florence.

———. 2002. "S. Rocco e la scuola scientifica della provincia veneta: il quadro storico (1600–1773)." In *Gesuiti e università*, 283–323.

———. 2005. "L'insegnamento fisico-matematico nella scuola di S. Rocco, 1600–1768: verso una ricognizione dei materiali didattici." *Annali di Storia delle Università italiane* 9: 65–90.

———. 2006a. "Luino (Luini), Francesco." DBI 66:518–22.

———. 2006b. "Magini, Giovanni Antonio." DBI 67:413–18.

Balsamo, Luigi. 1988. "Le biblioteche dei Gesuiti." In *Dall'isola alla città*, 183–92.

Bandini, Ottavio. In The Cardinals of the Holy Roman Church at www2.fiu.edu/~mirandas/bios1596.htm#Bandini.

Bangert, William V. 1985. *Claude Jay and Alfonso Salmerón. Two Early Jesuits*. Chicago.

———. 1986. *A History of the Society of Jesus*. Revised second edition. St. Louis, Mo.

Bangert, William V., SJ, and Thomas M. McCoog, SJ. 1992. *Jerome Nadal, S. J. 1507–1580. Tracking the First Generation of Jesuits*. Chicago.

Baptista, Javier. 2001. "Montoya, Juan de." DHCJ 3:2734–35.

Barsanti, Danilo. 1993. "I docenti e le cattedre dal 1543 al 1737." In *L'Università di Pisa*, vol. 1 in 2 parts: *1343–1737*, 1.2:505–66.

———. 2000. "I docenti e le cattedre." In *L'Università di Pisa*, vol. 2 in 2 parts: *1737–1861*, 2.1:269–416.

Bartlett, Dennis A. 1984. "The Evolution of the Philosophical and Theological Elements of the Jesuit *Ratio Studiorum*: An Historical Study, 1540–1599." PhD diss., University of San Francisco.

Barton, John. 1986. "The Faculty of Law." In *The Collegiate University*, 257–93.

Bascapé, Carla. 1931. *I Barnabiti e la Controriforma in Lombardia*. Milan.

Battlori, Miquel. 2012. *L'Università di Sassari e i Collegi dei gesuiti in Sardegna*. Saggio di storia istituzionale ed economia. First published in *Studi sassaresi* in 1969. No place.

Beales, Derek. 2003. *Prosperity and Plunder. European Catholic Monasteries in the Age of Revolution, 1650–1815*. Cambridge.

Bedini, Francesco S., and Giuseppe Mellinato. 2001. "Cabeo, Niccolò." DHCJ 1:589.

Bedoulle, Guy. 2008. "Attacks on the Biblical Humanism of Jacques Lefèbvre d'Etaples." In *Biblical Humanism and Scholasticism in the Age of Erasmus*, edited by Erika Rummel, 117–41. Leiden and Boston.

Bellomo, Manlio. 1995. *The Common Legal Past of Europe 1000–1800*. Translated from the second edition by Lydia G. Cochrane. Washington, D.C.

Belmonte, John M. 2006. "To Give Ornament, Splendor and Perfection: Diego de Ledesma and Sixteenth Century Jesuit Educational Administration." PhD diss., Loyola University Chicago.

Benet Perera. 2014. *Benet Perera (Pererius, 1535–1610). A Renaissance Jesuit at the Crossroads of Modernity. Quaestio* 14.

Benzoni, Gino. 1996. "Ferdinando Carlo Gonzaga Nevers, Duca di Mantova e del Monferrato." DBI 46:283–94.

Bernard-Maître, Henri. 1950. "Les fondateurs de la Compagnie de Jésus et l'humanisme parisien de la Renaissance (1535–1536)." *Nouvelle revue théologique* 72: 811–33.

Bernuzzi, Marco. 1982. "La facoltà teologica dell'Università di Pavia. Dalle riforme di Maria Teresa al Seminario Generale." In *Economia, istituzioni, cultura in Lombardia,* 3:549–59.

Berti, Giuseppe. 1967. *Lo studio universitario parmense alla fine del Seicento.* Parma.

Beylard, Hugues. 2001. "Pomey, François." DHCJ 4:3187.

Biblical Humanism. 2008. *Biblical Humanism and Scholasticism in the Age of Erasmus.* Edited by Erika Rummel. Leiden and Boston.

Bireley, Robert L. 1973. "The Origins of the 'Pacis Compositio' (1629): A Text of Paul Laymann, S. J." AHSI 42: 106–27.

———. 2001. "Laymann, Paul." DHCJ 3:2297–98.

Blum, Paul Richard. 2012. *Studies on Early Modern Aristotelianism.* Leiden.

Boffito, G. M. 1960. "Alessandro Sauli, Santo." DBI 2:234–36.

Borsetti. 1735. Ferrante Borsetti Ferranti Bolani. *Historia almi Ferrariae gymnasii, in duas partes divisa.* 2 vols. Ferrara.

Bösel, Richard. 1988. "La chiesa di S. Lucia. L'invenzione spaziale nel contesto dell'architettura gesuitica." In *Dall'isola alla città,* 19–30.

Bouwsma, William J. 1968. *Venice and the Defense of Republican Liberty. Renaissance Values in the Age of the Counter Reformation.* Berkeley and Los Angeles.

Brambilla, Elena. 2005. "Lecchi, Giovanni Antonio." DBI 64:267–69.

Brizzi, Gian Paolo. 1976. *La formazione della classe dirigente nel Sei-Settecento: I seminaria nobilium nell'Italia centrosettentrionale.* Bologna.

———. 1980. "Educare il Principe, formare le *élites:* I Gesuiti e Ranuccio I Farnese." In *Università, Principe, Gesuiti: La politica farnesiana dell'istruzione a Parma e Piacenza (1545–1622),* 133–211. Rome.

———. 1988a. "I Gesuiti e i seminari per la formazione della classe dirigente." In *Dall'isola alla città,* 145–55.

———. 1988b. "Matricole ed effettivi. Aspetti della presenza studentesca a Bologna fra Cinque e Seicento." In *Studenti e università degli studenti dal XII al XIX secolo,* edited by Gian Paolo Brizzi and Antonio Ivan Pini, 225–59. Studi e memorie per la storia dell'Università di Bologna, N. S., vol. 7. Bologna.

———. 1989. "Lo studio cittadino." In *Storia di Cesena,* vol. 3: *La dominazione pontificia (secoli XVI–XVII–XVIII),* edited by Adriano Prosperi, 219–63. Rimini.

———. 1994. "Scuole e collegi nell'antica Provincia Veneta della Compagnia di Gesù (1542–1773)." In *I gesuiti e Venezia,* 467–511.

———. 2001. *L'antica Università di Fermo.* Testo di Gian Paolo Brizzi, schedatura a cura di Maria Luisa Accorsi, fotografie di Alberto Lagomaggiore. Fermo.

———. 2008. "Lo Studio di Bologna fra *orbis academicus* e mondo cittadino." In *Storia di Bologna. Bologna nell'età moderna (secoli XVI–XVIII)*, vol. 2: *Cultura, istituzioni culturali, Chiesa e vita religiosa*, edited by Adriano Prosperi, 5–113. Bologna.

———. 2009. "La scolarité de Pietro Antonio Adami chez les jésuits de Bologne à la fin du XVIIe siècle." *Histoire de l'éducation* 124: 51–71.

Brockey, Liam Matthew. 2014. *The Visitor. André Palmeiro and the Jesuits in Asia*. Cambridge, Mass., and London.

Brodrick, James. 1961. *Robert Bellarmine, Saint and Scholar*. Westminster, Md.

———. 1998. *Saint Peter Canisius*. Chicago.

Brunelli, Giampiero. 1998. "Gagliardi, Achille." DBI 51:258–64.

Brunelli, Roberto. 1988. *Diocesi di Mantova*. Storia Religiosa della Lombardia 8. Brescia and Varese, 1986; reprinted in Varese.

Buscemi, Salvatore. 1900. "L'insegnamento del diritto civile nella antica Università di Messina." In *CCCL anniversario della Università di Messina (contributo storico)*, part 2, 57–78. Messina.

Cadoppi, Alberto. 2013. *Lo Studio di Ranuccio. La rifondazione dell'Università di Parma nel 1600. Con un inedito elenco di laureati dal 1527 al 1646*. Parma.

CHRP. 1988. *The Cambridge History of Renaissance Philosophy*. Edited by Charles B. Schmitt, Quentin Skinner, Eckhard Kessler, and Jill Kraye. Cambridge.

Cammarota, Marina Raffaeli. 1976. "Carafa, Carlo." DBI 19:513–17.

Cannavale, Ercole. 1980. *Lo Studio di Napoli nel Rinascimento (2700 documenti inediti)*. Naples, 1895; reprinted in Bologna.

Capasso, Gaetano. 1901. "Il Collegio dei Nobili di Parma. Memorie storiche pubblicate nel terzo centenario dalla sua fondazione (28 Ottobre 1901)." *Archivio storico per le provincie Parmensi*, N. S., 1: 1–285.

Capelo, António Cândido Simões. 2002. "La matematica nell'Ateneo pavese dalle origini alla riforma teresiana." *Bollettino della Società Pavese di storia patria* 102: 91–137.

Cappelletti, Vincenzo. 1979. "Belgrado, Iacopo." DBI 7:574–78.

Carafa, Giuseppe. 1971. *De Gymnasio Romano et de eius professoribus*. 2 vols. Rome, 1751; reprinted in Bologna.

Le cardinal Le Camus. 1974. *Le cardinal des montagnes Étienne Le Camus, Évêque de Grenoble (1671–1707)*. Actes du Colloque Le Camus, Grenoble 1971. Grenoble.

Cardinali, Alberta, and Tommaso Galanti. 1992. "Attività del collegio gesuitico di S. Rocco fino alla cacciata del 1768 alla luce della documentazione d'archivio." *Archivio storico per le provincie Parmensi*, Serie 4, vol. 43: 117–44.

The Cardinals of the Holy Roman Church. www2.fiu.edu/~mirandas/cardinals.htm.

Carella, Candida. 2003. "I lettori di 'filosofia naturale' della 'Sapienza' di Roma: I° Francesco Nazari." *Nouvelles de la Republique des Lettres* I/II, 7–35.

———. 2007. *L'insegnamento della filosofia alla "Sapienza" di Roma nel Seicento. Le cattedre e i maestri*. Florence.

Carlsmith, Christopher. 2012. "*Siam Ungari*: Nationalism, Students, and Misbehavior at the University of Bologna in the Late Seventeenth Century." *History of Universities* 26: 113–49.

Carpanetto, Dino, and Giuseppe Ricuperati. 1987. *Italy in the Age of Reason 1685–1789*. Translated by Caroline Higgitt. London and New York.

Casalini, Cristiano. 2012. *Aristotele a Coimbra. Il Cursus Conimbricensis e l'educazione nel Collegium Artium*. Rome.

————. 2014. "Pererio 'cattivo maestro': su un *cold case* nella storia della pedagogia gesuitica." In *Filosofia e religione. Studi in onore di Fabio Rossi*. Edited by Stefano Caroti and Alberto Siclari. *Quaderni di Noctua* 2, no. 2: 59–110. E-Theca On Line Open Access Edizioni. www.didaschein.net/ojs/index.php/QuadernidiNoctua.

————. 2015. "Benedictus Pererius and the *ordo doctrinae*. Lessons and Texts in the First Jesuits' Philosophy." *Noctua* 2, nos. 1–2: 204–32.

Casanovas, Juan. 2002. "Riccioli e l'astronomia dopo Keplero." In *Giambattista Riccioli*, 119–31.

Cascio Pratilli, Giovanni. 1975. *L'università e il principe. Gli Studi di Siena e di Pisa tra rinascimento e contoriforma*. Florence.

Casini, Paolo. 1971. "Boscovich (Bošković), Ruggero Giuseppe (Ruđer Josip)." DBI 13:221–30.

Castellani, Giuseppe. 1945. "Lo vocazione alla Compagnia di Gesù del P. Antonio Possevino da una relazione inedita del medesimo." AHSI 14: 102–24.

Catalano, Michele. 1916–1917. "La fondazione e le prime vicende del Collegio dei Gesuiti in Catania (1556–1579)." *Archivio Storico per la Sicilia Orientale* 13 (1916): 34–80; 14 (1917): 145–86.

————. 1934. "L'Università di Catania nel Rinascimento." In *Storia della Università di Catania dalle origini ai giorni nostri*, 3–98. Catania.

Catalano-Tirrito, Michele. 1975. *Storia documentata della R. Università di Catania nel secolo XV. Appendice*. Catania, 1913; reprinted in Bologna.

Catarinella, Annamaria, and Irene Salsotto. 1998. "L'università e i collegi." In *Storia di Torino*, vol. 3: *Dalla dominazione francese alla ricomposizione dello Stato (1536–1630)*, edited by Giuseppe Ricuperati, 523–67. Turin.

Catoni, Giuliano. 1991. "Le riforme del Granduca, le 'serre' degli scolari e i lettori di casa." In *L'Università di Siena. 750 anni di storia*, 45–66. Siena.

————. 1996. "Un nido di nobili: il Collegio Tolomei." In *Storia di Siena*, vol. 2: *Dal Granducato all'unità*, edited by Roberto Barzanti, Giuliano Catoni, and Mario De Gregorio, 81–94. Siena.

Catto, Michela. 2009. *La Compagnia divisa. Il dissenso nell'ordine gesuitico tra '500 e '600*. Brescia.

Cavanna Ciappina, Maristella. 2002. "Grimaldi, Ansaldo." DBI 59:475–78.

Cavazza, Silvano. 1987. "De Dominis, Marcantonio." DBI 33:642–50.

CCCL anniversario della Università di Messina (contributo storico). 1900. Messina.

Ceccarelli, Francesco. 1988. "Costruzione e trasformazione di un'isola cittadina: dalla fabbrica della chiesa e del noviziato di S. Ignazio agli interventi ottocenteschi." In *Dall'isola alla città*, 43–53.

Cecchi, Dante. 1979. *Macerata e il suo territorio: La storia*. Milan.

Cesareo, Francesco C. 2004. "The Jesuit Colleges in Rome under Everard Mercurian." In *The Mercurian Project*, 607–44.

Cesca, Giovanni. 1900. "L'Università di Messina e la Compagnia di Gesù." In *CCCL anniversario della Università di Messina (contributo storico)*, part 1, 3–36. Messina.

Cessi, Roberto. 1921–1922. "L'Università giurista dei Padova ed i Gesuiti alla fine del Cinquecento." *Atti del Reale Istituto veneto di scienze, lettere ed arti*, 18.2:585–601.

Chambers, David S. 1987. "The 'bellissimo ingegno' of Ferdinando Gonzaga (1587–1626), Cardinal and Duke of Mantua." *Journal of the Warburg and Courtauld Institutes* 50: 113–47.

Chiaudano, Mario. 1972a. "I lettori dell'Università di Torino ai tempi di Carlo Emanuele I (1580–1630)." In *L'Università di Torino nei sec. XVI e XVII*, 139–217. Turin.

———. 1972b. "I lettori dell'Università di Torino ai tempi di Emanuele Filiberto (1566–1580)." In *L'Università di Torino nei sec. XVI e XVII*, 69–137. Turin.

———. 1972c. "La restaurazione della Università di Torino per opera di Emanuele Filiberto." In *L'Università di Torino nei sec. XVI e XVII*, 51–67. Turin.

Chiellini, Sabrina. 1991. "Contributo per la storia degli insegnamenti umanistici dello studio ferrarese (XIV–XVII secolo)." In *La rinascita del sapere*, 210–45.

Chigi, Sigismondo. In The Cardinals of the Holy Roman Church. www2.fiu.edu/~mirandas/bios1667-ii.htm#Chigi.

Church, Culture & Curriculum. 1999. *Church, Culture & Curriculum. Theology and Mathematics in the Jesuit Ratio Studiorum.* Edited and translated by Frederick A. Homann. Philadelphia.

Codina Mir, Gabriel. 1967. "La ordenación y el doctorado en teología de Jerónimo Nadal en Aviñón (1537–1538)." AHSI 36: 247–51.

———. 1968. *Aux sources de la pédagogie des jésuites. Le 'Modus Parisiensis.'* Rome.

Cohen, Thomas M. 2004. "Nation, Lineage, and Jesuit Unity in Antonio Possevino's Memorial to Everard Mercurian (1576)." In *A Companhia de Jesus na Península Ibérica nos secs: XVI e XVII*, 1:543–61. 2 vols. Porto.

I collegi universitari. 1991. *I collegi universitari in Europa tra il XIV e XVIII secolo.* Atti del Convegno di Studi della Commissione Internazionale per la Storia delle Università. Siena-Bologna, 16–19 maggio 1988. Edited by Domenico Maffei and Hilde de Ridder-Symoens. Milan.

The Collegiate University. 1986. *The History of the University of Oxford,* vol. 3: *The Collegiate University.* Edited by James McConica. Oxford.

Colombo, Emanuele. 2014. "The Watershed of Conversion: Antonio Possevino, New Christians, and Jews." In *"The Tragic Couple."* In *Encounters Between Jews and Jesuits*, edited by James Bernauer and Robert A. Maryks, 25–42. Leiden and Boston.

Colpo, Mario. 2001. "Colegio Romano (Universidad Gregoriana desde 1873)." DHCJ 1:848–50.

Colpo, Mario, and José Martínez de la Escalera. 2001. "Casati, Paolo." DHCJ 1:688–89.

Congar, Yves Marie-Joseph. 1946. "Théologie." In *Dictionnaire de théologie catholique,* 15.1, cols. 341–502. Paris.

Coniglio, Giuseppe. 1960. "Acquaviva, Claudio." DBI 1:168–78.

———. 1967. *I Gonzaga.* Varese.

Constant, Eric A. 2002. "A Reinterpretation of the Fifth Lateran Council Decree *Apostolici regiminis* (1513)." *Sixteenth Century Journal* 33: 353–79.

Conte, Emanuele. 1985a. *Accademie studentesche a Roma nel Cinquecento. De modis docendi et discendi in iure.* Rome.

———. 1985b. "Università e formazione giuridica a Roma nel Cinquecento." *La cultura* 2: 328–46.

———. 1992. "Professori e cattedre tra Cinquecento e Seicento." In *Roma e lo Studium Urbis. Spazio urbano e cultura dal Quattro al Seicento,* Atti del convegno Roma, 7–10 giugno 1989, 186–99. Rome.

Cooper, Thompson. 1886. "Bower, Archibald." In *Dictionary of National Biography*, vol. 6: *Bottomley-Browell*, edited by Leslie Stephen, 48–51. London.

Corradino, Saverio. 2001. "Saccheri, Giovanni Girolamo." DHCJ 4:3457–58.

Cortese, Nino. 1924. *Lo Studio di Napoli nell'età spagnola*. Naples.

Cosentino, Giuseppe. 1982. "Il Collegio Gesuitico e le origini dell'Università di Genova." *Miscellanea storica ligure* 14: 57–137.

Costa, Emilio. 1912. "Contributi alla storia dello Studio bolognese durante il secolo XVII." *Studi e memorie per la storia dell'Università di Bologna* 3: 1–88.

Coyne, George V. 2001. "Asclepi, Giuseppe Maria." DHCJ 1:256.

Cozzi, Gaetano. 1958. *Il doge Nicolò Contarini. Ricerche sul patriziato veneziano agli inizi del Seicento*. Venice and Rome.

———. 1963. "Gesuiti e politica sul finire del '500. Una mediazione di pace tra Enrico IV, Filippo II e la Sede Apostolica proposta dal p. Achille Gagliardi alla Repubblica di Venezia." *Rivista storica italiana* 75: 477–537.

———. 1967. "Berinzaga, Isabella Cristina." DBI 9:103–5.

———. 1994. "Fortuna, e sfortuna, della Compagnia di Gesù a Venezia." In *I Gesuiti e Venezia*, 59 88.

Curi, Vincenzo. 1880. *L'università degli studi di Fermo. Notizie storiche*. Ancona.

D'Alessandro, Alessandro. 1980. "Materiali per la storia dello *Studium* di Parma (1545–1622)." In *Università, Principe, Gesuiti: La politica farnesiana dell'istruzione a Parma e Piacenza (1545–1622)*, 15–95. Rome.

Dall'isola alla città. 1988. *Dall'isola alla città: i gesuiti a Bologna*. Edited by Gian Paolo Brizzi and Anna Maria Matteucci. Bologna.

Dalmases, Cándido de. 1985. *Ignatius of Loyola, Founder of the Jesuits. His Life and Work*. Translated by Jerome Aixalá. St. Louis, Mo.

———. 2001a. "Bobadilla, Nicolás (Alonso) de." DHCJ 1:463–65.

———. 2001b. "Borja, Francisco de." DHCJ 2:1605–11.

———. 2001c. "Coduri (Codure), Jean." DHCJ 1:833.

———. 2001d. "España. Antiqua CJ. 1540–1615." DHCJ 2:1265–70.

———. 2001e. "Jay (Le Jay, Jayo), Claude." DHCJ 2:2142–43.

. 2001f. "Polanco, Juan Alfonso de." DHCJ 4:3168 69.

———. 2001g. "Torres, Baltasar de." DHCJ 4:3818.

Dal Nero, Domenico. 1991. "L'insegnamento della teologia in Europa e a Ferrara." In *La rinascita del sapere*, 246–63.

Davidson, Nicholas. 2015. "Hispanophobia in the Venetian Republic." In *The Spanish Presence in Sixteenth-Century Italy. Images of Iberia*, edited by Piers Baker-Bates and Miles Pattenden, 29–41. Burlington, Vt.

DBI. 1960–. *Dizionario biografico degli italiani*. Rome.

D'Amico, John F. 1988. *Theory and Practice in Renaissance Textual Criticism. Beatus Rhenanus Between Conjecture and History*. Los Angeles.

De Angelis, Carlo. 1988. "Il Collegio di S. Luigi dei Gesuiti: la costruzione, il restauro." In *Dall'isola alla città*, 55–64.

De Angelis, Carlo, and Roberto Scannavini. 1988. "L'insediamento dei Gesuiti nella zona di S. Lucia." In *Dall'isola alla città*, 13–18.

De Benedictis, Angela. 1995. *Repubblica per contratto. Bologna: una città nello Stato della Chiesa*. Bologna.

Debus, Allen G. 1977. *The Chemical Philosophy: Paracelsian Science and Medicine in the Sixteenth and Seventeenth Centuries*. 2 vols. New York.

De Caro, Gaspare. 1962. "Azzolini (Azzolino), Decio." DBI 4:768–71.

De Feo, Italo. 1987. *Sisto V: un grande papa tra Rinascimento e Barocco*. Second edition. Milan.

De Ferrari, Augusto. 1978. "Casati, Paolo." DBI 21:165–67.

De Lucca, Denis. 2012. *Jesuits and Fortifications. The Contribution of the Jesuits to Military Architecture in the Baroque Age*. Leiden and Boston.

Delattre, Pierre. 1955. "Paris. Le Collège. Collège de Clermont (1560–1682). Collège Louis-le-Grand (1682–1762)." In *Les établissements des Jésuites en France depuis quatre siècles*, vol. 3: *Macheville-Pinel*, edited by Pierre DeLattre, cols. 1101–1258. 4 vols. Enghien and Wetteren.

Dellacorna, Mila Amietta. 1972. "I lettori dell'Università dal 1630 al 1659." In *L'Università di Torino nei sec. XVI e XVII*, 219–346. Turin.

Del Monte, Giovanni. 1948. *Il collegio dei teologi dell'Università di Parma*. Parma.

Del Negro, Piero. 2002. "Il Settecento fino alla caduta della Repubblica." In *L'Università di Padova nei secoli (1601–1805). Documenti di storia dell'Ateneo*, edited by Piero Del Negro and Francesco Piovan, 149–340. Treviso.

———. 2006. "L'Università di Padova nei consulti di Paolo Sarpi." In *Ripensando Paolo Sarpi,* Atti del Convegno Internazionale di Studi nel 450° anniversario della nascita di Paolo Sarpi, edited by Corrado Pin, 417–37. Venice.

Del Soldato, Eva. 2010. *Simone Porzio. Un aristotelico tra natura e grazia*. Rome.

Demoment, Auguste. 1949. "Chambéry: Le Collège (1562–1729)." In *Les établissements des Jésuites en France depuis quatre siècles*, vol. 1: *Abbeville-Cyriacum*, edited by Pierre Delattre, SJ, cols. 1228–57. 4 vols. Enghien and Wetteren.

Derry, George H. 1913. "Canisius, Theodorich." In *The Catholic Encyclopedia*, 3:250. New York, 1908; reprinted in New York.

Devos, Roger, and Bernard Grosperrin. 1985. *La Savoie de la Réforme à la Révolution française*. Rennes.

DHCJ. 2001. *Diccionario Histórico de la Compañía de Jesús. Biográfico-temático*. Edited by Charles E. O'Neill, SJ, and Joaquín M. Domíngues, SJ. 4 vols. Rome and Madrid.

Di Napoli, Giovanni. 1963. *L'immortalità dell'anima nel Rinascimento*. Turin.

Dinis, Alfredo. 2002. "Was Riccioli a Secret Copernican?" In *Giambattista Riccioli*, 49–77.

Di Noto Marrella, Sergio. 2002. "Il collegio dei giuristi di Parma." In *Gesuiti e università*, 185–98.

Di Simone, Maria Rosa. 1980. *La 'Sapienza' Romana nel Settecento. Organizzazione Universitaria e Insegnamento del Diritto*. Rome.

———. 1982. "Il Collegio Romano nella prima metà del Seicento e la formazione di uno storico missionario." *Clio* 18: 36–56.

Donato, Maria Pia. 2007. "Manfredi, Paolo." DBI 7:729–33.

Donnelly, John Patrick. 1982. "The Jesuit College at Padua. Growth, Suppression, Attempts at Restoration: 1552–1606." AHSI 51: 45–79.

———. 1986. "Antonio Possevino and Jesuits of Jewish Ancestry." AHSI 74: 3–31.

———. 2001a. "Botero, Giovanni." DHCJ 1:502–3.

———. 2001b. "Broët, Paschase." DHCJ 1:552.

———. 2001c. "Comitoli, Paolo." DHCJ 1:874–75.

———. 2001d. "Fabro, Pierre." DHCJ 2:1369–70.

———. 2001e. "Hoffaeus, Paul." DHCJ 2:1932–33.

———. 2001f. "Mangioni, Valentino." DHCJ 3:2494.

———. 2001g. "Perpinyà (Perpiñá), Pedro Juan." DHCJ 3:3099–3100.

———. 2001h. "Toledo, Francisco de." DHCJ 4:3807–08.

———. 2004a. "Antonio Possevino: From Secretary to Papal Legate in Sweden." In *The Mercurian Project*, 323–49.

———. 2004b. *Ignatius of Loyola. Founder of the Jesuits.* New York.

Dossi, Luigi. 1964. *I Gesuiti a Parma.* Milan.

DSB. 1981. *Dictionary of Scientific Biography.* Edited by Charles C. Gillispie et al. 18 vols. New York.

Echarte, Ignacio. 2001. "Memorialistas." DHCJ 3:2615–16.

Economia, istituzioni, cultura in Lombardia. 1982. *Economia, istituzioni, cultura in Lombardia nell'età di Maria Teresa.* Edited by Aldo De Maddalena, Ettore Rotelli, and Gennaro Barbarisi. 3 vols. Bologna.

Edwards, Michael. 2013. *Time and the Science of the Soul in Early Modern Philosophy.* Leiden.

Emery, Jan. 1979. "Le renouveau et ses limites (1621–1715)." In *Le Diocèse de Grenoble,* edited by Bernard Bligny, 119–49. Paris.

ER. 1999. *Encyclopedia of the Renaissance.* Edited by Paul F. Grendler et al. 6 vols. New York.

Ermini, Giuseppe. 1971. *Storia della Università di Perugia.* 2 vols. Florence.

Fabrini, Natale. 1941. *Lo studio pubblico di Bologna ed i Gesuiti.* Bologna.

———. 1946a. *Le congregazioni dei Gesuiti a Bologna.* Rome.

Facciolati, Jacopo. 1978. *Fasti Gymnasii Patavini.* 3 vols. Padua, 1757; reprinted in Bologna (as one volume).

Fantini, Antonella. 1989. "Il collegio di Pavia. Profilo storico attraverso i documenti rinvenuti." AHSI 58: 329–54.

Farge, James K. 1985. *Orthodoxy and Reform in Early Reformation France. The Faculty of Theology of Paris, 1500–1543.* Leiden.

———. 1992a. *Le parti conservateur au XVIe siècle: Université et Parlement de Paris à l'époque de la Renaissance et de la Réforme.* Paris.

———. 1992b. "The University of Paris in the time of Ignatius Loyola." In *Ignacio de Loyola y su tiempo. Congreso internacional de historia (9–13 Setiembre 1991),* edited by Jan Plazaola, 221–43. Bilbao.

———. 1996a. "Cop, Nicolas." In OER 1:426.

———. 1996b. "Faculty of Theology of Paris." In OER 2:88–89.

———. 1999. "Paris, University of." In ER 4:403–6.

———. 2008. "Noël Beda and the Defense of the Tradition." In *Biblical Humanism,* 143–64.

———. 2014. "Scholasticism, Humanism and the Origins of the Collège de France." In *Neo-Latin and the Humanities. Essays in Honour of Charles E. Fantazzi,* edited by Luc Dietz, Timothy Kircher, and Jonathan Reid, 159–77. Toronto.

Farrell, Allan J. 1938. *The Jesuit Code of Liberal Education. Development and Scope of the Ratio Studiorum.* Milwaukee, Wis.

Favaro, Antonio. 1911. "Nuovi documenti sulla vertenza tra lo Studio di Padova e la Compagnia di Gesù sul finire del secolo decimosesto." *Nuovo archivio veneto,* serie 3, vol. 21: 89–100.

Feci, Simona, and Luca Bortolotti. 2001. "Giustiniani, Benedetto." DBI 57:315–25.

Fejér, Josephus. 1985–1990. *Defuncti secundi saeculi S. I. 1641–1740.* 5 vols. Rome.

Ferri, Edgardo. 1991. *Luigi Gonzaga 1568–1591*. Milan.

Figini, Carlo. 1938. "Il conferimento del grado di dottore in teologia in Milano da S. Carlo a noi." *Humiltas. Miscellanea storia dei seminari milanesi* 25: 1015–34.

Fiocca, Alessandra. 1991. "La formazione dei giudici e dei notai d'argine a Ferrara. Dai primi provvedimenti istituzionali alla scuola d'idraulica di Teodoro Bonati." In *La rinascita del sapere*, 367–84.

———. 2002a. "Ferrara e i gesuiti periti in materia d'acque." In *Gesuiti e università*, 339–59.

———. 2002b. "I gesuiti e il governo delle acque nel basso Po nel secolo XVII." In *Giambattista Riccioli*, 319–70.

———. 2004. "Studi matematici e regolazione delle acque." *Annali di Storia delle Università italiane* 8: 103–24.

———. 2011. "Galileiani e Gesuiti a Ferrara nel Seicento." In *Galileo e la scuola galileiana nelle Università del Seicento*, edited by Luigi Pete, 293–309. Bologna.

Fiocca, Alessandra, and Luigi Pepe. 1985. "La lettura di matematica nell'Università di Ferrara dal 1602 al 1771." *Annali dell'Università di Ferrara*, Sezione 7, Scienze matematiche, 31: 125–67.

Firpo, Luigi. 1971. "Botero, Giovanni." DBI 3:352–62.

Fisicaro Vercelli, Franca. 1972. "I lettori dell'Università di Torino dal 1659 al 1690." In *L'Università di Torino nei sec. XVI e XVII*, 347–456. Turin.

Foà, Simone. 2001. "Giraldi, Giovan Battista (Cinzio Giovan Battista)." DBI 56:442–47.

Fochessati, Giuseppe. 1930. *I Gonzaga di Mantova e l'ultima duca*. Edited by Riccardo Bacchelli. Milan.

Fois, Mario. 2001a. "Aquaviva, Claudio." DHCJ 2:1614–21.

———. 2001b. "Italia: Antigua Compañía de Jesús." DHCJ 3:2078–93.

Il fondo archivistico della Sapienza. 2006. *Il fondo archivistico del Collegio Pio della Sapienza di Perugia. Inventario*. Edited by Laura Marconi, Daniela Mori, and M. Alessandra Panzanelli Fratoni. Perugia.

Foschi, Paola. 1988. "La chiesa di S. Lucia e i collegi dei Gesuiti. Vicende costruttive." In *Dall'isola alla città*, 33–42.

Fosi Polverini, Irene. 1988. "Della Cornia, Fulvio." DBI 36:769–72.

Franci, Raffaella. 2006. "L'insegnamento della matematica nell'Università di Siena." *Annali di Storia delle Università italiane* 10: 191–204.

Francisco de Borja. 2011. *Francisco de Borja y su tiempo. Política, Religión y Cultura en la Edad Moderna*. Edited by Enrique García Hernán and María del Pilar Ryan. Valencia and Rome.

Frasson, Paolo. 1983. "Corner, Federico." DBI 29:83–85.

Freedman, Joseph S. 1985. "Philosophy Instruction within the Institutional Framework of Central European Schools and Universities during the Reformation Era." *History of Universities* 5: 117–66. Reprinted in Freedman, *Philosophy and the Arts in Central Europe, 1500–1700. Teaching and Texts in Schools and Universities*, study II. Aldershot, 1999.

Galeota, Gustavo. 2001. "Belarmino, Roberto." DHCJ 1:387–90.

Ganss, George E. 1956. *Saint Ignatius' Idea of a Jesuit University. A Study in the History of Catholic Education*. Including Part Four of the *Constitutions* of the Society of Jesus Translated from the Spanish of Saint Ignatius of Loyola with Introduction and Notes. Milwaukee, Wis.

García de Castro Valdés, José. 2012. *Polanco: el humanismo de los Jesuitas: (Burgos 1517–Roma 1576)*. Santander, Bilbao, and Madrid.

García Oro, José. 1992. *La Universidad de Alcalá de Henares en la etapa fundacional (1458–1578)*. Santiago de Compostela.

García-Villoslada, Ricardo. 1990. *Sant'Ignazio di Loyola. Una nuova biografia*. Translated by Anna Maria Ercoles, OSB. Milan.

Gardi, Andrea. 1995. "L'Università di Ferrara come terreno di scontro politico-sociale all'epoca di Benedetto XIV." In *'In supreme dignitatis ...' Per la storia dell'Università di Ferrara 1391–1991*, edited by Patrizia Castelli, 309–38. Florence.

Garms-Cornides, Elisabeth. 1997. "Firmian, Carlo Gottardo, Conte di." DBI 48:224–31.

Gavagna, Veronica. 2002. "I gesuiti e la polemica sul vuoto: il contributo di Paolo Casati." In *Gesuiti e università*, 325–38.

———. 2011. "Paolo Casati e la scuola galileliana." In *Galileo e la scuola galileiana nelle Università del Seicento*, edited by Luigi Pepe, 311–26. Bologna.

Gay, Jean-Pascal. 2011. *Morales en conflit. Théologie et polémique au Grand Siécle (1640–1700)*. Paris.

Gencarelli, Elvira. 1961. "Antonio Farnese, Duca di Parma e Piacenza." DBI 3:547–48.

Gerhartz, Johannes G. 2001. "Colegio Germánico-Húngarico, Roma." DHCJ 1:840–42.

Gerlich, Robert S. 2001. "Pirhing, Ehrenreich." DHCJ 4:3145–46.

I Gesuiti e la Ratio Studiorum. 2004. Edited by Manfred Hinz, Roberto Righi, and Danilo Zardin. Rome.

Gesuiti e università. 2002. *Gesuiti e università in Europa (secoli XVI–XVIII)*. Atti del Convegno di studi. Parma, 13–14–15 dicembre 2001. Edited by Gian Paolo Brizzi e Roberto Greci. Bologna.

I gesuiti e Venezia. 1994. *I gesuiti e Venezia. Momenti e problemi di storia veneziana della Compagnia di Gesù*. Atti del Convegno di Studi, Venezia, 2–5 ottobre 1990. Edited by Mario Zanardi. Padua.

Giachi, Gualberto. 2001. "Gonzaga, Luis." DHCJ 2:1779–80.

Giambattista Riccioli. 2002. *Giambattista Riccioli e il merito scientifico dei Gesuiti nell'eta barocca*. Edited by Maria Teresa Borgato. Florence.

Giard, Luce, 2012. "Les collèges jésuites des anciens Pays-Bas et l'élaboration de la Ratio Studiorum." In *The Jesuits of the Low Countries: Identity and Impact (1540–1773)*, Proceedings of the International Congress at the Faculty of Theology and Religious Studies Ku Leuven (2–5 December 2009), edited by Rob Faesen and Leo Kenis, 83–108. Leuven, Paris, and Walpole, Mass.

Gilbert, Neal. 1965. "Francesco Vimercato of Milan: a Bio-Bibliography." *Studies in the Renaissance* 12: 188–217.

Ginatempo, Maria, and Lucia Sandri. 1990. *L'Italia delle città: Il popolamento urbano tra Medioevo e Rinascimento (secoli XIII–XVI)*. Florence.

Giordano, Silvano. 2006. "Luigi (Alvigi) Gonzaga, santo." DBI 66:499–502.

———. 2014. "Pallavicino, Lazzaro." DBI 80:531–32.

Gliozzi, Giuliano. 1975. "Capodivacca (Capivaccio, Capivacceus), Girolamo." DBI 18:649–51.

Gonçalves, Nuno da Silva. 2004. "Jesuits in Portugal." In *The Mercurian Project*, 705–44.

Grafton, Anthony. 1983. *Joseph Scaliger. A Study in the History of Classical Scholarship*, vol. 1: *Textual Criticism and Exegesis*. Oxford.

Greci, Roberto. 1998. "Una duttile università 'di frontiera': lo Studio parmense nel XV secolo." In *Le università minori in Europa (secoli XV–XIX)*, Convegno Internazionale di Studi, Alghero, 30 ottobre–2 novembre 1996, edited by Gian Paolo Brizzi and Jacques Verger, 75–94. Catanzaro.

Grendler, Paul F. 1977. *The Roman Inquisition and the Venetian Press, 1540–1605*. Princeton, N.J.

———. 1979. "The *Tre Savii sopra Eresia*, 1547–1605: A Prosopographical Study." *Studi veneziani* N. S., 3: 283–340. Reprinted in Grendler 1981, study X.

———. 1981. *Culture and Censorship in Late Renaissance Italy and France*. London.

———. 1989. *Schooling in Renaissance Italy. Literacy and Learning, 1300–1600*. Baltimore and London.

———. 1990. "The Leaders of the Venetian State, 1540–1609: A Prosopographical Analysis." *Studi veneziani* N. S., 19: 35–85. Reprinted in Grendler 2006b, study XI.

———. 1998. "How to Get a Degree in Fifteen Days: Erasmus' Doctorate of Theology from the University of Turin." *Erasmus of Rotterdam Society Yearbook* 18: 40–69. Reprinted in Grendler 2006b, study II.

———. 2002. *The Universities of the Italian Renaissance*. Baltimore and London.

———. 2004a. "Italian Schools and University Dreams during Mercurian's Generalate." In *The Mercurian Project*, 482–522. Reprinted in Grendler 2006b, study V.

———. 2004b. "The Universities of the Renaissance and Reformation," *Renaissance Quarterly* 57: 1–42. Reprinted in Grendler 2006b, study I.

———. 2006a. "Gasparo Contarini and the University of Padua." In *Heresy, Culture, and Religion in Early Modern Italy. Contexts and Contestations*, edited by Ronald K. Delph, Michelle M. Fontaine, and John Jeffries Martin, 135–50. Kirksville, Mo.

———. 2006b. *Renaissance Education Between Religion and Politics*. Aldershot.

———. 2008. "Italian Biblical Humanism and the Papacy, 1515–1535." In *Biblical Humanism*, 227–76.

———. 2009a. "Fencing, Playing Ball, and Dancing in Italian Renaissance Universities." In *Sport and Culture in Early Modern Europe/Le Sport dans la Civilisation de l'Europe Pré-Moderne*, edited by John McClelland and Brian Merrilees, 295–318. Toronto.

———. 2009b. *The University of Mantua, the Gonzaga, and the Jesuits, 1584–1630*. Baltimore and London.

———. 2011a. "Italian Universities and War, 1494–1630." In *Le Università e le guerre dal Medioevo alla Seconda guerra mondiale*, edited by Piero Del Negro, 23–36. Bologna.

———. 2011b. "The Jesuit Education of Benedetto Pamphilj at the Collegio Romano." In *The Pamphilj and the Arts. Patronage and Consumption in Baroque Rome*, edited by Stephanie C. Leone, 85–94. Boston.

———. 2012a. "The Attempt to Found a Civic and Jesuit University in Chambéry, 1679–1681." In *Los jesuitas. Religión política y educación (siglos XVI–XVIII)*, edited by José Martínez Millán, Henar Pizarro Llorente, and Esther Jiménez Pablo, 1:407–32. 3 vols. Madrid.

———. 2012b. "Fifteenth-Century Catechesis, the Schools of Christian Doctrine, and the Jesuits." In *Prima di Carlo Borromeo. Istituzione, religione e società agli inizi del*

Cinquecento, edited by Alberto Rocca and Paola Vismara, 291–319. Studia Borromaica 26. Milan and Rome.

———. 2014. "The Attitudes of the Jesuits Toward Erasmus." In *Collaboration, Conflict, and Continuity in the Reformation: Essays in Honour of James M. Estes on His Eightieth Birthday*, edited by Konrad Eisenbichler, 363–85. Toronto.

———. 2015. "Laínez and the Schools in Europe." In *Diego Laínez (1512–1565) and his Generalate. Jesuit with Jewish Roots. Close Confident of Ignatius of Loyola. Preeminent Theologian of the Council of Trent,* edited by Paul Oberholzer, 649–78. Rome.

———. 2016. "The Culture of the Jesuit Teacher 1548–1773." *Journal of Jesuit Studies* 3: 17–41.

Grillo, Enzo. 1968. "Biancani, Giuseppe." DBI 10:33–35.

Gronda, Giovanna. 1980. "Ceva, Tommaso." DBI 24:325–28.

Grosso, Michele, and Maria Franca Mellano. 1957. *La controriforma nella arcidiocesi di Torino (1558–1610).* 3 vols. Vatican City.

Grzebień, Ludwik. 2001. "Polonia." DHCJ 4:3173–87.

Guderzo, Giulio. 1982. "La riforma dell'Università di Pavia." In *Economia, istituzioni, cultura,* 3:845–61.

Guidetti, Armando. 2001. "Ceva, Tommaso." DHCJ 1:743.

Gullino, Giuseppe. 1994. "Il rientro dei gesuiti a Venezia nel 1657: le ragioni della politica e dell'economia." In *I gesuiti e Venezia,* 421–33.

Hanlon, Gregory. 2000. *Early Modern Italy, 1550–1800: Three Seasons in European History.* New York.

———. 2014. *The Hero of Italy. Odoardo Farnese, Duke of Parma, his Soldiers, and his Subjects in the Thirty Years' War.* Oxford.

Haub, Rita. 2004. "From Peter to Paul: The Province of Upper Germany in the 1570s." In *The Mercurian Project,* 145–81.

Hellyer, Marcus. 2005. *Catholic Physics. Jesuit Natural Philosophy in Early Modern Germany.* Notre Dame, Ind.

Hengst, Karl. 1981. *Jesuiten an Universitäten und Jesuitenuniversitäten: zur Geschichte der Universitäten in der Oberdeutschen und Rheinischen Provinz der Gesellschaft Jesu im Zeitalter der konfessionellen Auseinandersetzung.* Paderborn.

Hexter, J. H. 1961. *Reappraisals in History. New Views on History and Society in Early Modern Europe.* New York.

Hierarchia Catholica. 1913–1978. *Hierarchia Catholica medii et recentioris aevi.* Edited by Konrad Eubel et al. 9 vols. Münster and Padua.

Hinnebusch, William A. 1973. *The History of the Dominican Order,* vol. 2: *Intellectual and Cultural Life to 1500.* New York.

Homann, Frederick A. 2001. "Clavius (Klau), Christophorus." DHCJ 1:825–26.

Ingegno, Alfonso. 1972. "Cabeo, Niccolò." DBI 15:686–88.

Iparraguirre, Ignacio, and André Derville. 1967. "Gagliardi, Achille." In *Dictionnaire de spiritualité,* vol. 6: *Gabriel-Guzman,* cols. 53–64. Paris.

Isnardi, Lorenzo. 1975. *Storia della Università di Genova.* 2 vols. Genoa, 1861–1867; reprinted in Sala Bolognese.

L'istituto di Celso Tolomei. 2000. *Nobile collegio - convitto nazionale (1676–1997).* Edited by Roberto Giorgi. Siena.

Jacobs, Hubert. 2001. "Lauretano, Michele." DHCJ 3:2293–94.

Jenkins, Allan K., and Patrick Preston. 2007. *Biblical Scholarship and the Church. A Sixteenth-Century Crisis of Authority.* Aldershot and Burlington, Vt.

The Jesuit Ratio Studiorum. 2000. *The Jesuit Ratio Studiorum. 400th Anniversary Perspectives.* Edited by Vincent J. Duminuco. New York.

Kainulainen, Jaska. 2014. *Paolo Sarpi: A Servant of God and State.* Leiden and Boston.

Kangro, Hans. 1978. "Sennert, Daniel." DSB 12:310–13.

Kessler, Eckhard. 1988. "The intellective soul." In CHRP, 485–534.

Knafla, Louis A., and Jean Dietz Moss. 1999. "Ramus, Petrus." ER 5:207–12.

Korade, Miko. 2001a. "De Dominis, Marcantonio." DHCJ 2:1054–55.

———. 2001b. "Tolomei, Giovanni Battista," DHCJ 4:3809–10.

Krajcar, Jan. 1965. "The Greek College under the Jesuits for the First Time (1591–1604)." *Orientalia Christiana Periodica* 31: 85–118.

———. 1966. "The Greek College in the Years of Unrest (1604–1630)." *Orientalia Christiana Periodica* 32: 6–38.

———. 2001. "Colegio Griego, Roma." DHCJ 1:842–43.

Kristeller, Paul Oskar. 1964. *Eight Philosophers of the Italian Renaissance.* Stanford, Calif.

Lachenschmid, Robert. 2001. "Gretser (Gretscher), Jakob." DHCJ 2:1814.

Lane, Frederic C. 1973. *Venice: A Maritime Republic.* Baltimore and London.

Lécrivain, Philippe. 2004. "The Struggle for Paris: Juan Maldonado in France." In *The Mercurian Project,* 295–321.

———. 2011. *Paris in the Time of Ignatius of Loyola (1528–1533).* Translated by Ralph C. Renner. St. Louis, Mo.

Legati e governatori. 1994. *Legati e governatori dello stato pontificio (1550–1809).* Edited by Christoph Weber. Rome.

Leijenhorst, Cees. 2002. *The Mechanisation of Aristotelianism. The Late Aristotelian Setting of Thomas Hobbes' Natural Philosophy.* Leiden.

Lenzi, Deanna. 1988. "Il teatro della Sapienza. La biblioteca di Giuseppe Antonio Ambrosi." In *Dall'isola alla città,* 85–92.

Lerda, Attilio. 1993. "Lo 'studio' di Mondovì, i primi docenti e le loro retribuzioni." *Studi piemontesi* 22: 183–88.

———. 1994. "San Roberto Bellarmino insegnante a Mondovì (1564–1567)." *Studi piemontesi* 23: 447–52.

Levi della Vida, Giorgio. 1960. "Albonesi, Teseo Ambrogio degli." DBI 2:39–42.

Lewis, Gillian. 1986. "The Faculty of Medicine." In *The Collegiate University,* 213–56.

Lewis, Mark. 2004. "The Rehabilitation of Nicolás Bobadilla, S.J., during the Generalate of Everard Mercurian." In *The Mercurian Project,* 437–59.

Liceo, Ginnasio. "Virgilio." www.liceoginnasiovirgilio.it.

Lines, David A. 2005. "Calendari del Seicento per l'Università "La Sapienza." Una integrazione dall'Archivio Segreto Vaticano." *Annali di Storia delle Università italiane* 9: 233–46.

———. 2011. "The University of the Artists in Bologna, 1586–1713." In *Galileo e la scuola galileiana nelle Università del Seicento,* edited by Luigi Pepe, 141–53. Bologna.

———. 2012. "Reorganizing the Curriculum: Teaching and Learning in the University of Bologna, c. 1560-c. 1590." *History of Universities* 25, no. 1: 1–59.

———. 2013. "Papal Power and University Control in Early Modern Italy: Bologna and Gregory XIII." *The Sixteenth Century Journal* 44: 663–82.

Lisson, Edwin L., Eduardo Moore, and James T. Bretske. 2001. "Teología: V. Moral." In DHCJ 4:3739–45.

Logan, Oliver. 2011. "San Luigi Gonzaga: Princeling-Jesuit and Model for Catholic Youth." In *Saints and Sanctity*, edited by Peter Clarke and Tony Claydon, 248–57. Woodbridge and Rochester, N.Y.

Lohr, Charles H. 1976. "Jesuit Aristotelianism and Sixteenth-Century Metaphysics." In *Paradosis. Studies in Memory of Edwin A. Quain*, 203–20. New York.

———. 1988a. *Latin Aristotle Commentaries*, vol. 2: *Renaissance Authors*. Florence.

———. 1988b. "Metaphysics." In CHRP, 537–638.

López-Gay, Jesús. 2001. "Javier, Francisco." DHCJ 3:2140–41.

Lovie, Jacques. 1974. "Le Cardinal Le Camus et le décanat de Savoie 1671–1707." In *Le cardinal des montagnes Étienne Le Camus, Évêque de Grenoble (1671–1707)*, Actes du Colloque Le Camus, Grenoble 1971, 171–77. Grenoble.

———. 1979. *Les diocèses de Chambéry Tarentaise Maurienne*. Paris.

Lucas, Thomas M. 1997. *Landmarking: City, Church & Jesuit Urban Strategy*. Chicago.

Lukács, Ladislaus, SJ. 1960–1961. "De origine collegiorum externorum deque controversiis circa eorum paupertatem obortis," AHSI 29: 189–245; 30: 3–89.

———. 1968. "De graduum diversitate inter sacerdotes in Societate Iesu." AHSI 37: 237–316.

———. 1970. "De primo diplomate doctoratus a Collegio Romano exarato (1558)." AHSI 39: 362–66.

———. 1999. "A History of the Jesuit *Ratio Studiorum*." In *Church, Culture & Curriculum*, 17–46.

———. 2001a. "Cardulo, Fulvio." DHCJ 1:658–59.

———. 2001b. "Frusius (Des Freux), Andreas." DHCJ 2:1537.

———. 2001c. "Ledesma, Diego de." DHCJ 3:2318–19.

Lupi, Regina. 2005. *Gli studia del papa. Nuova cultura e tentivi di riforma tra Sei e Settecento*. Florence.

———. 2014. "L'Università di Perugia in età moderna: una dialettica tra Stato e corporazioni urbane." *Annali di Storia delle Università italiane* 18: 185–93.

Luria, Keith P. 1991. *Territories of Grace. Cultural Change in the Seventeenth-Century Diocese of Grenoble*. Berkeley, Los Angeles, and Oxford.

Mack, Peter. 2011. *A History of Renaissance Rhetoric 1380–1620*. Oxford.

Maestri insegnamenti. 2009. *Maestri insegnamenti e libri a Perugia. Contributi per la storia dell'Università (1308–2008)*. Edited by Carla Frova, Ferdinando Treggiari, and Maria Alessandra Panzanelli Fratoni. Milan and Perugia.

Major, J. Russell. 1994. *From Renaissance Monarchy to Absolute Monarchy. French Kings, Nobles, & Estates*. Baltimore and London.

Mancia, Anita. 1985. "La controversia con i protestanti e i programmi degli studi teologici nella Compagnia di Gesù 1547–1599." AHSI 54: 3–43, 209–66.

Mango Tomei, Elsa. 1976. *Gli studenti dell'Università di Pisa sotto il regime granducale*. Pisa.

Maranini, Giuseppe. 1974. *La costituzione di Venezia*, vol. 2: *Dopo la serrata del Maggior Consiglio*. 1931; reprinted in Florence.

Marković, Žeijko. 1981. "Bošković, Rudjer." DSB 2:326–32.

Marongiu, Antonio. 1948. "L'Università di Macerata nel periodo delle origini." *Annali della Università di Macerata* 17: 3–23.

Martellozzo Forin, Elda. 1999. "Conti palatini e lauree conferite per privilegio: L'esempio padovano del sec. XV." *Annali di Storia delle Università italiane* 3: 79–119.

Martin, A. Lynn. 1988. *The Jesuit Mind. The Mentality of an Elite in Early Modern France*. Ithaca, N.Y., and London.

————. 2004. "The Jesuit Mission to France." In *The Mercurian Project*, 249–93.

Martin, Craig. 2014. *Subverting Aristotle. Religion, History, and Philosophy in Early Modern Science*. Baltimore.

Martini, Angelo. 1952. "Gli studi teologici di Giovanni de Polanco alle origine della legislazione scolastica della Compagnia di Gesù." AHSI 21: 225–81.

Maryks, Robert Aleksander. 2010. *The Jesuit Order as a Synagogue of Jews. Jesuits of Jewish Ancestry and Purity-of-Blood Laws in the Early Society of Jesus*. Leiden and Boston.

Massa, Paola. 2007. "Università degli Studi di Genova." In *Storia delle Università in Italia*, edited by Gian Paolo Brizzi, Piero Del Negro, and Andrea Romano, 3:371–78. Messina.

Matteucci, Anna Maria. 1988. "Alfonso Torreggiani architetto dei Gesuiti." In *Dall'isola alla città*, 69–83.

Mayer, Thomas F. 2014. *The Roman Inquisition on the Stage of Italy, c. 1590–1640*. Philadelphia.

Mazzoldi, Leonardo. 1963. "Da Guglielmo III Duca alla fine della prima dominazione austriaca." In *Mantova: La Storia*, vol. 3: *Da Guglielmo III Duca alla fine della Seconda Guerra Mondiale*, edited by Leonardo Mazzoli, Renato Giusti, and Rinaldo Salvadori, 3–257. Mantua.

McCoog, Thomas M. 2004. "'Striking Fear in Heretical Hearts': Mercurian and the British Religious Exiles." In *The Mercurian Project*, 645–73.

McGinness, Frederick J. 1995a. "The Collegio Romano, the University of Rome, and the Decline and Rise of Rhetoric in the Late Cinquecento." *Roma moderna e contemporanea* 3, no. 3: 601–22.

————. 1995b. *Right Thinking and Sacred Oratory in Counter-Reformation Rome*. Princeton, N.J.

Medina, Francisco de Borja, 2001. "Doménech, Juan Jerónimo." DHCJ 2:1135–36.

————. 2004. "Everard Mercurian and Spain: Some Burning Issues." In *The Mercurian Project*, 945–66.

Meessen, George. 2001. "Leunis, Jean." DHCJ 3:2342.

Mellinato, Giuseppe. 2001a. "Belgrado, Jacopo." DHCJ 1:401.

————. 2001b. "Biancani, Giuseppe." DHCJ 1:436.

The Mercurian Project. 2004. *The Mercurian Project. Forming Jesuit Culture 1573–1580*. Edited by Thomas M. McCoog. Rome and St. Louis, Mo.

Merlin, Pierpaolo. 1994. "Il Cinquecento." In Pierpaolo Merlin, Claudio Rosso, Geoffrey Symcox, and Giuseppe Ricuperati, *Il Piemonte sabaudo. Stato e territori in età moderna*, 3–170. Turin.

Merola, Alberto. 1963. "Bandini, Ottavio." DBI 5:718–19.

————. 1964. "Barberini, Francesco." DBI 6:172–76.

Minnich, Nelson H. 1986. "The Function of Sacred Scripture in the Decrees of the Fifth Lateran Council (1512–1517)." *Annuarium Historiae Conciliorum* 18: 319–29.

Mira, Giuseppe Maria. 1964. *Bibliografia Siciliana: ovvero gran dizionario bibliografico delle opere edite e inedite, antiche e moderne di autori siciliani o di argomento siciliano stampate in Sicilia e fuori*. 2 vols. Palermo, 1875; reprinted in New York.

Mobley, Susan Spruell. 2004. "The Jesuits at the University of Ingolstadt." In *The Mercurian Project*, 213–48.

Monti, Alessandro. 1914–1915. *La Compagnia di Gesù nel territorio della provincia torinese. Memorie storiche*. 2 vols. Chieri.

Moore, Eduardo. 2001a. "Casos de conciencia." DHCJ 1:691–94.

————. 2001b. "Teología: V.2. Casuismo." DHCJ 4:3747–48.

Moscheo, Rosario. 1991. "Istruzione superiore e autonomie locali nella Sicilia moderna: Apertura e sviluppi dello *Studium Urbis Messanae* (1590–1641)." *Archivio storico messinese* 59: 75–221.

Mousnier, Roland. 1973. *The Assassination of Henry IV. The Tyrannicide Problem and the Consolidation of the French Absolute Monarchy in the Early Seventeenth Century.* Translated by Joan Spencer. New York.

MP. 1965–1992. *Monumenta Paedagogica Societatis Iesu.* Edited by Ladislaus Lukács. 7 vols. Rome.

Mucci, Giandomenico. 2001. "Gagliardi, Achille." DHCJ 2:1547–48.

Muir, Edward. 2007. *The Culture Wars of the Late Renaissance. Skeptics, Libertines, and Opera.* Cambridge, Mass., and London.

Müller, Rainer. 1996. "Student Education, Student Life." In *A History of the University in Europe,* vol. 2: *Universities in Early Modern Europe (1500–1800),* edited by Hilde de Ridder-Symoens, 326–54. Cambridge.

Murphy, Paul V. 2007. *Ruling Peacefully. Cardinal Ercole Gonzaga and Patrician Reform in Sixteenth-Century Italy.* Washington, D.C.

Negruzzo, Simona. 1995a. "La formazione teologica e il sistema delle scuole nella Pavia spagnola." *Archivio Storico Lombardo* 121: 49–101.

————. 1995b. *Theologiam discere et docere. La facoltà teologica di Pavia nel XVI secolo.* Bologna and Milan.

————. 2001. *Collegij a forma di seminario. Il sistema di formazione teologica nello Stato di Milano in età spagnola.* Brescia.

————. 2003. "L'*Estado de Milan* e la sua università." *Annali di Storia delle Università italiane* 7: 51–69.

Nelles, Paul. 2007. "*Libros de papel, libri bianchi, libri papyracei.* Note-taking Techniques and the Role of Student Notebooks in the Early Jesuit Colleges." AHSI 76: 75–112.

Novarese, Daniela. 1994. *Istituzioni politiche e studi di diritto fra Cinque e Seicento: Il Messanense Studium Generale tra politica gesuitica e istanze egemoniche cittadine.* Milan.

————. 1998. "Policentrismo e politica culturale nella Sicilia spagnola. Palermo, una capitale senza *studium.*" In *Le Università minori in Europa (secoli XV–XIX),* Convegno Internazionale di Studi, Alghero, 30 Ottobre–2 Novembre 1996, edited by Gian Paolo Prizzi and Jacques Verger, 317–36. Soverino Mannelli (Catanzaro).

Nussdorfer, Laurie. 1992. *Civic Politics in the Rome of Urban VIII.* Princeton, N.J.

OER. 1996. *The Oxford Encyclopedia of the Reformation.* Edited by Hans J. Hillerbrand et al. 4 vols. New York.

Oettel, Herbert. 1981a. "Ceva, Giovanni." DSB 3:181–83.

————. 1981b. "Ceva, Tomasso." DSB 3:183–84.

Olivares, Estanislao. 2001. "Derecho Canónico." DHCJ 2:1090–93.

Olmi, Giuseppe. 2010. "Sulle presenza e rimarchevole attività dei gesuiti spagnoli espulsi nel ducato di Parma e Piacenza." In *La presenza in Italia dei gesuiti iberici espulsi. Aspetti religiosi, politici, culturali,* edited by Ugo Baldini and Gian Paolo Brizzi, 509–39. Bologna.

O'Malley, John W. 1993. *The First Jesuits.* Cambridge, Mass., and London.

————. 2000a. "From the 1599 *Ratio Studiorum* to the Present: A Humanistic Tradition?" In *The Jesuit Ratio Studiorum,* 127–44.

————. 2000b. "How the First Jesuits Became Involved in Education." In *The Jesuit Ratio Studiorum*, 56–74.

————. 2004. "Concluding remarks." In *I Gesuiti e la Ratio Studiorum*, 509–21.

O'Neill, Charles E., and Christopher J. Viscardi. 2001a. "Alejandro VII." DHCJ 3:2985–88.

————. 2001b. "Clemente X." DHCJ 3:2988–89.

Le origini dello Studio generale sassarese. 2013. *Le origini dello Studio generale sassarese nel mondo universitario europeo dell'età moderna*. Edited by Gian Paolo Brizzi and Antonello Mattone. Bologna.

Osbat, Luciano. 1982. "Clemente X." DBI 26:293–302.

Paci, Libero. 1977. "La decadenza e la controriforma." In *Storia di Macerata*, 5:108–246.

Padberg, John W. 2000. "Development of the *Ratio Studiorum*." In *The Jesuit Ratio Studiorum*, 80–100.

Paladino, Giuseppe. 1934. "L'Università di Catania nel secolo XVIII." In *Storia della Università di Catania dalle origini ai giorni nostri*, 215–71. Catania.

Il palazzo degli studi. 1998. *Il palazzo degli studi. Appunti per una storia dell'istruzione superiore a Mantova. Luoghi e vicende dal Collegio dei Gesuiti al Liceo Ginnasio "Virgilio."* Edited by Ugo Bazzotti and Daniela Ferrari. Second edition. Mantua.

Pasnau, Robert. 2012. "The Latin Aristotle." In *The Oxford Handbook of Aristotle*, edited by Christopher Shields, 665–89. Oxford.

Pastor, Ludwig von. 1891–1953. *The History of the Popes from the Close of the Middle Ages*. Translated by F. I. Antrobus et al. 40 vols. London and St. Louis, Mo.

Pedersen, Olaf. 1996. "Tradition and Innovation." In *A History of the University in Europe*, vol. 2: *Universities in Early Modern Europe (1500–1800)*, edited by Hilde de Ridde-Symoens, 451–88. Cambridge.

Pellistrandi, Benoît. 1990. "The University of Alcalá de Henares from 1568 to 1618: Students and Graduates." *History of Universities* 9: 119–65.

Pendola, Tommaso. 1852. *Il Collegio Tolomei di Siena e serie dei convittori dalla sua fondazione a tutto Giugno 1852. Cenni storici*. Siena.

Penuti, Carla. 1998. "Collegi professionali di giureconsulti con prerogativa di addottorare in area estense e romagnola." In *Le universitá minori in Europa (secoli XV–XVI)*, Convegno Internazionale di Studi, Alghero, 30 Ottobre–2 Novembre 1996, edited by Gian Paolo Brizzi and Jacques Verger, 337–52. Soverino Mannelli (Catanzaro).

Pepe, Luigi. 1995. "La crisi dell'insegnamento scientifico dei Gesuiti a Ferrara e l'inizio dell'attività didattica di Teodoro Bonati." In *'In supreme dignitatis ...' Per la storia dell'Università di Ferrara 1391–1991*, edited by Patrizia Castelli, 61–74. Florence.

Pereira, José. 2007. *Suárez: Between Scholasticism and Modernity*. Milwaukee, Wis.

Perry, Mary Elizabeth. 2011. "El legado de Francisco de Borja en las escuelas para niños moriscos." In *Francisco de Borja y su tiempo. Política, Religión y Cultura en la Edad Moderna*, edited by Enrique García Hernán and María del Pilar Ryan, 609–17. Valencia and Rome.

Pescasio, Luigi. 2000. *Ferdinando Carlo Gonzaga, decimo e ultimo Duca di Mantova e ottavo del Monferrato*. Suzzara (Mantua).

Piaget, Édouard. 1893. *Histoire de l'établissement des Jésuites en France (1540–1640)*. Leiden.

Piaia, Gregorio. 1973. "Aristotelismo, 'Heresis' e giurisdizionalismo nella polemica del P. Antonio Possevino contro lo Studio di Padova." *Quaderni per la storia del'Università di Padova* 7:125–45.

Piana, Celestino. 1986. "L'Università di Parma nel Quattrocento." In *Parma e l'umanesimo italiano*, Atti del convegno internazionale di studi umanistici (Parma, 20 ottobre 1984), edited by Paola Medioli Masotti, 97–120. Padua.

Pillat, Markus. 2004. "The Jesuits in the Rhineland Province." In *The Mercurian Project*, 77–114.

Pinotti, Chiara. 1983. "Riforme culturali a Mantova nella seconda metà del Settecento." In *Mantova nel Settecento. Un ducato ai confini dell'impero*, 92–97. Milan.

Pirri, Pietro. 1960. "Aguilera (Aquilera e Aghillera), Emmanuele." DBI 1:510–11.

Premoli, Orazio M. 1913. *Storia dei Barnabiti nel Cinquecento*. Rome.

Prodi, Paolo. 1959–1967. *Il Cardinale Gabriele Paleotti (1522–1597)*. 2 vols. Rome.

Prosperi, Adriano. 2013. "Il figlio, il padre, il gesuita. Un testo di Antonio Possevino." *Rinascimento* Serie 2, vol. 53: 111–55.

Quazza, Romolo. 1950. *Preponderanza spagnuola (1559–1700)*. Second edition. Milan.

Quondam, Amedeo. 2004. "Il metronomo classicista." In *I Gesuiti e la Ratio Studiorum*, 379–507.

Rahner, Hugo. 1960. *Saint Ignatius Loyola. Letters to Women*. Translated by Kathleen Pond and S. A. H. Weetman. Freiburg, Edinburgh, and London.

Raponi, Nicola. 1961a. "Archinto, Carlo." DBI 3:759–61.

———. 1961b. "Archinto, Filippo." DBI 3:764.

Renazzi, Filippo Maria. 1971. *Storia dell'Università degli Studj di Roma*. 4 vols. Rome, 1803–6; reprinted in Bologna.

Riminaldi, Giovanni Maria. The Cardinals of the Holy Roman Church. www2.fiu.edu/~mirandas/bios/1785.html#riminaldi.

La rinascita del sapere. 1991. *La rinascita del sapere. Libri e maestri dello studio ferrarese*. Edited by Patrizia Castelli. Venice.

Rizzi, Fortunato. 1948. *I professori dell'Università di Parma attraverso i secoli: Note indicative bio-bibliografiche*. Parma.

Roegiers, Jan. 2012. "Awkward Neighbours: The Leuven Faculty of Theology and the Jesuit College (1542–1773)." In *The Jesuits of the Low Countries: Identity and Impact (1540–1773)*, edited by Rob Raesen and Leo Kenis, 153–75. Leuven.

Romanello, Marina. 1993. "Elisabetta Farnese, regina di Spagna." DBI 42:486–94.

———. 1996. "Ferdinando Di Borbone, Duca di Parma, Piacenza e Guastalla." DBI 46:208–12.

———. 1997a. "Filippo Di Borbone, Duca di Parma, Piacenza e Guastalla." DBI 47:729–33.

———. 1997b. "Francesco Farnese, Duca di Parma e Piacenza." DBI 49:743–47.

Romano, Andrea. 1992. "'Primum ac prototypum collegium Societatis Iesù' e 'Messanense Studium Generale': L'insegnamento universitario a Messina nel Cinquecento." In *La pedagogia della Compagnia di Gesù*, Atti del Convegno Internazionale, Messina 14–16 novembre 1991, edited by F. Guerello and P. Schiavone, 33–72. Messina.

———. 1995. "Studenti e professori siciliani di diritto a Ferrara tra medioevo e età moderna." In *"In supreme dignitatis ...": Per la storia dell'Università dell'Università di Ferrara, 1391–1991*, edited by Patrizia Castelli, 107–36. Ferrara.

Romano, Giacinto. 1900. "Gli statuti dello studio messinese." In *CCCL anniversario della Università di Messina (contributo storico)*, part 1, 123–208. Messina.

Romeo, Giovanni. 1977. "Carpegna, Gaspare." DBI 20:589–91.

Rotondò, Antonio. 1969. "Boccadiferro, Ludovico." DBI 11:3–4.

Ruderman, David B. 1995. *Jewish Thought and Scientific Discovery in Early Modern Europe*. New Haven, Conn., and London.

Ruffino, Italo. 1975. "Canonici Regolari di Sant'Agostino di Sant'Antonio, di Vienne." In *Dizionario degli istituti di perfezione*, vol. 2, cols. 134–41. Rome.

Ruiz de Medina, Juan. 2001. "Morais (Morales), Sebastião." DHCJ 3:2737.

Ruiz Jurado, Manuel. 1986. "Polanco, Juan Alfonso de." In *Dictionnaire de spiritualité*, vol. 12, part 2: *Piatti-Quodvultdeus*, cols. 1838–43. Paris.

———. 2001a. "Nadal, Jerónimo." DHCJ 3:2793–96.

———. 2001b. "Negrone (Nigronius), Giulio." DHCJ 3:2806–7.

Rummel, Erika. 1995. *The Humanist-Scholastic Debate in the Renaissance and Reformation*. Cambridge, Mass., and London.

———. 2009. "The Renaissance Humanists." In *A History of Biblical Interpretation*, vol. 2: *The Medieval through the Reformation Periods*, edited by Alan J. Hauser, Duane F. Watson, and Schuyler Kaufman, 280–98. Grand Rapids, Mich.

Rurale, Flavio. 1992. *I gesuiti a Milano: Religione e politica nel secondo Cinquecento*. Rome.

———. 1997. "I gesuiti a Mantova (secoli XVI–XVIII)." In Gorzoni, 13–50.

———. 2002. "Milano e Mantova: conflitti politici e culturali nei collegi-università della Compagnia di Gesù." In *Gesuiti e università*, 53–68.

Sabbadini, Remigio. 1975. *Storia documentata della R. Università di Catania. Parte Prima: L'Università nel secolo XV*. Catania, 1898; reprinted in Bologna.

Saint-Genis, Victor de. 1978. *Histoire de Savoie d'après les documents originaux de puis les origines les plus reculées jusqu'a l'annexion*, vol. 2. Chambéry, 1869; reprinted in Marseille.

Sáinz y Zúñiga, C. M. Ajo G. y R. 1957–1958. *Historia de las Universidades hispánicas. Orígines y desarollo desde su aparición a nuestros días*, vol. 1: *Medievo y Renacimiento universitario*, and vol. 2: *El siglo de oro universitario*. Avila.

Salvo, Carmen. 1995. *Giurati, feudatori, mercanti. L'élite a Messina tra Medio Evo e Età Moderna*. Rome.

Salvo, Francesco. 2001a. "Aguilera, Emmanuele." DHCJ 1:21–22.

———. 2001b. "Salerno, Pietro." DHCJ 4:3470–71.

Sampolo, Luigi. 1888. *La R. Accademia degli Studi di Palermo. Narrazione storica*. Palermo.

Sander, Christoph. 2014a. "*In dubio pro fide*. The Fifth Lateran Council Decree *Apostolici Regiminis* (1513) and Its Impact on Early Jesuit Education and Pedagogy." *Educazione. Giornale di pedagogica critica* 3, no. 1: 39–62.

———. 2014b. "The War of the Roses. The Debate between Diego de Ledesma and Benet Perera about the Philosophy Course at the Jesuit College in Rome." In *Benet Perera*, 31–50.

Sanfilippo, Matteo. 1992. "Doria, Giannettino." DBI 41:345–48.

———. 1993. "Durazzo, Stefano." DBI 42:178–81.

Sangalli, Maurizio. 1996. "Università, scuole private, collegi d'educazione, accademie a Padova tra Cinque e Seicento: alcuni spunti per una storia 'integrata' delle istituzioni scolastiche." *Annali di storia dell'educazione e delle istituzioni scolastiche* 3: 93–118.

———. 1999. *Cultura, politica e religione nella Repubblica di Venezia tra Cinque e Seicento*.

Gesuiti e somaschi a Venezia. Istituto veneto di scienze, lettere ed arti. Memorie classe di scienze morali, lettere ed arti 84. Venice.

———. 2001. *Università Accademie Gesuiti. Cultura e religione a Padova tra Cinque e Seicento.* Padua.

Sanz de Diego, Rafale M. 2012. "Alcalá de Henares: presencia de Ignacio y primeros pasos de la Compañía de Jesús en la ciudad." In *Los Jesuitas. Religión, Política y Educación (Siglos XVI–XVIII),* edited by José Martínez Millán, Henar Pizarro Llorente, and Esther Jiménez Pablo, 2:671–713. 3 vols. Madrid.

Scaduto, Mario. 1948. "Le origini dell'Università di Messina." AHSI 17: 102–59.

———. 1959. "Le missioni di A. Possevino in Piemonte. Propaganda calvinista e restaurazione cattolica 1560–1563." AHSI 28: 51–191.

———. 1964. *Storia della Compagnia di Gesù in Italia,* vol. 3: *L'epoca di Giacomo Lainez, 1556–1565. Il governo.* Rome.

———. 1968. *Catalogo dei Gesuiti d'Italia 1540–1565.* Rome.

———. 1974. *Storia della Compagnia di Gesù in Italia,* vol. 4: *L'epoca di Giacomo Lainez, 1556–1565: L'azione.* Rome.

———. 1984. "Palmio, Benoit." In *Dictionnaire de spiritualité,* vol. 12, part 1: *Pacaud–Photius,* cols. 142–44. Paris.

———. 1992. *Storia della Compagnia di Gesù in Italia,* vol. 5: *L' opera di Francesco Borgia, 1565–1572.* Rome.

———. 2001a. "Adorno, Francesco." DHCJ 1:16.

———. 2001b. "Laínez, Diego." DHCJ 2:1601–5.

———. 2001c. "Palmio, Francesco." DHCJ 3:2963.

———. 2001d. "Possevino, Antonio." DHCJ 4:3201–3.

———. 2001e. "Salmerón, Alfonso." DHCJ 4:3474–76.

Scaglione, Aldo. 1986. *The Liberal Arts and the Jesuit College System.* Amsterdam and Philadelphia.

Scalvanti, Oscar. 1910. *Cenni storici della Università di Perugia.* Perugia.

Schmidt, Peter. 1984. *Das Collegium Germanicum in Rom und die Germaniker. Zur Funktion eines römischen Ausländerseminars (1552–1914).* Tübingen.

Schmitt, Charles B. 1981. "Zabarella, Jacopo." DSB 14:580–82.

———. 1983. *Aristotle and the Renaissance.* Cambridge, Mass., and London.

———. 1984. "Cremonini, Cesare." DBI 30:618–22.

———. 1988. "The rise of the philosophical textbook." In CHRP, 792–804.

Schurhammer, Georg, SJ. 1973. *Francis Xavier: His Life, His Times,* vol. 1: *Europe 1506–1541.* Translated by M. Joseph Costelloe, SJ. Rome.

Sebes, Joseph. 2001. "Ricci, Matteo." DHCJ 4:3351–53.

Selmi, Elisabetta. 2007. "Maggi, Vincenzo." DBI 67:365–69.

Serangeli, Sandro, and Raffaella Zambuto. 2005. "Sui rapporti tra Gesuiti e Università di Macerata: una fonte male intesa." *Annali di Storia delle Università italiane* 9: 269–72.

Shields, Christopher. 2012. "Shadows of Beings: Francisco Suárez's *Entia Rationis.*" In *The Philosophy of Francisco Suárez,* edited by Benjamin Hill and Henrik Lagerlund, 57–74. Oxford.

Sievernich, Michael. 2001. "Bidermann, Jakob." DHCJ 1:446–47.

Signorotto, Gian Vittorio. 1994. "Il rientro dei gesuiti a Venezia: la trattative (1606–1657)." In *I gesuiti e Venezia,* 385–419.

Simeoni, Luigi. 1987. *Storia della Università di Bologna*, vol. 2: *L'età moderna (1500–1888)*. Bologna, 1940; reprinted in Sala Bolognese.

Simioni, Elisa. 1934. "I professori della facoltà teologica dell'Università di Padova nel Cinquecento." *Padova: Rivista mensile del Comune* 8: 59–70.

Sola, Francisco de Paula. 2001. "Perera, Benito." DHCJ 3:3088–89.

Solari, Giovanna R. 1968. *The House of Farnese*. Translated by Simona Morini and Frederic Tuten. Garden City, N.Y.

Sommervogel, Carlos. 1960. *Bibliothèque de la Compagnie de Jèsus. Nouvelle Edition.* 11 vols. Paris, 1890, reprinted in Louvain.

Sorbelli, Albano. 1987. *Storia della Università di Bologna*, vol. 1: *Il medioevo (secoli XI–XV)*. Bologna, 1940; reprinted in Sala Bolognese.

Sorgia, Giancarlo. 1986. *Lo studio generale cagliaritano. Storia di una Università*. Cagliari.

Spada, Fabrizio. In The Cardinals of the Holy Roman Church. ww2.fiu.edu/~mirandas/bios1675.html#Spada.

Sperelli, Sperello. In The Cardinals of the Holy Roman Church. www2.fiu.edu/~mirandas/bios1699.htm#Sperelli.

Spinucci, Domenico. In The Cardinals of the Holy Roman Church. www2.fiu.edu~mirandas/bios1816.htm#Spinucci.

Springhetti, Emilio. 1961. "Un grande umanista messinese, Giovanni Antonio Viperano (Cenni biografici)." *Helikon: Rivista di Tradizione e Cultura Classica* 1: 94–117.

Stella, Aldo. 1960. "Altieri (Paluzzi degli Albertoni), Paluzzo." DBI 2:561–64.

Stolarski, Piotr. 2010. *Friars on the Frontier. Catholic Renewal and the Dominican Order in Southeastern Poland, 1594–1648*. Farnham and Burlington, Vt.

———. 2011. "Dominican-Jesuit Rivalry and the Politics of Catholic Renewal in Poland 1564–1648." *Journal of Ecclesiastical History* 62: 255–72.

Storia dell'Università di Pisa. 1993–2000. *Storia dell'Università di Pisa*, vol. 1 in 2 parts: *1343–1737*, and vol. 2 in 3 parts: *1737–1861*. Pisa.

Storia di Macerata. 1971–1977. *Storia di Macerata*. Edited by Aldo Adversi, Dante Cecchi e Libero Paci. 5 vols. Macerata.

Strilič, Ivan. 2001. "Bošković, Rudjer [Ruggero] Josip." DHCJ 1:499–500.

Strømholm, Per. 1976. "Valerio, Luca." DSB 13:560–61.

Struik, D. J. 1981. "Saccheri, (Giovanni) Girolamo." DSB 12:55–57.

Stumpo, Enrico. 1979. "Cenci, Baldassare." DBI 23:510–11.

———. 1989. "Della Rovere, Girolamo." DBI 37:350–53.

———. 1993. "Emanuele Filiberto, Duca di Savoia." DBI 42:553–66.

Symcox, Geoffrey. 1983. *Victor Amadeus II: Absolutism in the Savoyard State 1675–1730*. London.

Szilas, László. 2001. "Austria. Antigua." DHCJ 1:277–92.

Tacchi Venturi, Pietro. 1931. *Storia della Compagnia di Gesù in Italia*, vol. 1, part 2: *Documenti*. Rome.

———. 1951a. *Storia della Compagnia di Gesù in Italia*, vol. 2, part 1: *Dalla nascita del fondatore alla solenne approvazione dell'Ordine (1491–1540)*. Second improved edition. Rome.

———. 1951b. *Storia della Compagnia di Gesù in Italia*, vol. 2, part 2: *Dalla solenne approvazione dell'Ordine alla morte del fondatore (1540–1556)*. Rome.

Tamalio, Raffaele. 2004. "Isabella Clara d'Asburgo, Duchessa di Mantova e del Monferrato." DBI 62:637–39.

Tellechea, José Ignazio. 2001. "Maldonado, Juan." DHCJ 3:2484–85.

Terpstra, Nicholas. 1995. *Lay Confraternities and Civic Religion in Renaissance Bologna.* Cambridge.

——. 2005. *Abandoned Children of the Italian Renaissance. Orphan Care in Florence and Bologna.* Baltimore.

Tocci, Giovanni. 1979. "Il ducato di Parma e Piacenza." In Lino Marini, Giovanni Tocci, Cesare Mozzarelli, and Aldo Stella, *Ducati padana, Trento, e Trieste,* 213–356. Turin.

Tomasini, Iacopo Philippo. 1986. *Gymnasium Patavinum ... libri V.* Udine, 1654; reprinted in Sala Bolognese.

Torrini, Maurizio. 1973. "Giuseppe Ferroni, gesuita e galileiano." *Physis* 15: 411–23.

Turrini, Miriam. 1990. "Le letture di casi di coscienza e di teologia morale nello Studio bolognese del Sei-Settecento. La definizione di una disciplina e la formazione del clero." In *Sapere e/è potere. Discipline, Dispute e Professioni nell'Università Medievale e Moderna. Il caso bolognese a confronto,* Atti del 4° Convegno, Bologna, 13–15 aprile 1989, vol. 3: *Dalle discipline ai ruoli sociali,* edited by Angela De Benedictis, 203–36. Bologna.

——. 1991. *La coscienza e le leggi. Morale e diritto nei testi per la confessione della prima Età moderna.* Bologna.

——. 2006. *Il 'giovin signore' in collegio. I gesuiti e l'educazione della nobiltà nelle consuetudini del collegio ducale di Parma.* Bologna.

——. 2008. "L'insegnamento della teologia." In *Storia di Bologna nell'età moderna (secoli XVI–XVIII),* vol. 2: *Cultura, istituzioni culturali, Chiesa e vita religiosa,* edited by Adriano Prosperi, 437–94. Bologna.

Turrini, Patrizia. 2000. "Il Nobile Collegio Tolomei." In *L'istituto di Celso Tolomei,* 17–52.

Turtas, Raimondo. 1986. *La Casa dell'Università. La politica edilizia della Compagnia di Gesù nei decenni di formazione dell'Ateneo sassarese (1562–1632).* Sassari.

——. 1988. *La nascità dell'università in Sardegna. La culturale dei sovrani spagnoli nella formazione degli Atenei di Sassari e di Cagliari (1543–1632).* Sassari.

——. 1995. *Scuola e Università in Sardegna tra '500 e '600. L'organizzazione dell'istruzione durante i decenni formativi dell'Università di Sassari (1562–1635).* Sassari.

Turtas, Raimondo, Angelo Rundine, and Eugenia Tognotti. 1990. *Università Studenti Maestri. Contributi alla storia della cultura in Sardegna.* Sassari.

Udías, Agustín. 2015. *Jesuit Contribution to Science. A History.* Cham.

Ulianich, Boris. 1994. "I gesuiti e la Compagnia di Gesù nelle opere e nel pensiero di Paolo Sarpi." In *I gesuiti e Venezia,* 233–62.

Vaccari, Pietro. 1957. *Storia della Università di Pavia.* Second revised edition. Pavia.

Vaini, Mario. 1980. "La società mantovana nell'età delle Riforme." In *La città di Mantova nell'età di Maria Teresa,* edited by Mario Vaini, 12–25. Mantua.

Vallauri, Tommaso. 1970. *Storia delle Università degli Studi del Piemonte.* 3 vols. Turin, 1845–46; reprinted in Bologna.

——. 1975. *Storia della Università degli Studi del Piemonte.* 3 vols. in one volume. Second edition. Turin.

Vaz de Carvalho, José. 2001a. "Álvares, Manuel." DHCJ 1:90.

——. 2001b. "Rodrigues, Simão R. De Azevedo." DHCJ 4:3390–92.

Venturi, Franco. 1976. *Settecento riformatore,* vol. 2: *La chiesa e la repubblica dentro i loro limiti 1758–1774.* Turin.

Vidori, Pietro. In The Cardinals of the Roman Church. www2.fiu.edu/~mirandas/ bios1660.html#Vidori.

Vigna, Guido. 1991. *Il santo dei Gonzaga: San Luigi e il suo tempo*. Milan.

Villaret, Emilio. 1960. *Storia delle congregazioni mariane*. Rome.

Villoslada, Riccardo G. 1954. *Storia del Collegio Romano dal suo inizio (1551) alla soppressione della Compagnia di Gesù (1773)*. Rome.

Visconti, Alessandro. 1950. *La storia dell'Università di Ferrara (1391–1950)*. Bologna.

Vocabulaire des collèges. 1993. *Vocabulaire des collèges universitaires (XIIIe-XVIe siècles*, Actes du colloque Leuven, 9–11 avril 1992. Edited by Olga Weijers. Turnhout.

Voelkel, Markus. 1992. "L'Università romana ed i Barberini nella prima metà del XVII secolo." In *Roma e lo Studium Urbis. Spazio urbano e cultura dal Quattro al Seicento,* Atti del convegno Roma, 7–10 giugno 1989, 323–40. Rome.

Volpi Rosselli, Giuliana. 1993. "Il corpo studentesco, i collegi e le accademie." In *Storia dell'Università di Pisa*, vol. 1 in 2 parts: *1343–1737*, part 1, 377–468. Pisa.

Wallace, William A. 1999a. "Soto, Domingo de." ER 6:47–48.

———. 1999b. "Zabarella, Jacopo." ER 6:337–39.

———. 2006. "Jesuit Influences on Galileo's Science." In *The Jesuits II: Cultures, Sciences, and the Arts 1540–1773*, edited by John W. O'Malley, Gauvin Alexander Bailey, Steven J. Harris, and T. Frank Kennedy, 314–35. Toronto, Buffalo, N.Y., and London.

Wicks, Jared W. 2001a. "Erasmismo." DHCJ 2:1248–50.

———. 2001b. "Teología Positiva." DHCJ 4:3723–25.

Wormald, Jenny. 1996. "Buchanan, George." OER 1:224–25.

Wright, Anthony D. 2004. "The Jesuits and the Older Religious Orders in Spain." In *The Mercurian Project*, 913–44.

Zaccagnini, Guido. 1930. *Storia dello Studio di Bologna durante il Rinascimento*. Genève.

Zanardi, Mario. 1994. "I «domicilia» o centri operativi della Compagnia di Gesù nello Stato veneto (1542–1773)." In *I gesuiti e Venezia*, 89–180.

———. 2001. "Tesauro, Emanuele." DHCJ 4:3874.

Zanetti, Ginevra. 1982. *Profilo storico dell'Università di Sassari*. Milan.

Zanfredini, Mario. 2001a. "Fazio, Giulio." DHCJ 2:1384.

———. 2001b. "Febei (Phaebeus), Francesco Antonio." DHCJ 2:1385.

———. 2001c. "Ferroni, Giuseppe." DHCJ 2:1411.

———. 2001d. "Lana-Terzi, Francesco." DHCJ 3:2275–76.

———. 2001e. "Lecchi, Giovanni Francesco." DHCJ 3:2314.

———. 2001f. "Palmio, Benedetto." DHCJ 3:2962–63.

———. 2001g. "Viperano, Giovanni Antonio." DHCJ 4:3985.

———. 2001h. "Zucchi, Nicola." DHCJ 4:4085–86.

Zapperi, Roberto, and Clare Robertson. 1995. "Farnese, Odoardo." DBI 45:112–19.

Zarri, Gabriella. 1988. "La Compagnia di Gesù a Bologna: dall'origine alla stabilizzazione (1546–1568)." In *Dall'isola alla città*, 119–24.

Ziggelaar, August. 2001. "Grimaldi, Francesco Maria." DHCJ 2:1817–18.

Zorzoli, Maria Carla. 1986. *Università, dottori, giureconsulti: L'organizzazione della "facoltà legale" di Pavia nell'età spagnola*. Padua.

———. 1995. "Università di Pavia (1535–1796). L'organizzazione dello Studio." In *Storia di Pavia*, vol. 4 in 2 parts: *L'età spagnola e austriaca*, part 1, 427–81. Milan.

INDEX

Absolutism: defined, 156–57

Accademia: many meanings, 35n82

Accademia dei Catenati (Macerata), 249

Accarisi, Giacomo, 199, 202

Acquaviva, Claudio (superior general), 132, 139, 141, 145, 409, 442; abolishes commands of Borja, 408; and Macerata, 244; and Messina, 81–83, 86; moves Messina upper school to Palermo, 87–88; opposes teaching canon law, 323; rejects dividing Sicily, 90; sends Luigi Gonzaga to Mantua, 190; studied at University of Perugia, 159; and University of Parma, 159–60; wants uniform teaching, 414

Adam, Jean, 26n47

Adorni, Francesco: teaches cases at Bologna, 308

Adorno, Francesco: and canon law, 323; teaches cases at Milan, 312–14

Adriatic Sea, 4, 224, 371

Affair of the placards, 26

Aghierre, Diego: teaches canon law, 330, 331

Agnadello (battle), 141

Albert II (emperor), 191

Albert the Great, 404

Alcalá de Henares, 36

Alcalá de Henares Jesuit college and school, 45

Alexander VII (pope): and Macerata, 246–47; and moral theology, 423; supports higher education, 247

Alexander de Villedieu: *Doctrinale*, 23n33

Alexander of Aphrodisias, 394, 407, 409

Alexandria, 128, 136

Alfonzo V of Aragon (king): gives permission for university, 69

Alma Mater Studiorum. See University of Bologna

Altieri, Paluzzo (cardinal), 310; favors Jesuits 314

Alvarez de Toledo, Juan (cardinal): wants university, 63–64

Ammonius, 394

Angelelli, Alberto Serpa, 316; donations, 287, 291

Antwerp, 19

Apennine Mountains, 242

Apostolic Camera. *See* Camera Apostolica

Apostolici regiminis (bull), 406, 417; explained 403; Jesuits invoke, 408, 409

Arcadius (Byzantine emperor), 69

Archiginnasio building (Bologna), 158, 310

Archinto, Carlo, 379–80

Archinto, Filippo, 379

Arezzo, Guglielmo, 345–46

Aristotelian philosophy: leads to medicine, 400

Aristotle, 11, 126, 170, 218; *Categories*, 396; Greek commentators on, 401; *Organon*, 16; *Physics,* 16; *Poetics*, 140; *Rhetoric*, 140, 243, 385; teaching, 393–99; works, 410, 413, 414

Arnauld, Antoine, 271, 274

Arnauld d'Andilly, Simon (marquis of Pomponne), 274, 279

Arriaga, Rodrigo de: *Cursus philosophicus*, 414

Arts: defined, 16

Arts rolls: in Italian universities, 48

Assunteria di Studio (Bologna), 287–89, 295–96; and brief of Urban VIII, 305; and Jesuit school, 293–95, 297–99, 301,

The Jesuits and Italian Universities: 1548–1773 was designed and typeset in Monotype Bembo by Kachergis Book Design of Pittsboro, North Carolina. It was printed on 60-pound House Natural Smooth and bound by Sheridan Books of Chelsea, Michigan.